THE NEAR EAST
UNDER ROMAN RULE

MNEMOSYNE

BIBLIOTHECA CLASSICA BATAVA

COLLEGERUNT

J.M. BREMER · L.F. JANSSEN · H. PINKSTER

H.W. PLEKET · C.J. RUIJGH · P.H. SCHRIJVERS

BIBLIOTHECAE FASCICULOS EDENDOS CURAVIT

C.J. RUIJGH, KLASSIEK SEMINARIUM, OUDE TURFMARKT 129, AMSTERDAM

SUPPLEMENTUM CENTESIMUM SEPTUAGESIMUM SEPTIMUM

BENJAMIN ISAAC

THE NEAR EAST
UNDER ROMAN RULE

THE NEAR EAST
UNDER ROMAN RULE

SELECTED PAPERS

BY

BENJAMIN ISAAC

BRILL
LEIDEN · NEW YORK · KÖLN
1998

This book is printed on acid-free paper.

DS
62.2
.I85
1998

Library of Congress Cataloging-in-Publication Data

Library of Congress Cataloging in Publication Data is also available.

Die Deutsche Bibliothek]– CIP-Einheitsaufnahme

[Mnemosyne / Supplementum]
Mnemosyne : bibliotheca classica Batava. Supplementum. – Leiden ;
New York ; Köln : Brill
    Früher Schriftenreihe
    Reihe Supplementum zu: Mnemosyne
177. The Near East under Roman rule. – 1998

The Near East under Roman rule / by Benjamin Isaac. – Leiden ;
New York ; Köln : Brill, 1998
    (Mnemosyne : Supplementum ; 177)
    ISBN 90-04-10736-3

ISSN   0169-8958
ISBN   90 04 10736 3

PRINTED IN THE NETHERLANDS

CONTENTS

LIST OF ILLUSTRATIONS

Map

Plates

Figures

PLACES OF ORIGINAL PUBLICATION

Hellenistic and Herodian Palestine

A Seleucid Inscription from Jamnia-on-the-Sea: Antiochus V Eupator and the Sidonians. *Israel Exploration Journal*, 41 (1991), 132–44.

A Donation for Herod's Temple in Jerusalem. *Israel Exploration Journal*, 33 (1983), pp. 86–92.

Judaea under Roman Rule

Two Greek Inscriptions from Tell Abu-Shusha. In: B. Mazar (ed.), *Geva: Archaeological Discoveries at Tell Abu-Shusha, Mishmar Ha-'Emeq* (Jerusalem, 1988, in Hebrew), pp. 224–5.

B. Isaac and I. Roll, A Milestone of A.D. 69 from Judaea. *Journal of Roman Studies*, 56 (1976), pp. 9–14.

Vespasian's Titulature in A.D. 69. *Zeitschrift für Papyrologie und Epigraphik*, 55 (1984), 143–44.

Milestones in Judaea: From Vespasian to Constantine. *Palestine Exploration Quarterly*, 110 (1978), 47–60.

M. Gichon, and B. Isaac, A Flavian Inscription from Jerusalem. *Israel Exploration Journal*, 24 (1974), 117–123.

Roman Colonies in Judaea: The Foundation of Aelia Capitolina. *Talanta*, 12–13 (1980–81), pp. 31–53 (English).

Judaea after A.D. 70. *Journal of Jewish Studies*, 35 (1984), pp. 44–50.

Bandits in Judaea and Arabia. *Harvard Studies in Classical Philology*, 88 (1984), pp. 171–203. By Permission of the President and Fellows of Harvard College.

The Babatha Archive: A Review Article, *Israel Exploration Journal*, 42 (1992), 62–75.

B. Isaac and I. Roll, Judaea in the Early Years of Hadrian's Reign. *Latomus*, 38 (1979), pp. 54–66.

B. Isaac and I. Roll, Legio II Traiana in Judaea. *Zeitschrift für Papyrologie und Epigraphik*, 33 (1979), pp. 149–156.

B. Isaac and I. Roll, Legio II Traiana in Judaea—A Reply. *Zeitschrift für Papyrologie und Epigraphik*, 47 (1982), 131 f.

Cassius Dio on the Revolt of Bar Kokhba. *Scripta Classica Israelica*, 7 (1983–4) [1986], pp. 68–76.

B. Isaac and A. Oppenheimer, The Revolt of Bar Kokhba, Scholarship and Ideology. *Journal of Jewish Studies*, 36 (1985), pp. 33–60.

Ethnic Groups in Judaea under Roman Rule, *Dor Le-Dor: Studies in Honour of J. Efron*, eds. A. Kasher and A. Oppenheimer (Jerusalem 1995), 201–9 (in Hebrew).

Orientals and Jews in the Historia Augusta: Fourth-Century Prejudice and Stereotypes, *Studies in Memory of Menahem Stern* (Zalman Shazar Center, Jerusalem), 101*–118*.

Eusebius and the Geography of Roman Provinces for D. Kennedy (ed.), *The Roman Army in the East* (Journal of Roman Archaeology, Supplementary Series, Ann Arbor, MI, 1996), 153–167.

Arabia and Syria

The Decapolis in Syria, a Neglected Inscription. *Zeitschrift für Papyrologie und Epigraphik*, 44 (1981), pp. 67–74.

Tax Collection in Roman Arabia: A New Interpretation of the Evidence from the Babatha Archive, *Mediterranean Historical Review*, 9 (1994), 256–66.

Review article: 'Inscriptions from Southern Jordan: M. Sartre, Inscriptions grecques et latines de la Syrie, Tome xxi, Inscriptions de la Jordanie, Tome iv: Pétra et la Nabatène méridionale, du wadi al-Hasa au golfe de 'Aqaba (Paris, 1993)', *Scripta Classica Israelica*, 13 (1994), 163–8.

The Roman Army, General

The Meaning of 'Limes' and 'Limitanei' in Ancient Sources. *Journal of Roman Studies*, 78 (1988), 125–147.

Hierarchy and Command Structure in the Roman Army in Y. Le Bohec (ed.), *La hiérarchie (Rangordnung) de l'armée romaine sous le Haut-Empire: Actes du Congrès de Lyon 1994* (Paris, 1995), 23–31.

An Open Frontier, in *Frontières d'Empire: Nature et signification des frontières romaines*, eds. P. Brun, S. van der Leeuw & C.R. Whittaker (Nemours, 1993), 105–114.

Military Diplomas and Extraordinary Levies in: *Heer und Integrations-politik, Die römischen Militärdiplome als historische Quelle*, Passauer Historische Forschungen 2, Köln-Wien 1986, eds. W. Eck und H. Wolff, pp. 258–64.

The Late Roman Army

The Army in the Late Roman East: The Persian Wars and the Defence of the Byzantine Provinces, in *The Byzantine and Early Islamic Near East III. States, Resources and Armies*. Papers of the Third Workshop on Late Antiquity and Early Islam. eds. A. Cameron, L. Conrad, G. King, (Darwin Press, Princeton, 1995), pp. 125–55.

INTRODUCTION

Over the past twenty-five years various topics that used to be marginal in the eyes of most ancient historians have begun to attract more attention. The scholarly output on the Roman Near East used to be less than ten percent of that concerned with N-W Europe, and the ratio of archaeological field-work was probably even more unequal. In the seventies a generation of historians and archaeologists began their careers with a conscious decision to explore the history of the eastern provinces of the Roman empire and this has resulted in intense activity. This is not only a matter of quantity, but also of quality. The days are gone when there were eminent archaeologists working in the East who made fun of others who insisted that stratigraphy is an elementary ingredient in every professional excavation. No archaeologist or historian now claims that one period deserves more attention than another. All historical periods are considered equal, from the Stone Age to the Ottoman period, with the concomitant result that people are more aware of the need to specialize. At the same time, forms of integration are now widening perspectives. Thus there is more interaction between those studying Judaism in the period of the Mishnah and the Talmud, and students of Roman and Late Roman history. There are regular workshops on the Byzantine and Early Islamic Near East. All of this has resulted in interesting forms of academic debate and in discussions of topics that are essential, although they were not even considered relevant in the past.

This is true not only for the study of the Roman Near East, but for Roman frontier studies in general, a field that has attracted scholars in N-W and Central Europe since the nineteenth century. It received a remarkable impetus after the Second World War. It was then, with a few notable exceptions, a field of study for archaeologists who excavated the remains of Roman army installations in the frontier regions and for Roman army specialists. Over the past ten years the nature of the Roman frontiers has attracted attention of a much wider circle of students, including social and economic historians and those interested in Roman imperialism and in ancient warfare. There is a good deal of debate about major questions, usually civil, sometime not. Another trend is, that on the Roman Near East several works of synthesis have now been published: G.W. Bowersock, *Roman Arabia*

(1983), M. Sartre, *L'Orient romain* (1991), F. Millar, *The Roman Near East: 31 B.C.–A.D. 337* (1993).

This is a collection of papers written during the past twenty-five years on the related themes describe above. They are concerned with Judaea, Jews in Judaea and with the Near East under Roman rule. The army as an instrument of control occurs in many of them and hence papers are included, dealing with the army in general. Some of the essays here re-published, appeared originally in less-accessible venues and it is hoped that the collection as a whole will be considered useful. To enhance its possible usefulness postscripts have been provided with up-to-date bibliography and some discussion of recent trends or new material. I have not included here articles that were clearly superseded by subsequent publications and a few which are no longer relevant.

It might be interesting briefly to consider one of the papers which I excluded, because it illustrates how quickly archaeology can make an apparently well-researched paper irrelevant.[1] At the time of writing it was generally accepted that the road from Gaza to Petra was not used in the second and third centuries, that is, it was used in the first century, when the region was part of the Nabataean kingdom and not after its annexation as a Roman province, in 106. The pottery found on the sites of the road was dated by all the archaeologists who studied it as material of the first century A.D. or a little earlier. There was no pottery dating after the first century.[2] Yet, along at least one section of this road milestones have been found (two milestones per milestation) and the road had all the characteristics of Roman roads in this region. This was sometimes explained by the assumption that the Nabataeans placed milestones along their road under Roman influence. I found this hard to believe and suggested another explanation, equally hypothetical, but more in line with my views on the difference between client kingdoms and Roman provinces. It seemed possible that there had been a temporary presence in Arabia, early in the first century, which had been responsible for the organization of at least one main road from the Mediterranean coast to Petra. This was not entirely original. Mommsen already observed that 'a centurion with troops' was reported to have been

---

[1] 'Trade Routes to Arabia and the Roman Army' in W.S. Hanson & L.J.F. Keppie, *Roman Frontier Studies, 1979* (Oxford, BAR, Int. Series, 1980), 889–901.

[2] A. Negev, *PEQ* 98 (1966), 89–98, whose conclusion was generally accepted. Doubts were expressed by G.W. Bowersock, 'A Report on Arabia Provincia', *JRS* 61 (1971), 219–42, at 239–40.

stationed in the Nabataean Red Sea port of Leuke Kome (*Periplus Maris Erythraei* 19) and, assuming this to have been a Roman centurion, he concluded that Roman troops patrolled the caravan-road from the Red Sea to Gaza via Petra.[3] Thus it seemed possible that what Mommsen deduced from a literary source, had been confirmed by archaeological evidence.

It is now clear that the question was correct, as was the feeling of unease that led to it, but my hypothesis was not. Several of the sites along the road were excavated, and it became absolutely clear that the road remained in use at least till the early third century.[4] It was true indeed that the milestones were not Nabataean, but Roman. Not true proved the speculation of an early, temporary Roman presence in the area, for the road was just as Roman and of roughly the same date as other Roman roads in the area, the second-third century, when they were laid out in well-established Roman provinces. Also, it should be noted that there is by no means a concensus that the centurion in Leuke Kome was indeed Roman. He probably was Nabataean. Another related development—in a field which is not mine—is a tendency now to reconsider the date of Nabataean pottery. In the past this was believed not to have been produced in the second century, but this is no longer accepted. There is a lesson in this for those who think it easy, as I did at the time, to use artefacts for historical interpretation. Historical interpretation of artefacts in the study of the Roman frontier areas is all to often fed by easy assumptions and chains of shaky hypotheses.

Many of the papers in this collection represent efforts to obtain with due caution and correct methodology significant information from inscriptions, archaeological material and literary documents. Not all may have been successful, and if there was criticism after publication, this is explicitly and fully cited in the postscripts (for instance: Nos. 7, 9 and 13). Other postscrips serve to reinforce or clarify specific points in matters of ongoing debate (Bandits, No. 10; the meaning of *Limes*, No. 23).

The preparation of this volume was one of the activities made possible by the tenure of a generous Overseas Fellowship at Churchill College, Cambridge.

Cambridge, July 1997

---

[3] T. Mommsen, *Römische Geschichte* (Berlin, 1845–46), 479 with n. 30.
[4] R. Cohen, *Biblical Archaeologist* 45 (1982), 240–7.

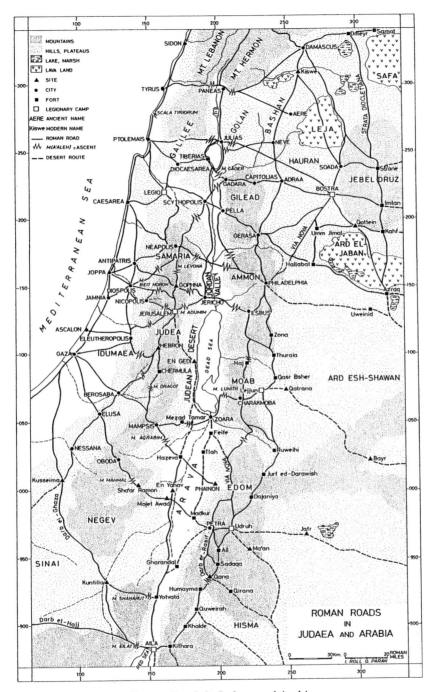

Roman Roads in Judaea and Arabia

HELLENISTIC AND HERODIAN PALESTINE

1

A SELEUCID INSCRIPTION FROM JAMNIA-ON-THE-SEA:
ANTIOCHUS V EUPATOR AND THE SIDONIANS*

In December 1986 a fragmentary inscription (Fig. 1) was discovered by Aharon Sadeh on the site of ancient Jamnia-on-the-Sea (Yavne-Yam), 1 km south of modern Kibbutz Palmahim.[1] The inscription is incised on a block of local limestone.[2] Two small fragments belonging to it were found shortly afterwards; these are also shown in the photograph. The inscription can be read easily and consists of 15 lines of fairly regular lettering marked by guidelines.[3]

Comments on the Reading

Line 2

Βασιλεὺς Ἀν]τίοχος. For the restoration, cf. C. Habicht, *HSCP* 8 (1976), 5 n. 7; Josephus: *Ant.* XII, 5, 5 (258); the Hefzibah inscription (below), 1.8, 18.

Line 3

τὸ κατακεχωρισμέ[νον ὑπόμνημα]: cf. Josephus: *Ant.* XII, 5, 5 (262); C.B. Welles: *The Royal Correspondence in the Hellenistic Period*, New Haven, 1934, No. 70, ll. 2–3.

  * Aharon Sadeh, who allowed me to publish this inscription, passed away suddenly while this article was in press. He spent many years actively exploring the site of Yavne-Yam and its vicinity, and this paper is dedicated to his memory.
  I further want to record the generous assistance afforded by Peter Fraser and Christian Habicht. I have also profited from conversations and correspondence with Bezalel Bar-Kochva, Moshe Fischer, Dov Gera, Aryeh Kasher, Fergus Millar, Israel Shatzman and Alla Stein.
  [1] The stone is now in the museum of the kibbutz and is registered as No. 583614 in the files of the Israel Antiquities Authority.
  [2] Maximum measurements 33 cm × 23 cm.
  [3] The average height of the lettering is 1 cm; the average distance between the lines is 0.5 cm.

Plate 1. A fragmentary inscription from Jamnia-on-the-Sea

1. —]αλμε[. . .
   [Βασιλεὺς ᾿Αν]τίοχος Νέσσωι χαίρειν· παρὰ [τῶν ἐν τῶι τῆς ᾿Ιαμνίας]
   λιμένι Σιδ]ωνίων ἐδόθη τὸ κατακεχωρισμέ[νον ὑπόμνημα. ἐπει-
4. δὴ . . . 6 . . κ]αί οἱ δεδηλωμένοι εἰσίν ἀτελεῖς [. . . . 14 . . . .]
   . . . ὅπω]ς καὶ οὗτοι τῶν αὐτῶν φιλανθρώπων [ἀπολαύωνται.
   ἔρρωσο] vac. 26–7 θμρ' Λωί[ου . . . .]
   Βασιλε]ῖ ᾿Αντιόχωι Εὐπατόρι ὑπόμνημα παρὰ [τῶν ἐν τῶι τῆς ᾿Ιαμ-]
8. [νίας λιμ]ένι Σιδωνίων· πολλὰς χρείας παρεισχημ[ένων . . . . . .]
   [. . . τῶ]ι πάππωι ἐν τοῖς κατὰ τὴν ναυτικὴν χρει[αν—]
   [—τοῖς] ἐπιτασσομένοις ἀόκνως αὐτοὺς ἐπ[ήνεσε . . . 9 . . .]
   . . . 7 . . . τὸν πατ]έρα σοῦ πρόαγον εἰς τοὺς καταιγ[—]
12. —]ΔΕΧΑΤ[. . . .]ΤΩΝΓΕΝ[—
    —]ΑΤΩΝΔ[—
    —]ΝΤΗΣΔ[—
    —]ΟΥ[—

Lines 4–5
For instance: [. . . 11. . . ., ἴδε] [οὖν ὅπω]ς or [. . . . 8 . . . . προνοή / θητι ὅπω]ς, for which cf. *ibid.*, 37.10.

Line 7
Βασιλε]ῖ ᾿Αντιόχωι: cf. Josephus: *Ant.* XII, 5, 5 (258).

Lines 7–8
Tentative restoration on the assumption that the Sidonians referred to resided where the inscription was found: τῶν ἐν τῶι τῆς ᾿Ιαμνείας λιμ]ένι Σιδωνίων; cf. Josephus: *Ant.* XII, 5, 5 (258): παρὰ τῶν ἐν Σικίμοις Σιδωνίων. *OGIS* 593: τῶν ἐν Μαρίσει Σιδωνίων.

Lines 8–9
Possibly: πολλὰς χρείας παρεισχημ[ένων τῶν προ-] / [γόνων τῶ]ι πάππωι ἐν τοῖς τὴν κατὰ τὴν ναυτικὴν χρε[ίαν, πειθομένων] / [πᾶσι τοῖς] (Habicht).

Line 11
[. . . 7 . . .]τὸν πατ]έρα σου προαγον εἰς τοὺς κατ᾿ Αἴγ[υπτον τόπους] (Habicht).

Partial Translation

'[King An]tiochus to Nessos, greetings. The recorded petition was submitted by [the Sid]onians [in the Port of Jamnia]. Since . . . the . . . referred to are [also] immune . . . so that they will also enjoy the same privileges. Farewell. Loos 149.'

'Petition to [King] Antiochus Eupator from the Sidonians in the [Port of Jamnia]. Since [their ancestors] rendered many services to his grandfather, promptly obeying [all] instructions regarding naval service. . . .'

The Lettering

Peter Fraser points out that the palaeography of the inscription is of interest since it reveals features not found in traditional hands of the Hellenistic period, and given the exact date, this is worthy of consideration. Note the θ, the high Ω, the tiny omicrons and the legless Υ. This confirms the point he has made about the hands of Hellenistic inscriptions of Syria and Palestine: that they foreshadow imperial styles (see: *Berytus* 13 [1960], 125 ff. à propos of *SEG* XX 665, there published).

Comments on the Text

The surviving text records fragments of a dossier consisting of a letter and a *hypomnema* (petition). Since Line 2 is the beginning of one letter, Line 1 may be all that survives of the end of a preceding document. Alternatively, this may be the end of the preamble to the entire text. Lines 2–6 form one letter; Lines 7 and following form a second. The original text may have contained any number of documents, but here there are only two that can be discussed.[4] From the contents it is obvious that they appear in inverse chronological order, for the first letter clearly refers to the second. For the sake of convenience I shall refer henceforth to Lines 1–6 as 'Letter A' and to Lines 7–15 as 'Letter B.' Letter A is dated to the month Loos of year 149 of the Seleucid calendar, i.e. June–July 163 B.C.E.[5] The second letter must therefore have been written before that date. If Line 1 is the end of another letter this must have been written afterwards. The date is further corroborated by the occurrence in Line 7 of the name of King Antiochus (V) Eupator, who ruled from 164 to 162 B.C.E.[6]

For the sake of clarity I shall discuss the documents in chronological order, i.e. starting with Letter B. It must be conceded at the outset that what survives of the inscription does not permit the reconstruction of a consecutive text and translation.

---

[4] The inscription from Hefzibah records nine letters written over a period of seven years: J.H. Landau: A Greek Inscription Found near Hefzibah, *IEJ* 16 (1966), pp. 54–70; J. and L. Robert: *Bulletin épigraphique* (1970), p. 627; *ibid.* (1971), p. 73; *ibid.* (1974), pp. 642, 642a; T. Fischer: Zur Seleukideninschrift von Hefzibah, *Zeitschrift für Papyrologie und Epigraphik* 33 (1979), pp. 131–138; J.M. Bertrand: Sur l'inscription d'Hefzibah, *Zeitschrift für Papyrologie und Epigraphik* 46 (1982), pp. 167–174.

[5] Loos is the tenth month of the Seleucid calendar and the equivalent of *Tammuz* (fourth month), which usually falls in June–July.

[6] For the dates, see E. Schürer in G. Vermes and F. Millar (eds): *The History of the Jewish People in the Age of Jesus Christ*, I, Edinburgh, 1973, p. 129; statements relating to the duration of his reign vary from a year and a half in Porphyry: *Fragmente der griechischen Historiker*, No. 244, in the summary of Eusebius: *Chronicon*, Schoene (ed.), I, 263–264, to two years in Josephus: *Ant.* II, 10, 1 (390). Antiochus IV Epiphanes, his father, died in the autumn of 164 B.C.E. The latest example of dating by his reign, in cuneiform tablets, is 16 October, 162 B.C.E. See R.A. Parker and W.H. Dubberstein: *Babylonian Chronology 626 B.C.–A.D. 75*, Chicago, 1956, p. 23.

Letter B
Lines 7–9. 'Petition to [King] Antiochus Eupator from the Sidonians in the [Port of Jamnia].[7] Since [their ancestors] rendered many services to his grandfather, promptly obeying [all] instructions regarding naval service. . . .'

Lines 10–11. Probably mentions the king's father, Antiochus Epiphanes, and his invasion of Egypt.

Letter A
This letter represents the reply from the King.

Lines 2–3. '[King An]tiochus to Nessos, greetings. The recorded petition was submitted by [the Sid]onians [in the Port of Jamnia].'

Line 4. In '. . . the . . . referred to are immune', the king mentions a group of people who enjoy immunity from some form of taxation. This serves as a precedent for the decision that appears in Line 5.

Line 5. '. . . they [the Sidonians in the Port of Jamnia] will also enjoy the same privileges'.

Line 6. The date: 'Loos 149.'

Any interpretation of the text will have to be based on these elements. Letter B is a petition from some Sidonians, probably those residing at 'the Port of Jamnia'—i.e. Jamnia-on-the-Sea—to King Antiochus V. It is not dated, but must precede the reply, Letter A, dating from June–July 163 B.C.E. The petitioners claim that [their ancestors] promptly assisted Antiochus III in naval matters.[8] They probably also mention their own services to the king's father, Antiochus Epiphanes. Letter A is addressed by the king to Nessos, an unknown official, and affirms that someone referred to enjoys immunity from taxation. This cannot refer to the petitioners, for the king then informs Nessos that 'they', presumably the petitioners, 'will also enjoy

---

[7] As noted in the comments above, the place name 'The Port of Jamnia' has been restored on grounds of probability. The name could in principle have been any ending in -ην. However, in view of the contents of the letter this must have been a settlement with a harbour, and I can think of no other suitable place name on the eastern Mediterranean shore; there is none in F.-M. Abel: *Géographie de la Palestine*, Paris, 1967 (3rd ed.), or M. Avi-Yonah: *Gazetteer of Roman Palestine*, Jerusalem, 1976.

[8] There is little point in speculating which naval campaign is meant, as there are several possibilities.

the same privileges'. These concessions are clearly connected with taxation. It is possible, but not certain, that the petitioners were to render naval services instead of levies in kind or cash. The extant part of the king's letter (A) does not mention the services to King Antiochus III, to which the petitioners themselves refer in Letter B.

Historical Comments

Late Seleucid texts are rare and the best parallel for these letters is the correspondence, recorded by Josephus, between the Sidonians in Shechem (*Sikhem*) and Antiochus IV.[9] There are expressions which occur in both the new inscription and the documents cited by Josephus. This is important because it reinforces the arguments of those who claim that Josephus' documents are basically authentic.[10] Both the petition of the Sidonians in Shechem and the king's reply begin with phrases similar to those in the new inscription:

> Josephus: *Ant.* XII, 5, 5 (258):
> βασιλεῖ Ἀντιόχῳ θεῷ ἐπιφανεῖ ὑπόμνημα παρὰ
> τῶν ἐν Σικίμοις Σιδωνίων.
>
> *Ibid.* (262):
> βασιλεὺς Ἀντίοχος Νικάνορι. οἱ ἐν Σικίμοις Σιδώνιοι ἐπέδωκαν τὸ
> κατακεχωρισμένον ὑπόμνημα.

The king's reply cited by Josephus states explicitly that the petition was submitted by a delegation of Sidonians which appeared in Shechem before the king sitting in council.[11] The same probably happened in the case of the Sidonians in Jamnia-on-the-Sea. More important is the recurrence of 'Sidonians in . . .' in both texts. In the documents quoted by Josephus this is the central element in the petition. The Sidonians in Shechem ask not to be treated like Jews

---

[9] Josephus: *Ant.* XII, 5, 5 (258–264).
[10] In favour of authenticity, see E. Bickerman: Un document relatif à la persécution d'Antiochos Épiphane, *Revue de l'histoire des religions* 115 (1937), pp. 188–223 (reprinted as *Studies in Jewish and Christian History* II, Leiden, 1980, pp. 105–135), followed by scholars cited below, n. 45.
[11] Josephus: *Ant.* XII, 5, 5 (263):

> ἐπεὶ οὖν συμβουλευομένοις ἡμῖν μετὰ τῶν φίλων παρέστησαν οἱ πεμφθέντες ὑπ' αὐτῶν. . . .

Also: (258).

because they are Sidonians by origin and have different customs.[12] The king grants their request because they 'live in accordance with Greek customs.'[13] It appears that a somewhat similar argument was used by the petitioners responsible for the new text: they were granted the same concessions as other people (Letter A), presumably because they had previously rendered (naval) services similar to those rendered by the others (Letter B). In any case, the essential fact remains that Sidonians are attested to in both Jamnia-on-the-Sea and Schechem, who claim and receive special favours from two Seleucid kings because of their loyalty towards two or three kings.

The next point to be considered is whether any of the events known to have taken place in this period are immediately relevant for an understanding of the inscription. It is natural to assume that there was some connection with the wars of the Maccabees, but the chronology of the events during the reign of Eupator is unclear because the accounts in I and II Maccabees diverge.[14] An episode of particular interest in this context is the attack of Judah on Jaffa and the Port of Jamnia, described only in II Maccabees.[15] As related there, the citizens of Jaffa treacherously killed the Jews residing in the town.[16] Judah then set fire to the harbour and ships, and killed anybody he

---

[12] *Ibid.* (260):

ὄντων ἡμῶν τὸ ἀνέκαθεν Σιδωνίων· . . . ἡμῶν καὶ τῷ γένει καὶ τοῖς
ἔθεσιν ἀλλοτρίων ὑπαρχόντων.

In *Ant.* XI, 8, 6 (344) they are cited as claiming to be 'Hebrews', called the Sidonians in Shechem, but not 'Jews'.

[13] *Idem: Ant.* XII, 5, 5 (263):

ὅτι μηδὲν τοῖς τῶν Ἰουδαίων ἐγκλήμασι προσήκουσιν, ἀλλὰ
τοῖς Ἑλληνικοῖς ἔθεσιν αἱροῦνται χρώμενοι ζῆν. . . .

[14] For discussion, see K. Bringmann: *Hellenistische Reform und Religionsverfolgung: Eine Untersuchung zur jüdisch-hellenistischen Geschichte, 175–167 v. Chr.*, Göttingen, 1983, pp. 51–60.

[15] II Macc. 12:3–9. This is followed by an account of Judah's campaign in Gilead, 12:10–31, described also in the parallel sources: I Macc. 5:18–19, 55–62; Josephus: *Ant.* XII, 8, 6 (350–352). Simon marched to Galilee, Judah to Gilead. In the same period Joseph son of Zekhariah and Azariah were repulsed by Gorgias at Jamnia. For the account in II Macc., cf. C. Habicht: *2 Makkabaerbuch, Jüdische Schriften aus hellenistisch-römischer Zeit*, I, Gütersloh, 1976, pp. 261–262. For the campaign in Gilead, see B. Bar-Kochva: *Judas Maccabaeus: The Jewish Struggle Against the Seleucids*, Cambridge, 1989, pp. 512–515.

[16] As observed by Habicht (above, n. 15), p. 261 on 12:3: the terminology τοὺς σὺν αὐτοῖς οἰκοῦντας Ἰουδαίους shows that the Jews in Jaffa were not citizens (*politai*), but resident aliens, and the same is true for the phrase used in II Macc. 12:8 to describe the Jews in Jamnia: τοῖς παροικοῦσιν Ἰουδαίοις.

caught outside the walls. Upon being informed that the Jamnites also intended to kill their Jews, he punished them in similar fashion.

The element which recurs in both II Maccabees and in the inscription is the reference to a fleet, but there is nothing in the inscription to suggest that Jamnia had suffered the loss of its fleet at that time, and there is no obvious connection between the text and the attack by Judah the Maccabee. The attacks on Jaffa and Jamnia-on-the-Sea may have taken place after June or July 163 B.C.E., i.e. after the inscription was set up.

It appears from the inscription that the Sidonians rendered services to the grandfather of Eupator, Antiochus III, and it is possible that the text implies that they did the same for Antiochus IV Epiphanes during his invasion of Egypt (around 170–168 B.C.E.),[17] and were to do so again for Eupator in 163 B.C.E.[18]

It seems advisable to conclude that although various possibilities may be legitimately considered, no precise connection can be found between the contents of the inscription and any of the known stages in the wars of Judah the Maccabee. No claim can be made, therefore, that the inscription provides new factual information on the course of events in those wars. The inscription is nonetheless instructive because of the light it sheds on the presence of Phoenician settlers in Judaea in general, and in Jamnia in particular.

Jamnia and the Sidonians

Philo of Byblos says that Jamnia was a city in Phoenicia,[19] and Philo of Alexandria describes Jamnia in the first century C.E. as 'one of

---

[17] See C. Habicht's restoration of Line 11 (above, n. 15).

[18] We know only the date of Eupator's reply, but not that of the petition, which was made some time before June–July 163 B.C.E. The inscription may have been set up quite some time after the dispatch of the royal letter. All this makes it doubtful whether we can establish any precise historical context for the inscription.

[19] Herennius Philo of Byblos, *ap.* Stephanus Byz., s.v. Ἰόπη (M. Stern: *Greek and Latin Authors on Jews and Judaism*, II, Jerusalem, 1980, p. 143, No. 327):

Ἰόπη πόλις Φοινίκης πλησίον Ἰαμνίας ὡς Φίλων, ὡς δὲ Διονύσιος

'Iope, according to Philo, is situated in Phoenicia in the vicinity of Jamnia. According to Dionysius it is situated in Palaestina.' On Jamnia, see Schürer (above, n. 6), II, pp. 109–110; Abel (above, n. 7), II, pp. 352–353; Stern, I, pp. 292–293. For Sidon in the Persian period, see J. Elayi: *Sidon, cité autonome de l'Empire Perse*, Paris, 1989.

the most populous towns of Judaea, inhabited by a mixed people, most of them being Jews, while others are gentiles, intruders from neighbouring communities. . . .'[20] Strabo also comments that the region 'was once so densely populated that the village of Jamnia and the settlements in the vicinity could provide forty thousand men'.[21]

These authors presumably meant inland Jamnia. As observed by Schürer, only Pliny and Ptolemy clearly distinguish between inland Jamnia and Jamnia on the coast.[22] The discovery of the new inscription on the site of Jamnia-on-the-Sea raises the question of the relationship between the two sites. Since an official inscription was set up near the harbour it must be asked whether there already existed two separate settlements with the Sidonian community being confined to the coast. This is not likely, however, for the Books of the Maccabees do not distinguish between the two. Jamnia appears to have been quite important as a centre of support for the Seleucid army, for it is mentioned three times as headquarters of base[23] and once again in II Maccabees as the target of the action of Judah, mentioned above. The description in II Maccabees mentions the town of Jamnia and its harbour without suggesting that the two are separate

---

[20] Philo: *Legatio ad Gaium* 30 (200):

τὴν Ἰάμνειαν—πόλις δέ ἐστι τῆς Ἰουδαίας ἐν τοῖς μάλιστα πολυάνθρωπος—[ταύτην] μιγάδες οἰκοῦσιν, οἱ πλείους μὲν Ἰουδαῖοι, ἕτεροι δέ τινες ἀλλόφυλοι παρεισφθάρεντες ἀπὸ τῶν πλησιοχώρων. . . .

Philo goes on to describe the hatred between Jews and gentiles in Jamnia at that time. He is mistaken in calling the gentiles 'intruders who had moved in to the detriment of the existing population' and *metoikoi*, for II Macc., as noted above (n. 16), describes the Jews as resident aliens in Jamnia. This, however, was before the conquest by Alexander Jannaeus, Josephus: *Ant.* XIII, 15, 4 (395), and the resettlement by Gabinius, Josephus: *War* I, 8, 4 (166). It is clear that by the first century the number of Jews had increased substantially.

[21] Strabo XVI, 2, 28 (758). It goes without saying that we should not take the number 40,000 seriously in itself. Strabo (followed by Stern [above n. 19], II, p. 293) also errs in calling Jamnia a village, for Philo (above, no. 20) refers to it as a town and Josephus: *War* III, 3, 5 (56), says that Jamnia and Jaffa 'administer the surrounding area.' The inscription cited below (n. 25) also proves that Jamnia had city status, as pointed out to me by Aharon Sadeh.

[22] Pliny: *NH* V 13: '*Iamneae duae, altera intus*'; Ptolemy V, 15, 2 (Nobbe):

Ἰάμνιτῶν λιμήν ξε' L' λβ'.

Ptolemy V, 16, 6 (Nobbe): Ἰάμνια ξε' γο" λβ' (Stern, II, pp. 166–167, No. 337a).

[23] First in 163 as the headquarters of Gorgias, the *strategos* of Idumaea, during an unsuccessful attack by Joseph son of Zekhariah and Azariah: I Macc. 5:18–19, 55–62; Josephus: *Ant.* XII, 8, 6 (350–352). Next as base of Apollonius in 147: I Macc. 10:69. Finally in 139–138 as the base of Cendebaeus, who incited the local population to make incursions into Judaea proper: I Macc. 15:40.

entities, although they were 8 km apart. As Bezalel Bar-Kochva pointed out to me, Sidonians in Jamnia-on-the-Sea almost certainly formed a *politeuma*, while it is possible that in inland Jamnia other *politeumata* were settled.

The gentile character of the place is emphasized in II Maccabees, where 'amulets of the idols from Jamnia' are mentioned as typical idol-atrous cult-objects,[24] and a dedication from Delos shows that these idols were related to the Phoenician cult: 'To Heracles and Hauronas, the gods who dwell in Jamnia, Zenodorus, Patron, Diodotus, Jamnitai, on behalf of themselves, their brothers, relatives and the citizens with them, a thank-offering. Everything may be sacrificed except goat.'[25] Heracles is familiar as the Hellenistic variant or equivalent of the Phoenician Melqart.[26] Hauron was apparently a local or regional deity.[27]

Neither inland Jamnia nor Jamnia-on-the-Sea has been excavated systematically. The discovery of the new inscription shows that the latter is a site of interest in its own right, and incidental exploration of this site and others in the vicinity confirm this impression. In the 1950s a survey of the area proved that the site was mainly occupied in three stages: the Middle Bronze Age, the Persian and Hellenistic

---

[24] II Macc. 12:40–45. Cf. Habicht (above, n. 15), 265; I. Lévy: Les dieux de Iamneia, in *Recherches esséniennes et pythagoriciennes*, Geneva and Paris, 1965, pp. 65–69.

[25] A. Plassart: *Les sanctuaires et les cultes du Mont Cynthe à Délos*, Paris, 1928, pp. 278–282; P. Roussel: *Corpus des inscriptions de Délos*, Paris, 1937, No. 2308; W.F. Albright: The Canaanite God Hauron (Hôrôn), *The American Journal of Semitic Languages and Literatures* 53 (1936), pp. 1–12; I. Lévy (above, n. 24); P. Bruneau: *Recherches sur les cultes de Délos à l'époque hellénistique et l'époque impériale*, Paris, 1970, p. 475:

Ἡρακλῆ καὶ Αὑρώνᾳ, θεοῖς Ἰάμνειαν κατέχουσιν, Ζηνόδωρος, Πάτρων, Διόδοτος Ἰαμνῖται ὑπὲρ ἑαυτῶν καὶ ἀδελφῶν καὶ συνγε[ν]ῶν καὶ τῶν συ[ν]όντων πολί[τ]ων χαριστήριον. θύειν πάντα πλὴν αἰγείου.

Another inscription (No. 2309) found on the same spot in Delos also mentions Heracles. Cf. C. Bonnet: *Melqart: Cultes et mythes de l'Héraclès Tyrien en Méditerranée* (Studia Phoenica VIII), Leuven-Namur, 1988, esp. pp. 129–131. See on this also A. Kasher: *Jews and Hellenistic Cities in Eretz-Israel*, Tübingen, 1990, p. 40. These discoveries attest to the commercial activity of the two citizens of Jamnia.

[26] Lucian: *de dea Syria*, p. 3; M.G. Guzzo Amadasi: *Le iscrizioni fenicie e puniche delle colonie in Occidente*, Rome, 1967, pp. 15–16, No. 1: a bilingual dedication in Malta made by two Tyrian brothers to Heracles/Melqart in Phoenician and Greek. On Melqart, see W. Röllig: *Wörterbuch der Mythologie* I, 2 Stuttgart, no date, pp. 297–298; Bonnet (above, n. 25).

[27] It occurs, for instance, in the place name Beth Horon, as first suggested by I. Lévy to A. Plassart (above, n. 25). A 'Beth Horon', i.e. a temple of Horon, is mentioned on an ostracon from Tell Qasile. See B. Maisler (Mazar): Two Hebrew Ostraca from Tell Qasile, *JNES* 19 (1951), pp. 265–267, esp. p. 266. Finally, a text from Ras Shamra mentions "Horon of Yavne': see C. Virolleaud: *CRAIBL*, 1936, p. 237.

periods, and the Roman and Byzantine periods.[28] Rescue excavations recently uncovered the remains of a Byzantine building near the seashore.[29] During further excavations on the same spot a trench was cut which uncovered the walls of a considerable building, occupied apparently in the Hellenistic period, quite close to the find-spot of the new inscription.[30] There is also some support for the insistence of several ancient authors on the populousness of the area: the survey carried out in the 1950s gave the impression of dense settlement from the Persian to the Byzantine periods. At Tel Yaʿoz (Tell Ghazza), 4 km north-east of Yavne-Yam, a survey and trial excavations uncovered another substantial settlement occupied in the Hellenistic period.[31] It may be assumed that the major site in the area was ancient Jamnia (Yavne) itself, but so far this has not been explored systematically.[32] To sum up, there is good reason to believe that archaeological excavation would produce information on the nature of Sidonian settlement in this particular area.

Finally, we must consider the presence of Sidonians in Judaea in a wider context. There is no need to discuss here the various cultural, administrative or commercial ties between the Phoenician cities and Judaea.[33] Grants of city status or the refoundation of cities are also

---

[28] M. Dothan: An Archaeological Survey of the Lower Rubin River, *IEJ* 2 (1952), pp. 104–117; note also the aerial photograph of the site published by A. Reifenberg: Archaeological Discoveries by Air Photography in Israel, *Archaeology* 3 (1950), pp. 40–46, esp. p. 45. For excavations of the Middle Bronze Age layers, see J. Kaplan: *IEJ* 17 (1967), p. 269; 19 (1969), pp. 120–122; *ZDPV* 91 (1975), pp. 1–17; summary in M. Avi-Yonah and E. Stern (eds.): *EAEHL*, IV, Jerusalem, 1978, 1216–1218, s.v. Yavneh-Yam. See also E. Stern: *The Material Culture of the Land of the Bible in the Persian Period 538–332 B.C.E.*, Warminster, 1982, p. 22.

[29] F. Vitto: Jamnitarum Portus, *Qadmoniot* 17 (1984), pp. 76–78 (Hebrew): a mosaic was uncovered, perhaps from a fifth-century bathhouse fed by an aqueduct seen nearby. Under the mosaic floor there was a wall dated by a Rhodian amphora-handle and a Hasmonaean coin.

[30] Y. Levi: *Ḥadashot Arkheologiyot* 92 (1988), pp. 33–34 (Hebrew). I am indebted to Aharon Sadeh for information on the site. He showed me sherds and coins, including Sidonian ones, collected on the surface, which reinforce the impression of occupation in the Persian period and afterwards.

[31] *Ḥadashot Arkheologiyot* 77 (1981), pp. 30–31 (Hebrew) and a forthcoming paper by I. Roll.

[32] The literary evidence for the importance of Yavne in the Roman period and archaeological remains of the later periods are not relevant here, but it is worth noting that a fort, established by settlers or traders of Greek origin in the last third of the seventh century B.C.E., was excavated at Meṣad Ḥashavyahu, 1.7 km south of Yavne-Yam: J. Naveh: Yavne-Yam, *EAEHL*, III, pp. 862–863; R. Reich: A Third Season of Excavations at Meṣad Ḥashavyahu, *EI* 20 (1989), pp. 228–232 (Hebrew).

[33] On all this, see Stern (above, n. 28).

irrelevant. What is pertinent is the presence of Hellenized people who called themselves Sidonians and who may therefore be considered to have been settlers, or the descendants of settlers, who established themselves in Judaea in sufficient numbers to preserve a common identity. For this purpose we may ignore sites in modern Israel which belonged to Phoenicia in antiquity.[34]

The first question is whether there is any evidence indicating when Phoenician settlers arrived in these parts. On his sarcophagus Eshmun'azar of Sidon claims that 'the Lord of Kings [the king of Persia] gave us Dor and Joppa, the mighty lands of Dagon, which are in the plain of Sharon, in accordance with the important deeds which I did. And we added them to the borders of our country, so that they would belong to Sidon forever.'[35] This inscription is now known to date from the Achaemenid period (late sixth century). It must be noted that this text does not tell us anything about settlement, but only about jurisdiction or possession.

The next piece of evidence is the fourth-century work known as the *Periplus* of Pseudo-Scylax. In the description of the Palestinian coast Dor is mentioned as a city of the Sidonians and Ashkelon as a city of the Tyrians, and seat of a royal palace.[36] Perhaps the wording of Pseudo-Scylax should be explained as a reference to actual settlement of Phoenicians. For Dor, indeed, there are other literary sources which describe it as a Phoenician town,[37] and two Phoenician inscriptions have been found on the site.[38] One other relevant piece

---

[34] On the coast the traditional boundary between Judaea and Phoenicia was Mt. Carmel. Josephus: *War* III, 3, 1 (35), assigns Mt. Carmel to Tyre while asserting that, in the past, it belonged to Galilee. The *Itinerarium Burdigalense* 584:8–585:4 (O. Cuntz [ed.]: *Itineraria Romana*, Leipzig, 1929, p. 94), explicitly marks the border between the provinces of Syria Phoenice and Palaestina at Certha (Kh. Kastri), 13 km south of Sicaminos (Shiqmona) and an equal distance north of Caesarea.

[35] H. Donner and W. Röllig: *Kanaanäische und aramäische Inschriften*, Wiesbaden, 1962, No. 14, l.20 (translation, F. Rosenthal in *ANET*, p. 662).

[36] Pseudo-Scylax in C. Müller (ed.): *Geographi graeci minores*, I, p. 79; Stern (above, n. 19), III, No. 558, pp. 8–12. The text is corrupt, but there certainly was a reference to Jaffa:

Δῶρος πόλις Σιδωνίων· ['Ιόππη πόλις· ἐκτε]θῆναί φασιν ἐνταῦθα τὴν
'Ανδρομ[έδαν τῷ κήτει·Ἀσκά]λων τόλις Τυρίων καὶ βασίλεια. Ἐνταῦ[θα ὄρος
ἐστὶ τῆς Κοίλης] Συρίας.

For a Phoenician inscribed weight from Ashkelon, see below, n. 42.

[37] Claudius Iolaus in Stephanus Byz., s.v.; Josephus: *Vita* 8 (31); *idem: Contra Apionem* II 9 (116).

[38] B. Delavault and A. Lemaire: Les inscriptions phéniciennes de Palestine, *Rivista*

of evidence is the original name of Caesarea: Straton's Tower, now usually explained as indicating that it was first established by one of the two Sidonian kings of that name, Straton ('Abd 'ashtart) I and II, who both reigned in the fourth century.[39] A Phoenician inscription of uncertain authenticity is said to have been found at Nebi Yunis (near modern Ashdod), between Jamnia-on-the-Sea and ancient Ashdod-on-the-Sea. It has been ascribed to the fifth or fourth century B.C.E.[40] Potsherds from Apollonia (Arsuf) incised with Phoenician characters seem to date to the same period.[41] Finally, a jar with a Phoenician inscription was found in a cave in modern Bat-Yam, south of Jaffa.[42] Yet it must be emphasized that isolated finds, however interesting in their own right, are not proof of organized or large-scale settlement by Sidonians.

This is all the evidence for the pre-Hellenistic presence of Phoenicians in Judaea. Admittedly, it does not get us very far, and, indeed, leaves us with a gap of several centuries.[43] Moreover, the Phoenicians

---

di Studi Fenici 7 (1979), pp. 18–19, No. 39; J. Naveh: Unpublished Phoenician Inscriptions from Palestine, *IEJ* 37 (1987), pp. 25–30, esp. p. 26, No. 2.

[39] Schürer (above, n. 6), II, p. 115 and cf. L. Levine: A propos de la fondation de la Tour de Straton, *RB* 80 (1973), pp. 75–81.

[40] B. Delavault and A. Lemaire: Une stèle 'molk' de Palestine dediée à Eshmoun? RES 367 reconsideré, *RB* 83 (1976), pp. 569–583; *idem* (above, n. 38), pp. 24–26, No. 48. The editors observe that Eshmûn was greatly honoured in Sidon. On the same site was found an Aramaic ostracon probably inscribed with a Phoenician personal name. See F.M. Cross: An Ostracon from Nebi Yunis, *IEJ* 14 (1964), pp. 185–186.

[41] S. Yizre'el: Appendix 2 in I. Roll and E. Ayalon: *Apollonia and Southern Sharon: Model of a Coastal City and its Hinterland*, Tel Aviv, 1989, pp. 259–267 (Hebrew). One of the two sherds contains a reference to Eshmûn (above, n. 40), perhaps as part of a theophoric name.

[42] B. Peckham: An Inscribed Jar from Bat-Yam, *IEJ* 16 (1966), pp. 11–17; Delavault and Lemaire (above, n. 38), p. 22, No. 45, dated on palaeographical grounds to the second half of the fourth century B.C.E.; ostraca from Eilat of the fifth or fourth century: *ibid.*, pp. 28–29, Nos. 56–57; an inscribed weight from Ashkelon: *ibid.*, p. 32, No. 60 (fourth century). To the second half of the fourth century jar inscriptions from Shiqmona are said to belong. See F.M. Cross: Jar Inscriptions from Shiqmona, *IEJ* 18 (1968), pp. 226–233; Delavault and Lemaire, pp. 14–16, Nos. 25–27; Naveh (above, n. 38), p. 28. However, Shiqmona at the foot of Mt. Carmel lies north of the traditional border between Palestine and Phoenicia as defined above (n. 34). Note also Delavault and Lemaire: Nos. 28–38 from other places north of the border of Phoenicia, such as Tel Dan, Akhzib, Hazor etc.; M. Dothan: A Phoenician Inscription from 'Akko, *IEJ* 35 (1985), pp. 81–94; cf. Naveh (above, n. 38) p. 27, citing a Phoenician jar inscription from Saqqara in Egypt which mentions a man from 'Akko. 'Akko was in Phoenicia and is identified as a Tyrian town by Pseudo-Scylax (above, n. 36). Inscriptions earlier than the fifth century need not be considered here.

[43] The impact and nature of Hellenization is hard to trace even in Phoenicia

attested to in this period were, of course, not Hellenized in language or social organization. On the other hand, the presence of Sidonians, but not that of Tyrians, in several places is well documented in later literary sources.

Turning to the Hellenistic period, the important town of Jaffa must be mentioned again.[44] The Sidonian settlement of Shechem can now be considered as more securely attested because the documents quoted by Josephus have features in common with the new inscription,[45] although the excavations carried out there have so far failed to produce unambiguous evidence of a Sidonian presence.[46] The Sidonian settlement at Maresha (Marissa) is known from archaeological and

---

itself. Cf. F. Millar: The Phoenician Cities: A Case-Study of Hellenisation, *Proceedings of the Cambridge Philological Society* 209/29 (1983), pp. 55–71; *idem*: The Problem of Hellenistic Syria, in A. Kuhrt and S. Sherwin-White (eds.): *Hellenism in the East*, London, 1987; pp. 111–133.

[44] Strabo I, 2, 35 (43): 'There are authors who also transfer Ethiopia to Phoenicia in our region and who say that the adventures of Andromeda took place in Iope, and yet these things are not told in ignorance of geography but in the form of a myth': Pliny V 14, 69; *Iope Phoenicum*; Philo of Byblos (above, n. 19); Dionysius Periegetes: Orbis Descriptio, ll. 910–912, in Stern (above, n. 19), III, p. 32, No. 563, first half of second century C.E.: 'Phoenicians inhabit Jaffa and Gaza' etc.; for the association of Jaffa with Andromeda, see Stern, III, index, p. 128. See also Conon the Mythographer, in Stern, I, No. 145, p. 353.

[45] Both A. Alt: *Kleine Schriften*, II, Munich, 1953, p. 398, n. 2, and M. Delcor: Vom Sichem der hellenistischen Epoche zu Sychar des Neuen Testamentes, *ZDPV* 78 (1962), pp. 34–48, argue that we should understand Josephus as referring to a Sidonian settlement in Shechem. Similarly, H.G. Kippenberg: *Gerizim und Synagoge*, Berlin, 1971, pp. 79, 85. This is undoubtedly correct and Bickerman's view (above, n. 10) that this was a reference to Samaritans (southern Canaanites) must be considered untenable. Against Alt/Delcor and in favour of Bickerman's theory, see A. Schalit: Die Denkschrift der Samaritaner an König Antiochos Epiphanes, *Annual Swedish Theological Institute* 8 (1972), pp. 131–183, esp. 134–135; Bringmann (above, n. 14), p. 142, n. 7; M. Mor: The Persian, Hellenistic and Hasmonaean Period, in A.D. Crown: *The Samaritans*, Tübingen, 1989, esp. pp. 14–15. All these authors accept Bickerman's arguments in favour of the authenticity of the document cited by Josephus. There are undoubtedly interpolations in the documents as reproduced by Josephus, but it is now clear that these were inserted in a genuine text of the second century B.C.E.

[46] Two ancient settlements have been found in the immediate vicinity of modern Nablus: at Tell Balāṭa, east of the city, and on Mt. Gerizim to the south. The excavations at Tell Balāṭa have uncovered a settlement occupied in early periods and also in the Hellenistic period until the end of the second century B.C.E. See *EAEHL*, IV, pp. 1083–1094, s.v. Shechem. Recent excavations on Mt. Gerizim have brought to light a town occupied in the second century B.C.E. See Y. Magen: A Fortified Town of the Hellenistic Period on Mount Gerizim, *Qadmoniot* 75–76 (1986), pp. 91–101 (Hebrew); *idem*, unpublished doctorate diss., The Hebrew University of Jerusalem, 1989; *idem*: Mount Gerizim—A Temple City, *Qadmoniot* 91–92 (1990), pp. 70–96 (Hebrew). This settlement was occupied in the period under discussion, but there is no unambiguous evidence as regards the identity of the population.

epigraphic material.[47] The study of the necropolis of this settlement has led to the conclusion that it was in use from the third century B.C.E. onwards.[48] Here again, evidence of pre-Hellenistic Phoenician settlement is lacking and the establishment of the settlers seems to go back to the period of Ptolemaic rule, in which several other settlements in the region were renamed or refounded: Philadelphia (Rabbat 'Ammon), Ptolemais ('Akko), Scythopolis (Beth She'an) and Philoteria (Beth Yeraḥ).[49] An interesting consideration, as pointed out by the editors of the material from Maresha, is that the onomastic material from the tomb inscriptions (all in Greek) contains many Semitic and Idumaean names. Together with the information on Sidonians and the substantial number of regular Greek names, this indicates that various groups co-existed in the area.[50]

Finally, we should note various inscriptions, such as Phoenician jar inscriptions found in Gaza or its vicinity and at Tel Anafa in Upper Galilee.[51] These, however, may be evidence of individual settlement on a private basis, or of import through merchant emporia. The evidence from Galilee is so far unique, and Gaza, being an important port city, could have attracted individual traders.[52] Moreover,

---

[47] *Dictionnaire de la Bible*, Supplément, pp. 336–339, s.v. Fouilles en Palestine; J.-P. Peters and H. Thiersch: *Painted Tombs in the Necropolis of Marissa*, London, 1905, pp. 36–37 (inscriptions); note in particular p. 66: Φιλώτιον Σιδωνίας *OGIS* 593: the tomb of Ἀπολλοφάνης Σεσμαίου ἄρξας τῶν ἐν Μαρίσηι Σιδωνίων. Sesmaios is a Phoenician name. Marissa was another target of Judah: I Macc. 5:66, and, if a textual correction is accepted, II Macc. 12:35. On Maresha, see also Josephus: *Ant*. XIII, 9, 1 (257); XIV, 13, 9 (364); G. Horowitz: The Town Planning of Hellenistic Marisa, *PEQ* 112 (1980), pp. 93–111; E.D. Oren and U. Rappaport: The Necropolis of Maresha-Beth Govrin, *IEJ* 34 (1984), pp. 114–153; G. Fuks: *Scythopolis—A Greek City in Eretz-Israel*, Jerusalem, 1983 (Hebrew), pp. 29–34. The presence of Phoenician settlers in Idumaea is reflected in the statement of an otherwise unknown author named Ptolemy that the Idumaeans were not Jews by origin and birth, but Phoenicians and Syrians: Stern (above, n. 19), I, p. 356, No. 146. Note, finally, the execration (?) text, *SEG* VIII 246; E. Gabba: *Iscrizioni greche e latine per lo studio della Bibbia*, 1958, pp. 33–35, No. X.

[48] Oren and Rappaport (above, n. 47), p. 149; cf. M. Hengel: *Judaism and Hellenism*, London, 1974, p. 43.

[49] Cf. Fuks (above, n. 47), p. 22. V. Tcherikover: *Hellenistic Civilization and the Jews*, New York, 1959 (repr. 1975) pp. 100–101, argued that there was a Tyrian settlement at Philadelphia. The evidence has been questioned by Fuks, pp. 25–26, but Melqart was worshipped there; cf. Bonnet (above, n. 25), pp. 145–148.

[50] Oren and Rappaport (above, n. 47), pp. 142–148, 151.

[51] Naveh (above, n. 38), pp. 25–26, No. 1 (Tel Anafa); pp. 26–30, Nos. 3–4 (Gaza).

[52] Note Phoenician inscriptions from near Eilat: J. Naveh: The Scripts of Two Ostraca from Elath, *BASOR* 183 (1966), pp. 27–28; Delavault and Lemaire (above, n. 38), pp. 28–29, No. 56. Phoenicians may have established themselves there in

it should be kept in mind that the Sidonian settlements discussed here were Hellenized and that their public monuments were inscribed in Greek.

To sum up, there is no way at present to determine when the introduction of settlers into Judaea started, or to what extent it was an ongoing process.[53] What can be said, however, is that there were several important Sidonian settlements in Judaea by the time of the wars of the Maccabees, when they were Hellenized subjects of, and loyal to, the Seleucid kings, rather than their mother-city Sidon. Nonetheless, the new inscription shows that they called themselves Sidonians and that their ties with other Sidonians were taken seriously by the Seleucid rulers, so seriously that they could determine the level and form of taxation. The literary sources show, and the new inscription vividly illustrates, that the presence of the settlers had tangible implications for social relations in Judaea, in times both of war and peace.

---

small numbers and it is conceivable that they maintained trade via the Gaza-Aela road. See, in general, C.A.M. Glucker: *The City of Gaza in the Roman and Byzantine Periods* (*BAR International Series*, 325), Oxford, 1987, Ch. 4: Trade, Industry and Population.

[53] It is sometimes claimed that I Macc. 3:36 shows that Antiochus IV sent settlers to Judaea. This passage, however, says only that Antiochus gave instructions to Lysias to do so, not that it actually happened. See also Daniel 11:39.

Postscript

This inscription was extensively discussed by P. Gauthier, *BE* (1992), no. 552.

Gauthier proposes the following alternative readings:

Line 1. [σύνταξον οὖν συντελεῖν κατὰ τὰ ἐπεστ]αλμεν[α

Line 2. Gauthier suggests: Νέσ[τορ]ι instead of Νέσ[σῳ, because the latter is rare, but Bingen in *SEG* (see below) observes that the fourth letter seems to be a S rather than a T. This is the correct reading.

In lines 4–5 he would prefer to restore: ἐπειδὴ . . . κ]αὶ οἱ δεδη-λωμένοι εἰσιν ἀτελεῖς—[φρόντισον (?) ὅπω]ς καὶ οὗτοι τῶν αὐτῶν φιλ-ανθρώπων [τυγχάνωσιν] or [μετέχωσιν] rather than [ἀπολαύωνται]. Furthermore, instead of κ]αὶ οἱ δεδηλωμένοι he would prefer a nom. plur., possibly ['Ιαμνῖτ]αι οἱ δεδηλωμένοι. This then would refer to the citizens of Iamnia in the interior, who already enjoyed the privi-lege which the Sidonians in the Port of Iamnia wanted to share. This is possible, but seems not quite necessary. The Sidonians in the Port of Iamnia could be comparing themselves with any group in the region who enjoyed priveliges which they, the Sidonians, felt they had earned as well. These could be, for instance, the Sidonians in Jaffa, or another community, unknown to us.

Line 8. Gauthier notes that 'Ιαμνείας is the only form on record, while there is no parallel for 'Ιαμνίας which I suggested. This is not quite true. Josephus, *Vita* 188.1 has 'Ιαμνία. The form occurs also in Herennius Philo ap. Stephanus Byz. s.v. 'Ιόπη; Pseudo-Herodianus 13.1.248; Epiphanius, *Haer.* iii 155, 26; on the Madaba Map, 70, 102. The *Onomasticon* of Eusebius has both 'Ιαμνία (22, 10; 50, 16; 72, 4) and 'Ιαμνεία (106, 21). It is found also on an undated mile-stone.[1]

Line 10. Gauthier does not find ἐπ[ήνεσε convincing and reads ἐπι[—Line 11. He finds it hard to understand what could be the subject of προάγον. I agree, but the reading is not in doubt.

Line 12.]ΔΕΚΑΤ[rather than]ΔΕΧΑΤ[. Gauthier is certainly right and suggests: [τὴν] δεκάτ[ην] *vel* [τῆς] δεκάτ[ης] τῶν γενημ[άτων]. We thus have an exemption from 'the tithe of the products' granted by predecessor of Antioch to some loyal community and asked for by

---

[1] Mentioned by Y.H. Landau, *Acta of the Fifth International Congress of Greek and Latin Epigraphy, Cambridge 1967* (1971), 389: ἔνθεν εἰς 'Ιαμνίαν μ(ίλια) δ᾽.

the petitioners (cf. above, ad 14). The king's reply will have been favourable, otherwise the correspondence would not have been inscribed in stone.

The inscription was listed also in *SEG* xli (1991), 1556.[2]

The inscription from the Sidonians in the Port of Iamnia contains formulae which immediately correspond with documents attributed by Josephus to the Sidonians in Shechem (Sikhem). After the publication of the article above, results of excavations on Mt. Gerizim above Nablus and in parts of the city below have been described in an article by the excavator.[3] The historical record suggests that there were separate communities of Sidonians and of Samaritans in Sikhem and it is therefore of interest to see whether the archaeological material throws any light on the manner in which these communities apparently lived side by side.

The excavator encountered imported pottery of the third century B.C. in Tel Balatah, in the valley east of Nablus and (chiefly) in the area of Neapolis-Mabartha; similar pottery is absent in the assemblages from Mt. Gerizim. Additional discoveries from Neapolis indicate that a foreign population dwelt there, perhaps since the Hellenistic period. In addition to the inscriptions attesting to tribes named for gods, the inscriptions found in the Roman theatre in Neapolis include to references to the tribes of Antiochus and Phlius.[4] The implication of this would seem to be that the Samaritans lived on the mountain, while the non-Samaritans, presumably the Sidonians in Sikhem lived below.

No new evidence has been discovered at Marisa/Maresha, the other Sidonian settlement on record in Judaea. Maresha, however, was not only a Sidonian settlement. It was also one of the two settlements of urban proportions in Idumaea.[5]

---

[2] With references to Gauthier and to A. Kasher, *SCI* 13 (1994), 161.

[3] Y. Magen, 'Mount Gerizim and the Samaritans', in F. Manns & E. Alliata (eds.), *Early Christianity in Context* (Jerusalem, 1993), 91–148, esp. 141 f.

[4] For these items Magen refers to his unpublished dissertation.

[5] Josephus, *Ant.* xiii (257): Ὑρκανὸς δὲ καὶ τῆς Ἰδουμαίας αἱρεῖ πόλεις Ἄδωρα καὶ Μάρισαν. 'Hyrkanos took the two towns of Judaea, Adora and Marisa'. See also *ibid.* (396).

2

A DONATION FOR HEROD'S TEMPLE IN JERUSALEM

The inscription published in the present paper (Pl. 3) was discovered by B. Mazar and his team in excavations south of the Temple Mount.[1] The find spot (Area 23, Locus 23005) lies 90 m south of the Triple Gate and 70 m south of the plaza which runs along the southern wall of the Temple Mount (Fig. 1). The inscription was found among debris which filled a pool in a palace of the Herodian period, destroyed in 70 C.E. A tower of the Byzantine city-wall (fourth century) was later built on the spot (Fig. 2). The fill which contained the stone ranged in date from the early Herodian period to the destruction of Jerusalem in 70 C.E. There were no objects postdating the destruction.[2] This accordingly is the archaeological *terminus ante quem* of the inscription.

The stone is hard local limestone. The size of the inscription suggests that it was a plaque inserted in a wall: extant measurements height 20 cm; width 26 cm; thickness 12 cm. The height of the lettering is 2 cm.

The stroke intervening between L and K is accidental damage, as on the surface below. The reading is not in doubt and does not require further comment.

The date may be established by what remains of line 1. L K, 'year 20', must be part of a regnal or similar formula. ἐπ' ἀρχιερέως shows that a high priest was mentioned. The lost part of line 2 contained his name and patronymic. L K and ἐπ' ἀρχιερέως cannot refer to the same dating system. We have here a very common formula of

---

[1] I am grateful to Prof. Mazar for permission to publish the inscription, for information on the circumstances in which the stone was found and for the photograph and figures which he provided. I further wish to record my thanks for the generous advice afforded by Mr. P.M. Fraser and Prof. M. Stern. I am likewise indebted to Profs. Chr. Habicht and C.P. Jones and to Dr. V. Kontorini for various suggestions.

[2] For the remains in Area 23. see B. Mazar: Herodian Jerusalem in the Light of the Excavations South and South-West of the Temple Mount. *IEJ* 28 (1978), pp. 236–237, Pl. 38. The fill also contained a few stray sherds of the Iron Age, a Hellenistic sherd and fragments of Herodian vessels.

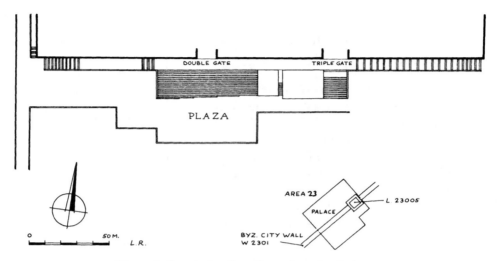

Figure 1. Inscription from Jerusalem: the find-spot

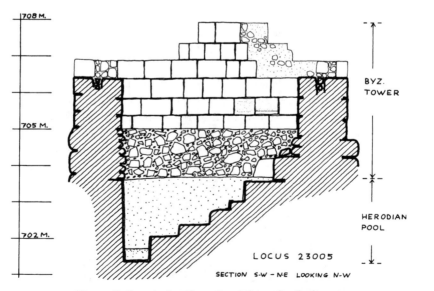

Figure 2. Inscription from Jerusalem: the find-spot

Plate 2. A fragmentary inscription from Jerusalem in the reign of Herod

Transcription

1 L ΚΕΠΑΡΧΙΕΡΕΩΣ
2 ΠΑΡΙΣΑΚΕΣΩΝΟΣ
3 ΕΝΡΟΔΩΙ
4 ΡΟΣΤΡΩΣΙΝ
5 ΡΑΧΜΑΣ

Reading

1](ἔτους) κ' ἐπ' ἀρχιερέως
2]Πάρις Ἀκέσωνος
3]ἐν Ῥόδωι
4 π]ροστρῶσιν
5 δ]ραχμάς

the type: βασιλεύοντος τοῦ δεῖνος ἔτους . . . ἐπὶ ἱερέως τοῦ δεῖνος.[3] In other words, 'year 20' does not refer to the high priest, but to a ruler mentioned by name in the missing part of line 1. The inscription, therefore, dates from the twentieth regnal year of a king who did not serve as high priest of the Jews. No Seleucid after Antiochus III ruled for 20 years and none of the Hasmoneans can be considered, since those whose reign lasted longer than 20 years were high priests themselves. The only possible candidate is Herod the Great,[4] whose regnal year 20 was probably 18/17 B.C.E.[5] This then must be the date of the inscription. The name of the high priest may accordingly be restored as Simon son of Boethus.[6]

The date is significant when seen in combination with the find spot and the contents of the inscription, for it falls within the period when Herod reconstructed the Temple in Jerusalem. The date of the commencement of the work is not entirely certain. According to Josephus' *Antiquities* it started in Herod's 18th regnal year, i.e. 20/19 B.C.E.,[7] but according to *War* it began in his 15th year, i.e. 23/22.[8] The evidence is not conclusive as to which is the correct date.[9] The construction of the Temple itself lasted a year and a half and that of the outer courts eight years.[10] It is not clear whether the building

---

[3] E.g. W. Dittenberger: *Orientis Graecae Inscriptiones Selectae*. Leipzig, 1910, Nos. 55–56, 90; *Berliner griechische Urkunden (Ägyptische Urkunden aus den Königlichen Museen zu Berlin)*. Berlin, 1904, Nos. 998, 1273. Cf., however, ἔτους πρώτου ἐπὶ Σίμωνος ἀρχιερέως (1 Macc. 13:41). Since this is Greek translated from a Hebrew literary text, it cannot be cited as an example of common epigraphic use.

[4] The combination of an emperor, i.e. Augustus or Tiberius, with a high priest cannot be considered, for King Herod or the Roman governor ought to be mentioned.

[5] There are two systems of reckoning Herod's regnal years. In Josephus' *Ant.* the year of Herod's conquest of Jerusalem, 37 B.C.E., is always taken as year 1. In *War* one finds the year of Herod's official appointment, 40 B.C.E., as year 1. Cf. H. Otto: *PWRE* Suppl. II (1913) s.v. Herodes, cols. 81–82. According to the latter system Herod's year 20 would be 21/20 B.C.E. See also O. Edwards: Herodian Chronology, *PEQ* 114 (1982), pp. 129–142.

[6] For Simon son of Boethus, see *Ant.* XV, 9, 3 (319–322); XVII, 4, 2 (78); XVIII, 5, 1 (109); XIX, 6, 2 (297).

[7] *Ant.* XV, 11, 1 (380).

[8] *War* I, 21, 1 (401).

[9] For various arguments and references see E. Schürer: *The History of the Jewish People in the Age of Jesus Christ*, I, revised ed. by G. Vermes and F. Millar, Edinburgh, 1973, p. 292, n. 12; E. Mary Smallwood; The Jews under Roman Rule², Leiden, 1981, p. 92, n. 112. T. Corbishley: The Chronology of the Reign of Herod the Great. *Journal of Theological Studies* 36 (1935), pp. 22–23 resolves the discrepancy by assuming that *Ant.* counts from 40 B.C.E. while dating the beginning in the 18th year and *War* from 37 while dating it in the 15th year. So both would date the commencement of the work in 23/22 B.C.E. Otto (above. n. 5) does not accept this theory.

[10] *Ant.* XV, 11, 5–6 (420–421).

period as a whole lasted eight years or whether the eight and one and a half years should be added together so as to make a total building period of nine and a half years. In any event, Herod's 20th year, the date of the present inscription, falls within the period of construction.

The find spot leaves no doubt that the inscription records a contribution for something connected with the Temple complex. The inscription may well support the earlier date for the start of the building, for Herod's year 20 would be very early if it marks the completion of part of a project which was commenced in year 18 and which lasted eight or nine and a half years.

From δ]ραχμάς in line 5 it is clear that the inscription records a donation by someone who is mentioned in lines 2 and 3, for something mentioned in line 4. The letter before the first Σ in line 4 must be O, as in line 3, and the previous letter cannot be other than P. There seems to be no alternative to π]ροστρῶσιν, a careless form of πρὸς στρῶσιν, two words written as one, like ἐστήλην.[11] στρῶσις is the common expression for 'pavement'.[12] Since the inscription was not found *in situ*, we cannot be certain what pavement is meant. It could have been somewhere near the find spot, south of the Temple Mount. Prof. Mazar has found abundant remains of fine Herodian paving in the area.[13] A pavement, however, for which a considerable sum was donated is more likely to be found on the Temple Mount itself, particularly since during the Herodian period the find spot was in the area of a palace. The spot is only 90 m from the southern retaining wall of the Temple Mount and it is therefore quite possible that the inscription derives from the superstructure, perhaps from the Royal Stoa. In the excavations south of the Mount architectural members have been found which certainly originate from the upper courses of the walls, from the gates and from the Royal Stoa.[14] The open,

---

[11] I have found no parallel for πρὸ⟨ς⟩στρῶσιν. In principle one might also read: π]ρό⟨σ⟩στρωσιν as one word, deriving from προσστρώννυμι. I have found only one example of the use of this verb (none of the substantive). In *Inscriptiones Graecae* (hereafter *IG*), VII, 3073, 11, 64–67 it signifies 'to place additional foundation courses' of a temple. The reconstruction of the Temple in Jerusalem certainly entailed the 'placing of additional foundation courses', but the expression is rare, unlike the alternative στρῶσιν which is therefore preferable.

[12] For στρῶσις see L. Robert: *Opera Minora*, II, Amsterdam, 1969, p. 900, n. 8; see also F.G. Maier: *Griechische Mauerbauinschriften*, II, Heidelberg, 1961, p. 89, n. 109.

[13] See B. Mazar: *The Excavations in the Old City of Jerusalem, Preliminary Report of the First Season*, Jerusalem, 1969, pp. 8, 12; idem, . . . *the Second and Third Seasons, 1969–70*, Jerusalem, 1971, p. 12.

[14] Mazar (above, n. 13, 1969), p. 12.

southern court of the Temple was, according to Josephus, 'completely
paved with a variety of all kinds of stones'.[15] It is quite possible that
this is the pavement to which the inscription refers.[16]

In line 2 the donor's name and patronymic are given. The name
could be Πάρις or [Σ]πάρις.[17] Σπάρις, however, is found rarely. The
father's name Ἀκέσων is attested at Rhodes and elsewhere.[18] The
obvious restoration of line 3 is [κατοικῶν] ἐν Ῥόδωι, which would
imply that he was a foreigner resident in Rhodes and not a Rhodian,
who would have been described as Ῥόδιος.[19] The Rhodian citizen
body was very small; the population consisted mainly of foreign residents and slaves.[20] The former would have played a very active role
in the flourishing Rhodian business life, which was affected but not
destroyed by Roman interference in the region.[21] The man who made
the benefaction in Jerusalem could therefore have been a wealthy
foreign resident from Rhodes. He must have been a Jew or a sympathizer, but since his name and the language of the inscription are

---

[15] *War* V, 5, 2 (192): τὸ δ' ὕπαιθρον ἅπαν πεποίκιλτο παντοδαπῷ λίθῳ κατεστρωμένον.

[16] If this is true, it reinforces the chronological argument for an early date of the
commencement of Herod's building project, for the southern court could not have
been paved, or the inscription set up, until the Temple Mount had been extended
south and west by building a huge artificial plateau. This certainly took more than
two years. For Herod's extension of the Temple platform, see *Ant.* XV, 11, 3 (393–
400); cf. J. Simons: *Jerusalem in the Old Testament*, Leiden, 1952, Chapter VI. For
further references see Schürer (above, n. 9), p. 309, n. 71.

[17] For Πάρις see *Supplementum Epigraphicum Graecum* (hereafter *SEG*), XXV, No. 591,
1.7; W. Pape and G.E. Benseler: *Wörterbuch der griechischen Eigennamen*, Braunschweig,
1911, p. 1138; F. Bechtel: *Die historischen Personnamen des Griechischen bis zur Kaiserzeit*,
Halle, 1917, p. 576; F. Preisigke: *Namenbuch*, Heidelberg, 1922, p. 280.

[18] For Σπάρις see Dittenberger (above, n. 3), No. 97, 1.10. For Ἀκέσων at Rhodes
see Chr. Blinkenberg: *Lindos, Fouilles de l'Acropole 1902–1914, Inscriptions*, II, Berlin-
Copenhagen, 1941, No. 378, 1.184; No. 51a II 14; No. 51c II 62. For Ἀκέσων
elsewhere, see *IG* XII 1 No. 764, 1.78; Callimachus, *Epigr.* LIV 2 (ed. Pfeiffer);
Preisigke (above. n. 17), p. 14; Bechtel (above, n. 17), p. 31.

[19] For the indications of civic status on Rhodian inscriptions see P.M. Fraser:
Rhodian Funerary Monuments, Oxford, 1977, pp. 46–47. A different possibility would
be that he was not a resident of Rhodes but had won a victory at the games there
and had made the benefaction on his return to celebrate his victory, e.g. | νικήσας
Ἄλεια | ἐν Ῥόδωι. However, if the man was a Jew from Jerusalem he probably would
not have participated in pagan games and he certainly would not proclaim his
participation on an inscription on the Temple Mount.

[20] See in general M. Rostovtzeff: *Social and Economic History of the Hellenistic World*,
Oxford, 1941, pp. 689–690, 1149. For the history of Rhodes, see H. van Gelder:
Geschichte der alten Rhodier, The Hague, 1900; H.v. Gaertringen: *PWRE* Suppl. V
(1931), s.v. Rhodos, cols. 731–840; M. Riemschneider: *Rhodos, Kultur und Geschichte*,
Vienna, 1974.

[21] See Rostovtzeff (above, n. 20), pp. 776–778, 1149 for an assessment of the
effect of the creation in 167 B.C.E. of the free port of Delos and pp. 689–690 for the

wholly Greek, only the benefaction as such indicates ties with Judaism. There is some evidence of the presence of Jews at Rhodes. In the mid-second century B.C.E. a letter about an alliance between Rome and the Jews was sent to various states including Rhodes.[22] Suetonius mentions a grammarian Diogenes in the time of Tiberius who lectured every Sabbath.[23] Inscriptions mention a sympathizer (θεοσεβής)[24] and one Menippos who probably came from Jerusalem.[25] There were many foreigners from the Near East living at Rhodes, but apart from Menippos these all came from the mixed or non-Jewish cities, mainly on the coast.[26] Their presence reflects Rhodian commercial contacts.

Rhodes is among the states which received benefactions from Herod. He rebuilt the temple of Apollo there and made donations for the maintenance of the Rhodian fleet.[27] These, of course, were the gifts of a monarch to another state, while the benefaction recorded in the inscription was made by a private individual.

The present inscription is not the first related to the Temple in Jerusalem. Literary sources mention inscriptions set up on the Temple Mount in the second century B.C.E.[28] Greek and Latin inscriptions warned Gentiles not to enter the sacred precinct. A complete copy and a fragment of the Greek text have been found.[29] Connected with

---

role of foreign residents in commerce, banking and industry. For the Rhodian banking system in this period, see P.M. Fraser: Notes on Two Rhodian Institutions. *Annals of the British School at Athens* 67 (1972), pp. 113–124.

[22] 1 Macc. 15:23.

[23] Suetonius, *Tiberius* 32, 4: 'Diogenes grammaticus, disputare sabbatis Rhodi solitus . . .' at the time of Tiberius' stay on the island (6 B.C.E.–2 C.E.). Cf. M. Stern: *Greek and Latin Authors on Jews and Judaism*, II, Jerusai .n, 1974, pp. 111–112.

[24] IG XII, 1, 593: Εὐφρο(σ)ύνα θεοσεβὴς χρηστὰ χαῖρε, mentioned by L. Robert: *Études Anatoliennes*, Amsterdam, 1970, p. 411, n. 5. J. Juster: *Les Juifs dans l'Empire Romain*, I, New York, 1914, p. 189, n. 4, suggests that the antisemitism of the authors Poseidonius and Apollonius Molon may reflect the presence of numerous Jews at Rhodes in the first century B.C.E., as both lived on the island in this period. Poseidonius' real views on the Jews and their religion are, however, not certain, as argued by Stern (above, n. 23), I, pp. 141–143.

[25] IG XII 1, No. 11, 1.6: Μένιππος Ἱερ . . . υμίτας.

[26] Cf. the list in D. Morelli: Gli Stranieri i Rodi, *Studi classice e orientali* 5 (1955), pp. 126–139, 148–150, 158–159, 169–170, 174: 4 men from Ascalon, 6 from Berytus, 1 from Damascus, 1 from Idumaea, 5 from Laodicea, 10 from Sidon, 6 from Tyre.

[27] *Ant.* XVI, 5, 3 (147); *War* I, 21, 2 (424).

[28] 1 Macc. 11:37; 14:26.

[29] J.B. Frey: *Corpus Inscriptionum Judaicarum*, II, Rome, 1952, No. 1400; Dittenberger (above, n. 3), p. 598; for photographs, see J.H. Iliffe: The ΘΑΝΑΤΟΣ Inscription from Herod's Temple: Fragment of a Second Copy, *QDAP* 6 (1938), Pl. I and A.H.M. Jones: *The Herods of Judaea*, Oxford, 1938, Pl. 4. The fragment: *SEG* VIII 169; Iliffe (above), Pl. II.

the reconstruction of the Temple are the ossuaries of a man 'who made the gates' and of 'Simon builder of the Sanctuary'.[30]

The Temple was very rich in dedications and votive gifts and these are frequently described in literary sources. Nowhere, however, is there any mention of contributions towards the actual costs of the building. On the contrary, Josephus describes the Temple emphatically as a project financed and carried out by Herod alone: 'and he surpassed his predecessors in spending money, so that it was thought that no one else had adorned the Temple so splendidly'.[31] Yet elsewhere he avoids naming Herod and depicts the Temple as the result of a collective effort.[32] No doubt this is partly a matter of sources. The pro-Herodian Nicolaos of Damascus will have described his master as the sole builder, while Josephus, speaking as an independent author of the Temple as he remembered it, saw it as a creation by the people. The construction of Greek temples, as of Jewish synagogues, was often supported by benefactions from various sources: private individuals, friendly cities and rulers.[33] The present inscription may not have been the only one of its kind on and around the Temple Mount.

In summary: the inscription records a benefaction made by Paris (or Sparis) son of Akeson, presumably a (Jewish) foreign resident at Rhodes, for a pavement somewhere on or near the Temple Mount. This may well have been the pavement of the southern court. The date is year 20 of a king who cannot be other than Herod, i.e. 18–17 B.C.E. This is the period in which the Temple was rebuilt. The inscription may support the earlier of the two dates given by Josephus for the commencement of the work. This is a rare record of a donation made for the building of the Temple complex and raises the question of whether such donations were more important as a means of financing the work than Josephus admits. The inscription is important as one of the few extant epigraphical documents related to the Temple in Jerusalem.

---

[30] Dittenberger (above, n. 3), p. 599; *SEG* VIII 200: Ὀστᾶ τῶν τοῦ Νεικάνορος Ἀλεξανδρέως ποιήσαντος τὰς θύρας. For the ossuary of 'Simon builder of the Sanctuary', see J. Naveh: The Ossuary Inscriptions from Giv'at ha-Mivtar. *IEJ* 20 (1970), pp. 33–34.

[31] *Ant.* XV, 11, 3 (396); cf. *War* I, 21, 1 (401) for a similar approach.

[32] *War* V, 5, 2 (189); cf. 5, 3 (205) where it is mentioned that nine gates of the temple court were overlaid with silver and gold plate by Alexander, the Alabarch of Alexandria, Philo's brother.

[33] For Greek temples, see Maier (above, n. 12), pp. 55 ff. For synagogues, see B. Lifshitz: *Donateurs et fondateurs dans les synagogues juives*, Paris, 1967.

JUDAEA UNDER ROMAN RULE

3

TWO GREEK INSCRIPTIONS FROM TELL ABU-SHUSHA

Inscription A

This is a well-dressed marble panel, found on the west slope of Tel Abu-Shusha, not *in situ*. It measures 31.1 × 22.7 cm. There is a six-line inscription engraved on the panel, which is broken at the bottom left corner. The panel was found by M. Linn. The inscription is as follows:

> ᾿Αβδαγον
> ᾿Αλέξανδρον
> τὸν τῆς πό-
> λεως πρῶτον
> [ἡ] πόλις
> [τὸν κ]τίστην

Translation:

> The city honours Abdagos, the son of Alexander, the first citizen[1] of the city and its founder.

This is an inscription put up to honour a respected citizen of the city, as was customary in Greek cities. The formula is also one which was usual in the Greek world. It was customary to describe such a citizen as the 'first citizen', i.e. the most important man in the city.[2] It was also customary to describe honoured citizens as 'founders of the city', but this description lost its original meaning and became merely an honorary title.[3]

The name Abdagos or Abdagon is not known. It is not found in any other inscriptions from Eretz Israel. A preliminary search showed that it is not found in Diaspora inscriptions either. It may be a Semitic

---

[1] The Hebrew version of this paper had 'guest', instead of 'citizen', due to a misprint.

[2] See, e.g. R. Cagnat (ed.), *Inscriptiones Graecae ad Res Romanas Pertinentes* (Paris 1906), IV, No. 666.

[3] Cf. W. Dittenberger, *Orientis Graeci Inscriptiones Selectae* (Leipzig 1903), Nos. 111, 9; 531, 4.

name made up of two elements: עבד (slave) and a further element, perhaps the name of a god. This could have been the early western Semitic Dagan, known from the Bible as the Philistine god Dagon, and as an element in the place-name Beit Dagon. In the Roman period there was a cult of this god in the city of Arados.[4] The name of Abdagos' father, Alexander, was, of course, an extremely popular name in the ancient world.

Plate 3. Inscription A from Tell Abu Shusha

---

[4] See: Pauly-Wissowa, *Realencyclopädie der Classischen Altertumswissenschaft*, IV, col. 1986 f.; *Der kleine Pauly*, I, 1360 f.

There are no internal criteria for dating this inscription.

The significance of this inscription is that we can infer from it that the city had the sort of institutions which were usual in the Greek world and related to its citizens in the usual way. The combination of Greek and Semitic names was common among the Hellenized peoples of the East.

Plate 4. Inscription B from Tell Abu Shusha

Inscription B

The second inscription was found near Inscription A. It contains a single line with just one word: ἀρχιερεύ[ς, ie 'high priest'. There can be no doubt that this refers to a local pagan cult. This shows that the city administration was not in Jewish hands.

Postscript

These inscriptions are recorded in *SEG* 1988.1586. The editors of
SEG add the following comments: 'Hellenistic period, ed. Pr. [the
letter forms point to a much later period, Pleket].' However, in my
Hebrew publication of these inscriptions I state that they are undated, not that they are Hellenistic.

For the identification of the site cf. A. Siegelman, *PEQ* 116 (1984),
89–93. The inscribed weight published by Siegelman and the present
inscriptions clearly prove that the site had the status of a polis named
Gaba. Siegelman and others concluded that this was also proof that
it was the town of Gaba Hippeon, settled by Herod. This conclusion
has not been accepted by Barag, followed by Shatzman.[1] Barag wants
to distinguish between two cities named Gaba, one at Tell Abu Shusha
and one at Sha'ar ha-'Amaqim (Khirbet el-Harthiyeh), further to the
north.[2] The editors of *TIR* tend to agree with Barag and Shatzman.[3]
Recent excavations have uncovered substantial remains of the Hellenistic period at Tel Harthiyeh. While I personally prefer to identify
this site with Gaba Hippeon it seems best to leave the matter open
at this stage. The inscriptions found at Tel Abu Shusha certainly
proved there was a *polis* there named Gaba, whether or not this was
the site occupied by Herod's colonists.

Dr. Alla Stein fixed the era of Gaba Philippi, on the basis of coins, to
60 B.C., from autumn to autumn.[4] The era appears also on the weight
found at Tel Shosh (Tel Abu Shusha), published by Siegelmann, which
bears the name of the city and the date, year 218 = A.D. 158/9.
Gaba was an episcopal see of Palaestina Secunda.

Some further comments on the god Dagon may be added. There
was a temple of Dagon at Azotus (Ashdod) which was destroyed by
Jonathan the Maccabee in 148/7 or 147/6 B.C.[5] Relevant is also the

---

[1] D. Barag, 'Geva and Geva Parashim' in B. Mazar (ed.), *Geva. Archaeological
Discoveries at Tell Abu-Shusha, Mishmar Ha-'Emeq* (Heb.) (1988), 4–12; 258. I. Shatzman,
The Armies of the Hasmonaeans and Herod (Tübingen 1991), 85 f.

[2] He disagrees in this with G. Schmitt, 'Gaba, Getta und Gintkirmil', *ZDPV* 103
(1987), 22–48.

[3] Y. Tsafrir, L. Di Segni and J. Green, *Tabula Imperii Romani. Iudaea-Palaestina*
(Jerusalem 1994), s.v. Gaba Hippeon, p. 125 and Gaba Philippi, Gabae in Palaestina
Secunda on p. 126.

[4] A. Kushnir-Stein, Unpublished Ph.D. dissertation, Tel Aviv, 1991, 53 f.

[5] 1 Macc. 10.84; 11.42.

sarcophagus of Eshmunazar of Sidon who claims to have received 'Dor and Joppa, the mighty lands of Dagon, which are in the plain of Sharon' from the Lord of Kings (the Persian king).[6] Philo of Byblos, who wrote in the reign of Hadrian, identifies Dagon with wheat.[7]

---

[6] *CIS* i 3, pp. 9–20, ll. 18–20; translation: *ANET*³ 662.

[7] Phylo of Byblos, fr. 809, 23 with comments by A.I. Baumgarten, *The Phoenician History of Philo of Byblos, A Commentary* (Leiden 1981), p. 15 and comm. on p. 190. For Dagon: E. Dhorme, 'Les Avatars du dieu Dagon', *Revue de l'Histoire des Religions* 138 (1950), 129–144; U. Oldenburg, *The Conflict between El and Baal* (Leiden 1969), 47–57; I. Singer, 'Toward an Identity of Dagon, the God of the Philistines', *Cathedra* 54 (1989), 17–42 (Heb.).

4

A MILESTONE OF A.D. 69 FROM JUDAEA: THE ELDER TRAJAN AND VESPASIAN

(with I. Roll)

In March 1973, a Roman milestone was discovered in a cultivated field, several hundred metres from the western edge of the town of Afula in the Valley of Jezreel.[1] The stone was found broken into two pieces.[2] The column was removed by a farmer belonging to the settlement of Balfouria, who transferred it to the garden of his home, where we had the opportunity to examine it.[3] The base and lower part of the column remained on the spot. The inscription, incised on the column above the fracture, consists of six lines of irregular lettering.[4]

```
1        IMP
      CAESAR[. .]SPA
      SIANVSAVGM[. .]
      PIOTR[. .]AN[.]LEG
5     LEGX FRET
           XXXIV
```

These may be restored as follows:

Imp(erator) / Caesar [Ve]spa / sianus
Aug(ustus) M(arco) [Ul] / pio Tr[ai]an[o]
leg(ato) / leg(ionis) X Fret(ensis) / XXXIV[5]

---

[1] Israel Grid reference number 17564.22356.

[2] Measurements of the column: height, 133 cm; diameter at top, 43 cm, at base, 45 cm; base: height, 66 cm; length, 44 cm; width, 42 cm.

[3] We wish to thank Mr. M. Kuriss for giving his permission to examine the stone, and for his co-operation. We also wish to thank Professor S. Applebaum of Tel-Aviv University and Mr. P. Porat of the Department of Antiquities for their generous assistance during the decipherment, and Professor S. Applebaum and Miss J. MacVeagh for reading the manuscript of this article. Finally we would like to record the great assistance afforded by Dr. F.G.B. Millar and the Editorial Committee.

[4] Height of the inscription, 65 cm; width, 65 cm. The height of the letters is not uniform, and varies between 7 and 9.5 cm: line 1 = 9.5 cm, lines 2–6 = 7–9 cm. Average distance between lines, 4 cm. Average depth of letters, 4 mm.

[5] The emperor appears in the nominative, the legate in the ablative without a verb like *curante*; cf. *CIL* viii 10016; see also 10048; 10114; 10210.

Plate 5. Milestone of A.D. 69

Plate 6. Milestone of A.D. 69: the lettering

The *terminus post quem* for the milestone must be the proclamation of Vespasian as emperor at the beginning of July 69.[6] The elder Traianus ceased to be *legatus* of X Fretensis by the campaigning season of 70.[7] A closer *terminus ante quem* is provided by Vespasian's nomenclature. He is described as *Imperator Caesar Augustus*, without any republican titles; these are never otherwise omitted on milestones before Antoninus Pius.[8] The inscription should therefore be dated in the period when Vespasian was not yet in possession of these titles. Suetonius confirms that Vespasian did not assume the *tribunicia potestas* immediately,[9] while Tacitus states that the senate endowed Vespasian with the usual imperial titles in December 69.[10] If we allow for an interval of time before the senate's vote was known in Judaea, the milestone can be dated between July 69 and the beginning of 70.

The milestone belonged to the road which led from Caesarea eastward along the narrow pass of Wadi Ara and through the valley of Jezreel to Scythopolis (Fig. 1). From there it led to Pella and Gerasa, cities of the Decapolis. It had been in use long before the Roman conquest.[11] It was an important route during Roman imperial rule, a fact which is attested by the numerous milestones discovered along it.[12] In the summer and autumn of 67 Vespasian quartered the 5th

---

[6] According to Suetonius, *Vesp.* 6, on 1 July by Tiberius Julius Alexander and the army in Egypt, and 11 July by the army in Judaea. Tacitus, *Hist.* ii 79 has the same date for Alexander and 3 July for Vespasian's own troops. Josephus, *BJ* iv, 10, 4 (601) ff. provides no exact date, but gives priority to the army in Judaea, followed by Mucianus, and, only after a personal appeal by Vespasian himself, by Alexander.

[7] See p. 19 below.

[8] Cf. M. Gichon and B.H. Isaac, *IEJ* 24 (1974), 120.

[9] *Vesp.* 12.

[10] *Hist.* iv 3. Evidence from coins confirms that Vespasian in 69 did not use the republican titles which he could not yet claim. See *BMC Emp.* ii, p. lxiii: mint of Asia, soon after 1 July 69, *Imp. Caes. Vespas. Aug.*; p. lxii: mint of Illyricum, August 69 onwards, *Imp. Caesar Vespasianus Aug.*; p. liv: Tarraco, about October, *Imp. Caesar Vespasianus*; p. xxviii: Rome, December onwards, *Imp. Caesar Vespasianus Aug.*

[11] See Y. Aharoni, *The Land of the Bible* (1967), 41 ff.

[12] (*a*) West of the pass: see n. 21 below. (*b*) The Wadi Ara pass: G. Schumacher, *Mitt. u. Nachr. des D.P.-V.* (1903), 4 ff., claimed to have seen several milestones. Since then, however, no one else has seen any of them, including the present authors who undertook a thorough search in the area. See also P. Thomsen, *ZDPV* 40 (1917), 69–70. (*c*) The section of the northern exit of the Wadi Ara pass to Scythopolis: M. Avi-Yonah, *QDAP* 12 (1946), 98–102. A complete account of this part of the road and its milestones is in preparation. (*d*) The section Scythopolis-Pella-Gerasa: Thomsen, *op. cit.* (n. 12), 65–7, and S. Mittmann, *Beiträge zur Siedlungsgeschichte des nördlichen Ostjordanlandes* (1970), 157–8. The authors wish to thank the Israel Milestone Committee for permission to use material in its possession.

and 10th legions in Caesarea, and the 15th legion in Scythopolis.[13] After the campaign in Gaulanitis, towards the end of 67, the 10th legion stayed at Scythopolis, and the 5th and 15th were sent to Caesarea.[14] The route must have been used again during the operations against Peraea, first by Vespasian, who set off from Caesarea early in 68,[15] then possibly by Placidus and Traianus.[16] It is clear how important it was to the Romans to possess a good road between the cities of Scythopolis and Caesarea Maritima. The new milestone furnishes proof that the Roman command took the necessary steps to construct and maintain such a road.[17] From Hadrian's time onward the legion VI Ferrata had its fort at Caparcotna near the road, not far from the northern entry of the Wadi Ara pass. The road thus formed the connection between the fort and Caesarea, the provincial capital, to the west, and provincia Arabia to the east.[18]

The presence of the name of the *legatus* of X Fretensis on the milestone suggests that the road was constructed by units of this legion. Josephus mentions that the Roman army in Judaea included special units of ὁδοποιοί whose task it was to straighten, to level and to broaden existing roads.[19] The date of the milestone from Afula indicates that at least one new road was constructed during the Jewish War. This must have been a project undertaken during the suspension of hostilities from July 69 till the spring of 70. The inscription shows an aspect of Roman activity in those parts of Judaea already subdued by the army.[20] Of course it should not be forgotten that

---

[13] *BJ* iii, 9, 1 (412).

[14] *BJ* iv, 2, 1 (87–8).

[15] *BJ* iv, 7, 3–4 (413–19).

[16] *BJ* iv, 8, 2 (450).

[17] It is very likely that the road constructed in 69 included the sections Scythopolis-Pella-Gerasa. Milestones of A.D. 112 discovered between Pella and Gerasa mention restoration of the road; cf. Thomsen, *ZDPV* 40 (1917), nos. 215, 216, 218a, 220; Mittmann, *loc. cit.* (n. 12). The emperor Trajan thus restored a road—possibly built by his father—in order to ensure communications between Caesarea and the Via Nova Traiana.

[18] Caparcotna = Caporcotani of the Tabula Peutingeriana (n. 22 below) = Kefar Otnay of the Jewish sources. Several inscriptions identify Caparcotna as the fort of VI Ferrata: *CIL* iii 6814–16; W.M. Ramsay, *JRS* 6 (1916), 129–31; B. Levick, *JRS* 48 (1958), 75–6. A rooftile-stamp of VI Ferrata, discovered on the site, was recorded by G. Schumacher, *Tell el-Mutesellim* i (1908), 175, fig. 261. See M. Avi-Yonah in P-W, Suppl. xiii (1973), s.v. 'Palaestina', cols. 400 and 419–20.

[19] Jos., *BJ* iii, 7, 3 (141–2); 6, 2 (118); see also v, 2, 1 (47).

[20] For a discussion of the development of the Roman road-system in Israel see

road-building was a useful employment for soldiers, kept idle in the midst of a civil war. This phase came to an end with the beginning of the siege of Jerusalem in 70.

The last line of the inscription indicates a distance of 34 miles. This number corresponds to the actual distance from the find-spot to Caesarea.[21] Moreover, it corresponds exactly to the distances given by the Tabula Peutingeriana for the Scythopolis-Caesarea road:[22] the section Scythopolis-Caporcotani as 24 miles and the section Caporcotani-Caesarea as 28 miles.[23] The milestone from Afula was discovered on the section Scythopolis-Caporcotani at the distances corresponding to 6 Roman miles from Caporcotani and 18 Roman miles from Scythopolis.[24] In other words the distance given by the milestone corresponds exactly to those of the Tabula and to actual distances as they appear on modern maps.

As has been mentioned above, because of the early date of the milestone, Vespasian appears without the republican titles which invariably follow the emperor's names on milestones of the first century. The present authors have found no epigraphical material dating to 69, which might furnish any parallel. The milestone seems to be not only the earliest record of Roman road-building in Judaea, but also the earliest official document relating to the Flavians.

M. Ulpius Traianus, father of the emperor Trajan, has been the subject of a number of studies.[25] Josephus describes some of his activities as commander of X Fretensis, the latest of which date to June 68.[26]

I. Roll, 'Routes romaines en Israel', *Actes du IXᵉ Congrès International d'Études sur les Frontières Romaines (Mamaïa, 6–13 Septembre 1972)* (1974), 505–6.

[21] One Roman mile = 1,482 m, so this gives 50 km. Four other known milestones indicate the distance from Caesarea: (*a*) a milestone of Marcus Aurelius, as yet unpublished, seems to have indicated the 7th mile from Caesarea on the road to Caparcotna; (*b*) a milestone of Septimius Severus, as yet unpublished, indicates the 2nd mile on the road to Ptolemais; (*c*) *AÉ* 1971, 471, of Pertinax, seems to have indicated the 5th mile on the same road; (*d*) S. Dar and S. Applebaum, *PEQ* (1973), 93 seems to have indicated a distance of 10 miles on the road to Antipatris.

[22] A facsimile of segment X can be found in *Atlas of Israel* (1970), map I/2. For a good copy, see G.A. Smith, *Historical Atlas of the Holy Land*² (1936), map on p. 27.

[23] Cf. n. 18.

[24] 24 − 6 = 18, i.e. the distance from the milestone to Scythopolis; and 28 + 6 = 34, i.e. the distance from the milestone to Caesarea.

[25] For a full bibliography: P-W, Suppl. X (1965), cols. 1032 ff., s.v. 'M. Ulpius Traianus (*pater*)' (R. Hanslik). See also F. Grosso, *Rend. Ac. Lomb.* 91 (1957), 318–42, and M. Durry, *Les Empereurs romains d'Espagne* (1965), 45–54. The most recent treatment is G.W. Bowersock, *JRS* 63 (1973), 133 ff.

[26] Jos., *BJ* iii, 7, 31 (289 ff.); 9, 8 (458); 10, 3 (485); iv, 8, 1 (450).

R. Syme has suggested that Traianus may have accompanied Vespasian from Judaea to Egypt after his proclamation as emperor in July 69,[27] while Hanslik assumed that he will have governed an additional minor province in 68/9.[28] But the milestone of 69 from Judaea shows that he remained there as *legatus* of X Fretensis at least until the second half of 69. As a consequence, his term as governor of Baetica must be dated before the Jewish War.[29] If so, he held his first provincial governorship in his country of origin. After the proconsulate of Baetica, he served as one of Vespasian's three legionary commanders. The other two were Titus, commanding the XV Apollinaris, and Sex. Vettulenus Cerealis the V Macedonica.[30] It should be noted that the two legates, Traianus and Cerealis, were in charge of the two legions which Josephus describes as τὰ ἐπισημότατα.[31] Vespasian was sole commander of the army, and neither Titus nor anybody else served as chief of staff. The three legionary commanders either acted under Vespasian's orders, or fulfilled independent missions: Cerealis marched against the Samaritans and Idumaeans,[32] Traianus subjugated Peraea.[33] Titus did not have sole command of any large-scale military operations before the siege of Jerusalem.[34] It has already been mentioned that the sources do not agree as to whether

---

[27] R. Syme, *Tacitus* (1958), 30.

[28] P-W, Suppl. x, col. 1033.

[29] Cf. W. Eck, *Senatoren von Vespasian bis Hadrian* (1970), 237.

[30] For Cerealis see Jos., *BJ* iii, 7, 32 (310 ff.). He retained his legionary command when Titus was in command of the whole army, see Jos., *BJ* vi, 2, 5 (131) and 4, 3 (237); after the latter's departure Cerealis was in charge of the army of occupation till the arrival of Lucilius Bassus: see Jos., *BJ* vii, 6, 1 (163). His full name appears in *CIL* x 4862. For his consulate, probably around 73/4, see R. Syme *Athenaeum* 35 (1957), 312–13. For Titus' command of XV Apollinaris, see Jos., *BJ* iii, 1, 3 (8) and 4, 2 (65); Suetonius, *Titus* 4: 'legioni praepositus'. See also E. Schürer, *The History of the Jewish People in the Age of Jesus Christ* I, ed. G. Vermes and F. Millar (1973), 492, n. 31.

[31] Jos., *BJ* iii, 4, 2 (65).

[32] Jos., *BJ* iii, 7, 32 (310 ff.) and iv, 9, 9 (552 ff.).

[33] Jos., *BJ* iv, 8, 1, (450).

[34] Titus did not take any town as sole commander: at Japha (in Galilee) Traianus was in command of the right wing, Jos., *BJ* iii, 7, 31 (298), at Jotapata Vespasian was in charge, 7, 33 (322). At Tarichaea Titus had to ask for support and, when Traianus joined him with 400 cavalry, Titus' men were vexed because their victory would be diminished because of this partnership, 10, 3 (485). At Gamala, finally, Vespasian joined his son in the course of the battle, iv, 1, 10 (70). Maybe as compensation for this lack of independent action, Josephus tends to mention Titus on every possible occasion, for example when he takes a legion from one place to another: e.g. *BJ* iii, 1, 3, (8); 4, 2 (64); 9, 7 (446).

Vespasian was first proclaimed emperor by his own troops or by the army in Egypt.[35] It is clear, however, that Vespasian could not possibly have aspired to the throne without being sure of the support of his own troops, whose commanders were Traianus, Cerealis and his own son. Among other things, he would have to be certain that these troops would remain loyal after he himself and Titus had left Judaea for Egypt. It is now apparent that the two legates remaining in Judaea were Traianus and Cerealis.[36] The construction of a road, attested by the milestone, shows that Traianus was not idle during Vespasian's absence. In setting up milestones naming Vespasian as emperor, Traianus showed himself as one of the earliest supporters of the new reign. There is an additional point of interest: Traianus added his own name on the milestone. This means that, apart from Vespasian, he had no superior in Judaea who might have claimed that honour. Between July 69 and the return of Titus, Traianus had a colleague in the area, Cerealis, commander of the V Macedonica, but no superior.[37] In 70 military operations in Judaea were resumed. Titus returned to Judaea with four legions for the siege of Jerusalem, where he arrived before Passover.[38] The structure of command was changed; it was apparently felt that Titus lacked the experience to be in sole command of his army. He was therefore assisted by Tiberius Julius Alexander, who had been among the first to proclaim Vespasian emperor, and now became chief of staff.[39] Traianus was superseded

---

[35] Cf. n. 6 above.

[36] Cerealis was still there during the siege of Jerusalem, Jos., *BJ* vi, 4, 3, (237).

[37] As R. Syme has noted, it happened more than once that *legati* took charge of the province when a governor died or departed: Cn. Pompeius Collega, a *legatus* in Syria, was apparently in charge there until the arrival of the consular legate L. Caesennius Paetus, late in 70, Jos., *BJ* vii, 3, 4 (58–60); see P-W xxi 2, cols. 2269–70. For a *legatus leg. IIII Scythicae, pro legato consulare provinc. Syriae* in 97/8, see *AÉ* 1908, 237, *CIL* viii 17891 = *ILS* 1055, cf. R. Syme, *JRS* 48 (1958), 6–7, and *Tacitus* (1958), App. 3. Later C. Julius Severus took over the administration of Syria as praetorian *legatus* while at the same time retaining command of his legion, when the governor, Publicius Marcellus, had to leave his province for Judaea at the time of the revolt of Bar Kochba (132–5), cf. *IGR* iii 174–5; see also Schürer, *op. cit.* (n. 30), 518–19, and 549, n. 151. For the significance of names of officials on milestones, see Th. Pekáry, *Untersuchungen zu den römischen Reichsstrassen* (1968), 77 ff.

[38] For Titus' march see Jos., *BJ* iv, 11, 5 (658); v, 1, 6 (41). He encamped before the walls of Jerusalem at Passover, on the 14th of the month Xanthicus, *BJ* v, 3, 1 (98–9) and 13, 7 (567).

[39] See Jos., *BJ* v, 1, 6 (46) and vi, 4, 3 (237); cf. Schürer, *op. cit.* (n. 30), 502, n. 85.

as legate of X Fretensis by (A.) Larcius Lepidus,[40] who came to his command straight from the quaestorship of Crete and Cyrenaica, and belonged to a group of officers who obtained promotion quickly under Vespasian.[41] Sex. Vettulenus Cerealis remained legate of V Macedonica, while M. Tittius Frugi took over the XV Apollinaris from Titus.[42] The commander of the 12th legion is not mentioned by name.[43] Traianus, as a veteran commander and early supporter of the new emperor, was apparently needed elsewhere in the empire. His suffect consulate early in the reign probably followed the command in Judaea.[44] As R. Syme has suggested, Traianus may have been *legatus* of Galatia-Cappadocia before 73.[45] He certainly governed the major province of Syria in 73/4–76/7, gaining *triumphalia ornamenta*, and was probably responsible for the ordering of the eastern frontier and its defences.[46] Finally, he came to the supreme provincial command, the proconsulate of Asia, in 79/80. He was also the first of his *gens* to be adlected into the patriciate.[47]

---

[40] Jos., *BJ* vi, 4, 3 (237); *CIL* x 6659 = *ILS* 987; see *PIR²* L 94.

[41] See D. Magie, *Roman Rule in Asia Minor* (1950), 1441, n. 33, and J. Morris, *JRS* 43 (1953), 79–80. Lepidus was decorated in the Jewish War and was afterwards governor of Bithynia-Pontus. It should be noted that the *terminus post quem* of the milestone proves the presence of Traianus in Judaea after 1 July 69. It furnishes no proof that he actually stayed there until the supreme command of Titus. This is, however, more than likely as Lepidus, a relatively inexperienced officer—cf. the rout of his legion described by Josephus, *BJ* v, 2, 4 (75 ff.—would hardly have been left in charge of X Fretensis without a senior officer responsible for the army as a whole.

[42] Jos., *BJ* vi, 4, 3 (237). For Tittius Frugi, see *PIR¹* T 208.

[43] Professor S. Applebaum notes that the legate of XII Fulminata is almost certainly not mentioned because the legion had disgraced itself at Beth Horon under Cestius Gallus, Jos., *BJ* vii, 1, 3 (18).

[44] Traianus may have held a consulate in absence, cf. R. Syme, *JRS* 48 (1958), 6–7. The date of the suffect consulate is not quite certain. June/July 70 was proposed by J. Morris, *JRS* 43 (1953), 79–80. The relevant fragment of the *Fasti Ostienses* has been re-discussed by F. Zevi, *Akten des VI. Internationalen Kongresses für griechische und lateinische Epigraphik, München 1972*, (1973), 438–9, and thence by L. Vidman in *Listy Filologické* 98 (1975), 66 ff.

[45] R. Syme, *Tacitus*, p. 31, n. 1.

[46] Syme, *op. cit.*, p. 31, supported by G.W. Bowersock, *JRS* 63 (1973), 133 ff.

[47] Pliny, *Pan.* 9 2.

It seems legitimate to conclude that the milestone has done much to clarify the important role of Traianus in Judaea under Vespasian as general and afterwards as emperor.[48] The years 68 and 69 decided the ultimate success of Traianus, and thus saw the real *incunabula et rudimenta* of his son's career as well.[49]

---

[48] Bowersock, *op. cit.* (n. 25), 134–5, proposed a restoration of the inscription from Miletus, containing Traianus' *cursus honorum*, which would make him a *legatus* of Titus, as well as of Vespasian, in the Jewish War (cf. Th. Wiegand, *Milet* i 5 (1919), 53, a corrected version of *ILS* 8970; see also Syme, *loc. cit.* (n. 35); G. Alföldy, *Fasti Hispanienses* (1969), 157, with n. 49). The following should be observed: (1) In 69, as argued above, Titus certainly was not higher in rank than Traianus. Accordingly, Titus is not named on the milestone of that year. (2) There is no reason to assume that Traianus remained in Judaea after Titus took over command of the army. (3) Other inscriptions relating to the Jewish War name only Vespasian as commander, e.g. *ILS* 2544 = *CIL* v, 7, 07; *ILS* 987 = *CIL* x 6659, describing someone who is probably Lepidus as legate of Vespasian only. On official inscriptions in general Vespasian and Titus do not appear as colleagues before 73 (*AÉ* 1903, 256). (4) In 70 Titus was indeed hailed as Imperator, gained a triumph which he celebrated in 71, and was awarded decorations (*ILS* 988; *CIL* iii 2917; *AÉ* 1903, 386). Significantly, there is no record of Traianus ever having received such decorations.

[49] The emperor Trajan later deified his natural father at the same time as his father by adoption, which did not, however, lead to his enrolment among the established *divi*, see *BMC* iii 498–508; Pliny, *Pan.* 89. The honours of *Divus Pater Traianus* may have stressed the fact that he, as much as *Divus Nerva*, was responsible for the present fortune of the emperor Trajan. In a similar vein Pliny insists that Nerva's sole claim to deification was based on his adoption of Trajan, cf. *Pan.* 6–10, esp. 10, 5. See also J.H. Oliver, *Harv. Theol. Rev.* 42 (1949), 36–7.

Postscript

Syme observes that Traianus, as suffect (A.D. 70), followed the second consulate of the great Licinius Mucianus. Like another legionary legate, Aurelius Fulvus, who commanded *III Gallica* in Moesia, Ulpius Traianus had a hand in the intrigue which made Vespasian emperor. Both were legates of some seniority. Fulvus is attested in 64, under Domitius Corbulo in Armenia (*ILS* 232).[1]

The Scythopolis-Legio road is the subject of a monograph: B. Isaac and I. Roll, *Roman Roads in Judaea*, I, *The Scythopolis-Legio Road* (B.A.R. Oxford 1982).

---

[1] R. Syme, 'Antoninus Saturninus', *JRS* 68 (1978), 12–21, at p. 12.

5

VESPASIAN'S TITULATURE IN A.D. 69

A milestone-inscription from Judaea refers to Vespasian as 'Imp. Caesar Vespasianus Aug.'[1] When publishing the stone we argued that this milestone can be dated between July of A.D. 69 and the beginning of 70. In a recent study a correction is suggested for the proposed terminus ante quem.[2] It is claimed that the milestone could have been set up any time before Passover of 70. At that time M. Ulpius Traianus, who is also mentioned on the inscription as legate of the Legion X Fretensis, certainly was superseded by (A.) Larcius Lepidus, Titus' legate of that legion.[3] Passover was celebrated in the month Xanthicus (Nisan), i.e. in April and I would not cavil about a correction of possibly one or two months at most. However, a matter of principle is involved.

The point at issue is the omission on the inscription of the emperor's 'republican' titles: tribunician power, consul and Pontifex Maximus. Buttrey notes that coins of A.D. 70 still bear the legend IMP CAESAR VESPASIANVS AVG. That, however, is beside the point for, as we indicated, the emperor's republican titles are, in this period, never otherwise omitted on milestone-inscriptions. Buttrey assumes that we were referring to milestones from Judaea only, but he has misread our text. The tribunicia potestas and consulate are invariably mentioned on milestones anywhere in the empire until the reign of Severus. I know of only three exceptions from Africa which mention Antoninus Pius.[4]

---

[1] B.H. Isaac and I. Roll, 'A Milestone of A.D. 69 from Judaea: The Elder Trajan and Vespasian', *JRS* 66 (1976), 15–19 and Pl. I. *idem*, Roman Roads in Judaea I, The Legio—Scythopolis Road (1982), 66; 91; Pl. Xa, b.

[2] T.V. Buttrey, Documentary Evidence for the Chronology of the Flavian Titulature (1980), 8 f.

[3] Titus encamped before the walls of Jerusalem at Passover, on the 14th of the month Xanthicus, cf. Jos. BJ v, 3, 1 (98–9) and 13, 7 (567). Buttrey accepts this as the terminus ante quem of the inscription.

[4] For the African inscriptions see: *CIL* viii 10327 f.; 22391. The republican titles are regularly omitted from 198 onwards. For the formulation of milestone-inscriptions of Septimius Severus in general, see: B. Isaac, 'Milestones in Judaea, from Vespasian to Constantine', Palestine Exploration Quarterly 110 (1978), 52 f.; Isaac and Roll, Roman Roads (*supra*, n. 1), 76.

There can be no doubt that the milestone-inscription here discussed is an exception which proves the rule. The republican titles are omitted because the stone was set up after Vespasian's proclamation as emperor by the army, but before the senate confirmed him in his office. Vespasian did not on his own authority assume the titles and offices which were granted by the senate in December 69.[5]

In summary, milestones invariably record the emperor's republican titles until 198. These are omitted on the milestone of 69 in recognition of the fact that Vespasian formally was a usurper at the time.

[5] Suetonius, Vesp. 12 (in a passage describing Vespasian's modesty): Ac ne tribuniciam quidem potestatem statim nec patris patriae appellationem nisi sero recepit. Buttrey considers this a mysterious statement which stands in need of correction. I can only repeat that the milestone of 69 makes it perfectly clear what Suetonius meant and that he was right: Vespasian did not immediately lay claim to titles which were to be endowed by the senate in December (Tacitus, Hist. iv, 3). If Vespasian waited until late in 70 before assuming the title pater patriae that may well have seemed surprisingly long to an author who lived through the reign of Domitian.

6

MILESTONES IN JUDAEA: FROM VESPASIAN
TO CONSTANTINE*

The first persons to explore the Roman road-system in Palestine were Conder and Kitchener, who published their results in *The Survey of Western Palestine*, (1881). The Survey's *Map of Western Palestine* (1880), recording much evidence now lost, has remained an important instrument for the restoration of the ancient road-system. The chronological development of the system has been sketched on several occasions. Kuhl and Meinhold were the first (1928 and 1929), basing themselves on Thomsen's comprehensive survey of all milestones known in his day (Thomsen, 1917). M. Avi-Yonah devoted several articles to the subject (1940, 1950, 1966, 1973). The activities of the Israel Milestones Committee have brought to light new evidence. Avi-Yonah's survey was brought up to date by I. Roll (1974). The aim of all these publications was to reconstruct the chronology of the road-system, based on dated milestones and on induction from historical events. The purpose of the following survey is to present, in advance of final publication of all the milestone-inscriptions, historical evidence derived from the study of material in the inventory of the Israel Milestones Committee.

The policy determining the setting up and formulation of milestone-inscriptions varied from province to province. Material has therefore been arranged according to its origin from different provinces. The evidence from Judaea has been treated systematically. Milestones from the provinces of Arabia and Syria have been used for comparison. First, the distribution in time of milestones in Judaea will be discussed, as well as the historical conclusions to be drawn from it. Second, the formulation of milestone-inscriptions will be dealt with, and third, the selection of *capita viarum*.

---

* This paper was written in the framework of the activities of the Israel Milestones Committee. Wherever I refer to numbers of unpublished milestones I cite from the Committee's inventory. I am grateful to Prof. S. Applebaum, Prof. M. Gichon, Prof. F.G.B. Millar and Dr. I. Roll for various suggestions and corrections. Prof. P. Salama kindly provided me with information on milestones in Africa.

The Distribution in Time

Vespasian

Vespasian is represented by one milestone-inscription of the year 69 (Isaac and Roll, 1976). It marks the construction of the Caesarea-Scythopolis road in that year. This was a war-time project and cannot be regarded as an aspect of the re-organization of the province after the First Jewish Revolt. No further Flavian inscriptions have been discovered as yet in Judaea. North of Ptolemais (Acco) and therefore outside the Roman province of Judaea a milestone of Domitian was found.[1]

Nerva and Trajan

One fragmentary inscription, possibly mentioning Nerva and Trajan or Hadrian, has been discovered in Judaea (Thomsen, no. 263a). Both its decipherment and its identification as a milestone are questionable. It may be relevant that in Pannonia some of the Hadrianic milestone are memorial stones to Nerva, which had been renewed (Mócsy, 1974, 107–108).

Hadrian

Milestones of Hadrian were found on the following roads:

1. Caparcotna—Diocaesarea (Sepphoris) (a) 120 and (b) 129/30 or 135.[2]
2. Caparcotna—Neapolis (Hadrian, fragment) (Thomsen, no. 242).
3. Caparcotna—Scythopolis (129. *IMC*, no. 431).
4. Scythopolis—Jericho (Hadrian, fragment. *IMC*, no. 415).
5. Aelia—Eleutheropolis (Beth Govrin) 130. (Thomsen, no. 282).
6. Aelia—Hebron (fragment, probably 130. Thomsen, no. 296).

Hadrianic activity has been inferred by Avi-Yonah and Roll for two other roads:

1. Aelia—Nicopolis (Emmaus)—Diospolis (Lydda).
2. Jericho—Esbus (in Arabia).

---

[1] W.J. Phythian-Adams, *PEQ* (1924), 94–95; A. Alt, *ZDPV* 51 (1928), 253–64.
[2] The relevant milestones are to be republished shortly, see also below.

Their argument is based on milestones of Marcus Aurelius, mentioning the repair of these roads. This entails their construction at an earlier date (Roll, 1974, 507–508; Thomsen, nos. 230a and 272). Three roads leading from Caparcotna seem to have been constructed and repaired under Hadrian. It is not impossible that the roads from Caparcotna to Caesarea also saw Hadrianic activity, so far unattested. In Arabia the road from Gerasa via Adra'a to Bostra was constructed in 120 (Mittman, 1964). Milestones record repair of the Gerasa—Philadelphia and Philadelphia—Bostra roads in 129 (Thomsen, nos. 110 and 211a). In Syria a milestone on the *Via Maris* dates to the same year (Goodchild, 1948, 121). A milestone of the Ptolemais—Diocaesarea road dates to 135 (Iliffe, 1933, 120).

In 129/30 Hadrian was present and active in the area. The decision to found Col. Aelia Capitolina at Jerusalem seems to have been taken at that time.[3] In 120 and 129/30 an extensive road-network was constructed around the new legionary fortress at Caparcotna, around the new colony and between other key-points. This is the earliest regular series of milestones found in Judaea. The milestones cited above are associated with years of specific importance in the military history of the province. All of them mark roads essential at the time when the stones were erected. It is therefore likely that the earliest *miliaria* on these roads reflect their first construction in accordance with Roman standards. There is, in other words, no need to believe that these *miliaria* were erected on roads previously made. As long as new milestones are being found no conclusion is final, but at present it can be said that there is no evidence of a Roman road-network existing in Judaea before Hadrian. Up to that time the local standard may have been thought sufficient, while in war-time, the legions brought with them units whose task it was to straighten, to broaden and to level existing roads.[4]

---

[3] See, Schürer, 1973, 540–42; 548. For the evidence concerning Hadrian's travels, see Weber, 1907. For the Second Revolt, see now Applebaum, 1976.

[4] Prof. Applebaum pointed out to me that in 4 B.C. Quinctilius Varus marched to Jerusalem through the countryside of Samaria with two legions and auxiliary troops (Jos. *BJ* ii, 5, 1 (66–76); *Ant.* xvii, 10, 9 (286–92)). He must have been able to use the existing roads. For units of ὁδοποιοί in Vespasian's army, see *BJ* iii, 7, 3 (141–42); 6, 2 (118); see also, v, 2, 1 (47).

Marcus Aurelius

All datable milestones of Marcus Aurelius in Judaea are of the year 162. They are found on the following roads:

1. Aelia—Neapolis (Thomsen, no. 261).
2. Aelia—Diospolis (Lydda) (Thomsen, no. 272; *IMC*, no. 307).
3. Aelia—Eleutheropolis (Beth Govrin) (Thomsen, nos. 288, 289).
4. Aelia—Beth Shemesh (modern town situated on the ancient Eleutheropolis—Diospolis road) (Thomsen, no. 305).
5. Aelia—Hebron (Thomsen, no. 303).
6. Eleutheropolis—Hebron (*IMC*, no. 410).
7. Eleutheropolis—North (*IMC*, no. 411).
8. Scythopolis—Jericho (*IMC*, no. 214).
9. Scythopolis—North (*IMC*, no. 416).
10. Scythopolis—Caparcotna (Avi-Yonah, 1946, 98 nos. 17; 18; *IMC*, no. 203).
11. Caparcotna—Caesarea (*IMC*, no. 246).
12. Caparcotna—Diocaesarea (Avi-Yonah, 1946, 96 no. 13; 97 no. 14; Hecker, 1961, 182).
13. Gophna—Jericho (uncertain) (Thomsen, no. 266).
14. Caesarea—Ptolemais (Avi-Yonah, 1960, 37 = *AÉ*, 1971, 470).

In Arabia:

1. *Via Nova Traiana*, several sections (Thomsen, no. 78b; 101a; 126a1; 136; 143c).
2. Scythopolis—Gerasa (continuation of above no. 10) (Thomsen, nos. 221; 222; 225b; 226).
3. Jericho—Esbus (Thomsen, no. 230a).

In Syria:

1. *Via Maris*, 161 (Goodchild, 1948, ref. 215).
2. Heliopolis—Damascus, 163–65 (Thomsen nos. 31; 32; 33).[5]

This is by far the most extensive series attested in Judaea. With the discovery of additional milestones the list may yet be supplemented. On published milestones in other parts of the empire the name of

---

[5] These are not milestones because the emperor's republican titles are missing. Note also the elements which would not be found on milestones in Syria: the information that the legate was *amicus Caesaris*, the name of the centurion in charge and the town which paid for the work. Cf. Thomsen, no. 28.

Marcus is rarely found. Although definite conclusions of this sort have to wait for the publication of *CIL* xvii, the evidence available at present seems to point to two conclusions: first, the series of mile-stones of 161–62 in Judaea and Arabia is not the result of routine road-repair. Second, we must assume that *SHA, Vita Marci* 11.5 '*vias etiam urbis atque itinera diligentissime curavit*', if true, refers to Rome and Italy alone. It is interesting to note, that milestones in Judaea and Arabia have a uniform text, apart from the name of the legate on Arabian milestones.[6] Without doubt this programme was associated with the Parthian war which started in the winter of 161/62, as al-ready noted by Avi-Yonah (1966, 76). Following the defeat of Attidius Cornelianus, legate of Syria, the emperor Lucius Verus came to the East as head of the expeditionary force (cf. Birley, 1966, 161 for the chronology). Of the legions in Judaea VI Ferr. certainly took part in this campaign (*PIR*², A 754). Verus himself stayed behind at Antiochia and Laodicea, leaving the fighting to his generals. The similarities between the milestone-inscriptions in two different provinces indicate that the programme discussed here must have been initiated by his staff. The man in charge of the programme may have been the freed-man Nicomedes, Lucius Verus' foster-father, who began his eques-trian career as *proc. ad silices* (the paving of the streets in Rome). Before the war he was *praefectus vehiculorum*. He went with Verus to the East in charge of the commissariat of the expeditionary force (Pflaum, 1960, no. 163).

Pertinax

Pertinax reigned from 1 January until 28 March 193. Milestones bear-ing his name are rare. In Judaea three are found on the Scythopolis—Caparcotna road (Avi-Yonah, 1946, 99 nos. 20; 21; 22; to be re-published) and one belonging to the Caesarea—Ptolemais road (Avi-Yonah, 1960, no. 2 = *AÉ*, 1971, 471). A fragmentary inscription of the Caparcotna—Diocaesarea road is, because of its spacing, likely to refer to Pertinax rather than Severus (Hecker, 1961, 181). In Arabia

---

[6] Compare Thomsen, no. 261 with no. 221 (Welles, 1938, nos. 258–59) and with Thomsen, no. 78b. Minor differences such as the absence of certain titles may be explained by the assumption that drafts were sent to officials in charge of different sectors. Copyists' mistakes must have caused such elements to be missing on all milestones of a sector.

Pertinax is met with along several sections of the *Via Nova Traiana* (Thomsen, no. 77a 1 etc.).

In Judaea, these are the first milestones since 162, in Arabia since 181 (Thomsen, no. 86a 2 etc.). In Numidia too, milestones are recorded bearing the name of Pertinax and of the legate L. Naevius Quadratianus (*CIL* viii, 10238; 22337).[7] In other provinces I could find no milestones of his reign. Those studied by us were all in secondary use. Two Arabian milestones also are reported to show traces of a second inscription (Thomsen, no. 88b 1–2; Mittmann, 1964, 125–27, Tafel 5b = *AÉ*, 1969–70, 618). The re-use of older milestones suggests that these inscriptions served a political purpose and do not record actual road-reconstruction. Of interest is the presence, on the Arabian milestones of the younger Pertinax as Caesar and *princeps iuventutis*. The sources stress the fact, that Pertinax refused his son the title of Caesar and did not allow his own children to live in the palace.[8] On coins the absence of the wife and son of the emperor is remarkable in its contrast to the behaviour of his predecessors and successors, as noted by Mattingly, who also observes that the coin-types of Pertinax make up a series almost unparalleled in the whole imperial coinage (*BMC Emp*, v, lxiii; lxv). Consequently there is good reason to suspect that the milestone-inscriptions of Pertinax in Arabia and Judaea were put up not by order from Rome, but on initiative of legates, friendly to the new emperor. They may have been influenced by the news of two coups, attempted by praetorians.[9] An interesting point is the identity of the emperor whose names were replaced by those of Pertinax. The milestone recorded by Thomsen, no. 88b 1–2, leaves little doubt that it was Commodus, who is as yet not otherwise attested in Judaea. Aelius Severianus, legate of Arabia,[10] and his unknown colleague in Judaea apparently responded to the desire of the senate to strike Commodus's name from all public and private records (*SHA, Vita Comm.* 20, 5; also: 18–19 and Dio lxxiii 2 (307)).

---

[7] For the legate, see Birley, 1971, 350; Barbieri, 1952, no. 378.

[8] Dio 73.7.1 (311); *Vita Pert.* 6.9; 13.4; Herodian 2.4.9; cf. a dedication to Pertinax in Gerasa, Welles, 1938, 148; also: a dedication in Mediomatricum, *CIL* xiii 4323 = *ILS* 410 and Millar, 1964, 135 n. 6.

[9] *Vita Pert.* 6.3–5 and 10.1–7; Crook, 1955, 78–9; F. Cassola, *PP*, 20 (1965), 451–77; Birley, 1971, 104–14; 1967, 7–13.

[10] Cf. Birley, 1971, 337. *CIL* iii 13614 and Thomsen, p. 28 cannot be right in ascribing to Pertinax and Aelius Severianus a milestone of the Palmyra-Sura road. Obviously a governor of Arabia cannot have put up milestones in Syria, where Niger was legate.

Septimius Severus

Milestones dated to several years of his reign have been found on various roads:

194. Aelia—Hebron (Thomsen, nos. 300; 304).
198. Scythopolis—Caparcotna (Avi-Yonah, 1946, 100 no. 25; *IMC*, nos. 334; 337).
   Scythopolis—North (Thomsen, no. 255a).
199. Neapolis—Phasaelis (*IMC*, no. 393).
   Aelia—Eleutheropolis (Landau, 1964, 232; 234–35, Pl. 23.2).
210. Antipatris-Diospolis (Lydda) (Thomsen, no. 20).

Fragmentary, certainly Severan:

198–201. Caesarea—Ptolemais (*IMC*, no. 330).
198–210. Scythopolis—Neapolis (Thomsen, no. 291; Landau, 1964, 232–33).

The milestones of 194 must, like those of Pertinax, be seen against the background of the civil war. We found published milestones of 194 on record in Arabia (Thomsen, no. 76b etc.), Judaea and in the newly created province of Syria-Phoenice (*AÉ*, 1930, 141; Thomsen, no. 29).[11] It seems no coincidence that the first two are the provinces which provided us with milestones of Pertinax as well. The milestones of 194 in Judaea and Arabia will have been declarations of loyalty by provincial governors, who supported first Pertinax and then his former legionary legate Severus (cf. *SHA, Vita Sev.* 4.4; Birley, 1971, 104–105). The legate in Arabia, Severianus Maximus, was the same as in 193. The governor of Judaea is not known for these years. Of the legions in Judaea the VI Ferr. supported Severus (Ritterling, *Legio*, 1312–13; 1593) and X Fret. his competitor Niger (*ibid.*, 1312 ff.; 1675). In 195 we find at least 17 centurions of X Fret. in charge of construction works at an aqueduct near Jerusalem.[12] Apparently Severus trusted the legionaries more as masons than as combatants in Mesopotamia.

---

[11] Thomsen, no. 29 has to be read '[Ma]nilium [F]u [scum]' instead of '[Ve]nidium [R]u[fum]' as proposed by the editors. See also a milestone of December 194 from the neighbourhood of Sitifis, Mauretania: *CIL* viii 10351 = 22407.

[12] Vetrali, 1967, 149–61, figs. 1–5; for the date, *Échos d'Orient*, 4 (1900–1901), 134–36. The consul mentioned in the inscription should be Q. Tineius Clemens, *ordinarius* in 195 (Degrassi, no. 948) rather than M. Herennius Faustus [Ti?] Iulius Clemens Tadius Flaccus, suffect shortly before 205 (Degrassi, p. 57; W. Eck, *Historia*, 24 (1975), 329 ff.).

Milestones of 198 and 199 must be associated with the emperor's presence in the area. After the Parthian expedition he came to Palestine in the autumn of 198.[13] Milestones of that year can be dated to several months before Severus's arrival.[14] To the same time belongs the well-known Jewish dedication to Severus, to his sons (Caracalla not yet Augustus) and—as a sensible afterthought?—to Julia Domna (*IGR* iii, 1106 = Frey, 1952, 157–59, no. 972).

In 199 Severus went on to Egypt, perhaps accompanied by a detachment of the VI Ferr. (*IGR* i, 1089). Generally much road-building and repair in Severus's time was connected with his movements and those of his armies. This is clear from a comparison of the location of dated milestones with the imperial itineraries.[15] Remarkable is too that there seem to be hardly any milestones anywhere of the years 202–207, when the emperor was at Rome, apart from a visit to Africa (for which, see, *CIL* xiii 2705). Thereafter the campaign in Britain is marked again by milestones.[16]

The Formulation of Milestone-Inscriptions of Severus

The formula of the milestone-inscriptions, the most rigidly controlled category of official inscriptions (see above, n. 5, and below, p. 56), changes gradually between 194 and 198. In 194 the inscriptions are completely traditional (e.g. Thomsen nos. 29 and 300).[17] In 195 Caracalla appears on milestones when he was not yet elevated to the rank of Caesar.[18] Albinus, on the other hand, does not appear on

---

[13] For the chronology, see Millar, 1964, 143; Hasebroek, 1921, 119–20. Z. Rubin, *Chiron*, 5 (1975), 432 ff. has pointed out that Caracalla appears on coins as Augustus late in 197. He argues that Ctesiphon was captured at this time rather than in 198.

[14] *IMC*, nos. 334; 337; 393. The date will be discussed in a forthcoming road-report. For milestones of 198 on the Via Maris in Syria, see Goodchild, 1948, 121.

[15] See, Hasebroek, 1921, 95; 111; 127–28; Magie, 1950, 1543–45; M.H. Ballance, *Anatolian Studies*, 8 (1958), 232; note also Severus's march in 197 through Cilicia and Syria (*Vita Sept. Sev.* 15.2; Hasebroek, 1921, 111), marked by milestones, *CIL* iii 12120; 12123; *AÉ*, 1965, 325; Thomsen, nos. 34; 35. For the famous inscription, recording the setting up of Forum Pizus in 202, Mihailov, 1964, no. 1690, 103 ff.

[16] Hasebroek, 1921, 141; *RIB*, 2266 and Sedgley, 1975, no. 52; *RIB*, 2228.

[17] For the formula of Severan *miliaria* in Mauretania Caes., see P. Salama, *Libyca*, 1 (1953), 233–34. For the subject in general, see Hammond, 1959.

[18] E.g. *CIL* iii, 5704; 5745; 5980. For the date of Caracalla's elevation to the rank of Caesar, see *ILS* 8805 = *IGR* iv 566 and *Vita Sept. Sev.* 10.3 and 14.3; cf. Birley, 1971, 185, n. 1; 187 and 191–92. Caracalla's coinage as Caesar begins summer 196, cf. Mattingly, *BMC Emp.*, v, lxv.

milestones, even in the years when he was recognized as Caesar by Severus (an exception, *AÉ*, 1926, 144). In 197 Severus appears with his predecessors as ancestors without having been adopted legally (Hasebroek, 1921, 90 ff.; Hammond, 1959, 77). In the same year the military cognomina are introduced on milestones (e.g. *CIL* iii 1210). Henceforward these are hardly ever omitted. Severus was the first to bestow upon his wife the title of *mater castrorum* and to permit her to be mentioned on milestones (e.g. *CIL* iii 13689) from 198 onward. Until Severus's reign milestones invariably contained all or part of the emperor's 'republican' titles, referring more especially to the consulate and *tribunicia potestas*. The omission of these titles is an innovation of the Severan period and is found on milestones of 198 onward, since Caracalla is usually mentioned as Augustus.[19] Imperial propaganda thus shows a sudden and outspoken shift from the formal constitutional and traditional elements of the monarchy to the military aspects. F. Millar has shown the unimportance of the constitutional forms of the monarchy to Cassius Dio, a senator writing in the Severan period (Miller, 1964, 98–100). The changes noted in official inscriptions appear thus to be in accordance with the attitude of a representative of the senatorial class. Previously the formal recognition of the 'republican' origin of the principate may well have been considered an expression of the emperor's relationship with the senate (cf. Pertinax's *princeps senatus*). The imperial formula, as published on a milestone, may be said to represent first and foremost the recognition or the rejection by the emperor of those who gave him power: the senate, the army, his predecessors and his family.

Caracalla

1.	+	212	Scythopolis—North (Thomsen, no. 244; *IMC*, no. 392).
2.			Eleutheropolis—Nicopolis (Thomsen, no. 276).
3.	+	213	Scythopolis—Caparcotna (Avi-Yonah, 1946, 99, no. 23; *IMC*, no. 209).
4.			Scythopolis—Jericho (*IMC*, no. 414; Avi-Yonah, 1966, 75).
5.	+		Caparcotna—Ptolemais (Avi-Yonah, 1946, 96, no. 12).
6.	+		Caesarea—Ptolemais (Avi-Yonah, 1960, 38 = *AÉ*, 1971, 472).

---

[19] E.g. *CIL* ix, 8022; 8025, iii, 14200. For milestones without republican titles and Caracalla still 'Aug. n. fil.', see *CIL* iii 10616; viii 22579. However, irregularities in the titulature of Severus are frequent on inscriptions, see W.F. Snyder, *MAAR*, 15 (1938), 62–9 and P. Salama, *Libyca*, 1 (1953), 233. Cf. also M. Gichon and B. Isaac, *IEJ* 24 (1974), 118.

7.   213?   Eleutheropolis—Hebron (*IMC*, no. 412).
8.   +   215   Caesarea—Ptolemais (Avi-Yonah, 1960, 38, no. 4 = *AÉ*, 1971,
                 473).
9. Probably Caracalla: Eleutheropolis—Ascalon (*IMC*, no. 413).
'*vias et pontes restituit*' on milestones of all roads except Caesarea—Ptolemais
and Eleutheropolis—Hebron.
+   Means milestones of Septimius Severus attested on the same road.
Total: Thirteen milestones on seven different roads, two being dated to
     212, five dated to 213, one to 215.

The year 214/5 marked Caracalla's Parthian campaign.[20] There is
evidence of long-term planning for this expedition, reflected, among
other things, by road-making and by the preparation of *mansiones*.[20a]
However, these preparations can hardly have started as early as 212,
the year in which Caracalla's first milestones appear in Judaea and
in Syria (Thomsen, nos. 43; 46 and, possibly, no. 44). As indicated
above, three of the seven roads which have milestones of Caracalla
also have milestones of Severus. Moreover, one road has milestones
dating to 213 and 215. This shows, that the inscriptions do not mark
extensive road-construction in that year, but were meant to be an
affirmation of the emperor's authority (see also above, p. 51). The
formula '*vias et pontes restituit*' on the other hand, claims that roads
and bridges were indeed repaired. This phrase is found in Judaea
only on Caracallan milestones and on one milestone of Elagabalus
or Severus Alexander (*IMC*, no. 414). The phrase occurs under
Caracalla on milestones of specific areas.[21] We may conclude, that
from 198 onward down to the death of Caracalla both road-repair
and the provision of milestones were a matter of provincial routine,
rather than an extraordinary initiative, as under Hadrian and in 162
and, possibly, in 198 itself. Goodchild (1948, 114) has pointed out
that the date 198 represents the first major overhaul of the road-
system in Syria.

Milestones After Caracalla

217.   Macrinus   Antipatris—Lydda (Thomsen, no. 21).
                                    Aelia—Hebron (Thomsen, no. 295).[22]

---

[20] For the chronology of the campaign, see, A. Maricq, *Syria*, 34 (1957), 297–302.
[20a] See Millar, 1964, 152 with notes 3 and 4; Rickmann, 1971, 280–81.
[21] Pannonia Superior (*CIL* iii 4639), Helvetian territory (*CIL* xiii, 9061; 9068;
9072), Narbonensis (*CIL* xii 5430).
[22] For an inventory of inscriptions of Macrinus, see, P. Salama, REA, 66 (1964),
334 ff.

222–35.	Severus Alexander	Scythopolis—Caparcotna (*IMC*, nos. 294; 333).
(?)		Eleutheropolis—Ascalon (*IMC*, no. 257).
(?) 235–38.	Maximinus Thrax	Scythopolis—North (Thomsen, no. 246a).
		Scythopolis—Jericho (*IMC*, no. 313).
		Scythopolis—Neapolis (Thomsen, nos. 248; 249; 255b).
		Caesarea—Ptolemais (Avi-Yonah, 1960, 39 = *AÉ*, 1971, 474).
		Ptolemais—Caparcotna (*IMC*, no. 421).
		Aelia—Nicopolis—Diospolis (Roll, 1972).
		Aelia—Eleutheropolis (A. Alt, *PJb*, 25 (1929), 124–26).
		Eleutheropolis—Diospolis (*ibidem*).
238.	Gordian I	Caesarea—Ptolemais (Avi-Yonah, 1960, 39 = *AÉ*, 1971, 475).
286–305.	Diocletian + Maximian/Scythopolis—Caparcotna (*IMC*, no. 340).
324–46.	Constantine + Crispus/Scythopolis—Caparcotna (Avi-Yonah, 1946, 100 no. 25), secondary use.
333–37.	Constantine	Caparcotna—Diocaesarea (Avi-Yonah, 1946, 97 no. 16), secondary use.[23]
undated	Constantine	Scythopolis—Neapolis (Thomsen, no. 255c.).
undated	Constantine	Ptolemais—Diocaesarea (Iliffe, 1933, 120–21).

Severus Alexander

Severus Alexander's milestones on the Scythopolis—Legio road and, possibly, the Eleutheropolis—Ascalon road are probably associated with his Persian campaign, 231–33. Two Greek inscriptions, dating to 233, seem to have belonged to a series of milestone-inscriptions, marking the coastal road in Sinai, from Pelusium to the frontier of Syria-Palaestina.[24] In Arabia milestones of the same emperor are probably dated to 230 (Thomsen, nos. 126e 1; 157; 164a 2).[25] In Gerasa two pedestals or bases with dedications to Severus Alexander are dated to 231/2 (Welles, 1938, nos. 157–58). Preparations for his

---

[23] Many milestones of these years have been found in Arabia and Syria, see Thomsen, 93 and Goodchild, 1948, 127.

[24] D. Barag, *IEJ* 23 (1973), 50–52; *AÉ*, 1973 (1976), 559; 559 bis.

[25] The lost inscription, *CIL* iii 166, dated to 214 is not likely to have been a milestone, as suggested by Goodchild, 1948, 120. In Syria there is no parallel before the fourth century of a milestone mentioning a city otherwise than as *caput viae* (above n. 5 and p. 56).

Persian campaign are reflected by widespread road-repairs.[26] Alexander himself did not visit Judaea and Arabia. His presence is recorded at Antioch and, with part of the army, at Palmyra (*IGR* iii, 1033; Herodian, 6.4.3. ff.). Road-reconstruction in Judaea and Arabia may have served the Egyptian troops taking part in the expedition (Wilcken, *Chrestomathie*, no. 41). Attention to logistics and the provision of Alexander's armies is commented upon by the *Historia Augusta, Vita Sev. Alex.* 45.2; 47. Preparation of *mansiones, stativae* and *annona* two months in advance is mentioned in a well-known decree quoted there. It is very likely that there is a connexion of road-building and milestones with the collection of *annona* for this expedition. As regards both Caracalla's campaign and Severus Alexander's, Professor Millar pointed out to me that there is good evidence for the collection of supplies elsewhere in the East.[27] As suggested regarding Marcus Aurelius's Parthian campaign, the official in charge of the commissariat may also have been responsible for the roads (above, p. 50). At the time of Alexander's campaign this was again a friend of the emperor and his family, C. Furius Sabinus Aquila Timesitheus, later praetorian praefect and father-in-law of Gordian III (Pflaum, 1948, 53–62; 1960, 811–21). In 231–32 he served in an interesting dual function as financial procurator of Syria-Palaestina and *exactor reliquorum annonae sacrae expeditionis.*

Maximinus Thrax and Gordian I

Numerous milestones, found in most provinces of the empire, date to Maximinus' reign (Bersanetti, 1940, 23–36). Many of them bear phrases indicating that roads were indeed repaired (*op. cit.*, 32–34). As regards Judaea this series must be considered an extraordinary initiative of the central government in years when otherwise no milestones were erected in the province. A matter of controversy has been the significance of erasure in many provinces of the names of Maximinus and his son as an indicator of support for either Maximinus

---

[26] *CIL* iii, 10628; –30; –33; –50 ff.; –55; –57; 11331; –35; H.U. Instinsky, *Sitz. ber. Preuss. Akad. Wiss., Ph.-h.Kl.* (1938), 421–22 (not accessible to me); Magie, 1950, 694; 1560; *AÉ*, 1905, 132–33; D. Wilson, *An. Studies*, 10 (1960), 135; D. Oates, *Sumer*, 11 (1955), 34–43. Cf. Whittaker's comments on Herodian, 6.4 (Loeb).

[27] For Caracalla's expedition, see J. Schwartz in *Chronique d'Égypte* (1939) and now *P. Oxy*, 3091. For Severus Alexander, see the Cilician inscription, *AÉ*, 1972, 626–28.

or his enemy Gordian I.[28] In Judaea none of the extant milestones of Maximinus has been touched and yet two milestones bearing the titles of Gordian indicate support for this emperor and the senate.

Diocletian, Constantine and After

Thomsen's list for Syria and Arabia is rather poor for the years of crisis in the third century (Thomsen, 91–92). In these provinces, however, evidence for 284–335 is very extensive, while in Judaea few milestones are listed throughout the third century and none after Constantine.[29] This is remarkable, since Diocletian's reign saw much activity in the Negev and his stay in Tiberias in 286 is better attested in the Jewish sources than any other emperor's visit (for the evidence, Avi-Yonah, 1962, 127). The Diocletianic reforms left only three army-units north of Hebron (*Not. Dig. Or.* (Seeck), 34.21; 47; 48). The other formations were moved to the Negev and the Arabian *limes*.

Consideration of the distribution in time of milestones thus allows the following conclusions: the introduction into Judaea of milestones coincided with the arrival under Hadrian of the second legion based in the province. It should be noted that in Britain and Pannonia too the first milestones date to Hadrian's reign. In Pannonia they are associated with the building activity on the *limes* from 124 onward (Mócsy, 1974, 107–108). In Britain they are considered part of the many reforms said to have been instituted by Hadrian.[30] Apart from the milestones of 193–94 and a group of 199–215, milestones in Judaea were seen to be connected with specific military campaigns involving troop-movements and the collection of *annona*. After the two legions had been removed from Judaea, at an uncertain date in the third century, hardly any milestone-inscriptions were added. The conclusion of all this is, that in Judaea milestones were set up, first of all, to serve the military.[31] Interestingly, Jewish sources do not seem to refer to Roman roads before the third century.[32]

---

[28] See Bersanetti, 1940, Chapter 4 and comments by Barbieri, *Epigraphica*, 4 (1942), 90–93; P. Townsend, *YCS*, 14 (1955), 17 ff.

[29] In Arabia an extensive series of milestones bears the name Julian; Thomsen, nos. 126; 127 etc.

[30] *SHA, Vita Hadr.* 11.2; cf. S. Frere, 1974, 147 ff. Milestones, *RIB*, 2244; 2265; 2272; cf. Sedgley, 1975, 2.

[31] More than 320 anepigraphic milestones are, of course, undatable. Comparison with dated milestones by petrographic analysis and classification of forms may eventually help in this matter.

[32] I owe this point to Mr. I. Ben Shalom of Tel-Aviv University. Alon, 1954, 42

After the distribution in time of milestones in Judaea, two other subjects need to be studied, namely the formula of the inscriptions and the selection of *capita viarum*.

The Formula

While in the first part of this discussion characteristics were noted of Severan milestone-texts all over the empire (above, pp. 52–3), attention will now be paid to the formulation of milestone-inscriptions as found in Judaea from Hadrian onward. The names of governors are usually mentioned on milestones in Syria and Arabia. On milestones of Hadrian, however, these names are lacking in both provinces as well as in Judaea (Syria: Thomsen, no. 11; 30a 1; Arabia: Thomsen, no. 110; Mittmann, 1964, 122–25). When the emperor's name appears and the governor's is ignored, this may be an expression of Hadrian's efforts to achieve efficiency by centralized direction. As noted, the first regular series of milestones in Judaea dates to Hadrian's reign. It is a feature peculiar to all later milestones in Judaea, that on none of them is the governor ever mentioned. This is one of the reasons why we do not know the identity of many *legati* of the province. The omission, for which Hadrian's series constituted the precedent, should tell us something about the organization of road-building in Judaea. It might be mentioned in this connexion that in Britannia and Pannonia legates are mentioned on milestones, even though in these provinces Hadrian also was the first to set up *miliaria*. Pekáry (1968, 77–86) has shown that the governor is not usually mentioned in the West. He has further collected evidence of road-construction by officials who were not governors, among them financial procurators. It should be noted that rules were more stringent for milestone-texts than for other inscriptions. Milestones in Syria, for example, never mention military units or towns. But Thomsen, nos. 5 and 28, both commemorative inscriptions, mention *leg. III Gallica* and *Col. Heliopolitana* respectively. There are important regional differences. In Numidia the *III Augusta* is regularly mentioned on milestones (e.g. *CIL* viii 10335). In Mauretania Caesariensis Sitifis is often named (e.g. *CIL*

---

considered *Mekhilta of R. Ishmael* (ed. Horovitz and Rabin), 202 as containing an authentic first century reference to forced road-repair and construction. However, E.E. Urbach, *Beḥinot bebikoreth hasifruth*, 4 (1953), 70 has pointed out that these references are missing in all parallel sources.

viii, 10337; 10384) and the *Coh. Breucorum* (*ibid.*, 22598; −9; 22600) and *i Pannon.* (*ibid.*, 22602/4) are found. Regional studies are needed to explain the significance of such features.

We should ask then which official was in charge. The extensive series of *miliaria* in Judaea and Arabia of 162, the first since Hadrian, was discussed above, as well as its connexion with the Parthian expedition of Lucius Verus. It was suggested that the man in charge may have been the freedman Nicomedes, who was responsible for transport facilities. In Severus Alexander's Parthian campaign another equestrian official, Timesitheus, may have been responsible for the setting up of *miliaria* as proculator of Syria-Palaestina and *exactor reliquorum annonae* (above, p. 55). Timesitheus, as official in charge of *annona*, may have been responsible for the roads in several provinces. It is also quite possible that, as procurator, he supervised the roads in Judaea himself. In the absence of other evidence the formulation of Judaean milestone-inscriptions might be taken to indicate that, ever since Hadrian, the procurator, rather than the legate was responsible for the roads and milestones. While there is no proof of this, the omission of the legate certainly strengthens the conclusion, based on the distribution in time of the *miliaria*, that these were set up at special occasions, on the initiative of the central government.

The Selection of Capita Viarum

A third subject for discussion is the indication of distance on Judaean milestones. *Miliaria*-inscriptions have preserved indications of distance on 16 roads. This provides us with an opportunity to clarify the system, which determined the choice of *capita viarum*.

It is important to note that the system did not remain uniform throughout the period under consideration. This has caused errors in interpretation by scholars, who did not notice this fact. The system, conceived as static, has been thought to furnish information on the provincial and municipal administrative boundaries.[33] Evidence to the contrary has been collected from several parts of the empire

---

[33] Avi-Yonah, 1973, cols. 416, 419, 420, 426, 427; *The Holy Land* (1966), 128–29. Mommsen stated clearly that the selection of *capita viarum* was worth studying while rejecting any connexion between *territoria* and counting of miles, *Hermes*, 12 (1877), 486 ff. = *Gesammelte Schriften*, v, 66–67.

by Pekáry and need not be recapitulated (Pekáry, 1968, 138–48). However, much of what has been written on the territorial history of Roman Judaea has been based on this fallacy and will therefore have to be reviewed. Avi-Yonah likewise assumed that the indications of distance in Eusebius's *Onomasticon*, perhaps based on road-maps, reflect the territorial division of the province (Avi-Yonah, 1966, 128–29; cf. Alt, 1931, 213 ff.). This assumption has led to many speculative boundary-lines which cannot be accepted. For Arabia S. Mittmann (1964, 132–36) has argued that milestones furnish information concerning territoria. Here too a change of the system of reckoning will have caused this misconception.

In Arabia, Judaea and Syria distances are indicated either in Latin or in Greek, or in both languages. As the town, serving as *caput viae*, is often mentioned, identification is no problem. In Judaea milestones giving the distance in both Latin and Greek either reckon from the same spot or from two different points. Milestones reckoning from two different points never give those distances in only one language. Latin is not found after Caracalla. This shows that the Greek is often a later addition on older milestones which had at first only Latin inscriptions. Considerations of lettering and layout confirm this observation. It is likely that Greek was added under Severus. Both Greek and Latin often reckon from the same *caput viae*. When two different places are mentioned we may infer that the place from where miles were counted was changed and with it the reasons for choosing it. Three instances of such changes in the system of counting may be cited.

A milestone of 69 on the Caesarea—Scythopolis road marks the 34th mile from Caesarea (Isaac and Roll, 1976, 17). This shows that in 69, miles were counted from Caesarea all along the road, since there was no town of significance between the milestone and Scythopolis. However, on milestones of Marcus Aurelius onward miles were counted from Caesarea along the section west of Caparcotna, *castra* of VI Ferr., and from Scythopolis east of Caparcotna (Isaac and Roll, 1976, 16). The second instance, two Hadrianic milestones on the Caparcotna—Diocaesarea road are to be re-published shortly. One milestone gives the distance from Caparcotna as six miles in Latin only (Avi-Yonah, 1946, 97, no. 15, incorrectly ascribed to Caracalla). The other gives the distance from Caparcotna in Latin as five miles and in Greek from Diocaesarea as eleven miles (Hecker, 1961, 175–76; Lifshitz, 1960, 109–11). The Greek lettering is cut only half as deep as the Latin inscription. This road was first paved when a

legionary fortress was established at Caparcotna and the Hadrianic
milestone shows that miles were then counted from there. Apparently the distance from Diocaesarea was added later on the Hadrianic
milestone. A milestone of Caracalla gives the distance from Diocaesarea only (Avi-Yonah, 1948, 96, no. 12). It should be noted that the
legionary fortress never appears on later milestones, although seven
are known on roads around the fortress. Legionary territories are
often difficult to define, but VI Ferr. will have had territory somewhere. This serves as additional proof that there is no connexion
between territory and milestones.

The third instance of a change in the system is taken from the
South of the province. On the road from Eleutheropolis (Beth Govrin)
to Jerusalem a milestone of the year 162 gives the distance from
Beth Govrin in Latin as six miles and from Col. Aelia Capitolina
(Jerusalem) as twenty-four miles (Landau, 1964, 232–33, Pl. 23.2;
here the Latin numeral VI was unnecessarily considered to be a
stonecutter's mistake for [XX] IV). Re-examination of the stone again
showed that the Greek lettering is cut only half as deep as the Latin
numeral reckoning from Beth Govrin. When the milestone was set
up, in 162, the town of Beth Govrin did not yet have municipal
status and the name of Eleutheropolis, which it received in 199/200
(Hill, *BMC Palestine*, xxiii; cf.: Hasebroek, 1921, 120). In 162 there
was no apparent reason for its being *caput viae* rather than Aelia.
Moreover, a milestone of the year 199 reckons the distance in Greek
from Aelia only (Landau, 1964, 232; 234–35, Pl. 23.2). The explanation must be the presence in or near Beth Govrin of a vexillation
of VI Ferr., according to an inscription, dated on palaeographical
grounds to the second third of the second century (Iliffe, 1933, 121 =
AÉ, 1933, 15). A similar inscription was found in the northern Jordan valley near Tel-Shalem, 11 km south-south-east of Beth-Shean
(N. Tsori, *IEJ*, 21 (1971), 53–54; Applebaum, 1976, 30). Excavations
at the site revealed fragments of a bronze statue of Hadrian and
remains of a military installation (G. Foerster, *Qadmoniot*, 3 (1975)
38–40).[34] To the West of this site passes the road from Scythopolis
through the Jordan valley to Jericho. It cannot be a coincidence that
on this road no milestones were found south of Tel-Shalem, even

---

[34] Eusebius, *Onomasticon*, ed. Klostermann, 153, 6 (Hieronymus), '*in octavo quoque
lapide a Scythopoli in campo vicus Salumias appellatur*'. See also John 3.23; Epiphanius,
de mens. et pond. 72, 74.

though the desert conditions in the Jordan valley would have been favourable for the preservation of *miliaria* (Avi-Yonah, 1966, 75; *IMC*, no. 213). The distance is given in both Latin and Greek.

We thus see two systems of counting miles in Judaea. The earlier (in Latin) belongs mainly to the series of Hadrian and 162. This system is based on military key-points in the province. It was superseded by a later system in Greek, probably dating to Severan times. This system, based on the six most important towns in the province, had a 'civilian' character (maintained by rather than for civilians). A change of *capita viarum* along the coastal road from Antioch to Ptolemais has been noticed by R.G. Goodchild (1948, 91 ff.; Pekáry, 1968, 146–47). This change can be dated to 198. This would be an acceptable date for the change in Judaea as well. The importance of this year has been noted above (p. 52). Further study may clarify the reasons for the introduction of a new system of counting miles. In other provinces milestone-inscriptions are found recording those who executed the work, towns or, more rarely, military units.[35] This is not the case in Judaea. Pekáry (1968, 146–47) emphatically denies the feasibility of any connexion between counting of miles and assignation of duties concerning road-repair. Evidence from Judaea, however, may suggest differently. A comparison of errors and anomalies, found in milestone-inscriptions of several roads in the neighbourhood of Scythopolis, shows that the inscriptions were the work of local stonecutters from Severus onward.[36] Further evidence may help us to ascertain whether the towns, mentioned as *caput viae*, were normally responsible for the setting up of milestones.

Conclusion

Milestones were set up in Judaea from Hadrian onward and as long as Judaea remained a military province. Their dates link many of them with the great eastern expeditions of the second and third century. G. Rickmann has argued recently that what is known of the

---

[35] E.g. *CIL* viii, 10335; –40; –41; xiii, 9116 (towns); *RIB* 2313 and *JRS* 56 (1966), 230; *CIL* viii, 10114 = 22173 (military units). See also above n. 5 and p. 56.

[36] ἀπὸ τῆς πόλεως instead of ἀπὸ Σκυθοπόλεως (*IMC*, no. 337); the abbreviation 'ADI' for '*Adiabenicus*' on Severan milestones of several roads around Scythopolis (*idem* and *IMC*, no. 393).

annona militaris and the creation of the *Itineraria* in this period should be seen in the same light (1971, ch. viii and esp. 280–81). The formula of the milestones suggests that they were erected mainly on the initiative of the central government. Until Severus military key-points served as *caput viae*. From Severus onward miles were counted from the six most important towns in the province, a reform which will have been connected with his policy of urbanization and which may, among other things, reflect responsibility for milestones and roads at the time. However, further study is needed to clarify these matters, especially in other provinces with similar phenomena, such as Arabia and Syria.[37] Pekáry has emphasized the connexion between road-repair and the organization of the *cursus publicus*.[38] While it might be argued that the first series of milestones in Judaea marks the first systematic construction of Roman roads in the province (above, p. 49), there is, of course, no reason to suppose that roads were made or repaired only when milestones were set up. Nevertheless, if milestones are an indication of such things, Judaea may be suspected of having had a provincial government with little initiative of its own.

Bibliography

This is not a full bibliography of the subject concerned, but solely a list of the works to which abbreviated reference has been made in the text or the notes. Standard works of reference and periodicals are not included.

Alon, G., 1954. *The History of the Jews in the period of the Mishnah and the Talmud*, I–II (Hebrew).
Alt, A., 1931. *ZDPV* 54, 213 ff.
Applebaum, S., 1976. *Prolegomena to the study of the Second Jewish Revolt.*
Avi-Yonah, M., 1940. *Map of Roman Palestine.*
——, 1946. *QDAP* 12, 84–102.
——, 1950. *IEJ* 1, 54–60 = 1966, 181–87.
——, 1960. *BIES* 24, 37–39, (Hebrew).
——, 1962. *Geschichte der Juden im Zeitalter des Talmud.*
——, 1966. *The Holy Land.*
——, 1973. P-W, Suppl. xiii, s.v. 'Palaestina', cols. 321–454.
Barbieri, G., 1952. *L'albo senatorio de Settimo Severo a Carino, 193–285.*
Bersanetti, G.M., 1940. *Studi sull'Imperatore Massimino il Trace.*
Birley, A., 1966. *Marcus Aurelius.*

---

[37] For a recent study of the measurements of distances on milestones and the Antonine Itinerary in Britain, see W. Rodwell, *Britannia*, 6 (1975), 76–101.

[38] Pekáry, 1968, 146; for literature on the *cursus*, see bibliography on pp. 173–75.

——, 1967. *Roman Frontier Studies*, 1967 (1971), 7–13.

——, 1971. *Septimius Severus*.

Crook, J., 1955. *Consilium Principis*.

Degrassi, A., 1952. *I fasti consolari dell'impero romano dal 30 av.C. al 613 d.C.*

Frere, S., 1974. *Britannia* (²1974).

Frey, J.-B., 1952. *Corpus Inscriptionum Iudaicarum*, I–II (1936–52).

Goodchild, R.G., 1948. *Berytus*, 9 (1948–49), 91 ff.

Hammond, M., 1959. *The Antonine Monarchy*.

Hasebroek, J., 1921. *Untersuchungen zur Geschichte des Kaisers Septimius Severus*.

Hecker, M., 1961. *BIES* 25, 175–86 (Hebrew).

Iliffe, J.H., 1933. *QDAP* 2, 120–21.

Isaac, B.H. and Roll, I., 1976. *JRS* 66, 15–19.

Kuhl, C., and Meinhold, J., 1928. *Palästina Jahrbuch*, 24, 113–40.

——, 1929. *Palästina Jahrbuch*, 25, 95–124.

Landau, Y., 1964. *BIES* 28, 232 ff. (Hebrew).

Lifshitz, B., 1960. *Latomus*, 19, 109–11.

Magie, D., 1950. *Roman Rule in Asia Minor*, I–II.

Mihailov, G., 1964. *Inscriptiones Graecae in Bulgaria repertae*, III.

Millar, F., 1964. *A Study of Cassus Dio*.

Mittmann, S., 1964. *ZDPV* 80, 113 ff. (German) = *ADAJ* 11 (1966), 65 ff. (English).

Mócsy, A., 1974. *Pannonia and Upper Moesia*.

Pekáry, T., 1968. *Untersuchungen zu den Römischen Reichsstrassen*.

Pflaum, H.-G., 1948. *Le Marbre de Thorigny*.

——, 1960. *Les Carrières procuratoriennes équestres sous le Haut-Empire romain* (1960–61).

Rickmann, G., 1971. *Roman Granaries and Storage Buildings*.

Ritterling, *Legio*, P-W xii, s.v. 'Legio'.

Roll, I., 1972. *Eretz Binyamin*, 272–4 (Hebrew).

——, 1974. In *Actes du IXᵉ Congrès International d'Études sur les Frontières Romaines, 1972* (1974), 503–11.

Schürer, E., 1973. *The History of the Jewish People in the Age of Jesus Christ*, I, ed. G. Vermes and F. Millar.

Sedgley, J.P., 1975. *The Roman Milestones of Britain*.

Thomsen, P., 1917. *ZDPV* 40, 1–103.

Vetrali, L., 1967. *Liber Annuus*, 17, 149–61, figs. 1–5.

Weber, W., 1907. *Untersuchungen zur Geschichte des Kaisers Hadrianus*.

Welles, C.B., 1938. C.H. Kraeling (ed.), *Gerasa*. The inscriptions, by C.B. Welles, 355–494.

Wilcken, U., 1912. L. Mitteis and U. Wilcken, *Grundzüge und Chrestomathie der Papyruskunde*.

Abbreviations

AÉ   = *l'Année Épigraphique*.

BMC Emp.   = H. Mattingly, *Coins of the Roman Empire in the British Museum* (1933–).

BMC Palestine	=	G.F. Hill, *Catalogue of the Greek Coins in the British Museum: Palestine* (1914).
CIL	=	*Corpus Inscriptionum Latinarum.*
JRS	=	*Journal of Roman Studies.*
IGR	=	R. Cagnat, ed. *Inscriptiones Graecae ad Res Romanas Pertinentes*, Vols. I, III and IV (1911–27).
ILS	=	H. Desau, *Inscriptiones Latinae Selectae*, Vols. I–III (1892–1916).
IMC	=	Israel Milestones Committee inventory.
Not. Dig., Or.	=	*Notitia Dignitatum Orientis* in *Notitia Dignitatum* ed. Seeck, (1876).
PIR	=	*Prosopographia Imperii Romani.*
RIB	=	R.G. Collingwood and R.P. Wright, *The Roman Inscriptions of Britain*, I (1965).
SHA	=	*Scriptores Historiae Augustae, vitae Hadriani* etc. ed. Hohl, (1927).

Postscript

Since the publication of this article quite a few milestone-inscriptions have been discovered and most of them have been published. It cannot be said, however, that the general impression of the distribution in time has been affected significantly by the new discoveries. It remains true that the discovery of individual and unique inscriptions, such as that on the milestone of A.D. 69 (above, article no. 4) remains a possibility. Such discoveries could make an impact. However, in spite of regular and frequent surveys throughout the country, the numbers of inscribed milestones discovered in recent years is too small to affect the pattern described in the present article, which was published in 1978. A volume that will contain all milestone-inscriptions, known so far, is now in preparation. For the moment some additional bibliography will have to suffice.

Y. Tsafrir, Leah Di Segni and Judith Green, *Tabula Imperii Romani. Iudaea-Palaestina* (Jerusalem 1994). The Roman roads on the accompanying maps (1:250,000) are the responsibility of Israel Roll. The locations of milestone-stations are indicated on the maps.

B. Isaac and I. Roll, *Roman Roads in Judaea*, I, *The Scythopolis-Legio Road*, (B.A.R., International Series, 1982).

M. Fischer, B. Isaac and I. Roll, Israel. *Roman Roads in Judaea*, II, *The Jaffa-Jerusalem Roads* (B.A.R. International Series, Oxford 1996).

For historical discussion: B. Isaac, *The Limits of Empire: The Roman Army in the East* (Oxford, Second ed. 1992), esp. 108–112.

Vespasian?

A Flavian milestone from Jerusalem may have been discovered and will be published soon, one hopes. If this is the case the inscription from Jerusalem, dated to 72–79 and discussed below in article no. 7, may also have been a milestone. It is not clear, as yet, which roads this milestone, or these milestones could have marked. In any case, the existence of one or more Flavian milestones in the vicinity of Jerusalem would mean that we have here the first real evidence of Roman road-construction along any of the roads to this city, which became the headquarters of the *Legion X Fretensis* after the First Jewish revolt. So far the earliest milestones along roads to and from Jerusalem were Hadrianic (A.D. 130).

Commodus

As observed in the article above, no milestones of Commodus have been found in Judaea, but there can be little doubt that his name was removed from some, on which the name of Pertinax was incised in 193. It is worth noting that a milestone recently discovered bears Commodus names and titulature of A.D. 181 (*SEG* 1991.1592). It was set up between Bostra and Philadelphia, and the names of Commodus have not been erased.

Severus Alexander

Above it has been suggested that the milestones of Severus Alexander without a specific date might be attributed to the years of his Persian campaign. Among other arguments it was observed that there are milestones in the province of Arabia dated to 230. While this is true, it should be added that recently another milestone of this Emperor from Arabia was published, dated to 222 (*AÉ* 1991.1589).[1]

Vaballathus

Two milestones were found on the road from Scythopolis to the north, a road which leads to Tiberias but also branches off, first across the Jordan towards Gadara, while further north a second branch makes for Damascus via Hippos. Both inscriptions are fragmentary, but the two combined leave no doubt as to the formula:

> *Vaballatho / Athenodoro / V(iro) C(larissimo) Regi Cons(uli) / Imp(eratori) Duc(i) Roma / norum.*

Two series of milestones of Vaballathus have been found along the *Via Nova Traiana* in Arabia, an earlier series, which omits the title Augustus and fails to mention any other emperor:

> *[L.] Iulius Aurel[ius Septi]mius [Va]ballath[us Ath]enodorus Rex Co(n)s(ul) [Impe]rator Dux [R]omanorum.*[2]

On the later series Vaballathus bears the title Augustus and has a string of victory titles, often assumed by Roman emperors after Septimius Severus:

---

[1] *Imp(eratori) Caes(ari) M(arco) Aur(elio) / Severo A[[lexandro]] / Pio Fel(ici) Aug(usto) pon / tif(ici) max(imo) trib(unicia) po / test(ate) imp(eratori) II co(n)s(uli) / [p]roco(n)s(uli) p(atri) p(atriae) per / Trebonium For / tunatum leg(atum) / pr(o) pr(aetore).*

[2] T. Bauzou, 'Deux milliaires inédits de Vaballath en Jordanie du Nord', pp. 1–8 in P. Freeman and D. Kennedy (eds.), *The Defence of the Roman and Byzantine East* (BAR Int. Series, Oxford, 1986).

Imp(eratori) Caesari L. Iulio Aurelio Septimio Vaballatho Athenodoro Persico Maximo Arabico maximo Adiabenico maximo pio felici invicto Aug(usto).[3]

Palmyra in those years has attracted a good deal of attention in recent literature.[4] This is not the place to try and interpret the wider significance of these events, the aims and ambitions of the Palmyrene rulers, and the hopes of their supporters. For present purposes it will be relevant to note that the formula encountered in the area of Scythopolis/Beth Shean and the earlier series in Arabia reflect Vaballathus' titulature between December 270 and Spring 272. The Palmyrene expedition to Egypt probably took place in 270. There is good evidence of Palmyrene destruction in Bostra.[5] It is therefore clear that these stones mark Palmyrene movement to Egypt through the northern parts of the provinces of Arabia and Palaestina. Although this has been observed before, it is worth mentioning again that the Latin texts on these milestones show us Palmyrene rulers claiming Roman dignities, rather than oriental or Arab rebels hostile to the Roman empire.

Tetrarchic Milestones
A Tetrarchic milestone indicating the third milestation from Ashkelon, is reported to have been found.

Tetrarchic Inscriptions from the Southern Aravah
A series of three groups of milestones with Tetrarchic inscriptions has been found in the southern Aravah.[6] One of these, found at Yahel, gives a distance of 12 m *ABOSIA* which could be read '*Ab Osia*' or '*A Bosia*'. The distance is clearly measured from the site of the fort at Yotvetah, where a Tetrarchic inscription has been found with a phrase of uncertain meaning: '*alam Costia constituerunt*'.[7]

---

[3] P. Thomsen, *ZDPV* 40 (1971), 38, no. 73 b; 44, no. 96 b; *ILS* 8924.

[4] B. Isaac, *Limits of Empire*, 220–8; F. Millar, *The Roman Near East: 31 B.C.–A.D. 337* (Cambridge, MA 1993), 159–73; D.F. Graf, 'Zenobia and the Arabs' in D.H. French and C.S. Lightfoot (ed.), *The Eastern Frontier of the Roman Empire, Colloquium at Ankara, September 1988* (1989), 143–67; E. Equini Schneider, *Septimia Zenobia Sebaste* (Rome 1993), 61–75; J. Long, 'Two Sides of a Coin: Aurelian, Vaballathus, and Eastern Frontiers in the Early 270s', in R.W. Mathisen & H.S. Sivan, *Shifting Frontiers in Late Antiquity* (Altershot, Hampshire, 1995), 59–71; D. Potter, 'Septimius Odenathus', *ZPE* 113 (1996), 271–85.

[5] Malalas, 299; H. Seyrig, *Syria* 22 (1941), 46 (*IGLS* xiii 1, no. 9107)

[6] U. Avner, *Hadashot Arkheologiyot* 104 (1995), 120 f.; S.R. Wolff, 'Archaeology in Israel', *AJA* 100 (1996), 725–68, esp. 762–4 (with photographs): three milestations, 16056.93645; 16230.93868; 16145.93765.

[7] Ed. princeps: I. Roll, *IEJ* 39 (1989), 239–260, who interprets this as architectural

The first conclusion, and an important one, to be drawn from this discovery is that there was a Roman road through the Aravah, at least northwards to Moa, as suggested by Eusebius' *Onomasticon*. This is significant, for doubts have been expressed in the past as to the feasibility of maintaining a public road through the Aravah, even though this was the shortest link between Aela/Elath and Judaea/western Palestine in the north. The existence of Roman milestones now confirms that there was a public road. This particular Roman road quite possibly was a new one, laid out in the Tetrarchic period, in connection with the transfer of *Legio X Fret.* to Aela. It would have been part of the measures which accompanied the transfer of the legion to the Red Sea shore. Since the early second century there had been a road from Aela, but this connected the Red Sea with Transjordan. It is described on milestones as a *via nova Traiana*. It linked the southern part of the province of Arabia with the northern part, more specifically with the legionary headquarters and provincial centre at Bostra. With the transfer, in the Tetrarchic period, of the legion from Jerusalem to Aela on the Red Sea, another public highway was laid out and organized through the Aravah, linking the new legionary base with the region of the abandoned legionary headquarters in Jerusalem. This shows that Aela was now considered part of Western Palestine rather than Transjordan, a conception which was expressed administratively by the transfer of the Negev to the province of Palaestina in the same period. It may be added that this is merely one of a number of desert roads organized or re-organized in the Tetrarchic period. Other roads elsewhere are the *Strata Diocletiana*, roads in the desert area south and south-east of Bostra, at Hallabat,[8] the road from Umm el-Jemal to Umm el Qottein (A.D. 293–305),[9]

---

terminology. I prefer to read this as a reference to a unit of horsemen and the name of the unit (*Constantianam?*): *Limits of Empire*, 188; similarly: *AÉ* 1990.1015. W. Eck, 'Alam costia constituerunt: Zum Verständnis einer Militärinschrift aus dem südlichen Negev', *Klio* 74 (1992), 395–400, sees *Costia* as a place-name in the abblative. For the site: Z. Meshel, *IEJ* 39 (1989), 228–238; for the coins, A. Kindler, *ibid.*, 261–6; *Limits of Empire*, 188–91. The inscription mentions a governor of Palaestina, Aufidius Priscus, who now occurs also on inscriptions from Caesarea: B. Purrell, *ZPE* 99 (1993), 287–95, 296; *AÉ* 1993.1621; 1624.

[8] D.L. Kennedy, *Archaeological Explorations on the Roman Frontier in North-East Jordan: The Roman and Byzantine Military Installations and Road Network on the Ground and from the Air* (BAR, International Series, Oxford 1982), 162.

[9] S.T. Parker, 'A Tetrarchic Milestone from Roman Arabia', *ZPE* 62 (1986), 256–8.

the Bostra-Qottein road,[10] and the road from Bostra, through the Wadi Sirhan to Jawf.[11]

The second conclusion to be drawn from the discovery is that it must now be considered uncertain indeed whether Yotvetah is to be identified with *Ad Dianam* of the Peutinger Table. The Roman fort at Yotvetah certainly was named '*Osia*' or '*Bosia*' in the Tetrarchic period. Furthermore there is the question whether the same place would have been called '*Costia*' on another official Roman inscription of the same date, as argued by W. Eck. If this is believed to be the case, then the inscription from the fort at Yotvetah records the establishment of an unnamed *ala* at a named place,[12] 'Costia' (as suggested by W. Eck), which elsewhere is named 'Osia' or 'Bosia'.[13]

Costia, Osia or *Bosia*, none of them are mentioned in any ancient source: the *Tabula Peutingeriana*, Ptolemy, Eusebius or on other inscriptions. It has not been attested before. *Ad Dianam* appears on the Peutinger map as a station 16 m (c. 24 km) north of Aela. Yotvetah, formerly named Ghadiyan, is 39 km (c. 20 m) north of Aela, i.e. further away than it should be. If we give up the identification of Yotvetah with *Ad Dianam* the latter site must be sought somewhere else and that is not simple in this barren area. There are therefore two possibilities: 1) *Osia/Bosia* was previously named *Ad Dianam*, possibly a Semitic name for the same site. This is archaeologically convenient and requires a minor correction in the distance given on the Peutinger Table, from XVI to XXVI, not a drastic step, given the numerous proven errors for these parts.[14] 2) Alternatively *Ad Dianam*

---

[10] D.L. Kennedy and H.I. MacAdam, 'Latin Inscriptions from Jordan', *ZPE* 65 (1986), 231–6.

[11] *Limits of Empire*, 163–71.

[12] The *Notitia* lists many unnamed units, but these are locally recruited cavalry formations (*Equites Indigenae*), not auxilia. It also lists named auxiliary units as '*constituta*' without naming their bases, e.g. *Ala Idiota Constituta*, or *Ala Prima Praetoria nuper Constituta*.

[13] S.R. Wolff in his brief report on these inscriptions cryptically refers to Stephanus Byzantinus, without giving a location or citation, as being relevant for the present problem. Possibly he means the following lemma: Κοσίανα, φρούριον Παλαιστίνης. Χάραξ δεκάτῳ. ἐν τῇ παραλίᾳ τῆς Συρίας. No one could claim that the southern Aravah is ἐν τῇ παραλίᾳ τῆς Συρίας.

[14] The relevant section of the map requires far more drastic engineering in various places. For instance, the only way in which we can understand the road from Emmaus (Amavante) to Jerusalem, is to assume that three separate roads were conflated. See Fischer, Isaac and Roll, *Roman Roads in Judaea*, II, *the Jaffa-Jerusalem*

is where the Peutinger Table in fact says that it is: a point 16 m north of Aela brings us somewhere at the height of Timna. There was Late Roman copper smelting in the area, but there is no site along the road that has a proper source of water.[15]

Between Yotvetah and Elath two other sites have been recorded:

Beer Orah, 17 km (ca. 12 m) north of Elath. B. Rothenberg, *Tsephunot Negev*, p. 148: 'The water is known as bad, most travellers in the 'Aravah did not trouble to visit the site at all.' Ancient remains destroyed. Pottery apparently early (i.e. pre-Roman).

Horvat Evronah, M.R. 15009.9001, 16 km north of Elath. *Op. cit.*, 150: small square building, measuring 20 × 18, Nabataean pottery. Rothenberg suggests that this was a small road-station. The distance does not make it an attractive candidate for identification with *ad Dianam*.

To sum up, the new inscriptions provide us with conclusive information about the existence of a Roman road through the Aravah in the Tetrarchic period, and of a contemporary fort at Yotvetah, where an *ala* was based. It is also certain that this fort was named *Osia* or *Bosia* on milestones of this period. The expression '*alam Costia constituerunt*' on the inscription from Yotvetah and the related problems seem to remain unresolved.

Recent Publications on Roads in Arabia Provincia

AÉ 1991. 1585–93.

T. Bauzou, 'Les voies romaines entre Damas et Amman', pp. 293–99 in P.-L. Gatier and J.-P. Rey-Coquais (eds.), *Géographie Historique au Proche-Orient* (Paris, CNRS, NMT 23, 1990).

——, 'Les fastes de la Provincia d'Arabia et les inscriptions des milliaires', *Syria* 68 (1991), 145–7.

——, 'La Via Nova de Trajan entre Bostra et Philadelphie: étude archéologique et épigraphique', in A. Desrumeaux & J.-B. Humbert (eds.), *Khirbet es-Samra I* (Paris, forthcoming).

Roads (1996), 298. An immediate parallel: the distance from Ascalon(e) to Betogabri (Beth Guvrin) is indicated as XVI, while the actual distance is ca. 40 km.

[15] B. Rothenberg, *Tsephunot Negev* (Jerusalem, 1967, Heb.), 145–150. Note site no. 37 (for which: p. 16) at M.R. 1459.9056, 36 km n. of Aela. Two soldiers of III Cyr are mentioned on inscriptions from the region: A. Alt, 'Aus der Araba', *ZDPV* 58 (1935), 1–78, at 62 f.

D.F. Graf, 'The *Via Nova Traiana* in Arabia Petraea', *The Roman and Byzantine Near East: Some Recent Archaeological Research* (*JRA* Supp. 14, Ann Arbor, MI, 1995), 241–67.

A.G. al-Husan & D. Kennedy, 'New Milestones from Northern Jordan', *ZPE* 13 (1996), 257–62. Umm el-Quttein (tetrarchic) and al-Qihati (tetrarchic and 305/6). These belong to the main road to the north and these stones should be seen in combination with the evidence previously known regarding the Tetrarchic period.

D. Kennedy, 'The *Via Nova Traiana* in Northern Jordan: a cultural resource under threat', *ADAJ* 39 (1995), 221–7.

A.-M. Rasson-Seigne & J. Seigne, 'Notes préliminaires à l'étude de la voie Romaine Gerasa/Philadelphia', *ADAJ* 39 (1995), 193–210.

7

A FLAVIAN INSCRIPTION FROM JERUSALEM

(with M. Gichon)

Among the wealth of interesting material excavated by Prof. Mazar and his team west and south of the Temple Mount, is a Latin inscription engraved on a pillar (Pl. 7).[1] The stone was discovered in secondary use in the southern part of a large Umayyad building. This building, situated at the foot of the western part of the Temple Mount's southern retaining wall, was constructed mainly of Herodian masonry originally from this wall.[2]

The pillar reminded the excavator of a milestone,[3] but in a discussion with the authors, Mazar expressed the opinion that it had not served this purpose. Mazar has read the inscription as follows:

1. IMP CAESAR	5. L
2. VESPASIAN[VS]	6. AVG PR PR
3. AVG IMP T[CAE]	7. LEG X FR
4. SAR VESP AVG	

The excavator comments: 'In the first four lines . . . the Emperor Caesar Vespasianus Augustus . . . and Titus Caesar Vespasianus Augustus . . . are mentioned. The last three lines mention a commander of the *legio X Fretensis*. It is most plausible that this commander is none other than Lucius Flavius Silva, commander of the legion and governor of the Provincia Iudaea between 73–79/80 A.D. . . . .'

It should be observed that Titus had never been made Augustus during his father's lifetime. Line 4 should therefore end: Aug(usti) [f(ilius) or f(ilio)].

The diameter of the column (at top) is 42 cm, and its present height is 1.2 m. The top of the column shows a rather crude disfiguration

---

[1] See B. Mazar, *Qadmoniot* 5 (1973), pp. 83–84 (Hebrew). The authors wish to thank Prof. Mazar most cordially for his permission to study this object in the Jerusalem City Museum, Jerusalem.

[2] *Loc. cit.*

[3] *Loc. cit.*

VA
IMPCAESA
VESPASIAN
AVC IMPT
SARVESPAVC
L
AVC PR PR
ᴵᴱᴄ ᶜᴿ

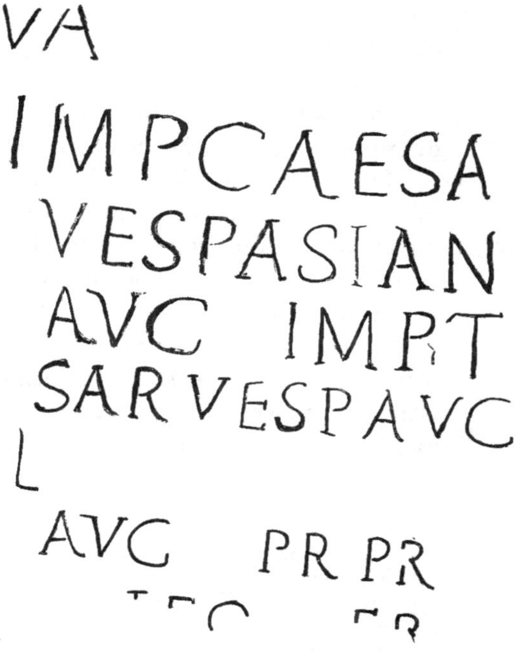

Plate 8. Inscribed pillar from Jerusalem: the lettering

Plate 7. Inscribed pillar from Jerusalem

and exactly the same weathering as the rest of the surface. It seems unlikely that the column served as a base or was part of any structure; more probably it was free-standing. The letters are incised to an average depth of 4–6 mm.[4] The Umayyad builders chipped off a strip, 16 cm wide, at the right-hand edge of the inscription. As a result, the last letters of several lines were effaced. Mortar is still sticking to the stone. Above and on the left of IMP in 1.1, the two letters VA are visible. These two letters are covered by mortar and are probably not part of the Flavian inscription.[5] The inscription shows a rather high standard of engraving. The letters are slender. Line 5, except for the first letter L, seems to have been erased deliberately. The fact that Titus bears the title 'Imperator' as praenomen, *patre vivo*, seems to date the inscription within the years A.D. 72–79.[6] The inscription provides no clue for a closer date.

Mazar's identification of the missing name in 1.5 with L. Flavius Silva is probably correct, though L[ucilius Bassus] could be substituted. Bassus was legatus from the end of 71 until his death in A.D. 73. However, since Bassus' praenomen was probably Sextus,[7] the identification of the missing name as Flavius Silva seems more credible.[8]

The erasure is either the result of official *damnatio memoriae* or the work of local enemies. The official condemnation of many magistrates was marked by the removal of their names from public monuments.[9] However, it is difficult to find instances of illegal erasure of

---

[4] The average height of the letters is: in 1.1: 9–9.5 cm; in 11.2–3: 8–8.5 cm; in 1.4: 6.5–7 cm; letter L in 1.5: 6.5 cm; the erasure: 7–8 cm; 1.6: 5–6 cm.

[5] Other letters could well be hidden under the remains of the mortar.

[6] See *PWRE* VI[2] s.v. Flavius, col. 2709 (Weynand).

[7] On Lucilius Bassus, see H.G. Pflaum: *Les carrières procuratoriennes équestres sous le haut-empire romain*, Paris, 1960–61, No. 39; *PWRE* XIII[2], col. 1640, s.v. Lucilius 22 (Stein).

[8] There is, of course, a theoretical possibility that there was another legatus Iudaeae, so far unknown, between A.D. 73 and 79/80. However, a tenure of office of six or seven years was not at all uncommon. It seems preferable, therefore, to adhere to the proposal of Silva as the legatus concerned. For new evidence concerning Flavius Silva, see W. Eck: *Senatoren von Vespasian bis Hadrian*, München, 1970, pp. 93–111. Here two inscriptions are discussed in detail, which provide us with information on Silva's origin and *cursus honorum*. For Silva's tenure of office in Judaea, cf. *ibid.*, pp. 101–102 and n. 41.

[9] In the provinces, too, the names of condemned officials were removed from inscriptions: C. Silius, legatus of Germania Superior, condemned in A.D. 24 (*CIL* XIII 11515). The case of C. Asinius Gallus is of interest. He was consul in 8 B.C., proconsul of Asia in 6/5, and condemned in A.D. 30. In Rome his name was erased and later reinserted (cf.: *Prosopographia Imperii Romani* [hereafter, *PIR*], I, Berlin, 1952–

the name of an unpopular provincial official. Moreover, if Silva's name was removed by Jewish enemies, and not on imperial orders, it would be difficult to explain why the name *legio X Fretensis*, surely just as unpopular, had been left untouched. In the same year and after comparable events, the name of the *legio XXI Rapax* was effaced from several inscriptions from the Helvetian territory.[10]

There is no direct information concerning when and why Flavius Silva may have been condemned. Little is known about his career after A.D. 74,[11] but it is well known that Vespasian started assembling a faction of supporters for his reign immediately after his accession. Among other things, he took special care to designate strong and reliable men as provincial governors, in order to prevent a repetition of the events which had, ultimately, brought himself to power.[12] The office of consul was offered to important allies of the new dynasty. The emperor's principal supporters, like Mucianus and Eprius Marcellus, were honoured with repeated consulates.[13] Titus continued this policy and his attitude towards the senate was, like his father's, based on respect and consideration.[14] As a gesture of good will towards the senate he renounced the consulate in A.D. 81. During only two years of the reigns of Vespasian and Titus, 78 and 81, were no Flavians *consules ordinarii*. In 81 Silva and Asinius Pollio Verrucosus were made consuls. Pollio's exact position within his family is unknown.[15] Most probably a descendant of the famous Pollio, he sprang from a powerful family of consulares, not always known for their good relationship with the emperors. Accordingly, we may assume that in 81 Asinius Pollio was appointed *ordinarius* as a representative of the senatorial

---

1966, 1229; F. Dessau: *Inscriptiones Latinae Selectae*, Berlin, 1954, 165, 5923, 8894; *CIL* XII 2623, among other instances). On several inscriptions in Ephesos, however, his name was erased and not reinserted (e.g. *CIL* III 6070; 7118). For other cases, see: *CIL* III 3385; VIII 2581; *CIL* III, p. 285; XIII 8150; *L'Année Épigraphique* (hereafter, *AÉ*) (1946), 202.

[10] Cf. *CIL* XIII 11514, 11524.

[11] See Eck, *op. cit.* (above, n. 8) and *PIR* III 368.

[12] Cf. Tacitus: *Hist.* II 82; III 52.

[13] On the supporters of the Flavian dynasty, see J.A. Crook: *Consilium principis*, Cambridge, 1955, pp. 48 ff.; B. Grenzheuser: *Kaiser und Senat in der Zeit von Nero bis Nerva* (diss.), Münster, 1964, p. 80; G. Townend, *Journal of Roman Studies* 51 (1961), pp. 54 ff. See also R. Syme: *Tacitus*, Oxford, 1958, pp. 592 ff. and appendix B 12.

[14] Cf. Suetonius: *Titus* 7; 9; 11; *Cassius Dio: Hist. Rom.* (hereafter, *Dio*), LXVI 18; 19.

[15] Cf. Borghesi: *Oeuvres complètes*, Vol. III, Paris, 1862–1893, p. 352; *PWRE* II², col. 1603, s.v. Asinius 27 (v. Rohden).

establishment. Silva, one of Vespasian's associates, must therefore have
been the consul, representing the supporters of the emperor. Domitian,
immediately after his accession in the same year, quarrelled with
his father's and brother's friends and councillors. There must have
been some sort of insurrection against Domitian's anti-senatorial policy as early as 83–84.[16] According to Eusebius (a. mundi 2099 =
A.D. 82–83) '(. . .) *plurimos senatorum Domitianus in exilium mittit*'.[17] Silva,
consul ordinarius in the year of Domitian's accession, was clearly a
prominent representative of the old order and most probably one of
the conspirators or their sympathizers. This could very well have led
to the condemnation to which the inscription from Jerusalem may
testify.

Prof. Mazar and the present authors agree that the inscription
does not appear to be a milestone. The fact that its shape is peculiar
to milestones, however, makes its study essential. First, the site of its
discovery should be taken into account. The Umayyad builders had
at their disposal an abundance of building material from the ruins of
Aelia Capitolina, and thus had no reason to stray a mile from town
in search of such material. It is possible that the stone served as the
'zero-marker' for the counting of miles. There is evidence from Byzantine Jerusalem for the existence of such a stone near the present-
day Damascus gate.[18] However, a similar arrangement has not been
recorded for earlier periods. Moreover, the inscription on this 'zero-
marker' would have been set according to the same rules as those on
milestones (see below).[19]

Of equal importance is the fact that the total number of miliaria
presently registered by the Israel Milestone Committee is 395. Of
these, 91 bear inscriptions. No milestone antedating Domitian has

---

[16] On the early opposition against Domitian, see Grenzheuser, *op. cit.* (above,
n. 13), pp. 109–113; also Eck, *op. cit.* (above, n. 8), pp. 108–9.

[17] See also *Dio* LXVII, 2 ff., especially 3, 3.

[18] H. Guthe, *ZDPV* 28 (1905), p. 127; A. Jacoby: *Das geographische Mosaik von Madaba*,
Leipzig, 1905, p. 73; M. Giesler, *Das Heilige Land* (1912), p. 4; M. Avi-Yonah: *The
Madaba Mosaic Map*, Jerusalem, 1954, Pl. 7, pp. 50–52. Avi-Yonah accepted a pre-
Byzantine origin of the column, but proposed seeing it as a base for the statue of
an emperor. This possibility cannot be ruled out. However, a mediaeval tradition
existed, quoted by, among others, Avi-Yonah himself, which saw this column as a
geographical marker (centre of the Holy Land, centre of the world), and thus points
to an identification as a 'zero-marker'.

[19] For example, in the centre of Theveste a big stele marked the beginning of the
road to Carthage (*CIL* VIII 10114). The text of this monument is identical to inscriptions on milestones of this road (*CIL* VIII 10048; 10056–8 etc.).

been recorded and only one bears this emperor's name.[20] This makes the identification of an inscribed pillar from Vespasian's reign as a milestone very questionable.

The text of the inscription does not fit the pattern of contemporary milestones. In Judaea as well as in other provinces the year of the emperor's reign, consulship or *tribunicia potestas* were not omitted from milestones before the reign of Severus. Only a few African milestones from the reign of Antoninus Pius appear to antedate the Severan examples.[21] During the third century, the 'republican' elements among the emperor's titles were frequently omitted.

Finally, no inscriptions bearing the name of a military unit have been found on milestones in Judaea and they are rare on milestones from other provinces. In Judaea only one milestone is known which mentions a legatus.[22] Milestones are never signed by a provincial governor and a military unit at the same time.[23] Assuming that the pillar from Jerusalem is a milestone, the only solution for this dilemma would be to read '*leg. X Fr.*' as a genitive. The dedicator of the inscription would then style himself: '*legatus Augusti pro praetore legionis X Fretensis*'. This, however, is an impossible title for a provincial governor. In Judaea the governor's title was '*legatus Augusti pro praetore provinciae Iudaeae et legionis X Fretensis*' or '*legatus Augusti legionis X Fretensis et legatus pro praetore provinciae Iudaeae*'.[24] These titles indicate that the provincial governor (*legatus pro praetore*) was at the same time commander of the legion (*legatus legionis*). To the best of our knowledge, the *legatus legionis III Augustae* in Africa was the only one in the empire having the rank of *legatus pro praetore* in his position as commander of a legion.[25] One must therefore conclude that the inscription from Jerusalem mentions both a legatus and a legion.

In summary, both the location where the pillar was discovered and the fact that in Judaea no milestones prior to Domitianus' reign have yet been found, make its designation as a milestone difficult. Milestones of the first century A.D. never lack an indication of the emperor's regnal year. Only one milestone has been found in this

---

[20] W.J. Pythian-Adams, *PEFQSt* 56 (1924), pp. 94–95.
[21] *CIL* VIII 10327–8; 22391.
[22] See above, n. 20.
[23] Africa again provides an exception to the rule (*CIL* VIII 10018; 10023; 10048).
[24] Dessau, *op. cit.* (above, n. 9), 1035, 1036 (= *CIL* III 12117).
[25] *Ibid.*, 5872. See *PWRE* XII, s.v. Legio, col. 1495 (Ritterling).

province signed by a legate. Milestones signed by a legate and a legion have been recorded only in Africa.

The pillar inscription must have served a different purpose. Again the place of discovery may help in clarifying matters. Between A.D. 70 and Hadrian's building of Aelia Capitolina—and especially between A.D. 70 and 80—all Roman activity in the city must have been connected with the Tenth Legion and its camp.[26] As Broshi's recent excavations in the Armenian Quarter of the Old City have confirmed, the eastern wall of the camp ran parallel to and west of the rocky precipice which marks the western side of the Tyropoeon valley.[27] Vespasian's monumental inscription could thus have come from a building connected with the legion, outside the camp, in the Tyropoeon. At the foot of the campsite, late Roman-Byzantine *thermae* have been excavated by Mazar.[28] Earlier *thermae* might still come to light under this complex.[29] Another possibility is that the column belonged to the campsite itself and later rolled down the cliff into the valley. Mazar pointed out to the authors that the column was discovered 70 m from the Hulda (Double) Gate in the southern wall of the Temple Mount and that the current excavation has given credibility to the well-known talmudic passage indicating the survival of this gate after the destruction of the Temple.[30] This was in accordance with official imperial policy, which kept the Temple Mount in ruins but did not prevent Jews from praying there.[31] Mazar therefore

---

[26] L.H. Vincent and A.M. Steve: *Jérusalem de l'Ancien Testament*, Paris, 1956, pp. 753–4; L.H. Vincent and F.M. Abel: *Jérusalem*, II, Paris, 1926, Pl. I; C.N. Johns, *QDAP 14* (1950), pp. 148–150; S. Yeivin: *The Bar-Kokhba War*, Jerusalem, 1946, pp. 131–138 (Hebrew).

[27] Paper read on 15th March 1973 at the Second Archaeological Convention in Jerusalem.

[28] Not yet published.

[29] Topographical considerations made the area south-west of the Temple Mount the natural site for sport and recreational installations in Jerusalem. Cf. maps based on the most recent research in D. Bahat: *Jerusalem—its Epochs*, Jerusalem, 1970, pp. 3, 5, 7 (Hebrew); see also Vincent and Steve, *op. cit.* (above, n. 26), pp. 708–9. *Thermae*, though in legionary fortresses mostly *intra muros*, were in auxiliary establishments more often than not *extra muros*. Cf. A.S. Robertson: *The Antonine Wall*, Glasgow, 1968, p. 28; J. Collingwood Bruce: *Handbook to the Roman Wall*, Newcastle, 1957, pp. 29 ff.; W. Schleiermacher: *Der römische Limes in Deutschland*, Berlin, 1966, pp. 32 ff. The location of an extramural legionary bathhouse in Flavian Jerusalem, at the site of the Byzantine *thermae* excavated by Mazar, would have made it possible for the Romans to use the existing system of aqueducts.

[30] Shir Hashirim Rabba, 2.9.4, p. 17a.

[31] See A. Schlatter: *Synagoge und Kirche bis zum Barkochba-Aufstand*, Stuttgart, 1966, pp. 69–86, including the Talmudic sources. See also Vincent and Steve, *op. cit.*

suggested that a connection between the inscription and the refurbished Double Gate might be considered. Only further archaeological investigation may provide us with more concrete information concerning the Jerusalem column's original function. A column like the one discussed here could be of one of four types: (a) a funerary monument; (b) a boundary stone; (c) an honorary inscription; (d) a building inscription commemorating the completion or restoration of a public building. Since types (a) and (b) are not relevant to this discussion, only the latter two are to be considered. Building inscriptions are composed in the same general style as 'honorary inscriptions'. They are distinguished and characterised by the fact that they are inscribed *on* the buildings and not usually on free-standing columns. Thus if our column was free-standing, it must have been an honorary inscription. If, on the other hand, it was part of a building, both types (c) and (d) should be considered as possibilities. Donor's inscriptions, a variety of building inscriptions, are found on columns of synagogues and churches throughout the Holy Land and other areas. Honorary inscriptions on columns were fairly common throughout the empire,[32] and in Judaea honorary inscriptions are frequently encountered. In the Roman period private citizens as well as emperors were thus honoured.[33] Many honorary inscriptions signed by military units have been found in Judaea.[34] Moreover, honorary inscriptions without the emperor's regnal year are not at all unusual in the first and second centuries A.D.[35] The combination of a military unit and a legate as signatories is very common on building inscriptions.[36] On

---

(above, n. 26), pp. 756–58; P. Prigent: *La fin de Jérusalem*, Neuchatel, 1969, pp. 77–80. Cf. Epiphanius: *De mens. et pond.* 14, one of the references indicating continuation of settlement in Jerusalem after A.D. 70 and before the building of Aelia Capitolina.

[32] See Plinius: *Natural History* XXXIV 27; Dessau, *op. cit.* (above, n. 9), 211; *AÉ* (1927), 11; (1924), 102. Emperors especially were often honoured in this way (e.g. *CIL* VI 950; 1051; *AÉ* [1907], 130; [1924], 133, with a cretan *quaestor pro praetore* being honoured on the other side of the column).

[33] Private citizens: *Supplementum epigraphicum Graecum* (hereafter, *SEG*) 7 (1934), 822 = *IGR* III 1368 = *PEFQSt* 60 (1928), pp. 187–188; see also *SEG* 7 (1934), 824; 827.

Emperors: *AÉ* (1939), 255 = C.H. Kraeling: *Gerasa*, New Haven, 1938, p. 428, No. 153; Geta; *AÉ* (1964), 198 = *Coll. Latomus* 58 (1962), pp. 1063–64: Galerius. A column from Caesarea has three honorary inscriptions from different periods, two for provincial governors and one for Diocletianus, see M. Avi-Yonah, *IEJ* 16 (1966), pp. 135–141 and B. Lifshitz, *Coll. Latomus* 65 (1969), pp. 462–68.

[34] For example: *AÉ* (1894), 131; (1896), 54.

[35] E.g. Augustus: *AÉ* (1936), 18; Nero: *CIL* VI 913; Vespasian and Titus: *AÉ* (1930), 126, etc.

[36] *CIL* III 11194–6, according to the editor marking the dedication of the *castra*

honorary inscriptions, not connected with any building, this combination does not seem to have been customary before the third century.[37] The Jerusalem inscription therefore shows all the characteristics of honorary and building inscriptions. The combined signature of a legate and a legion seems to fit best a building inscription, but these are not usually encountered on columns. In the absence of further evidence both possibilities must remain open.

A specimen from Scotland may form an interesting parallel to the inscription from Jerusalem. Along the 'Antonine Wall', commemorative tablets, also called 'distance slabs', have been found. These recorded the exact distance covered by the work of each respective army unit.[38] One of these inscriptions was not engraved on a slab, but on the 'upper part of a rounded pillar with rectangular panel (. . .)':[39] *Imp(eratori) Caes(ari)/ T(ito) Ae[l(io)] Hadr(iano)/Antonino/Aug(usto) Pio p(atri) p(atriae)/vexillatio[ne]s/ ////.*

In *Roman Inscriptions of Britain* this pillar has been classified as a milestone. However, it has the same text as the distance slabs, and the 'republican part' of the emperor's nomenclature is completely omitted (see above, p. 120). Consequently, there might be reasons to consider the possibility that this pillar, like its counterpart from Jerusalem, is not a milestone, but either an honorary or a building inscription. Another inscription of this group was signed by both a legion and a legate.[40]

Concerning the case of the emperor's names, the dative seems to be preferable to both nominative and ablative.[41] Nominative and ablative are generally followed by a specification of the emperor's

---

stativa in Carnuntum; *CIL* III 6741 = Dessau, *op. cit.* (above, n. 9), 232. Identical: *CIL* III 6742 and 6742a; see also *CIL* II 2447 (below, n. 43). *AÉ* (1936), 18.

[37] For example: *CIL* III 797; cf. 798; 14429; 14430.

[38] See G. Macdonald: *The Roman Wall in Scotland*, Oxford, 1934, esp. pp. 359 ff.; Robertson, *op. cit.* (above, n. 29), pp. 14 ff. The inscriptions are published in R.G. Collingwood and R.P. Wright: *Roman Inscriptions of Britain* (hereafter *RIB*), Oxford, 1965.

[39] *RIB* 2312, p. 726 = *CIL* VII 1109; cf.: 1110a. '(. . .) seen in or before 1726 at Bar Hill (. . .)'.

[40] *RIB* 2191 = *CIL* VII 1125.

[41] A parallel to the form of the ruler's names on the inscription from Jerusalem might be:

[I]mp. Caesari Vespasiano [Aug.]
[I]mp. T. Caesari Vespasiani [Aug. f.]

(*AÉ* [1930], 126). For the form 'Caesar' as abbreviation, see below: *CIL* VIII 10116; see also M. Avi-Yonah, *QDAP* 12 (1946), p. 99, Nos. 20 and 22.

regnal year.[42] The cases of the *legatus* and the *legio* could well be ablative and nominative respectively.

The inscription from Jerusalem would then be read as follows:[43]

VA (?)
1. *Imp(eratori) Caesar(i)*
2. *Vespasian[o]*
3. *Aug(usto); Imp(eratori) T(ito) [Cae]*
4. *sar(i) Vesp(asiano) Aug(usti) [f(ilio)]*

5. *L(ucio) [Flavio Silva leg(ato)]*
6. *Aug(usti) pr(o) pr(aetore)*
7. *legio(io) X Fr(etensis)*

---

[42] Nominative, for example: *AÉ* (1951), 205 (Tiberius); *CIL* III 6741 (Claudius), see above, n. 36. Ablative, for example: *CIL* III 11194 (above, n. 36).

[43] Cf. the following building inscriptions from Vespasian's reign: *CIL* III 11194, II 2477 = Dessau 254; *CIL* VIII 10116. A clear parallel for the legion in the nominative is found in Dessau 261, where provincia Lusitania' can only be a nominative; see also *AÉ* (1936), 18.

Postscript

This inscription was the starting point for an extensive discussion by R. Syme of the identity of the legate whose name had been erased.[1] As regards the date, Syme remarks that 'imp. Titus Caesar' occurs on several inscriptions set up between 76 and 79.[2] An earlier and sporadic instance dates from 72/3.[3] Syme argues that this cannot have been Flavius Silva as we suggested. Suetonius, *Dom.* 10.2 f. (add 11.1; 15.1) lists ten men of consular rank who were put to death by Domitian. Silva, who was *ordinarius* in 81 is not on the list. Syme then argues that the erased legate was L. Antonius Saturninus. The stone may have read: 'L.Ant Saturnin.', or 'L.Ant.Sat.' or 'L.Antonio leg.' It is a brilliant suggestion, entirely possible and more attractive than that of Flavius Silva, but it remains an hypothesis and as yet no proof has been discovered.

Saturninus was probably consul in 82 and *could* have been legate of Judaea in 78–81 (he rebelled as legate of Germania Superior in 89). Syme's list of Judaean governors after Titus is then: Sex. Vettulenus Cerealis (70–), Sex. Lucilius Bassus, Flavius Silva (73 or 74–?), followed by Lucius Antonius Saturninus.

A new and very similar inscription on a pillar has now reportedly been found in Jerusalem. The name of the legate apparently has been erased on this inscription as well and cannot be read. Otherwise, apparently more of the new inscription has been preserved and it is definitely bearing the numeral 'I' under the title of the Legate. It must therefore be a milestone and, if so, the pillar discovered by Mazar in his excavations also was a milestone. This raises various questions: What was the original location of both stones? Were there two identical stones side by side on one spot? If so, why? What road did the stones mark? If the new inscription gives all of the titles of the legate, and if these are, again, 'Leg. Aug. Pr. Pr. Leg. X Fr.' then we have two inscriptions in which a Flavian legionary legate of *X Fretensis* fails to describe himself as legate of Provincia Judaea. It can only be hoped that the newly discovered inscription will be published soon.

---

[1] R. Syme, 'Antoninus Saturninus', *JRS* 68 (1978), 12–21.
[2] In note 8 he refers to *ILS* 8904; 253 f.; *AÉ* 1974.653.
[3] *ILS* 260: *Imp. T. Caes. Aug. f. Vespasian. Pont. Tribun. Pot. ii Imperat. iiii Cos ii design. iii Censori D D.*

8

ROMAN COLONIES IN JUDAEA:
THE FOUNDATION OF AELIA CAPITOLINA*

The Foundation of Aelia Capitolina and its connection with the outbreak of the Second Jewish Revolt have been discussed by many
scholars.[1] It is now usually accepted that the decision to found a
colony of Roman Citizens at Jerusalem was taken during Hadrian's
visit in the area 129/130.[2] The city may not have been built until
after the war which lasted from 132–135.[3] Whether a start was made
before, we do not know. There is less agreement on Hadrian's motives
and intentions, since this involves a judgement of Hadrian, of the
Roman Empire and of the Jewish people. Any evaluation of Hadrian's
religious policy should now take into account W. Den Boer's paper
on the subject.[4] It is instructive precisely because it does not primarily deal with Hadrian's treatment of the Jews. As regards Aelia there
is yet another question to be asked, namely what were Hadrian's
reasons for founding a *Colonia Civium Romanorum* rather than a Greek
πόλις according to the pattern prevalent in the Eastern Roman provinces.[5] There is no easy answer but some observations may be made.

---

* An earlier version of this paper appeared in Hebrew in *Chapters in the History
of Jerusalem in the Second Temple Period—Abraham Schalit Memorial Volume*, edited by
A. Oppenheimer, U. Rappaport and M. Stern (Jerusalem, 1981). I am grateful for
suggestions and comments by Professors S. Applebaum, J.E. Bogaers, G.W. Bowersock,
Dr. J. Matthews and Dr. M.M. Roxan.

[1] Dio lxix, 12, 1–2; see: Schürer i (1973), 540–2; Applebaum, 1976, 8; Smallwood,
1976, 432–34 and older literature cited in these works. See also: B. Lifshitz, *ANRW*
ii, 8, 444–89, 'Jérusalem sous la Domination Romaine'.

[2] Prof. Gichon will argue for a later date in his forthcoming study on the Second
Revolt (in *ANRW* ii). For the foundation in 129/130, see Schürer, I (1973), 541–2;
Applebaum (1976), 8.

[3] See above, n. 1 and esp. Schürer i (1973), 553–54; Smallwood, 1976, 559 ff.

[4] Den Boer, 1995; see also: J. Beaujeu, *La Religion Romaine à l'apogée de l'empire* i
(1995), 180 ff.; A.S. Benjamin, *Hesperia* 32 (1963), 57–86. M. Guarducci, in: *Les
Empereurs Romains d'Espagne* (1965), 209–222.

[5] For the establishment of colonies in the eastern provinces, see Millar, 1977,
395–410; also: Jones, 1940, 61–5; Bowersock, 1965, Chapter v; Grant, 1946; Levick,
1967, Chapter xiv; Vittinghoff, 1952; Sherwin-White, 1973, 228–29; 275 ff. The
present paper is concerned with the establishment of colonies up to Hadrian. The
cities founded by Severus and his successors are not discussed.

Considering why a Roman colony instead of a Greek city was founded we should, first of all, note that, in one respect, it was a creation without precedent. I do not know of any other Roman colony, existing at this time, which also served as legionary headquarters.[6] In the East two or, possibly, three communities where a legion was quartered acquired city-status before Hadrian's reign.[7] In the western prov-

---

[6] The archaeological evidence for the legionary fortress in Jerusalem is, so far, very unsatisfactory. For the period after 70, Josephus, *BJ* vii, 1, 1 (1–2); cf.: 1, 3 (17), records that the garrison was encamped in the western part of the city. Inscriptions from this period indicate that the fortress was in the city: *ILS* 9059 (diploma of A.D. 93); M. Gichon and B. Isaac, *IEJ* 24 (1974), 117–23 (Flavian inscription from Jerusalem); *CIL* iii 13587 = *ILS* 4393 (inscription of 116/7 set up by a detachment of the III *Cyr.* in Jerusalem). From the period after the Second Revolt and the foundation of Aelia we have one legionary inscription found in the city: *CIL* iii 12080a = 6641 = *AÉ* 1888. 50. Tombstones of veterans of the legion were found in Jerusalem, but this only shows that they settled in Aelia after their discharge, cf.: *CIL* iii, 14155, 3; M. Avi-Yonah, *QDAP* 8 (1938), 54–7 = *AÉ* 1939.157; see also: Lifshitz, *ANRW* ii, 8, 470–71; E. Birley, *Roman Britain and the Roman Army* (1953), 115 attributes this inscription to the Hadrian-Antonine period. Fragmentary but probably relating to the presence of army units in town are: *AÉ* 1904.91; cf.: Thomsen, *ZDPV* 64 (1941), no. 3; *AÉ* 1904, 201; *CIL* iii 6638; G.B. Sarfatti, *IEJ* 25 (1975), 151. A piped drain with stamps of the legion was excavated in the citadel, cf.: C.N. Johns, *QDAP* 14 (1950), 152–53; 156. Stamped bricks of the legion were found at this and many other sites in the city, e.g. *CIL* iii 12090; A.D. Tushingham, *PEQ* 99 (1967), 73; B. Mazar, *The Excavations in the Old City of Jerusalem, Preliminary Report of the Second and Third Seasons* (1971), 5; 22. For brick-stamps of the legion, see: D. Barag, *Bonner Jahrbücher* 167 (1967), 244–67 (English) = *Eretz Israel* 8 (1967), 168–82 (Hebrew). Remains of brick ovens of the legion were excavated (but never adequately published) at Giv'at Ram (Sheikh Bader), c. 1 km from Jerusalem near the Roman Road to Emmaus, cf.: M. Avi-Yonah, *BIES* 15 (1950), 19–24, Pl. 6–7. Legionary bricks were produced primarily for military installations (see below, n. 13). Although the relationship between legion and colony is unclear at Jerusalem, it may be assumed that here too the stamps of the legion indicate a military presence. There is therefore no reason to doubt that both before and after 135 the legionary fortress was in Jerusalem. It must be emphasized, however, that no excavated site has been published, furnishing evidence of what can be described as legionary structures. Only Mazar claims to have excavated a building, w. of the Western Wall, in use as barracks of the legion from the foundation of Aelia down to the time when the legion left Jerusalem (*loc. cit.*). Scholarly literature is full of plans of the *castra* and of confident statements concerning its site, all as contradictory as they are speculative, see: C.W. Wilson, *PEFQSt* (1905), 138–44; L.H. Vincent and F.M. Abel, *Jérusalem nouvelle* ii, (1926), 19–21, Pl. i; M. Avi-Yonah, *Enc. Arch. Exc.* ii, 610–11; Y. Tsafrir, *Zion* (unpublished Ph.D. thesis, Jerusalem, 1975), 286–301. In the last mentioned work the archaeological evidence is conveniently compiled, pp. 50–78.

[7] The era of Samosata dates from 71, it issued coins as Flavia Samosata from Hadrian onwards, see: *BMC, Galatia* etc., 117 ff.; for Bostra in Arabia, cf.: Bowersock, 1971, 231–2. It had already become a major city before it became the legionary headquarters, cf.: Bowersock, *JRS* 63 (1973), 139; A. Negev, *ANRW* ii, 8, 660 ff. For Melitene in Cappadocia, see: Procopius, *de Aed.* iii, 4; cf. Josephus, *BJ* vii, 1, 3 (18) who still describes it as a district rather than a town. It seems not to have

inces we know two sorts of civilian settlements near camps: a) civil settlements that grew up around camps and were somehow attached to them (*canabae* and *vici*); b) independent communities a little distance off.[8] In Pannonia civilian settlements developed into *municipia*, but these are found to be situated at some distance from the camp.[9] It may be noted that here too it was Hadrian who put the final touches to urban development near the legionary fortresses, begun under the Flavians. He created three municipia near camps on the Danube.[10] Military control of civilian settlements near camps (*canabae legionis* and *vici* of auxiliary units) and the physical separation of *municipia* and legionary bases are thought to have prevented conflicts between civilian and military administration in the area closest to the fortress. In several western provinces these matters have been clarified by years of digging and the study of numerous inscriptions.[11] It is clear that the practice of quartering army-units in urban centres in the eastern provinces must have created completely different patterns, but we know, in fact, nothing of their working.[12] As regards Aelia, it seems

---

issued coinage; see also: Magie, 1950, 1436; 1464. For Cyrrhus and Zeugma, cities since Hellenistic times, see below, n. 12.

[8] E.g.: Chr.B. Rüger, *Germania Inferior* (1968), 74 ff. for the situation in this province, see also: J.E. Bogaers and Chr.B. Rüger, *Der Niedergermanische Limes* (1974), s.v. Nijmegen and Xanten. In Britain the relevant case is York, where the *canabae* remained under military control, while the separate civil settlement (across the river) eventually was granted the status of a *colonia*, cf.: I.A. Richmond, *Eburacum* (1962), xxxiv–xxxix. See also on this subject: F. Vittinghoff in: *Legio VII Gemina* (1970), 339–352.

[9] For Pannonia and Upper Moesia, see: Mócsy, 1974, 126–28; 139 ff. F. Vittinghoff in: *Festschrift H. Jankuhn* (1968), 132–42. As observed by Dobson and Mann, 1973, 196 'one effect of the so-called "vallum" on the Hadrianic frontier of Britain (whatever its main function) was certainly to keep the early civilian settlement along its line well clear of military installations.'

[10] Mócsy, *loc. cit.*; Millar, 1977, 399–406 has argued that the title of *municipium* was not formally conferred by the emperor.

[11] No legionary fortress has been excavated even partly in the eastern provinces. H. v. Petrikovits, *Die Innenbauten römischer Legionslager der Principatszeit* (1975), Bild 1, lists 66 permanent legionary fortresses, 15 of those are in the Near East, but not one could be discussed in this book. In Israel the only plans of a legionary establishment published (but not excavated), are those of Masada, cf.: I.A. Richmond, *JRS* 52 (1962), 141–55. Even here some thirty little buildings belonging to a civilian settlement near camp F can be seen scattered on the hillside (Pl. xvii and p. 151).

[12] Archaeological evidence of military camps in cities is so far available only from Dura (third century): M.I. Rostovtzeff (ed.), *The Excavations of Dura* (1934) (report on the fifth season, 1931–2), 201 ff. A military camp excavated in Palmyra dates to the late third century: Th. Wiegand, *Palmyra* (1932), 82 ff., Pl. 9–10. Syrian cities known to have been quarters of legions are: Raphanaeae (Jones, 1971, 267 with n. 53) *IGLS* 1399; 1400; J.-P. Rey-Coquais, *Arados et sa perée aux époques grecque romaine et*

quite certain that the legionary base was part of the city, but we have no evidence at all about the division of authority between the colony's administration and the legionary command. We know nothing of the territorial situation. What was military territory and what belonged to the colony? Was there a division between the two or not? These are questions which cannot be answered until more evidence becomes available.[13] In general it must be said that we know nothing about the consequences of the eastern practice of quartering the army in cities, apart from the observation of Tacitus and Fronto that it was bad for discipline.[14] Concerning Aelia it must be noted that not until the third century was there another colony serving as legionary headquarters.[15]

---

byzantine (1974), 167 f.; Samosata (above, n. 7, Jones, 1971, 263–64; 267); J. and L. Robert, *Bull. épigr.* 1949, 190; *AÉ* 1950, 190; Zeugma (J. Wagner, *Seleukia am Euphrat—Zeugma*, Beiträge zum Tübinger Atlas des Vorderen Orients, Reihe B. Nr. 10, 1976; id in: *Studien zu den Militärgrenzen Roms* ii (Beih. BoJb 38, 1977, 517–39); Cyrrhus (Tact *Ann.* ii, 57; E. Frézouls in: *ANRW* ii, 8, 164–97, esp. 182–83). All these cannot properly be compared with Aelia, since they were existing cities in which army units were quartered, rather than bases around which a city was built. Comparable with Aelia might be Melitene (above, n. 7) and Satala in Armenia Minor (Magie, 1950, 1436; 1465; T.B. Mitford, *JRS* 64 (1974), 160 ff.). Both were fortresses around which cities developed. The site of the *castra* known to have been at Bostra has not been located as yet, cf.: A. Negev, *ANRW* ii, 8, 663.

[13] For the territory of Aelia, cf.: Avi-Yonah, 1966, 155–56; 1974, 421. It must be said, however, that much of what is written there is based on unreliable sources. Apart from the incorrect use of milestones and Eusebius' *Onomasticon*, there is, e.g., no reason why a road-station ('Maledomnei') should mark the border of a territorium. The same sources were, apparently, used by Jones, 1971, 277 and *JRS* 21 (1931), Pl. vii, which therefore cannot be accepted at face value, cf.: Isaac, 1978, 57. The territorial history of Judaea needs revision. Worthless evidence should be rejected and no attempt should be made to draw a map of Roman Judaea which includes territorial borders, since this serves only to present a misleading picture of the state of our knowledge. In Germania Superior and Inferior the spread of military brick-stamps has been used as an indicator of military territory, since it has been shown that such bricks were used first of all in military installations or in civilian buildings constructed by the military (cf.: Rüger, 1968, 56 ff.). This will not get us very far in Judaea since finds of stamped bricks are rare in this country, apart from substantial finds in Jerusalem. For the subject in general (in the western provinces), see: F. Vittinghoff, *Ac. Naz. Lincei* 194 (1974), 109–124.

[14] *Ann.* xiii 35; Fronto, *ad Verum imp.* ii, 1 (128 Naber). Cf.: Mommsen, *Römische Geschichte* (⁵1904), v, 448–9. Part of the tasks of the army units encamped in cities will have been to control these cities themselves and their surrounding territory. Josephus indicates that the legions stationed in Alexandria were used to suppress fighting between Jews and Greeks (*BJ* ii, 18, 8 [494]). In Jerusalem, before 67, *auxilia* were established in two permanent camps, one in the royal palace, the other in the Antonia fortress: *BJ* ii, 15, 5 (328–9); 17, 8 (439). Josephus extensively describes the way these troops were used in town.

[15] It has been suggested that Bostra received the status of colony at the same

Returning to the question why Aelia was made a Roman colony rather than a Greek city, we must keep in mind that, at the time, it was an unusual creation which does not fit the general characteristics of Roman colonies of the period. First I shall try to clarify matters by looking at earlier citizen-colonies in the East, next by considering contemporary foundations in other provinces.

The foundation of Roman colonies in the East started with Caesar and Augustus. This period has been subject of extensive research. Jones dealt with cities in the East founded at this time. Vittinghoff devoted a monograph to the study of colonisation and citizenship under Caesar and Augustus. Barbara Levick has much to say on the period in her book on Roman colonies in Southern Asia Minor and G.W. Bowersock, *Augustus and the Greek World*, contains a chapter on eastern colonies. Cities which issued coinage in this period are discussed by M. Grant. Most recent is the second edition of Sherwin-White, *The Roman Citizenship* with a new discussion of the *ius Italicum*.[16]

In Syria Augustus planted veteran-colonies at Berytus and possibly also at Heliopolis (Baalbek).[17] Jones (for Berytus only) and Bowersock (for both) pointed out that they must have served to control the territory of the Ituraeans, who were notorious brigands.[18] There were comparable groups of colonies elsewhere, discussed in the studies mentioned above. For the present paper it may be relevant to mention the Caesarian colonies garrisoning the s. coast of the Propontis and the Black Sea and the chain of Augustan veteran-colonies along the coast of Mauretania, protecting communications on the North African coast.[19] The group of colonies in Pisidia were studied by

---

time as Petra, i.e. under Elagabalus, 221/2, cf.: S. Ben Dor, *Berytus* 9 (1948–9), 430. Head, *Hist. Num.*², p. 812 dates the grant in Severus Alexander's reign.

[16] *V. supra* n. 5. For the *ius italicum* see also the discussions by F.T. Hinrichs, *Die Geschichte der gromatischen Institutionem* (1974), 147–57 and by J. Bleicken, *Chiron* 4 (1974), 367 ff.

[17] For Berytus, see now: J. Lauffray in: *ANRW* ii, 8, 135–63; for the foundation of the colony, 145–47. Heliopolis was made a colony by Augustus according to Sherwin-White, 1973, 229; H. Seyrig, *Bull. Musée de Beyrouth* 16 (1961), 111–12 = *AÉ* 1964, 55; Bowersock, 1965, 66; Vittinghoff, 1952, 135. However, Jones, 1940, 72–3; 1971, 287–88 with n. 85 and Grant, 1946, 258 opt for Severus. For a somewhat different hypothesis, see: J.-P. Rey-Coquais, *JRS* 68 (1978), 52.

[18] Jones, *JRS* 21 (1931), 266–67; Bowersock, 1965, 71.

[19] For Caesar's foundations in Asia, see: Levick, 1967, 4–5; Bowersock, 1965, 62–4 and literature listed there; Vittinghoff, 1952, 87–9 denies their military function. For the colonies in Mauretania, see: S. Gsell, *Histoire ancienne de l'Afrique du Nord* viii (1928), 199–205; Grant, 1946, 222 ff.; Vittinghoff, 1952, 116–18; Syme, *op. cit.* (below, n. 21A), 218 f.

Barbara Levick. In her book she has shown that these colonies, founded at the same time, threw a cordon round the whole of Pisidia as part of a program meant to tame and civilize the entire region.[20] In 6 B.C., nineteen years after the foundation of these colonies an extensive road-network was constructed linking them, as shown by Dr. Levick. This, it appears, was part of the preparation for the Homanadensian war, in which a rebellious tribe which hindered communications and the development of the area was subjugated. The colonies were meant to garrison the area and to serve as base of operations. The roads made the conquest easier. Besides, as observed by Dr. Levick, 'the soldiers (brought perhaps from Syria) who were to fight the war must have been those who built the roads. The building of roads is a valuable act in itself but it serves another purpose: it toughens those who take part. The Syrian legions were not always maintained at fighting pitch.'[21]

In Numidia the nomadic Musulamii were subjugated by the same method, but here the process took longer, as shown by Sir Ronald Syme.[21a] A start was made under Augustus but the organization was not completed until the reign of Trajan. This entailed the construction of the colony of Thamugadi by the legion III Augusta, the transference of this legion to Lambaesis, road-building, the delimitation of Musulamian territory and the establishment of *municipia* at Calama and Thubursicu.

Claudius planted one colony in the East, Ptolemais (Acco) in Phoenice, a foundation which required our attention.[22] In Judea the reign of Claudius was marked by a series of popular uprisings of increasing violence and bitterness. Most dangerous were the troubles between Jews and Samaritans which were investigated on the spot by Ummidius Quadratus, governor of Syria and cost the prefect of Judaea his office (c. 52).[23] Under Felix, the next prefect, rebellion

[20] Levick, 1967, 6; 38–40: 187 ff. Recently it has been argued that Col. Archelais and Iconium were founded in the same period: D. French, *ZPE* 27 (1977), 247–49.

[21] Levick, 1967, 40; see above, n. 14.

[21a] R. Syme, 'Tacfarinas, the Musulamii, and Thubursicu', *Roman Papers* I, Chapter 16, 218–230 = *Studies in Economic and Social History in Honor of Allen Chester Johnson* (1951), 113–30.

[22] For Ptolemais (Acco), see: Kadman, 1961; N. Makhouly and C.N. Johns, *Guide to Acre* (1946); H. Seyrig, *Rev. Num.* (1962); *Syria* 39 (1962), 193–207; Schürer ii (1907), 141–48; also: *Enc. Arch. Exc.* i, 14–23 (Z. Goldmann); Avi-Yonah, 1976, 89.

[23] See: Schürer, i (1973), 458–60.

continued.[24] Clearly as a response to these events veterans of the four
Syrian legions were settled in a new colony at Ptolemais, c. 52–54.[25]
The decision will have been taken by Claudius in accordance with
advice of Ummidius Quadratus, who remained governor of Syria
from 50 till 60.[26] Next the coastal road from Antioch down to
Ptolemais was constructed and provided with milestones, dated A.D.
56. The inscriptions mention Ummidius Quadratus and record the
paving of the road 'from Antioch to the new colony of Ptolemais'.[27]
The site of the Claudian colony was well chosen, just outside the
province but at the 'gateway' to it. In 67 it served as Vespasian's
base of operations and only after the subjugation of Galilee did he
move his headquarters to Caesarea.[28] The veteran-colony at Ptolemais
and the road to it assured the Romans of a convenient spot for their
rear-headquarters and marshalling area in any action against Judaea.[29]

All colonies discussed so far were veteran-settlements serving as *ad
hoc* garrisons. Their sites were chosen out of military considerations,
a fact which detracts nothing from the reality that this was a way to
dispose of a surplus of veteran-soldiers. Their siting at locations con-
trolling communications was, in many instances, a factor contribut-
ing to eventual economic growth. As pointed out by Levick, they
were both garrison-colonies and *poleis*. Their foundation and the
construction of a road-network in the surroundings must be explained

---

[24] *Op. cit.*, 462 ff.

[25] The date of the foundation is determined by coins of A.D. 52 which name the
city without its colonial titles; Kadman, 1961, nos. 88–90. The foundation by Claudius
(i.e. 54 at the latest) is recorded by Pliny, *NH* v, 19, 75: '*Colonia Claudi Caesaris
Ptolemais quae quondam Acce*'. Milestones of 56 mention the city as the 'new colony of
Ptolemais': Thomsen, 1917, no. 9a2; R.G. Goodchild, *Berytus* 9 (1948), 112–23; 120.
See also: M. Avi-Yonah, *QDAP* 12 (1946), 85–6: '*col. Ptol. Veter(anorum)*'. For the
legions, see the founder's coins with *vexilla*, A.D. 66: Kadman, 1961, nos. 88–90.

[26] For Ummidius Quadratus, see: Schürer i (1973), 264.

[27] *V. supra*, n. 25.

[28] Jos. *BJ* iii, 2, 4 (29); *ibid.* 4, 2 (64 ff.); *ibid.* 9, 1 (409). Ptolemais was a military
base under the later Seleucids, cf.: *SEG* xx 413; xix 404; S. Applebaum in: *Essays
in honour of C.E. Stevens*, ed. B. Levick (1975), 64–5, n. 48.

[29] Ulpian, *Dig.* L 15, 1, 3: '*Ptolemaeensium enim colonia, quae inter Phoenicen et Palaestinam
sita est, nihil praeter nomen coloniae habet*' is a good indication of the strategic siting of
Ptolemais. The last part of the sentence shows that the colony did not have any
additional privileges, such as *ius Italicum* or freedom from taxes. This has been misunderstood by several scholars, e.g.: Schürer ii (1907), 148; Avi-Yonah, 1974, 382
and 1976, 89. For the purpose of Claudius' colonies, see: A. Momigliano, *Claudius,
the Emperor and his Achievement* (1961), 65 (partly political, partly military function); see
also p. 64: 'a great builder of roads', with references. For Claudian road-building,
see also: E.M. Smallwood, *Documents illustrating the Principates of Gaius, Claudius and
Nero* (1967), 87–91.

as an attempt 'not only to pacify the country but permanently to alter its character.'[30]

The next colony to be founded in the East was Caesarea, capital of Judaea, with the titles '*Colonia Prima Flavia Augusta Caesarea*' or '*Caesarensis*'.[31] The previous history of the city is well known and need not be recapitulated here.[32] What must be emphasized is that this was an entirely different sort of foundation. This is clear from all available evidence and can be explained by the background of, and the history leading up to, the foundation. Till the reign of Claudius there were two sorts of colonies: 1) entirely new foundations on sites where no earlier community existed at the time of colonization; 2) veteran-settlements superimposed upon existing towns, the result being a community consisting of an upper class formed by new settlers and an original population of mostly lower status.[33] The eastern colonies mentioned so far, including Ptolemais, belong to the second class. Claudius, apparently, was the first to create colonies of a third kind, purely native communities elevated to the rank of a Roman colony, without any *deductio* of veterans taking place. The first towns to be granted the honorary title of colony were prosperous communities in Gaul.[34]

---

[30] Levick, 1967, 187–89. The territory of Col. Ptolemais was divided into *pagi* as appears from an inscription published by M. Avi-Yonah, *QDAP* 12 (1946), no. 3, p. 86. This is an indication of the city's organization as a Roman colony. The function of veteran colonies is described in a number of well known passages in ancient sources: Cicero, *de Lege Agraria* ii, 73; *Pro Fonteio* 5; 13; Tac. *Ann.* xi, 24; xii, 32; xiv, 31; *Hist.* i, 65; iv, 64; *Agric.* 16, 1; Appian, *BC* v, 12 ff.

[31] Pliny, *NH* v, 13, 69: '*Stratonis turris, eadem Caesarea ab Herode rege condita, nunc colonia prima Flavia a Vespasiano imperatore deducta.*' See also sources quoted below, p. 97 and coins mentioned below, n. 43; *CIL* iii 12082 = *ILS* 7206 (see below, n. 39). On Caesarea there exists an extensive literature: Kadman, 1957; recently, J. Ringel, 1975; L.I. Levine, *Caesarea under Roman Rule* (1975); *id. roman Caesarea, an archaeological-topographical Study* (1975). Bibliographies of older literature can be found in these works. See also G. Foerster in: R.J. Bull (ed.), *The Joint Expedition to Caesarea Maritima*, I (*BASOR*, Supp. No. 19, 1975), pp. 9 ff.; Schürer II (1979), 115–8.

[32] For a convenient survey: Ringel, 1975, 81 ff. The archaeological remains are described on pp. 28–78. See also: Schürer ii (1907), 134–38; Avi-Yonah, 1976, 44; *Enc. Arch. Exc.* i, 270 ff.; B. Lifshitz in: *ANRW* ii, 8, 490–518. It must be said that, in this paper, the late Prof. Lifshitz again failed to acknowledge sources of information (cf.: p. 505 and Y. Kaplan, *JQR* 54 (1963), 111–113) or even previous publication of inscriptions (cf.: p. 499, n. 54; p. 517 and J. Olami and J. Ringel, *IEJ* 25 (1975), 148–50, esp. n. 44; *id. Qadmoniot* 7 (1974), 44–46, 3 figs. (Hebrew); *id. RB* 81 (1974), 597–600, pl. xiii).

[33] To this group belong Antioch in Pisidia and her sister-colonies, cf.: Levick, 1967, 189–90. See also: Vittinghoff, 1952, 23–27.

[34] See: Sherwin-White, 1973, 244; 350–52. For a different opinion: Vittinghoff, 1952, 27 ff.

In the second century this honorary title became a popular and important institution as a reward for loyalty. A brief survey of the facts will show that Caesarea must have belonged to this group, the first in the East to be founded according to this pattern.

1) *Digest.* L, 15, 8: '*Divus Vespasianus Caesarienses colonos fecit*'. 'The Divine Vespasian made the Caesarienses *coloni*.' This suggests a formal change in status without settlement of veterans.[35]

2) Josephus, *BJ* vii, 6, 6 (217) records that Vespasian, after the fall of Machaerus, allotted land property in Emmaus near Jerusalem to some eight hundred veterans. From this passage it may be understood that there were no other settlements of veterans in the province.[36]

---

[35] Paulus, *Dig.* L, 15, 8, 6: '*Divus Antoninus Antiochenses colonos fecit salvis tributis.*' Antioch obviously was an honorary colony, cf.: G. Downey, *A History of Antioch in Syria* (1961), 243 ff.; Sherwin-White, 1973, 276 and Millar, 1977, 409.

[36] Jos. *BJ* vii, 6, 6 (216–17):

Περὶ δὲ τὸν αὐτὸν καιρὸν ἐπέστειλε Καῖσαρ Βάσσῳ καὶ Λαβερίῳ Μαξίμῳ, οὗτος δὲ ἦν ἐπίτροπος, κελεύων πᾶσαν γῆν ἀποδόσθαι τῶν Ἰουδαίων. οὐ γὰρ κατῴκισεν ἐκεῖ πόλιν ἰδίαν αὐτῷ τὴν χώραν φυλάττων, ὀκτακοσίοις δὲ μόνοις ἀπὸ τῆς στρατιᾶς διαφειμένοις χωρίον ἔδωκεν εἰς κατοίκησιν, ὃ καλεῖται μὲν Ἀμμαοῦς, ἀπέχει δὲ τῶν Ἱεροσολύμων σταδίους τριάκοντα.

Schürer i (1901), 640 already pointed out that, according to Josephus, Jewish land was leased and not sold. Momigliano, 1934, 85–6 concluded that the passage must refer to Jewish land everywhere in the province of Judaea and not only to land of the Jews in Judaea in its narrower and proper sense (thus e.g. Schürer i (1973), 520; Jones, 1971, 276–77). There would be no reason to treat Jews in the area around Jerusalem differently from those in Galilee or Peraea. The Emmaus mentioned here did not have city-status—it was much too small for that with only 800 veterans. It was certainly no citizen-colony. Our sources, particularly the *Digest*, would say something about it. (For the site, see: Schürer i (1973), 512, n. 142.) A regular veteran-colony received at least 3000 settlers (Levick, 1967, 92–3 with statistics down to the Augustan age). Emmaus must have been one of the many similar communities of veterans called κολωνίαι but lacking city-status (Jones, 1940, 64). Josephus, in this passage, wants to emphasize that Vespasian did not give away Jewish land and, especially, that no settlements of foreigners were planted on territory taken from the Jews, apart from the minor κατοίκησις at Emmaus, which is the exception confirming the rule. Caesarea is not mentioned, precisely because no foreign settlers were planted there. Similarly, Joppa and Neapolis are ignored. Both appear from coins to have received city-status from one of the Flavians (for Flavia Joppa, *BMC, Palestine*, 44 nos. 1–2, cf.: xxiv–xxv; for Flavia Neapolis, see: *ibid.*, 45–7, nos. 1–19, cf.: xxvi–xxvii. See Schürer i (1973), 520–21 for further evidence). Both were previously existing communities which were ravaged in the war (Joppa: Jos. *BJ* ii, 18, 10 (507–09); iii, 9, 2–4 (414–31); Neapolis, formerly Ma'abartha, at the foot of Mount Gerizim, for which see: iii, 8, 32 (307–15)). There is good evidence implying that in neither of these two towns the original community of respectively Jews and Samaritans was disenfranchised. These may have formed joint municipalities together with pagans living in the two cities (for Joppa, see S. Klein, *Sepher Hayishuv* i (²1977), 79 ff. (Hebrew); Frei, *CII* ii, nos. 892–960; stamps of a Jewish *agoranomos* have been found by Y. Kaplan, *JQR* 54 (1964), 111–13 (Trajan). Neapolis issued coinage under

3) Veteran-colonies invariably issued coinage marking the military origins of the settlers and the units from which they were discharged.[37] The coins of Caesarea never refer to a military origin of the colony.[38]

4) No inscriptions referring to veteran-colonists are known, although we have a considerable number of inscriptions mentioning inhabitants of the town and army-units stationed there.[39]

5) Veterans used to be sent to colonies where they could fulfil a military task as *ad-hoc* garrison. Caesarea, as provincial capital and residence of the governor, had a detachment both before and after the first Jewish Revolt.[40] As noted above, the foundation of veteran-colonies with a military purpose usually was accompanied by the construction of a Roman road-system in the area. I have shown elsewhere that the reorganization of Judaea after the First Revolt did not involve road-building.[41]

6) The *Digest*, as quoted above, adds: '*non adiecto, ut et iuris Italici essent, sed tributum his remisit capitis: sed divus Titus etiam solum immune factum interpretatus est.*' 'without adding the *ius Italicum*, but remitting

---

Domitian which avoided pagan types). Josephus' statement can therefore serve as indirect confirmation that no veterans were settled in Caesarea and no foreign communities planted in Joppa, Neapolis or elsewhere in the province.

[37] For example: Berytus, *BMC, Phoenicia*, nos. 55 ff. and above, n. 17; Lugdunum, Grant, 1946, 209; Caesaraugusta (Saldusia), *op. cit.* 217 no. 10; Patricia (Corduba), *op. cit.* 220; Pisidian Antioch and sister-colonies, Levick, 1967, 35–6; Grant, 1946, 250–51; Tyrus, *BMC, Phoenicia*, pp. cxxvi; cxxix; Jones, 1971, 287 and n. 85. As observed by Sherwin-White, 1973, 228: to trace the settlement of veterans is a comparatively easy matter, since they usually left abundant traces of themselves in their personal inscriptions or in the titles of their colonies (and in their coinage). The *vexilla* with legionary numbers usually kept appearing on successive issues long after the foundation.

[38] A coin of Trebonianus Gallus mentions the legion III *Gall.*: Kadman, 1957, no. 213, but this, of course, has nothing to do with the first century colonization. Not only are the *vexilla* with legionary numbers missing on Caesarea's coinage, Kadman, p. 69 also noticed that the military reverse types, so important at Aelia, are almost insignificant in the coinage of Caesarea. This must reflect a lasting difference in the character of the two communities and not a mere technicality relating to the foundation of the two colonies. Caesarea did not strike colonial coinage until Domitian. This can be explained by the fact that Caesarea after the First Revolt minted coins of the ΙΟΥΔΑΙΑ ΕΑΛΩΚΥΙΑ series. It has no bearing on her status at the time. For the coins, see H. Hamburger, *IEJ* 20 (1970), 87.

[39] For a bibliography of inscriptions from Caesarea, see: Ringel, 1975, 179–83. Compare the inscriptions of X *Fret.* at Jerusalem (above, n. 6).

[40] Cf. Schürer i, 1973, 363 ff. For the governor's military staff, see: A. von Domaszewski, *Die Rangordnung des Römischen Heeres* (ed. Dobson, 1966), 29 ff.; D. Breeze, *Bo Jb.* 174 (1974), 245–92; for the *officium consulare* in Arabia, see: M.P. Speidel, *ANRW* ii, 8, 695–97; in Pannonia: A. Dobó, *Die Verwaltung der römischen Provinz Pannonien* (1968), 155–68.

[41] Isaac, 1978, 47–9 = above, ch. 6.

the poll-tax: but the divine Titus decided that the soil had been made immune also.' The nature of the *ius Italicum* recently was analyzed anew by Sherwin-White, by F.T. Hinrichs and by Bleicken.[42] Its practical significance—and the reason why it was rarely granted—was that it meant freedom from poll—and land-tax. This raises the question what prevented Titus from granting the *ius Italicum* to Caesarea, since he gave it the substance of this status.[43] The explanation must be that, at that time, it was considered undesirable to recognize as 'Italians' the first eastern community which enjoyed the status of 'Colony of Roman Citizens' without a nucleus of ex-legionaries. Sherwin-White suggested that *ius Italicum* was granted to the eastern foundations of Caesar and Augustus, such as Berytus and Antioch in Pisidia precisely in order to emphasize the non-Greek character of these communities.[44]

It may therefore be concluded that the citizens of Caesarea were granted the honorary title of a Roman colony without accompanying settlement of veterans, as a reward for past services towards the empire.[44a] These services are extensively described by Josephus. Until 67 troops stationed in Judaea consisted mostly of Caesareans and Sebastenes. In A.D. 67 Vespasian enlisted in his army 5 cohorts and one ala from Caesarea.[45] These troops took active part in the suppression of the Revolt.[46] The citizens of Caesarea enthusiastically supported the Romans at the same time and, among other things, provided the troops with winter-quarters. 'The inhabitants received

---

[42] Sherwin-White, 1973, 276–77; 316–22; Hinrichs and Bleicken (*supra*, n. 16).

[43] Cf. *op. cit.*, 276, n. 4. Millar, 1977, 409 observes that 'we can be reasonably sure that when Titus 'interpreted' Vespasian's conferment in a wider sense, this was either a response to a request from the city, or a decision in a dispute about tribute.' A. Kindler, *Museum Haaretz, Bulletin* 10 (1968), 9–11 attributes to Caesarea a founder's coin of 81/2 on which a 'T' is clearly visible. According to Kindler this would refer to Caesarea's era, counting from the year of Titus' ruling, which would then be 78/9.

[44] Sherwin-White, 1973, 276. Hinrichs (*supra*, n. 16) has argued that the concept did not exist before the end of the Flavian period. See also Bleicken (*supra*, n. 16), pp. 375–6.

[44a] Pliny's phrase on Caesarea (above, n. 31) shows that to him the '*deductio*' of a colony had lost its original meaning and represented merely a formal measure relating to the charter of a town. Pliny obviously does not mean to say that Caesarea was 'founded by king Herod and now "led forth" or "conducted" by Vespasian as a colony.'

[45] Jos. *BJ* iii, 4, 2 (66).

[46] For these units, see: Schürer i (1973), 360–63. Prof. Applebaum pointed out to me that during the second revolt the *coh. I Vindelicorum* recruited local inhabitants of Caesarea (*CIL* vi, no. 107).

the army and its general with blessings and congratulations of every description, prompted partly by goodwill towards the Romans, but mainly by hatred of the vanquished.'[47] Furthermore Josephus records that Vespasian was first proclaimed Emperor by his own troops at Caesarea.[48] This almost certainly explains the *cognomen* 'Prima', indicating that Vespasian founded the first Flavian colony where he had been first proclaimed Emperor.[49]

We may therefore assume that Caesarea was made an honorary colony because of its good behaviour in the first Revolt.[50] There may have been an additional reason, discussed below. Other measures in the province, apart from the quartering of the X *Fret.* at Jerusalem and the planting of veterans at Emmaus, included the grant of city-status and the name 'Flavia' to Neapolis and Joppa.[51] As mentioned above, there is no evidence of road-building.[52] No other indications of activities resulting from government-initiative can be traced as yet, until Hadrian's reign.

In other eastern provinces I can find no colony-foundation during the reigns of Titus through Trajan.[53] Trajan's reign, on the other hand, was marked first by the annexation of Arabia as a province in

---

[47] *BJ* iii, 9, 1 (409–13) transl. Thackeray, Loeb; iv, 2, 1 (88).

[48] *BJ* iv, 10, 4 (601 ff.), but cf. Suetonius, *Vesp.* 6; Tac. *Hist.* ii, 79.

[49] B. Galsterer-Kröll, *Epigraphische Studien* 9 (1972), 74, agrees that there could be a connection with the proclamation of Vespasian as emperor but denies that 'Prima' could signify that Caesarea was the first Flavian colony as there was no '*Col. Secunda Flavia*', '*Tertia Flavia*' etc. This seems somewhat formalistic. The only parallel is Col. Comama which, long after its foundation, was styled '*Prima Fida*' (from Caracalla onwards, see *ILS*, 7203) B Levick, *Numismatic Chronicle* 7 (1967), 34–5 prefers to see this as an unconvincing claim for primacy and precedence in the region. The case of Caesarea, a century and a half before Comama, is different. She received the title 'Prima' from the emperor at the time of her elevation to the rank of a colony (cf. Pliny, above n. 31).

[50] For a similar conclusion, see: Kadman, 1957, 64; Ringel, 1975, 145. *Deductio* of veterans a.o. according to F. Hampl, *Anzeiger für die Altertumswissenschaft* 3 (1950), 39; *Rheinisches Museum* 95 (1952), 60; 70 f.; L. Haefeli, *Caesarea am Meer* (1923), 31; 74. L.I. Levine, *Caesarea under Roman Rule* (1975), 35.

[51] Above p. 95, and no. 36.

[52] *V. supra*, n. 41. The road from Caesarea to Scythopolis and probably onwards to Gerasa was constructed in 69, during the war; see: B. Isaac and I. Roll, *JRS* 66 (1976), 15–9. There is no further evidence of building activity on this road until 129. The coastal road in Syria, from Antioch to Ptolemais, constructed in 56, has milestones of 72, Domitian and Trajan (before 116); see: R.G. Goodchild, *Berytus* 9 (1948–49), 120; 124–125 and nos. 234A (ii); 235 (ii).

[53] Col. *Ninica Claudiopolis* in Cilicia began to coin under Trajan, cf.: Jones, 1971, 209 and n. 32. According to Vittinghoff, 1952, 132, however, her titles '*Iulia Augusta*' would point to an earlier foundation. Levick, 1967, Appendix ii, tends to accept Ninica as a foundation of Trajan.

106 and the subsequent construction of a road from Bostra, legionary fortress and new capital to the Red Sea.[54] Both this and the Parthian War of 114–7 must have changed the position of Judea drastically.[55] When Hadrian became emperor he had to organize the withdrawal from Mesopotamia and the reorganization of the eastern frontier. Judaea was no longer a territory on the fringes of the empire but an interior province which controlled vital lines of communication.[55a] The damage Jews could cause by an insurrection became clear in 117.[56]

The nature of Hadrian's activities in Judaea, as in other provinces, is gradually being clarified by excavation, numismatics and epigraphy.[57] The general characteristics of his reign, marked by centralization, unification and an increasing absolutism have been studied from various points of view.[58] We now know that in Judaea a second legion was quartered before the Second Revolt, probably immediately after the withdrawal from Mesopotamia.[59] Jones argued

---

[54] Cf. Bowersock, 1971, 228 ff.; see also, below n. 65.

[55] For the Parthian expedition, see F.A. Lepper, *Trajan's Parthian War* (1949). A. Maricq, *Syria* 36 (1959), 254–263 = *Classica et Orientalia* (1965), 103–112.

[55a] Cf. Applebaum, 1976, 3–4.

[56] For the Jewish Revolt of 115–17, see: Schurer i (1973), 529–34; Smallwood, 1976, 421–27 and bibliographies there; see now M. Pucci, *Scripta Classica Israelica* 4 (1978), 63–76.

[57] The best survey of Hadrian's work in the provinces is still W. Weber, *Untersuchungen zur Geschichte des Kaisers Hadrianus* (1907); see also: De Ruggiero, *Diz. Epigr.* iii, 640 ff. (De Vaglieri). Two evaluating chapters: Rostovtzeff, *SEHRE*, 362–71; R. Syme, *Tacitus* (1958), chapter xx. See also: R. Syme, 'Hadrian the Intellectual' in *Les Empereurs Romains d'Espagne*, Colloques Internationaux du Centre National de la Recherche Scientifique, Madrid-Italica 1964 (1965), 243–54. For Judaea in the early years of Hadrian's reign, see Isaac and Roll, 1979a below, ch. 12.

[58] For Hadrian as an administrator, see: J. Crook, *Consilium Principis* (1955), 56 ff. Of great interest is a recent study of the changes in the witnesses to military *diplomata*: J. Morris and M. Roxan, *Arheološki Vestnik* 28 (1977), 299–333. The authors have shown that Hadrian introduced changes in administrative practice which must have concerned the whole of the administration. See also: W. Williams, 'Individuality in the Imperial Constitutions', *JRS* 66 (1976), 69–74; P.J. Alexander, 'Letters and Speeches of the Emperor Hadrian', *HSCPh* 49 (1938), 141–77. Den Boer, in his study of Hadrian's religious policy, 1955, concludes that Hadrian had 'the one purpose to put everything in the melting pot and so to produce one official religion presenting all the various elements' (p. 130). He further emphasizes the importance of the ruler-cult, leading to extreme forms of divine honour equalled only under Caracalla (p. 140).

[59] B. Isaac and I. Roll, 1979a and b. The legion was the II Traiana, according to a milestone published in 1979b. J.P. Rea, *ZPE* 38 (1980), 220 f. does not accept our reading of this milestone. Our reply in *ZPE* is forthcoming. Note that this does not affect the other indications that there was a second legion in Judaea by 120. A vexillation of *II Traiana* in Judaea is also attested on a Hadrianic inscription from Caesarea (A. Negev, *IEJ* 14 (1964), 245).

that Hadrian transferred the local government in Sepphoris, Tiberias and Neapolis to pagans.[60] This happened in Tiberias before 120, i.e. soon after the accession.[61] Hadrian was an active road-builder in many provinces.[62] The road-network in Syria had been developed since Nero and, especially, under Vespasian by his legate, the elder Trajan.[63] In Arabia roads were constructed by the emperor Trajan, shortly after the annexation. This left a gap in Judaea, to be filled by Hadrian. The significance of Hadrian's road-building in Judaea was noted in two previous publications.[64] Starting from 120 roads were constructed connecting key-sites in the province both with each other and with neighbouring provinces. The roads were built first of all to serve the military. The army is likely to have been involved and this, as noted above, was one of the customary methods of toughening soldiers in the Roman army.[65] It is of some interest for the history of the Second Revolt that, shortly before it broke out, the army (i.e. the legions, which were responsible for engineering projects, rather than auxiliary units)[66] had constructed roads all over the province.[67]

Jerusalem too was linked with other towns by new roads, one of

---

[60] Jones, 1971, 278.

[61] A. Kindler, *The Coins of Tiberias* (1961), no. 7b and pp. 48–9; Hill, *BMC, Palestine*, p. xv, cf. Isaac and Roll, 1979a, 62 ff.

[62] Weber, 1907, *passim*; Ruggiero, 621 ff.

[63] For the Elder Trajan as governor of Syria, see: G.W. Bowersock, *JRS* 63 (1973), 133 ff. For roads of Vespasian in Syria, see also above, n. 52 and two milestones of 72, recently discovered: *AÉ* 1974, 652; 653. For milestones of 109 from the region of Palmyra, see: Smallwood, 1966, 136, no. 421 and A. Bounni, *Annales Archéologiques de la Syrie* 10 (1960), 159–60.

[64] Isaac, 1978, 49 and above, n. 59. Meanwhile an additional milestone of Hadrian, A.D. 129, came to my notice, published in 1962, but unidentified for what it was because of its fragmentary state: N. Zori, 'An Archaeological Survey of the Beth Shean Valley' in: *The Beth Shean Valley, The 17th Archaeological Convention* (1962), 182, no. 120, now lost. It marked the road from Scythopolis to Sussita (Hippos) and thence to Damascus. Dr. I. Roll has now informed me of the discovery of a Hadrianic milestone on the road from Lydda and Antipatris to Gophna and thence to Aelia Capitolina. So far eight major routes in Judea appear to have been marked first by Hadrianic milestones.

[65] A Soldier's letter home of 107 shows that units of the legion in Arabia were working in quarries, apparently for the construction of the *via Traiana* (*P. Mich.* viii, 465; cf.: 466 = Smallwood, 1966, 307a; b; cf.: C. Préaux, *Phoibos* 5 (1950–1), 123 ff.; M.P. Speidel, *ANRW* ii, 8, 691 ff.). From this we can learn that the construction of the road started immediately after the annexation of the province in 106. The setting up of milestones in 111 and 114 must have formed the last stage.

[66] For legionary road-building, see also: Thomsen, 1917, no. 5; *CIL* viii 10335; Jos. *BJ* iii, 7, 3 (141–42); 6, 2 (118); v, 2, 1 (47); Isaac and Roll, 1976, 17, 1979b.

[67] When Hadrian inspected the army in Africa in 128, practice field-works formed part of the manoeuvres, see: *ILS* 2487 = Smallwood, 1966, 328.

them certainly, another probably dated to 130.[68] This was the year of Hadrian's visit and, apparently, of the decision to found *Colonia Aelia Capitolina*. As indicated above, the combination of road-building and foundation of colonies was a familiar pattern in Roman history.[69] Programs such as these, in the words of Barbara Levick, were meant, not only to pacify a country but permanently to alter it. Whether these observations apply to Judaea also, depends, to a certain extent, on the nature of the new colony in Jerusalem. The veteran-colonies of Caesar and Augustus were planted in order to serve as garrison-towns. Aelia Capitolina was founded a century and a half later on the ruins of a city, where a legionary fortress already existed. The colony itself can not have been intended to serve as a fort. Moreover, it was founded at a time when the systematic establishment of colonies by settlement—as opposed to honorary ones—had already come to an end.[70] For the identity of the first colonists we have two indications. Late christian sources inform us that they were Ἕλληνες which need not signify more than that they were Gentiles.[71] Second there are founder's coins with *vexilla* of the *X Fret.*[72] These have been taken to indicate the close relationship between colony and legion. This, however, is never the purpose of such coins. They invariably indicate the units from which colonists in a new colony were discharged.[73] And this should be their meaning in Aelia as well. As noted above, when Aelia was founded, no other colony attached to a legionary fortress was known. We may perhaps accept Jones' suggestion that the *canabae legionis* (or whatever was left of them after 135) formed the nucleus of Aelia Capitolina.[74] If this is true,

---

[68] Thomsen, 1917, nos. 282; 296; *supra* n. 64.

[69] See above, p. 92 and, for the numerous cities founded by Hadrian during his travels: Weber, 1907. We may note Rostovtzeff's comment on Hadrian's urbanizing: 'His activity was devoted chiefly to the lands which by their position were destined to be the bases on which the most important military frontiers rested.' (*SEHRE*, 366). It has been suggested that the roads were constructed for the emperor's travels, i.e. to facilitate his passage (e.g. Avi-Yonah, 1974, 400; *IEJ* 1 (1950–1), 56–8). This might be true for the third century when, at such occasions, series of milestone-inscriptions would be set up on existing roads. It is not plausible that the whole road-network in a province was first constructed for the convenience of Hadrian and his *familia*.

[70] See Sherwin-White, 1973, 253; see also Vittinghoff, 1952, 29.

[71] Zonaras, *Ann.* xi, 23c; Malalas, *Chron.*, 279 (Dindorf).

[72] Kadman, 1956, nos. 53; 54; cf.: 55–60.

[73] See above, n. 37.

[74] 1940, 64. The suggestion is not repeated in 1971, 277, where he speaks only of 'foreign colonists'. Note the tombstones of legionaries found in Jerusalem (above,

then the citizens of the colony would be veterans of *X Fret.*, settling in the colony and inhabitants of the former *canabae* and *prata legionis*. This would make sense in terms of the history of Roman colonization, which furnishes no parallel for the settlement of a group of nondescript 'Syrians and Arabs', as has been suggested.[75]

The title of a colony would enhance the status of the city, since only this rank carried more prestige than that of a *polis*.[76] It would save the inhabitants taxes.[77] These privileges would make Aelia an attractive place to live in, at the cost of the imperial treasury. But the question why Hadrian decided to make his new city a colony remains to be answered. His religious policy could have been realized just as well in a *polis* without colonial status.[78] Moreover the

---

p. 88). Since we know nothing of the topography and organization of the legionary base at the time, it is not clear whether we should speak, in principle, of *canabae* or whether civil settlement would be the correct term or if there was no such distinction. *V. supra*, p. 89.

[75] Avi-Yonah, 1974, 404: 'Syrer and Araber wurden in der Stadt und ihrem Gebiet angesiedelt.' See also: Smallwood, 1976, 459; Lifshitz, *ANRW* ii, 8, 484. There is, in fact, no parallel for the *deductio* of civilian non-veterans, let alone non-citizens, after Caesar and Augustus, cf.: Jones, 1940, 61–3; Bowersock, 1965, 67–8; Sherwin-White, 1971, 228–29. J. Meyshan, *PEQ* 90 (1958), 19–26 published a founder's coin of Aelia with vexillum on the reverse on which, according to the author, 'LE V' can be read. Meyshan therefore attributes to the Leg. V *Macedonica* the recapture of Jerusalem in the Second Revolt and her subsequent colonization. As noted by Prof. Applebaum, 1976, n. 243, it seems altogether probable that we are faced with an error for 'LEX'. The reading 'LE V' was supported by Kadman, 1956, 2, but it must be said that the photograph in the article is too vague to show any lettering. Dr. A. Kindler of the Museum Ha'aretz, Tel-Aviv informed me that he could not identify any lettering on the original either. For the population of Jerusalem between 70 and 130, see: Smallwood, 1976, 433, Alon, vol. i, 35; Lifshitz, *ANRW* ii, 8, 471–73.

[76] This appears from the fact that Greek *poleis* requested the rank of *colonia* from emperors; however, it has been emphasized in literature on the subject that the *Colonia Civium Romanorum* was, in the East, a marginal phenomenon as compared with the status of *polis*. It was local status and the relative prestige of communities which mattered, i.e., that of *polis, mētropolis* and additional titles, cf.: B. Levick, *Numismatic Chronicle* 7 (1967), 34–5; Millar, 1977, 407–09; also: Jones, 1940, 64–5.

[77] According to Paulus, *Dig.* L, 15, 8, 7 Aelia had the same rights as Caesarea, i.e. freedom from land and poll-tax.

[78] Jewish resistance against the foundation of Aelia may not have been directed against the establishment of a colony as such. Jews were willing to live as citizens in *poleis* and there may be evidence that the status of a colony was, in their eyes, desirable. Agrippa I is on record as having claimed that he might have dared to ask on behalf of his native city, if not for the Roman citizenship (πολιτεία) then at least freedom or relief from taxes. (Philo, *Leg.* 36, 287). Millar, 1977, 407 pointed out that πολιτεία must refer to the status of a colony, since there was no other way of granting Roman citizenship *en bloc*. We can be reasonably sure that Agrippa I would not have considered involving Jerusalem in anything abhorrent to the Jews. Again,

foundation of a colony involved extra investments. A recent study has shown that the grant of colonial status to a city usually was accompanied by the building of a city-wall.[79] A second-century wall is not yet clearly attested in Jerusalem,[80] but evidence from other colonies leads one to suppose that Aelia was furnished with walls at the time of the foundation (similarly we should expect Flavian building-activity in Caesarea).[81]

A possible explanation for the grant of colonial status may be found by comparison with contemporary patterns in other provinces.[82] If it is accepted that the nucleus of Aelia Capitolina was formed by the legionary *canabae* and that many of the settlers were former legionaries this will have made Aelia, in a sense, one of the last real veteran colonies. In any event it is evident that the foundation of Aelia entailed the settlement of Roman citizens in a newly established town. In this respect it was fundamentally different from the honorary colonies which were existing communities elevated to the rank of a colony. Caesarea was one of the first colonies of this type, while Aelia was one of the last colonies established by settlement. As noted by Dobson and Mann, there were two main reasons for the discontinuance of veteran-colonies: new sites ceased to become available as the expansion of the empire came to an end and as legions ceased to move forward, but more important, they argue, was the fact that the veterans themselves did not like being moved away from what had become their real homes.[82a] Jerusalem was not a vacated legionary site, it was a military base in a ruined city. Both the site and the

---

almost two hundred years later, R. Jehuda Hanassi is represented as asking the emperor for colonial status on behalf of Tiberias (b. Abodah zarah 10a). The information itself is untrustworthy, because it is part of a series of stories on the close relationship between R. Jehuda and an emperor Antoninus. However, it shows that colonial status was considered desirable among Jews. (I am indebted to Dr. I. Ben Shalom and Dr. A. Oppenheimer for clarification on this point.) It is therefore quite possible that not the organization of Jerusalem as a colony provoked Jewish resistance, but the decision to make it a pagan city and the plans for the site of the temple.

[79] See the papers by P.-A. Fevrier in: *Omaggio à Fernand Benoit* iii (1972) = *Rivista di Studi Liguri* 35 (1969), 277–86 and H.-G. Pflaum, *ZPE* 17 (1975), 260–62.

[80] See Smallwood, 1976, 461; R.W. Hamilton, *QDAP* 10 (1944), 26; 35; 52 and above, n. 6.

[81] There is no reference to the possibility of Flavian building in Caesarea in archaeological literature e.g. *Enc. Arch. Exc.* i, 273; L.I. Levine, *Roman Caesarea* (1975), 9–11; Ringel, 1975, chapters ii–iv.

[82] See also: Isaac and Roll, 1979a, 65–6 = below, ch. 12.

[82a] Dobson and Mann, 1973, 196.

veterans for a colony were available. At Aelia they could settle in a new colony without being moved away from their real homes. Many of the settlers may have been veterans of the legion who had been discharged years ago and had not left Jerusalem. Aelia has, therefore, much in common with western veteran colonies. What sets it apart from these are the geographic proximity of, and close ties with the legionary headquarters. This was normal in the East but not, in this period, in the West.

Another consideration may also have played a role when the decision was taken to found Aelia. Mócsy has observed that under Trajan the number of *coloniae* corresponds to the number of legions in some of the European frontier provinces.[83] He concluded that new colonies were created as new recruitment areas for the provincial armies.[84] Many legionaries in these provinces came indeed from the colonies.[85] Dobson and Mann agree that the veteran colonies produced many recruits, but they deny that this was the reason for their foundation, for otherwise, they say, many more would have been founded. As a general statement this may be true, but, in the absence of any evidence, it is hard to distinguish between function and effect. Since emperors must have been aware of the effects of founding colonies some of them may have been founded to serve, among other things, as centres for the recruitment of legionaries.

Little is known about the origins of legionary recruits in Judaea. There are, however, facts which seem to indicate that in this province, too, the colonies played an important role. F. Millar has pointed out that an invariable consequence of acquiring the rank of *colonia* in the imperial period was that all the citizens of the town became Roman citizens. 'In the established empire it was the principal means by which the emperor gave the citizenship to communities, and as regards Greek cities it seems to have been the only means.'[85a] For Judaea this means that the citizens of Caesarea in the seventies and

---

[83] Mócsy, 1974, 94. I have found no discussion of this phenomenon in literature on other provinces. It happens to be true for Syria as well, if Heliopolis was a foundation of Augustus. However, the third colony in the province was founded by Claudius before the correspondence in numbers had any significance.

[84] Mócsy, 1974, 118. On recruitment, see Dobson and Mann, 1973; P.A. Brunt, *Scripta Classica Israelica* 1 (1974), 90 ff.

[85] Cf. A. Mócsy, *Gesellschaft und Romanisation in der Römischen Provinz Moesia Superior* (1970), 168; 170. For Britain, see Dobson and Mann, 1973, 202 f.

[85a] Millar, 1977, 407.

those of Aelia Capitolina in the thirties of the next century became Roman citizens.

Two Roman soldiers who came from Caesarea may be mentioned here as a matter of interest. First L. Cornelius Simon, who appears as a witness on diploma *CIL* XVI 15 of A.D. 71. He must have been a Caesarean Jew who fought in the Roman army during the First Jewish Revolt. Presumably he came to the West with the troops in 69. The other is the recipient of diploma *CIL* XVI 106 of A.D. 157: Barsimso Callisthenis f. He was recruited when the Second Jewish Revolt broke out in 132. He must have been one of the few Jews who helped to suppress that revolt. As noted above, the garrison of Judaea was, until 70, drawn mainly from Caesareans and Sebastenes.[86] These, being non-citizens, could serve in the auxilia only. These units, having behaved in an irresponsible manner before the outbreak of the First Revolt were, after the revolt, transferred to other provinces.[87] There is, however, no reason to assume that recruits for these units were drawn from Judaea for a long time afterwards. In Judaea, from 70 onwards, there was one legion along with units of auxilia.[88] The promotion of Caesarea to colonial status made Roman citizens of the Caesareans and consequently they could serve in the legions. Hadrian added a legion and a colony. The second legion was based at Caparcotna which did not see rapid urban development.[89] As a result of the foundation of *Colonia Aelia Capitolina* all male citizens of the city could serve in the legions. This, as in the case of Caesarea, would include inhabitants of the colonia territory.[90]

In summary, two points may be stressed: the nucleus of Aelia Capitolina seems to have been formed by veterans of the *X Fretensis* and by its *canabae*. One of the important consequences of the foundation of the colony was that its population received the Roman citizenship and thus could serve in the legions based in the province. The relationship between Aelia and *X Fret.*, however, is unclear and will remain so until more evidence is forthcoming on legionary

---

[86] Schürer i (1973), 362–65.

[87] Jos. *Ant.* xix, 9, 2 (366).

[88] For *X Fret.* in Judaea, *v. supra* n. 6; for the auxilia, see the diploma of 86, *CIL* xvi 33.

[89] It did not acquire city status until the reign of Diocletian (Maximianopolis): Hieronymus, *PL* 25, 1589; Hierocles, *Synecdemus*, 398, 25 (Niebuhr); *It. Burdigalense* (Geyer), 19:19; see also Jones, 1971, 279–80.

[90] See above, n. 13.

establishments in the eastern provinces.[91] If the Bar Kokhba revolt was caused partly or mainly by the foundation of Aelia, it is helpful to realize what kind of pagan city superseded Jerusalem. Hadrian decided in 130 to organize Aelia as a garrison town, dominated by the legionary headquarters and the veterans of the X Fretensis.

Roman administration in Judaea was marked by a combination of improvisation and traditional policy, both with unfortunate results. Reluctance to get involved more than necessary may account for the fact that Judaea was the first Roman province with an equestrian prefect, rather than a senator as governor.[92] The same may be true for the years after 70, when Judaea was the first province with an ex-praetor serving both as governor and as commander of the legion.[93] As argued above, Caesarea seems to have been the first honorary colony in the eastern provinces.[94] This will certainly have been a reward for past loyalty, but recruitment for the legion is likely to have been a factor as well. As formulated by Rostovtzeff: 'The first duty of the newly constituted (Flavian) cities was to send their youth to the legions.'[95] We are ill informed on the history of Judaea between the first and the second Revolt, but it is clear that, apart from these measures and those mentioned above things were left rather as they were. Of Hadrian's measures only an outline can be detected, but it is clear that he instituted drastic reforms in many fields. And it can no longer be doubted that a start was made in the first years of the reign. When more evidence becomes available we many be able to trace the development and extent of Hadrian's policy in Judaea, just as Den Boer has sketched succeeding phases in the development

---

[91] At present we can only point to two observations of a general nature, namely that Hadrian gradually introduced the system of local recruiting and thus created an army familiar with the needs of the provinces in which it was stationed (Rostovtzeff, *SEHRE*, 363; for recruitment policy, *v. supra*). Secondly, it has been observed that Hadrian's consistent policy of fostering town life in the provinces was, among other things, motivated by his desire to base the army on those elements regarded by Rome as civilized (Rostovtzeff, 365–66). This again was a tradition from earlier times. In Pseudo-Sallust, *Ad Caes.* ii, 5, 8 Caesar is advised to found colonies in order to enrich the army.

[92] H.-G. Pflaum, *Les Procurateurs Équestres sous le Haut-Empire Romain* (1950), 22–4. Egypt, of course, was also governed by an equestrian prefect.

[93] The second province was Arabia in 106. See B.E. Thomasson, 'The One-Legion Provinces of the Roman Empire during the Principate', *Opuscula Romana* 9 (1973), 63 f. Thomasson argues that these one-legion provinces are, in fact, each a legionary command removed from the jurisdiction of the senior legate of Syria.

[94] *V. supra*, p. 00.

[95] *SEHRE*, 107.

of Hadrian's religious policy.[96] In this connection it is worth noting that the year 130 clearly showed a progress towards absolutism.[97] By this time Hadrian's plans for Judaea had assumed a definite shape. Part was traditional, such as the combination of road-building and colonization as a prelude to the pacification of an area inhabited by an unwieldy people. Part was new, such as the nature of the new colony which formed part of a Legionary establishment rather than constituting a garrison-city by itself. Added to this there was Hadrian's religious policy, a peculiarity of this Emperor, which had its consequences for the colony and is reflected by its names.[98]

It can, perhaps, be said that the first revolt was the result of neglect by the central government, the second of over-interference.

List of Works to which Abbreviated Reference has been Made

Alon, vol. I	Along, G., *The History of the Jews in the period of the Mishna and the Talmud* (1952–). (Hebrew).
ANRW ii, 8	*Aufstieg und Niedergang der römischen Welt* (ed. H. Temporini and W. Haase), ii, Band 8 (1977).
Applebaum, 1976	Applebaum, Sh., *Prolegomena to the Study of the Second Jewish Revolt*.
Avi-Yonah, 1966	Avi-Yonah, M., *The Holy Land* (²1977 has an extensive toponymic index).
Avi-Yonah, 1974	Avi-Yonah, M., *P-W, Sup.* xiii, s.v. 'Palaestina' cols. 11–454.
Avi-Yonah, 1976	Avi-Yonah, M., *Gazetteer of Roman Palestine*.
BMC, Galatia etc.	Wroth, W., *Catalogue of Greek Coins in the British Museum: Galatia, Cappadocia and Syria* (1899).
BMC, Palestine	Hill, G.F., *id.: Palestine* (1914).
BMC, Phoenicia	Hill, G.F., *id.: Phoenicia* (1910).
Bowersock, 1965	Bowersock, G.W., *Augustus and the Greek World*.
Bowersock, 1971	Bowersock, G.W., *JRS* 61, 219–42.
Den Boer, 1955	Den Boer, W., 'Religion and Literature in Hadrian's Policy', *Mnemosyne* 8, 123–44.
Dobson and Mann, 1973	Dobson, B. and Mann, J.C., *Britannia* 4, 191–205.

---

[96] *V. supra*, 00.

[97] *Op. cit.*, 139.

[98] It may be noted that both elements of the name *Aelia Capitolina* refer to Hadrian himself. The latter is the Latin equivalent of *Olympios*, Hadrian's favourite epithet, Latin because a Roman colony ought to have a Roman name. In naming Jerusalem *Aelia Capitolina* he dedicated the city to himself as identified with the Capitoline Jupiter.

Enc. Arch. Exc.	Encyclopaedia of Archaeological Excavations in the Holy Land (ed. M. Avi-Yonah), vols. i (1975); ii (1976); iii–iv (1977–8 with E. Stern).
Grant, 1946	Grand, M., From Imperium to Auctoritas.
Head, Hist. Num.	Head, B.V., Historia Numorum (²1911).
Isaac, 1978	Isaac, B., PEQ 110, 47–60.
Isaac and Roll, 1979a	Isaac, B. and Roll, I., Latomus 38, 54–66.
Isaac and Roll, 1979b	Isaac, B. and Roll, I., ZPE 33, 149–56.
Jones, 1940	Jones, A.H.M., The Greek City.
Jones, 1971	Jones, A.H.M., Cities of the Eastern Roman Provinces (Second Edition).
Kadman, 1956	Kadman, L., The Coins of Aelia Capitolina.
Kadman, 1957	Kadman, L., The Coins of Caesarea Maritima.
Kadman, 1961	Kadman, L., The Coins of Akko-Ptolemais.
Kraft, 1951	Kraft, K., Zur Rekrutierung der Alen und Koherten an Rhein und Donau.
Levick, 1967	Levick, B., Roman Colonies in Southern Asia Minor.
Magie, 1950	Magie, D., Roman Rule in Asia Minor.
Millar, 1977	Millar, F., The Emperor and the Roman World.
Mócsy, 1974	Mócsy, A., Pannonia and Upper Moesia.
Momigliano, 1934	Momigliano, A., Ricerche sull'Organizzazione della Giudea sotto il Dominio Romano.
Ringel, 1975	Ringel, J., Césaree de Palestine, Étude Historique et Archéologique.
Rostovtzeff, SEHRE	Rostovtzeff, M., The Social and Economic History of the Roman Empire (Second Edition, revised by P.M. Fraser, 1957).
Rüger, 1968	Rüger, C., Germania Inferior.
Schürer i (1901)	Schürer, E., Geschichte des Jüdischen Volkes im Zeitalter Jesu Christi, Vol. i.
Schürer ii	Op. cit., vol. ii (1907).
Schürer i (1973) and ii (1979)	id., The History of the Jewish People in the Age of Jesus Christ (ed. G. Vermes and F. Millar).
Sherwin-White, 1973	Sherwin-White, A.N., The Roman Citizenship (Second Edition).
Smallwood, 1966	Smallwood, E.M., Documents illustrating the Principates of Nerva, Trajan and Hadrian.
Smallwood, 1976	Smallwood, E.M., The Jews in the Roman Empire.
Thomsen, 1917	Thomsen, P., ZDPV 40, 1 ff.
Vittinghoff, 1952	Vittinghoff, F., Römische Kolonisation und Bürgerrechts Politik.
Weber, 1907	Weber W., Untersuchungen zur Geschichte des Kaisers Hadrianus.

Postscript

The foundation of the three colonies Ptolemais-Acco, Caesarea, and Aelia Capitolina was rediscussed in my general work about the Roman army in the East.[1] F. Millar has published a general survey and discussion of the Roman citizen colonies in the East.[2]

The conclusions offered in this article about the nature of the three colonies: Ptolemais, Caesarea and Aelia Capitolina seem generally to have been accepted. Only on Caesarea have I seen implicit dissent.[3]

A. Kushnir-Stein has published a very interesting study, suggesting that an unidentified city, named Demetrias, in south Phoenicia, may in fact be identified with Strato's Tower, the predecessor of Caesarea.[4] One lead weight and several coins of Demetrias were issued from 154/53 to c. 40 B.C. This seems to imply a fairly important and properly organized polis. If the identification is correct, as it seems to be, this shows that Strato's Tower was rather more important than one would assume from Josephus. Following Nicolaus of Damascus, Josephus describes Strato's Tower as dilapidated when Herod re-founded and re-built it as Caesarea. This may easily be understood as partisan historiography.

Since the publication of this article large-scale excavations have been carried out at Caesarea. Much archaeological evidence concerning Caesarea may now be found in:

Holum *et al.*, *op. cit.* (above, n. 3).
R.L. Vann (ed.), *Caesarea Papers. Straton's Tower, Herod's Harbour, and Roman and Byzantine Caesarea* (*JRA*, Supp. 5, Ann Arbor, MI, 1992).

---

[1] *Limits*, chapter 7: 'The military function of Roman veteran colonies', at 322–5 and chapter 8: 'Urbanization', at 344, 347–9, 352–9.

[2] F. Millar, 'The Roman *Coloniae* of the Near East: A Study of Cultural Relations' in H. Solin and F.M. Kajave (eds.), *Roman Policy in the East and Other Studies in Roman History, Proceedings of a Colloquium at Tvärminne, 1987* (Helsinki, 1990), 7–57.

[3] K.G. Holum, R.L. Hohlfelder, R.J. Bull and A. Raban, *King Herod's Dream: Caesarea on the Sea* (New York, 1988), p. 113: 'Vespasian and his son settled veterans in the new colony . . . assigned land to the veterans in the territory of Caesarea.' These authors therefore either disagree with my conclusion that Caesarea was not a veteran colony, or they are unaware of it.

[4] A. Kushnir-Stein, 'The Predecessor of Caesarea: on the identification of Demetrias in South Phoenicia', in *The Roman and Byzantine Near East: Some Recent Archaeological Research* (JRA Supp. 14, Ann Arbor, MI, 1995), 9–14.

For Straton's Tower see two articles in this volume:
A. Raban, 'In Search of Straton's Tower', 7–22, a brief exposition presenting the archaeological evidence for the existence of a moderate-size fortified Hellenistic city with probably two harbours, dating to the second half of the second century B.C.
A. Raban and K. Holum (eds.), *Caesarea Maritima, Retrospective After 2,000 Years: A Symposium of Scholars Held at Caesarea, Israel, January 3–11, 1995* (Leiden, 1996).
D.W. Roller, 'Straton's Tower: some additional thoughts', 23–5.

Several publications deal with newly discovered inscriptions of the period under discussion.[5]

At Jerusalem, as at Caesarea, archaeological activity has proceeded at a pace, but the matters considered in this article have not been elucidated any further. The most intriguing question that might have come nearer a solution through archaeological discoveries, is still unsolved. Nothing more is known now about the physical organization of the *legio X Fretensis* in Jerusalem, than in the late seventies. This is a topic, important in itself, and essential if we want to understand the relationship between army and civilians in Aelia Capitolina. The excavations that have been carried out in the south-western and southern part of the city have not uncovered any remains that can clearly be assigned to a military base.[6] It has therefore been suggested that the legionary presence in the city may have consisted of headquarters and soldiers billeted in various parts of the city.[7] Since there is, so far, no evidence that this ever was Roman practice, it seems better to leave the matter open and assume that the unit was concentrated somewhere in the city.[8]

Not far north-west of the city kilnworks of the legion have been excavated, the first such installations uncovered in the Roman East.[9]

---

[5] W. Eck, 'Zu lateinischen Inschriften aus Caesarea in Iudaea/Syria Palaestina' *ZPE* 113 (1996), 129–143. This article rediscusses inscriptions first published by B. Burrell, *ZPE* 99 (1993), 229–337.

[6] H. Geva, 'The Camp of the Tenth Legion in Jerusalem' *IEJ* 34 (1984), 239–254.

[7] *Op. cit.*

[8] That is the view I expressed in *Limits*, 427 f. For military installations in the East see now the important work by Shelagh Gregory, *Roman Military Architecture on the Eastern Frontier*, (Amsterdam, 1995). So far two volumes of three have come out. For army units in cities, see pp. 60 f.

[9] B. Arubas and Haim Goldfuss, 'The Kilnworks of the Tenth Legion Fretensis', in *The Roman and Byzantine Near East*, 95–107.

These were situated immediately along one of the two main roads from Jerusalem to Jaffa. These roads have been surveyed extensively and are the subject of a monograph, recently published.[10]

Finally it may be noted that the recent publication of a corrected reading of an inscription of 308–311 proves that, by that time, the city of Scythopolis had received the status of a Roman colony.

---

[10] M. Fischer, B. Isaac and I. Roll, *Roman Roads in Judaea*, ii, *The Jaffa—Jerusalem Roads* (B.A.R. International Series, Oxford 1996).

9

JUDAEA AFTER A.D. 70*

The nature of Vespasian's treatment of Jewish land after the First Revolt is indicated by Flavius Josephus in a well known passage,[1] usually considered obscure and imprecise.[2] It is, however, generally agreed that Vespasian held the land as his private property and gave instructions to lease it out to his own advantage.[3] There are differences of opinion as to the extent of the area affected: Judaea proper or the whole province of that name.[4] It is agreed that Josephus fails to explain that only the land of insurgents will have been confiscated. It is further assumed that land around Jerusalem was assigned to the Tenth legion.[5]

I shall now attempt to show that Josephus' statements *BJ* vii, 6, 6 (216) have been misinterpreted in modern literature.

(1) Josephus,

Περὶ δὲ τὸν αὐτὸν καιρὸν ἐπέστειλε Καῖσαρ Βάσσῳ καὶ Λαβερίῳ Μαξίμῳ, οὗτος δὲ ἦν ἐπίτροπος, κελεύων πᾶσαν γῆν ἀποδόσθαι τῶν Ἰουδαίων. οὐ γὰρ κατῴκισεν ἐκεῖ πόλιν ἰδίαν αὐτῷ τὴν χώραν φυλάττων, ὀκτακοσίοις δὲ μόνοις

---

* I am grateful to Professor F.G.B. Millar and Dr. A. Oppenheimer for their comments on this paper.

[1] See the discussion by Th. Mommsen, *Römische Geschichte* V, 539 and n. 29; A. Momigliano, *Ricerche sull'organizzazione della Guidea sotto il dominio romano, Annali della R. Scuola Normale Superiore di Pisa* 2/3 (1934), 85–9; G. Alon, *The Jews in their Land in the Talmudic Age* I (1980), 59–64; E. Schürer, *The History of the Jewish People in the Age of Jesus Christ* I, ed. G. Vermes and F. Millar (1973), 512; 520; E.M. Smallwood, *The Jews under Roman Rule* (²1981), 340; S. Applebaum in *Aufstieg und Niedergang der römischen Welt* II 8, 385 ff.

[2] Mommsen saw internal contradictions due to a mistake or textual corruption. Momigliano considers Josephus' statement exaggerated, Schürer calls it vague, Smallwood brief and imprecise, Alon misleading.

[3] Only P. Baldacci, *La Parola del Passato* 24 (1969), 366–7 concludes that the land was partly sold and partly made *ager publicus* and farmed out, but it is not quite clear how he deduces this from Josephus' text.

[4] Mommsen interprets Josephus as referring to Jerusalem and its territory alone. Schürer assumed that Josephus meant all of Judaea in its narrower and proper sense. Momigliano argues that Jews in Gallilee and the Peraea cannot have been treated differently from those in Judaea proper. Applebaum, *op. cit.*, 386–393 extensively discusses the area affected.

[5] See below, n. 14.

ἀπὸ τῆς στρατιᾶς διαφειμένοις χωρίον ἔδωκεν εἰς κατοίκησιν ὃ καλεῖται μὲν Ἀμμαοῦς, ἀπέχει δὲ τῶν Ἱεροσολύμων σταδίους τριάκοντα.

αὐτῷ Dindorf, Bekker, Naber, Niese, Thackeray; αὐτῷ L; αὐτῶν PAMVRC.

Thackeray's translation:[6] About the same time Caesar sent instructions to Bassus and Laberius Maximus, the procurator, to farm out all Jewish territory. For he founded no city there, reserving the country as his private property, except that he did assign to eight hundred veterans discharged from the army a place for habitation called Emmaus, distant thirty furlongs from Jerusalem.

Michel and Bauernfeind's translation:[7] Um diese zeit erteilte der Kaiser dem Bassus und dem Liberius Maximus, letzterer war der derzeitige Schatzmeister, den schriftlichen Befehl, das ganze Land der Juden zu verpachten. Denn die Gründung einer eigenen Stadt unternahm der Kaiser dort nicht, er behielt sich also das Land persönlich vor. Nur 800 verabschiedeten Angehörigen des Heeres gab er einen Siedlungsraum, der Emmaus hiess und 30 Stadien von Jerusalem entfernt war.

Mommsen translates ἀποδόσθαι as 'to sell' and considered this as contradicting the next sentence, which he too assumed to refer to confiscation of Jewish land by the Emperor. Schürer resolves the contradiction by translating the verb as 'to lease', 'to farm out'. Josephus is then represented as asserting that Vespasian kept all Jewish land and farmed it out to his own advantage. This is now the generally accepted interpretation.

There are, however, several problems. First, Josephus uses the verb ἀποδόσθαι fifteen times for 'to sell' and twice for 'to return', 'to give back', but nowhere for 'to lease'.[8] Should we then prefer Mommsen's 'to sell' and accept that Josephus' text contains a contradiction or a scribal error? That would be a last resort. It must be noted, moreover, that the next sentence, as usually interpreted, is bad Greek and uncharacteristic of Josephus. Josephus states that Vespasian did not found a city (οὐ γὰρ κατῴκισεν ... ind. aorist.). What Vespasian did instead of founding a city would then be expressed by a participle

---

[6] H.St.J. Thackeray, Loeb Classical Library ed. of Josephus, III, 567.

[7] O. Michel and O. Bauernfeind, *Flavius Josephus, De Bello Judaico, Der jüdische Krieg, griechisch und deutsch*, II 2 (1969), 115 with comments on p. 258.

[8] To sell: *Ant.* ii, 1, 3 (3); 3, 3 (33); 6, 1 (94); 6, 2 (98); iii, 12, 3 (283); viii, 12, 5 (312); 13, 8 (355); ix, 3, 2 (50); xiii, 5, 10 (179); xiv, 9, 5 (180); xv, 9, 2 (305); xvi, 1, 1 (1); xvii, 13, 5 (355); xviii, 1, 1 (2); 2, 1 (26). To return: *BJ* vi, 2, 1 (101); *Ant.* xiv, 10, 22 (249). Cf. K.H. Rengstorf (ed.), *A Complete Concordance to Flavius Josephus*, I (1973), 181–2. 'To lease', is not even mentioned in F. Preisigke, *Wörterbuch der griechischen Papyrusurkunden* (1924), s.v.

(φυλάττων), followed by δὲ and another aorist (ἔδωκε). I could find no parallel for such a sentence in Josephus' work. Further, αὐτῷ φυλάσσειν is an awkward expression to indicate appropriation of property by the Emperor. There is a common phrase, ἀναλαμβανεῖν, 'to take up', used also by Josephus.⁹ This point should perhaps not be pressed. More important is the fact that the usual interpretation accepts without discussion a rather significant emendation. All manuscripts have αὐτῶν, apart from L which has αὐτῷ. All editors read αὐτῷ.¹⁰ A far more satisfactory interpretation leaves αὐτῶν as it stands and recognizes δὲ as adversative particle, expressing opposition between οὐ . . . κατῴκισεν . . . πόλιν and χωρίον ἔδωκεν. φυλάττων then serves as a modal participle, also negated by οὐ. This may be translated as follows:

> About the same time Caesar sent instructions to Bassus and Laberius Maximus, the procurator, to dispose of all Jewish land. For he founded there no city of his own while keeping their territory, but only to eight hundred veterans did he assign a place for settlement called Emmaus. . . .

Interpreted in this manner, all elements in the statement are well balanced.¹¹ The sentence is perfectly comprehensible without resorting to emendation. The verb ἀποδόσθαι causes no problem if Vespasian did not keep any land and may be translated as 'to dispose of', 'to sell', the normal use in this period. The verb is used three times to indicate the liquidation of the private estate of Archelaus

---

⁹ *BJ* vii, 11, 2 (446). Elsewhere Josephus uses ἀποφέρειν (*Ant.* xiii, 13, 2 (446)) and ἐγκαταστάσσεται (*BJ* ii, 7, 3 (111)). For confiscation of property and the terminology employed in ancient literature see F. Millar, *The Emperor in the Roman World* (1977), 158; 163 ff.

¹⁰ Niese, in his critical apparatus, gives 'ei' as the reading of the Latin translation. This presumably is taken from the Baseler edition of 1524 which is presently inaccessible to me. It is hard to see how *ei* (rather than *sibi*) could justify reading αυτῷ. The Kölner edition of 1691 which I consulted reads: Eodem vero tempore Caesar etiam ad Liberium Maximum scripsit (erat autem procurator) ut omnem terram venderet Judaeorum. nec enim civitatem in ea condidit proprium servans sibi eorum agrum. Solis autem octingentis militibus illic relictis locum dedit quem incolerent, qui vocatur Ammaus. distat autem ab Hierosolymis triginta stadiis. There is no indication whether *eorum* is the translation of αὐτῶν or *sibi* of αὐτῷ. In any event, not the ancient Latin translation, whatever its reading, should determine our interpretation of this passage, but a proper understanding of the Greek text as preserved in the manuscripts. On the Latin translation of Josephus see: H. Schreckenberg, *Die Flavius-Josephus-Tradition in Antike und Mittelalter* (1972), 59.

¹¹ ἰδίαν is taken as attribute referring to πόλιν as in the German translation cited above. Most editors take ἰδίαν αὐτῷ τὴν χώραν φυλάττων together as a pleonastic phrase.

after confiscation.[12] That is the context of the present passage as well. The only element missing in the statement, needed to make it absolutely clear, is a note explaining that 'all Jewish land' refers only to confiscated property. Josephus takes it for granted that the reader realizes that communities and individuals who had not taken part in the revolt were, as a rule, not punished. Furthermore, land which had been confiscated could be given as a present to others.[13] Josephus himself received such a gift:

(2) *Vita* 76 (422)
Ἐπεὶ δὲ κατέπαυσεν τὰς ἐν τῇ Ἰουδαίᾳ ταραχὰς Τίτος, εἰκάσας τοὺς ἀγροὺς οὓς εἶχον ἐν τοῖς Ἱεροσολύμοις ἀνονήτους ἐσομένους μοι διὰ τὴν μέλλουσαν ἐκεῖ Ῥωμαίων φρουρὰν ἐγκαθέζεσθαι, ἔδωκεν ἑτέραν χώραν ἐν πεδίῳ

From this passage it has been concluded that land in the vicinity of Jerusalem became legionary territory.[14] It must be noted, however, that Josephus does not say that his lands were confiscated or taken up by the army. Titus thought that the possessions of Josephus might become unprofitable because of the presence of the garrison in town. He therefore gave him other lands in the plain. It may be conjectured that land was assigned for the use of the army, but Josephus does not say so.[15] The present passage only expresses what Josephus meant to convey: that, after 70, Jerusalem was dominated by the army and that he himself received gifts from Titus.

What conclusions may be drawn from the texts as reinterpreted? First, Josephus does not say that Jewish land was held as private property by the Emperor. Any reference to crown land in this passage exists only in the imagination of those who have emended the text. Second, Vespasian, according to Josephus, did not keep any territory in Judaea, but gave instructions to dispose of all confiscated

---

[12] *Ant.* xvii, 13, 5 (355): ... πέμπεται Κυρίνιος ὑπὸ Καίσαρος, ἀνὴρ ὑπατικός, ἀποτιμησόμενος τὰ ἐν Συρίᾳ καὶ τοῦ Ἀρχελάου ἀποδωσόμενος οἶκον. xviii, 1, 1 (2) ... ἀποδωσόμενος τὰ Ἀρχελάου χρήματα. xviii, 2, 1 (26). The confiscation of Archelaus' estate is mentioned in *Ant.* xvii, 13, 2 (344).

[13] Cf. Millar, *op. cit.*, 168 f.

[14] Mommsen, *loc. cit.* (*supra*, n. 1); Schürer-Vermes-Millar, *op. cit.* 512, n. 141; Momigliano, *op. cit.*, 85; M. Avi-Yonah, *The Holy Land* (²1977), 112 and F.-M. Abel, *Géographie de la Palestine*, II (³1967), 162 assign a huge territory to the legion on no evidence at all. Cf. B. Isaac and I. Roll, *Roman Roads in Judaea* I (1982), 108, n. 12.

[15] Mommsen, *loc. cit.*, refers to Tacitus, *Ann.* xiii 54. That is definitely not a good parallel, for it refers to a border-area of the Empire kept clear of inhabitants as a buffer zone. Jerusalem was no frontier-town and Judaea was not kept clear of inhabitants. On military land in general see: F. Vittinghoff, Acc. Naz. Lincei 194 (1974), 109–124.

land. That would not apply to crown land which had that status before the revolt, of course.[16] Josephus means to emphasize that Vespasian did not introduce foreigners into any newly-founded Flavian city, intended to replace Jerusalem.[17] He stressed therefore that only a limited number of veterans was established at the modest settlement of Emmaus. The Flavian cities of Caesarea, Jaffa and Neapolis are not mentioned because no foreigners were settled there.[18] Moreover, they were outside the area of Judaea proper which would have been affected by the refoundation of Jerusalem as a pagan city. By not founding a city, Vespasian made it possible for Jews to buy land, if they could afford it, a possibility which the establishment of a large veteran-colony would have precluded. The difference between selling and leasing the land is obvious: after the sale the land became, once again, privately owned property. According to the usual interpretation of the text, all the land would have been farmed out by the Emperor to tenants who could never own their land and had to pay rent. Josephus' statement emphasizes Vespasian's moderation in his treatment of the Jews and to a certain extent this may be considered a pro-Flavian description of the state of affairs.

Josephus' information corresponds with the facts as we know them. Talmudic sources leave no doubt that the Jews owned land in Judaea after 70.[19] Eusebius and others cite Hegesippus as their authority for

---

[16] The famous Balsam-plantations (Pliny, *NH* xii 112; cf. M. Stern, *Greek and Latin Authors on Jews and Judaism*, I (1974), no. 213; P. Baldacci, *La Parola del Passato* 24 (1969), 349–367); Jamnia and its toparchy (*Ant.* xvii, 8, 1 (189); *BJ* ii, 9, 1 (167) cf. Millar, *op. cit.* (*supra*, n. 9), 178)); land in the Valley of Jezreel (cf. Isaac and Roll, *op. cit.*, Appendix, pp. 104–106).

[17] πόλιν ἰδίαν, a city of his own, i.e. named after him like Aelia Capitolina (Hadrian's city).

[18] For Caesarea see Isaac, *Talanta* 12–13 (1980–81), 38–43; for Neapolis and Jaffa, *ibid.*, n. 36. Caesarea was made a titular colony, while Jaffa and Neapolis were previously existing communities ravaged in the war.

[19] Dr. A. Oppenheimer writes to me: Numerous Talmudic sources deal with the sale, mortgaging and inheritance of landed property and with related subjects. It can not be assumed that all are purely theoretical. In a number of instances the events referred to are firmly dated in the period following the destruction of the Second Temple. For instance, the sale of land and related activities which prove ownership of landed property by Baitos ben Zonin, a wealthy resident of Lydda in the time of R. Gamaliel of Javneh (*mBaba Mezi'a* 5, 3; *bBaba Mezi'a* 63a); R. Eliezer ben Hyrcanus owned a vineyard east of Lydda near Kefar Tavi (*bRosh Hashanah* 31b); R. Akiba undertook to buy land on behalf of R. Tarfon (*Wayyikra Rabbah* 34, 17, ed. Margolies, 812; this is indeed a legendary story, but it may be interpreted as reflecting a reality of free trade in landed property). Various ordinances of the

a story about relatives of Jesus in the reign of Domitian, smallholders who possessed 'only thirty-nine plethra of land on which they paid taxes and on which they lived by their own work'.[20] In the Second Jewish Revolt, the governor Tineius Rufus 'enslaved the territory of the Jews', according to Eusebius.[21] This implies that the Jews owned their land, for Tineius Rufus could not have enslaved crown land. Titus promised prominent Jewish refugees from Jerusalem to restore to them their property after the war.[22] It is clear that Jews possessed land in Judaea in fact and by right after the First Revolt. While the property of those condemned for participation in the revolt was undoubtedly confiscated, this was not taken up by the treasury, but sold again. It could then be bought by Jews and gentiles.

The status of the land seems clear in outline. A related problem is the legal status of the Jews after 70.[23] Mommsen's theory that the Jews ceased to exist legally as a nation and permanently remained *peregrini dediticii* is not now accepted. Yet we know that the Jews were punished in various ways. Most serious for the people as a whole was the fact that Jerusalem and the Temple were left in ruins.[24] Vespasian founded the *fiscus Iudaicus* as a form of collective punishment

---

Jewish leadership at Javneh and Usha prove that Jews owned land and that the Sages took steps to preserve this situation: it was prohibited to sell to gentiles land or slaves and large cattle—which formed the work-force in agriculture; it was also prohibited to change over from agriculture to the raising of small cattle. All these ordinances originated in the period subsequent to the First Revolt and were further established during the crisis following the Second Revolt. In this connection must be mentioned the enactments concerning '*sikarikon*' which deal with the acquisition of landed property expropriated by the Romans. These are testimony of land-expropriation but they do also indicate that Jews could acquire land. Finally there are the sources regarding the observation of precepts connected with the produce of the land, such as the Sabbatical year (*shebi'ith*) or tithes (*ma'aseroth*) which show clearly that landed property played an important role in Jewish life after the First Revolt. See A. Büchler, *The Economic Conditions of Judaea after the Destruction of the Second Temple* (1912), 30–39; Alon, *op. cit.* (*supra*, n. 1), 59–64; 152–168; 277–287; S. Safrai, *Tarbiz* 35 (1965), 306–310 (Hebr.).

[20] *HE* iii 19–20; Georgius-Syncellus, p. 652 (Dindorf); Zonaras, p. 504 (Niebuhr). The reliability of the source is uncertain, but the details seem realistic.

[21] Eusebius, *HE* iv, 6, 1: τὰς χώρας αὐτῶν ἐξανδραποδιζόμενος. Cf. Momigliano, *op. cit.*, 86.

[22] *BJ* vi, 2, 2 (115).

[23] Cf. Mommsen, *Historische Zeitschrift* 64 (1890), 424–6; J. Juster, *Les Juifs dans l'Empire romain* II (1914), 19–27; Momigliano, *op. cit.*, 84–9; Alon, *op. cit.* (*supra*, n. 1), 71 with n. 45a; 122–3; S.W. Baron, *A Social and Religious History of the Jews* II (²1952), 103–4; S.L. Guterman, *Religious Toleration and Persecution in Ancient Rome* (1951), 103–8; Smallwood, *op. cit.* (*supra*, n. 1), 342.

[24] *BJ* vii, 1, 1 (1–4) records Titus' decision regarding the city.

of all Jews wherever they lived in the Empire.[25] All this is recorded
by Josephus and in other sources, but no source has anything to say
about the legal status of the Jews, an indication, perhaps, that there
was nothing worth saying.[26] It may confidentially be assumed that
those who had not participated in the revolt did not suffer any further punishment. Large numbers of insurgents were deported as slaves.
It is not clear what legal status was conferred on those who had
surrendered and who remained free men. It has been suggested that
they remained *dediticii* for a relatively long period.[27] There is, however, no evidence showing that Jews were kept in a class inferior to
that of other provincials. Momigliano has argued that there must
have been a connection in fact, though not in law, between the status of the people and that of the land.[28] That there was such a connection is suggested by Cicero: 'cum . . . senatus et populus Romanus
Thermitanis . . . urbem agros legesque suas reddidisset'.[29] We now
know that Vespasian did not keep large tracts of Jewish land as his
own property. If Momigliano's assertion is accepted, we have no reason
to believe that large numbers of free Jews were kept in an inferior
condition. The text of Josephus would seem to support this assertion.
Following the statement on Jewish land, Josephus describes the institution of the *Fiscus Iudaicus*, ending with the sentence: 'Such was the
state of Jewish affairs at this time'.[30] Apparently these were the two
important decisions regarding the Jews.

Apart from the establishment of legionary headquarters at Jerusalem, Josephus makes no mention of any reorganization of Judaea as
a Roman province. As argued elsewhere, archaeology confirms this
impression. There is no trace of road-building or of the introduction
of foreign settlers anywhere in the province.[31] No further measures

[25] *BJ* vii, 6, 6 (218); cf. V.A. Tcherikover and A. Fuks, *Corpus Papyrorum Judaicarum*
I (1957), 80 ff.; Schürer-Vermes-Millar, *op. cit.*, I, 513, n. 143; Smallwood, *op. cit.*,
371–6. See also: Tcherikover, *The Jews in Egypt in the Hellenistic and Roman Periods in
the Light of Papyrology* (²1963), 86–94; 112 (Hebr.).

[26] Christian sources would not have omitted any decision seriously embarrassing
to the Jews.

[27] See literature cited above, n. 23. On *dediticii* see Gaius, *Inst.* I 14 and cf. A.H.M.
Jones, *JRS* 26 (1936), 229–31. Momigliano first pointed out that a distinction will
have been made between participants in the revolt and those who remained loyal
to Rome, such as the Jews of Sepphoris. For the treatment of those who surrendered see *BJ* iv, 3, 2 (130); 8, 1 (444) and *supra*, n. 22.

[28] *Op. cit.*, 86.

[29] *Verr.* 37, 90; cf. Jones, *loc. cit.*

[30] *BJ* vii, 6, 6 (218): καὶ τὰ μὲν Ἰουδαίων τότε τοιαύτην εἶχε κατάστασιν.

[31] B. Isaac, *PEQ* 110 (1978), 47; *Talanta* 12–13 (1980–81), 38–43, above, ch. 8.

were taken actively to suppress the Jews. The contrast with Hadrian's
policy is obvious. Hadrian initiated the construction of a road-network
and reinforced the garrison.[32] He seems to have interfered in local
affairs.[33] He may not have made the Jews *dediticii*, but he certainly
took steps aiming at the suppression of their religion, and transformed
Jerusalem into a pagan city inhabited by foreigners.[34]

---

[32] See n. 31. For the reinforcement of the garrison see: Isaac and Roll, *Latomus*
38 (1979), 54–66; *ZPE* 33 (1979), 149–155; J.R. Rea, *ZPE* 38 (1980), 220 f.; Isaac
and Roll, *ZPE* 47 (1982), 131 f., below, ch. 12, 13, 14.

[33] *Latomus, op. cit.*, 62–4.

[34] See Schürer-Vermes-Millar, *op. cit.*, 555; Alon, *Toldot ha-Yehudim* II (⁴1975), 55 f.

Postscript

After publishing this article I checked the ancient Latin translation of Josephus, to see whether this supported my interpretation or not. The Augsburg edition of 1470 and the Paris edition of 1514 have the following:

Eodem vero tempore Caesar tempore Caesar etiam ad Liberium Maximum scripsit (erat autem procurator) ut omnem terram venderet Iudaeorum. Neque ei civitatem in ea condidit propria [sic] servans & patriam suam [sic]. Solis vero octingentis illic relictis locum dedit quem incolerent qui vocat Massada. . . .

The one element that stands out here is 'venderet', which shows that the Latin translator understood Greek ἀποδόσθαι as meaning 'to sell'. Otherwise this translation does not get us very far, but it shows that all later editions of the Latin Josephus, tried to make sense of the Latin by looking at the Greek. A good edition of the Latin Josephus is definitely a desideratum.

The site of Emmaus, which Vespasian assigned to eight hundred veterans, should almost certainly be identified with Motza, on the road from Jerusalem to Emmaus-Nicopolis. At Motza various remains have been found, but these are inadequately published. Whatever is to be seen there suits a modest settlement of veterans.[1]

The interpretation of this passage in the work of Josephus has again been discussed by G. Veltri.[2] Whether Veltri has understood the Greek better than I do is for others to determine, but there can be no doubt that he has failed to understand my English. He misrepresents my arguments at least three times. The details are not of interest here. He also cites me as writing nonsense instead of Greek: αὐτῶν (*sic, twice!*) τὴν χώραν φυλάττων, and cites the Basler edition of the Latin Josephus (1559) as an authority, although it has no independent value, as observed above.

---

[1] M. Fischer, B. Isaac and I. Roll, *Roman Roads in Judaea*, ii, *The Jaffa-Jerusalem Roads* (B.A.R. International Series, Oxford 1996), see geographical index s.v. Motza and, especially, the Gazetteer, site no. 99. Motza (Colonia; Kalonia; Qaluniya).

[2] G. Veltri, 'Enteignung des Landes oder Pax Romana? Zur politischen Geschichte der Juden nach 70 (Josephus, Bell 7 §§216–218)' *Frankfurter Judaistische Beiträge* 16 (1988), pp. 1–23.

Veltri argues for the following interpretation: Vespasian instructed his procurator

1. *das ganze Land der Juden zurückzugeben*
b. *Er unternahm nämlich keine Gründung einer eigenen Stadt*
a. *um die Region für sich selbst zu beaufsichtigen*

Veltri thus understands Josephus as saying that Vespasian 'ordered to give back the entire land of the Jews in order to supervise (control?) the region for himself, for he founded there no city of himself. . . .' All this rests, naturally, on the interpretation of ἀποδόσθαι. Here it remains a fact that 'to sell' is abundantly attested, while there is almost no evidence at all for 'to return', 'to give back'. There is no problem in assuming that the land concerned was sold after it had been confiscated. Josephus only does not say so because it was self-evident to his readers who knew Roman practice. There is at least a hint in his vocabulary, for instance the contrast between γή = 'land' in the sense of 'landed property' and χώρα = territory, an administrative concept: Vespasian sold all land . . . for he did not keep (their) territory.

10

BANDITS IN JUDAEA AND ARABIA*

A member of a band of *listim, leistai,* bandits was arrested in Cappadocia.[1] Before he was executed he had a last request, as we are told in a rabbinical source relating to the second century: 'Go to the wife of Shimon ben Cahana and tell her that I killed him as he entered the town of Lydda.' Thus the murderer saw to it that his victim's wife was legally declared a widow and could marry again. Rabbi Shimon ben Cahana was a well-known scholar who studied in the school at Lydda in the period between the First and the Second Jewish Revolt.[2] The period, the identity of the victim, and the behavior of the murderer all combined leave no doubt that this was a case of political murder.

Another well-known scholar in the same period was R. Ḥanania ben Teradion, one of the wealthiest men in Galilee and treasurer of a fund for the poor. His son, we are told, first joined a band of *listim* and then proceeded to betray them.[3] This was discovered and he was killed by these bandits. After three days they gave his body up for burial out of respect for the father. We are told, however, that

---

* The substance of this paper was presented as a lecture at the Institute for Advanced Study on 4 February 1981 and at the annual meeting of the Association of Ancient Historians in Ann Arbor, Michigan, on 9 May 1981. First of all I should like to record the great assistance afforded by A. Oppenheimer, who provided me with references to rabbinical sources on banditry and commentary, where needed. I am indebted to G.W. Bowersock for very helpful comments. Further, I have profited from conversations with T. Barnes, J. Eadie, J.F. Gilliam, D. Graf, P. Hyams, M.M. Roxan, and Z. Rubin.

[1] *tos. Yebamoth* 4.5; cf. the parallel passages: *y Yebamoth* 2.4 b; *b Yebamoth* 25 b. The *Yerushalmi* says he was arrested in Caesarea in Cappadocia, the *Babli* mentions Magiza, i.e., Mazaca.

[2] Shimon ben Cahana was a pupil of R. Eliezer ben Hyrcanus (c. 100–130), who taught at Lydda, and a teacher of Raban Simeon ben Gamaliel II (c. 130–160); cf. *tos. Parah* 12.6. This establishes the chronology. The rabbinical sources discuss when a confession of murder may serve as evidence to allow the widow of the victim to remarry.

[3] *Ekhah Rabbah* 3.6; cf. ed. Buber 128 and the parallel source *semaḥot* 12.13, ed. Higger 199 f. For R. Ḥanania as treasurer of a fund for the poor see a.o. *b. Baba Bathra* 10b. His execution as a leader in the revolt of Bar Kokhba is recorded in *b'Abodah Zara* 17b–18a.

the family cursed the son in exquisite terms which need not be repeated. R. Ḥanania was executed by the Romans after the Revolt of Bar Kokhba. The background of the son and the behavior of these *listim* show that they were political bandits, guerilla fighters, or terrorists, according to one's point of view.

These are two instances of political banditry in the years before the Revolt of Bar Kokhba. Before proceeding, the problems discussed in this article may be indicated. Archaeologists working in Jordan and Israel have, in recent years, resumed the systematic study of the remains of Roman army installations in these countries. As a result many papers have appeared which offer historical interpretations based on the exploration of numerous forts, roads, and other structures in the Negev and in the desert area of Jordan.[4] The primary question, of course, is what function the army fulfilled in both the Roman and Byzantine periods. The army's function often is explained without further discussion in terms of frontier defense.[5] The point I want to make here is that it may be unwise to take such an explanation for granted. Before we can define the role of the Roman army in Judaea and Arabia there are various questions to be asked. First, what do we know about the threat of invasion in the region throughout the Roman and Byzantine period? Was nomadic pressure equally strong at all times? Was it continuous, almost continuous or sporadic? Second, are the army installations discovered best explained in terms of frontier defense? Third, what other functions could the army have fulfilled? We should have an idea of the extent to which Roman government in the province was based on force; whether subject peoples fully consented to Roman rule; whether they were doubtfully

---

[4] The Roman military sites in the Negev have been explored by M. Gichon, whose views can be found in many articles, most recently: *Roman Frontier Studies, 1979*, ed. W.S. Hanson and L.J.F. Keppie (1980) 843–864. The Roman army installations in Jordan are being explored by several archaeologists, all of whom acknowledge their indebtedness to G.W. Bowersock, *JRS* 61 (1971) 219–242. For southern Jordan see D. Graf, *BASOR* 229 (1978) 1–26; *Annual of the Department of Antiquities of Jordan* 23 (1979) 121–127. Many sites were visited in 1976 by a survey team directed by S. Thomas Parker. See his preliminary report in *ADAJ* 21 (1976) 19–31; also *Roman Frontier Studies, 1979*, 865–878. New epigraphical evidence has been collected by D. Kennedy in *Roman Frontier Studies* 879–888, *HSCP* 83 (1960) 289 ff., and see now his *Archaeological Explorations on the Roman Frontier in North-East Jordan* (1982).

[5] A. Alt, *ZDPV* 58 (1935) 37, 43–51, F.-M. Abel, *Géographie de la Palestine* (³1967) 178–184, 187–191. See M. Avi-Yonah, *The Holy Land* (²1977) 119 f. (for the *limes* in the Negev); Parker; E.W. Gray, *Proc. Afr. Class. Ass.* 12 (1973) 27; Speidel, *ANRW* II.8.688, for Arabia.

loyal or actively hostile. What was the degree of social, political, and economic stability? My question, in short, what military problems were the Romans facing in these provinces?

First, the threat allegedly posed by nomad invasions. Even those who assume that the primary function of the Roman army in the region here discussed was the protection of the provinces against invading nomads have to admit that not a single literary source mentions major difficulties caused by nomadic tribes before the Byzantine period.[6] Such silence is significant, for Judaea is exceptional as a Roman province in that it produced a substantial body of local literature. Josephus is the only historian of antiquity who has left us a running account of the transformation of an independent kingdom into a Roman province, stage by stage. Rabbinical and early Christian sources, while having different aims, certainly reflect major contemporary troubles but make no mention of nomad raids.

Many undated graffiti have been found in Sinai, in the Negev desert, and in the desert regions of Transjordan.[7] These reflect the presence of Bedouin tribes.[8] Some of the graffiti in southern Syria mention raids and fighting with the Romans, presumably in the first three centuries A.D.[9] However, there is no evidence that these tribes formed a serious threat to the stability of the Roman province. It is conceivable that we have here evidence of Roman efforts to oversee the movements of nomads and sporadic resistance to these measures. It is important to distinguish between Roman police activities in a desert area and military action to defend the province against invasion. The Thamudic graffiti of North Arabia do not mention the

---

[6] M. Gichon has discussed this problem at length in his various articles. From parallels in the biblical and other periods he concludes that the primary task of the installations in the Negev was the protection of Judaea against Nomad raids and invasions, besides other functions such as the encouragement of trade and supervision of traffic. See below, note 79. For the relationship between Rome and the Nomads see now M. Sartre, *Trois Études sur l'Arabie romaine et byzantine* (1982) chap. 3.

[7] See now Graf, *BASOR* with extensive bibliography; *op. cit.* (below, n. 79, forthcoming); F.V. Winnett and G. Lankaster Harding, *Inscriptions from Fifty Safaitic Cairns* (1978).

[8] These graffiti are hard to date and to interpret. It is very likely that careful study may uncover patterns of tribal movements, but by themselves they can not be taken as evidence of great pressure on the Roman provinces, unless one takes it for granted that there was such pressure.

[9] Cf. Graf, *BASOR* 5–6. The inscriptions present these conflicts from the perspective of tribesmen, which will have been quite different from that of the Romans. It is important to remember that there are various kinds of fighting, from a minor camel raid to massive migrations.

Romans at all. A famous bilingual text, most recently discussed by David Graf and M. O'Connor, shows that, in the reign of Marcus Aurelius, the Thamudians formed a confederation that recognized the authority of the Roman emperor and the governor of Arabia.[10] An inscription of 328 refers to a 'lord of all the Arabs.'[11] It is hard to say how much this meant at the time. The first classical author who describes Saracens as a nuisance is Ammianus.[12] The first real crisis caused by Bedouin tribes we know of was the Revolt of Queen Mavia in 378, recently discussed by various scholars.[13] We have, therefore, no literary references to nomad incursions during the four and a half centuries which followed Pompey's appearance in the region.

There is, on the other hand, no lack of information on various forms of internal unrest. Apart from the major wars which are studied again and again, there are ever recurring references to banditry.

---

[10] D.F. Graf and M. O'Connor, *Byzantine Studies* 4 (1977) 52–66; G.W Bowersock in *Le monde grec: Hommages à Claire Préaux* (1975) 513–522. This is a Greek-Nabataean bilingual text recording the building of a temple in the reign of Marcus and Lucius, 166–169 under the governorship of L. Antistius Adventus (166) by the Θαμουδηνῶν ἔθνος. Another inscription there mentions L. Claudius Modestus as governor. The Nabataean texts speak of a federation (*šrkt*), called Thamud, governed by elders (*qdmy šrkth*). The sanctuary of Rawwafa was a central shrine and meeting place on a major trade route. Graf and O'Connor propose that the name *Saraceni* derived from the early Arabic term for confederation *šrkt*, attested in these inscriptions.

[11] Bowersock 520–522. The inscription was found near Nemara in southern Syria and marks the tomb of Imrū al-Quays, *mlk* (lord or king) of all the Arabs. It has been suggested that this man was identical with Imrū al-Quays, son of 'Amr, the second king of the Lakhmid dynasty of Al Hira in southern Babylonia. We do not know the real significance of the term *mlk* at that time. R.E. Brünnow and A. v. Domaszewski, *Die Provincia Arabia* III (1909) 283–284 note that we need not accept the grandiose language of the text at face value. On the inscription see most recently A.F.L. Beeston, *BSOAS* 42 (1979) 1–6; I. Shahid, *JSS* 24 (1979) 33–42. See also Sartre (above, n. 6) 136–139.

[12] Some are mentioned as paid allies of the Romans: XXIII.5.1; others were allies of the Persians (XXIV.2.4). Dr. John Matthews notes that the description of the Arab chief may be colored to emphasize the contrast with the distinguished Persian Surena. The most extensive description of the Saracens is XIV.4. They are described as raiders, not as an invading force. A few references relating to the third century may be mentioned: *SHA* Niger 7.8 need not be taken seriously. Campaigns against southern Arabia by Severus (Herodian III.913) and Macrinus (*SHA* Macrinus 7.8) may similarly be ignored. Diocletian fought the Saracens (*Panegyrici Latini* 11 [3].5.4.). That will have been in northern Mesopotamia, where he fortified Circesium (cf. Ammianus XXIII.5.1–2; Procopius, *De Aed.* II.6; *Bell* II.4). All this is not to deny that there were tribal movements and that the Arabs may have troubled the Romans. I want to point out that we have no evidence of great pressure before the Byzantine period.

[13] *Studien zur antiken Sozialgeschichte, Festschrift F. Vittinghoff*, ed. W. Eck, H. Galsterer, and H. Wolff (1980) 477–495. Bowersock 486–487 returns to 378 as the date of the revolt, first suggested by Brünnow and Domaszewski II.286. See also P. Mayerson, *IEJ* 30 (1980) 123–124; Sartre (above, n. 6) 140–144.

Agatharchides of Cnidus, through Strabo and Diodorus, informs us that the Nabataeans practiced piracy in the Red Sea, attacking merchant vessels in the second century B.C. These activities were suppressed by the Ptolemaean fleet.[14]

Josephus and Strabo extensively describe the regions which suffered from brigandage at the time of Pompey's eastern campaign in 63 B.C.[15] The mountains of the Lebanon were inhabited by Ituraeans and Arabians. Strabo gives a long list of strongholds which served as bases of operation for robbers, all of them destroyed by Pompey.[16] That, of course, caused hardship for the robbers but did not stop them robbing. In the reign of Augustus further steps were taken to bring the situation in the Lebanon under control.[17]

The lava plateau between Damascus and Bostra, modern El Leja (= 'a refuge'; a place in which to hide), was, in antiquity, called Trachonitis.[18] Here too lived Ituraeans and Arabians. They made incursions into the territory of Damascus. Strabo states: 'For the most part indeed, the barbarians have been robbing the merchants from Arabia Felix, but this is less the case now that the band of robbers under Zenodorus has been broken up through the good government established by the Romans and through the security established by the Roman soldiers that are kept in Syria.'[19] That view was too

---

[14] Diodorus III.43.5; Strabo VI.4.18 (777).

[15] Strabo XVI.2.37 (761) mentions bands of robbers that arose in revolt against 'the tyrannies.' These bands plundered both their own country and that of their neighbors. Other groups cooperated with the established rulers and attacked only the neighboring countries. For Pompey's route see Josephus, *Ant.* XIV.3.2 (38–40). See also Pompeius Trogus, *Hist. Philippicae*, Prologus, L. XXXIX (for comments see M. Stern, *Greek and Latin Sources on Jews and Judaism* [Jerusalem 1974] no. 138) and cf. Justinus (Pompeius Trogus) XI.2.4: *ne rursus Syriam Iudaeorum et Arabum latrociniis infestam reddat.*

[16] Strabo XVI.2.18 (755). Strabo says that the mountains are inhabited by Ituraeans and Arabians, all of whom are κακοῦργοι. Their victims are unidentified γεωργοί, living in the plains, who cannot help themselves. For the history of Ituraea see E. Schürer, *The History of the Jewish People in the Age of Jesus Christ*, ed. G. Vermes and F. Millar, I (Edinburgh 1973) app. I, 561–573. For such raiding in modern times and in the same region see, e.g., the Great Britain Admiralty *Handbook of Syria* (*including Palestine*), 1920 229–231.

[17] Notably the establishment of a veteran colony at Berytus, cf. A.H.M. Jones, *JRS* 21 (1931) 266–267. For Berytus, see now J. Lauffray in *ANRW* II.8.135–163; for the foundation of the colony, 145–147.

[18] For the geography of Trachonitis see Schürer (above, n. 16) 336–338. For a description of the region see, e.g., the Admiralty *Handbook* (above, n. 16) 562 f. For air photographs see A. Poidebard, *Syria* 9 (1928) 114–123.

[19] Strabo XVI.2.20 (756). Cf. again the Admiralty *Handbook* 563: 'The passes, fissures, and caverns in this black and desolate region are so inaccessible that the Bedouin robbers by which El-Leja has been infested for centuries, continue to find

optimistic, as we shall soon see. The merchants from Arabia Felix were the traders who brought aromatics and spices from Yemen along the old King's Highway, which was to become a Roman road, re-named *via Traiana*.[20] Incidentally, it is of interest to see that part of this traffic went to Southern Syria rather than the ports of Gaza and Alexandria.

On the Mediterranean coast we find robbers and pirates in Berytus, Byblos[21] on Mt. Carmel, and in the plain of Sharon, inhabited by Jews and Syrians.[22] Josephus quotes the Hasmonaean Hyrcanus as accusing his rival Aristobulus before Pompey of having 'instigated raids against neighbouring peoples and acts of piracy at sea.'[23] All this gives us a picture of endemic piracy, condoned or even organized by local leaders at the time of the Roman conquest.

It was Herod's task as client king to suppress banditry. His first act as governor of Galilee in 47–46 B.C. was an attack on a bandit leader (ἀρχιληστής) Ezekias, who harassed Tyrian villages. Ezekias was killed, the Syrians were satisfied and so was the governor of Syria, Sex. Julius Caesar.[24] There was more to it, however, for Herod was called to account before the sanhedrin in Jerusalem. We do not know the first Zealots and many of his descendants were active in the resistance to Rome before and during the First Revolt, all of them called ληισταί by Josephus. The last was Eleazar ben Yair, commander of the defendants of Masada.[25] This is not the occasion to discuss the

---

secure refuge from the law. . . . At only a few points are the rocky borders pen-etrable and, there, the tracks are hewn out of the rock. The secrets of internal communication are carefully guarded by the inhabitants. Tracks over and around deep fissures or through narrow passes and confused masses of fallen or upheaved rocks, can only be followed in daylight with the help of local guides whose knowl-edge is confined to particular localities.' All this amply illustrates what the Romans were up against in this region. Later they constructed a road from Damascus to Bostra (see below).

[20] For Roman control over the trade routes in the region see B. Isaac in *Roman Frontier Studies, 1979* (above, n. 4) 889–901.

[21] Strabo XVI.2.18 (755).

[22] Strabo XVI.2.28 (759).

[23] *Ant.* XIV.3.2 (43); cf. Diodorus XL.2 with Stern's comments (above, n. 15) 187.

[24] Josephus, *Ant.* XIV.9.2 (159); *BJ* I.10.5 (204).

[25] For Judas, the son of Ezekias, who was active between 4 B.C. and A.D. 9 see *Ant.* XVII.10.5 (271–272): 4 B.C.; *Ant.* XVIII.1.1 (4–11); 23 (6); *BJ* II.8.1 (117–118); cf.: Hengel, *Die Zeloten* 336–340, 343 f. The sons of Judas, James, and Simon were crucified in the governorship of Tiberius Alexander A.D. 46?–48: *Ant.* XX.5.2 (102); cf. *Acts* 5.37 and the comments in Schürer I.381 f. A relative, Menahem, was one of the leaders early in the First Jewish Revolt: *BJ* II.433–448; see also below, p. 179 and n. 45. For Eleazar the son of Yair see *BJ* II.17.9 (447). Cf. Schürer (above, n. 16) 275 f.; S. Applebaum, *JRS* 61 (1971) 159; M. Hengel, *Die Zeloten* (1961) 219–222.

ideology or social origin of the Zealot movement. There is no lack of works on the subject.[26] Here it will suffice to note that Judaea, from Herod's rise to power until the outbreak of the First Jewish Revolt, saw the emergence of groups refusing to accept the order imposed by Rome on her clients.[27] These groups are all described as bands of robbers by Josephus. Rabbinical sources, on the other hand, regularly describe representatives of the Roman government as bandits (*listim*).[28] The frequence of political banditry in this period both resulted from and increased instability. In the words of R. Acha: 'Where the empire takes over government, there appear bands and bands of *listim*.'[29]

After discussing political banditry for the period up to the First Revolt, it remains to indicate what can be learned about the causes of nonpolitical banditry, about the tactics of bandits, and the methods used by the government to combat them.

In 23 B.C., Augustus gave Trachonitis, Batanaea, and Auranitis to Herod. His task was to suppress the robber bands in Trachonitis.[30] Josephus explains: 'It was not easy to restrain people who had made brigandage a habit and had no other means of making a living, since they had neither city nor field of their own but only underground shelters and caves where they lived together with their cattle.' Fourteen years later the people of Trachonitis are said to have revolted without success.[31] Some of them fled to Arabia where they were received and provided with a base of operations. This led to conflicts

---

[26] See the previous note and R. Horsley, *Journ. for the Study of Judaism* 10 (1979) 37–63; *Catholic Biblical Quarterly* 43 (1981) 409–432; D.M. Rhoads, *Israel in Revolution: 6–74 C.E.* (1976) *passim*, esp. 72–76, 159–162.

[27] Note also Herod's campaign against the brigands who dwelt in caves near Arbela in Galilee (38 B.C.): Josephus, *Ant.* XIV.15.4 (415); 15.5 (420–430); *BJ* I.16.2 (305); 16.4 (309–313). The description of an old man who cut down his family and jumped down the cliff, 'submitting to death rather than slavery,' foreshadows Masada: *Ant.* XIV.15.5 (429–430). For the location of the caves see Schürer I (above, n. 16) 282 n. 6.

[28] Many sources describe tax collectors and customs officials as *listim*: tos. *Baba Mezi'a* 8.25; tos. *Shebu'oth* 2.14; *y Baba Mezi'a* 6.11a; *b Shebu'oth* 39a; *Sifra* on Leviticus 8, ed. Weiss 101, p. 3; *Sifre on Deuteronomium* 1, ed. Finkelstein 6.

[29] *Wayyikra Rabbah* 9.8, ed. Margolies 196.

[30] *Ant.* XV.10.1 (342–348); *BJ* I.20.4 (398–400); see above, n. 16. Banditry here was encouraged by Zenodoros, who received a share of the profit, according to Josephus. See also Schürer I (above, n. 16) 291, 565.

[31] *Ant.* XVI.9.1 (271). According to Josephus the inhabitants revolted and resumed their practice of robbing neighbors. They were suppressed by Herod's generals. Forty chiefs are said to have fled to Arabia.

between Herod and the Nabataeans.[32] In an effort to suppress banditry Herod settled 3,000 Idumaeans, his own countrymen, in Trachonitis[33] and attacked the Nabataeans. He was reprimanded by Augustus, following which both the inhabitants of Trachonitis and the Nabataeans resorted to brigandage. Herod, in the end, obviously failed to gain control of Trachonitis, for in the last years he planted settlers in a colony in Batanaea to serve as a buffer between Trachonitis and Galilee.[34] This was a serious matter, for an important caravan route ran through this territory from Bostra to Damascus.[35]

I have described Herod's problems in Trachonitis at some length because Josephus makes explicit statements about the causes of brigandage in that region and because it can be seen how difficult it was to put a stop to this brigandage without moving in with an army and establishing permanent centers of authority.

Following Herod's death many royal residences and houses of wealthy people were destroyed and plundered in Judaea and the Peraea.[36] Among the brigand leaders in these years we find a former shepherd,[37] a former royal slave,[38] and ex-soldiers.[39] This suggests that the Herodian administration had been economically oppressive.[40] Josephus, in fact, more than once points out that banditry was a result of economic oppression. In 39/40 Jewish leaders ask the governor of Syria to point out to Caligula 'that, since the land was unsown, there would be a harvest of banditry because the requirements

---

[32] According to Josephus, *loc. cit.*, they operated both in Judaea (i.e., Galilee) and Coele-Syria (i.e., the territory of Damascus). Herod first attacked the home base of the bandits in Trachonitis, which was ineffective, since they had their base of operations on Nabataean territory. There they 'numbered about a thousand' (*ibid.*, 2 [283]). Herod attacked them there also which led to Nabataean intervention and political problems for Herod (*ibid.*, 287).

[33] *Ibid.*, 285.

[34] *Ant.* XVII.2.1 (23–30). The settlers were Jews from Babylonia, mounted archers, who had crossed the Euphrates. The settlers are mentioned again in connection with events which took place later. Varus, administrator of Agrippa II, planned to cooperate with the people of Trachonitis in an attack on the 'Babylonian Jews.' See Josephus, *Vita* 54–58; cf. *BJ* II.18.6 (481–483). Their presence is attested by carvings found at Neve, cf. Schürer 1.338 n. 3; II.14 n. 46.

[35] See above, p. 127.

[36] *Ant.* XVII.10.6 (274); *BJ* II.4.2 (57, 59).

[37] *Ant.* XVII.10.7 (278–284); *BJ* II.4.3 (60–65).

[38] *Ant.* XVII.10.6 (273–277); *BJ* II.4.2 (57–59). Both had messianic ambitions. Cf. Hengel, *Die Zeloten* 298.

[39] *Ant.* XVII.10.4 (270).

[40] Cf. S. Applebaum, *JRS* 61 (1971) 158.

of tribute could not be met.' In other words, poverty and oppressive taxation led to banditry.[41]

Targets specifically mentioned are, on one occasion, an entire Roman company which was engaged in conveying corn and arms to the troops which occupied Jerusalem.[42] This happened on the highway from Emmaus to Jerusalem. On the same road a slave of Caesar was once attacked and robbed of his baggage.[43] In 4 B.C. the arsenal of the royal palace at Sepphoris in Galilee was attacked and the arms stored there were seized.[44] The same happened in the first stage of the First Jewish Revolt when the Royal armory at Masada was plundered by Menahem.[45] The Romans, in turn, would attempt to capture the bandit leaders, sometimes with success. The towns or villages near the spot where the attack had taken place were held responsible, evacuated, and set on fire.[46] There is, indeed, evidence in some instances of popular support for or collaboration with brigands. The Barabbas released at the time of Jesus' trial was, according to Mark, 'among the rebels who had committed murder in the insurrection.'[47] John calls him a ληστής.[48] Around the middle of the century there was serious trouble between Jews and Samaritans. 'The masses . . . took up arms and invited the assistance of Eleazar ben Dinai—he was a brigand who for many years had had his home in the mountains.' Eleazar is also known from rabbinical sources.[49] He is said to have inspired so many murders that the regular sacrifice of atonement for an unknown murderer was discontinued, and he began to be called Ben Harazhan, son of the murderer.[50] Elsewhere he

---

[41] *Ant.* XVIII.8.4 (274). In another passage, *Ant.* XVIII.1.1 (8), Josephus says that famine strengthens the zealots. Cf. Schürer I (above, n. 16); Hengel, *Die Zeloten* 352.
[42] *BJ* II.4.3 (63). Under Felix (c. 52–?60) bandits fought both Romans and wealthy Jews: *BJ* II.13.6 (264–265).
[43] *Ant.* XX.5.4 (113 ff.); *BJ* II.12.2 (228).
[44] *Ant.* XVII.10.5 (271–272).
[45] *BJ* II.17 (433–434); see above, n. 25.
[46] Following the attack on the Roman company mentioned above Emmaus was burned at the order of Varus: *Ant.* XVII.10.9 (291); *BJ* II.5.1 (71). In revenge for the attack on the arsenal at Sepphoris, Varus burned the city and reduced its inhabitants to slavery: *BJ* II.5.1 (68); *Ant.* XVII.10.9 (289). After the attack on the imperial slave, Cumanus sent troops to the neighboring villages to bring up the inhabitants to him and reprimanded them because they had let the robbers escape: *Ant.* XX.5.4 (113 ff.); *BJ* II.12.2 (218).
[47] Mark 15.7; cf. Luke 23.18 f.
[48] John 18.40; cf. Hengel, *Die Zeloten* 344–348.
[49] *Ant.* XX.6.1 (121 ff.); *BJ* II.12.4 (235 ff.).
[50] *m Sotah* 9.9.

is described as 'one who prematurely tried to free the Jews.'[51] Following the fighting between Jews and Samaritans the governor of Syria, Ummidius Quadratus, had many leaders and participants executed,[52] but Eleazar ben Dinai was caught only some years afterward.[53]

Two concrete steps were taken between 52 and 56: a Roman veteran colony was planted at Acco-Ptolemais and a military road was constructed from the Syrian capital to the new colony, obviously in anticipation of new troubles. Josephus does not mention these actions, but any historian of the Roman empire will recognize them for what they were: preparation for drastic measures.[54]

The *sicarii*, Zealots who practiced political murder must be mentioned here but need not be discussed.[55]

One story concerning Josephus' own activities as commander of the Jewish insurgents in Galilee is worth dwelling upon. Josephus 'summoned the most stalwart of the brigands and, seeing it would be impossible to disarm them, persuaded the people to pay them as mercenaries, remarking that it was better to give them a small sum voluntarily than to submit to raids upon their property.'[56] Elsewhere, describing his army, he states that it was the mercenaries in whom he placed most confidence.[57] The term 'mercenary' is misleading. These bandits would rob anyone, but they would support only an army fighting the Romans and their allies. They would not join the Romans, whatever the reward.

All that has been said so far on brigandage in the first century A.D. concerns Judaea proper. There is some evidence concerning Nabataea as well. Cuspius Fadus, procurator in the mid-forties, captured

---

[51] *Midrash Rabbah on Song of Songs* 2.18. For Ben Dinai cf. Hengel, *Die Zeloten* 356–357.

[52] XX.6.2 (122–124, 129–130); see especially 124 ἐξ ἐκείνου τε ἡ σύμπασα Ἰουδαία λῃστηρίων ἐπληρώθη; *BJ* II.12.5 (236, 241 ff.).

[53] By Felix (c. 52–?60); cf. *Ant.* XX.8.5 (160–161); *BJ* II.13.2 (253).

[54] On the foundation of Roman colonies in Judaea see Isaac in *Jerusalem in the Second Temple Period, A. Schalit Memorial Volume*, ed. A. Oppenheimer, U. Rappaport, M. Stern (1980) 340–360 (Hebrew); *Talanta* 12–13 (1980–81) 31–54 (English).

[55] See Hengel, *Die Zeloten* 47–54.

[56] *Vita* 14 (77–78); cf. *BJ* II.20.7 (581–582) where Josephus refers to these men's habitual κλοπῆς τε καὶ λῃστείας καὶ ἁρπαγῆς κτλ.

[57] *Ibid.* (583) μισθοφόροι (. . .) οἷς ἐπεποίθει μάλιστα. They were 4,500 in number. The enemies of Josephus also hired bandits to fight for them. The people of Sepphoris promised Jesus, a brigand chief active in the hills of western Galilee, a reward if he would attack Josephus (*Vita* 22.104–111). Probably the same Jesus later stayed at Jerusalem with a force of 600 men. There he was paid by leading Pharisees to assist those who were to depose Josephus (*ibid.*, 40 [200]).

a brigand leader named Tholomaeus, who operated in Idumaea and among the Arabs.[58]

An inscription set up at Canatha on the slopes of rebel Druze, southeast of Trachonitis, in the reign of one of the two Agrippas, mentions people who hide in holes like animals. This almost certainly is a reference to the bandits in that region, already familiar to us.[59]

The elder Pliny, writing before A.D. 79, says of the Arabs that an equal part of them were engaged in trade or lived by brigandage.[60]

Banditry did not come to an end with the suppression of the First Jewish Revolt. I have already quoted two sources referring to the same kind of political banditry after the First Revolt and before the Revolt of Bar Kokhba. There are other sources as well clearly referring to this phenomenon in the same period. A rabbinical source describes *listim* who met with pupils of R. Akiba making for the south on their way to Acco. They traveled together for a while, and when they separated the bandits expressed their admiration for R. Akiba and his pupils.[61] R. Akiba was one of the leaders of the Revolt of Bar Kokhba. To the same period belongs the story of Galileans who had killed a man. They fled to Lydda and there appealed to R. Tarfon to hide them. R. Tarfon, influential in the years before the Second Revolt, did not help them, but he did not betray them either.[62] That, again, suggests that they cannot have been ordinary murderers.

Jewish sources, in fact, describe banditry as endemic in the second century and afterward. A source of the second century mentions the possibility that a *nazirite* (who is not allowed a shave) is shaved by *listim*.[63] It is not clear why anyone would do that, but it certainly would not be the work of regular robbers. To the same period belongs the rule concerning payment of ransom for a wife taken captive. If she was imprisoned by the authorities, the husband was not obliged

---

[58] *Ant.* XX.1.1 (5).

[59] *OGIS* 424 = *IGR* III.1223; for Canatha see *Syria* 11 (1930) 272–279. See Waddington's extensive comments on the inscription (Le Bas-Waddington, no. 2329). During the revolt of the Samaritans in the sixth century, part of the insurgents fled to Trachonitis (see below, n. 112).

[60] *NH* VI.32 (162).

[61] *b Abodah Zarah* 25b. This source was first interpreted as referring to guerilla fighters by G. Alon, *A History of the Jews in the Period of the Mishna and the Talmud* II (1961) 1–2 (Hebrew); cf. Isaac and Roll, *Latomus* 38 (1979) 64 n. 56.

[62] *b Niddah* 61a; Alon, *loc. cit.* Comparable is the reference to a conspirator, sought by the authorities, who was hidden by R. Judah ben Levi (early third century): *Bereshith Rabbah* 94.9, ed. Theodor and Albeck, 1184 f.; *y Terumoth* 8.6b.

[63] *m Nazir* 6.3; cf. *Sifre on Numbers* 25, ed. Horovitz, 31.

to pay ransom; if she was taken by *listim* he was. The reason for this distinction was that a wife in the hands of the authorities might have consented to having sexual relations with her captors. When she was the prisoner of *listim* there was no such risk.[64]

Other sources describe *listim* in connection with the imperial authorities. In the third century R. Jose bei R. Bun predicted that *listim* would occupy the throne of Israel 'in the fourth generation.'[65] Another source of that period discusses wives of *listim* and *listim* who are condemned to death, namely, whether sexual relations between them are still permitted.[66] As in the discussion on payment of ransom for captive women, described above, the question which determines the ruling is how the women were thought to behave toward the Roman authorities. It is important that there is no indication here of any condemnation of the bandits as such; the question considered is how their wives were likely to behave when they were in the hands of Roman soldiers and officials. The same source goes on to discuss similar problems as regards towns taken by, respectively, the Roman authorities or 'another power like *listim*.' Only in the first case were women likely to have been violated.[67] The *listim* in both cases must be ideologically motivated guerilla fighters.

There are many more references to *listim* in rabbinical sources,[68] too numerous to list them all. Often they cannot be dated accurately, and it is not always possible to determine whether the examples reflect historical reality or purely academic dispute. Where this is not in doubt it is not always clear whether the *listim* mentioned in the sources were regular robbers and, when they were not, whether they were part of the imperial establishment or belonged to its enemies.[69] Since the Roman authorities were not considered a legitimate government by the Jews, any representative of it could be considered a bandit by them. The term 'bandit' could be applied to

---

[64] *tos. Ketubboth* 4.5; cf. *b Ketubboth* 51b.

[65] *y Horayoth* 3.7c. The source ostensibly discusses the biblical period, but there is no reason to assume that R. Jose here refers to a tradition from biblical times. The statement reflects the realities of his own time, marked by anarchy and political banditry.

[66] *y Ketubboth* 2.26d. The ruling is ascribed to R. Joḥanan, who was head of the Sanhedrin in the middle of the third century.

[67] The ruling is ascribed to R. Judah Nesi'ah who was patriarch in the same period.

[68] They appear 12 times in the mishna, 17 times in the tosephta, 20 times in the Jerusalem talmud, and 40 times in the Babylonian talmud.

[69] See the statement of R. Acha quoted above, p. 177.

anyone who used force to achieve his aims, whether on behalf of the Romans or in the struggle against them. The sources discussed above as well as the great number of other references to bandits in rabbinical sources leave no doubt that terrorism and ordinary brigandage were endemic in Judaea throughout the second and third centuries.

Now, to return to classical sources: Ammianus describes the emperor Marcus Aurelius as traveling through Palestine on his way to Egypt. The Jews are described in terms that might—but need not—refer to civil unrest.[70]

Achilles Tatius, writing in the second half of the second century, describes robbers active between Gaza and Pelusium. His novel *Leucippe and Clitophon* contains an interesting description of an attack by robbers in the Nile delta. The attack is beaten off by fifty infantry with cavalry support.[71]

In the reign of Severus, according to Dio, a bandit named Claudius, 'who was overrunning Judaea and Syria and was being very vigorously pursued in consequence, came to the emperor one day with some horsemen like a military tribune, and saluted and kissed him, and he was neither discovered at the time nor caught later.'[72]

The father of the emperor Philip the Arab was a most notable leader of brigands, according to the *epitome de Caesaribus*.[73] That would have been early in the third century. It is an attractive story, but I do not know whether we should believe it. The location is familiar, for Philip was born in a town near Trachonitis, refounded by him as Philippopolis.[74]

Something must be said on banditry in the Byzantine period as well, but first the Roman army and its organization in the area during the previous period have to be considered.

---

[70] Ammianus XXII.5.5.

[71] Achilles Tatius, *Leucippe and Clitophon* 3.9.2 ff.; 3.5.5 (on the coast of Sinai): καὶ ἦγ ταῦτα τῆς Αἰγύπτου τὰ παράλια κατεῖχον δὲ τότε λῃσταὶ πᾶσαν τὴν ἐκεῖ χώραν. The author describes events which took place during a trip along the coast from Berytus to Pelusium, certainly one of the most important routes in the eastern Mediterranean. He was an Alexandrian and may be assumed to know what he was describing—and this was the second half of the second century, not a period notorious for instability. Cf. E. Vilborg, *Achilles Tatius, Leucippe and Clitophon: A Commentary* (1962) 9–10. In 172 the βουκόλοι in the Nile Delta staged a dangerous revolt (Dio LXXII.4).

[72] Dio LXXV.2.4. Note that these were mounted robbers.

[73] *Epitome de Caesaribus* 28.4: *is Philippus humillimo ortus loco fuit, patre nobilissimo latronum ductore.* I do realize that anyone earning an honest living may be called a bandit by his enemies. In the present article I attempt to collect unambiguous evidence.

[74] Cf. *RE* X s.v. Iulius (Philippus) 386, 755 ff.; XIX s.v. Philippopolis (2) 2263. A. Spijkerman, *The Coins of the Decapolis and Provincia Arabia* (1978) 258–261.

After the First Jewish Revolt the garrison of Judaea consisted of one legion and an undetermined, possibly equally strong force of auxiliaries. The legionary headquarters were at Jerusalem—for obvious reasons. There is no evidence of large-scale construction anywhere in the province.[75]

Arabia too had one legion and auxiliaries after the annexation of the Nabataean kingdom.[76] There a major project was carried out immediately, namely, the construction of the *via nova Traiana*. This road is often called a *limes* or fortified frontier line. That is a misconception, as pointed out by Bowersock.[77] It was precisely what the milestones say: a road between Bostra in the north of the province and the Red Sea in the south.[78] The road did not serve to keep out nomads. A road is not a barrier. In the south the sites are approximately 20 kilometers, almost a day's march, apart.[79] This was convenient for

---

[75] Cf. B. Isaac, *Pal. Explor. Quart.* 110 (1978) 47–49; *op. cit.* (above, n. 54); Isaac and Roll, *Roman Roads in Judaea* I (1982) 66 f., 91. M. Gichon has concluded that road stations and installations in the northern Negev were manned in the second half of the first century. So far there is no proof that Roman troops rather than Nabataean allies were involved, although there is evidence of Roman military organization on the Petra-Gaza road as I have argued elsewhere (above, n. 20). If we assume that the Roman army guarded the roads in the northern Negev, there is still no reason to believe that the troops engaged were numerous, for the forts are small. See most recently Gichon (above, n. 4) with extensive bibliography. The first to argue for a Roman presence in the Negev in the Flavian period was S. Applebaum, *Zion* 27 (1962) 1–10 (Hebrew). However, I do not know of any site having furnished actual proof that it was first occupied in the Flavian period and not before.

[76] For the Roman army in Arabia, see M. Speidel in *ANRW* II.8.687–730.

[77] *HSCP* 80 (1976) 219–229. It must be noted that the road was not constructed between 111 and 114, as is sometimes said. That is the date of the milestones that mark the completion of the road. Construction must have started immediately after the annexation. Military construction activity in 107 is referred to in the letter written by Iulius Apollinaris on March 26 of that year (P. Mich 466, cf. 565, 571, 562), recently discussed by Speidel, *ANRW* II.8.691–692 and by Kennedy (above, n. 4). Professor Bowersock points out to me that the coins of the *Arabia adquisita* series were also minted between 111 and 114, cf. W.E. Metcalf, *American Numismatic Society Museum Notes* 20 (1975) 104 ff.; Spijkerman (above, n. 71) 240.

[78] The milestones give Trajan's titles and continue: *redacta in formam provinciae Arabia viam novam a finibus Syriae usque ad mare rubrum aperuit et stravit.* . . . The texts known at the time are collected in P. Thomsen, *ZDPV* 40 (1917) 1 ff. *Aperuit* is true only to a certain extent. Many of the road stations have Nabataean predecessors, and the road itself more or less corresponded with the old Transjordanian caravan route, the King's Highway.

[79] The Nabataean and Roman military sites in southern Jordan have been surveyed by David Graf. See his preliminary reports in *ADAJ* 23 (1979) 121–127 and in *The Word of the Lord Shall Go Forth: Essays in Celebration of the 60th Birthday of D.N. Freedman* (forthcoming). Full report forthcoming in *Damaszener Mitteilungen*. I am grateful to Dr. Graf for information on the results of his survey in advance of publication.

travelers along the road. It was equally convenient for nomads who might have wanted to cross it, since there was nothing to prevent them from doing so. Farther north the forts are farther apart.[80] In the northern part of the province Arabia, the cities had garrisons.[81] The extant forts are mostly rather small and of later date. So far we have little information on the plans of the forts and road-stations existing in the second century. If the second-century forts were as small as their later successors—which seems most likely—far more troops were stationed in the cities in the north than in the forts on or near the road. Since the forts along the road were limited in number and rather small, the duty of the troops must have been to keep the road safe.[82] To do so it was essential to fortify wells and water reservoirs and deny potential bandits access. There is no lack of memoirs of colonial officers of the nineteenth century which explain

---

Graf concludes that Roman presence in this region was minimal and consisted essentially only of the string of road stations between 'Aqaba and the plateau at Ras en-Naqb. The region east of this line provides evidence for only local occupation (Nabataean and Thamudic Arabs). Moreover, all the Roman sites along the *Via Traiana* have produced Nabataean pottery. Further west the 'Arabah was once thought to have been a corridor lined with Diocletianic castella. Here Graf's investigation of the eastern side have confirmed the conclusions of Beno Rothenberg for the western side, namely, that there was no continuous line of *castella* in the 'Arabah from the Dead Sea to the Red Sea, let alone a double line. The only Roman sites in the northern and central part are those found on roads that crossed the 'Arabah, running east-west. Cf. B. Rothenberg, *Tsephunot Negev* (Archaeology in the Negev and the 'Arabah; Hebrew, 1967) 211 ff.; and in: *Roman Frontier Studies, 1967*, ed. S. Applebaum (1971) 160 ff. For recent discoveries in the western part of the 'Arabah, see Gichon (above, n. 4) 850–852.

[80] For the region north of that covered by Graf's survey, we have that of Parker (see above, n. 4; final report in preparation). He has sketched the increase and decrease of the Roman presence east of the River Jordan on the basis of ceramic evidence from surface finds. It remains to be seen whether these data are sufficiently reliable and whether they allow of an accurate reconstruction of the development of the system. Cf. Graf, *BASOR* and Kennedy (above, n. 4) *passim*. Six sites have been surveyed both by Parker and by Graf. On two of these, Graf claims to have found quantities of Nabataean pottery that are missing in Parker's survey (Quweira and Khirbet al-Kithara). D. Kennedy has shown that the Roman military presence east of the line Bostra-Philadelphia dates to the reign of Septimius Severus (*Roman Frontier Studies 1979* [1980] 879–887; *Roman Frontier* [above, n. 4]).

[81] For the evidence of vexillations in cities see Kennedy, *HSCP* 83 (1980) 289, 292, 297–299, 299–302 (evidence from Petra, Gerasa, and Philadelphia). As a legionary base, Bostra, of course, also had troops.

[82] M. Gichon pointed out that this was a function of the installations in the Negev which he surveyed: *Actes IXe Congrès International d'Études sur les Frontières Romaines, 1972* (1974) 535 f. Gichon devoted several papers to the tactics of intercepting raiders in the desert; see also *Roman Frontier Studies 1967* (1971) ed. S. Applebaum, 191–200; *Provincialia, Festschrift für R. Laur-Belart* (1968) 317–334.

the procedures in detail.[83] The legionary headquarters were in Bostra in the far north of the province.[84] As Trachonitis could most easily be controlled from this city, the need to suppress banditry there is perhaps the best explanation for the choice of this site as legionary fortress. A Roman road ran through the Leja, presumably from Bostra to Damascus.[85] Roman roads were constructed, in this period, not for defense, but for determined and sustained attack. It can perhaps be said that Transjordan was annexed in order to provide caravan traffic from the Arabian peninsula to Syria and the Palestinian coast with a safe road free from banditry.

The Roman authorities, it would seem, were interested primarily in the urbanized areas of southern Syria, Palestine, and Transjordan. They would move into the desert slowly and reluctantly and only when necessary. In the desert the roads were the focus of attention. Elsewhere diplomacy and occasional police action had to suffice.

West of Jordan the garrison was doubled under Hadrian.[86] It was

---

[83] See, for example, the interesting observations of James Felix Jones, 'Researches in the vicinity of the Median Wall,' *Selections from the Records of the Bombay Government*, n.s. 43 (1857) 238 f. Jones criticizes the inefficiency and corruption of the Turkish authorities who went to great trouble to build a fort at Waneh on the Tigris at a considerable distance from the nearest source of water. The garrison was soon withdrawn. 'Had the fortress, indeed, been built around the well above mentioned, the Arabs would have been deprived of the article so much needed in their predatory excursions, and this alone would have effectually deterred them from making any stay on the spot. A casual visit even to their hiding place, the tomb of Kef Ali would have been attended by risk to themselves, for the well is within point-blank range of the building.' Jones goes on to describe the grave consequences of Turkish ineffectiveness. As a result of increased daring of the desert tribes, the direct road to the Diyala was closed to caravans because of the danger and the local, smaller tribes lived in almost constant fear for the safety of their flocks. For a similar situation in antiquity, see below, p. 199.

[84] It is uncertain what was the strength of the troops actually stationed in the city, cf. Kennedy (above, n. 77) 885 f.

[85] For the Roman road that ran from Bostra to Damascus through the Leja, cf. A. Poidebard, *Syria* 9 (1928) 114 (air photographs); M. Dunand, *Mem. Ac. Inscr.* 13.2 (1930) 521–557. As pointed out by Bowersock, *JRS* 61 (1971) 221–222, Bostra lay at a nodal point where the caravan route from Wadi Sirhan joined the main north-south road. Provincial boundaries make it appear as if the city was away from the center. In actual fact it was at about equal distance from Damascus and from Scythopolis (Beth Shean), whence the important port of Caesarea could be reached. At approximately the same distance to the southwest was Philadelphia, and to the southeast there was Wadi Sirhan. Bostra's position near Trachonitis and that of Damascus immediately north of that region is recognized by Eusebius, *Onomastikon*, ed. Klostermann, 110.27–29: 167.1–4. Rabbinical sources emphasize the connection between Bostra and Trachonitis (Schürer I.337).

[86] Cf. Isaac and Roll, *Latomus* 38 (1979) 54–66; *ZPE* 33 (1979) 149–156. Our reading of one of the relevant milestones is doubted by J.P. Rea, *ZPE* 38 (1980) 220 f.

Hadrian, too, who first developed the road system in Judaea.[87] The legionary headquarters were at Jerusalem and Legio, near Megiddo. There is evidence of army units at or near cities which formed the nodal points of the road system. In the Negev a cohors was stationed in the town Mampsis (Kurnub).[88] There is a fort at Oboda, said to date to the second century.[89] Those said to be early are very small. Most known forts and towers in the Negev are of the second half of the third century.[90] In the second century only very limited forces can have been active in the Negev. These most probably were drawn from the army of the province Arabia.[91] From all this it appears that the Roman army in Judaea and Arabia in the second century nowhere was organized in such a manner that it could defend these provinces against serious pressure from the southeast or the east.

Consider for comparison Hadrian's Wall: there is an auxiliary fort at least every 7 kilometers. Small forts control gates every mile, with interval towers in between. Even so it is not now thought that the wall ever served as a fighting platform. It was not built to withstand large-scale attack but as a means to control traffic.[92] The same

---

This does not affect the evidence that Legio was a legionary base by 120. Cf. our reply, *ZPE* 47 (1982) 131 f. and pl. XI, b, c.

[87] Isaac (above, n. 75); Isaac and Roll (above, n. 86).

[88] Inscription discussed by J. Mann, *IEJ* 19 (1969) 211–214; M. Speidel, *ANRW* II.8.710; first published by A. Negev, *IEJ* 17 (1967) 52–54, pl. 8 A, 9 C. The tombstone of a centurion who served in the legion *III Cyr.* and the *II Traiana Fortis* was also found at Mampsis according to A. Negev, *ANRW* II.8.645, 658. I have not found any photograph or published text of the latter inscription. For the cemetery see also A. Negev, *IEJ* 21 (1971) 124 f., pl. 25 A–C.

[89] See R. Cohen, *Qadmoniot* 13 (1980) 44 f., plan and figs. Measuring 100 by 100 meters it is, to my knowledge, the largest pre-Byzantine military installation in the Negev. Even if it was built before A.D. 106—which is uncertain—there is no need to assume that this was a Nabataean fort. The published notes do not indicate whether there were any later modifications in the plan of the fort.

[90] Gichon (above, n. 4) 852 ff.; *Studien zu den Militärgrenzen Roms* (1967) 186–193, and (above, n. 82) 317–334. Gichon has argued that not all the installations of that period necessarily belong to the reign of Diocletian, as assumed by several scholars, most recently by M. Avi-Yonah, *The Holy Land* (²1977) 120; also *RE* Suppl. XIII s.v. Palaestina (1973) col. 408. Avi-Yonah also denied that there was a Roman military presence in the Negev before Diocletian, because it 'would have been unparalleled to have a *limes* insides the imperial borders.' Avi-Yonah thus ignores archaeological facts because they do not suit his twentieth-century terminology. Military installations may have served a purpose 'inside the imperial borders.'

[91] This appears from the inscriptions found at Mampsis. An inscription of a soldier of the *III Cyr.* was found west of Aila, in Sinai: *AÉ* (1936) 131 = *SEG* VIII.345; *AÉ* (1972) 671; E.D. Kollmann, *IEJ* 22 (1972) 145–46, pl. 17 B; Rothenberg, *Roman Frontier Studies 1967* (1971) 221, fig. 110. Cf. Speidel, *ANRW* II.8.694 f.

[92] See D.J. Breeze and B. Dobson, *Hadrian's Wall* (1976). The purpose of Hadrian's Wall was first seen in this light by R.G. Collingwood, *The Vasculum* 8 (1921) 4–9.

hypothesis has been advanced for the Hadrianic *fossatum Africae* in Numidia.[93] In a recent study Elizabeth Fentress has shown that there actually is no evidence of very serious nomad pressure in Numidia before the second half of the third century. For various reasons the *fossatum* seems of little military value.[94] It is, therefore, suggested that the *fossatum*, like the road system in Numidia, was designed to control and direct the flow of traffic into and out of the occupied areas. The *fossatum*, by rerouting trade, served as a customs boundary through which the movement of flocks, trade, and people could be carefully overseen.[95] The comparison is of interest, for even to carry out this task the army installations in Numidia are far greater in number and larger in size than those in the Negev and southern Jordan. This is not to deny that there were troops in these regions, carrying out important functions. My point is that, in this period, these were essentially police duties along the roads and not meant to resist serious pressure from nomads intent on penetrating Roman territory. The annexation of a province such as Arabia worked in two different but complementary ways to suppress banditry: first, by the permanent presence of foreign troops in the region, and second, by the removal of potential bandits through recruitment into the army.[96] The units recruited originally from Arabia number at least 5,000 men. That represents a substantial number of able-bodied men withdrawn from the province. These could be used to suppress their former colleagues in other areas (for example, the *ala I Ulpia Dromedariorum* was well qualified for such duties).[97] The Ituraeans whom I mentioned several

---

[93] E.W.B. Fentress, *Numidia and the Roman Army* (1979) 66, 98 ff. Pol Trousset has formulated comparable conclusions for southern Tunisia in *Roman Frontier Studies, 1979*, ed. W. Hanson and L. Keppie (1980) 931–942.

[94] Cf. D. van Berchem, *L'Armée de Dioclétien et la réforme Constantinienne* (1952) 42–49.

[95] A similar change in outlook is now defended by some scholars as regards the function of crusader castles. These have been most often explained in terms of defending the frontiers. R.C. Smail, *Crusading Warfare* (1956) 204 ff., has argued that the castles were ill equipped to restrain the passage of an invading force when warfare was fought on a scale likely to endanger the occupation of the country. 'They served as residences, as administrative centres, as barracks, and as police posts. Above all, they were centres of authority. The commander of a castle and its garrison was master of the surrounding district and had means at his disposal to meet any challenge to his authority' (*ibid.*, 60 f.).

[96] Cf. Speidel, *ANRW* II.8.719 f.; Cichorius, *RE* IV s.v. Cohors, 324 f.

[97] Not listed by Cichorius as recruited in Arabia, but cf. G.L. Cheesman, *The Auxilia of the Roman Imperial Army* (1914) 182; *CIL* XVI no. 106. There were units of *dromedarii* in Arabia as well, recruited from Arabs. A detachment was based at a road station between Madā'in Ṣāliḥ and Al Ulā in the Ḥijāz. These patrolled the

times were greatly esteemed as archers. There were at least six or seven cohorts and one *ala Ituraeorum*.[98]

Later in the third century, troops were transferred to southern Transjordan. The *Legio X Fretensis* moved from Jerusalem to Aila,[99] and there are two legionary fortresses of Byzantine date farther north.[100] Far more forts and towers from that period are found both in the Negev and in Jordan. That shows that there was, indeed, a need for increased security measures.[101] It is, however, less clear what the aim of these measures was. For southern Jordan Graf's survey has shown that 'none of the *castella* in either the Ḥismā or the Arabah appear to have originated in Diocletianic times or in the fourth century. . . . In fact, in the southern Arabah, the reverse seems to be the case.'[102] The regions strengthened appear to be the northern Negev and, especially, the desert road east of the *via Traiana*, between Esbus and Lejjūn (i.e., east of the Dead Sea),[103] an indica-

---

caravan route as pointed out by H. Seyrig, *Syria* 22 (1941) 218–223 = *Antiquités Syriennes* III (1946) 162–167. Another inscription of a veteran of the *ala dromedariorum*, possibly the same unit, was found in the southern Leja (Trachonitis) where it will have served in a similar capacity (*ILS* 2541) cf. Speidel 703 f.

[98] Cf. Schürer I (above, n. 16) 562, 570; M.M. Roxan, *Roman Military Diplomas, 1954–1977* (1978) nos. 9, 53.

[99] Eusebius, *Onomastikon* (Klostermann) 8.1; *Not. Dig. Or.* 73.30. An inscription probably of 253/259 from Al Hadid mentions troops transferred from Palaestina (rediscussed by Speidel 725). The latest evidence of the *X Fret.* in Jerusalem is a coin of Herennius Etruscus (c. 250) with boar and inscription XF on vexillum, see L. Kadman, *The Coins of Aelia Capitolina* (1956) no. 182.

[100] The *Legio IV Martia* was based at Betthoro according to the *Not. Dig. Or.* 37.22. This is generally identified with Lejjūn. The date of the formation of the legion and its establishment there are uncertain, cf. Speidel, *ANRW* II.8.699; Graf, *BASOR* (above, n. 4) 19. The fortress is now being excavated by S. Thomas Parker. Farther south and east of Petra is the legionary fortress Udruḥ of uncertain date (cf. Bowersock [above, n. 77] 228). Graf found the site continuously occupied, with Iron Age 2 and Nabataean ware represented.

[101] For the Negev see above, n. 90. For Jordan see Parker, *ADAJ* (above, n. 4) 23–25, 27; *Roman Frontier Studies, 1979*, 871–874; Graf, *BASOR* 13. Graf points out for Jordan—as Gichon does for the Negev—that there is no archaeological evidence of any specific association of this development with the Diocletianic reforms (*contra* Parker).

[102] Graf (above, n. 79). Graf has revisited some of the sites, first surveyed by F. von Frank, *ZDPV* 57 (1934) 191–280, and identified as Diocletianic *limes* forts by A. Alt, *ZDPV* 58 (1935) 25 ff. Graf found only Nabataean and late Roman pottery on these sites and no Byzantine ware but notes that further exploration is necessary.

[103] Professor Bowersock deserves gratitude for clarifying the meaning of the term *limes* in Byzantine sources (see above, n. 77). He pointed out that there never were two fortified lines, one being the *via Traiana*, the other running along the edge of the desert. However, he goes too far, I think, when he states that there was no continuous road east of the *via Traiana*. The 1:100.000 maps in volume I of

tion that this road had become more important[104] but also that the local Bedouins formed a threat.

In or before 307 all of southern Arabia became Palaestina Salutaris, later Palaestina Tertia. The province Arabia was extended northward so as to include Batanaea and Trachonitis.[105] Speidel has shown that, in this period, the army of Arabia was drastically reinforced.[106] The most important effect of the reorganization of Arabia was that its army no longer had to patrol the huge desert area, now the responsibility of the army of Palaestina Tertia.[107] Consequently, there were more troops available for a smaller area. There is, however, no evidence of any kind that the steps taken by the Romans in this period were a response to pressure from the southeast.

Queen Mavia's revolt in 378 is the first indication that confederated desert tribes could be very dangerous. Several nomad incursions are mentioned in the following two and a half centuries. Even the

---

R. Brunnow and A. von Domaszewski, *Die Provincia Arabia* (1904), clearly show that the forts from Udhruḥ in the south past Zīzā in the north were part of a 'route system,' linked with the *via Traiana* by series of watchtowers, particularly along wadis. The whole series of forts in this sector makes no sense otherwise. There may be no continuous paved road, but that should not surprise us in the desert. There are many parallel cases which we have surveyed in Israel. The main route from Jerusalem to Petra is elaborately constructed in the Hebron mountains and where it descends into the 'Arabah over the Scorpion's pass, but it disappears altogether in the plain around Malḥata and in the 'Arabah. We have to think of Roman roads in terms of organization, whether paved or not.

[104] In 106 the Romans paved the Old King's Highway, which ran through fertile and settled land. Travelers suffered the major disadvantage of having to negotiate deep wadis. There seems to have been an initial reluctance on the part of the Romans to move in the desert. The road farther east, roughly parallel to the Darlb el-Haj, would have been preferred by those who had no fear of the desert, for it ran across easier terrain. The forts and towers controlled the movements of Bedouins, who, in the second century, may have been able to move freely east of the *via Traiana*. It is this zone and the region farther east which was meant by the term 'inner limes,' *interior limes*, for in Greek and Roman Christian texts inner desert (ἐσωτέρα ἔρημος, *interior heremus*) means the remote desert, e.g., Sinai; see Antoninus Placentinus, ed. Geyer, *Corpus Scriptorum Ecclesiasticorum Latinorum* 39.181–182; Malalas, *Chron.* XVIII.165c (Dindorf 434–435); cf. W. Liebeschuetz, *Studien zu den Militärgrenzen Roms* (1977) 487–499, esp. 488 for other passages illustrating the meaning of the term 'inner limes.'

[105] Brünnow and Domaszewski, *Die Provincia Arabia* III (1909) 266 ff.; for the date see T.D. Barnes, *ZPE* 16 (1975) 277. The southern boundary between Arabia and Palaestina Tertia was Wadi Hesa.

[106] Speidel (above, n. 76) 724–727, cf. 701.

[107] The description of Arabia, studded with strong fortresses, etc., by Ammianus XIV.8.13 refers to the province of his days, consequently Bostra, Gerasa, and Philadelphia are mentioned, but not Petra; moreover, Arabia is *Nabataeis contigua*; it does not include the Nabataean region.

Byzantine sources, however, which tend to describe such events in apocalyptical terms, clearly suggest that usually the disturbances are local.[108] In Palestine there was a Jewish revolt possibly under Constantine, and another of some importance in 351.[109] In 418 again the Jews are said to have been rebellious. The man who suppressed this revolt became consul next year.[110] In 484 the Samaritans revolted.[111] In 530 again there was a dangerous Samaritan insurrection.[112] It was

[108] The first serious disturbances caused by Saracens are described by Ammianus XXIV.2.4 (above, p. 174): *Malechus Podosacis nomine, phylarchus Saracenorum Assanitarum, famosi nominis latro, omni saevitia per nostros limites diu grassatus.* This tribal chief was an ally of the Persians with the title of phylarchus and engaged in irregular warfare (*latro*, for this use of the term cf. A. Alföldi, *Arch. Artesitö* 3 [1941] 40–48 on *CIL* III.3385). Major incursions are described by Jerome c. 410: *Ep.* 126.2 (*PL* 22.1086); under Anastasius I: Theophanes, A.M. 5990, ed. de Boor 141; Evagrius, *Historia Ecclesiastica* III.36; *Vita Abramii, apud* Schwartz, *Kyrillos von Skythopolis* (1939) 244; John of Nikiu, *Chronicle,* chap. 89 (trans. R.H. Charles, 1916) 338; for the date, see E. Stein, *Histoire du Bas-Empire* II (1949) 91 n. 4: A.D. 499; another *razzia* reached Palestine in 502: Theophanes, A.M. 5994, de Boor 143; Nonnosus, *FHG* IV.179; *v. Euthym., apud* Schwartz 67 f., cf. Stein 92 and n. 1; I. Kawar, *Der Islam* 33 (1958) 232 ff.; Sartre 159 f. After A.D. 528 the Lakhmid chief Al-Mundhir, being a vassal of the Persians, made two of his most destructive inroads; cf. Procopius *Bell.* I.17, 29 ff.; Malalas 434–435. These, however, seem not to have reached southern Syria, Arabia, and Palestine. See also below, p. 194 and n. 118.

[109] For the revolt under Constantine, see John Chrysostom, *Adv. Judaeos* V.11 (*PG* 48.900); Cedrenus, ed. Bonn I.499; Syriac Chronicle of 848, *CSCO* (SS) IV, II; the two last mentioned depend on John Chrysostom. Cf. M. Avi-Yonah, *The Jews of Palestine* (1976) 173 f. For that in 351 see M. Stern, *Greek and Latin Sources on Jews and Judaism* II (1980) 500 f. for the sources and bibliography. For a different view of the events in 351, see S. Lieberman, *JQR* 36 (1946) 337–341; J. Geiger, *SCI* 5 (1979–80) 250–257; for skepticism regarding the rebellion under Constantine, *ibid.,* 257, n. 29.

[110] For the revolt in 418 see Marcellus Comes, *Chronicon ad a. 418,* ed. Mommsen, *Monumenta Germaniae Historica* (1894). The revolt was suppressed by the Goth Plinta, *deletus est* says the chronicle, but the text must be corrupt, since the same source lists him as consul for 419, as pointed out by O. Seeck, *Geschichte des Untergangs der antiken Welt* VI (1920–21) 484 n. 1. In that year many Palestinian cities and settlements were destroyed in an earthquake. The chronicle may wish to indicate that there is a connection with the revolt of 418.

[111] *Chronicon Paschale,* ed. Dindorf 603–604; Procopius, *De Aed.* V.7.5–9; Malalas XV.5.53–54 (Dindorf 382); cf. *RE* XIV.2395, s.v. Mauropappos (Ensslin); J.A. Montgomery, *The Samaritans* (1907) 111–113, 305–308, 319; M. Avi-Yonah, *Eretz Israel* 4 (1956) 127–132 (Hebrew). The revolt was suppressed by the *dux Palaestinae* assisted by a ληστοδιώκτης. The leader of the revolt, Ioustasa, is called ληστάρχος in our sources, and it is added that the Samaritans crowned him (ἔστεψαν). Both the terminology used by the Romans and the messianic tendency of the revolt are familiar from Josephus, four centuries earlier (*Chron. Paschale,* Dindorf 603–604). Procopius, *De Aed.* V.7.10–14 reports continued unrest at Neapolis in the reign of Anastasius (491–518).

[112] Malalas XVIII (ed. Bonn 445–447); *Historia Miscella* XVI (*PL* XCV.981); Cyrillus of Scythopolis, *Vita S. Sabae,* E. Schwartz, *Texte und Untersuchungen* 49/2 (1939) 172; Eutychius, *Ann.* 160–167 (*PG* 111.1071 f.). Cf. E. Stein, *Histoire du Bas-Empire* II

so bad that Christians could not travel on the public roads, and it had to be suppressed by the army. Judaea obviously remained a tense and unstable province for centuries after the Revolt of Bar Kokhba. Major disturbances caused by nomads, however, were rare and, usually, were concentrated in the north. Most important, there is no evidence of serious trouble in Palaestina Tertia between Mavia's revolt and the Muslim conquest.[113]

There is, again, a good deal of evidence regarding local disturbances and banditry. These often took the form of raids, but they were carried out by local people, not by nomads migrating and trying to infiltrate into the empire. The story of Nilus and his son Theodolus gives us a vivid picture of incursions and banditry in Sinai and the Negev in the late fourth century and of the agreements made by small communities with bedouin sheikhs for protection.[114] Jerome mentions highwaymen on the Jerusalem-Jericho road.[115] Early in the fifth century monks were killed near Teqoa in the Judaean desert in a bedouin raid.[116] Sabas asked Anastasius (491–518) to construct a *Kastron* in the same desert, near his lavra on the Kidron, in order to protect it against Saracen incursions.[117] The request was granted, but the order was not carried out. In the same period and in the same region a settlement of sedentary Bedouins, christianized by Euthymius, was attacked by nomads. It was then transferred to a place closer to

(1949) 287 f.; Montgomery 114–117; Avi-Yonah; Sartre (above n. 6) 168–170. Again, in 556, Samaritans and Jews are said to have rebelled in Caesarea. See Theophanes, A.M. 6048; Malalas, *ibid.*, 487 f., ed. Bonn, I.675; *Historia Miscella* XVI (*PL* XCV.991); Michel le Syrien, ed. Chabot, II.262. Between 565 and 578 Christians complained about Samaritan aggression in churches at the foot of Mt. Carmel. See Hardouin, *Acta Conc.* (Nicaea 787) IV.290; cf. Montgomery 121 f.; Avi-Yonah 132.

[113] This has already been observed by Ph. Mayerson, *Transactions of the American Philosophical Association* 95 (1964) 155–199, esp. 168, 178; *idem, Proceedings of the American Philosophical Society* 107 (1963) 160–172. In these two articles the relationship between Bedouins and the settled area of southern Palestine and Sinai is seen in the right perspective.

[114] Nilus, *Narrationes* (*PG* 79.589–693). The historicity of the story has been doubted, but, as observed by Mayerson, *Proc. Am. Phil. Soc.* (above, n. 113) 162 and *Journal Am. Research Center in Egypt* 12 (1975) 51–74, there is no doubt that the setting is historically true.

[115] *Onomastikon*, ed. Klostermann, 24; and Jerome's trans., *ibid.*, esp. 25.10–14; Jerome, *Ep.* 109.12 (*Vita S. Paulae*), *PL* XXII.888.

[116] John Cassianus, *Collatio* VI, 1 (ed. Petschenig [1886] 153 = *PG* 49.645a = *CSEL* XIII.2).

[117] Cyrillus of Scythopolis, *loc. cit.* (above, n. 112); cf. A.A. Vasiliev, *Dumbarton Oaks Papers* 9/10 (1956) 310 and Sartre (above, n. 6) 159, who suggests that there was a connection with the raids in 499 mentioned above, n. 108.

Jerusalem, where it was attacked once again.[118] Later in this century John Moschus has more cheerful stories to tell, for his monks, by their very piety, could immobilize Saracen robbers.[119] John Moschus lived northeast of Jerusalem from 568/579. It is worth listing these sources here, for a glance at the map will show that all these bandits were operating west of the mighty *limes Arabicus*. That should make it clear enough that this was not a barrier which could keep the settled lands to the west free of Saracens.[120] It may be added that not the *limes Palestinae* protected Hilarion against robbers near Gaza, but his persuasive piety, as well as the fact that he was already naked when the robbers met him (early fourth century).[121]

Literary sources of the Byzantine period tell us more about countermeasures than those of the principate. Cities were strongly fortified only in the area of conflict between Persia and Rome, for, as Procopius observes, the Saracens were incapable of storming a wall.[122] We have, in fact, no reference to Bedouins attacking a town.[123] They formed a danger to travelers and isolated monasteries. Saba's request to build a fort near his lavra on the Kidron has been mentioned above. The imperial promise to do so was not carried out. At the time of the Persian capture of Jerusalem in 614, the monks were massacred by Arabs.[124] However, the wall of the monastery of St. Catherine in

---

[118] See Cyrillus of Scythopolis, *Vita Euthymii* (Schwartz, above, n. 108) 67–68. There is no evidence that the second attack was carried out by al-Mundhir in 529 as suggested by Raymond Génier, *Vie de Saint Euthyme le Grand* (1909) 116, and P. Henri Charles, *Le Christianisme des Arabes Nomades sur le limes* (1936) 46. As pointed out by Charles, this community still had bishops in 536 and 556. The raids, therefore, cannot have been as devastating as suggested by our source and may well have been carried out by other tribes living in the area. See also F.-M. Abel, *Géographie de la Palestine* II (³1967) 273: Sartre (above, n. 6) 149–153.

[119] *Pratum spirituale*, *PG* 87.3.2851–3112; see chaps. 99, 133, 136, 155. Cf. Vasiliev 315 f. For Christian, Jewish, and Samaritan bandits in the area of Emmaus-Nikopolis, see *Pratum spirituale* 95 (col. 3032).

[120] According to Parker, *Frontier Studies, 1979* (above, n. 4) 871: 'The *limes Arabicus* was at its height of effectiveness and strength in the period from Diocletian to the death of Theodosius II in 450.'

[121] Jerome, *Vita Hilarionis* 12 (*PL* XXIII.34). Jerome emphasizes (*ibid.*, 3–4, col. 31) that the desert of Gaza was full of robbers.

[122] *De Aed.* II.9.4–5. Mayerson, *Trans. Am. Ph. Ass.* (above, n. 113) 183 ff. has observed, in this connection, that the settlements in the Negev all have modest walls or no walls at all.

[123] Vasiliev (above, n. 117) 309 n. 10 cites the Syriac chronicle of Arbela for a reference to an attack by Bedouins on Arbela in Adiabene. However, the chronicle is now known to have been composed by its first 'editor' Alfonse Mingana. This has been shown by J.-M. Fiey, *L'Orient Syrien* 12 (1967) 265–302.

[124] Antiochus Monachus, *Ep. ad Eustathium* (*PG* 89.1423). Cf. Vasiliev (above, n. 117) 311 n. 21.

Sinai still stands.[125] Egeria found a group of monks living unprotected near the site of the burning bush.[126] In 373 Saracens attacked hermits living there.[127] In the reign of Justinian a new church and fortress were built to defend the monks against bedouin raids.[128] Procopius' comments on this project are of interest.[129] He did not know that the site of the monastery was determined by the tradition concerning the burning bush, nor does he mention the harassment of hermits there by Bedouins. He describes the building as 'a very strong fortress,' an obvious overstatement. It was built, he says, to prevent the Saracens from making incursions into Palestine from that region, which he calls uninhabited. A modern historian without knowledge of the site or background information and with no detailed maps at his disposal could have given the same erroneous explanation. In fact, no Saracen with any sense would pass the monastery if he wanted to plunder Palestine.[130]

Monasteries sometimes enjoyed imperial protection if they were lucky. Small and isolated communities might organize a paid militia of their own, or they might make private arrangements for protection against incursions with bedouin sheikhs.[131] The acropoleis of Oboda and Nessana were converted into incongruously massive forts in the fifth century.[132] It is usually accepted that these are instances

---

[125] For the sixth century remains see G.H. Forsyth, *Dumbarton Oaks Papers* 22 (1968) 3–19, plates; G.H. Forsyth and K. Weitzmann, *The Monastery of Saint Catherine at Mount Sinai* (1973). The relative weakness of the site and the walls is emphasized (above, n. 124). For the monastery see also Y. Tsafrir, *IEJ* 28 (1978) 218–229.

[126] *Itinerarium Egeriae* I.1 ff.

[127] Nilus, *Narratio* IV, *PG* 79.625 ff. For the problems concerning this source, see above, n. 114. See Evagrius V.6 (*PG* 86 bis, 2804) for an attack on the monastery c. 563. This attack was successfully beaten off by the abbot Gregory.

[128] Eutychius, *Annales PG* III.1071–72. For references to the Arabic version which I have not seen, cf. Vasiliev (above, n. 117) 308 n. 5. Other monasteries fortified by Justinian were at Klysma and Raithou. For an inscription from St. Catherine's in honor of Justinian see I. Ševčenko, *Dumbarton Oaks Papers* 20 (1966) 262, no. 5, with photograph.

[129] Procopius, *De Aed.* V.8.9. Cf. Ph. Mayerson, *BASOR* 230 (1978) 33–38.

[130] Mayerson, *Trans. Am. Phil. Ass.* (above, n. 113) 156 ff. argues that the Muslim conquest of Palestine followed an unexpected march from Aïla through southern Sinai to Gaza. Even so they would not have passed the monastery.

[131] See the description of the town of Pharan (modern Feiran) in south Sinai with its ineffective (?) Saracen militia by Ps.-Antoninus Placentinus, *Itinerarium* 40 (*CCSL* 175.150).

[132] For Nessana, see H.D. Colt *et al.*, *Excavations at Nessana* I (1962). For the date see C.J. Kraemer, *Nessana: Non-literary Papyri* III (1958) 16. Colt notes that the Nessana fort and the smaller one at Oboda are so alike in plan and construction that it is certain they were erected about the same time.

of centralized planning with no consideration of local needs.[133] In fact, this was a period of unparalleled prosperity for the Negev. Apart from flourishing towns many rural settlements have been found.[134]

Major trouble—of which we hear very little in the south—obviously was the responsibility of the authorities. At the end of the fifth century the *dux Palaestinae*, Romanus, undertook a punitive expedition against the Ghassanids who had raided Palestine.[135] Next he expelled Arabs who had taken possession of the island Jotaba (Tiran or, more likely, Jeziret el-Far'un), which controlled the gulf of Aila.[136] This is an interesting episode. At Jotaba was a Byzantine customhouse where dues on commercial shipping were collected. This was seized by a Persian bandit of Arab origin named Amorcesus.[137] Thus far this man had lived in Arabia where he made raids, not on Romans, but on Saracens. Now he rather than the imperial government collected dues at Jotaba. Nevertheless he became acceptable to the authorities in Constantinople by his conversion to Christianity, and he was granted an audience with Leo I (457–474) and made phylarch of Arabia Petraea. The story recalls that of the Jewish brothers Asinaeus and Anilaeus in Babylonia, in the first century.[138] They too started as bandits and attained royal recognition of their control over a region against the will of powerful personalities at court. In 534 another *dux Palaestinae*, Aratius Kamsarakan, recaptured Jotaba. This time it had been occupied by Arab Jews.[139] In the same period a governor named

---

[133] Colt 6 f.; L. Woolley and T.E. Lawrence, *The Wilderness of Zin* (1914–15) 118 f.; Mayerson, *Trans. Am. Phil. Assoc.* (above, n. 113) 185. According to Colt, 'The arrangements of both forts, large rectangular enclosures with very few internal rooms, clearly show that they were not built to house large garrisons, but were more in the nature of armories and, in the case of a mounted unit, a place where horses or camels could be quartered.' Woolley and Lawrence note that 'fortresses are of no avail against a mobile enemy in a desert country where roads run everywhither.' As noted, the towns had no walls or a modest one. Woolley and Lawrence (p. 73) comment that 'a blank dry-stone wall can stop a Bedouin raid.'

[134] See Gichon (above, n. 4) 857, with references to the brief reports published in Hebrew by Mr. R. Cohen; P. Mayerson in Colt (above, n. 132) 231 ff.; Woolley and Lawrence, 32.

[135] See above, n. 108.

[136] Theophanes, A.M. 5990, de Boor 141. Cf. F.-M. Abel, *Revue Biblique* 47 (1938) 512 ff.; Vasiliev (above, n. 111) 313; *IGLS* XIII.9046 with comments and Sartre (above, n. 6) 154 f. For Jotabe see also Procopius, *Bella* I.19.3.

[137] The story is told in fragment 1 of Malchus Philadelphensis, ed. Bonn, 231–234, *FHG* IV.113.

[138] Josephus, *Ant.* XVIII.9.1 (310)–7 (370).

[139] Choricius Gazaeus, *Laud. Arat. et Steph.* 66–67, ed. Foerster and Richtsteig 65–66. Cf. Stein 300 n. 1; Abel (above, n. 136).

Stephen acted to check Saracen incursions from Egypt which troubled border cities,[140] although the citizens of Gaza apparently saw no cause for alarm.[141] All this does not amount to very much. When Justinian dismissed the *limitanei* as border guards and started paying bedouin chiefs to keep order, the system worked well in the south, mainly, one suspects, because there were no grave problems anyway.[142] The reform was instituted, of course, because of the collapse of existing arrangements farther north.[143]

So far we have seen that, in the Byzantine period as in the centuries before, there is no evidence that urban communities, whether in the desert or in the fertile region, were really threatened by nomads. Small settlements appear to have flourished, even in the desert. The central government interfered rarely and only in special cases. An interesting building inscription from the Syrian desert, dated 334, may be cited here: 'Vincentius, who was acting as *protector* . . ., observing that many of the *agrarienses* had been ambushed and killed by the Saracens while fetching water for themselves, laid out and constructed a reservoir for the water.' The stone was found on a site along the Roman road from Salkhad to Azraq and shows that firm control of the water supply along the roads was needed to prevent hostile Bedouins from causing trouble.[144]

---

[140] Choricius 33–49. Choricius elsewhere mentions intertribal conflicts which needed Roman intervention (*Laud Summi* 20.75).

[141] As pointed out by Mayerson, *Trans. Am. Phil. Ass.* (above, n. 113) 181. Choricius, *Laud Marc.* 16 (p. 32), relates that the city wall had been allowed to deteriorate to such an extent that it had ceased to function as any kind of barrier. It was repaired at the initiative of the civil head of Gaza, even though no enemy threatened the town.

[142] For Justinian's reform in the east see A.H.M. Jones, *The Later Roman Empire* (1964) 661 ff.; I. Kawar, *JAOS* 77 (1957) 79–87; Mayerson, *Trans. Am. Phil. Ass.* (above, n. 113) 188–190. Mayerson plausibly argues that the sphere of action of these phylarchs was limited to areas beyond the settled territory and that payments were designed primarily for the prevention of raids carried out by tribes under the authority of the phylarch.

[143] For the disastrous raids of Mundhir the Lakhmid as ally of the Persians in northern Syria, see Procopius, *Bella* I.17.29 ff.; *Hist. Arc.* 24.12 ff.; Malalas XVIII (ed. Bonn) 446. For the reform, see *Hist. Arc.* 24.12 ff. Procopius, *Bella* I.19.7 ff. states that Abocharabes (Abū Karib) was effective as *phylarch* in Palestine; cf. Kawar 85 f.

[144] *Cum pervidisset Vincentius protector agens Basie plurimos ex agrariensibus, dum aqua(s) sibi in uso transfererent, insidiatos a Saracenos perisse, receptaculum aqua(rum) ex fundamentis fecit, Optato et Paulino vv cc conss.* J.H. Iliffe, *QDAP* 10 (1942) 62–64; *AÉ* (1948) 136. For the *protectores* see Stein (above, n. 106) 1.80 ff.; Jones (above, n. 142) 636 f. For the *agrariae stationes*, cf. D. van Berchem, *L'armée de Dioclétien et la réforme constantinienne* (1952) 30 n. 1. It would be interesting to know more about the site. We may assume that there was a *statio agraria* along the road which, originally, did not control an adequate water supply. For the site (Basie = Basie[nsa]?), cf. Kennedy (above,

Special care was taken, however, to ensure the safety of travelers. We have evidence on measures taken on the main roads and desert routes frequented by pilgrims. There is no specific evidence on the means by which caravan traffic was protected in the desert beyond Aila. We may assume that both diplomacy and the legion based at Aila had a role to play. Whether there was a Byzantine fleet in the Red Sea we do not know. The other major Red Sea port, Clysma (Suez) had a fortified harbor, 'a defence and deterrent against Saracen raids.'[145] The *Itinerarium Egeriae* describes a trip, made c. 380, from Jerusalem to Mount Sinai and back through Clysma, Pelusium, and the coastal road. *Mansiones* were available for the entire journey. At these *mansiones* soldiers and officers were based who escorted the travelers from one fort to the next.[146] As the pilgrims reached the public road there was no need for their protection any more and the soldiers were dismissed.

In the fourth century the *mansiones* or *xenodocheia* were kept up by the state.[147] Later in 570 another pilgrim traveled to the monastery of St. Catherine. His account is incorrectly ascribed to Antoninus Placentinus. He mentions three *xenodocheia*, two described as forts that contained churches and *xenodocheia*, the third a *castellum modicum, infra se xenodochium.*[148] The pilgrim does not describe them as manned with

---

n. 4) 184. Vincentius presumably constructed a reservoir which was more easily accessible. In Egypt Hadrian constructed ὑδρεύματα, σταθμοί, and φρούρια along the desert road from the Red Sea to the Nile (*OGIS* 701; *IGR* I.1142). Along the Roman road to Coptus *lacci* and *castra* were constructed (*ILS* 2483; Pliny, *N.H.* VI.26.102–103; see also *CIL* III.6123). At Abu Gosh, a site on the Jaffa-Jerusalem road, a reservoir was constructed by the *Legio X Fret.*, which has been partially preserved in the crypt of a crusader church; cf. R. de Vaux and A.-M. Steve, *Fouilles à Qaryet el-'Enab = Abū Gôsh* (1950) 36–39. See also above, p. 186.

[145] Petrus Diaconus (derived from the lost part of the *Itinerarium Egeriae*) Y 6, *CCSL* 175.101. For a modern translation see J. Wilkinson, *Egeria's Travels* (1971).

[146] *Op. cit.*, 9.3, *CCSL* 175.49: *milites qui nobis pro disciplina Romana auxilia pre-buerant . . . iam autem, quoniam agger publicum erat per Egyptum quod transiebat per Arabiam civitatem*, etc. For the date see Wilkinson 237–239.

[147] Leontios, bishop of Antioch in 350, is mentioned as one who took special interest in the organization of *xenodocheia*: *Chronicon Paschale*, ed. Dindorf 535–536; the same source (ad A.D. 365) states that Constantius Augustus spent much money on the church, the orphans, and the *xenodocheia*. In 402 the Empress Eudoxia gave money for a hospice to be built in Gaza. Pilgrims were to receive three days of free lodgings in the city; cf. Marcus Diaconus, *Vita Porphyrii* 53 (ed. Grégoire and Kugener) 44.

[148] (1) Antoninus Placentinus 35 (*CCSL* 175.146–147): twenty miles from Elusa was the *castrum in quo est xenodochius S. Georgi in quo habent quasi refugiam transeuntes vel heremitae stipendia*. It has been argued that this was the fort of Nessana (Mayerson, *Proc. Am. Phil. Soc.* [above, n. 107] 170). (2) and (3) Antoninus Placentinus 41 (*CCSL* 175.150).

soldiers and that may well be proof that they were not.[149] The connection with the church is clear. Commercial caravans had to stay
at Caravanserais.[150] Ps.-Antoninus traveled through Sinai to the monastery. Saracens are described only in Sinai. At that time the Bedouins
were celebrating a festival which precluded trading and raiding. When
the pilgrims returned from Mt. Sinai, the festival was over and therefore they traveled a different route on their way back.[151] No mention
is made of soldiers accompanying the pilgrims from one *mansio* to
the next. All this may reflect the situation after Justinian's reform
which did away with the *limitanei*. The same is true for P.Colt 89 of
the same period, which lists an amount of 3 *solidi*, paid by a small
company of traders 'to the Arab escort who took us to the Holy
Mountain.'[152] Even so a camel was taken by Saracens, the *bani al-
Udayyid*.[153] The excavators of Nessana have concluded that a period
of great prosperity which started in the fifth century lasted until after
the Arab invasion.[154]

While there is no lack of evidence pointing to banditry as a problem for travelers, it is clear that this did not prevent pilgrims and
traders from traveling through the desert, thanks partly to fairly
effective measures taken by the government as late as the sixth century
A.D. On the main public roads far more intensive security arrangements
were in force. It appears from the statement in the *Itinerarium Egeriae*
that on the public road there was no need for an escort of soldiers.
Half way between Jerusalem and Jericho a very considerable fort is
still visible. According to Eusebius its purpose was the protection of
travelers against bandits, who had caused frequent bloodshed on the
Jerusalem-Jericho road.[155]

---

[149] The mounted company of the 'Most Loyal Theodosians' was based at Nessana
during part of the sixth century; see Kraemer, *Excavations at Nessana* III.5. The date
of arrival and demobilization of the unit is unknown. It was a unit of camel riders
(P.Colt 37).

[150] At sixth-century Nessana one is certainly mentioned in P.Colt, no. 31. At
Mampsis a khan has been recognized outside the town wall: A. Negev, *ANRW* II.8.648,
and fig. 24, no. 8, said to be Byzantine on remains of an earlier structure; cf. *Enc.
Arch. Excavations in the Holy Land* III.732.

[151] Antoninus Placentinus 39 (*CCSL* 175.149). Cf. Mayerson, *Trans. Am. Phil. Assoc.*
(above, n. 113) 185–188.

[152] Kraemer, *Excavations at Nessana, 3: The Non-Literary Papyri* (1958) II.22–23:
δοθ(έντα) τῷ Σαρακαινῷ τῷ σικοφαντέσαντι ἐμᾶς ἰς τὸ ἅγιον ὄρος. As noted (259), the
amount is considerable—more than half that of a camel.

[153] *Ibid.*, 1.35.

[154] H.D. Colt (above, n. 132) 17 ff.

[155] Eusebius, *Onomastikon* in Jerome's translation, Klostermann 25.10–14 (above,

The situation in the frontier zone in Mesopotamia in the sixth century is vividly described by J.B. Segal,[156] who refers to local, Syriac sources. The frontier was 'closed' in time of war. That, however, could mean no more than that the passage of large companies of men was made impossible. 'Between the villagers living on either side there was constant and friendly intercourse.' Moreover, with the help of Bedouin friends anyone could move in and out of Persia by taking the desert route. Only merchants were forced to travel along the main road, for on both sides of the border travelers were robbed and carried into slavery by the Bedouins, who 'had not come to fight, but in search of booty.'[157] Segal refers to sources which describe collaboration between the Persian and Byzantine army, between 485 and 491 and in 575/6, to suppress these activities, but to little effect.[158] In order to be safe, travelers had to use the main public road, which was patrolled at great expense—or not, as Malchus and his companions found out.

Instructive are the wise words addressed by John Chrysostom to Stagirius, harassed by a demon.[159] He explained that there was no

n. 115): *Maledomni . . . ubi et castellum militum situs est ob auxilia viatorum et Graece dicitur* ἀνάβασις πυρρῶν *Latine autem appellari potest ascensus ruforum sive rubrantium, propter sanguinem illic crebro a latronibus funditur.*

[156] *Proc. Brit. Ac. 1955*, 127 f., 133.

[157] Jerome, *Vita Malchi* 4, *PG* 23.58, speaking of the road from Beroea to Edessa: *vicina est publico itineri solitudo, per quam Saraceni incertis sedibus huc atque illuc vogantur.* Palladius, *The Book of Paradise or Garden of the Holy Fathers* (trans. E. Wallis Budge, 1904) II, chap. 15; Segal 127 n. 6 also refers to the Chronicle of Arbela, for which, however see above, n. 123.

[158] Chabot, *Synodicon Orientale* 526 f., 529; John of Ephesus, *Ecclesiastical History* III.6.12. Compare the description in the Babylonian Talmud, of life in the town of Nehardea on the Euphrates: 'In the town that was close to the border, they [the Bedouins] did not come with any intention of taking lives but merely straw and stubble, but the people are permitted to go forth with their weapons and desecrate the Sabbath on their account' (*Eruvin* 45a). And, again (in *Bava Kamma* 83a): 'The rabbis taught that a man should not raise a dog unless it is chained, but if he raises it in a border town, he ties it up by day and releases it by night.' From other sources (*b Eruvin* 6b; *b Ta'anit* 20b) it appears that the town wall of Nehardea was badly neglected. A sword and an unchained dog were sufficient to keep those who came 'to take straw and stubble' away. In 259 Nehardea was destroyed by Odainat of Palmyra.

[159] *Ad Stagirium* II.189–190, *PG* 60.457. The routes from Palestine to Mesopotamia are well known. Frequently used was the road to Sura on the Euphrates by way of Damascus and Palmyra. The earliest milestone, discovered on the section Palmyra-Sura, was set up in Vespasian's reign. Cf. H. Seyrig, *Syria* 13 (1932) 270–272; also G.W. Bowersock, *JRS* 63 (1973) 133 ff. For later milestones see P. Thomsen, *ZDPV* 40 (1917) nos. 49–55. In the Byzantine period there was a direct Roman road through the desert to Palmyra. It is named *Strata Diocletiana* on milestones. Cf.

need to envy Abraham, for think what it meant to travel from Babylon to Palestine in those days, as compared with the late fourth century. The distance had not changed, but the conditions of travel were completely different. In Chrysostom's days there were road stations, towns, and villas. The roads were paved, and the towns maintained groups of armed men, well disciplined under officers of their own. Their sole duty was to guarantee the safety of the road. Moreover, every mile there was a building, where guards were stationed at night. Thanks to their vigilance travelers were fully protected against attacks by robbers. John Chrysostom was content; the more so since he never had to travel to Babylon himself. The bandits and the robbers did not leave us their record. Modern historians, nevertheless, should not assume that the enemies of the empire all lived across an imaginary border which they desperately wanted to cross.

M. Dunand, *Revue Biblique* 40 (1931) 227–248; van Berchem (above, n. 144) 10–15 and map; Kennedy (above, n. 4). For banditry on this road, see the inscription discussed above, p. 199. It was probably found on the section of this road which ran into Arabia. For the road and forts in Syria see A. Poidebard, *La Trace de Rome dans le désert de Syrie* (1934). Here again the roads and forts are described as a *limes* designed to defend the frontier. John Chrysostom describes its function in antiquity.

Postscript

In the same year as this paper, a wide-ranging article on banditry in the Roman Empire was published by Brent Shaw.[1] This was the first of several interesting publications on the subject by this author.[2] As Shaw observed in his first article (p. 18): 'The whole role of the army as an internal police force in the empire remains one of the most neglected of subjects in works devoted to the institution.' This was precisely the point the article on bandits in Judaea and Arabia also intended to make: it was argued, firstly, that there was internal unrest, much of it social and economic in origin, but some of it with ideological motives; secondly, that the threat posed by nomads living inside or outside the zone of nominal or actual Roman control was not of such a kind that the stability or Roman rule in the provinces was seriously threatened, thirdly that the Roman army was therefore more engaged in internal police duties and less in foreign defence than was often assumed. These topics were later discussed in my book, *The Limits of Empire*. There would be no point in taking up all the arguments and questions, belonging to the wider field of Roman frontier studies, that have come up in recent years. For the present it may be useful to discuss some of the recent developments in the study of the Roman presence in the Negev, the development of settlement there and the relationship with the nomadic population.

The most remarkable feature of the northern Negev in the period under discussion is the development of a group of substantial and prospering settlements and towns in this arid environment. While they were first established in the Nabataean period, it is now clear that the stage of their greatest expansion was the Late Roman/Early Byzantine period. These settlements are the subject of a very interesting architectural study by Shereshevski.[3] The first point to be made is that only one of these, Mampsis, had a wall. While the presence of a city-wall in itself does not prove that there was a threat to security,

---

[1] B.D. Shaw, 'Banditry in the Roman Empire', *Past and Present* 105 (1984), 3–52.

[2] B.D. Shaw, 'Bandit highlands and lowland peace: the mountains of Isauria-Cilicia', *JESHO* 33 (1990), 199–233; 'The Bandit' in A. Giardina (ed.), *The Romans* (Chicago and London, 1993), 300–41.

[3] J. Shereshevski, *Byzantine Urban Settlements in the Negev Desert* (Beer Sheva 1991); cf. the favourable review by Clive Foss, 'The Near Eastern Countryside in Late Antiquity', in *The Roman and Byzantine Near East: Some Recent Archaeological Research* (*JRA* Supplement 14, Ann Arbor, MI 1995), 213–34, at 225–31.

the absence of one surely is a sign of stability and relative peace.[4] This is an important conclusion, given the views of many scholars that the depredations of the desert nomads formed a constant threat to the security of the eastern provinces of the Later Roman Empire.[5] Much of Shereshevski's study views the desert architecture in relation to the climate and reaches the conclusion that planning and execution of the settlements and individual buildings exhibit an absence of adaptation to desert conditions. They follow the traditions of the Mediterranean climate.

Another significant conclusion is that the Byzantine towns were not created by the Byzantine state, but grew organically as the local economy flourished and the population in the country as a whole expanded.[6] This conclusion is essential for any interpretation of the role of the state in Roman and Byzantine society. It is still not unusual for scholars to believe in massive state intervention in the development of the arid zone. They assume that the construction of elaborate systems of terraces in the wadis and the emergence of settled areas in the desert is attributable to the policy of the Byzantine Empire.[7] This is, in a manner of speaking, a civilian counterpart to the old interpretations of a massive military presence in the frontier zone[8] and should, for similar reasons, be viewed with healthy scepticism. Like the old military theories, it again wants to attribute to the imperial will developments for which we have no evidence of state interference at all. One should hesitate in accepting without further proof the assumption that complex social and economic developments in antiquity were the result of direct imperial interference.

---

[4] Shereshevski, 184–9; cf. the similar observations in an earlier paper by A. Lewin, 'Roman Urban Defences in the East in Antiquity: the Case of the Negev', in D.H. French & C.S. Lightfoot, *The eastern frontier of the Roman empire: colloquium Ankara, September 1988* (Oxford, 1989), 295–309.

[5] For a review of various opinions, including my own, see *Limits of Empire*, 68–77.

[6] Shereshevski, chap. 5; pp. 217–22.

[7] M. Haiman, 'Agriculture and Nomad-State Relationship in the Negev Desertin the Byzantine and Early Islamic Periods', *BASOR* 97 (1995), 29–53. See also R. Rubin, *The Negev as a Settled Land* (Jerusalem 1990, in Hebrew); and a brief summary in article form: 'Urbanization, Settlement and Agriculture in the Negev Desert—The Impact of the Roman-Byzantine Empire on the Frontier', *ZDPV* 112 (1996), 49–60.

[8] This is the view of Haiman, p. 32: 'This policy aimed toward defending the borders by establishing an agricultural frontier even beyond the natural capacity of the area and support of the frontier during drought years.' He refers to J. Schaefer, *The Ecology of Empires: An Archaeological Approach to the Byzantine Communities of the Negev Desert* (Ann Arbor: University Microfilms, 1980); Rubin, 1990, 187–80.

Since the publication of this article much has been written about nomadism that has a bearing on our understanding of relations between the settled populations and the pastoralists. Processes of nomadization and sedentarization are better understood, or have at least been more carefully studied. Those who believe in the efficacy of massive state-intervention may profitably consider the observation that 'policies of enforced sedentarization are likely to be ineffective while the underlying factors giving rise to nomadism remain unaltered. Even radical restructuring of systems of land tenure and agricultural policy are likely to be effective as a means of sedentarization policy only so long as such systems remain in operation. . . .'[9] A recent study of nomadism in the Central Jordan Valley describes various and distinct patterns of sedentarization.[10] Rich tribe-members may settle down because they have too much wealth, while poor members, because of lack of resources also may settle down, but in the marginal areas, and/or in the service of the rich pastoral nomads. The reason for settling in a marginal zone is usually population pressure.

This, however, goes beyond the scope of this postscript to an article on banditry. It should suffice to observe that, archaeologically, the Negev is now far better known than it was a few years ago, thanks to the publication of a series of excavations, detailed surveys and studies.

Mention should also be made of the major paper by MacDonald about nomadism in the Hawran in antiquity.[11] He is concerned with the information to be derived from the Safaitic inscriptions,[12] almost all of them found in the desert east of the Hauran. They are the work of nomadic people, predominantly camel-breeders who migrated annually between the Harra, east of the Hawran and the Hamad. As MacDonald observes—and that is important for the present study—there is no evidence that the Romans faced constant pressure from

---

[9] R. Cribb, *Nomadism in Archaeology* (Cambridge 1991), 61.

[10] E. van der Steen, 'Aspects of Nomadism in the Central Jordan Valley', *PEQ* 127 (1995), 141–58. Note the major work on sedentarization and nomadization in the Hesban area, cited below.

[11] M.C.A. MacDonald, 'Nomads and the Hawran in the Late Hellenistic and Roman Periods: a Reassessment of the Epigraphic Evidence', *Syria* 70 (1993), 303–413.

[12] MacDonald observes that Safaitic is a modern term. It is a misnomer, for the texts are not found in the Safa. It refers only to a script and dialect. It is not an ethnic label.

nomads trying to enter the settled regions. Other points of interest are that a tribal social structure in itself does not entail a nomadic lifestyle. Villagers can have a tribal society.[13]

To be noted here, apart from works already cited:

For the towns:
Y. Tsafrir *et al.*, *Excavations at Rehovot-in-the-Negev*, i, *The Northern Church* (Jerusalem, 1988).

For the countryside:
Yehuda D. Nevo, *Pagans and Herders* (Midreshet Ben Gurion, Negev, 1991); an interesting, but highly idiosyncratic work with valuable material about the central Negev.[14]

Gideon Avni, *Nomads, Farmers, and Town-Dwellers: Pastoralist-Sedentist Interaction in the Negev Highlands, Sixth–Eighth Centuries* c.e. (Israel Antiquities Authority, Jerusalem, 1996).

P. Mayerson, 'Some Observations on the Negev Archaeological Survey', *IEJ* 46 (1996), 100–105.

The publications of the Survey of Israel, cited in the works above.

East of the Jordan:
G. King, 'Prospection de sites Byzantins et Islamiques en Jordanie, 1980–3', *Syria* 60 (1983), 326–9.

Ø.S. La Bianca, *Hesban 1, Sedentarization and Nomadization: Food System Cycles at Hesban and Vicinity in Transjordan* (Berrien Springs, MI: Andrews University 1990).

B. MacDonald, 'Evidence from the Wadi el-Hasa and southern Ghors and north-east Arabah archaeological surveys', in P. Bienkowski (ed.), *Early Edom and Moab, the beginning for the Iron Age in Southern Jordan* (Sheffield Archaeological Monographs 7), 113–42.

Relevant for the presence of nomads in the Negev are recently published Thamudic inscriptions:
M. Halloun, 'New Thamudic Inscriptions from the Negev' in *Archaeological Survey of Israel: Ancient Rock Inscriptions, Supplement to Har Nafha* (Israel Antiquities Authority, Jerusalem, 1990).

---

[13] Cf. also van der Steen, cited above; Cibb, p. 119.
[14] C. Foss, 'The Near Eastern Countryside', 1995, at 231–4, for a negative review, particularly regarding the author's belief that many presumed dwellings were pagan shrines.

Y.D. Nevo, Z. Cohen and D. Heftman, *Ancient Arabic Inscriptions from the Negev*, I (Jerusalem 1993).

Nurit Tsafrir, 'New Thamudic Inscriptions from the Negev', *Le Muséon* 109 (1996), 137–67.

Some recent publications:

For Trachonitis: M. Sartre, in *L'epigrafia del villaggio*. Actes du VIIᵉ colloque international Borghesi à l'occasion du cinquantenaire d' *Epigraphica* (Forli, 27–30 septembre 1990), A. Calbi *et al.* (edd.) (Faenza 1993), 133–5; *AÉ* 1993.1636 uit Dhunaybeh (Danaba): Οἱ ἐν Δαναβοις Ἕλληνες Μηνοφίλῳ εὐνοίας ἑνεκεν. Could this be connected with the Herodian settlers?

For Trachonitis see now extensively I. Shatzman, *The Armies of the Hasmonaeans and Herod: From Hellenistic to Roman Frameworks* (Tübingen 1991), 170–80, for Herod's activities in Trachonitis and Batanaea; Chapter VII, for Herod and the Nabataeans.

P. Freeman, 'Recent Work on a Roman Fort in South Jordan', in: H. Vetters & M. Kandler (eds.), *Akten des 14. internationalen Limeskongresses 1986 in Carnuntum* (Wien 1990), 179–91: discussion of a survey of the fort of Da'janiya in Arabia. Note the corrected plan on p. 191 and the discussion of the date which remains inconclusive.

P.M. Bikai & V. Egan, 'Archaeology in Jordan', *AJA* 100 (1996), 28–30; esp. 529: *Humaima*, excavated by J.P. Oleson: 'the very substantial corpus of ceramics found in the barracks area in 1995 indicates without a doubt that the fort was active by the first half of the second century A.D., possibly early in the century. The barracks, at least may have been abandoned for some time in the third century, then reoccupied in the fourth. This makes Humaima the first and, so far, only military installation in Arabia, south of Wadi Hasa, that can with certainty be dated to the second century.'

Cf. J.P. Oleson *et al.*, 'Preliminary Report of the Humayma Excavation Project, 1993', *ADAJ* 39 (1995), 317–49. Measurements: 206 × 148 = 500 × 700 R. feet. Dating.

R.P. Harper, *Upper Zohar: an Early Byzantine Fort in Palaestina Tertia. Final Report of Excavations in 1985–86* (Oxford 1995) provides firm proof that this little post was not occupied before the fifth century.[15]

---

[15] Cf. the observations in *Limits of Empire*, 191–3.

M. Gichon, *En Boqeq: Ausgrabungen in einer Oase am Toten Meer*, vol. I (Mainz a/R 1993).

Bikai & Egan, *op. cit.*, p. 531: Latin inscriptions found in secondary use in Petra (no text is given. The inscriptions are to be published by Z.T. Fiema): a *signifer* to the *praefectus* of the *Ala II Ulpia Auriana*, a unit stationed in Cappadocia.

An interesting inscription was discovered on a site along the Gaza-Petra road.[16] It represents a dedication to Athena (Allat) The dedicant's name An[tonios?] is given in Greek and he is identified in Latin as a *mil(es) coh(ortis) vi Hisp(anorum)*.[17] The unit is attested at Hallabat in A.D. 212-3 and an ala of that name is mentioned in the *Notitia Dignitatis Orientis*.[18] The editor draws conclusions that are quite unwarranted. He assumes without good reason that the inscription proves the find-spot to have been a permanent military base. It should be emphasized again that an isolated inscription does not justify such assumptions. A dedication made by a soldier proves an occasional visit by a soldier, not the existence of a local garrison for any length of time, especially if the site is on a major road. The inscription is undated.

An important study in three volumes, two of which have so far come out:

S. Gregory, *Roman Military Architecture on the Eastern Frontier* (Amsterdam 1995).

P. Mayerson, *Monks, Martyrs, Soldiers and Saracens: Papers on the Near East in Late Antiquity (1962-93)* (Jerusalem 1994), particularly relevant are two recent papers, re-published in this volume:
'The Saracens and the *Limes*', *BASOR* 262 (1986), 35-47, reprinted as pp. 271-83. 'The Island of Iotabê in the Byzantine Sources: A Reprise', *BASOR* 287 (1992), 1-4, reprinted as pp. 352-5; for Iotabe, note also:
P. Mayerson, 'A Note on Iotabê and other Islands in the Red Sea', *BASOR* 298 (1995), 33-5: Mayerson emphatically restates that the island cannot possibly be identified with Tiran. He gives examples

---

[16] P. Figueras, 'The Roman Worship of Athena-Allat in the Decapolis and the Negev', *ARAM* 4 (1992), 173-83; cf. *AÉ* 1993. 1652; *SEG* 1992. 1455. The findspot is Ein Saharonim (no map reference given); *AÉ* 1992.1652.

[17] Τῇ Κυρίᾳ Ἀθηνᾷ ἐπόησεν ἐκ τῶν ἰ(δίων) Μ(ᾶρκος) ΑΙΝΓΟΛ *mil(es) coh(ortis) VI Hisp(anorum)*.

[18] M. Speidel, *ANRW* II 8, 709.

of offshore islands with fordable access and suggests that Iotabe will have been an island close to the Arabian coast, south of the outlet of the Gulf of Aqaba.

On the African frontier:

A. Rushworth, 'North African deserts and mountains: comparisons and insights', in D. Kennedy (ed.), *The Roman Army in the East* (*JRA* Supplement, Ann Arbor, MI, 1996), 297–316.

Pol Trousset, 'Signification d'une frontière: nomades et sedentaires dans la zone du lime d'Afrique' in W.S. Hanson and L.J.F. Keppie (eds.), *Roman Frontier Studies 1979* (BAR, Oxford, 1980), 9331–43. Trousset emphasizes the zonal character of the frontier. It is not a line, but an area where the Romans controlled the course of seasonal migrations. The zonal character of the frontiers in general is brought out also in the indispensable work:

C.R. Whittaker, *Frontiers of the Roman Empire: A Social and Economic Study* (Baltimore and London, 1994).

11

THE BABATHA ARCHIVE[1]

'In the consulship of Manius Acilius Glabrio and Torquatus Teba-
nianus one day before the nones of May, in En-gedi village of lord
Caesar, Judah son of Elazar Khthousion, En-gedian, to Magonius
Valens, centurion of *Cohors I Miliaria Thracum*, greeting. I acknowledge
that I have received and owe to you in loan sixty denarii of Tyrian
silver. . . .'

This is the opening sentence of document No. 11 from the Babatha
archive. It records a minor transaction between a military officer and
a civilian in a village in one of the eastern provinces of the Roman
empire. The loan referred to in this document, and the conditions
attached to it, made no impact on Imperial history. Like all the other
events recorded in these documents it was a private matter, of interest only to those immediately involved. The texts found in the Cave
of Letters are without literary value, and the personal and financial
affairs of a Jewish woman called Babatha constitute random information that would never have been considered worthy of comment
by a Roman historian. For the modern reader, however, the volume
discussed here offers a unique impression of daily life in the Roman
provinces of Judaea and Arabia. This is particularly important as the
literary sources regarding this period—the years between the First
Revolt and the Bar Kokhba War—are very poor. Moreover, the
impression it provides is of rural life, far more representative of contemporary society in this region than, for example, the picture obtained
from Josephus and Philo.

The transaction mentioned above between the centurion and Judah
son of Elazar, for instance, allows us to conclude that there was in
En-gedi, in 124 A.D., a *praisidion*, i.e. a *praesidium*, a police station or
guard post, manned by part of the *Cohors I Miliaria Thracum*.[2] It follows

---

[1] N. Lewis (ed.), *The Documents from the Bar Kokhba Period in the Cave of Letters,
Greek Papyri*, ed. by N. Lewis, *Aramaic and Nabatean Signatures and Subscriptions*, ed. by
Y. Yadin and J.C. Greenfield (Jerusalem, 1989). I am grateful to Jonas Greenfield
for comments and suggestions.
[2] Cf. B. Isaac, *The Limits of Empire: the Roman Army in the East* (Oxford, 1990), 137;
174; 430.

that the entire unit was transferred from Syria to Judaea before that date. The presence of this cohort in Judaea reinforces our impression that the garrison of the province was strengthened well before the Bar Kokhba War (132–5). Another conclusion to be drawn is that the village of En-gedi with its royal estate, which was destroyed in the First Revolt, was resettled by Jews after the war. From documents Nos. 19 and 20 it is clear that the unit had left En-gedi by April 128, for the sites occupied in 124 by the *praisidion* and soldiers' quarters were now empty or in private hands.[3] This shows how mobile Roman army units were in this period.

Furthermore, we have here at least one example of a military officer lending money to a local man—possibly at a usurious rate of interest, as suggested by the editor. A courtyard in the village served as security for the loan, and would have become the property of the officer were the loan not repaid (it was repaid, as documents 19 and 20 indicate). Another military man, a soldier of the *Legio X Fretensis*, was also involved in a financial transaction with a civilian, in a document from Murabba'at, published earlier.[4] This then informs us of the relationship between soldiers and civilians in the countryside of Judaea.

The present volume contains the Greek papyri discovered almost thirty years ago by Yigael Yadin and his team of archaeologists in the Cave of Letters near En-gedi. The Greek texts have been edited in exemplary fashion by Naphtali Lewis, the Aramaic and Nabatean signatures and subscriptions by Yigael Yadin and Jonas C. Greenfield. The Nabatean and Aramaic documents will be published by Jonas Greenfield in a forthcoming volume. The immediate publication of the present volume is most welcome, for the extraordinary delay in publication of these important texts had become a matter of concern to all scholars interested in the discoveries.

The book will undoubtedly become a classic work for consultation and debate. It contains a General Introduction, transcriptions of the documents with translation, comments and good photographs. A minor disadvantage of the arrangement is that the General Introduction will remain spread over two volumes with part remaining inaccessible for the time being. An attempt has been made here to sum up

---

[3] Cf. Lewis, p. 83.

[4] P. Benoit *et al.*, *Discoveries in the Judaean Desert*, ii, *Les grottes de Murabba'at* (Oxford, 1961), no. 114 (A.D. 171?). Apparently there was a unit somewhere near Murabba'at thirty-five years after the end of the Bar Kokhba War.

the historical information gained by the publication of the documents. Technical and specialist matters beyond the competence of the present reviewer have been left for the papyrologists.

Roman Provincial Organization in Arabia and Judaea

The Courts

The history of the Roman provinces of Judaea and Arabia between the First Revolt and the Bar Kokhba War is very poorly documented in literary sources. The new documents add interesting information on the Roman administration in Judaea after the First Revolt, and in Arabia following the formation of the province in 106. Some unexpected aspects of the Roman military presence in Judaea have been discussed above. The first observation to be made here is that Roman organization in Arabia had an immediate and drastic impact. This is shown, for instance, by document No. 12 (first half A.D. 124): an extract from the council minutes of the city of Petra regarding the appointment of two guardians for Babatha's son Jesus. It is remarkable that the council (boule) of Petra should have decided such matters. Petra was 'capital' of the hyparchia i.e. the subdivision of the province, but the village of Maoza was far from Petra and closer to another town, Rabbath-Moab which like Petra served as an assize city (document No. 25, l. 22) and as financial centre for the area (No. 16). The boule of Petra apparently had direct jurisdiction in family legal and financial affairs throughout the territory of the huge hyparchia. Was the territory of the hyparchia in this instance the same as that of the city? There clearly was no bearer of authority in Zoara, centre of the subdivision of the hyparchia to which Maoza belonged. We have here a striking reminder of the importance of city-status in the Roman empire: the city council made decisions regarding personal status of all those living in the territory of the city and its influence was certainly not restricted to city affairs.

Further on No. 12, Lewis notes: 'From beginning to end this document reads like the Greek translation of a Latin original.'[5] He also notes, however, that the assignation of two guardians (one Jew

---

[5] Lewis, p. 48 (and cf. pp. 16 f.).

and one Nabataean) was a local custom, for in Greek and Roman law one guardian was sufficient. In document No. 27, a receipt of 19 August 132, there is another instance of two guardians being assigned; one of the two is a woman and Roman citizen, Julia Crispina, mentioned below. The Latin form of this and other documents has been discussed by Wolff in his article based on preliminary publications.[6] Wolff points out that they reflect Roman, not Hellenistic legal procedure. Document No. 27, in particular, is entirely Roman.[7]

The immediate impact of the Roman administration on the private life of the inhabitants of the province is further illustrated by the ensuing conflicts between Babatha and the two guardians of her son, a Nabatean and a Jew (documents Nos. 13–15). No. 13 is a petition to the governor by Babatha (second half of 124), in which she complains that her guardians do not pay sufficient money from the estate for the living expenses of her son. It is remarkable that this disagreement was brought before the court of the governor himself. Later one of the two guardians is summoned before the governor's court at Petra (document No. 14, 11 or 12 October 125).

In November 130 Babatha is summoned to the court of Haterius Nepos in Petra 'in the matter of a date orchard devolving to the said orphans . . . to attend every hour and day until judgment' (No. 23), while in July 131, she is again summoned to travel to Petra for the same purpose and 'to attend in Hadrianic Petra until we are heard' (No. 25). Babatha, however, summoned her adversary first 'before his Excellency the governor in Rabbath—Moab'.[8] This demonstrates the hardships caused by the Roman judicial system which forced provincials to travel to assize cities and wait till they were heard on relatively minor matters by the governor himself. We note, too, that the governor of Arabia, a praetorian legate, was expected to give judgment on the ownership of a single date orchard. The serious defects of this sort of organization are clearly visible also in a recently published document from the third century from the Middle Euphrates area.[9] The absence of any reference to Jewish courts or local officials who might have settled financial disputes between Jews

---

[6] H.J. Wolff, 'Römisches Provinzialrecht in der Provinz Arabia', *Aufstieg und Niedergang der römischen Welt* II 13, pp. 763–806.

[7] Note also the judiciary rules in Nos. 28–30.

[8] See also No. 26: with another summons regarding yet another quarrel.

[9] D. Feisel & J. Gascou, *Comptes-rendus de l'Académie des Inscriptions et Belles-lettres* 1990, pp. 535–61, esp. 546–8.

is striking. Indeed, Jewish institutions are nowhere mentioned in the Babatha archive. There is far more evidence of local institutions and officials from the large province of Egypt, where there was therefore less need for recourse to the governor's court.

We are also reminded of the comments of the geographer Strabo, who was told by his friend Athenodorus 'that he found many Romans and many other foreigners sojourning there [at Petra], and that he saw that the foreigners often engaged in lawsuits, both with one another and with the natives, but that none of the natives prosecuted one another, and that they in every way kept peace with one another.'[10] This, however, dates to the period of Augustus, when Petra was still the capital of the Nabatean kingdom. The point at issue here is the far reaching impact which the Roman annexation had on the daily lives of the inhabitants of the new province.

Taxation

Babatha also had to travel in person to Rabbath-Moab to file returns for the provincial census.[11] Document No. 16 enables us to reconstruct the relevant procedure.[12] It is particularly interesting that the declaration was received by a cavalry commander (*eparchos hippeon*). Nothing is known of the unit under his command, but it is likely to have been an *ala* (a battalion).

It is notable that only two decades after the organization of the province of Arabia a military officer was engaged in administrative duties in a town, and that his attestation had to be translated from the Latin. This concrete example of the involvement of military officers in financial administration is significant, but not unique. The role of centurions at the time of the annexation of the kingdom of the Iceni in Britain is emphasized by Tacitus.[13] In western provinces the *centurio regionarius* is well attested from the late first century onward.[14] According

---

[10] Strabo XVI, 4, 21 (779).

[11] Document No. 16, census declaration, 2 and 4 December 127. Cf. M. Broshi, 'Agriculture and Economy in Roman Palestine in the Babatha Papyri', *Zion* 55 (1990), pp. 269–281; on taxation, *ibid.*, pp. 276–79 (Hebrew).

[12] Cf. Lewis' comments on p. 65.

[13] Tacitus, *Annales* xiv 31.

[14] E.g. R.G. Collingwood and R.P. Wright, *Roman Inscriptions of Britain* i (Oxford 1965), 152, 583, 587, *Corpus Inscriptionum Latinarum* (henceforth: *CIL*) XIII 2958, *l'Année Epigraphique* 1944.103 (and 1950.105); cf. I.A. Richmond, 'The Sarmatae *Bremetennacum Veteranorum* and the *Regio Bremetennacensis*', *Journal of Roman Studies* 35 (1945), 15–29,

to Richmond such officers were charged with police duties and some administrative tasks in their districts. Richmond thinks these were imperial domain lands, but one could also think of less urbanized districts, such as the southern part of the province of Arabia.[15]

The declaration contains a verbal description of the landed properties concerned: an identifying name, the size, the taxes to be paid, and the abutters. It is clear that there was no plan or map in existence, comparable to those found at Orange in Gaul.[16] Babatha registered three orchards, two of which paid share of produce and the crown tax in money, the other paying a share of the produce alone. The reference to crown tax is interesting, for this is usually known as an extraordinary supplementary tax,[17] and not a regular income tax. In the present document, however, it appears as a fixed amount to be paid in money.

Double Documents

Babatha and the other refugees took with them a few prized possessions and their personal papers (but no money) to their hiding place; this is a clear indication that they considered these papers irreplaceable, an impression reinforced by the care with which the documents were hidden in the cave (pp. 3–4). The importance of the papers to the owners is all the more remarkable when one considers that many are copies, or rather transcripts, of originals kept in a public archive. Document No. 12, ll. 1–2, for instance, reads: 'Verified exact copy of one item from the minutes of the council of Petra the metropolis, minutes displayed in the temple of Aphrodite in Petra . . .', which is, incidentally, another instance of the assimilating influence exerted by the Roman administration. Were Babatha to have lost her copy of document No. 12, it should have been possible to obtain another copy from Petra; she apparently did not trust the efficacy or reliability of the system.

In this connection it is of particular interest that most of Babatha's

---

esp. 20; A.K. Bowman and J.D. Thomas, *Vindolanda, the Latin Writing Tablets* (1983), no. 22, l. 8 and comments on p. 110.

[15] Richmond (above, n. 13). Further on these military matters: Isaac, *op. cit.* (above, n. 1), index s.v. centurio.

[16] A. Piganiol, *Les documents cadastraux de la colonie romaine d'Orange. Gallia*, Suppl. 16 (Paris 1962).

[17] Isaac, *op. cit.* (above, n. 2), pp. 301 f.

papers are double documents, a relatively rare form of certificate, extensively discussed by Lewis in the Introduction (pp. 6–10). This form of document was produced in cases where the owner was not certain that he would have access to authoritative archives in case of need, and were suspicion existed of fraudulent tampering with the document. The most widely found type of double document is, therefore, the military diploma, a bronze certificate of the grant of Roman citizenship to Roman auxiliaries who had served twenty-five years or more. Since the original texts were kept in Rome, it was useful for veterans to have authorized copies in the provinces. In Roman Egypt, on the other hand, the double document was no longer customary at this period.

The fact that most of Babatha's papers were double documents, despite the existence of official archives at Petra and Rabbath-Moab, may have been merely a local bureaucratic habit, or it may indicate that the rural population did not wish to rely on archives and also demanded protection against falsification of documents.[18]

Administrative Division and Boundaries

The new documents furnish important new information on the administrative division of Judaea and Arabia in this period. It merits a detailed discussion because it shows that after the First Revolt the system in Judaea was basically left intact, with only minor modifications, and because the new evidence gives an impression of how the system functioned.

For Judaea proper there are two lists of districts which existed before the First Jewish Revolt.[19] The organization probably dates from the Roman period, but it is clear that a similar system already existed during the period of Greek domination.[20] This is clear from the terminology used. The term 'toparchy' is used both by Josephus and

---

[18] There were double documents at Dura Europos, and even as far afield as Avroman. It is also clear that their use was widespread from talmudic sources as well. The question is whether one can learn anything from their existence about attitudes.

[19] Josephus, *Jewish War* iii, 3, 5 (51–8) and Pliny, *Naturalis Historia* v 70; cf. E. Schürer, *The History of the Jewish People in the Age of Jesus Christ*, ed. G. Vermes and F. Millar, ii (Edinburgh 1979), 190–6; M. Stern, *Latin Authors on Jews and Judaism* i (Jerusalem 1974), 474–8; E. Mary Smallwood, *The Jews under Roman Rule* (Leiden ²1981), 344.

[20] Schürer, (above, n. 18), 196.

Pliny, but it occurs first in 1 Macc. 11, 28, where Jonathan is represented as asking the king for exemption from taxation on behalf of Judaea and 'the three toparchies of Samaria' [sc. Aphairema, Lydda and Ramathaim which had been attached to Judaea]. This was apparently already an administrative subdivision in Seleucid Palestine. These subdistricts, however, are called *nomoi* in 1 Macc. 10, 28 and again in 11, 34. Both terms were common in Ptolemaic Egypt cf. L&S s.v.] and had apparently been taken over by the Seleucid administration. The term 'toparchy' survived into the Roman period, but the question is what it represented then.

Josephus lists the districts as follows: '[Judaea] is divided into eleven *klerouchiai* of which Jerusalem is the capital. The other parts, after Jerusalem, are divided into *toparchiai*: Gophna is the second, then Acrabeta, Thamna, thereby Lydda, Emmaus, Pella, Idumaea, En-gedi, Herodion, Jericho. Following these Jamnia and Jaffa administer the surrounding areas. . . .' Jamnia and Jaffa are mentioned at the end of the list and apparently considered distinct from the others, as 'having jurisdiction over their surrounding districts'.[21] The places named in the first part of the list were the only real Greek cities with a constitution. Josephus describes as *toparchies* places which had no city status; hence Jamnia and Jaffa are separately mentioned. This explanation is preferable to that which claims they were not in Judaea proper. The meaning of the phrase 'to have jurisdiction over the surrounding districts' is now clearly illustrated by the Babatha documents, as already noted in the case of Petra. The arrangement was made for administrative reasons, served as basis for the collection of taxes, and was connected with, although not identical to, the judicial circuit.

Pliny's list shows some differences. It reflects the situation after the First Revolt in several respects: Caesarea is mentioned as a colony; Neapolis as a new city which superseded 'Mamortha' (Mabartha in Josephus). Jerusalem is referred to as having been destroyed. It is, therefore, reasonable to assume some significance in the absence of En-gedi and Idumaea, which appears as a toparchy in Josephus.

An important difference between Josephus' list and that of Pliny is the absence of Idumaea and En-gedi in the latter. From document

---

[21] However, as noted in Schürer (above, n. 18), elsewhere, in connection with Salome's bequest to Livia, Josephus refers to Jamnia as a *toparchy* (*Ant.* xviii, 2, 2, [31]).

No. 16, l. 16, it is now clear that En-gedi was incorporated into the toparchy of Jericho, as appears from the new document No. 16, l. 16: κώμης Αἰνγαδδῶν περὶ Ἱερειχοῦντα τῆς Ιουδαίας. Thus En-gedi, which was destroyed in the war, was no longer a toparchy, while Jericho remained one. This may therefore be taken as confirmation that Pliny's list reflects post-70 reorganization rather than antiquated information, as assumed by some authors. It may then be assumed that Pliny's omission of Idumaea as a toparchy represents the reality following the First Revolt. The district disappeared, just as the people of that name disappears in this period. The toparchy was perhaps attached, at least partly, to the neighbouring districts of *Oreine* and Herodion.

It is to be noted that the papyri use the term 'toparchy' only once.[22] The repeated references to villages as belonging to the district of places which themselves did not have city status, however, clearly shows that the organization existed in the second century. Jericho is not the only district mentioned in the papyri.

Further evidence that the system was preserved after A.D. 70 is the fact that Herodion appears as a toparchy on papyri from Murabba'at.[23] The case of Herodion is interesting because the Aramaic documents from Murabba'at show that Bar Kokhba made it one of his regional headquarters and treasuries.[24] P. Mur. 114 (A.D. 171?, well after the Bar Kokhba War), mentions Jerusalem and *Oreine*, the latter being listed by Pliny as the district in which Jerusalem had been. P. Mur. 115 ll. 2–4 also mentions Gophna and Acrabeta as centres of territories, or rather, it mentions two villages as lying respectively περὶ Ἀκραβάττων and περὶ Γοφνοῖς. The term 'toparchy' is not used here, but both places are described as toparchies by Josephus and Pliny. There can be no doubt that the structure described by Josephus and Pliny survived in essence far into the second century. Toparchies were normally abolished only when their chief settlements received city status. What we do not understand—and the new documents do not shed any light on this—is functioning of the internal administration of a toparchy. To mention only one example, it is clear that the council of Petra appointed guardians for minors throughout

---

[22] P. Mur. 115, l. 2.

[23] P. Mur. 115, dated 124, l. 2.

[24] P. Mur. 24 mentions Ben Kosba in camp there and, elsewhere, refers to the treasury at Herodion.

the city territory, but we do not know what body fulfilled similar functions in toparchies.

Finally, No. 37 mentions Jesus son of Menahem who lives in the village of 'Soffathe . . . in the district of the city of Livias in the region of P[—] (Σοφφαθε[.] . . . περὶ πόλιν Λιουιάδος τῆς π[—). There can be little doubt that P[—] should be restored P[eraia], the region of Judaea east of the Jordan, since the only city of the name Livias in the wider region was in Peraia. Lewis hesitates: 'as [this is a document] drawn up in the province of Arabia the text would normally add the specification τῆς Ἰουδαίας . . . for which there is no room in the lacuna . . .' (p. 132, n. to l. 3). There was only one Peraia in the entire region, however, so this argument may not be compelling. It seems uncertain whether Peraia is more than a geographical notion, like Galilee, Samaria and Judaea, since there is no evidence that cities were incorporated into subdivisions of provinces, or that a city would be described as 'belonging to' a specific administrative region within a province, as assumed by Lewis.

The administrative division of Arabia apparently was organized on different lines from that of Judaea. Document No. 26, ll. 5–6, refers to a division of the province (*eparcheia*) as *hyparcheia*. This is not a common term for the subdivisions of a province.[25] In the same document, l. 18, a subdivision of a *hyparcheia* appears as περίμετρον (the *perimetron* of Zoara). The village where Babatha lived, Maoza, is described as lying in the *perimetron* of Zoara in 21, 5; 22, 5; 27, 3–4. It would appear, therefore, that Arabia was divided into districts called *hyparcheia*, while Judaea was divided into *toparcheiai*. For the subdivision called *perimetron* in Arabia we have no name in Judaea, nor is it clear whether the different terminology reflects actual differences in practice. Moreover, the terminology in Arabia is not always adhered to in the various documents, for in No. 16, 14 Babatha is described as a woman 'of Maoza in the Zoarene [district] of the *perimetron* of Petra' (Μαωζηνὴ τῆς Ζοαρηνῆς περιμέτρου Πέτρας). This is a census declaration and thus a document of official standing. In other words, what is called a *hyparcheia* in No. 26, a legal document of 131, is described as *perimetron* in No. 16, an administrative document of 127. As already noted, for Judaea the papyri do not use the term *toparchy*, which is current in Josephus and Pliny. An exception is P. Murabbaʿat,

---

[25] Lewis, p. 115 n. gives as parallel P. Dura, p. 111 and n. 13, but that reflects Parthian organization.

No. 115 ll. 2–4, which uses the term once. All this raises the question whether there was any fixed bureaucratic terminology.

As indicated above, the *boule* of Petra had direct jurisdiction in family legal and financial affairs throughout its territory. The inhabitants of this territory, however, could turn to the governor's court either in Petra or in Rabbath-Moab, which also served as an assize city. Babatha submitted her census declaration not in Petra but in Rabbath-Moab.

In my book *The Limits of Empire* I have put forward the proposal that the borders of the Roman empire were not only less firmly delineated in practice but also less relevant conceptually than is commonly assumed. Were the boundaries within provinces as fluid as the external borders of the provinces of the empire?

Crown Property and En-gedi

In document No. 11, ll. 1 (inner text) and 13 (outer text) En-gedi is described as 'a village of the Lord Caesar' (κώμη Κυρίου Καίσαρος). Lewis notes that the village had been part of the crown domain under both the Hasmonaean and Herodian dynasties (p. 42). It would, therefore, appear inappropriate to describe this expression as an honorific appellation (p. 44, n. to l. 1). It is a formal expression, indicating crown property, as can be seen from the parallel in No. 16, l. 24: μοσχαντικὴ Κυρίου Καίσαρος which definitely refers to an estate belonging to the crown. Before 106 land was purchased in Maoza by Shimon, Babatha's father: 'to the south is the orchard of our lord, Rabbel the King, king of the Nabataeans, who maintained life and brought deliverance to his people, and to the north the water.' This clearly refers to the same property and, like the case of En-gedi, is good evidence of the transformation of crown land into imperial possessions.

While it is thus clear that En-gedi was crown property, it is also a fact that there was private property in the village, amply attested in documents 11, 19 and 20. It is therefore likely that the imperial possessions here were restricted to the famous balsam-trees that have been described by the elder Pliny as 'belonging to Rome'.[26] Elsewhere Pliny describes how, in the Jewish Revolt, Jews attempted to destroy the orchards while the Romans defended them 'and now

---

[26] Pliny *Naturalis Historia* xii 112: '*servit nunc haec ac tributa pendit cum sua gente*'.

they are being cultivated by the fiscus'.[27] Josephus relates that rebels from Masada raided En-gedi. Later sources still refer to balsam plantations there.[28] The Jews apparently failed to cause any permanent damage and En-gedi was still a flourishing centre of production in the fourth century although it no longer had the status of a toparchy. The garrison temporarily stationed at En-gedi may also have been placed to guard the orchards in the Dead Sea area. The main point of interest in this context, however, is the fact that we have further confirmation of the transformation of crown property into imperial domains.[29] J.C. Greenfield pointed out to me that in the Hebrew documents from the revolt, Bar Kokhba is described as giving land in lease, including palm groves. It is possible that these too were crown property, and thus devolved to Bar Kokhba.

Rural Society

As already noted, the new documents are extremely interesting because of the information they provide about Jewish rural society in the Dead Sea area, even though it is true that there are limitations to what can be learned from financial and legal papers. It would obviously be incorrect, for instance, to assume that people were constantly engaged in litigation, merely because of evidence of conflict in one family. Notwithstanding our strictures in interpretation, however, they contain information that is unique and worthy of consideration, such as the evidence of polygamy, discussed by Lewis, pp. 22–4.

The papyri give an impression of the settlement of Jews around the Dead Sea: in the Babatha archive Jewish settlements are found at En-gedi, at Maoza, the Dead Sea port of Zoara (Mahoza means 'port' in Aramaic), in Mazraa, east of the lake, and, in document No. 37, near Livias to the north-east. The number of Jews at Maoza is clear also from the names of witnesses on e.g. nos. 20–23; 26 for

---

[27] Pliny, *ibid.* 113, see also *ibid.*, V 71–73.

[28] Josephus, *BJ* iv, 7, 2 (402 f.), see also *Ant.* ix, 1, 2 (7). Galen, *De Antidotis* i 4, Stern, *op. cit.* (above, n. 19) ii, no. 391 with n. on p. 326; Eusebius, *Onomastikon* (ed. Klostermann), 86; Jerome, *Comm. in Hiezechielem* xxvii 17 (*Patrologia Latina* xxv, col. 256); Jerome, *epistola* 108, *ad Eustochium* 11.

[29] For imperial property see now K. Wiegels, '"Solum Caesaris"—Zu einer Weihung im römischen Walheim', *Chiron* 19 (1989), 61–102.

example; G.W. Bowersock, on the basis of preliminary publications, studied at the personal names of property owners and observed that estates formerly owned by people with Nabatean names were in the course of time taken over by Jews.[30] The Jews mentioned in the documents in this area cultivated figs, dates, olives and vines (No. 5, ll. 10–11) and were quite affluent. Economic historians will find the precise description of their properties useful.

A good deal can be learned about the status of women. Babatha always had to be represented by a guardian in her contacts with the authorities. The only woman who could act in her own right and serve as a guardian herself was Julia Crispina, daughter of Bernicianus, almost certainly a Roman citizen (see above). This illustrates the importance of Roman citizenship for the inhabitants of the new province. As observed by Lewis, the presence of this woman in Maoza and her active participation in local affairs 'are remarkable in themselves, and all the more remarkable if, as seems likely, she was the same Julia Crispina who appears in a papyrus, BGU 53, as the absentee owner, in the years 131–3, of two houses in the village of Euhemeria in the Arsinoite nome of Egypt' (p. 111, n. to l. 2).

The conclusions to be drawn from the various marriage contracts will presumably be discussed in Part V of the General Introduction, to appear in Volume II. One point of general interest should, however, be raised briefly. Lewis comments on the Greek marriage contract No. 18 of A.D. 128 that it is governed in part by Greek rather than Jewish, custom; he views this as a 'social trend towards the adoption of gentile ways', which is seen also 'in the bridegroom's supplementation of his Hebrew name with a Roman name, Cimber' (p. 77). It is by no means clear that we are faced here with a trend towards the adoption of Gentile ways as such. We have no way of knowing if a *ketubba* was not written as well.[31] The impression is that the people concerned were guided mostly by practical considerations. Babatha did not hesitate to swear an oath by the '*Tyche*' of the Lord Caesar' (document No. 16, l. 34) although we would not normally expect observant Jews to do this. In the second century Christians were willing to die a martyr's death, merely to avoid swearing this oath.[32] Any social changes in this period must be seen against the

---

[30] G.W. Bowersock, *Roman Arabia* (Cambridge, Mass., 1983), 78.

[31] As observed by Professor Greenfield. Babatha received a *ketubba* from Yehuda (*P.Yadin* 2).

[32] Eusebius, *Ecclesiastical History* iv, 15, 18; 21.

background of the imposition of Roman provincial administration. If Jews in Arabia preferred Greco-Roman marriage contracts to traditional *ketubbot* the most likely explanation is that the former offered advantages that had been unavailable under Nabatean rule. The position of the woman, for instance, is more favourable in 'Greek law' (document No. 18, ll. 16, 51). One of the features which enhance the interest of the documents for historians is precisely the fact that they reflect the period of transition from Nabatean rule to Roman provincial administration.

Interesting observations are made throughout the work about the level of culture. Babatha cannot write and only spells her own name (No. 16). Judah, Babatha's second husband writes himself in Aramaic in a hand which 'may be described as that of a practiced, experienced writer' (p. 136). The hands of his son-in-law and of various others 'may be described as unpractised and clumsy'. 'Abd'obdath son of Elloutha, one of the guardians, writes Nabatean in a formal and legible manner. The cavalry officer at Rabbath-Moab who was involved in receiving census declarations wrote Latin, which had to be translated for the local population. The editors comment extensively on the quality of the Greek and other languages in the documents (Introduction, chapter III; pp. 136 f.).

Librarii

Many documents were written by local scribes, clearly Jews, two of whom sometimes call themselves '*liblarius*.' The fact that Jews fulfilled a function with a Latin title in the new province of Arabia is of interest and it is therefore worth establishing what kind of function the title 'liblarius' could have represented. Lewis (p. 64, n. to l. 38) rightly concludes that it cannot derive from '*libellarius*' which is a Byzantine title.[33] He suggests the possibility that they were temporarily employed as bi-lingual or multi-lingual scribes by the local unit of the Roman army of occupation in Arabia. This is not a very likely theory, for there is hardly any evidence of Jews serving in the Roman army. *Librarii* were professional, serving soldiers in the standing army and the position had its place in the military hierarchy.

Librarii are well attested in literature and epigraphy: full treatment

---

[33] *Thesaurus Linguae Latinae* s.v.; F. Preisigke, *Wörterbuch der griechischen Papyrusurkunden* iii, s.v.

may be found in Ruggiero.[34] Documents or inscriptions that mention military *librarii* invariably mention the unit or office to which they belonged, which is not the case in the Babatha documents. They were never simply *librarii*: they were clerks who belonged to some unit, office, or official. For comparison we may refer to the well-known letters written by Julius Apollinaris to his father in Egypt. He was *librarius legionis*, or rather *librarius* of the legionary legate, in the new province of Arabia.[35] This man clearly belonged to a different social class from Theenas and Germanos, the scribes of the Babatha documents. There is no evidence anywhere that the Roman army hired temporary workers, let alone Jews, who were granted the same ranks as professional soldiers. It is therefore unlikely that the two *librarii* of the Babatha archive were soldiers or civilians working for the Roman army.

The term '*librarius*' is used also to indicate commercial copyists of formal documents, which could be applicable here, but the evidence is confined to Italy and most of it seems to be later in date than the Babatha archive. The term seems to occur on an unpublished act of sale from the third century from the Middle Euphrates area.[36] This scribe also bears a Semitic local name. The use of a Latin title by a Jewish scribe of Greek documents in a village in the province of Arabia clearly suggests that his function belongs to the sphere of the Roman administration and it is likely that Babatha's scribes were local people with an official function. It is worth noting that 'liblar' became a normal term for copyist, clerk, scribe in Talmudic sources.

One of Babatha's orchards in Maoza bordered on an imperial estate (No. 16, l. 24). Imperial estates in the provinces were administered by procurators. *Librarii* are attested in the offices of procurators, e.g. that of the procurator of the *tractus Carthaginiensis*[37] or those serving in the gold mines near Ampelum.[38] They are also encountered in toll stations and stations of the imperial post. Their status varied in accordance with the function they fulfilled.[39] The *librarii*

---

[34] Ruggiero, *Dizionario Epigrafico* iv, cols. 955–65 (R.F. Rossi); also: Pauly-Wissowa-Kroll, *Real-Encyclopaedie* xiii, cols. 137–9, s.v. *librarius* (Bilabel).

[35] *P. Michigan* VIII 466 of A.D. 107 and cf. 465.

[36] D. Feisel & J. Gascou, *CRAI* 1990, p. 559.

[37] *CIL* viii 12615; 12616–9; 24688.

[38] *CIL* iii 1314, more evidence in de Ruggiero, *DE*, 960.

[39] *IGLS* vi 2859 from Heliopolis: a personal secretary and barber in the staff of the governor.

from the Babatha archive may have been low-ranking clerks in a local government office, possibly the one administering imperial possessions in the region. In any case, it is clear that we have here evidence of local Jews functioning in the lower ranks of the imperial administration at a local level, and that is of interest.

The Bar Kokhba Revolt

The archive contributes one unambiguous new item of information regarding the Bar Kokhba War, namely a point of chronology. Until now, the only certainty was that war broke out in A.D. 131/2.[40] The latest document of the series, No. 27, bears the date of 19 August 132, which shows that the revolt had not broken out by that time, at least not to the extent that normal daily life was interrupted in this particular area. Further confirmation of this may perhaps be found in fragment No. 35, dating c. Aug./Sept. 132.

The documents were all written before the war of 132–5; something should be said about the circumstances in which they reached the cave in which they were discovered. Lewis notes that Babatha was born and lived at Maoza on the south shore of the Dead Sea in the province of Arabia. This raises the question why she fled to a cave near En-gedi. Lewis writes, pp. 4–5: 'The sad irony is that they may [might?] well have remained untouched by the war if they had stayed in their village in the province of Arabia.' However, there is no reason to assume that the boundary between two provinces would have served as a barrier for the rebels or the Roman army in times of war. The documents show that Jews had settled in substantial numbers in this part of the province of Arabia. It is clear that not only Babatha, but also her stepdaughter (No. 18) and others from the same village (No. 37) fled to the same cave. The obvious conclusion is that at least this village, but probably the entire area, was to some extent affected by the revolt.

We can only speculate why they fled to caves near En-gedi. En-gedi was closer to the heartland of the revolt, was held by Bar Kokhba's men and may have appeared safer to non-combatant Jews than the Zoara district in the initial, successful, stages of the revolt.

---

[40] Cf. Schürer, *op. cit.* (above, n. 19), vol. i (Edinburgh, 1973), 542, n. 126.

The Jews from Maoza may first have moved to En-gedi and only in a later stage of the revolt to the cave in Nahal Hever.

Finally, a few minor comments:

Document 16, l. 21: The road mentioned is the Roman highway which ran throught Mampsis and Zoara and joined the Trajanic road through Rabbath-Moab.

Documents 21 and 22: Is this the sale of the date crop (thus Lewis), or rather a lease of the right of working the orchard in exchange for a share in the produce? Babatha is to receive dates or money. Who would sell a crop of dates in exchange for dates?

Lewis suggests that L. Haterius Nepos, the governor of Arabia mentioned in 23, 25 and 26, may be identified with the prefect of Egypt in A.D. 120–124 or with his son (p. 104, n. to l. 4). There can be no doubt that he was the son, suffect consul in A.D. 134, governor of Pannonia Superior in A.D. 138.[41] The prefecture of Egypt was almost the top of the equestrian career, the governorship of Arabia a position for a middle ranking senator. The latter post would never have followed the former.[42]

These notes merely constitute an attempt to formulate a number of issues of historical interest raised by the Babatha archive. The publication of the Greek papyri from the Cave of Letters is a rare event because it makes accessible to the public an entirely new and interconnected series of texts which will continue to be read and discussed for many years to come.

---

[41] *CIL* xvi 84.

[42] M. Sartre, *Trois etudes sur l'Arabie romaine et byzantine* (Bruxelles, 1982), 82, observes that the name of the Arabian governor Haterius Nepos is found erased on inscriptions in Gerasa.

Postscript

Since the publication of this article many new documents have been published and the Babatha archive has been the subject of numerous studies. It might be reasonable to argue that this article has indeed been superseded by all that came afterwards. However, it seems true to say that a number of issues that matter are here clearly defined. Since there would be no point in re-publishing part of the article it seemed best to offer all of it, for whatever it is worth, with some elementary bibliography pointing to essential recent work.

The Cohors I Milliaria Thracum

J. Russell has discussed the presence of the *Cohors I Milliaria Thracum* in En-gedi.[1] He observes that a large bathhouse has been excavated at En-gedi, assigned by the excavator, B. Mazar, to the period between the two revolts.[2] Russell deduces that the entire cohort, and not merely a part of it, was based there for some time, as had been assumed by other scholars. He then goes on to observe that a similar but smaller building has been excavated at Capernaum.[3] Furthermore he observes that also at En-gedi (Tel Goren) have been found, a public building, traces of destruction, and coins from year 2 of the First Revolt. Finally, it is worth mentioning that the synagogue there dates to the late second—early third century, followed by several stages, to be destroyed in the sixth century.

Administrative Division and Boundaries

In a critical response, the editor of the work under review, Prof. N. Lewis, raises various points of disagreement with my article.[4] I accept part of his remarks and disagree with others. The aim of my review article, however, was to raise matters of historical interest that were not discussed in Lewis' publication of the documents. Having raised them, I will not now enter into a prolonged discussion with the editor of the texts, especially since so many matters of genuine

---

[1] James Russell, 'A Roman Military Diploma from Rough Cilicia', *BJb* 195 (1995), 67–133.
[2] *NEAEHL* ii, 399–409.
[3] V. Tzaferis (ed.), *Excavations at Capernaum 2*. 1983–88, currently in preparation.
[4] N. Lewis, 'The Babatha Archive: A Response', *IEJ* 44 (1994), 243–6.

importance have been dealt with in numerous recent publications. However, there is one point of particular interest that warrants attention, namely the information about the administrative division of Judaea, contained in the documents. The question to be considered in this connection, is the organization of those parts of Judaea that were not urbanized, for one of the essential elements of city-status is that the city controlled its surrounding territory, or 'had jurisdiction over it', in the words of Josephus. In other words: a city cannot belong to the territory of another city, but a village can belong to the territory of a city. The question is then, how villages were organized where there was no city nearby, as in most of Judaea proper in the first century A.D. It is clear that the documents help in clarifying this matter. A term frequently encountered in Judaea is 'toparchy'. The terms 'toparchy' and *nomos*, I observed, were common in Ptolemaic Egypt and had apparently been taken over by the Seleucid administration. It is worth noting that the term 'toparchy' is not found in the Seleucid empire outside Judaea. It is then my suggestion that, in Judaea proper, the term represents an administrative district not headed by a city but, in the absence of a city, by a village.[5]

One of the phrases which I considered interesting, occurs in *P.Yadin* 16: κώμης Αἰνγαδδῶν περὶ Ἱερειχοῦντα τῆς Ἰουδαίας. I deduced from it that, after the First Jewish Revolt, En-gedi was incorporated into the toparchy of Jericho. Lewis considers my observations irrelevant for two reasons: the term 'toparchy' does not occur in the Babatha archive and he disagrees with my claim that the preposition περί as used in the documents is instructive. 'All that *peri* tells us is that En-gedi was in the *territorium* of (and administered from) Jericho,' says Lewis. This, however, ignores the elementary point that in Roman provinces, apart from Egypt, villages like Jericho did not normally have territories. If the documents show, as they do, that there was a hierarchy of villages, the village of En-gedi being dependent on the village of Jericho, this is noteworthy. The literary evidence shows that En-gedi and Jericho were both toparchies before the First Jewish Revolt. Now the documents show also that, thereafter, En-gedi was somehow administered from Jericho. The obvious conclusion is that

---

[5] J.-M. Bertrand, 'Le statut du territoire attribué dans le monde grec des Romains', in E. Frézouls (ed.), *Sociétés urbaines, Sociétés rurales, Actes du colloque organisé à Strasbourg* (Strasbourg, 1987), 95–106.

En-gedi lost the status which Jericho preserved. Further confirmation of these suggestions may now be found in other documents:

1) DJD ii, no. 115, ll. 2–3.[6] The text of the document was drawn up 'at Bethbassi in the toparchy of Herodium', while Eleaios son of Simon is 'from the village of Galoda in the district of (περί) Akrabatta, but resides in the village of Batharda in the district of (περί) Gophna'.[7] Here we have a document dated to 124, roughly half a century after the end of the first revolt, post-dating both Josephus and Pliny. It describes Herodium as a toparchy, which it is also in the list of Josephus. The villages of Gophna and Akrabatta, which were also toparchies in Josephus' list are not described as such, but there are other villages described as being dependent on them. We have therefore three first-century toparchies, one of which is still described as a toparchy, while the other two for all practical purposes had the same capacity. It is quite likely that the term went out of use gradually. It is clear, in any case, that Professor Lewis' statement that the term 'toparchy' does not occur in the Babatha archive is not to the point, for it occurs in a similar document of the same period.

2) In a cancelled marriage contract published recently by Hannah Cotton,[8] we find a reference to the village of Aristobulias 'in Ziphene' (line 3) and to the village of 'Yaqim [in Ziphene]'.[9] Aristobulias and

---

[6] P. Benoit, J.T. Milik and R. de Vaux, *Discoveries in the Judaean Desert*, II (Oxford, 1961), No. 115: Contrat de remarriage (124 ap. J.-C.), text on pp. 248 f.

[7] ... ἐν Βαιτοβαισσαιας ... τοπαρχείας Ἡρωδείο[υ] ... Ἐλεαίος Σίμωνος τῶν ἀπὸκ(ώμης) Γαλωδῶν τῆς περὶ Ἀκραβαττῶν οἰκῶν ἐν κώμῃ Βαιτοαρδοις τῆς περὶ Γοφνοῖς. Cf. lines 21 f.

[8] H.M. Cotton, 'A Cancelled Marriage Contract from Judaea', *JRS* 84 (1994), 64–86, at 67, line 3: ἐν Ἀριστοβουλιάδι τῆς Ζειφηνῆς with comments on pp. 73–7. Line 5: the groom comes 'from the village of Yaqim [of the Zephênê]. H.M. Cotton, 'The archive of Salome Komaïse daughter of Levi: another archive from the Cave of Letters', *ZPE* 105 (1995), 171–208, now forthcoming in final publication: M. Cotton and A. Yardeni, *Aramaic and Greek Texts from Naal ever (the Seiyl Collection II), Discoveries in the Judaean Desert* XXVII, in press. For further references to documents published in recent years: H.M. Cotton, W.E.H. Cockle and F. Millar, 'The Papyrology of the Roman Near East: a Survey', *JRS* 85 (1995), 214–235. See further: E. Tov with S.J. Pfann, *The Dead Sea Scrolls on Microfiche, Companion Volume*, Revised ed., Leiden, 1995. The Aramaic and Nabataean papyri from the Babatha archive and the Hebrew, Aramaic and Greek Bar Kokhba material will be published in Y. Yadin, J.H. Greenfield, B. Levine and A. Yardeni, *Judean Desert Studies. The Documents from the Bar Kokhba Period in the Cave of Letters*, II.

[9] For the identification of Aristobulias and Ziph, see, respectively, *TIR*, p. 67 and 262. Abel, *Géographie*, ii, 490, identifies Aristobulias with Kh. Istabul. Zif is undoubtedly to be identified with Kh. Zif, M.R. 163.098. For Ziph see also V. Guérin,

Ziph were villages in the area south of Hebron. That means they were in the area which Josephus still calls Idumaea, usually as a rather loose term indicating a geographical area,[10] and once as a toparchy.[11] In the period represented by the cancelled marriage contract, after the First Revolt, Idumaea apparently was not an administrative unit. In any case, it is not mentioned as such. This may be compared with the entry on Ziph in Eusebius' Onomasticon: 'This is now a village in Daroma, in the territory of Eleutheropolis, near Hebron, 8 miles to the North, where David hid.'[12] (On. 92, 15). Thus the village of Ziph was, by that time, in the territory of the city of Eleutheropolis (Beth Guvrin), which had received city-status in 199/200. Before the assignment of this territory to a city it was a region of villages. The phrase in the document, 'Aristobulias in Ziphene', might suggest that Aristobulias was somehow attached to Ziph, which would then represent a hierarchy of villages. This is likely, but not entirely certain, however, for Josephus uses the name 'Ziphene' in the early books of the Antiquities as a purely geographical notion.[13]

To conclude this point, I would repeat that the documents give us a glimpse of the administrative organization of the non-urban parts of Judaea and Arabia.

So far my reaction to Prof. Lewis' response.

Taxation

About this subject more has been said in the article reproduced below, no. 21.

Description géographique, historique et archéologique de la Palestine Paris, 1868–75), *Judée* iii, 159 f.; *SWP* iii 315 379. M. Avi-Yonah, *Gazetteer*, s.v. Aristobulias, M.R. 163.097, refers to L.S. en E.A. Mader, *Altchristliche Basiliken und Lokaltraditionen in Süd-Judäa*, 168–176 [non vidi]. For a bilingual Greek and Aramaic inscription from this site: L.Y. Rahmani, 'A Bilingual Ossuary-Inscription from Khirbet Zif', *IEJ* 22 (1972), 113.

[10] For instance in *BJ* ii, 6, 3 (96): τῆς Ἀρχελα/ου δ' ἐθναρχίας Ἰδουμαία τε καὶ Ἰουδαία πᾶσα καὶ Σαμαρεῖτις ἦν κεκουφισμένη τετάρτῳ μέρει τῶν φόρων εἰς τιμὴν τοῦ μὴ μετὰ τῶν ἄλλων ἀποστῆναι.

[11] *BJ* iii, 3, 5 (55), discussed in the article, above.

[12] Onomasticon 92.15 Ζίφ. κώμη νῦν ἐστιν ἐν τῷ Δαρωμᾷ ἐν ὁρίοις Ἐλευθεροπόλεως πλησίον Χεβρὼν ἀπὸσημείων ηέ πρὸς ἀνατολάς, ἔνθα ἐκρύπτετο Δαυίδ. {Βασιλειῶν.}

[13] Josephus, *Ant.* vi, 13, 2 (275) Δαυίδης δὲ ἐκεῖθεν ἄρας εἴς τινα τόπον Καινὴν καλουμένην τῆς Ζιφήνης παραγίνεται.... See also *ibid.* (277).

Rural Society

It is to be noted that Priscus the Prefect, whose name appears on the census declaration *P.Yadin* No. 16, is now found mentioned also in another land declaration.[14]

In an article about agriculture and the economy as seen through the Babatha archive, M. Broshi has a number of interesting observations.[15] He notes that there is ample evidence that life continued without interruption in the territory controlled by the rebels into the third, or even fourth year of the revolt. He agrees with the usual identification of Zoara with Oasis of Ghor es-Safi. Furthermore he learns from *P.Yadin* 21–22 that Babatha sold the yield of her palm groves in a sort of share-cropping arrangement, in which the share cropper pays a certain amount of yield.

The weights, measurements and yields occurring in the documents have now been extensively treated in an article by Weiser and Cotton.[16]

Many other topics have been studied since the publication of the above review-article. For the present a brief bibliography will have to suffice.

Selected Additional Literature

G.W. Bowersock, 'The Babatha Papyri, Masada and Rome', *JRA* 4 (1991), 336–44 (reprinted in: *Studies on the Eastern Roman Empire* (Goldbach, 1994).
M. Broshi & E. Qimron, 'A House Sale Deed from Kefar Baru from the Time of Bar Kokhba', *IEJ* 36 (1986), 201–214, for which, see also the postscript to article No. 16, below.
H.M. Cotton, 'The Guardianship of Jesus son of Babatha: Roman and Local Law in the Province of Arabia', *JRS* 83 (1993), 94–113.
H.M. Cotton and J.C. Greenfield, 'Babatha's Property and the Law of Succession in the Babatha Archive', *ZPE* 104 (1994), ...

---

[14] H. Cotton, *ZPE* 105 (1995), 171–208, no. II on p. 176.
[15] M. Broshi, 'Agriculture and Economy in Roman Palestine: Seven Notes on Babatha's Archive', *IEJ* 42 (1992), 230–40.
[16] W. Weiser and H.M. Cotton, 'Die Geldwährungen im syrisch-nabatäischen Raum', *ZPE* 114 (1996), 237–87; for preliminary observations, Broshi, p. 234.

H.M. Cotton, 'A Cancelled Marriage Contract from the Judaean Desert', *JRS* 84 (1994), 84–6.

E. and H. Eshel, 'Fragments of two Aramaic Documents', *Eretz Israel* 23 (1992), 276–85 (Heb.; English summary: 155*).

F. Millar, *The Roman Near East*, (1993), Appendix B: 'Documents from the Bar Kochba War', 545–52.

A. Wasserstein, 'A Marriage Contract from the Province of Arabia Nova: Notes on Papyrus Yadin 18', *JQR* 80 (1989), 92–130.

Id., 'Non-Hellenized Jews in the semi-Hellenized East', *Scripta Classica Israelica* 14 (1995), 111–37.

Y. Yadin, J.C. Greenfield and A. Yardeni, 'Babatha's Ketubba', *IEJ* 44 (1994), 75–99.

12

JUDAEA IN THE EARLY YEARS OF HADRIAN'S REIGN*

(with I. Roll)

Mommsen doubted that the legion VI *Ferrata* was in Judaea at all, questioning the truth of Dio's statement that it was based there.[1] Ritterling has shown that, not later than 152, it was in garrison in Galilee, at Caparcotna, called 'Legio' by Eusebius.[2] The arrival of the legion was dated by von Rohden from the time of the Second Jewish Revolt, 132–5.[3] Mc Elderry preferred to make it earlier, A.D. 117, noting that Lusius Quietus, Trajan's governor of Judaea in that year was a *consularis*.[4] The date at which Judaea became a consular province with two legions has remained a problem ever since.[5] If we

---

* This paper was written in the framework of the activities of the Israel Milestones Committee. For various suggestions and comments we are grateful to Prof. S. Applebaum and Prof. M. Gichon. Further we would like to record the great assistance afforded by Mr. I. Ben-Shalom and Dr. A. Oppenheimer in interpreting Jewish sources.

[1] Note on *CIL* iii 6641. Dio IV 23 (113).

[2] *Rheinisches Museum*, 58 (1903), 633–5; *P-W*, xii, s.v. 'Legio', col. 1591. Caparcotna is mentioned as *castra* of VI *Ferr.* in *CIL* iii, 6814–16; W.M. Ramsay, *JRS* 6 (1916), 129–31; B. Levick, *JRS* 48 (1958), 75–6; *AÉ* 1920.78. See: 'Caporcotani' on the *Tabula Peutingeriana* (ed. Miller, segm. x, 1–2); Καπαρκοτνεῖ in Ptolemy, v, 15, 4. The name is derived from Kefar 'Otnay, a village mentioned in Jewish sources, inhabited both before and after the Second Revolt by Jews and Samaritans: *Mishna, Gittin*, 1:5; 7:7; *Tos. Gittin*, 1:4 (ed. Zuckermandel, 323) and 7:9 (331); *Tos. Demai*, 5:3 (56); *Tos. Bekhoroth*, 7:3 (541); cf.: *b Bekhoroth*, 55a. Named 'Legio' by Eusebius, *Onomasticon* (ed. Klostermann), 14, 21; 28, 26 *et passim*. Later: *urbs Maximianopolis*, cf.: Hieronymus *ap.* Migne, *Patr. Lat.*, xxv, 1589; Hierocles, *Synecdemesis*, 720, 10; *Itinerarium Burdigalense* (ed. Geyer), 19:19. Ultimately Arabic 'el-Lejjûn'. For further references, see: M. Avi-Yonah, *Gazetteer of Roman Palestine* (1976) s.v. 'Legio', 74. See also: S. Applebaum, *Prolegomena to the Study of the Second Jewish Revolt* (1976), 29. For a rooftile-stamp of VI *Ferr.* discovered on the site, cf. G. Schumacher, *Tell El Mutesellim*, i (1908), 175, fig. 261; for a plan of the area: *ibid.*, Tafel i.

[3] *de Palestina et Arabia prouinciis Romanis, quaestiones selectae* (1885), 30 ff.

[4] *CQ* 2 (1908), 110–3; 3 (1909), 53.

[5] Judaea was the first province with a praetorian legate who served both as governor and as commander of a legion. The legion was based at Jerusalem while the residence of the governor was in Caesarea. This raises the question how the legate could fulfil both tasks adequately. He must have had deputies in Caesarea and Jerusalem. By the time of the outbreak of the Second Revolt the provincial governor was

are not mistaken, at least 20 scholars have expressed opinions on this question and on the related problem of the identity of the first legion, stationed in the province of Arabia after its formation.

The present state of the debate has been set forth by G.W. Bowersock and there is no need to recapitulate what he has written.[6] Before presenting new evidence we shall briefly review some of the facts. Mc Elderry, followed by M. Avi-Yonah, attached importance to the fact that Lusius Quietus was of consular rank while serving as Governor of Judaea in 117 after he had suppressed the Jewish rebellion in Mesopotamia.[7] It has rightly been observed that under the special circumstances of the time his rank did not necessarily reflect the formal status of the province.[8] It may be added that there is no reason to believe that he had two legions at his disposal.[9] Q. Tineius Rufus, governor of Judaea at the outbreak of the Second Revolt in 132, had been suffect in 127.[10] This indicates that the change of the rank of the legate to that of a consular must have occurred before this time. Pflaum has shown that the rank of the *procurator* of Judaea had risen by 123. This entails a rise in the rank of the legate as well.[11] L.J.F. Keppie has argued convincingly that there appears to

---

no longer in personal command of the legion in Jerusalem, where, according to Dio, the new colony, cause of the revolt, was being built.

[6] *JRS* 65 (1975), 184.

[7] *CQ* 2 (1908), 111; M. Avi-Yonah, *IEJ* 23 (1973), 212–3.

[8] E. Schürer, *The History of the Jews in the Age of Jesus Christ*, i, ed. G. Vermes and F. Millar (1973), 518; L.J.F. Keppie, *Latomus*, 32 (1973), 859–60. For Lusius Quietus, see: Groag, *P-W*, xiii, col. 1874 ff.; *PIR²*. L. 439; consul in absence: R. Syme, *JRS* 48 (1958), 9. See also: E.M. Smallwood, *The Jews under Roman Rule* (1976), 550.

[9] The X *Fret.* took part in Trajan's campaign, cf.: *CIL* vi 1838 = *ILS* 2727; *AÉ* 1935.167; for Trajan's forces, see: F.A. Lepper, *Trajan's Parthian War* (1948), 173–8. In Judaea Lusius Quietus certainly had with him his *Mauri* and vexillation of III *Cyr.*, for which see: *CIL* iii 13587 = *ILS* 4393. It is not impossible that he had other troops as well, cf. E.M. Smallwood, *Historia*, 11 (1962), 509 with n. 36 and *op. cit.* (*supra*, n. 8), 422, n. 136 and 426–7. An inscription of an *eques numerorum Maurorum* from Neapolis (Shechem) is generally believed to belong to the Severan period: M. Avi-Yonah, *QDAP* 12 (1946), 93–4 = *AÉ* 1948, 148; M. Speidel, *ANRW* ii, 3, p. 214. However, Applebaum, *op. cit.*, (*supra*, n. 2) does not exclude the possibility that it belongs to Trajan's time (pp. 47–8).

[10] Schürer, *op. cit.* (*supra*, n. 8), 518. The publication of the relevant fragment of the *Fasti Ostiensis* (*Inscr. Italiae*, xiii, i, 205) provided the first indication that Judaea became a consular province before the Second Revolt, cf. R. Syme, *JRS* 52 (1962), 90; Smallwood, *op. cit.* (*supra*, n. 8), 550. W. Eck, *Senatoren von Vespasian bis Hadrian* (1970), 18, n. 88 suggested that the 'Aquila' mentioned by Epiphanius, *de mens. et pond.*, 14 might be L. Statius Aquila (cos. suffect 116); cf. *AÉ* 1936, 97.

[11] *IEJ* 19 (1969), 232–3; cf. J.-P. Rey-Coquais, *Mel. Univ. St. Joseph*, 46 (1970–1), 243.

be one legion too many in the East after 117. This legion, whatever its identity, would fit best in Judaea.[12]

In 1960 B. Lifshitz re-published a reading of a milestone first published by M. Hecker.[13] The milestone records the construction of the road leading from Caparcotna to Diocaesarea (Sepphoris) and marks the fifth mile from the former place, as shown by Hecker's road-report. The date given by Hecker and Lifshitz was 130. Lifshitz argued that the milestone shows Caparcotna to have existed as a military base at the time and that the unit stationed there was the VI *Ferr.* We have examined this milestone again. Our reading is as follows:[14]

> *Imp(erator) Caesar Diui / Trai(a)ni Parthici /*
> *fil(ius) Diui Nervae nepos / Hadrianus Aug(ustus) pontif(ex) /*
> *max[i]m(us) trib(unicia) potestas* (sic) /
> *i͞i͞i͞i co(n)s(ul) i͞i͞i fecit / V /*
> *ἀπὸ Δ[ι]ο[κ]αισαρί /*
> *ας μίλ(ια) /*
> *ια᾽ //*

This reading is confirmed by a fragment of another milestone of the same road, published by Hecker but not by Lifshitz.[15] In addition we examined another milestone which reads as follows:[16]

> *Im[p(eratori)] / [Ca]esa[ri Diui Traiani Parthici f.] /*
> *[Di]ui Nervae [n(epoti)] / Traiano Hadr[iano] /*

---

[12] *Op. cit.* (*supra*, n. 8), 859–64.

[13] First published in *Lamerḥav* of 10–4–1959 (Hebrew); thence by B. Lifshitz, *Latomus*, 19 (1960), 110–111 and published again by M. Hecker in a road-report: *BIES* 25 (1961), 175–86 (Hebrew).

[14] The inscription was seen also by Prof. S. Applebaum. Now in Qibbutz Yif'at, Jezreel Valley, broken into two pieces. Both milestone and inscription are of finer quality than any other seen by us in this country. Base: h. 0.50, w. 0.64, l. 0.66; total height of pillar c. 1.50; moulding at base: 0.10; upper diam. 0.40 × 0.46. Inscription: h. 0.65; w. 0.65; height of lettering: c. 0.06. The upper part of the stone is now embedded in a ring of mortar, covering the numeral V, seen by Hecker. The Greek inscription indicating the distance from Diocaesarea seems not to be contemporary with the Latin inscription. This is suggested by a distinct difference in the depth of the lettering, 2–4 mm for the former as opposed to 5–6 mm for the latter. The indication of *capita uiarum* on milestones in Judaea will be discussed by B. Isaac in a paper to be published in *PEQ*, 1978.

[15] Hecker, *op. cit.* (*supra*, n. 13), 178; cf. 182. In his reading of the fragment, published on p. 178, Hecker, apparently unaware of the implications, gives the correct numeral iiii of Hadrian's tribunician power. For an undated fragment of the same series, see: M. Avi-Yonah, *QDAP* 12 (1946), 96, no. 13.

[16] *Ibid.*, 97, no. 15, Pl. xxvii, 15; according to Avi-Yonah found c. 1.5 km SSW of Sarid settlement and almost illegible. He suggested that it might date to Caracalla's reign.

Aug(usto) pontif(ici)[max(imo)] /
trib(unicia) potest(ate) [---] co(n)s(uli) /
$\overline{iii}$ *p(atri) p(atriae)* / $\overline{VI}$ / /

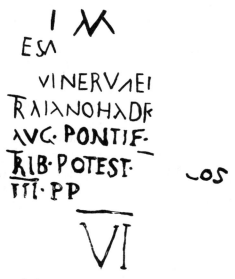

Figure 3. Later Hadrianic milestone: the lettering

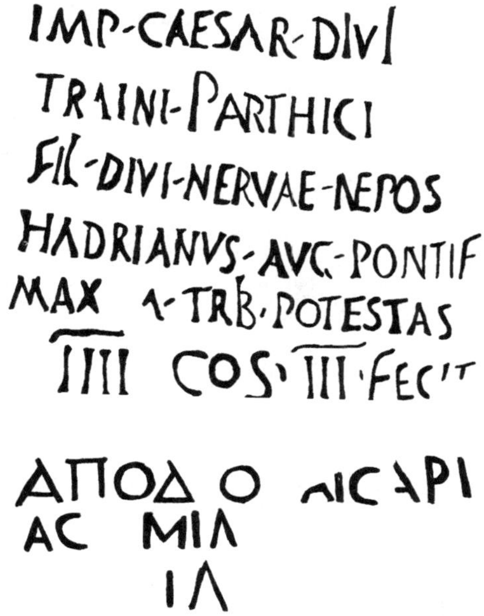

Figure 4. Milestone of A.D. 120: the lettering

This milestone marks the sixth mile from Caparcotna on the road to Diocaesarea, as pointed out by Avi-Yonah. Both the text of the inscription and the shape of the stone show that it belongs to a different series recording repair of the road under Hadrian. Hadrianic milestones of other roads in the area bearing the same formula are dated to 129 and 135.[17]

We may conclude that the road from Caparcotna to Diocaesarea (Sepphoris) was first build in A.D. 120 and repaired again under Hadrian, probably in 129 or 135. In both cases Caparcotna served as *caput uiae* and not Diocaesarea, a city of importance (see below, p. 192), unlike the village of Kefar 'Otnay. This shows that the *terminus ante quem* of Caparcotna as a permanent military base is 120 (rather than 130 as thought previously).[18] The milestones do not help in establishing the identity of the unit stationed there. They show, however, that by 120 Caparcotna had become the headquarters of a newly established Galilean command. Since this must have involved extra troops, it is clear that a second legion was in garrison in Judaea at the time. As noted above, the rank of the governor of Judaea is known to have risen before 132 and the rank of the procurator by 123. The new date of the reinforcement of the provincial garrison, as indicated by the milestones discussed above, moves back the *terminus ante* of these interrelated changes. The date of their institution might well be 117 as we shall now attempt to show.

---

[17] J.H. Iliffe, *QDAP* 2 (1933), 120–1; first discovered by A. Saarisalo, *JPOS* 9 (1929), 33–4; for the find-spot, see: A. Alt, *Palästinajahrbuch* 25 (1929), 42–3. A fragment of a milestone dating to 129 has recently been found on the Scythopolis-Caparcotna road (as yet unpublished). This will reflect preparations for the imperial visit of 130. It is more than likely that Hadrian travelled from Gerasa to Caparcotna (cf. Schürer, *op. cit., supra,* n. 8, 541, nn. 119 and 120). A milestone of 130 was found on the Aelia-Eleutheropolis road, cf. J. Germer-Durand, *RB* 3 (1894), 613 = Thomsen, *ZDPV* 40 (1917), no. 282; seen also by A. Alt in 1926, cf. *Pjb* 23 (1927), 9–10. For a fragment, probably of 130, see: Thomsen, *op. cit.,* no. 296 (Aelia-Hebron road). For undated fragments, *ibid.,* no. 242 (Caparcotna-Neapolis road); I. Roll, *Qadmoniot* 9 (1976), 46 (Scythopolis-Jericho road). Hadrian's road-making will also be considered in the forthcoming paper referred to above n. 14. See also pp. 61–62 and n. 44.

[18] From the site itself there is at present no datable evidence. Schumacher, *op. cit. (supra,* n. 2) is so far the only publication providing information on the site of the *castra* and its surroundings.

After Trajan's death in August 117 Hadrian abandoned Trajan's plans for yet another Mesopotamian campaign.[19] This made the expeditionary force available for redistribution in the provinces. The Jewish rebellion of these years seems not to have ended completely until the beginning of Hadrian's reign.[20] Palestine had shown some measure of unrest, reported by the *Historia Augusta* and indicated in Jewish sources. One of Hadrian's first acts as emperor was to depose Lusius Quietus and to send his *Mauri* home.[21] Hadrian probably stayed in Syria, where he had been legate at the time of Trajan's death, till about October.[22] These arrangements for the Eastern provinces must have been completed by that time. He was not to return to there until 123 and there are no indications of unrest in the following years. With the year 120 as *terminus ante* and in the absence of all evidence of a reason for the shuffling of troops in 118 or 119 it seems very likely that Judaea became a consular province with two legions in 117.

L.J.F. Keppie discussed the disposition of all the Eastern legions at this time.[23] He argued that there was one legion too many in the East after 117. This was based on the likely but unproven assumption that the legion XV *Apollinaris* was already in Cappadocia at the time, although it is not attested there until c. 135.[24] The new evidence may help to clarify this matter. If two legions were indeed based in Judaea, the presence of XV *Apollinaris* in the East, probable in itself, is required in order to make up for the total number of legions known to have been there. As regards the identity of the second legion in Judaea, Keppie has shown that no single legion was available for service in Judaea throughout the 117–132 period.

---

[19] Cf. W. Weber, *Untersuchungen zur Geschichte des Kaisers Hadrianus* (1907), 25; 34 ff.; F.A. Lepper, *Trajan's Parthian War* (1949), 7; 148–50; 210–13; R. Syme, *Tacitus* (1958), 239–43.

[20] Schürer, *op. cit.* (*supra*, n. 8), 529–34 with bibliography on p. 529; Smallwood, *op. cit.* (*supra*, n. 8), 421–7.

[21] Weber, *op. cit.*, 33–4; 51–3; Groag, *P-W*, xiii, col. 1886; Syme, *op. cit.* (*supra*, n. 19). See also: A. v. Premerstein, *Klio Beiheft*, viii (1908), 29–30; 62–7.

[22] Weber, *op. cit.*, 56. Weber (pp. 51–2) properly rejects the theory of an imperial visit to Judaea and Egypt in 117, based exclusively on Epiphanius, *de mens. et pond.*, c. 14. See also Schürer, *op. cit.* (*supra*, n. 8), 540.

[23] *Op. cit.* (*supra*, n. 8).

[24] See Ritterling, *P-W*, xii, s.v. 'Legio', col. 1738–9; 1754; R. Syme, *Laureae Aquincenses*, i, 280 and *Historia*, 14 (1965), 343; cf. *CIL* iii 4491, perhaps the latest record of XV *Apollinaris* at Carnuntum. Attested in Cappadocia, A.D. 134, see Arrian, *Tactica*, 5, 15 and 24; cf. *CIL* xi 383.

The III *Cyrenaica* and XXII *Deiotariana* are attested in Egypt in 119.[25] VI *Ferr.* was in Arabia under Hadrian, as pointed out by Prof. Bowersock.[26] It is not attested in Judaea before the Second Revolt.[27] In 117 in fact only II *Traiana* seems to be available. A vexillation is attested in Judaea and a soldier of the legion was buried at Sidon in 117/8.[28] In or before 127 it was certainly transferred to Egypt.[29] Since it was one of the two legions serving under Claudius Quartinus and accompanying Hadrian to the Euphrates in 123, Ritterling's sugges- tion that it will have arrived in Egypt after this expedition may well be right.[30] Here it must have released either III *Cyr.*, or XXII *Deiot.* for service in Judaea or Arabia.[31] In the latter case VI *Ferr.* would have moved to Judaea at the time. The XXII *Deiot.* attested in Egypt in 119, is missing from the list of legions of c. A.D. 145.[32] Its disap- pearance has been thought due to total destruction or disbandment in the Second Jewish Revolt. Concrete evidence for this was sug- gested to be S. Julius Africanus' remark that the legion's wine was said to have been 'poisoned by the Pharisees'.[33] The fact that it ceases

---

[25] *BGU* i, 140 = E.M. Smallwood, *Documents illustrating the Principates of Nerva, Trajan and Hadrian*, 333; *CR* 33 (1919), 49. Cf. A. Stein, *Die Präfekten von Ägypten* (1950), 61–3. See also: *AÉ* 1951.88 with comments by M.G. Jarrett and J.C. Mann, *BJ* 170 (1970), 181.

[26] *ZPE* 5 (1970), 42–3; M. Sartre, *ZPE* 13 (1974), 85–9.

[27] The Hadrianic vexillationary inscriptions from Caesarea are, in fact, the only proof that the legion was in Judaea before Pius (below n. 35). Similarly III, *Cyr.* is not firmly attested in Arabia before 162 (cf. Keppie, *op. cit., supra*, n. 8, p. 862, n. 22).

[28] E. Ritterling, *Rheinisches Museum*, 58 (1903), 476. For two legates of the legion, see: *CIL* iii 6813 = *ILS* 1038 and *IGR* iii 615. The legion is possibly mentioned on a fragmentary inscription from Jerusalem: Clermont-Ganneau, *CRAI* 1903 490 = *AÉ* 1904.91; R. Savignac, *RB* 1 (1904), 94–8; P. Thomsen, *ZDPV* 44 (1921), 2, no. 3. For the vexillation, see below, n. 35.

[29] *CIL* iii 42; 79; cf. 14476.6. The legion certainly served in Judaea during the Second Revolt, cf. Schürer, *op. cit. (supra*, n. 8), 548. In 132–3 the legion was brought up to full strength and recruits were drawn from more distant areas than usual, see J.F. Gilliam, *AJP* 77 (1956), 358–65.

[30] For Claudius Quartinus, see G. Alföldy, *Fasti Hispanienses* (1969), 79–81; Ritterling, *P-W*, xii, col. 1486–7; 1795; see also H.M.D. Parker, *The Roman Legions* (1958), 162.

[31] The *cursus*-inscription of Q. Voconius Saxa Fidus (suffect 146) shows him to have been *tribunus laticlauius* of III *Cyr.*, in the mid 120's (*IGR* iii 763 = *ILS* 8828). This may not be conclusive evidence that the legion had its base outside Egypt at the time. Voconius Saxa may have served with the legion during the campaign in 123 (above n. 30) or he may have commanded a vexillation outside Egypt.

[32] *CIL* vi 3492a, b = *ILS* 2288. See also S. Applebaum, *op. cit. (supra*, n. 2), 26–7 and 36 with n. 296.

[33] A. v. Harnack, *Texte und Untersuchungen der altchristlichen Literatur* (1882), 4, 44; F.-M. Abel, *Histoire de la Palestine*, ii (1952), 93 with n. 1 takes the story seriously.

to be mentioned in Egypt in the early 120's might point to its transfer to Judaea before the Revolt.[34] A neglected piece of evidence justifies
further discussion of these matters. A series of 8 inscriptions records
repair of the Caesarea high-level aqueduct by vexillations of II *Tra.*,
VI *Ferr.* and X *Fret.*[35] Several of these are dedicated to Hadrian.
One additional inscription proved to be illegible. A. Negev, who
published it, tentatively attributed it to the VI *Ferr.*[36] S. Applebaum
noted its importance for the present discussion and, following an earlier
suggestion by A. Negev, speculated that the unknown legion might
have been XXII *Deiot.*[37] Reexamination of the stone established that
the lettering has been deliberately and carefully erased, as shown by
the diagonal marks of a stonecutter's chisel.[38] None of the other 13
inscriptions of this type found in Judaea show any sign of having
been damaged intentionally.[39] It is therefore likely that the erased

---

[34] Ritterling, *P-W*, xii, col. 1795.

[35] 1) X *Fret.*: Z. Vilnay, *PEFQSt.* (1928), 45–7 = *AÉ* 1928. 136 = Saxer, *Epigrafische Studien*, 1, no. 291; republished by D. Barag, *IEJ* 14 (1964), 250–2. 2) X *Fret.*: B. Lifshitz, *Latomus*, 22 (1963), 784 (first published in Hebrew newspaper) and A. Negev, *IEJ* 14 (1964), 244. 3) X *Fret.*: A. Negev, *IEJ* 22 (1972), 52–3 = *AÉ* 1972, 670. 4 and 5) X *Fret.*: I. Olami and J. Ringel, *IEJ* 25 (1975), 148 ff. (two adjoining inscriptions). 6) VI *Ferr.*: B. Lihshitz, *Latomus*, 19 (1960), 110 (first pub-lished in a Hebrew newspaper). 7) VI *Ferr.*: Z. Vilnay, *op. cit.*, 108–9 = *AÉ* 1928. 137 = Saxer, *op. cit.*, no. 290. 8) II *Traiana Fortis*: A. Negev, *IEJ* 14 (1964), 245.

[36] *IEJ* 14 (1964), 244–5.

[37] *Supra*, n. 32; A. Negev, *Ḥadashot Arheologiot*, 7 (1963), 1–2 (Archaeological News of the Department of Antiquities and Museums, in Hebrew).

[38] It is very difficult to make out the difference between these incisions and the traces of original lettering. The inscription is cut in a limestone block, bearing a moulded *tabula ansata*, 0.47 h. and 0.95 w. The panel measures 0.25 h. and 0.375 w. The inscription consists of three lines:

[---]
L̰E[---]I
D̰[---]T̰ [---]A

The 'D' in 1.3 which would be decisive is not certain. The letter 'A' still bears traces of red paint. There is no space for an emperor's name in the first line. This is the only one of the vexillation-inscriptions in Judaea on which the name of the unit is spread over three lines, leaving so much space for number and *cognomen*. This would fit a legion with a long number and name.

[39] Apart from those found in Caesarea, the following inscriptions record legionary vexillations in Judaea: 1) VI *Ferr.*, Samaria-Sebaste: *Harvard Excavations*, i, 251 no. 1. 2) VI *Ferr.*, Eleutheropolis-Beth Govrin: J.H. Iliffe, *QDAP* 2 (1933), 121–2. 3) VI *Ferr.*, Tel-Shalem: N. Tzori, *IEJ* 21 (1971), 53–4. 4) X *Fret.*, Abu-Gosh: Two in-scriptions, H. Vincent, *RB* 1 (1902), 430 = *AÉ* 1902.230 = Saxer, *Epigrafische Studien*, i, no. 293; F.M. Abel, *RB* 35 (1925), 580–1 = *AÉ* 1926. 136. The unit at Tel-Shalem is dated by the discovery of a bronze statue of Hadrian: G. Foerster, *Qadmoniot*, 7 (1975), 38–40 (Hebrew). This inscription and the one from Eleutheropolis had

number and name do not belong to a legion mentioned on any of the extant inscriptions, but to another which was indeed disbanded in disgrace. The Hadrianic date of the inscriptions from Caesarea strongly suggest a connection with the Second Revolt. The XXII *Deiot.* is therefore the most likely candidate and the erased inscription may strengthen the theory of its removal from the list of legions because of events in the Second Revolt.

The most likely conjecture as to the identity of the legions in Judaea seems therefore to be that II *Tra.* arrived in 117 and was superseded after its return from the Euphrates in or shortly after 123 by III *Cyr.* or XXII *Deiot.* However, it remains a fact that there is no datable evidence establishing the presence of either legion in Judaea before 132, while VI *Ferr.* may have left Arabia anytime under Hadrian.[40] Various possibilities have been suggested by Keppie. On the other hand, there is little doubt that two legions were in Judaea from 117 onwards.

We now have to consider the implications of the new evidence for the organization of Judaea as a province.

First of all it should be noted that the change in the status of the province at the time suggested here, came at the moment when Hadrian abandoned Mesopotamia. The new Judaean legion was stationed at Caparcotna, a site commanding the Valley of Jezreel. Military geographers have always held that through this plain and across the Jordan was the natural access from the Mediterranean coast to Damascus, from Damascus to the Euphrates and thence to India.[41] The upheavals in Judaea during Trajan's Parthian campaign will have convinced Hadrian of the necessity of safeguarding this route. Important, in this connection, is the evidence of the only other road known to have been constructed in this region in 120, a road from Gerasa via Adra'a to Bostra.[42] This road provided the legion in

---

already been dated in this period on palaeographical grounds, cf. Iliffe and Tzori, *loc. cit.* For a vexillation of III, *Cyr.*, in Jerusalem in 116/7, see *CIL* iii 13587 = *ILS* 4393. For vexillations in Judaea during the Second Revolt, see Schürer, *op. cit. (supra,* n. 8), 548 and Applebaum, *op. cit. (supra,* n. 2), 45.

[40] That III, *Cyr.*, took part in the war appears from *CIL* xiv 3610 = *ILS* 1071 and *CIL* x 3733 = *ILS* 2083. The participation of VI *Ferr.* is suggested by the inscriptions cited above nn. 35 and 39.

[41] The classic description: G.A. Smith, *The Historical Geography of the Holy Land,* chapter xx; see also: A. Alt, *Palästinajahrbuch,* 35 (1937), 80–2. The Valley of Jezreel is named by Eusebius, *Onomasticon,* 14, 21 (ed. Klostermann) τὸ μέγαλον πεδίον τῆς λεγεῶνος = *grandis campus legionis* or *maximus campus* in Hieronymus' translation.

[42] See the road-report on the section Gerasa-Adra'a by S. Mittmann, *ZDPV* 80 (1964), 113 ff. = *ADAJ* 11 (1966), 65 ff.

Bostra with direct access into the Decapolis. The highway through the Valley of Jezreel linking the coastal plain with the Decapolis was constructed in 69 by M. Ulpius Traianus the Elder, while milestones of Trajan and Hadrian record repair of the road, the section Gerasa-Scythopolis in 112 and the section Scythopolis westward in 129.[43] From this it appears that immediately after the installation of a legionary command in the Valley of Jezreel direct communication was provided with the legion in Bostra.[44] The next fact to be noted about the Valley of Jezreel is, of course, the passage it affords across Palestine from Ptolemais (Acco), from the coastal plain, the Samarian hills, the River Jordan and Galilee. As noted by Prof. Applebaum, the legion at Caparcotna was in a position to check any attempt at coordination between the Jews of Galilee and those of Judaea.[45] While X *Fret.* had been stationed in the Judaean mountains since 70, Galilee until 117 did not come under control of a legion which from its

---

[43] See B.H. Isaac and I. Roll, *JRS* 66 (1976), 15–19; see also above n. 17. The construction of a proper road was particularly important because the Valley of Jezreel is very muddy in winter. We may note that Traianus also was responsible for the construction of the Palmyra-Sura road, cf. H. Seyrig, *Syria*, 13 (1932), 270–2; also G.W. Bowersock, *JRS* 63 (1973), 133 ff.

[44] An alternative route linking Scythopolis and Bostra via Gadara is marked on the *Tabula Peutingeriana*. As yet there is no evidence for its existence as a Roman road in the 2nd century, see S. Mittmann, *Beiträge zur Siedlungsgeschichte des nördlichen Ostjordanlandes* (1970), 133–8, see also 162–3. In 129 another road linking Gerasa and the *uia noua Traiana* was either made or repaired (P. Thomsen, *ZDPV* 40 (1917), no. 211: Gerasa-Philadelphia). In the same year a milestone records repair of the *uia noua* itself between Philadelphia and Bostra (Thomsen, *op. cit.*, no. 110). For Hadrianic road-making, see also above n. 17. All this is evidence of the attention paid to communications between the legions and the major cities between them on both sides of the Jordan.

[45] *Op. cit.* (*supra*, n. 2), 23. For Galileans seeking refuge in the South at this time, see below n. 56. West of the Jordan there exist three lines of communication between Galilee and Judaea. The first runs through the coastal plain and S. of the Carmel or around it, the second through the mountains of Samaria via Neapolis (Shechem) and the third through the Jordan-valley. Those travelling via Samaria or the Jordan-valley have to pass through narrow gorges just at places known to have been occupied by legionary vexillations (above n. 39). The highway S. of the Carmel through wadi 'Ara was controlled by the fortress at Caparcotna. From Jewish sources it appears that the usual route for Jews travelling from Galilee to Judaea was via Kefar 'Otnay mentioned explicitly, see *Tos. Gittin*, 7:9 (ed. Zuckermandel, 331). Hadrianic road-making is attested by milestones on the Caparcotna-Neapolis road (above n. 17), the Caparcotna-Scythopolis road (report forthcoming) and the road from Scythopolis to Tel Shalem (above n. 17). It may be noted that no milestone-inscriptions have been found on the Scythopolis-Jericho road, south of Tel Shalem, where desert-conditions would have been favourable for their preservation. The section Scythopolis-Tel Shalem (Salem of Eusebius, *Onomasticon*, 6 (ed. Klostermann): see also Epiphanius, *de mens. et pond.*, c. 72; John 3:23) is marked by milestones from Hadrian down to Caracalla. This might date the period of occupation of the fort.

base at Caparcotna, could command all its parts. We must therefore consider the function of the new road linking Caparcotna and Sepphoris. Sepphoris was, according to Josephus, situated in the heart of Galilee, being its largest city and strongest fortress, adapted to stand guard over the entire region.[46] It was the capital of Galilee, apart from the period lasting from ca. A.D. 18 till Nero when the new city of Tiberias held this rank.[47] During the first Jewish revolt it was notably pro-Roman.[48] Information on its history in the 2nd century has to be derived from coins which, as noted by Hill, acknowledged obligations to the Emperor Trajan.[49] On a later series, before or early in the reign of Pius its name was changed to 'Diocaesarea' with the additional titles ἱερά, ἄσυλος καὶ αὐτόνομος.[50] Hill suggests that this will have been connected with Hadrian's visit in 130. He points to Hadrian's identification with Zeus Olympios. The events reflected by coins of Diocaesarea may be further clarified by coin-issues of other cities. Hadrianic coins of Tiberias, second largest city of Galilee, represent Zeus seated in a temple, possibly the 'Αδριανεῖον mentioned by Epiphanius.[51] These coins remind of issues from

---

[46] Jos., *BJ* iii, 2, 1 (34); *Vita*, 34. See also *BJ* i, 8, 5 (170); 16, 2 (304): abundant provisions; ii, 4, 1 (56): βασιλικαὶ ὁπλοθῆκαι; *Vita*, 38: Βασιλικὴ τραπέζα καὶ τὰ ἀργεῖα (see also below n. 52). See further: E. Schürer, *Geschichte des Jüdischen Volkes im Zeitalter Jesu Christi*, ii (1907), 209–13 and references in Avi-Yonah, *op. cit.* (*supra*, n. 2), 95–6. For the excavations, see L. Waterman, *Preliminary Report of the University of Michigan Excavations at Sepphoris* (1937).

[47] Jos., *Vita*, 37–8. Herodes Antipas fortified the town to be πρόσχημα τοῦ Γαλιλαίου and named it 'Autocratoris' (*Ant.* xviii, 2, 1 (27)).

[48] *BJ* ii, 18, 11 (511); 21, 7 (629); 21, 10 (645–6); iii, 2, 1 (30–4); 4, 1 (59 and 61); *Vita*, 31 ff.; 373 ff.; 394.

[49] Hill, *BMC Palestine*, xi. Of the garrison presumably quartered at Sepphoris at this time nothing is known. Josephus mentions troops sent here by Cestius Gallus (XII *Fulm.* under Caesennius Gallus): *Vita*, 394 and *BJ* ii, 18, 11 (510–11); iii, 2, 4 (30–3). Later Vespasian sent a thousand cavalry and six thousand infantry under the command of Placidus ἐν τῷ μεγάλῳ πεδίῳ στρατοπεδευσάμενοι (at Caparcotna?) διαιροῦνται καὶ τὸ μὲν πεζόν ἐν τῇ πόλει πρὸς φυλακὴν αὐτῆς, τὸ δ'ἱππικὸν ἐπὶ τῆς παρεμβολῆς αὐλίζεται. (*BJ* iii, 4, 1 (59)). A passage instructive for the later military situation as well. An 'old castra' (fort) at Sepphoris is mentioned in Jewish sources not later than the end of the second century: *Mishna 'Arakhin*, 9:6, cf. *b 'Arakhin*, 9:32a; *Torat Kohanim ba-Har*, 4:1. See also *Tos. Shabbath*, 13:9 (ed. Zuckermandel, 129); *j Shabbath*, 16:7 (15d); *b Shabbath*, 16:121a.

[50] Hill, *loc. cit.* The milestone of 120 does not help to establish an early date for the new name, since the Greek phrase indicating the distance from Diocaesarea was added later and is missing on the later Hadrianic milestone (*supra*, n. 14).

[51] Hill, *op. cit.*, xv; A. Kindler, *The Coins of Tiberias* (1961), no. 7b and p. 21. Epiphanius, *Haer.*, 30, 12 *ap.* Migne, *Patr. Gr.*, xli, 426.

Neapolis.[52] The date of the coins from Tiberias is c. 119–120 (year 101 of the city).[53] It is clear that Jews would have had no part in the issue of coins with Zeus, Nike and Tyche represented. Jones discussing these matters suggests that Hadrian disenfranchised the Jewish and Samaritan aristocracies which had hitherto ruled these three cities and entrusted their government to pagans.[54] If we accept the interconnection between the events reflected by coin-issues in three cities the date would seem to be the same for all of them, namely 119–120.[55] The conclusion seems to be that after 117 the strengthening of the garrison in the North of Judaea was combined with the handing over of local administration to non-Jewish elements. These measures must have been taken after the dismissal of Lusius Quietus and after order had been restored in the province following the unrest of 115–7.[56] The steps seem to have been effective as there is no evidence

---

[52] Hill, *op. cit.*, xxviii. See also the coins of Aelia Capitolina with the capitoline trias in a temple: Hill, *op. cit.*, xliv; L. Kadman, *The Coins of Aelia Capitolina* (1956), no. 3.

[53] See above n. 51; for the date, see also Kindler, *op. cit.* (above, n. 51), 48–9. For the date of the foundation of Tiberias, see: M. Avi-Yonah, *IEJ* 1 (1950–1), 160–9; cf. Smallwood, *op. cit.* (*supra*, n. 8), 184, n. 13. Other coins of Tiberias, issued c. 119/120, represent Tyche holding a bust of what is likely to be Hadrian, symbolizing the allegiance of the city to the Emperor (Hill, *op. cit.*, nos. 29–31; Kindler, *op. cit.*, no. 9 and p. 38). A third issue represents *Nike* (Hill, nos. 32–3; Kindler, no. 8b). Smallwood, *op. cit.*, p. 423, noted the possibility that this coin refers to a recent victory over the Jews. Of interest, in this connection, is Mattingly's observation that in Rome in 117 no coins were minted of the Victory Type. 'The mint-master may have been waiting for the Eastern situation to clear' (*BMC Empire*, iii, p. cxxviii).

[54] A.H.M. Jones, *The Cities of the Eastern Roman Empire* (²1971), 278; see also *JRS* 21 (1931), 82. There is little reason to doubt that these events are, in the case of Sepphoris, reflected by *Mishna, Qiddushin*, 4:5, referring to the 'old law-court' of Sepphoris which, according to R. Jose (*flor.* in Sepphoris under Hadrian), confirmed the Jewish identity of everybody registered as a legal witness. Schürer, *op. cit.* (*supra*, n. 46), ii, 211, n. 495, considering when local government will have been taken out of Jewish hands, suggests the time of Herod Antipas or Hadrian and prefers the former. However, the source as it stands is far more likely to refer to events of recent date.

[55] A Roman road linked Sepphoris and Tiberias, marked by an undated milestone, as yet unpublished. A 2nd century source mentions towers on the road between Sepphoris and Tiberias: *Tos. 'Erubin*, 6:8 (ed. Zuckermandel, 145); cf. *J. 'Erubin*, 5:1 (22b) where the term '*burganin*' (*burgi*) is used, both ascribed to R. Simon bar Yoḥai (*flor.* under Hadrian, survived the Second Revolt). It is not unlikely that the Sepphoris-Tiberias highway was a patrolled line in the time of the Second Revolt, provided with towers, similar to the road in Judaea from Bethlehem southwards noted by M. Kochavi, *Judaea, Samaria and the Golan, Archaeological Survey 1967–8* (1972), 26 and map 3 (Hebrew).

[56] Jewish sources might reveal some of the reasons for the removal of Jewish leaders from the local administration. G. Alon, *A History of the Jews in the Period of the*

for large-scale participation of Galilee in the Second Jewish Revolt.[57]
On the other hand, Hadrian's attested activities in Judaea proper,
the main centre of the revolt: the decision to found *Colonia Aelia
Capitolina* and milestones in the area seem to be associated with
Hadrian's visit of 130.[58] It is not impossible that there was a connec-
tion between the reinforcement of the garrison early in the reign

---

Mishna and the Talmud, ii (1961), 1–2 (Hebrew) discussed 'political brigandage' in the
years before the Second Revolt. Three testimonies cited by him are of particular
interest: 1) *b Abodah Zarah*, 25b described brigands ('listim') in Galilee who met with
pupils of R. Akiba making for the South and who expressed their admiration for
him and his pupils. R. Akiba was one of the leaders of the Second Revolt. 2) *Ekhah
Rabbah* 3:6: the son of R. Hananiah ben Teradion (a wealthy Galilean, killed in the
Second Revolt) joined a group of brigands, betrayed them and was killed by them.
Out of respect for the father the brigands gave up the body for burial. The son was
then cursed by all his family. 3) *b Niddah* 61a: Galileans who had killed a man fled
to Lydda and there appealed to R. Tarfon (influential in the years before the 2nd
revolt) to hide them. This he did not but neither did he deliver them to the authorities. Alon cited these stories as testimony of political brigandage in the years before
the Second Revolt. Dr. Oppenheimer has pointed out to us that they also show that
these activities were tolerated or even encouraged by Jewish leaders. Furthermore
the three sources are all associated with Galilee. Also associated with Galilee is
another important testimony cited by Alon, vol. i (1954), 262 and 292: *Tos. Kelim,
Baba Bathra*, 2:2 (ed. Zuckermandel, 591); cf. S. Liebermann, *Tosefeth Rishonim* (1939),
74. According to R. Joshua (or R. Jose, for whom see above n. 54) five Rabbis, all
of them members of the supreme law-court, were meeting in secret in Sepphoris.
Among the five were R. Eleazar ben Azariah (who had been temporary president
of the supreme court) and R. Halafta of Sepphoris, father of R. Jose. The number
of scholars present, 5, gives the gathering the quorum needed for a rabbinical court.
The language of the source indicates that it refers to times of trouble and persecution and from the dates of the participants it appears that these must have been the
disturbances under Trajan. The place of the meeting, Sepphoris, is significant for
the present discussion.

[57] The geographical scope of the Second Revolt is discussed by A. Büchler, *JQR*
16 (1904), 143–205; G. Alon, *op. cit. (supra,* n. 56), 19 ff. For the Jewish sources on
Galilee during the Revolt, see: A. Oppenheimer, in *The Roman Period in Israel, Publications of the Dept. of Local Studies of the Qibbutz Movement* (1973, Hebrew), 227–34.
Important numismatic evidence is cited by Applebaum, *op. cit (supra,* n. 2), 22–5;
34–5; for a Bar Kokhba coin from Sepphoris, see n. 208. Mr. I. Ben Shalom has
pointed out to us that it appears from Jewish sources that coins of the Second
Revolt were in peoples' hands after its suppression; see: *Tos. Ma'aser Sheni*, 1:5–6 (ed.
Zuckermandel, 86); *j Ma'aser Sheni*, 1:2 (52d); *b Baba Kamma*, 4:3; 4–5. Not too much
value should therefore be attached to isolated coin finds.

[58] For the date of the foundation of Aelia, cause of the Second Revolt according
to Dio lxix, 12, 1–2, see: Schürer, *op. cit. (supra,* n. 4), 540–2; Applebaum, *op. cit.
(supra,* n. 4), 8; Smallwood, *op. cit. (supra,* n. 8). 432–4; for a different opinion, see
Gichon's forthcoming study. For milestones, see above n. 17. There is not much
evidence as regards the organization of the colony. It would be interesting to know
more about the administration of a citizen-colony with a *castra* in its midst. Nothing
is known of the territorial situation. For the colony, see A.H.M. Jones, *JRS* 21
(1931), 82 and *op. cit. (supra,* n. 54), 279. Coins emphasize the connection between

and the foundation of a second colony sometime afterwards.[59] As noted by Mócsy, under Trajan there was a principle applied in the European frontier provinces: the number of *coloniae* corresponded to the number of legions in the province.[60] In the East the same is true for Syria.[61] In Judaea we have seen the foundation of Caesarea as a Roman colony at the time when X *Fret.* was first established at Jerusalem. Similarly there may be a connection between the two decisions taken by Hadrian: to assign a second legion to the province and to found another colony.[62, 63]

---

legion and colony, cf. Hill, *op. cit. (supra, n. 49)*, 7; L. Kadman, *op. cit. (supra, n. 52)*, nos. 1; 5; 6, etc. According to *SHA, Vita Hadr.*, 14, 2 the cause of the revolt was a ban placed on circumcision. Several scholars have accepted this statement and concluded that the ban and the foundation of Aelia combined caused the revolt, cf. E.M. Smallwood, *Latomus*, 18 (1959), 334–47 and 20 (1961), 93–6; *Idem, op. cit. (supra, n. 8)*, 428–38; Schürer, *op. cit. (supra, n. 8)*, 536–40; see also Gichon, *op. cit.* Recently J. Geiger, *Zion* 41 (1976), 139–47 (Hebrew, English summary) has re-discussed the sources. He argued that there is no evidence of a general ban on circumcision under Hadrian before the Revolt. This would leave the foundation of Aelia as the only cause.

[59] Alon has argued that at the very beginning of Hadrian's reign plans did exist to rebuild Jerusalem. The sources, however, are unreliable (*op. cit., supra, n. 56*), vol. i, 272–89.

[60] A. Mócsy, *Pannonia and Moesia Superior* (1974), 94. Recruiting policy seems to have been involved, cf. *Gesellschaft und Romanisation in der Römischen Provinz Moesia Superior* (1970), 168; 170.

[61] See *Dig.* 1, 15, 1 ff.: 8, 3–7 for the colonies. For the colonies in Judaea, cf. *Dig.* 1, 15, 1, 6: '*In Palaestina duae fuerunt coloniae, Caesariensis et Aelia Capitolina, sed neutra ius italicum habet*'.

[62] Before the First Revolt part of the local auxilia were recruited in Caesarea, cf. Schürer, *op. cit. (supra, n. 8)*, 326–7. Eck, *op. cit. (supra, n. 10)*, 5–6 raises the question what was Vespasian's motive for the creation of the type of province with a praetorian legate who was both governor and commander of its single legion. It should be noted that Judaea was not only the first province of this type but also (previously) the first governed by an equestrian officer, as expounded by H.-M. Pflaum, *Les procurateurs équestres sous le Haut-Empire romain* (1950), 22–4. Pflaum emphasized that it remained the only instance during Augustus' reign. As regards praetorian one-legion provinces: the second of this type was Arabia (106). Augustus and Vespasian may be said to have created precedents rather than types. They must have sought a solution for a specific problem: whom to send to a place as difficult to handle as Judaea, with no appeal for senators, let alone *consulares*. The aim was to send as few senators as possible to Judaea. The solution as such proved applicable to other provinces. Hadrian when raising the rank of the legate of Judaea may have had plans for drastic re-organization. According to *SHA, Vita Hadr.*, 14, 1 he wanted to sever Phoenicia from Syria. R. Syme, *JRS* 52 (1962), 96, n. 39 suggested that there was a notion of adding it to Judaea, i.e. to a new Syria-Palaestina.

[63] After this paper had been prepared for the press, a milestone was discovered, set up in A.D. 120 on the Ptolemais-Sepphoris road. It was signed by the Legion II *Traiana*. The inscription will be published in *ZPE* 1979.

Postscript

The early garrison of the province of Arabia has been extensively discussed by D. Kennedy.[1] There is now more evidence of the presence of (detachments) of the legion *VI Ferrata* in Arabia. A limestone slab found at Gadara reads: *Vex [Le]g VI F.*[2] In this connection it may be noted that several veterans are on record as originating from Gadara.[3] This further reinforces the impression one gets of a substantial Roman army presence in the Near Eastern cities and, to be more precise, a presence of Roman legionary vexillations.[4]

In 1984 W. Eck suggested that Judaea might have become a consular province with two legions early in the second century.[5] However, he himself does no longer support this view.

A. Zertal has published an interesting discussion of a road surveyed by him which apparently ran from Caesarea to Ginae (modern Jenin). This would form a parallel connection between Caesarea and the interior, south of the Caesarea-Legio road. Zertal also proposes an alternative site for Legio-Caparcotna which, however, does not fit with the facts presented in our article above.[6] It would render inex-

---

[1] D.L. Kennedy, '*Legio VI Ferrata*: The Annexation and Early Garrison of Arabia', *HSCP* 84 (1980), 283–309. See also: Isaac, *Limits*, 123–125 and, recently, P. Freeman, 'The annexation of Arabia and imperial Grand Strategy', in D.L. Kennedy (ed.), *The Roman Army in the East* (Ann Arbor, MI, 1996), 91–118, at 94–102. Note also L. Keppie, 'Legions in the East from Augustus to Trajan', in P. Freeman and D.L. Kennedy, *The Defence of the Roman and Byzantine East, Proceedings of a Colloquium Held at the University of Sheffield in April 1986*, (B.A.R. International Series, Oxford, 1986), 411–29; M. Mor, 'The Roman Army in Eretz Israel in the Years A.D. 70–132', *ibid.*, 575–602.

[2] T. Batayneh, W. Karasneh & T. Weber, 'Two New Inscriptions from Umm Qeis', *ADAJ* 38 (1994), 379–84, esp. 380 f. Note also two inscriptions from Gadara set up by centurions: one by Marcus Iulius Secundus, a *primus pilus* (Trajan), P.W. Herz, 'Gadara in der Dekapolis', *Archäologischer Anzeiger* 1990, 260, fig. 40; the other an anonymous centurion of the *leg. IV Scyth.*

[3] M. Calpurnius Germanus, veteran of *leg. II Traiana*: *AÉ* 1969/70.633a vi; *Leg. XIV Gem.*: *CIL* III 12091 =; T. Flavius Pudens, a veteran from the territory of Gadara: S. Mittmann, *Beiträge zur Siedlungsgeschichte des nördlichen Ostjordanlandes* (Wiesbaden, 1970), 173 no. 10.

[4] Isaac, *Limits*, chapter 3, *passim*.

[5] W. Eck, 'Zum Konsularen Status von Iudaea im frühen 2. Jahrhundert,' *Bull. Am. Soc. Papyr.* 21 (1984), 55–67. Discussion by K. Strobel, 'Zu Fragen der frühen Geschichte der römischen Provinz Arabia und zu einigen Problemen der Legionsdislokation im Osten des Imperium Romanum zu Beginn des 2. Jh. n. Chr.' *ZPE* 71 (1988), 251–80.

[6] A. Zertal, 'The Roman Road Caesarea-Ginae and the Location of Capercotani', *PEQ* 122 (1990), 21–33.

plicable, for one thing, the name of *Legio*, still attached to the village of Lajjûn in the beginning of the twentieth century. The legionary base may not have been identified through excavation, so far, but there can be no doubt as to its approximate site. Further confirmation has been published by Z. Tsuk, who discovered a segment of an aqueduct leading to the site.[7] While examining the remains of the aqueduct he also found cremation cooking-pot burials of the 1st– 2nd c. This is not a local type of burial and has been found in Israel so far only in Jerusalem and vicinity, where it clearly is associated with Roman military sites.

Note also: L.J.F. Keppie, 'Legions in the East from Augustus to Trajan', in P. Freeman and D. Kennedy (eds.), *The Defence of the Roman and Byzantine East: Proceedings of a Colloquium Held at the University of Sheffield in April 1986* (BAR, International Series, Oxford, 1986), 411–29.

M. Mor, 'The Roman Army in Eretz Israel in the Years A.D. 70– 132', *ibid.*, 575–602.

Plate 9. Milestone of A.D. 120: upper part

---

[7] T. Tsuk, 'The Aqueduct to Legio and the Location of the Camp of the VIth Roman Legion', *Tel Aviv* 15–16 (1988–89), 92–7.

13

LEGIO II TRAIANA IN JUDAEA

(with I. Roll)

In recent years several scholars have argued for the presence of a second legion in Judaea before the Second Jewish Revolt.[1] Their argument was based on deductions from indirect evidence,[2] since there was no direct reference to a Judaean legion other than the *X Fretensis* before the reign of Antoninus Pius. Although there were indications that the garrison of Judaea was strengthened before 132, probably by 117, there was no evidence establishing the identity of the second legion in those years.[3] As regards the VI Ferrata, certainly stationed in Judaea after the Second Revolt, two inscriptions suggest a stay in Arabia some time under Hadrian.[4] This does not necessarily exclude a transfer of the legion early in the reign. However, it may have stayed in Arabia till the Second Revolt. On the other hand, it was pointed out that the legion II Traiana Fortis seems to have been available for service in Judaea from 117 till 127 at the latest, when it is attested in Egypt.[5]

---

[1] See most recently: G.W. Bowersock, *JRS* 65 (1975), 184 and a forthcoming article in Latomus by the present authors.

[2] a. The legate of Judaea at the outbreak of the Second Jewish revolt, Q. Tineius Rufus, was a consular, see: E. Schürer, The History of the Jewish People in the Age of Jesus Christ, i (ed. G. Vermes and F. Millar, 1973), 518. b. The procurator was a ducenarius by 123, cf.: H.-G. Pflaum, *IEJ* 19 (1969). 232–33. c. L.J.F. Keppie, Latomus 32 (1973), 859–64 argued that there appeared to be one legion too many in the East after 117, which would fit best in Judaea. d. A milestone of A.D. 120 on the Caparcotna-Diocaesarea road marked the fifth mile from the former place, an indication that it served as a military base at the time (see below p. 153 and n. 26). For further discussion, see n. 1.

[3] B. Lifshitz, Latomus 19 (1960), 110–111 and M. Avi-Yonah, *IEJ* 23 (1973), 212–3 assumed that the VI Ferrata was transferred to Judaea before the revolt. Keppie, *op. cit.* (*supra*, n. 2), pointed out that this legion seems to be attested elsewhere at the time and that the II Traiana apparently was available.

[4] See most recently: M.P. Speidel, *ANRW* II, 8, 697–98. Speidel notes that the presence of the legion in Arabia is very likely but not attested beyond doubt.

[5] For the legion, see: Ritterling, *RE* xii 1280–81; 1484–93; H.M.D. Parker, The Roman Legions (1928), 109 ff.; R. Syme, *JRS* 18 (1928), 53–4; Danubian Papers

A recently discovered inscription clarifies part of these problems. On the 4th of July, 1978 a survey was made of the Roman road from Ptolemais (Acco) to Diocaesarea (Sepphoris) in Galilee by the authors of the present paper and students of the Absalom Institute, Tel-Aviv University.[6] A site in the valley of Acco, c. 13 km SE of this city, was known to have been the find-spot of a milestone in the nineteen hundred twenties.[7] Since mile-stations in this country are often found to produce more than one stone, we made a search for more and, as a result, fragments of three inscribed columns were discovered in secondary use in field-walls. One of these bore, in clearly legible lettering, the following inscription:[8]

1   ]AIANI   Pl. VI
        PARTICI · FIL · D[-]NEPOS
        HADRIANVS · AVG · PONTIF ·
        MAX · TRIB · (vac) POTESTAS
5   IIII COS · (vac) III LEG II T
        [IX

This may be restored as follows:

    [Imp(erator) Caesar Divi Tr]aiani
    Part<h>ici fil(ius) D[ivi Nervae] nepos
    Hadrianus Aug(ustus) pontif(ex)
    max(imus) trib(unicia) potestas (sic)
    iiii co(n)s(ul) iii Leg(io) ii T(raiana)
        (mp) ix

The inscription is dated by Hadrian's fourth tribunician power to 120. The titulature occurs in the same form on a milestone of the

---

(1971), 91–2; J.C. Mann, Hermes 91 (1963), 483–85; Keppie, op. cit. (supra, n. 2), 862–63. For its presence in Egypt, see below, n. 29.

    [6] Thanks are due to Mr. G. Horowitz, director of the Absalom institute and to all participants in the survey for their enthusiastic cooperation. The survey will be published as a road-report, by the Israel Milestones Commitee, whose activities are made possible by a generous grant of the Thyssen Foundation.

    [7] First discovered and published by A. Saarisalo, JPOS 9 (1929), 33–4. Seen on the spot by A. Alt, Palästina Jahrbuch 25 (1929), 42–3; re-published by J.H. Iliffe, QDAP 2 (1933), 120–21. See also below, p. 151. The site is at Israel Grid ref. 1660. 2513, 2.5 km west of the village of Tamra, a little distance west of the modern road from Yagur to Ahihud. The spot is registered under the heading 'Kh. et Tira', G.R. 166. 250 in the Department of Antiquities, Geographical List of the Record Files (1976), p. 21.

    [8] Fragment of a pillar, total h. 1.65; diameter, upper: 0.46; lower: 0.48; lettering, h.: 0.04; the number ix: 0.12; depth of lettering: 0.001–0.002. Dr. M. Prausnitz of the Department of Antiquities and Museums has kindly informed us that the milestones will be taken to the Museum in Acco.

Plate 10. Milestone of A.D. 120

same year from the Caparcotna (Legio)-Diocaesarea road, previously published.[9] The latter, however, has no ligatures, has a later addition, indicating the distance from Diocaesarea in Greek, and the word 'fecit' instead of the name of the legion. Both inscriptions have the unabbreviated 'potestas' in the nominative instead of the genitive or ablative.

The milestone marks the ninth mile, undoubtedly from Colonia Claudia Ptolemais (Acco) on the road to Diocaesarea (Sepphoris). A milestone from the same site, referred to above, certainly Hadrianic and possibly of 135, marks the tenth mile from Diocaesarea.[10] Col. Ptolemais belonged to the Roman province of Syria, Sepphoris to Judaea.[11] In the plain of Acco the boundary between the two provinces skirted the hills of w. Galilee and must have passed close by the find-spot of the milestones here discussed.[12] Whether the provincial boundary passed the spot to the West or to the East is unknown, but either way it was ignored by one of the two milestones. This is additional proof that the counting of miles was a matter of utility, entirely unconnected with boundaries.[13]

It is clear from the milestones now known that in 120 the construction of a road was completed from the military base at Caparcotna (Legio) to Diocaesarea (Sepphoris) in the hills of w. Galilee and thence to Col. Ptolemais in the coastal plain.[14] This was undoubtedly a

---

[9] B. Lifshitz, *op. cit.* (*supra*, p. 149, n. 3); M. Hecker, *BIES* 25 (1961), 175 ff. (Hebrew); for the date, see a forthcoming article (above, p. 149, n. 1).

[10] *Supra*, p. 150, n. 7. Alt, *loc. cit.* and M. Avi-Yonah, *QDAP* 12 (1946), 100–101 incorrectly assumed that the milestone counted from Ptolemais.

[11] For Ptolemais, e.g. Josephus, Vita 8, 31 (where Dora, south of modern Haifa is described as belonging to Phoenice); Pliny, *NH* 15 75 described Ptolemais among Phoenician cities; Itin. Burdigalense (ed. Geyer and Cuntz), 584–5. A stone marking the boundary between Gaba (in Judaea) and Ptolemais has been found at Qiriat Bialik, see: Sh. Applebaum, B. Isaac and Y. Landau, Scripta Classica Israelica 4 (1978), forthcoming; for the earlier period, see: Diodorus, xix, 93, 7 (312 B.C.). Ptolemais did not belong to Herod's realm (*BJ* I, 21, 11 (422)). See also: Dig. 1, 15, 1, 3; Galling, *ZDPV* (1938), 66 ff.; BMC, Phoenicia lxxviii. It is noteworthy that the fortress of Caparcotna itself was sited right on the boundary between Judaea and Phoenice, since the valley of Jezreel belonged to the former, but the Carmel to the latter province (e.g. Pliny, *loc. cit.*). The legion at Caparcotna must have been on duty in Syria at times, cf.: the soldier buried at Sidon, (below, p. 154, n. 28).

[12] For the border of Ptolemais to the East, see: Josephus, Vita 24, 118; 43, 213; M. Avi-Yonah, *QDAP* 12 (1946), 85–6, no. 2 and the cippus mentioned above, n. 11.

[13] For the choice of capita viarum in Judaea, see: B. Isaac, *PEQ* 110 (1978), 57–9.

[14] The erection of milestones formed the last stage of the construction of a road. In Arabia the last milestones were set up at least seven years after the beginning of

military road. There was a shorter and easier Roman road between Caparcotna and Ptolemais through the plain, skirting the Carmel, which saved c. 9 km and a climb and decent of 250 m each way.[15] The purpose of the road via Sepphoris must have been to make that town and its surroundings accessible from two directions as reflected by the counting of miles on the milliaria of 120.[16] The strategic importance of Sepphoris and the road to it from Caparcotna has been noted elsewhere.[17] Sepphoris was pro-Roman in the First Jewish Revolt. The surrounding villages, however, and especially those of the valley of Asochis (Emeq Beth Netufah) took active part in the revolt against the Romans, providing men,[18] serving as battleground[19] and, repeatedly, as the headquarters of Josephus,[20] commander of

the construction of the via Traiana, cf.: Th. Pekáry, Untersuchungen zu den Römischen Reichsstrassen (1968), 140–42. Colonia Claudia Ptolemais (Acco) was founded A.D. 52–4 (the date is determined by its foundation by Claudius, cf.: Pliny, *NH* v, 19, 75, i.e. 54 at the latest, and by non-colonial coins of Ptolemais, dated to 52, cf.: L. Kadman, The Coins of Akko-Ptolemais (1961), nos. 88–90). Milestones marking the construction of the road from Antioch to the new colony are dated A.D. 56, i.e. between two and four years after the foundation of the colony were milestones set up mentioning the construction of a road to it (for the road, see: R.G. Goodchild, Berytus 9 (1948–9), 112–23; 120).

[15] The road from Ptolemais to Caparcotna through the plain was part of the network of major Roman roads in the province and gave access to all parts of it via the cross-roads at Caparcotna (Legio), cf. P. Thomsen, *ZDPV* 40 (1917), 69.

[16] The counting of miles from two opposite directions may also reflect the progress of the paving of the road, as has been suggested for the via Traiana in Arabia, cf.: Pekáry, *loc. cit. (supra*, p. 151, n. 14). The road from Ptolemais to Sepphoris was the western section of the old caravan route from Damascus to Acco, the 'Darb el Hawârneh'. The greater part of this route, east of Sepphoris, was never paved as a Roman road. For the Darb el Hawârneh, see: A. Saarisalo, The Boundary between Issachar and Naphtali (1927), 22–26; B. Oded, Eretz Israel 10 (1971), 191–97 (Hebrew) and for roads in Galilee in general: W. Schwöbel, *ZDPV* 27 (1904), 105–51.

[17] Isaac and Roll, *op. cit. (supra*, p. 149, n. 1). Note, for example, Josephus' description of the battle near Simonias (= Semûnieh, Tel Shimron), a site on the Caparcotna-Diocaesarea road where milestones, including a fragment of Hadrian, have been found, cf.: M. Hecker, *op. cit. (supra*, p. 151, n. 9), 182–3. For the importance of Sepphoris, see especially: Josephus, *BJ* iii, 2, 4 (30–4); administrative center: *BJ* i, 7, 5 (170) = *Ant.* xiv, 5, 4 (91); garrison: *BJ* i, 16, 2 (304) = *Ant.* xiv, 15, 4 (414); royal arsenals: *BJ* ii, 4, 1 (56) = *Ant.* xvii, 10, 5 (271); see also: Vita 71, 394–6; *BJ* iii, 4, 1 (59–61); a fort at Sepphoris is mentioned in Jewish sources not later than the end of the second century, e.g. Mishna 'Arakhin 9, 6,' a later Jewish source refers to 'numeri' of Sepphoris: jer. Pesahim 30a, 70b; Sepphoris issued coins during the First revolt, in A.D. 67/8, bearing the name of Vespasian as commander and governor of the province: cf.: H. Seyrig, Numismatic Chronicle 10 (1950), 284–89; 15 (1955) 157–59.

[18] See: Josephus, Vita 45, 233; *BJ* iii, 7, 21 (233).

[19] Vita 43, 213–14; 71, 395.

[20] Vita 41, 207; 68, 384; *BJ* iii, 6, 3 (129); see also: v, 11, 5 (474).

the Jewish forces in Galilee. The road from Ptolemais to Sepphoris passed through this area and through the hilly borderland of Ptolemais where, at the beginning of the First Revolt, we find Jesus, τὸν ἀρχιληστήν, with a force of 800 men.[21]

The road, therefore, was built for local, military traffic by soldiers of the legion II Traiana, as appears from the milestones marking its construction.[22] This is the first instance in Judaea of a milestone-inscription containing a reference to a military unit.[23] As noted above, the milestone of the road from Caparcotna to Sepphoris has the same formula (including the irregular 'potestas'), but there the reference to the legion is missing. It is therefore not altogether certain that the legion was supposed to be mentioned in the inscription according to the officially authorized draft of the formula.[24]

There is no doubt as to the identity of the legion. 'Leg. II' is very clearly readable and no doubt part of the original inscription. The 'T' of 'T(raiana)' is shaped irregularly, but the two other Legiones II existing at the time are firmly established elsewhere, the Augusta at Caerleon and the Adiutrix at Aquincum.[25] The inscription mentions the legion as such and there is therefore no reason to assume that only a legionary vexillation was in the province at the time. We may conclude that some time before 120 the legion was transferred to Caparcotna in Judaea.[26] The II Traiana probably was a participant

---

[21] Vita 22, 104–111. The last recorded military use of the Roman road from Acco to Sepphoris was by Napoleon in April, 1799, according to Jacotin's Map, no. 46, see: Atlas of Israel (1970), map no. 1/4.

[22] Strictly speaking we have one milestone marking the construction ('fecit') and one mentioning the builders ('Leg. II T.'). As the inscriptions obviously belong to the same series the evidence of the two may be combined. It must be added that the road has stretches running through formerly marshy country, where a mound and ditches on both sides can be observed. At the time such a project could only be carried out by legionary engineers. A Roman road also existed between Sepphoris and Tiberias; so far one anepigraphic milestone has been found. There may be indications that it was constructed under Hadrian, cf.: S. Applebaum, Prolegomena to the Study of the Second Jewish Revolt (1976), 23.

[23] The *X Fret.* is mentioned on a milestone of 69 as part of the titulature of its commander, cf.: B. Isaac and I. Roll, *JRS* 66 (1976), 15. See also: Isaac, *op. cit.* (*supra* p. 151, n. 13), 56–7.

[24] With the emperor's name in the nominative it would have been more regular to find the legion mentioned in the accusative with the preposition 'per', e.g.: *SEG* ix, 251; xiii, 619; *ILS* 5834; –5; or cf.: *CIL* viii 22598; –9: 'a coin. Breuc.'

[25] Cf.: Ritterling, *RE* xii, cols. 1446; 1460 f.

[26] From the milestone referred to above p. 149, n. 2, it appears that Caparcotna was caput viae in 120 and, as a consequence, must have been a military base (it certainly was no city before the late third century); full references will be found in

in Trajan's Parthian war and thus because available for service in Judaea from the second half of 117 onward.[27] An inscription of a soldier of the legion, buried at Sidon in 117/8 could be connected with the legion's stay in Galilee.[28] It left Judaea in or before 127, when it is attested in Egypt.[29] It is further known to have been moved to the Euphrates under Claudius Quartinus during the trouble with the Parthians in 123.[30] This may have been an occasion for the reshuffling of units in the eastern provinces.[31]

In the years after 117 the redistribution of legions in Arabia, Egypt and Judaea is likely to have been as follows: at Bostra most probably the VI Ferrata,[32] at Nicopolis the III Cyrenaica and XXII Deiotariana,[33] in Jerusalem the *X Fretensis*[34] and at Caparcotna (Legio) the II Traiana Fortis. It is possible that detachments of the Judaean legions were based elsewhere in the province.[35] The situation after

---

Isaac and Roll, *supra*, p. 149, n. 1; M. Avi-Yonah, Gazetteer of Roman Palestine (1976), 74 s.v. 'Legio'; Applebaum, *op. cit.* (*supra*, n. 22), 29. Since the Leg. II Traiana constructed a road from the later fortress of VI Ferrata at Caparcotna to Acco, it is very likely that the former place served as headquarters already in 120.

[27] See: Ritterling, *op. cit.*, col. 1486; F. Lepper, Trajan's Parthian War (1948), 173; 175; 178; Mann, *loc. cit.* (*supra*, p. 149, n. 5). The year 120, of course, is merely a terminus ante quem for the arrival of the legion in Judaea and only marks the completion of the road (*v. supra*, p. 151, n. 14).

[28] *CIL* iii 151 and p. 1139; Ritterling, Rheinisches Museum 58 (1903), 476; cf.: Mann, *loc. cit.* (*supra*, p. 149, n. 5); see also above, p. 151, n. 11.

[29] *CIL* iii 42; 79; cf.: 14476.6.

[30] See: G. Alföldy, Fasti Hispanienses (1967), 79–81; Ritterling, *RE* xii, cols. 1486–7; 1795.

[31] As suggested by Ritterling, *loc. cit.* The legion appears to have returned to Judaea in the Second Revolt, cf.: *CIL* x 3733 = *ILS* 2083; J.F. Gilliam, *AJP* 77 (1956), 358–65; J.C. Mann, *op. cit.* (*supra*, p. 149, n. 5), 488. An inscription from the Caesarea aqueduct mentions a vexillation of the legion: A. Negev, *IEJ* 14 (1964), 245. This may belong to the period of the Second Revolt or to the legion's earlier stay in the province, see also: Schürer, *op. cit.* (*supra*, p. 149, n. 2), 548. The legion is mentioned on a fragmentary inscription from Jerusalem, see: P. Thomsen, *ZDPV* 44 (1921), 2 no. 3; cf.: Applebaum, *op. cit.* (*supra*, n. 22), 27.

[32] See most recently: M.P. Speidel, *ANRW* ii, 8, 691 ff. and 697–8.

[33] *BGU* I 140 = Mitteis and Wilcken, Chrestomathie, 373; A. Stein, Die Präfekten von Ägypten in der römischen Kaiserzeit (1950), 62; Cl. Préaux, Phoibos 5 (1950), 123 ff.

[34] The headquarters of *X Fret.* were in Jerusalem after the First Revolt, according to Josephus, *BJ* vii, 1, 1 (1–2); cf.: 1, 3 (17). See also: *ILS* 9059.

[35] Inscriptions of vexillations of the legion have been found at Abu Gosh: *AÉ* 1902.230; 1926.136 and in Caesarea; cf. J. Ringel, Césarée de Palestine (1975) and Isaac and Roll, *op. cit.* (*supra*, p. 149, n. 1) for the evidence from Caesarea. Vexillations of VI Ferr. have been found at Samaria-Sebaste: Harvard Excavations i, 251, no. 1; Eleutheropolis (Beth Govrin): *AÉ* 1933.15; Tel Shalem: N. Tsori, *IEJ* 21 (1971), 53–4 and at Caesarea (*v. supra*). On some of the Caesarea-inscriptions Hadrian is

the transfer of the II Traiana, not later than 127 and possibly in 123 remains unresolved. However, there can be no doubt that it was replaced in Judaea by another legion.[36] Accordingly it is no longer in doubt that some 15 years before the Second Jewish Revolt broke out the legionary garrison in the province was augmented to twice the strength thought sufficient after the suppression of the First Revolt.[37]

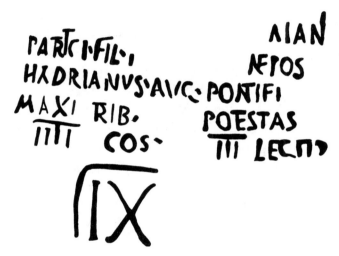

Figure 5. Milestone of A.D. 120: the lettering

mentioned, the others are undated, but it seems altogether possible that legionary vexillations were based in various towns in the province. See also the evidence of military sites collected by Applebaum, *op. cit.* (*supra*, p. 153, n. 22), 28–31. As for the undated inscriptions, it is, of course, uncertain whether they reflect a temporary military presence in times of trouble or permanent camps. However, the fact that they are monumental inscriptions may be an indication in favour of the latter alternative. For inscriptions of vexillations in Judaea during the Second Revolt, see: Schürer, *op. cit.* (*supra*, p. 149, n. 2), 548 and Applebaum, *op. cit.*, 45.

[36] As noted above, p. 149, n. 2, the rank of the legate in 132 proves that he must have governed a province with two legions.

[37] We have no information on the auxilia in the years preceding the Second Revolt.

Postscript

J.R. Rea, 'The Legio II Traiana in Judaea?', *ZPE* 38 (1980), 220 f. referred to the milestone text, revised by I. Roll and me in the article published in *Latomus* 38 (1979), 54–66, with Pl. II, figs. 3–4 and Pl. IV (Article No. 12: Judaea in the Early Years of Hadrian's Reign). He compared our reading of this inscription critically with the text published by us in the article re-printed above, No. 13: 'Legio II Traiana in Judaea'. It seems proper to cite his comments in full.

'These inscriptions look as if they ought to agree, but one has 'fecit' where the other has 'Leg(io) ii T(raiana)', which is alleged to be the first definite evidence that this legion was stationed in Judaea before being transferred to Egypt in or before A.D. 127.

Diplomatic transcripts juxtaposed for comparison suggest even more that we ought to read the same in both places:

FECIT

LEGIIT

The photo in Latomus 38 (1979) Pl. II, fig. 4 (between pages 64 and 65) shows the first two letters clearly as FE, and an earlier photo in Bull. Israel Explor. Soc. 25 (1961), 185 shows the back of a rounded letter following. We can accept 'fecit' as the reading of one of the stones, and look for the same on the other.

The photographs show a very badly weathered surface, in a not too suitable light. It is only with the aid of the drawing in *ZPE* 33 (1979) 155 that we can interpret this passage on the photo, *ibid.*, Pl. VI (lower photo). The last trace, interpreted as "= T(raiana)"—odd enough in itself—is a deep incision concave on the left and convex on the right. It looks like no letter at all. It might be a decorative hedera or it might be accidental damage. Discarding this, we can compare FECIT and LEGIIT. The photo shows an upright from the first letter, with no trace of the crossbars of F or the foot of L, which, however, does appear in the authors' drawing. Noting of E is visible, but it is common to both versions and therefore credible. An edge curved to the left could represent either C or G, though the top appears to be very flat. The uprights of the next two elements are clear, and there is a faint horizontal line at the top, which seems not to extend to the left of the first upright, but to be visible to right and left of the second.

The little that can be seen is entirely compatible with FECIT, which is recommended by the other stone, and is certainly not sufficient to compel us to accept LEGIIT. Unless a photo taken in a more suitable raking light can be published, we should not accept this as the only solid evidence of the activity of the legio II Traiana in Judaea at this period.'

So far J.R. Rea's comments. In response we published the following paper with a new and better photograph.

14

LEGIO II TRAIANA IN JUDAEA—A REPLY

(with I. Roll)

In *ZPE* 33 (1979), 149–156 we published a milestone which records the construction in A.D. 120 of a road from Ptolemais (Acco) to Diocaesarea (Sepphoris) (fig. 1). The inscription, as we read it, mentions the '*Leg. II T.*' This then would prove that the legion was in Judaea at the time, based almost certainly at Caparcotna (Legio) near Megiddo. Our reading was questioned by J.R. Rea who pointed out that our photographs of the inscription do not prove the reading (*ZPE* 38 (1980), 220 f.). Rea suggests that instead of LEG II Ṭ one might read FECIT, which appears on a milestone of the same year and the same region published by us in *Latomus* 38 (1979) (fig. 2). It is true indeed that the photographs do not prove anything and the alternative reading might therefore seem plausible to anyone who has not seen the stone.[1] We are grateful to Dr. Rea for encouragement to clarify this matter.

The first letter clearly is an *L*. The horizontal stroke at the base of the leg is visible and can be felt without any doubt. The two bars needed to make it an *F* simply are not there. Had they existed they should have been well pronounced, like those of the *F* in ll. 2 and 3. The *E* is visible and causes no problem anyway. The third letter is not a *C* but a *G*, marked by a slanting tail at the bottom of the half circle (like its parallel in l. 3). The numeral II is produced by two upright strokes connected at the top by a horizontal bar which is not continued to the right of the second leg.[2] On the other hand,

---

[1] The stone has now been moved to Tel Aviv University and may be inspected near the main entrance to the campus.

[2] It may be noted that the I's on the inscription are formed by a vertical line only. The horizontal bars of the T's have tendency to protrude to the right because they were cut from left right. We agree with Dr. Rea that the two inscriptions look as if they ought to agree. It is, however, a fact that one has fecịt where the other has Leg. ii.

Plate 11. Milestone of A.D. 120: detail

we agree that the following sign which we interpreted as a Ṭ really
looks like no letter at all. It could be a misshapen ivy leaf. That,
however, is irrelevant for the interpretation of the inscription, since
no other Legio II could be a candidate for service in the East in
those years.

We do not claim, as suggested by Dr. Rea, that the present inscription is the only document establishing the presence of this legion
in Judaea. As we pointed out, a vexillation of the legion is mentioned
on a Hadrianic building inscription from the Caesarea-aqueduct.[3] The
legion is mentioned again on a fragmentary inscription from Jerusalem.[4] The milestone, however, is so far the only proof that the legion
was based in Judaea around A.D. 120.

---

[3] A. Negev, *IEJ* 14 (1964), 245.

[4] P. Thomsen, *ZDPV* 44 (1921), 2, no. 3.

Postscript

Eighteen years later, no further milestone texts or other inscriptions have come to light that could resolve this problem. Any further milestones of the same year along this road might reinforce J.R. Rea's doubts or confirm our reading, but no such stones have been found, in spite of intensive survey activity along this and other roads in the region. The milestone published in article No. 13 and discussed again in No. 14 now stands near the main entrance to the campus of Tel Aviv University.

The discussion about the reference to the Legion has perhaps tended to obscure the other contribution this milestone has made and which is not in doubt, namely the fact that this is a second milestone, firmly dated to A.D. 120 and related to the same road as the one which we re-published in Latomus (above, article No. 12). Thus we have conclusive evidence that a Roman road was constructed in that year from Legio to Sepphoris and thence to Acco. This is indubitably connected with the establishment of a legionary base at Legio and the link it maintained with the city of Ptolemais-Acco in Syria.

15

CASSIUS DIO ON THE REVOLT OF BAR KOKHBA*

The *epitome* of Dio's text describes a dangerous revolt caused by
Hadrian's decision to transform Jerusalem into a Roman colony and
a pagan cult-centre. The insurgents were motivated by religious fervour
and ideology. Their rebellion was well-planned. After Hadrian's departure they fought a guerilla-war, avoiding open battle. The Romans
were slow to react. Only when the rising had assumed major proportions were reinforcements sent against the Jews. Their commander,
Julius Severus, also avoided open battle, isolating Jewish strongholds
and reducing them systematically. Losses were very high on both
sides. Much of Judaea was destroyed.

These are the main points of the only consistent survey of the
Revolt as abridged by Xiphilinus. This account forms the basis for
every modern discussion. Its credibility has been evaluated on internal
grounds and by comparison with additional information from literary and epigraphical sources relating to the revolt. In this paper I
shall approach Dio's text in a somewhat different manner, namely by
comparison with the description in ancient literary sources of other
insurrections against Roman rule in this period. The material, it must
be noted, is found mainly in Dio's History and in the works of Tacitus.
This might help us to judge whether Dio has properly brought out
the specific character of this war. We should establish whether the
text contains features which recur in other descriptions of native rebellions as opposed to elements peculiar to this text.

First, the cause of the uprising: Hadrian's measures regarding Jerusalem. I do not know of any other insurrection said to have been caused
directly by the actions of an emperor,[1] nor have I found any which

* The substance of this paper was presented as a lecture at a symposium on the
Bar Kokhba Revolt at Tel-Aviv University in March 1982.
[1] The revolt of Vindex aimed at overthrowing Nero. However, as pointed out
by P.A. Brunt, this was not a native rebellion against Roman rule, but a general
uprising against Nero's oppressive regime ('The Revolt of Vindex and the Fall of
Nero,' *Latomus* 18 (1959) 531–9). Cf. J.B. Hainsworth, 'Verginius and Vindex,'
Historia 11 (1962) 86–96. For a different view see S.L. Dyson, 'Native Revolt Patterns

arose primarily from religious and ideological motives. In the first
and second centuries A.D. every rebellion is somehow attributed to
anger about taxation in one form or another and to the behaviour
of those responsible for its collection. To mention only a few examples:
In 21 the Treveri revolted because of the magnitude of their foreign
debt.[2] The Frisians successfully rebelled in 28.[3] They used to pay a
moderate tribute in kind. Their rising was prompted by excessive
demands made by the officer in charge of the region.[4] Dio attributes
the rebellion of Arminius to the imposition of taxes.[5] The first Jewish
revolt was, according to Tacitus, caused by the bad government of the
procurators.[6] The insurrection of the Iceni under Boudicca in 60–1
is ascribed by Tacitus to the rapacity of the financial procurator and
his collaborators at the time of incorporation in the Roman province.[7]
It may be noted that, when the revolt broke out, the provincial governor was engaged in the suppression of the cult-centre of the Druids
at Mona (Anglesey). That, however, is not described as a cause of the
rebellion. This uprising is of particular interest for our purpose,
since we have both Tacitus' account and that of Dio, abridged by
Xiphilinus.[8] Tacitus provides far more information[9] and Dio is, by

---

in the Roman Empire,' *ANRW* II, 3, 158–61. In this study (*ibid.*, 138–75) and in an
earlier paper: 'Native Revolts in the Roman Empire,' *Historia* 20 (1971) 239–74,
Dyson formulates general conclusions on such revolts. This is not the aim of the
present paper, which evaluates Dio's report on the Second Jewish Revolt through
comparison with other literary sources on native revolts. It may be noted that one
emperor, Caligula, *almost* caused a revolt when he ordered that a statue with his
effigy be set up in the Temple in Jerusalem, cf.: E. Schürer, *The History of the Jewish
People in the Age of Jesus Christ*, I, revised by G. Vermes and F. Millar (Edinburgh
1973), 394–7. It is, of course, no coincidence that this too was a case involving the
Emperor-cult and Jewish religion.

[2] Tacitus, *Ann.* 3, 40–6, esp. 40, 1. In 40, 4 this is further specified as: continuous
taxation, the burden of debt and the cruelty and arrogance of the governor. The
revolt in Illyricum, A.D. 6–9 is also ascribed to tribute and maladministration, cf.
Dio 55.29, 1; 56. 16, 3. See however Syme, *CAH* X 369.

[3] Tacitus, *Ann.* 4.72–4.

[4] *Ibid.*, 72, 1–2.

[5] Dio 56.18, 3; Tacitus, *Ann.* 1.59. Both Dio and Velleius hold the governor
Quinctilius Varus responsible for the outbreak of the revolt in A.D. 9, but Velleius,
2.117 and Florus, 2.30, 31 say that the cause was the introduction of Roman
jurisdiction.

[6] *Hist.* 5.9, 3–10, 1.

[7] *Ann.* 14.31 and 32, 7; Dio 62.2.

[8] The sources for the revolt are Tacitus, *Ann.* 14.29–39; *Agricola* 15–16, 2; Dio 62.
1–12 (Xiphilinus). For the revolt see G. Webster, *Boudicca, the British Revolt against
Rome A.D. 60* (London, 1978); S. Frere, *Britannia* (1974²) pp. 104–8; Salway, *Roman
Britain* (Oxford, 1981) 100–23.

[9] For an evaluation of the sources see R. Syme, *Tacitus* (Oxford, 1958), 762–6.

comparison, 'verbiose and miserable'—the words of Sir Ronald Syme.[10] Dio's description of the outbreak of the revolt at least agrees with that of Tacitus in ascribing its primary cause to Roman exactions.[11]

Another factor mentioned by Tacitus were the outrages suffered by the Queen and her daughters and the nobility of the Iceni at the hands of centurions and fiscal agents.[12] This too is a recurrent theme. Personal grievances of native leaders are also mentioned as a significant motive in connection with the insurrections of the Batavians,[13] of the Brigantes,[14] and in Pontos in Asia Minor, all in 69.[15]

Tacitus gives a third reason which prompted the Britons to revolt under Boudicca, namely resentment at the conscription of their men into auxilia of the Roman army.[16] In two other cases the levy was the primary cause of a revolt, according to Tacitus. Until the reign of Tiberius the Thracians served under their own officers and only in neighbouring lands. They revolted in 26 when it was decided to incorporate the Thracian forces as regular units in the Roman army under Roman officers, which would serve in all parts of the Empire.[17] Similarly the Batavians, until 69, raised for themselves the troops Rome required. They served under their own officers. They enjoyed fiscal immunity in return for these contingents and revolted when a new levy was conducted in a brutal manner by Roman officers.[18]

The religious motives for the rebellion which Dio ascribes to the Jews appear to be unique in this period. On the other hand, Aelia Capitolina was not the only Roman colony which provoked resistence.

---

[10] *Op. cit.*, 763.

[11] Like Tacitus, Dio singles out the procurator as responsible for the course of events (above, n. 8). Dio also states that Roman money lenders, chief among them Seneca, had extracted repayment of the vast sums they lent to the Iceni. These felt themselves facing ruin. Tacitus does not mention this and it is uncertain whether the two accounts may simply be combined. Syme (*loc. cit.*) suggests that Dio was biased by his dislike of Seneca and dismisses the item about him.

[12] Tacitus, *Ann.* 14.31.

[13] Tacitus, *Hist.* 4.13. For this revolt see: P.A. Brunt, 'Tacitus on the Batavian Revolt,' *Latomus* 19 (1960) 494 ff. against G. Walser, *Rom, das Reich und die fremden Völker* (Basel 1951) 86 ff.

[14] Tacitus, *Hist.* 3.45.

[15] *Ibid.*, 47 f.

[16] *Agricola* 15, 3. Cf. P.A. Brunt 'Conscription and Volunteering in the Roman Army,' *SCI* (1974) 107.

[17] Tacitus, *Ann.* 4.46; cf. K. Kraft, *Zur Rekrutierung der Alen und Cohorten an Rhein und Donau* (Bern 1951) 35 ff.; Brunt, *op. cit.*, 106.

[18] Tacitus, *Hist.* 4.14; cf. Brunt, *op. cit.* (above, n. 13); *op. cit.* (above, n. 16), 106 f.

A parallel case is the rising of the Trinovantes who took up arms in support of Boudicca in 60–1.[19] Tacitus gives a striking description of the hatred engendered by the arrogance and rapacity of the colonists at Colonia Camulodunum (Colchester). They were supported by the military, themselves prospective citizens of the colony after their discharge. Camulodunum also was the centre of the imperial cult in Britain, both a symbol of slavery and ruinously expensive to the local nobility. Another Roman colony which aroused fierce enmity among the neighbouring tribes was Colonia Agrippinensis (Cologne).[20] However, here too the primary motive for resistance was material rather than religious, according to our source.

To sum up: in their description of native insurrections our sources blame local officers, fiscal agents and, sometimes, the governor, but never the emperor personally. Revolts broke out because of excessive demands made upon money, men or goods of the provincials. The desire for liberty might be mentioned as a significant factor or an effective slogan, but religious elements were never considered in this context.[21]

Bar Kokhba is not mentioned in the *epitome* of Dio's text. This is highly remarkable, for in ancient descriptions of native revolts in this period the leader usually plays a central role. Without a leader there was no revolt and the end of the revolt was marked by the death or capture of the leader. Such is the impression we get when reading our sources. Rome, apparently, tended to see a native uprising not so much as a mass-movement, but as an affront to her dignity suffered at the hands of an individual.[22] To mention only a few famous names: Jugurtha, Vercingetorix, Arminius, Boudicca, Civilis. I must mention one exception: the revolt of the Frisians in 28. Only Tacitus relates their success, but he gives no names of any chiefs, perhaps because they were successful? The case of Boudicca is particularly significant

---

[19] Tacitus, *Ann.* 14.31. See also 1.59, 8, an oration put into the mouth of Arminius in A.D. 15: 'si patriam parentes antiqua mallent quam dominos et colonias novas. . . .' 'Masters and colonies' sums up Arminius' view of Roman rule, according to Tacitus. As suggested by Brunt, there may have been a rumour that colonies were projected (*op. cit.*, above, n. 13, p. 498, n. 3).

[20] *Hist.* 4.63–6.

[21] The great revolt of the Gauls in 52 B.C. (Caesar, *BG* 7) was, in fact, part of the struggle against the Roman occupation and broke out before the country had been organized as a province. The revolt of Arminius was a response to Varus' efforts to introduce provincial organization in Germany. Religion played a role in the Thracian revolt of 11 B.C.; cf. Dio 51.25; 54.34, who does not tell us much. See also Dyson, *ANRW* II, 3 (1975) 172.

[22] For the case of Jugurtha cf. Syme, *Sallust* (Berkeley, 1964) 150 f.

since much of Dio's account, as abridged by Xiphilinus, is taken up by a description of the Queen and her oration inciting the Britons to rebellion. She is clearly perceived as a leader without whom there could have been no rising. The insurrection ended with her death. Similarly the revolt of the Treveri and Haedui in 21 ended with the suicide of their leaders and, we may add, that of Arminius with the suicide of Quinctilius Varus. Civilis started the Batavian rebellion and brought it to an end.[23] Caesar describes the uprising of the Gauls in 52 B.C. very much as a personal contest between himself and Vercingetorix.[24] These were all native noblemen most of whom had Roman citizenship.[25] Most of them are said to have rebelled for personal reasons and, while each rising was an affront to Roman dignity, these men certainly are described as worthy enemies.

A different kind of rebel-leader is represented by Musulamian Tacfarinas,[26] a plain soldier who had deserted from the Roman auxilia. He was a formidable enemy, in full control of his men. Yet his inferior social status stamped him a bandit (*latro*) who could never be an acceptable partner in negotiations.[27] In Roman eyes Tacfarinas belonged to the same class of rebels as Spartacus.[28] In this connection must be mentioned two leaders of the Jewish rising in Cyrene, Egypt and Cyprus in the reign of Trajan. Dio, in the *epitome* of Xiphilinus, mentions 'a certain Andreas' and 'a certain Artemion.'[29]

---

[23] Tacitus' account breaks off in the fifth book of the Histories. It is, however, clear from 5.26 that Cavilis negotiated a settlement on behalf of the Batavians.

[24] Nevertheless it must be noted that the revolt of the Gauls broke out before Vercingetorix took over the general command and went on after his defeat and surrender at Alesia.

[25] Jugurtha was king and had served in the Roman army. Arminius is said to have been an *eques* (Velleius 2.118, 2). Florus and Sacrovir, leaders of the Treveri and Aedui, both were noblemen with Roman citizenship, cf. Tac., *Ann.* 3.40. Civilis was *regia stirpe* (*Hist.* 4.13). Civilis was supported by the Treveri, led by Iulius Classicus and Iulius Tutor and by the Lingones under the leadership of Iulius Sabinus (4.55). They all belonged to families which received Roman citizenship before Claudius. In Britain the Brigantes caused trouble in 69 when the pro-Roman Queen Cartimandua fell out with her anti-Roman husband Venutius (Tacitus, *Hist.* 3.45), cf. I.A. Richmond, *JRS* 44 (1954) 43 ff.; Frere, *op. cit.* (above, n. 8) 116 f. For the leaders of native revolts see also Dyson, *Historia* 20 (1971) 267–70.

[26] Cf. R. Syme, 'Tacfarinas, the Musulamii, and Tubursicu,' *Studies in Roman Economic and Social History in Honor of Allen Chester Johnson* (1951) 113–130 = *Roman Papers* I, 218–30.

[27] The Roman attitude towards Tacfarinas contrasts with their treatment of Civilis with whom the provincial governor was willing to negotiate (*Hist.* 5.26).

[28] The comparison is made by Tacitus himself, *Ann.* 3.73.

[29] Dio 68.32, 1–3; Eusebius has Lukuas instead of Andreas, *HE* 4.2, 3. Cf. M. Stern, *Greek and Latin Authors on Jews and Judaism*, II (Jerusalem, 1980) 386 ff.

These are to us mere names, but it is clear that they were popular leaders of low social status. They are probably best compared with the brigand-chiefs active in Judaea after Herod's death: a former shepherd,[30] a former royal slave,[31] and ex-soldiers.[32] Their activity reflects a combination of economic hardship and messianic expectations.[33]

To sum up: the omission of the leader's name in Dio's report of the Second Jewish Revolt is exceptional, even in an *epitome*, for the first question an ancient reader would have asked regarding any insurrection was: 'who was the leader?'[34]

The third subject for comparison is the description of the war itself. As regards preparations carried out in secret, the Gauls in 52 B.C. concealed their plans[35] and in A.D. 21 they also managed to keep their arms-production hidden.[36] The Germans under Arminius and the Batavians and Britons in 69 likewise disguised their intentions.[37] Nor was there anything exceptional in the slowness of the Roman response to the Revolt of Bar Kokhba. That seems to have been a familiar pattern, usually interpreted in our sources as cavalier indifference.[38] Dio explains that in the Second Jewish Revolt both

---

[30] Jos. *AJ* 17.10, 7 (278–84); *BJ* 2.4, 3 (60–5).

[31] *AJ* 27.10.6 (273–7); *BJ* 2.4, 2 (57–9).

[32] *AJ* 17.10, 4 (270).

[33] In 68 a lowborn prophet ('e plebe Boiorum') who claimed to be the liberator of Gallic lands and a god succeeded in gathering a following of 8000 men about him (Tacitus, *Hist.* 2.61). He was suppressed by the Aedui. At another level there was a rebellion in Pontos in 69 (*Hist.* 3.47–8), led by a freedman of ex-king Polemo. Before the annexation this man was commander of the royal fleet and very powerful. Yet Tacitus calls him a 'barbarian slave' and speaks of a 'slave-war'.

[34] The brief note on the Second Jewish Revolt in the *SHA*, v., *Hadriani* 14, 2, Stern, *op. cit.* (above, n. 28), n. 511, does not mention Bar Kokhba either. This source, however, does not usually mention names of rebel-leaders. Talmudic and Christian sources do mention Bar Kokhba (Eusebius, *HE* 4.6, 1: Eusebius, *Chron.* (ed. Schoene, II) 166–7; Jerome, *Chron.* (ed. Helm²) p. 200; Syncellus I (ed. Dindorf), p. 660; *TB Ta'anit*, 29a). It should be noted that these also mention Tineius Rufus, but not Severus as Roman commander, while Dio mentions Severus but not Tineius Rufus. The role of Severus in the Bar Kokhba revolt is attested independently (see *ILS* 1056 and cf. Schürer I (above, n. 1) 519; for Q. Tineius Rufus, *ibid.* p. 518). Christian and Talmudic sources—but not Cassius Dio—mention the final siege of Bethar. It is clear that the information in Jewish and Christian literature on the one hand and in Cassius Dio's work on the other derives from different but basically trustworthy traditions.

[35] Caesar, *BG* 7.1.

[36] *Ann.* 3.40, 3; 41, 1.

[37] For the Germans under Arminius see: Dio 56.18, 5–19; Velleius 2.118. For the Batavians see: Tac., *Hist.* 4.13. For the Britons see: *Ann.* 14.31.

[38] See Sallust on Jugurtha; Tacitus on the revolts of Tacfarinas (*Ann.* 4.23); of the

sides refrained from open battle. In the literature of this period I could find no comparable description of a revolt which entailed guerilla-activity on the one hand and the systematic isolation and reduction of mountain strongholds on the other. The closest parallels might be Corbulo's Armenian expedition[39] and the Homanadensian war in Southern Asia Minor.[40] These, however, were wars of conquest, not campaigns against insurgents. Dio refers to subterranean passages as places of refuge for the Jews. These are attested through archaeology.[41] Josephus described caves used in this manner in other areas: early in his reign Herod suppressed brigands who lived in caves near Arbela in Galilee.[42] Bandits who lived in caves in Trachonitis and on the Phoenician coast are described by Josephus and Strabo.[43]

Dio's description of the fighting certainly reflects local reality. His statement that both sides suffered heavy losses is confirmed by other sources.[44] One element is remarkable by its absence. There is no charge of excessive cruelty such as Dio himself brings against the Britons in the Revolt of Boudicca[45] and against the Jews in the Revolt of the Diaspora.[46] That may be taken as an indication that the rebellion in

---

Frisians (*ibid.*, 4.73 f.); of the Treveri and Aedui (*ibid.*, 3.41; 44); of Civilis (*Hist.* 4.12).

[39] See Tacitus, *Ann.* 13.34–41; 14.23–26, esp. 23.

[40] Cf. B. Levick, *Roman Colonies in Southern Asia Minor* (Oxford, 1967), esp. chapter iv and Appendex v. The Roman conquest of NW Spain will have seen similar fighting, cf. R. Syme in: *Legio VII Gemina* (1970) = *Roman Papers* II, 825–54. Sallust and Tacitus, in their treatment of the wars against Jugurtha and Tacfarinas give striking descriptions of desert warfare, but the revolt of Bar Kokhba was not fought in the desert.

[41] Evidence for Second Revolt occupation was uncovered in northern Judaea at Wadi ed-Dalieh by G.W.E. Nickelsburg, Jr. Cf. P.W. and N.L. Lapp, *Annual of the American Schools of Oriental Research* 41 (1974) 49 ff.; in a cave at 'Ein el-'Arub between Bethlehem and Hebron, cf.: Y. Tsafrir, *Qadmoniot* 8 (1975) 24–75 (in Hebrew); in a cave at Khirbet el-'Aqed, east of Emmaus, see: M. Gichon, *Cathedra* 26 (1982) 30–42 (in Hebrew). In recent years scores of subterranean hiding places have been discovered in the foothills of southern Judaea and part of these can with certainty be ascribed to the Second Revolt. See a preliminary report by A. Kloner, *Cathedra* 26 (1982) 4–23 (in Hebrew).

[42] Josephus *AJ* 14.15, 4 (415); 15.5 (420–30); *BJ* 1.16, 2 (305); 16, 4 (309–13).

[43] Strabo 16.2, 20 (756); Jos. *AJ* 15.10, 1 (342–8); *BJ* 1.20, 4 (398–400); *AJ* 16.9, 1 (271). See on this B. Isaac, 'Bandits in Judaea and Arabia,' *HSCP* (1984) 171–203. See also the inscription from Canatha, *OGIS* 424 = *IGR* III 1223 (Waddington 2324).

[44] For Roman losses see Fronto, *de bello Parthico* 2; Stern, *op. cit.* (above, n. 29), nr. 342.

[45] Dio 62.1; Tacitus, *Ann.* 14.33.

[46] Dio 68.32, 1–3. See the parallel sources cited by Stern, *op. cit.* (above, n. 29), 387. Italian merchants were slaughtered in the first Mithridatic war (88 B.C.), cf. Appian, *Mithr.* 22 f.; Plutarch, *Sulla* 24; Memnon, *FGH* 434 F 22, 9); in the *bellum*

Judaea had, at least in Dio's eyes, a different character. This also appears from the fact that he calls the Bar Kokhba revolt a *polemos*, while he does not use this term in speaking of the Revolt in the Diaspora. Another point worth mentioning is that the victims of the atrocities in these rebellions were civilian non-combatants. That may perhaps be taken as indirect support for the assumption that the Second Jewish Revolt did not extend to the mixed cities outside Judaea proper.

We may conclude that Dio's description of the Revolt of Bar Kokhba, even it is abridged form, clearly brings out the distinctive nature of the war. While specific information concerning its duration is sadly lacking, its cause, general character and conclusion are not really paralleled elsewhere in the literature covering these centuries. That may strengthen our trust in the reliability of the source.

Jugurthinum, cf. Sallust, *Jug.* 26; in the great revolt of the Gauls in 52 B.C., cf. Caesar, *BG* 7.3; and by the Treveri in 21, cf. Tacitus, *Ann.* 3.42, 1. Roman citizens were overpowered and traders massacred in Illyricum in A.D. 6; cf. Velleius 2.110, 6.

Postscript

For a different view: M. Gichon, 'New Insights into the Bar Kokhba War and a Reappraisal of Dio Cassius', *JQR* n.s. 77 (1986), 15–43.

16

THE REVOLT OF BAR KOKHBA:
IDEOLOGY AND MODERN SCHOLARSHIP

(with Aharon Oppenheimer)

Jewish armed resistance against Roman rule in Judaea reached its culmination and exhausted itself in the Revolt of Bar Kokhba. Great numbers of rebels participated in the insurrection, employing guerilla-tactics, and large reinforcements were needed to suppress it. The rebels were united under the leadership of one man: Bar Kokhba. The revolt resulted in the emergence of a kind of independent state, marked by the organization of local authorities, the issue of coinage and the leasing of state-land.

Whereas in the past this war was often ignored in scholarly litera-ture, great and even excessive attention is now being paid to the revolt. For the lack of interest of past generations two basic reasons may be mentioned. (1) No extant literary source gives a comprehen-sive description of the revolt, its causes and course. We have conse-quently to depend on a variety of testimonies found in talmudic and Roman literature, in the writings of the Church Fathers, and in Samaritan chronicles. These sources contain partial and isolated state-ments only, sometimes contradictory and often tendentious, which must then be interpreted in combination with the archaeological evidence. However, all the available combined information still does not produce a clear picture of the course of the revolt, and essential problems cannot be solved, such as the geographical scope of the rising, the question of whether Jerusalem was conquered by the rebels, and if so whether the Temple was rebuilt. (2) Historians used to assume that the Jewish diaspora began after the destruction of the Second Temple. This view was determined by a theological concept, for in the nineteenth century and the beginning of the twentieth scholars wished to represent the destruction of the Second Temple as divine punishment of the people of Israel since they saw the rise of Christianity as the true continuation of Judaism.[1] Obviously such

---

[1] See e.g. H. Graetz, *Geschichte der Juden* ([5]1908), pp. 1–9. Christian authors followed

an attitude precluded serious consideration of the Revolt of Bar Kokhba and its impact, for in this rebellion the Jews displayed impressive military and political activity some sixty years after the suppression of the First Revolt.

In recent decades various factors have heightened interest in the Revolt of Bar Kokhba. (1) A critical and balanced scrutiny of Jewish history in the period of the Mishnah has made it clear that after the destruction of the Second Temple the Jews in Judaea still showed many of the characteristics of an independent people. This follows in particular from the study of the independent Jewish authorities and their relationship with the Roman government and with the Jewish people in the country and in the diaspora. The Jewish leadership was actively involved in the rehabilitation of the people after the suppression of the First Revolt and the destruction of the Temple. The Jewish authorities created in this period the basic conditions for a continued religious and national life without Jerusalem and the Temple.[2] The unity of the nation during the revolt of Bar Kokhba, and the military and political strength it displayed, formed the apogee of this process and showed the vitality of the people generations after the destruction of the Second Temple.

(2) Popular interest in the two Jewish revolts against Rome in Judaea has greatly increased as a result of the spectacular archaeological discoveries of recent decades. The excavations at Masada have produced what may almost be called a monument to the First Revolt. In 1952, documents and objects from the time of the Bar Kokhba uprising were found in Wadi Murabba'at. In 1960 and 1961, further

---

patristic historiography (see below). In doing so, they ignored the historical context of the war and represented it as the last part of the First Jewish Revolt. They express a negative opinion on Jewish nationalism and messianism. See e.g. F.-M. Abel, *Histoire de la Palestine*, ii (1952), pp. 83–104. These scholars therefore conceive the period of the Mishnah as the beginning of the diaspora and see the Bar Kokhba revolt as a sort of epilogue to the First Revolt. In their view, the two wars together plunged the Jewish people into the darkness of exile, as illustrated by the final quotation in Schürer's account of the war: E. Schürer, *Geschichte des jüdischen Volkes im Zeitalter Jesu Christi*, i (⁴1909), pp. 703 f. Cf., however, the new English version revised and edited by G. Vermes and F. Millar (1973), p. 557. Here the quotation from Jerome is followed by the sentence: 'Yet the tears of mourning concealed hope, and hope refused to die'.

[2] This approach was first developed by Gedalyahu Alon, who was followed by many students of the period of the Mishnah and the Talmud. See in particular: G. Alon, *The Jews in their Land in the Talmudic Age*, i (1980), pp. 1–17. See also the recent treatment (with different views on the subject) by M. Goodman, *State and Society in Roman Galilee, A.D. 132–212* (1983), esp. parts iii and iv.

discoveries were made in the Judaean desert, notably of documents including letters from Bar Kokhba, found in Naḥal Ḥever (see below). In addition a systematic exploration was undertaken in several areas of caves and underground hiding-places, at least some of which were constructed in the period under consideration. All these finds have attracted attention to the revolt and its leader and given fresh impetus to the study of the subject.

(3) A recent development which does not in fact belong to the realm of scholarship must briefly be noted. There is today in Israel a tendency to identify with the rebels.[3] It might have been expected that the generation which saw the establishment of the Jewish state would identify with past periods of national prosperity, with the Kingdom of David and Solomon or that of the Hasmonaeans. Instead, there is clearly an inclination to feel closer to those who fought a foreign empire unsuccessfully. This has become the subject of polemic writings in recent years. Bar Kokhba's revolt is now described as an inexcusable failure which could have been foreseen and avoided.[4] Y. Harkabi and others assume that contemporary political controversies may be clarified by the study of the revolt, a supposition that has made the study of the revolt itself a subject of debate. These publications have again excited popular curiosity in regard to this war in Israel.

Once scholars turned their attention to the Bar Kokhba revolt, they depicted it in various ways, depending to a large extent on personal conceptions of the Roman empire, the Jewish people, Greek and Roman culture, and Jewish religion. We find in scholarly literature discussions which wholly identify with a presumed Roman point of view or, conversely, with that of the Jews. A third group attempts to understand historical reality by giving both the supposed Roman and Jewish perspectives. Roman actions are described as basically

---

[3] See, for example, the expressions of such sentiment in Y. Yadin's popular accounts of his discoveries: *Masada* (1966), p. 201; *Bar Kokhba* (1971), p. 15: Bar Kokhba 'the last President of Israel 1800 years ago'; p. 253: 'we found that our emotions were a mixture of tension and awe, yet astonishment and pride at being part of the reborn State of Israel after a Diaspora of 1800 years'.

[4] Y. Harkabi, *Facing Reality* (1981) *Vision, no Phantasy* (1982; both in Hebrew); *The Bar Kokhba Syndrome* (1983); cf. the highly nationalistic response by I. Eldad, *A Controversy: Our Perceptions of the Destruction of the Second Temple and of Bar Kokhba's Revolt* (including Historical Reflections by D. Rokeaḥ) (1982, in Hebrew). For a critical review of this pamphlet, see: M. Broshi, 'Revolting Thesis', in *The Jerusalem Post* of 3 December, 1982.

benevolent (but shortsighted); Jewish resistance as comprehensible. An example of the first attitude is that of Wilhelm Weber,[5] 'Finally his (Hadrian's) serious war, that against the Jews, was in essence purely defensive. In it he was fully justified in taking drastic and relentless measures'. Through the foundation of Aelia Capitolina, 'new life was to blossom forth from the ruins. But the break with the past was unavoidable. . . . Graeco-Roman culture was henceforth to prosper' etc.[6] As so often, this extreme statement has something in common with the opposite point of view expressed in the publications of several Israeli scholars.[7] These agree with Weber that Hadrian consciously intended to destroy Jewish life and culture in Judaea and elsewhere. The difference, of course, is that Weber considered this a laudable plan, accepting the brutal repression of Jewish resistance as unavoidable, while Israeli scholars often see the revolt as an heroic struggle against Roman oppression. In contrast to those who manifestly take sides, others prefer a balanced view that attempts to explain what happened without blaming either the Jews or the Romans unduly.[8] These assume that Hadrian's intentions were essentially benevolent. He did not want to destroy Jewish culture in Judaea and he was unaware of the significance of his reputed decision to ban circumcision. It is held that on the one hand no active aggression against the Jews was intended, and on the other that the Jews cannot be blamed for their violent response.

There exists now a new trend towards critical re-examination. In a recent book P. Schäfer denies the historical relevance of many literary sources relating to the revolt.[9] Elsewhere Bar Kokhba is

---

[5] W. Weber in: *Cambridge Ancient History* xi (1936), pp. 313 ff.

[6] See also: B.W. Henderson, *The Life and Principate of the Emperor Hadrian* (1923), pp. 213–231 esp. 213 f.; 220 f. Henderson, however, has harsh words for Hadrian as well: 'Not even Caligula in all his madness could have devised a provocation more sure of its result'. Like some Israeli authors, Henderson considers 'Hadrian's work linked with post-war Zionism' (for which he has no sympathy). Henderson's negative judgement of Judaism after the revolt of Bar Kokhba echoes that of Th. Mommsen, *Römische Geschichte*, v, pp. 551 f. and of many others.

[7] S. Yeivin, *The War of Bar Kokhba* (²1957), pp. 58–61 (in Hebrew); G. Alon, *The History of the Jews in Eretz-Israel in the Period of the Mishnah and the Talmud*, ii (1956, in Hebrew), pp. 9–13; S. Applebaum, *Prolegomena to the Study of the Second Jewish Revolt* (1976), pp. 5–9; *id.*, in: U. Rappaport (ed.), *Judea and Rome—The Jewish Revolts* (1983, in Hebrew), pp. 220–4; 253.

[8] Mommsen (above, n. 6), pp. 545–7; Schürer (above, n. 1), p. 679 (German ed.); p. 540 (revised ed.); E.M. Smallwood, *The Jews under Roman Rule* (²1981), pp. 431; 433 f.

[9] P. Schäfer, *Der Bar Kokhba-Aufstand* (1981).

described as a 'pious thug'.[10] It has been suggested that the Jewish war was not as disastrous from the Roman perspective as Cassius Dio and modern authors claim.[11] The messianic or zealot character of the revolt has been denied.[12] It is argued that no evidence exists of any tension in the 120's or of underground preparations for war.[13] In the past, it was generally held that the revolt spread over the whole of the Roman province of Judaea. Now, many scholars argue that only a limited area was affected and that Jerusalem was never captured.[14]

Critical scrutiny of the evidence is necessary, of course. Yet since there is always room for disagreement on specific subjects, it cannot lead to decisive revision. The most substantial contribution to our information on the revolt has been made by archaeological exploration, epigraphy, and numismatics. The present paper presents an account of the development of modern thinking on the revolt and of the impact of archaeological discoveries.

The Evidence

Talmudic Sources

The revolt of Bar Kokhba is mentioned rather extensively in talmudic literature for several reasons, one of them being that, apart from the deep impression made by the events themselves, the final editing of the Mishnah took place not very long after the war ended. Sages active in the period c. 140–180 played a crucial role both in the redaction of tannaitic literature and in the development of the oral law. Most references to the revolt are found in three groups of tradition[15]

---

[10] G.W. Bowersock, 'A Roman Perspective on the Bar Kokhba Revolt' in: *Approaches to Ancient Judaism*, ii, by W.S. Green (*Brown Judaic Studies* 9, 1980), pp. 131–141; or cf. Broshi (above, n. 4): 'a despotic leader, cruel and arrogant' and Mommsen (above, n. 6): 'Rauberhauptmann'. This is, in fact, the judgement of Eusebius, *HE* iv, 6, 2: Φονικὸς καὶ λῃστρικός τις ἀνήρ.

[11] Bowersock, *op. cit.*, pp. 132; 138.

[12] M.D. Herr, 'The Causes of the Bar-Kokhba War', *Zion* 43 (1978), pp. 10–11 (in Hebrew).

[13] *Idem*, 'The Participation of Galilee in the "War of Qitos" (= Quietus) or in the "Ben Kosba Revolt"', *Cathedra* 4 (1977), pp. 67–73 (Hebrew) Bowersock, (above, n. 10), pp. 132–4. See below, p. 49.

[14] Below, pp. 54 f.

[15] yTa'anit iv 68d–69b; Lamentations Rabbah ii 4; *ibid.*, ed. Buber, pp. 100–109; bGittin 57a–58a.

focussing on (1) the quality of Bar Kokhba's leadership; (2) the attitude of the sages towards the rebellion and Bar Kokhba personally; and (3) the fall of Bethar and the aftermath of the revolt. Little information exists on the causes and course of the war, but talmudic sources must be taken into account when considering its geographical scope, the possible conquest of Jerusalem and the reconstruction of the Temple by the rebels.

The evaluation of the Talmud as an historical source is problematic in general, and this is particularly true of the evidence relating to the revolt. The character of talmudic literature is such that historical facts are mentioned incidentally only. The aim of the Talmud is not historiography. It concentrates on legislation (*halakhah*) and on theological didactics (*aggadah*). One may find there in juxtaposition sources from the period of the revolt itself; sources dating to the years after the revolt showing the deep impression made by failure and defeat; anachronistic descriptions of historical situations clearly reflecting a later period; sources which attempt to solve in a historiosophic manner problems connected with the revolt. All these are bound to have been distorted by later editors for whom the revolt was a nebulous event which took place in ancient history.

The revolt of Bar Kokhba was at first studied by scholars who did not seriously examine talmudic material or considered it as of only marginal importance.[16] Others accepted each talmudic source at its face value, as authentic information. Where they encountered internal contradictions, they tended to resolve them by reconciliation.[17] G. Alon laid the foundations of the modern study of the period of the Mishnah and the Talmud through critical examination of talmudic literature. He took it upon himself to separate the authentic historical kernel from the mass of halakhic and aggadic material, while combining this with evidence from Greek and Latin literature. Alon, in his treatment of the revolt, attempted to analyze basic problems such as the geographic scope of the war, involvement of the Samaritans and the attitude of the sages towards the rebellion.[18]

Recently, two methods of analysis have been developed which go much further than Alon's in their critical evaluation of talmudic sources. The first emphasizes that the rebellion must be studied in

---

[16] See e.g. F. Gregorovius, *Der Kaiser Hadrian* ([3]1884), pp. 188–216.
[17] For instance, I. Halevy, *Dorot ha-Rishonim*, iv ([2]1967), pp. 574–672.
[18] G. Alon, (above, n. 7), i (1953), pp. 265–289; ii (1956); pp. 1–47; 263.

the light of the preceding period, through comparative analysis of the
talmudic sources regarding the First Revolt.[19] The authenticity of the
sources is analyzed, particularly the respective reliability of the Jerusalem and the Babylonian Talmuds, their background, the way in which
they were edited, and their particular tendencies. These scholars are
highly critical of the Babylonian sources, which are remote chrono-
logically and geographically, and were later distorted for extraneous
purposes, such as the preservation of good relations with the gentile
authorities. On the other hand, they consider the Palestinian sources
as containing authentic historical evidence in addition to a mass of
legendary material. The second method dissects talmudic sources into
their component parts and studies each source separately, considering its historical relevance, if any.[20] This approach might seem to be
the most precise of all. Its strength lies in the elimination of speculation prevalent in previous research, but a fundamental weakness is
that it fails to consider the sources in combination, and this sometimes results in conjecture that is no better founded than that which
it criticized in the first place.

Greek and Latin Sources

The relevant Greek and Latin sources are discussed in various works
dealing with the revolt.[21] It is generally admitted that Dio's account
provides the sole consistent survey, but the text is preserved only in
the Byzantine epitome of Xiphilinus.[22] Moreover, it is a general description, not an account of the course of the war. For its causes, the
Historia Augusta is important as the only source to mention a ban on

---

[19] J. Efron, 'Bar-Kokhva in the Light of the Palestinian and Babylonian Tal-
mudic Traditions', in: *The Bar Kokhba Revolt—New Studies*, ed. A. Oppenheimer and
U. Rappaport (1984), pp. 47–105; I. Ben-Shalom, 'Events and Ideology of the Yavneh
Period as indirect Causes of the Bar-Kokhva Revolt', *ibid.*, pp. 1–12; *id.*, 'The Sup-
port of the Sages for Bar-Kokhba's Revolt', *Cathedra* 29 (1983), pp. 13–28 (all in
Hebrew).

[20] Schäfer (above, n. 9); D. Goodblatt, 'Did the *Tannaim* support Bar-Kokhva?',
Cathedra 29 (1983), pp. 6–12; *idem*, 'The Title *Nasi* and the Ideological Background
of the Second Revolt' in: *New Studies* (above, n. 19), pp. 113–132 (both papers in
Hebrew).

[21] See in particular: M. Stern, *Greek and Latin Authors on Jews and Judaism*, ii (1980),
nos. 332; 342; 343; 353; 440; 511. Patristic sources are mentioned in the commentary but not cited in full.

[22] *Dio* LXIX 12, 1–14, 3: 15, 1. Cf. Stern (above), no. 440 and F. Millar, *A Study
of Cassius Dio* (1964), pp. 60–72.

circumcision preceding the revolt.[23] The *Historia Augusta* is, of course, a most unreliable and problematic work. We may add that the statement there gives the impression of being a hostile pronouncement, disparaging circumcision and providing the reputed reason for the revolt. This does not mean that it is untrue; but Dio, even in Xiphilinus' version, is not hostile. Christian sources are remote in time and antagonistic towards the Jews, yet it cannot be denied that they and the Jewish sources have features in common which they do not share with Dio: references to Bar Kokhba, Tineius Rufus and the fall of Bethar, as opposed to the statement regarding Julius Severus in the latter source. This may partly be explained by the circumstance that Jewish and Christian sources are, in fact, local sources, while Dio presumably based himself on Roman material. However, it is also possible that talmudic literature and the Church Fathers reflect, to a certain extent, a common tradition, even though they have no common sympathy. We have, altogether, four contemporary references to the war. Three are isolated sentences (Appianus, Fronto and Pausanias).[24] The fourth does not even mention the revolt specifically (Apollodorus of Damascus).[25] Our sources are deficient, however they are interpreted.

Samaritan Chronicles

There exists no systematic discussion of the Samaritan chronicles related to the revolt, but various scholars mention them in their works.[26] The chronicles date to the Middle Ages and they are very

---

[23] *Scriptores Historiae Augustae, vita Hadriani* 14, 2. Cf. Stern. (above, n. 21), no. 511.

[24] Appianus, *Syriaca* 50, 252. Cf. Stern (above, n. 21), no. 343; Fronto, *de bello Parthico*, 2; cf. Stern, no. 342; Pausanias, *Graeciae descriptio* I, 5, 5; cf. Stern, no. 353. Fronto refers to the great number of Roman soldiers killed under Hadrian in Britain (c. A.D. 118) and in the Jewish rebellion. Bowersock (above, n. 10), p. 132, singles out Fronto as the only author who gives us the contemporary Roman perspective, because no other writer mentions the British revolt as comparable with the Jewish one. The Jewish revolt received more publicity afterwards. Pausanias, however, another contemporary of Hadrian, mentions the Jewish war as the only event to disturb the peace in Hadrian's reign. It may be argued that Pausanias rather than Fronto gives us the Roman perspective, for Fronto listed as many disasters as he could. E. Champlin, *Fronto and Antonine Rome* (1980), p. 95, points out that 'an astonishing note of bitterness pervades Fronto's attitude to Hadrian'. The present passage is characteristic of the author's disparagement of that emperor.

[25] Apollodorus of Damascus, ed. R. Schneider 8, 10. Cf. Stern, (above, n. 21), no. 322.

[26] See e.g.: A. Büchler, 'The participation of the Samaritans in the Insurrection

probably influenced by the relationship between Jews and Samaritans as it developed in the period after the revolt.

Archaeological Exploration

Archaeological evidence gains in importance when literary sources are scarce. Accordingly, archaeology has more to contribute, relatively speaking, to our understanding of the Bar Kokhba revolt than to that of the First Revolt. The excavations at Masada, for instance, are valuable because among other things they confirm much of what Josephus relates; but they add comparatively little to what can be learned from the literary source. As regards the Bar Kokhba revolt, part of what we know derives exclusively from archaeological evidence, and elementary problems can be solved only—if at all—by systematic field-work.

Archaeological exploration has thrown light on the activities of both the Roman army and the Jewish insurgents. Despite the sensational discoveries of the past decades, much of what we now know is due to patient and systematic exploration begun in the nineteenth century. Of general importance and still invaluable is the *Survey of Western Palestine*.[27] Much of the network of Roman roads in the country was first indicated on the map of the *Survey*. French scholars first published two important inscriptions from Bethar: (1) a Roman milestone which shows that the Jerusalem–Beth Govrin road was constructed in 130, two years before the revolt broke out, when Hadrian visited the province;[28] (2) a military inscription recording troops which presumably took part in the siege of Bar Kokhba's last stronghold.[29] Bethar has not been excavated, but surface exploration has produced plans of the extant remains of the Roman siege-works and of the walls of the Roman camps near the site.[30]

---

of Bar Kokhba', *Magyar-Zsidó Szemle* 14 (1897), pp. 36–47 (in Hungarian) = *The Bar-Kokhva Revolt*, ed. A. Oppenheimer (1980), pp. 115–121 (in Hebrew); S. Yeivin (above, n. 7), index; Alon (above, n. 7), ii, pp. 24–26.

[27] C.R. Conder and H.H. Kitchener, *Survey of Western Palestine, Memoirs*, i–iii (1881–3). Roman roads and milestones are indicated on the map which was published in 1880.

[28] J. Germer-Durand, *RB* 3 (1894), 613; P. Thomsen, 'Die römischen Meilensteine der Provinzen Syria, Arabia und Palaestina', *ZDPV* 40 (1917), no. 282.

[29] *CIL* iii, no. 14155.2.

[30] Ch. Clermont-Ganneau, *Archaeological Researches in Palestine*, i, (1899), pp. 463–470; E. Zickermann, 'Chirbet el-jehūd (bettīr)', *ZDPV* 29 (1906), pp. 51–72; W.D.

Relevant to the history of the revolt is, further, the continued exploration of the Roman road network in the country. It is now known that most Roman roads were first constructed in the reign of Hadrian, before the revolt broke out.[31] On the other hand, archaeology has so far failed to uncover any traces of military construction (roads or camps) dating to the years of the war, apart from the remains at Bethar. Roads and forts had been tentatively ascribed to the period of the revolt,[32] but there is no evidence for this, and at least part of these forts are now known to be of Byzantine date.[33] Abel and others attempted to trace strategic roads which allegedly encircled the area of the revolt and their idea found wide acceptance.[34] However, this is definitely a misconception.[35]

Our knowledge concerning the Roman troops in the country before and during the revolt derives from Greek and Latin inscriptions found in Israel and in other countries. Important, too, is our familiarity

---

Carroll, 'Bittîr and its Archaeological Remains', *AASOR* 5 (1923/24), pp. 77–103, A. Alt, 'Römerstrasse Jerusalem-Eleutheropolis', *PJb* 23 (1927), pp. 9–15; A. Schulten, 'Masada, die Burg des Herodes und die römischen Lager, mit einem Anhang: Beth-Ter', *ZDPV* 56 (1933), pp. 180–184; A. Reifenberg, *Archaeology* 3 (1950), p. 41, fig. 3; Yeivin (above, n. 7), pp. 105–119, plates vi–xi; M. Kochavi (ed.), *Judaea, Samaria and the Golan, Archaeological Survey 1967–1968* (1972) (Hebrew), map 2 and sites nos. 4–6; 8; 10; 16–18; 23–26 on pp. 36–41.

[31] For the Roman road network in Judaea, see Thomsen (above, n. 28), pp. 1–102; B. Isaac, 'Milestones in Judaea, from Vespasian to Constantine', *PEQ* 110 (1978) pp. 47–60; I. Roll, 'The Roman Road System in Judaea', *The Jerusalem Cathedra* 3 (1983) pp. 136–161; Isaac and Roll, *Roman Roads in Judaea* i, *The Legio-Scythopolis Road* (1982).

[32] Kochavi (above, n. 30), p. 26, map 3.

[33] Y. Hirschfeld, 'A Line of Byzantine Forts along the Eastern Highway of the Hebron Hills', *Qadmoniot* 12 (1979), pp. 78–84 (Hebrew).

[34] C. Kuhl, 'Römische Strassen und Strassenstationen in der Umgebung von Jerusalem, i', *PJB* 24 (1928), p. 127, noted the importance of the construction of a Roman road past Bethar in 130, but asserted that Hadrian's road-building had only cultural and administrative significance and no military purpose. F.-M. Abel, *Géographie de la Palestine*, ii (1938), pp. 222 f., states incorrectly: 'La révolte des Juifs sous Barko-kèba, en 132–135, eut pour corollaire la création des voies de l'Idumée, d'Aelia à Hébron, d'Aelia à Éleutheropolis'. Yeivin (above, n. 7) followed this mistake and imagined that during the war a road from Eleutheropolis (Beth Govrin) to Lydda was also constructed. This formed the basis for his theory of strategic encirclement. M. Avi-Yonah, *The Holy Land from the Persian to the Arab Conquest* (²1977), pp. 184 f., misquoting and misinterpreting a midrashic text and archaeological evidence, confidently states that the line should be extended further northwards. Kochavi (above, n. 32) was influenced by this theory when he assigned road-construction to the years of the revolt. See also Smallwood (above, n. 8), p. 452, and M. Avi-Yonah, *Carta's Atlas of the Period of the Second Temple, the Mishnah and the Talmud* (1964), p. 83.

[35] For the evidence see: Isaac and Roll (above, n. 31), pp. 91 f. and n. 12 on p. 100.

with the physical setting in which the war was fought. Only an understanding of the nature of the terrain helps to explain its suitability for guerilla warfare.[36]

Coinage is part of the archaeological material discussed in any treatment of the revolt,[37] and the contribution of numismatic evidence towards our understanding of the revolt cannot be over-estimated. Coin-hoards help to determine the geographical scope of the revolt.[38] Here, recent discoveries are particularly important. As noted by Mildenberg, two-thirds of the total number of coins known have come to light after 1965.[39] The size of the Bar Kokhba coinage, and the quantities of coins issued, tell us something of the population and the economy of Judaea at the time of the revolt.[40] The legends and symbols on them embody the only extant contemporary pronouncements of the values and objectives of the insurgents.[41] Interpretation, however, became possible only after the chronology of the coinage was established in recent years. Finally, with the help of the coinage, specific problems may be solved such as the date of the foundation of Aelia Capitolina and the chronology of the revolt.

The hiding-places of the insurgents are, of course, among the most spectacular discoveries of recent times. The documents discovered give a sense of immediacy rare in the study of antiquity. The letters

---

[36] See the discussion by Applebaum (above, n. 7) pp. 25 ff., and cf. the original edition of Schürer (above, n. 1), which describes a revolt that, theoretically speaking, could have taken place anywhere in the world.

[37] G. Hill, *British Museum Catalogue of Coins, Palestine*, pp. civ–cviii; M. Narkiss, *The Coins of Palestine* i, *Jewish Coins* (1936), pp. 40 f.; 20–128; A. Reifenberg, *Ancient Jewish Coins* (²1947) pp. 33–8; 60–6; L. Mildenberg, 'The Eleazar Coins of the Bar Kokhba Rebellion', *Historia Judaica* 11 (1949), pp. 77–108; A. Kindler, 'The Coinage of the Bar Kokhba War', in: *The Dating and Meaning of Ancient Jewish Coins and Symbols*, Publications of the Israel Numismatic Society (1958), pp. 62–80; Y. Meshorer, *Jewish Coins of the Second Temple Period* (1967), pp. 92–101; 159–169; Kindler, *Coins of the Land of Israel; Collection of the Bank of Israel, A Catalogue* (1974), pp. 58–93; L. Mildenberg, 'Bar Kokhba Coins and Documents', *HSCP* 84 (1980), pp. 311–335: U. Rappaport, 'The Coins', in: Rappaport (above, n. 7), pp. 132–135. Note also: M. Philonenko, 'Observations sur des monnaies juives de la seconde révolte (132–125)', *CRAI* 1974, pp. 193–9; B. Kanael, 'Notes on the Dates used for the Bar Kokhba Revolt', *IEJ* 21 (1971), pp. 39–46, both highly speculative. For Roman coins relating to the revolt see: H. Mattingly, *Coins of the Roman Empire in the British Museum*, iii (1936), p. cxlii.

[38] Mildenberg, *HSCP* (above), pp. 320–5; D. Barag, 'A Note on the Geographical Distribution of Bar Kokhba Coins', *INJ* 4 (1980), 30–3.

[39] Mildenberg (above), pp. 311 f.

[40] *Op. cit.*, p. 327.

[41] See below, p. 46.

from the leader of the revolt have no parallel among ancient sources. Many of the texts discovered by Prof. Yadin are as yet unpublished, more than twenty years after they were found.[42] The documents throw a partial light on the organization of the revolt, on the personality of the leader and his priorities, but they add hardly anything to our knowledge of the causes and the course of the war.[43]

Hardly less spectacular is the find in recent years of great numbers of subterranean hiding-places, some of which can with certainty be assigned to the revolt of Bar Kokhba. Most occur within ancient settlements. They are caves cut from the rock, linked by low and narrow horizontal passages and by vertical shafts which connect different levels. The entrances are usually low and narrow and can be blocked from the inside. The hiding-places are provided with ventilation-shafts, water-tanks, store-rooms and niches for lamps.

These archaeological discoveries correspond in a remarkable manner to Dio's description of the Jewish refuges in the Bar Kokhba revolt: 'To be sure, they did not dare try conclusions with the Romans in the open field, but they occupied the advantageous positions in the country and strengthened them with mines and walls, in order that they might have places of refuge whenever they should be hard pressed, and might meet together unobserved under ground; and they pierced these subterranean passages from above at intervals to let in

---

[42] When this paper was sent to the press, shortly after Yigael Yadin's death, it was not clear to us whether there were any concrete plans regarding the unpublished documents. For the finds from the Murabba'ât caves see P. Benoit, J.T. Milik and R. de Vaux, *Discoveries in the Judaean Desert*, ii, *Les grottes de Murabba'ât* (1961); for the Nahal Hever finds, see Y. Yadin, *Judaean Desert Studies, The Finds from the Bar Kokhba Period in the Cave of Letters* (1963); for a preliminary report on the Bar Kokhba letters found there, see Yadin, 'Expedition D', *IEJ* 11 (1961), 36–52; for the Babatha archive, see the preliminary reports by Yadin: 'Expedition D', *IEJ* 12 (1962), pp. 227–57; esp. 235 ff. (on the Aramaic, Hebrew and Nabataean documents); see also *id.*, 'The Nabataean Kingdom, Provincia Arabia, Petra and En-Gedi in the Documents from Nahal Hever', *Ex Oriente Lux* 17 (1963), pp. 227–41; for a preliminary account of the contents of the Greek documents, H.J. Polotsky, *IEJ* 12 (1962), pp. 258–62; three documents published in full: *id.*, 'The Archive of Babatha', *Eretz-Israel* 8 (1967), pp. 46–50 (in Hebrew); N. Lewis, 'Two Greek Documents from Provincia Arabia' *Illinois Classical Studies* 3 (1978), pp. 100–114; H.J. Wolff, 'Römisches Provinzialrecht in der Provinz Arabia' *ANRW* ii 13 (1980), pp. 763–806; two letters from Bar Kokhba's headquarters to Ein Geddi: B. Lifshitz, 'Papyrus grecs du désert de Juda', *Aegyptus* 42 (1962), pp. 204–256. For the finds from other caves, see Y. Aharoni, 'Expedition B', *IEJ* 11 (1962), pp. 11–24; B. Lifshitz, 'The Greek Documents from Nahal Seelim and Nahal Mishmar', *ibid.*, pp. 53–621 (lists of names). Finally, Yadin's popular account, *Bar Kokhba* (1971).

[43] Cf. Applebaum's observations (above, n. 7), p. 1.

air and light' (Dio lxix 12:1(3); Loeb). Talmudic sources which deal
with the revolt contain descriptions of people hiding in caves.

Several archaeologists are of the opinion that these refuges are all
related to the Bar Kokhba revolt, an assumption that rests basically
on three arguments. First, in part of the subterranean strongholds
finds have come to light which must indubitably be assigned to the
revolt (Bar Kokhba coinage). Second, the refuges and the measures
taken to prevent their discovery and penetration from the outside
are so similar as to be virtually identical. This, it is argued, indicates
that there was a uniform plan behind their construction. Third,
emphasis is laid on the conformity of the archaeological evidence
with the words of Cassius Dio and talmudic sources.

Other archaeologists and historians doubt that all these hide-outs
are exclusively related to the period of the Bar Kokhba revolt. In
their view, they were prepared and used from the Hellenistic until
the Byzantine period. From a number of inscriptions and literary
sources it appears that the use of caves as bases and refuges by bandits
and terrorists in their fight against the authorities was common in
various periods.[43a] This, of course, is not to deny the use of subterranean hiding-places during the Bar Kokhba revolt also, as proved by
archaeological evidence and indicated by Cassius Dio. It must be
noted, however, that the talmudic sources relate only to the last stage
of the revolt and the period of persecution that followed.

First discovered was the cave in Wadi Daliyah, south-west of
Phasaelis in the Jordan valley.[44] Then followed the caves at Khirbat
al-'Arrub between Bethlehem and Hebron,[45] and at Khirbat al-'Aqed,
east of Emmaus (Nicopolis).[46] Of particular interest is the evidence
at Herodion of occupation during the two Jewish revolts,[47] since a

---

[43a] See in general B. Isaac, 'Bandits in Judaea and Arabia', *HSCP* 88 (1984),
171–203.

[44] N.L. Lapp and G.W.E. Nickelsburg, Jr., 'Discoveries in the Wâdī ed-Dâliyeh',
AASOR 41 (1974), pp. 49 ff.

[45] Y. Tafsir, 'A Cave of the Bar-Kokhba Period near 'Ain-'Arrub', *Qadmoniot*
8 (1975), pp. 24–7 (in Hebrew).

[46] M. Gichon, 'Military Aspects of the Bar-Kokhba Revolt and the subterranean
Hideaways', *Cathedra* 26 (1982), 30–42 (in Hebrew); see also E. Damati, 'Four Bar
Kokhba Coins from Khirbet el-'Aqd', *INJ* 4 (1980), pp. 27–9.

[47] See: V. Corbo, 'L'Herodion Di Giabal Fureidis', *SBF, Liber Annuus* 17 (1967),
pp. 113–116; G. Foerster, *IEJ* 19 (1969), pp. 123 f.; *id.*, in *Encyclopaedia of Archaeological Excavations in the Holy Land*, ii, ed. M. Avi-Yonah and E. Stern (1976), pp. 509 f.;
E. Netzer, *Greater Herodium* (1981), p. 9. For the coinage of the Second Revolt from
Herodion, see A. Spijkerman, *Herodion*, iii, *Catalogo delle monete* (1972).

rebel camp there is mentioned in one of the documents from Wadi Murabba'at.[48] Many rock-cut hiding-places have now been found in the *Shephelat Yehudah* (the foothills of Judaea) and elsewhere. New discoveries are being made regularly as systematic exploration continues. Some of these—if not all—were occupied in the time of the revolt of Bar Kokhba.[49] A number of similar artificial caves have now been explored in Lower Galilee as well.[50]

The Causes of the War

No subject relating to the war has been more discussed than its causes, but it can scarcely be said that progress has been made. It is remarkable how many scholars admit that this is a matter of controversy and then claim to produce a decisive argument in favour of their own opinion. The aim of the present paper is not to suggest a solution however, even though we too may have our personal preference. It will suffice here to indicate the current state of the debate.

---

[48] See Milik (above, n. 42), no. 24; Yadin, *IEJ* 11 (1961), pp. 51 f.; E.-M. Laperrousaz, 'L'Hérodium, quartiér général de Bar Kokhba?', *Syria* 41 (1964), pp. 347–358; Schäfer (above, n. 9), pp. 122–4.

[49] See A. Kloner, 'The subterranean Hideaways of the Judean Foothills and the Bar-Kokhba Revolt', *The Jerusalem Cathedra* 3 (1983), pp. 83–96 (a preliminary account); see also Y. Dagan, *Shephelat Yehudah* (1982, in Hebrew), pp. 32–4. Dagan argues that these hiding-places were used from the Hellenistic till the Byzantine periods; for a similar argument, see G. Foerster, *Cathedra* 28 (1983), pp. 155–7 (Hebrew). Note also Dagan's brief note in *Hadashot Arkheologiyot* 82 (1983), p. 58, with a sketch-map indicating the location of 69 caves prepared as hide-outs. The same issue contains reports on recent discoveries: Y. Patrich and R. Rubin, *ibid.*, pp. 40 f. on caves found in Wadi Suweinit, c. 6 km SE of Ramallah; D. Alon, *ibid.*, pp. 64–6, on the partial excavation of a small fort and rock-cut cave system in Nahal Yattir. The fort is said to have been built after the First Revolt, while the cave system has produced coins of the period of the Bar Kokhba revolt. Additional sites, also on the southern edge of the Hebron Mountains, are now being explored. For a discussion of the talmudic sources referring to refugees in caves in the period of the revolt, see A. Oppenheimer, *Cathedra* 26 (1982), pp. 24–29 (in Hebrew).

[50] Discussion and plans by Y. Tepper and Y. Shahar, *Jewish Settlements in Galilee in the Revolts against the Romans and the underground Hiding-Places* (published by the Department of Local Studies of the Qibbutz Movement, 1983, in Hebrew). In several caves, pottery ascribed to the second century has been found; in a cave at Shunem (Valley of Jezreel) coins from A.D. 59 to 76/7 have been collected. Several other caves have failed to produce any datable material. For a cave previously explored, see D. Bahat, 'A Roof Tile of the Legio VI Ferrata and Pottery Vessels from Horvat Hazon', *IEJ* 24 (1974), pp. 160–169.

The following causes or combination of causes are found in modern literature:

(1) The revolt was caused by Hadrian's decision to transform Jerusalem into a pagan city, as stated by Cassius Dio.

(2) It was caused by a ban on circumcision as indicated in the *Historia Augusta*.

(3) These sources may be combined. The revolt was caused by the decision to found Aelia Capitolina and by a ban on circumcision.

(4) Hadrian decided, or was believed to have decided, that the Jewish Temple in Jerusalem might be rebuilt. When it appeared that he would not permit this the Jews rebelled.

(5) Various scholars have suggested that the destruction of the Temple created a psychological climate which led to renewed violence, irrespective of any decisions which may have formed the immediate cause of the revolt.[51]

(6) It has been suggested that the economic situation contributed to the outbreak of the revolt.[52] S. Applebaum argues that the revolt took its initial impetus from peasant discontent engendered by expropriation and oppressive tenurial conditions.[53]

Most scholars advocate the third alternative in one form or another.[54] Several consider the foundation of Aelia Capitolina the sole

---

[51] Mommsen (above, n. 6), p. 543; Henderson (above, n. 6), pp. 213 f. Smallwood (above, n. 8), p. 438, speaks of endemic nationalism; Applebaum (above, n. 7), p. 9, and in Rappaport (above, n. 7), pp. 211–5. See also L. Huteau-Dubois, 'Les sursauts du nationalisme Juif contre l'occupation Romaine; de Massada à Bar Kokhba', *REJ* 127 (1968), pp. 172 f. The value of such arguments is denied by Bowersock (above, n. 10), pp. 132 f.; 138 and by Mildenberg (above, n. 37), pp. 332–4. See also below, p. 16.

[52] Alon (above, n. 7), ii, pp. 2–4.

[53] Applebaum (above, n. 7), pp. 9–17; *id.*, 'Judaea as a Roman Province', *ANRW* ii 8 (1977), pp. 385–95; *id.*, in Rappaport, *loc. cit.* For a different view, see Mildenberg, *loc. cit.*

[54] Mommsen (above, n. 6); Schürer in the German and in the revised versions (above, n. 1), pp. 671–9; and pp. 535–40 respectively. Similarly Abel (above, n. 1), pp. 83–6; Alon (above, n. 7), ii, pp. 9–15; Applebaum, (above, n. 7), pp. 7–9 and in Rappaport (above, n. 7), pp. 220–5; Herr (above, n. 12), pp. 1–11 lays emphasis on the ban on circumcision but considers it possible that the foundation of Aelia also was a factor; for the opposite view, see Henderson (above, n. 6), pp. 213 f.; Yeivin (above, n. 7), pp. 58–61. Yeivin's account of the outbreak of the war is otherwise wholly speculative. See also B. Lifshitz, 'Jerusalem sous la domination romaine', *ANRW* ii 8 (1977), pp. 473–5; Huteau-Dubois (above, n. 51); P. Prigent, *La fin de Jérusalem* (1969), pp. 94–101. Smallwood (above, n. 8), pp. 428–38, considers these causes complementary to the evidence for continuous and increasing unrest in the years preceding the revolt.

cause of the revolt.[55] Only Bowersock and Mildenberg altogether reject Dio's statement that the foundation of Aelia Capitolina was the reason for the rebellion.[56] Bowersock argues that two years elapsed between Hadrian's visit to Judaea and the outbreak of the revolt there. That need not be decisive. Parallels show that the development of a Roman colony might proceed very slowly once the decision to found one had been taken.[57] The alleged permission given by Hadrian to rebuild the Jewish Temple, subsequently withdrawn, is not now considered a primary cause of the revolt by anyone.[58] Some contemporary

---

[55] Gregorovius (above, n. 16), pp. 188–91; Grätz (above, n. 1), pp. 133–5; Weber (above, n. 5), pp. 313 f.; M. Avi-Yonah, *RE* xiii *Suppl.* s.v. Palaestina, col. 403. Gregorovius assumes that the ban on circumcision followed the revolt. The other authors ignore the evidence for the ban. The ban is specifically rejected as cause of the revolt by H. Strathmann, 'Der Kampf um Beth-Ter' *PJb* 23 (1927), p. 99, n. 1; H. Bietenhard, 'Die Freiheitskriege der Juden unter den Kaisern Trajan und Hadrian und der messianische Tempelbau', *Judaica* 4 (1948), pp. 92–4; D. Rokeaḥ, 'Comments on the Revolt of Bar Kokhba', *Tarbiz* 35 (1966), pp. 127–130 (in Hebrew); J. Geiger, 'The Ban on Circumcision and the Bar-Kokhba Revolt', *Zion* 41 (1976), pp. 139–47 (in Hebrew).

[56] Bowersock (above, n. 10), pp. 135 f.; Mildenberg (above, n. 37), pp. 332–4. A. Schlatter, *Die Tage Trajans und Hadrians* (1897), pp. 1 f.; 11 f.; 31; 40; 88–99, argued that the revolt was not caused by any provocation on the part of the Romans. 'Hadrian hat nicht durch Bedrückung sondern durch sein Entgegenkommen die Leidenschaft des Volkes zu diesem furchtbaren Ausbruch gebracht'. Schlatter considered this the final battle of the Jewish people. He was first of all interested in the confrontation between Jews and Christians. This preoccupation is even more apparent in his brochure: *Wird der Jude über uns siegen? Ein Wort für die Weihnachtszeit* (Velbert im Rheinland, 1935). H. Mantel, 'The Causes of the Bar Kokhba Revolt', *JQR* 58 (1967–1968), pp. 224–242; 274–296, also rejects both the cause given by Dio and that mentioned in the *Historia Augusta*. He argues that Eusebius describes the true state of affairs: 'It was not the decrees of Hadrian that caused the revolt, but Hadrian's decrees constituted a reaction to the Jewish revolt'. See also Mantel's 'Postscript', *ibid.*, 59 (1968–1969), pp. 341–2. Mantel's theory is basically the same as that of Schlatter. A similar approach to a different conflict may be found in a recent study of the American War of Independence: R.W. Tucker and D.C. Hendrickson, *The Fall of the British Empire: Origins of the American Independence* (1982). The authors attempt to show that the colonies were the challenging power, while Britain's attitude was too passive and conciliatory. Britain's policy 'was one of appeasement' and this, according to the authors, was the real cause of the conflict.

[57] The walls of Aquileia were built in 169 B.C., twelve years after the foundation of the colony (Livy xliii 1; 17). Note also the early history of Placentia and Cremona, cf. B. Isaac, *Talanta* 3 (1971), pp. 20 f. There were military colonies built in hostile territory. For the Roman colonies in Judaea see Isaac, 'Roman Colonies in Judaea: The Foundation of Aelia Capitolina', *Talanta* 12–13 (1980–1981), 31–54, = ch. 8.

[58] It was considered an immediate cause of the revolt by several scholars in the 19th century, notably Grätz (above, n. 1), pp. 125 ff.; J. Derenbourg, *Essai sur l'histoire et la géographie de la Palestine* (1867), pp. 412–420; Schlatter (above, n. 56), 59–67 states without hesitation that the temple was virtually completed when the revolt broke out.

studies, however, are not prepared to reject the story absolutely and assume there may be some truth in it.[59]

A few additional observations may be made. The coin legends, 'Jerusalem' and 'For the Freedom of Jerusalem', and the design of the Temple on the coinage, are not mint indications but programmatic declarations.[60] Accordingly, they cannot decide whether Jerusalem was taken by the insurgents. They provide, however, the only extant contemporary pronouncements in regard to the values and objectives, both of the leadership of the revolt and of the recipients of the coins. Jerusalem clearly was of central importance to the rebels, whether they temporarily captured the city or not.

Several studies refer to the praise of Hadrian in the fifth Sibylline Oracle (11.46–50), composed by a Jew before the end of Hadrian's reign. It has been variously interpreted:

(1) as confirmation that Hadrian was popular among the Jews early in his reign;[61]

(2) as an indication of the attitude of the Jews toward Hadrian at the time of his visit to Judaea in 130, before the presumed ban on circumcision.[62]

(3) Schäfer goes much further. He considers this passage evidence of support among Hellenizing Jews in Palestine for Hadrian's policy regarding Judaism. As in the time of the Maccabees, the ruler was encouraged to impose Hellenism by a group of Jews in the country, and the revolt was started by their rivals, who remained unnoticed until it was too late. This is an artificial transfer of the situation in the second century B.C. to that three centuries later, and the Sibylline Oracle is no sufficient basis for such a theory.[63]

---

[59] Bietenhard (above, n. 55), pp. 85–108: Alon (above, n. 7), i, pp. 276–89; Yeivin (above, n. 7), pp. 52 ff.; M.D. Herr, 'Persecutions and Martyrdom in Hadrian's Days', *Scripta Hierosolymitana* 23 (1972), p. 91; Smallwood (above, n. 8), pp. 434–6; M. Gichon, 'The Bar-Kochba War: A Colonial Uprising against Imperial Rome', *Revue International d'Histoire Militaire* 42 (1979), pp. 82–97; Applebaum, in Rappaport (above, n. 7), p. 209. The story is rejected by Schürer (above, n. 1), (⁴1909), pp. 671–3; (1973), pp. 535 f.; Strathmann (above, n. 55), pp. 103–5; Schäfer (above, n. 9), pp. 29–34.

[60] Mildenberg, *HSCP* (above, n. 37), p. 325.

[61] Gregorovius (above, n. 16), pp. 37 f.; Grätz (above, n. 1), pp. 126–8; Alon (above, n. 7), i, pp. 1; 282–4; Rokeah (above, n. 55), p. 130.

[62] Bowersock (above, n. 10), p. 134.

[63] Schäfer (above, n. 9), pp. 48–50, a surprising speculation for an author whose declared aim is to combat the uncritical use of literary sources.

As for Hadrian, it is hard to determine what he knew or what he could have known, what he felt about the Jews and what he hoped for in Judaea. It is true that he did not wage wars of conquest, but all that we know about his religious policy shows him to have been intolerant and an activist.[64]

It may now be considered certain that Aelia Capitolina was formally founded before the outbreak of the war for it has been shown that foundation coinage of the colony was issued before the end of the revolt.[65]

As noted above, it is not our aim to offer a solution for problems which, on the evidence available, apparently remain debatable. Something may however be said about the nature of the debate. Without demeaning the importance of the various questions discussed, it may be observed that two major issues are, in fact, at stake: the ultimate responsibility for and justification of the revolt; and the credibility of the ancient sources, Graeco-Roman, Jewish and Christian respectively. The discussion is essentially about the values, morals and achievements of both sides, according to ancient norms and those of our own times. Summing up, we shall now list again modern views on the causes and background of the revolt.

A. *The Romans*

(1) The Romans consciously intended to suppress Judaism in Judaea. Some authors consider such a policy laudable or necessary, others condemn it as imperialist oppression.

(2) An activist and intolerant policy threatened values fundamental to the Jews.

(3) The Jews felt themselves threatened by actions which were not aimed at Judaism in particular and hence cannot be considered anti-Jewish.

---

[64] Cf. W. den Boer, 'Religion and Literature in Hadrian's Policy', *Mnemosyne* 8 (1955), pp. 123–144 = *Syngrammata* (1979), pp. 197–218.

[65] Meshorer (above, n. 37), pp. 92 f., reports on a coin-hoard which contained foundation coins as well as coins of the revolt. Mildenberg, *HSCP* (above, n. 37), p. 333, observes that coins of Aelia bear the legend 'Imp. Caes. Traiano Hadriano', a legend impossible after the Bar Kokhba war. Other coins bear the early legend 'Imp. Caesar Had. Aug.' with a head of Sabina and the inscription 'Sabina Augusta' (not: Diva Sabina) on the reverse. Sabina died in 136. Cf. L. Kadman, *The Coins of Aelia Capitolina* (1956).

B. *The Jews*

(1) There is disagreement as regards the situation preceding the revolt. Was there prolonged unrest before 132? If so, this would show that they were acting in response to the climate created by the Roman occupation. Among those who assume that this was the case, some conclude that it explains, or even justifies, their rebellion. Others, on the contrary, assert that it justifies strong Roman action against the rebels.

(2) Should one sympathize with the ideology of the insurgents (itself a matter of debate)?[66] Were Bar Kokhba and his followers fanatic bandits or heroic freedom-fighters, or both?

(3) Schäfer's view: there were Jews who supported Hadrian's Hellenizing policy, which itself was not hostile in character.

As regards the sources, these are usually interpreted so as to confirm a specific conception of the events. However, a matter of disagreement in its own right is the evaluation of talmudic sources. On the one hand, there are those who assume that judicious interpretation will find much that is of value to the historian. On the other, there is a conviction that no authentic history can be drawn from these sources unless the contrary can be proved.

Prior Unrest

It is clear that the Bar Kokhba revolt did not erupt spontaneously. The question is, how far can its origins be traced? Not much is known about the period between the wars, but according to some scholars

---

[66] See below, p. 49, for views of the ideology of the rebels. One example of total rejection of their aims may be cited: 'Kein fühlender Mensch wird dem Schicksal des Judenvolk seine Teilnahme versagen, aber kein ruhig denkender sich vorstellen, dass der Sieg eines Akiba und Barkocheba einen Fortschritt in der geschichtlichen Entwicklung auch nur Asiens würde bezeichnet haben. Die Herstellung eines selbständigen Judenstaates war undenkbar und unmöglich. Er hätte die ganze Schöpfung Roms in Syrien, vom Euphrat bis zum roten Meer zersprengt, und an die Stelle der hellenistisch-römischen Cultur den beschränkten semitischen Fanatismus und die religiöse Unduldsamkeit gesetzt. Die kosmopolitische Idee des Römerreichs hatte keinen gleich hartnäckigen Feind als das Judenvolk, und deshalb wurde dieses als Staatsprincip umgebracht' (Gregorovius, above, n. 16, p. 204). Gregorovius has no doubt that it was a blessing to be part of the Roman Empire. Those who thought otherwise were fanatics in his opinion. Similar or opposite assumptions, even though expressed in less peremptory or explicit form, still influence the debate about Bar Kokhba.

talmudic sources when properly analyzed allow a partial insight in the political development of Judaism in Judaea. It is argued that the activities of the Jewish authorities must be studied from the years of recovery after the First Revolt up to the revolt in the diaspora in the reign of Trajan. Some even see a connection between the ideology that gave the Bar Kokhba revolt its impetus and the attitudes of the zealots in Pharisaic circles in the period before the First Revolt. These are said to have been among the followers of Beth Shammai.[67] In any event, it is intrinsically likely that a connection existed between the activities of the Jewish authorities at Yavneh and the revolt of Bar Kokhba.

Two different effects of their endeavours may be mentioned. In reshaping the life of the nation after the loss of Jerusalem and the Temple, the authorities went to great effort to prevent the people from being wholly cut off from religion as practised in the days of the Second Temple. Thus they repeatedly emphasized that the Temple would soon be rebuilt. This was not an abstract phrase, but a firm expectation which formed the basis of the development of *halakhot* and the routine of daily life.[68]

Second, the leaders at Yavneh did much to intensify the unity of the nation. In this period many of the parties and sects disappeared which had typified the life of the people before the destruction of the Temple. At the same time, many groups, including the Jewish Christian sects, were expelled from the Jewish community. It is likely that there was a connection between this policy, which actively sought to unite the people, and the undivided resistance to Rome under the leadership of Bar Kokhba. This unity certainly contributed to the impact of the rebellion, as did the fact that there was no Jewish party at that time opposed to the revolt.[69]

The fierce rebellion of the Jews in the diaspora in 115–117 is well attested in various sources. It is a subject of debate whether the Jews in Judaea participated. The literary sources do not convince everybody.[70] It has been argued that there was unrest in Judaea in the

---

[67] I. Ben-Shalom, *Cathedra* (above, n. 19), pp. 13–19; *id.*, *The Shammai School and its Place in the Political and Social History of Eretz Israel in the First Century* A.D. (Ph.D. Thesis, Tel Aviv, 1980).

[68] Alon (above, n. 2), pp. 111–118; 253–265; Ben-Shalom, in *New Studies* (above, n. 19), p. 11.

[69] Alon (above, n. 2), pp. 288–307. Note, however, Schäfer's suggestion (above, p. 48).

[70] Several authors believe there was a large scale war: Grätz (above, n. 1), pp.

subsequent period preceding the Bar Kokhba revolt.[71] Epigraphical
and archaeological evidence has now shown that the Roman army
in Judaea was reinforced before 120, probably in 117, an indication
that there must have been trouble in those years.[72] The evidence for
the strengthening of the army in Judaea is as follows. It is certain
that the rank of governor[73] and that of procurator[74] rose in importance before the Bar Kokhba revolt, a change which must have
entailed the addition of a second legion to the provincial army. In
120, a road was constructed from Legio (Caparcotna, Kefar 'Otnay)
to Sepphoris, proof of the location of a military camp at the former
site, later the fortress of the legion VI Ferrata. In the same year a
road was constructed from Ptolemais (Acco) to Sepphoris. On a
milestone of that year, the Leg(io) II (Traiana) is mentioned, which
proves that it was in the area together with the X Fretensis, based

112–6; M. Avi-Yonah, 'When did Judea become a Consular Province?', *IEJ* 23 (1973),
p. 213; M. Pucci, *La rivolta ebraica al tempo di Traiano* (1981), pp. 104–119; Bietenhard
(above, n. 55), pp. 69–73. The majority assume that there were upheavals but no
war in the full sense of the term: Gregorovius (above, n. 16), pp. 24–7 (the only
scholar, so it seems, who repeats without scepticism Dio's story about Jewish canni-
balism); Alon (above, n. 7), i, pp. 255–263; Schürer (above, n. 1), (1973), pp. 533 f.;
Smallwood (above, n. 8), pp. 421–7, and her earlier paper: 'Palestine c. A.D. 115–
118', *Historia* 11 (1962), pp. 500–10; Applebaum, *Prolegomena* (above, n. 7), p. 18 and
in Rappaport (above, n. 7), pp. 208; 211 f.; D. Goodblatt, 'The Jews of Eretz Israel
in the Years 70–132', *ibid.*, p. 182; I. Shatzman, 'Armed Confrontation between
Romans and Jews', *ibid.*, pp. 324 f. There was no revolt in Palestine according to
Derenbourg (above, n. 58), pp. 404–8; Schlatter (above, n. 56), pp. 88 f. D. Rokeaḥ,
'The War of Kitos', *Scripta Hierosolymitana* 23 (1972), pp. 79–84, argues that 'Kitos'
of the talmudic sources is not Lusius Quietus, governor of Judaea, but Quintus
Marcius Turbo, who suppressed the Jewish rebellion in Egypt. According to this
theory, the sources would not refer to a war in Judaea but only to the revolt in the
diaspora. The theory, however, is not convincing, for Roman citizens were not usually
referred to by their first name (*praenomen*).

[71] Strathman (above, n. 55), p. 107; Alon (above, n. 7), ii, pp. 1–15; Mantel
(above, n. 56); Smallwood (above, n. 8), pp. 421–7; Applebaum, *Prolegomena* (above,
n. 7), p. 18, and in Rappaport (above, n. 7), pp. 211–215; Goodblatt, *ibid.*, p. 182;
Shatzman, *ibid.*, pp. 324 f. Bowersock (above, n. 10), p. 133, rejects their argument
and states that there is no evidence for prior unrest.

[72] For references, see B. Isaac and I. Roll, 'Judaea in the early Years of Hadrian's
Reign' *Latomus* 38 (1979), pp. 54–66.

[73] Tineius Rufus, legate of Judaea when the revolt broke out, was suffect consul
in 127. The significance of this was first pointed out by R. Syme, *JRS* 48 (1958),
p. 1 with n. 5.

[74] H.-G. Pflaum, 'Remarques sur le changement de statut administratif de la
province de Judée: à propos d'une inscription récemment découverte à Sidé de
Pamphylie', *IEJ* 19 (1969), pp. 225–233, observed that in 123 the procurator of
Judaea was a *ducenarius*. Consequently the legate must have been of consular rank
by that time.

on Jerusalem.[75] At least one other unit was transferred to Judaea between 91 and 124.[76] Furthermore the construction of military roads in Galilee is significant in itself. Long ago it was pointed out by A.H.M. Jones that the coinage of Tiberias of 119/120 had, for the first time, a pagan character, an indication perhaps that the local administration had been transferred to non-Jewish elements. The same may have happened at Sepphoris and Neapolis.[77]

All this is best explained as the Roman response to local unrest in 117/8. Something may also be said about the subsequent period in this connection. It has gradually become clear that most Roman roads in Judaea were first constructed in 129/130.[78] It has been assumed that the roads were built in preparation for Hadrian's visit to the province.[79] Parallels from other provinces suggest, however, that such a programme was military in character and part of plans for taking drastic measures.[80] If this is true, it is possible that they were a response to unrest in the preceding years; but there is no proof for this assumption.

In sum, it may be concluded that there is evidence of increased Roman military activity in the area, both in the years following Trajan's death and in 129/130, which may reflect a response to local

---

[75] B. Isaac and I. Roll, 'Legio II Traiana in Judaea', *ZPE* 33 (1979), pp. 149–156, Pl. vi. Our reading has been questioned by J.R. Rea, *ibid.*, 38 (1980), pp. 220 f.; for our reply, see *ibid.*, 47 (1982), p. 131, Pl. xi. For the date of the Legio-Sepphoris road, see the article cited above, n. 72. Before the publication of these papers L.J.F. Keppie studied the disposition of the legions in the East in this period and concluded that there probably were two legions in Judaea: 'The Legionary Garrison of Judaea under Hadrian', *Latomus* 33 (1973), pp. 859–864. Cf. the recent paper by D. Kennedy, 'Legio VI Ferrata: The Annexation and Early Garrison of Arabia', *HSCP* 84 (1980), pp. 283–309.

[76] The Cohors I milliaria Thracum was in Syria in 91 (M. Roxan, *Roman Military Diplomas 1954–77* (1978), no. 4) and is mentioned in a document from the 'Babatha archive', referring to 124, which shows that it was in Judaea by that time. Cf. H.J. Polotsky, *IEJ* 12 (1962), p. 259. The unit was still in the province in 139 (*CIL* xvi 87) and in 186 (Roxan, *RMD*, no. 69). See Smallwood (above, n. 8), p. 422, n. 136; M. Speidel, 'A tile-stamp of the Cohors I Thracum milliaria from Hebron', *ZPE* 35 (1979), pp. 170–2; D. Kennedy, 'Milliary Cohorts', *ZPE* 50 (1983), p. 257.

[77] A.H.M. Jones, *The Cities of the Eastern Roman Provinces* (²1971), p. 278; *JRS* 21 (1931), p. 82; Isaac and Roll (above, n. 72), pp. 63 f.; A. Oppenheimer, 'The Jewish Community in Galilee during the Period of Yavneh and the Bar Kokhba Revolt', *Cathedra* 4 (1977), pp. 53–66 (in Hebrew).

[78] See Isaac, *Talanta* 12–13 (above, n. 57), pp. 44–6; Isaac and Roll (above, n. 31), pp. 91 f.

[79] Avi-Yonah, *The Holy Land* (above, n. 34), pp. 183 f.; *RE Suppl.* xiii, s.v. Palaestina, col. 400; Bowersock (above, n. 10), p. 134.

[80] As argued by Isaac, *Talanta* 12–13 (above, n. 57), p. 46.

unrest, or preparations for the suppression of anticipated hostilities, or both.[81]

Pertinent to the period preceding the revolt is further talmudic testimony regarding Bethar, the last fortress of the insurgents. A number of sources indicate that this was an important Jewish town in the years between the two major wars and during the revolt of Bar Kokhba. Evidence shows that the Jewish authorities had their seat established at Bethar.[82] Rabban Simeon ben Gamaliel stated that he had been taught there as a pupil. We cannot assume that he was a student during the war, for he was appointed patriarch shortly afterwards. He will therefore have studied in this place before the revolt and it follows that the patriarchal family was settled there at the time. The transfer of the seat of the leadership to Bethar near Jerusalem is significant and reflects the hope that after its liberation the centre of Jewish authority would again be established there.[83] If excavations were to be carried out at Bethar, it might help to clarify the importance of the town before the revolt.

It has been claimed that the many travels of R. Aqiva to the diaspora were associated with preparations for the war. R. Aqiva is known as one of the leaders of the revolt and it is suggested that the aim of his journeys to the diaspora was to procure financial support or to recruit men for the war.[84] This theory lacks support. The sources do not suggest that these were other than conventional journeys to visit Jewish communities, to preach, solve halakhic problems and so forth. Moreover, R. Aqiva made some of his trips as member of a mission headed by Rabban Gamaliel, who travelled to the diaspora before the revolt in the reign of Trajan. R. Aqiva cannot, of course, have planned the revolt of Bar Kokhba before 115.[85]

---

[81] See also Smallwood (above, n. 8), pp. 436 f.; Shatzman (above, n. 70).

[82] See Alon (above, n. 7), ii, pp. 38–40; A. Oppenheimer in *Eretz Israel from the Destruction of the Second Temple to the Muslim Conquest*, i, ed. Z. Baras (1982, in Hebrew), pp. 48–50. The sources led Alon to assume that the Jewish leadership was established at Bethar only at the time of the revolt itself, while Oppenheimer concludes that part of these sources refer also to the years before the war.

[83] It is likely that the Jewish authorities were also established at Lydda for some time in the years between the revolt under Trajan and the Bar Kokhba revolt, see: Alon (above, n. 7), i, pp. 291–4.

[84] See e.g. Graetz (above, n. 1), pp. 135–6; I.H. Weiss, *Dor Dor we-Doreshaw*, ii (⁴1904), p. 3; Z. Frankel, *Darkei ha-Mishnah* (photostatic repr. 1959), p. 128; Avi-Yonah, *Carta's Atlas* (above, n. 34), p. 81.

[85] Cf. Halevy (above, n. 17), pp. 622–6; S. Safrai, *Rabbi Aqiva b. Yosef, Ḥayaw u-Mishnato* (1970), p. 30. It should be noted that, on general grounds, it is unlikely

Cassius Dio states explicitly that preparations for the war were made during the period between Hadrian's visit (in 130) and the outbreak of the revolt (in 132). The underground hiding-places which are now being explored may partly have been prepared in those years.[86]

The Course of the War

The literary sources and archaeological evidence do not allow of a description of the course of the war. In fact, we know nothing at all of the first stage of the rebellion; Cassius Dio passes it over in silence, possibly because the Jews were successful at that point. Talmudic sources, by contrast, refer again and again to the end of the war, impressed as they were by the ultimate failure of the rising and the fall of Bethar. Efforts in scholarly literature to give a full or partial account of the war are inevitably speculative.[87] In this connection, only three subjects can be debated: the geographical scope of the revolt, the question of whether Jerusalem was captured, and the size of the Roman forces which suppressed the rebellion.

(1) The Geographical Scope of the Revolt

The available evidence relates mainly to Judaea in the narrow and proper sense, and it appears that this is where most of the fighting took place. There is no consensus about whether the war spread at

---

that the Jews of the diaspora supported the Bar Kokhba revolt in a significant manner. The grave results of the revolt in the diaspora in the reign of Trajan will have precluded active participation of the Jews living in nearby countries. The persecution after the revolt of Bar Kokhba was aimed at the Jews in Judaea alone. This is indirect proof that the diaspora was not involved in the war on a large scale. Dio states that 'all Judaea had been stirred up, and the Jews everywhere (ἀπανταχοῦ γῆς) were showing signs of disturbance' (lxix 13:1, Transl. Cary, Loeb). This must be interpreted as referring to Judaea proper and the country as a whole. Cf. Oppenheimer (above, n. 82), p. 68.

[86] Above, pp. 43 f.

[87] See e.g.: Yeivin (above, n. 7), pp. 67–104; Avi-Yonah, *Carta's Atlas* (above, n. 34), pp. 82–4 with maps 123–8. In these works one may find detailed discussions and maps describing troop-movements and battles which are partly the product of the author's imagination and partly the result of over-interpretation (or misinterpretation) of literary sources and archaeological evidence. Recently M. Gichon (above, n. 46) has suggested that the discovery and excavation of subterranean hiding-places now allows the reconstruction of an outline of the course of the war.

all to Galilee[88] though admittedly a number of references in literary sources may point toward incidents in that region.[89] In any event, it cannot be presupposed that the revolt in Galilee resembled that in Judaea. All hoards containing coins of the second Jewish revolt were discovered in Judaea, notably in the Hebron mountains, west of Jerusalem, and in the Judaean desert.[90] The same is true of the underground hiding-places recently explored, although admittedly not many of those are firmly dated and some have now been found in Lower Galilee as well.[91]

Talmudic sources on the aftermath furnish additional information. Enactments dealing with the acquisition by Jews of landed property, confiscated by the Romans (*siqariqon*), were temporarily annulled in Judaea. The most likely explanation of this is that it was a response to large-scale land-expropriations by the Romans. The sages apparently wanted to preserve Jewish occupation of the land. On the other hand, it is stated in regard to Galilee that the enactments concerning *siqariqon* were always in force there.[92]

---

[88] The most comprehensive study has been that of A. Büchler, 'Die Schauplätze des Bar-Kochbakrieges und die auf diesen bezogenen jüdischen Nachrichten', *JQR* 16 (1904), pp. 143–205. Büchler concludes that the war was on the whole confined to Judaea proper. This had earlier been the view of Derenbourg (above, n. 58), pp. 427–9. On the other hand, Schlatter (above, n. 56); Schürer (above, n. 1), in the German edition, p. 685 (the revised ed., p. 545, is ambiguous); Yeivin (above, n. 7), pp. 67–74; 89–96; Gichon (above, 59), pp. 86–7; assert that Galilee took part in the rebellion. Yeivin even maintains that this is where the war broke out. Alon (above, n. 7), ii, pp. 19–23, accepts Büchler's view that Judaea was the main focus of hostilities, but he concludes that there is evidence in talmudic sources for manifestations of revolt in Galilee and in part of Transjordan. It must be noted, however, that talmudic sources testifying to economic hardship in Galilee after the war are not necessarily evidence of fighting there, as assumed by Alon. The cause may just as well have been the arrival in Galilee of great numbers of refugees or oppressive taxation after the war. In two recent papers it has been suggested that Roman military and administrative re-organization in Galilee and the Valley of Jezreel successfully prevented the outbreak of large-scale hostilities there: Isaac and Roll (above, n. 72), pp. 62–5; Oppenheimer (above, n. 77), pp. 53–66. It is suggested that the Roman re-organization in Galilee was prompted by events in the reign of Trajan (the 'War of Quietus'). See also the discussion on Oppenheimer's paper in the same issue, pp. 67–83, and, most recently, Applebaum, in Rappaport (above, n. 7), pp. 237–242.

[89] See A. Oppenheimer, 'Galilee during the Bar Kokhba Revolt: Collected Sources', *The Roman Period in Israel* (Published by the Department of Local Studies of the Qibbutz movement, 1973, in Hebrew), pp. 227–234.

[90] Above, p. 230 and n. 38.

[91] Above, p. 233 and nn. 49–50.

[92] yGiṭṭin v 47b. See S. Safrai, 'Siqariqon', *Zion* 17 (1952), pp. 56–64; Rokeaḥ (above, n. 55), pp. 125–131.

The focus of Jewish life was transferred to Galilee and the authorities established Ushah in Lower Galilee as their centre.[93] Refugees moved from Judaea to Galilee, as is illustrated by the organization of priestly courses in settlements in Galilee. Most of these courses were in Judaea in the period of the Second Temple.[94]

(2) The Conquest of Jerusalem

It is not clear whether Jerusalem was captured by the Jews in the revolt of Bar Kokhba. Appianus and Christian authors lend support to the view that the city fell into the hands of the Jews and was reconquered by Roman troops.[95] Those who adopt the opposite point of view explain that Cassius Dio, the best source, is silent on the subject.[96] The coin legend 'For the Freedom of Jerusalem' has been

---

[93] See Alon (above, n. 7), i, pp. 69–83; E.E. Urbach, 'From Judaea to Galilee', *J. Friedman Memorial Volume* (1974), pp. 59–75 (Hebrew); A. Oppenheimer, 'The Restoration of Jewish Settlement in Galilee' in *Eretz Israel* (above, n. 82), pp. 75–92.

[94] S. Klein, *Galilee* (²1967), pp. 62–8 (Hebr.); M. Zulai, 'The History of the Piyut in Eretz Israel', *Yediyot ha-Makhon le-Heker ha-Shirah be-Ivrit* 5 (1939), pp. 107–108 (in Hebrew); R. Degen, 'An Inscription from the Yemen of the Twenty-Four Priestly Courses', *Tarbiz* 42 (1972/3), pp. 302 f. (Hebrew), E.E. Urbach, 'Mishmarot and Ma'amadot' *ibid.*, pp. 304–327; M. Avi-Yohan, 'A List of Priestly Courses from Caesarea', *IEJ* 12 (1962), pp. 137–9; 'The Caesarea Inscription of the Twenty-Four Priestly Courses', *The Teacher's Yoke: Studies in Memory of Henry Trentham* (1964), pp. 45–57; Z. Ilan, 'A Fragmentary Inscription containing the Names of the Twenty-Four Priestly Courses discovered in the Vicinity of Kissufim', *Tarbiz* 43 (1973/4), pp. 225 f.; T. Kahane, 'The Priestly Courses and their geographical Settlements', *Tarbiz* 48 (1978/9), pp. 9–29 (both in Hebrew).

[95] Appianus (above, n. 24); Eusebius, *Demonstratio Evangelica* vi, 18, 10; *HE* iv, 5, 2; v, 12, 1. Two documents from Wadi Murabba'at may be relevant: Benoit, Milik and de Vaux (above, n. 42), no. 29, recto 1.9 and 11 (p. 142); no. 30, 1.8 (p. 145), cf. the *addendum* on p. 205. In the *addendum* Milik suggests that these documents, acts of sale, were signed in Jerusalem in August 133 and in the autumn of 134, which would imply that Jerusalem was occupied by the Jews at the time. However, the reading is uncertain and proceeds from the *a priori* assumption that Jerusalem was indeed occupied by the rebels. In fact, on p. 143 Milik proposes a different reading instead of the crucial 'at Jerusalem', which he later preferred. See also Applebaum (below, n. 98). See Smallwood (above, n. 8) for further patristic sources.

[96] Jerusalem was captured in the opinion of Schürer (above, n. 1), pp. 685–7 with n. 112; 691; (German edition, with references to older literature); 545 f.; 550 f. (revised edition); Abel (above, n. 1), pp. 92 f.; Avi-Yonah (above, n. 55); Derenbourg (above, n. 58), p. 431; Gichon, (above, n. 59), pp. 86 f.; Henderson (above, n. 6), p. 218; Huteau-Dubois (above, n. 51), pp. 180–3; Lifshitz (above, n. 54), p. 482; Mommsen (above, n. 6); Prigent (above, n. 54), p. 109; Smallwood (above, n. 8), pp. 443–5; Stern (above, n. 21), p. 180; Strathmann (above, n. 55), pp. 109–112; Weber (above, n. 5), pp. 313 ff.; Yeivin (above, n. 7), pp. 80–6. The latter even states that the Jews started rebuilding the walls. Abel, Avi-Yonah, Huteau-Dubois, Prigent, and

explained as celebrating the capture of the city, and the legend 'Jerusalem' has been interpeted as a mint indication. According to others, however, these legends describe war aims or hopes rather than achievements.[97] The evidence from Appian and Christian sources would seem decisive. However, as pointed out by Applebaum, the archaeological evidence, as it stands, raises grave doubts, for in the excavations carried out since 1967 in the Old City of Jerusalem almost no coins of the Second Revolt came to light.[98]

It may be added that a number of Midrashim speak of Hadrian as 'the destroyer of the Temple'.[99] This is a peculiar statement, and the late date seems to disqualify them as trustworthy sources for the problem here discussed.

The geographical scope of the rising in general, and the reconquest of Jerusalem, are important subjects in their own right, and yet, as so often in the discussion relating to the war, a significant element of ideology lies behind the arguments. At issue are the achievements of the rebels. If Bar Kokhba controlled the greater part of the province of Judaea and the capital Jerusalem for a considerable period, it is easier to justify his effort. Increased achievement enhances, in our view, the stature of Bar Kokhba and his men. If he did not control more than part of Judaea proper, excluding its centre, Jerusalem, he nowhere near approached success in modern eyes. There would be more reason to assert that the Jews should have known in advance that theirs was a lost cause. Total failure is hard to justify, easy to condemn.

Strathmann believe that a start was made with the reconstruction of the Temple. For the opinion of Milik see n. 95. Against Jewish capture of the town have argued Bowersock (above, n. 10), pp. 136 f.; Mildenberg, *HSCP* (above, n. 37), pp. 320–5; Schäfer (above, n. 9), and older works, cited by Schürer. See also n. 101 below.

[97] See Mildenberg, *loc. cit.*

[98] See Applebaum (above, n. 7), p. 27; Mildenberg, *HSCP* (above, n. 37), p. 323. This observation is true for the excavations conducted by B. Mazar west and south of the Temple Mount and for those conducted by N. Avigad in the 'Upper City', cf.: N. Avigad, *Ha'ir Ha'elyonah* (1980), pp. 205–7. Applebaum, in his more recent study, follows Milik (see n. 95) in asserting that Jerusalem was indeed captured by the rebels and held at least until September/October 134 (in Rappaport (above, n. 7), pp. 242; 245 f.; 254).

[99] See Deuteronomy Rabbah, *eqev* iii 13 (ed. Lieberman, based on the Oxford MS, p. 89); Tanḥuma *bereshit* vii; cf. Exodus Rabbah li 5; Tanḥuma *pequde* iv; Tanḥuma, ed. Buber, p. 128. Cf. Alon (above, n. 7), ii, p. 31.

(3) *The Roman Forces*

While significant discoveries have been made regarding the strength of the garrison in Judaea before the war, the same cannot be said about the Roman troops which participated in the war itself. This is not for want of interest. It merely shows that our knowledge depends on chance discoveries of inscriptions. When we compare recent lists of units known to have been sent to Judaea with one compiled more than eighty years ago we notice that they are virtually identical.[100]

Most of the new evidence is inconclusive, e.g., the numismatic evidence regarding the legion V Macedonica.[101] The participation of the XXII Deiotariana and its possible disbandment or destruction are uncertain.[102] Some new evidence has come to light regarding the legion II Traiana, and we now know that the praetorian cohorts probably fought in this war. This is of special interest because it indicates that the emperor himself was in Judaea at the same time. It could, however, already be inferred from literary sources and other inscriptions.[103]

---

[100] Compare Schürer's list in the original edition (above, n. 1), n. 116 on pp. 687–9, with that in the revised edition, n. 150 on pp. 547–9. See also the lists in Applebaum (above, n. 7), pp. 44–9; 65–8; Smallwood (above, n. 8), pp. 446–9; Stern (above, n. 21), pp. 397–400. Shatzman (above, n. 70), p. 327, lists the Legion I Italica as having dispatched a vexillation to Judaea. This is possible, since the two other legions from Moesia Inferior, the V Macedonica and the XI Claudia, are attested, but there is no evidence for the participation in the war of the I Italica.

[101] J. Meyshan, 'The Legion which reconquered Jerusalem in the War of Bar Kochba (A.D. 132–5)', *PEQ* 90 (1958), pp. 19–26 = *Essays in Jewish Numismatics* (1968), pp. 143–150, has published a foundation coin of Aelia Capitolina with the legend: 'LE V'. It has, however, been suggested that we are faced with an error for 'LE X': Applebaum (above, n. 7), n. 243 on pp. 83 f.; Isaac (above, n. 57), *Talanta* 12–13, p. 47, n. 75.

[102] The legion was in Egypt in 119 (*BGU* i, no. 140). It is missing from a list of legions from the period of Antoninus Pius (*ILS* 2288). Its disappearance may have been the result of events in the Bar Kokhba war. Cf. Ritterling, *RE* xii, s.v. Legio, cols. 1292; 1795; H.M.D. Parker, *The Roman Legions* (1928), pp. 162 f; J.F. Gilliam, *AJP* 77 (1956), p. 362; Smallwood (above, n. 8), pp. 446 f.; Applebaum (above, n. 7), pp. 26 f.; 36 with n. 296; Isaac and Roll (above, n. 72), pp. 59 ff. The possibility is mentioned with strong reservations by Schürer (above, n. 1, revised edition), p. 548; Keppie (above, n. 75), p. 863; Stern (above, n. 21), p. 398; Shatzman (above, n. 70), n. 153 on p. 437. Bowersock (above, n. 10), pp. 133 f., and Schäfer (above, n. 9), pp. 12–14 reject the theory.

[103] Cf. Dio lxix, 14, 3; the letter of Apollodorus of Damascus to Hadrian (*ap*. Stern, above, n. 21, no. 322 with introduction and comments on pp. 134 f.); also Jerome, *In Joel* i 4; *Chronicon Paschale* i (Dindorf, p. 474); for inscriptions see *ILS* 1065 which mentions Q. Lollius Urbicus as legate of Hadrian in the war and possibly *CIL* vi 974 referring to Hadrian himself. Gregorovius (above, n. 16), p. 197, denies that Hadrian was in Judaea during the war.

Tineius Rufus is known as governor of Judaea at the outbreak of the war from Jewish and Christian sources only,[104] but he is attested as suffect consul in 127.[105] Julius Severus is not mentioned in Jewish and Christian sources. Dio mentions his transfer from Britain to Judaea for the suppression of the revolt.[106] This is confirmed by an inscription which lists his career.[107]

Bar Kokhba, Leader of the Revolt

It is no coincidence that the revolt of Bar Kokhba was the only Jewish war fought against foreign rule in antiquity to have been named after one leader,[108] for a major contribution to the impact of the rising was the unity of the rebels under Bar Kokhba's leadership. In talmudic sources he is given the title 'Nasi and Messiah', and the years of his reign are described as kingship.[109] In his letters he assumes the title 'Nesi Yisrael', and on coins he appears as 'Simeon Nesi Yisrael'. The title 'Nasi' may be interpreted in various ways. It has been explained as denoting a limited form of authority lower in status than that of king and comparable to that of ethnarch, the title of the first Hasmonaean rulers.[110] Others assume that it refers to the ideal king as in Ezekiel's vision of the End of Days.[111]

R. Aqiva declared of Bar Kokhba: 'This is the King Messiah'.[112] The role of messiah, attributed to him has also been variously interpreted: as a divine and supernatural saviour and redeemer,[113] or as

---

[104] Eusebius, *HE* iv, 6, 1; *Chron.* Hadr. xvi (Schoene ii, pp. 166 f.).

[105] Schürer (above, n. 1, revised ed.), p. 518; Smallwood (above, n. 8), p. 550. See also n. 73, above.

[106] Dio lxix, 13, 2.

[107] *ILS* 1056. Cf. Schürer, p. 519 (revised ed.); Smallwood, p. 551; A. Birley, *The Fasti of Roman Britain* (1981), pp. 106–9.

[108] The Bar Kokhba revolt is referred to under that name in talmudic literature. See Seder 'Olam Rabbah xxx (ed. Ratner, p. 146): 'the war of Ben Koziba'.

[109] See for example bSanhedrin 97b: 'and the kingship of Ben Koziba two years and a half'.

[110] See Alon (above, n. 7), ii, p. 36.

[111] See Oppenheimer (above, n. 82), p. 51.

[112] yTa'anit iv 68d; cf. Lamentations Rabbah ii 4 (ed. Buber, p. 101).

[113] An extreme example of this view can be found in Y. Devir, *Bar Kokhba, the Man and Messiah in the light of Talmudic Literature and the Dead Sea Scrolls* (1964, in Hebrew). Devir sees Bar Kokhba as acting under the influence of the Dead Sea sect and inspiration from the desert, while the people considered him the messiah.

a general and leader of ordinary human stature whose title merely emphasizes his royal rank.[114]

Bar Kokhba is not mentioned by Cassius Dio or in the *Historia Augusta*. He is referred to only in talmudic and Christian sources. The latter describe him as a murderer and a bandit but at the same time attribute to him miracles and supernatural signs.[115] We cannot know whether these sources reflect authentic traditions regarding Bar Kokhba's status and deeds. Their aim may simply have been to blacken his image and to represent him as 'antichrist'.

Talmudic sources refer to Bar Kokhba ambivalently. On the one hand, they emphasize his legendary strength, R. Aqiva's admiration for him and even his obedience to the sages. On the other, they criticize his addresses to God, 'Do not help and do not humiliate', and it is said that he was put to death by the sages when it appeared that he was a false messiah.[116] There are diverse explanations for this ambivalent attitude, namely, that it reflects differences of opinion among the sages during the revolt, or a change of mind after the failure of the rising. Others wish to differentiate between an authentic attitude at the time of the war, and anachronistic opinions which actually date to the period of the redaction of talmudic literature.[117]

Bar Kokhba's letters give a partial but genuine impression of his personality. He seems to have been an aggressive general and ruler who occupied himself in person with details of discipline and daily life in his army units.[118] His leadership moreover extended beyond the sphere of military matters, for part of his letters deal with the

---

[114] See A. Oppenheimer, 'The Messianism of Bar Kokhba', in *Messianism and Eschatology* (The Historical Society of Israel, 1983, in Hebrew), pp. 153–165 with further references.

[115] See Eusebius, *HE* iv, 6, 2; Jerome, *Apol. in Libr. Rufini* iii 31 (*PL* xxiii, col. 480) and cf. Alon (above, n. 7), ii, p. 34.

[116] Disrespect for God can be found also in Palestinian sources, e.g. yTaʿanit iv 68d. Similar expressions are ascribed to the brothers from Kefar Ḥarivah (*ibid.*, 69a and parallel sources). See also the words of Bar Daroma (bGiṭṭin 57b). The execution of Bar Kokhba by sages occurs only in the Babylonian Talmud (bSanhedrin 93b).

[117] See Alon (above, n. 7), ii, p. 42; Oppenheimer (above, n. 114), pp. 156 f.; Goodblatt, *Cathedra* (above, n. 20), pp. 6–12; Ben Shalom, *Cathedra* (above, n. 19), pp. 19–28.

[118] Note e.g. the threats and reproaches in Bar Kokhba's letters to Masabala and Yehonatan, rebel commanders in the area of En Gedi, Yadin, *IEJ* 11 (1961) (above, n. 42), pp. 41 f.; 46 f.; or the threats addressed to men of the unit of Yeshua ben Galgoula: Benoit, Milik and de Vaux (above, n. 42), pp. 159–162.

leasing of lands on his behalf.[119] It appears that he insisted on the observance of religious commandments such as those of the sabbath, and precepts connected with the produce of the land. He even gave instructions concerning the supply of the four species of sukkoth.[120]

The Aftermath

Talmudic literature gives vivid and extensive descriptions of the horrors of the Jewish defeat, and much is written about the bitter fate of the besieged at Bethar.[121] Cassius Dio emphasizes the extent of the destruction and lists the numbers of those fallen in battle, and of forts and settlements destroyed. The accounts and the establishment of the Jewish authorities in Galilee have led some scholars to assume that all of Judaea was laid waste.[122] However, a closer look at the sources, and the archaeological evidence, clearly shows that Judaea was not permanently depopulated and that it certainly recovered within a few generations.[123] But the centre of authority did not return to the region nor did it regain the predominant position which is enjoyed among the Jews in other parts of the country and—to a certain extent—in the diaspora.

After the revolt, the Romans issued a number of decrees of religious persecution against the Jews there, but although they interfered with several aspects of religious life, their purpose was not the suppression of Jewish religion as such. Their tendency was to suppress those elements in the Jewish religion which were of national significance and to abolish the autonomy of the Jewish people. M.D.

---

[119] See e.g. Benoit, Milik and de Vaux, *op. cit.*, no. 24, pp. 124–128.

[120] Cf. A. Oppenheimer, 'Bar Kokhba and the Observation of Religious Precepts', *New Studies* (above, n. 19), pp. 140–146 (in Hebrew).

[121] yTa'anit iv 69a; Lamentations Rabbah ii 4. Talmudic literature contains a graphic description of the bitter fate of the refugees who hid in caves in the Judaean desert. The midrash tells of people who concealed themselves in caves and consumed the bodies of their friends until one of them found out that he had been eating the flesh of his father's corpse (Lamentations Rabbah i 45). This picture has been corroborated by archaeological evidence in the 'Cave of Horrors' where at least forty men took refuge, finally burning their possessions and dying while under siege (Y. Aharoni, 'Expedition B—The Cave of Horror', *IEJ* 11 (1962), pp. 186–199).

[122] E.g.: M. Avi-Yonah, *Geschichte der Juden im Zeitalter des Talmud* (1962), pp. 16–18.

[123] J. Schwartz, 'Judea in the Wake of Bar-Kokhba Revolt', *New Studies* (above, n. 19), pp. 215–223 (in Hebrew).

Herr emphasized in his study of the decrees of persecution that they did not include demands to violate religious prohibitions, such as idolatry or the consumption of prohibited food, but entailed only measures against religious injunctions.[124] S. Lieberman argues that they were not issued all at once, but that a gradual development may be discerned. He analyzes details of the decrees and the methods by which they were put into effect, and proves that they were in accordance with customary practice in the Roman Empire.[125] Schäfer disagrees with the total number of oppressive measures listed by Lieberman and Herr. He discusses each source separately and concludes that the terminology found in part of the sources does not necessarily refer to the period of the revolt or its aftermath.[126] As with other subjects, Schäfer's analysis of sources in isolation does not lead to results more logical than those reached in previous publications. Studying the sources in combination and against the background of what is known of Roman practice in parallel situations, Lieberman and Herr appear to formulate more convincing conclusions.

The response of the people and the sages to the decrees was not uniform. There were those who attempted to continue living according to Jewish law with modifications or in secret, while others openly ignored them and willingly faced execution. We may recognize here patterns of Jewish response to persecution which were to become familiar in later periods. Historical literary expression of such attitudes can be found in the traditions concerning the 'Ten Sages', martyred by the Romans, in religious *piyutim* of the Middle Ages, although not all the sages mentioned there were in fact killed for their faith during the persecutions following the revolt.[127]

---

[124] M.D. Herr, 'Persecutions and Martyrdom in Hadrian's Days', *Scripta Hierosolymitana* 23 (1972), pp. 82–125.

[125] S. Lieberman, 'The Martyrs of Caesarea' *Annuaire de l'Institut de Philologie et d'Histoire Orientales et Slaves*, 7 (1939–1944), pp. 395–446; *id.*, 'Religious Persecution of the Jews', *Studies in Honour of Salo Baron* (Hebrew section, 1975), pp. 213–245.

[126] Schäfer (above, n. 9), pp. 194–235.

[127] See S. Krauss, 'Ten Martyrs executed by the Romans', Ha-Shiloaḥ 44 (1925), pp. 10–22; 106–117; 221–223 (Hebrew); L. Finkelstein, 'The Ten Martyrs', *Essays and Studies in Memory of Linda Miller* (1938), pp. 29–55.

Progress and Controversy

It is the aim of this paper to trace the development of the study of the Bar Kokhba revolt during the past century. We have found both progress and controversy is fiercest. Progress depends on a patient analysis of sources and systematic archaeological exploration. Controversy, on the other hand, is instructive in that it clarifies modern attitudes towards Jewish resistance and towards the Roman empire, the object of this resistance.

Postscript

In the twelve years since the publication of this article scholarly activity has proceeded steadlily. Much of the published work consists of efforts at re-interpreting the previously available evidence. Several major publications of important new material should be mentioned here, however. Other publications are listed in the postscript to article 11, above.

Mildenberg, L., *The Coinage of the Bar-Kokhba War* (Aarau, 1984). This work appeared before our article, but unfortunately too late for us to take into account.

The Documents from the Bar Kokhba Period ed. by N. Lewis, (Jerusalem, 1989), discussed in article no. 11 in this volume.

H.M. Cotton and A. Yardeni, *Aramaic and Greek Texts from Naḥal Ḥever (the Seiyl Collection II), Discoveries in the Judaean Desert* XXVII, in press.

The Aramaic and Nabataean papyri from the Babatha archive and the Hebrew, Aramaic and Greek Bar Kokhba papyri will be published in: *Judaean Desert Studies. The Documents from the Bar Kokhba Period in the Cave of Letters*, II, by Y. Yadin, J.C. Greenfield, A. Jardeni (in press).

Broshi and Qimron have published a double document recording the sale of a house, written in year 3 of the revolt (A.D. 134–5).[1] The provenance is uncertain. The authors note (p. 207) that Kefar Baru, mentioned in the text, probably was a settlement east of the Dead Sea, Manyat Umm Hasan above the springs of Hammam ez-Zarqa, some 5 km N-W of Machaerus.[2] If this identification is correct (p. 214) and if this is also Kefar Bebayu of another document, published by Milik,[3] then Bar Kokhba's territory included the area east of the Dead Sea. This would explain very well why people like Babatha, Jews who had lived under, and presumably cooperated with Bar Kokhba's administration, felt the need to flee to Judaea when the Jewish forces lost control of the area where they lived.

---

[1] M. Broshi & E. Qimron, 'A House Sale Deed from Kefar Baru from the Time of Bar Kokhba', *IEJ* 35 (1986), 200–214.

[2] [Βα]αρου on the Madaba map, Βαάρας in Jos., *BJ* VII (181).

[3] J.T. Milik, 'Deux documents inédits du Désert de Juda', *Biblica* 38 (1957), 245–268, at 264–8.

M. Broshi, 'Agriculture and Economy in Roman Palestine: Seven Notes on Babatha's Archive', *IEJ* 42 (1992), 230–40.
231: ample evidence that life continued without interruption in the territory controlled by the rebels into the third, or even fourth year of the revolt (references in docs).

Additional Bibliography

D. Amit, and H. Eshel, 'A Tetradrachm of Bar-Kochba from a Cave in Nahal Hever', *INJ* 11 (1993), 33–35.

S. Applebaum, 'The Second Jewish Revolt', *PEQ* 116 (1984), 35–41.

R. Bauckham, 'Jews and Jewish Christians in the Land of Israel at the Time of the Bar Kochva War, with Special Reference to the Apocalypse of Peter', in G. Stanton and G. Stroumsa, (eds.), *Tolerance and its Limits in Early Judaism and Early Christianity* (Cambridge, 1995).

R. Fishman-Duker, 'Anti-Jewish Arguments in the Chronicon Paschale', in O. Limor and G. Stroumsa, *Contra Iudaeaos: Ancient Medieval Polemics between Christians and Jews* (Tübingen, 1996), 105–17.

G. Foerster, 'A Cuirassed Bronze Statue of Hadrian', *'Atiqot* 17 (1985), 139–60.

M. Gichon, 'New Insights into the Bar Kokhba War and a Reappraisal of Dio Cassius', *JQR* n.s. 77 (1986), 15–43.

D. Goodblatt, 'A Contribution to the Prosopography of the Second Revolt: Yehudah bar Menasheh', *JJS* 38 (1987), 38–55.

M. Hengel, 'Hadrians Politik gegenüber Juden und Christen', *JANES* 16–17 (1984–5) *Ancient studies in Memory of E. Bickerman*, 153–82 = Hengel, *Judaica et Hellenistica: Kleine Schriften*, I (Tübingen, 1996), 358–91.

B. Isaac, and A. Oppenheimer, 'The Bar Kokhba Revolt', *Anchor Bible Dictionary* (ed. D.N. Freedman), I (1992), 598–601.

L.J.F. Keppie, 'The History and Disappearance of the Legion XXII Deiotariana', in A. Kasher *et al.* (eds.), *Greece and Rome in Eretz Israel: Collected Essays* (Jerusalem, 1989), 54–61.

Y. Meshorer, 'A Coin Hoard of Bar-Kokhba's Time', *Israel Museum News* 4 (1985), 43–50.

L. Mildenberg, 'Der Bar-Kokhba Krieg im Lichte der Münzprägungen', in H.-P. Kuhnen, *Handbuch der Archäologie, Vorderasien ii/2, Palästina in griechisch-römischer Zeit* (Munich, 1990), 357–66.

——, 'Rebel Coinage in the Roman Empire', in *Greece and Rome in Eretz Israel*, 62–74.

M. Mor, 'Two Legions—The Same Fate? (The Disappearance of the Legions IX Hispana and XXII Deiotariana), *ZPE* 62 (1986), 267–78.

——, 'The Roman Army in Eretz-Israel in the Years A.D. 70–132', in P. Freeman and D. Kennedy (eds.), *The Defence of the Roman and Byzantine East* (Oxford, 1986), 575–602.

——, 'The Roman Army in the Province of Judaea, A.D. 132–5', in A. Kasher (ed.), *Greece and Rome in Eretz Israel* (Jerusalem, 1989), 98–130 (Heb.).

——, 'The Samaritans and the Bar-Kokhba Revolt', in A.D. Crown (ed.), *The Samaritans* (Tübingen, 1989), 19–31.

——, 'The Bar-Kokhba Revolt and Non-Jewish Participants', *JJS* 36 (1985), 200–9.

A. Oppenheimer, 'Shabat and the Bar Kokhba Revolt', in: A. Oppenheimer *et al.*, *Jews and Judaism in the Period of the Second Temple, the Mishnah and the Talmud: Studies in Honour of S. Safrai* (Jerusalem, 1983), 226–34.

——, 'Talmudic Literature as a Historical Source for the Bar-Kokhba Revolt', in F. Parente (ed.), *Aspetti della storiografia ebraica* (Rome, 1987), 139–52.

P. Schäfer, 'Hadrian's Policy in Judaea and the Bar Kokhba Revolt: A Reassessment', in P.R. Davies and R.T. White eds., *A Tribute to G. Vermes: Essays on Jewish and Christian Literature and History* (Sheffield, 1990), 281–3.

D. Schwartz, 'On Barnabas and Bar-Kokhba', in D. Schwartz, *Studies in the Jewish Background of Christianity* (Tübingen, 1992), 147–53.

I. Shatzman, 'The Military Confrontation between Rome and the Jews', in U. Rappaport (ed.), *Judaea and Rome—the Jewish Revolts* (Jerusalem, 1983), 323–9; 436–8.

For the site of Bethar: David Ussishkin, 'Archaeological soundings at Betar, Bar-Kochba's Last Stronghold', *Tel Aviv* 20 (1993), 66–97.

For the Roman siege works around Bethar: D. Kennedy, & D. Riley, *Rome's Desert Frontier from the Air* (London, 1990), 100.

The Second Jewish Revolt appears also in various works with a different or wider perspective:

D. Mendels, *The Rise and Fall of Jewish Nationalism* (New York, 1992).

F. Millar, *The Roman Near East 31 B.C.–A.D. 337* (Cambridge, MA, 1993), esp. Appendix B: 'Documents from the Bar Kochba War'.

A Collection of Articles in Hebrew

A. Oppenheimer, and U. Rappaport, (eds.), *The Bar Kokhba Revolt— New Studies* (Jerusalem, 1984, Hebr.).

The Roman roads between Jaffa and Jerusalem: Fischer, Isaac and Roll, *Roman Roads in Judaea*, ii, (BAR, Oxford, 1996).

The underground hiding-places: *Cathedra* 26 (1983), collection of articles (Hebr.) A. Kloner, and Y. Tepper (eds.), *The Hiding Complexes in the Judaean Shephelah* (Tel Aviv, 1987, Hebr.).

17

ETHNIC GROUPS IN JUDAEA UNDER ROMAN RULE

In Wadi Mukatteb in Sinai a traveller left the following graffito: 'Cessent Syri ante Latinos Romanos'.[1] This, then, reflects the opinion of a Latin speaking Roman who expressed the superiority of his people over the Syrians. The implication of the pronouncement is that only those who spoke Latin were Romans and that Syrians were not. The graffito is undated, naturally. However, there is no lack of dated literary passages reflecting similar sentiments. Thus we find the emperor Marcus Aurelius encouraging his western troops when they were about to fight the eastern army of Avidius Cassius—in the words of Cassius Dio:

> You, at least, fellow soldiers, ought to be of good cheer. For surely Cilicians, Syrians, Jews and Egyptians have never proved superior to you and never will, even if they should muster as many tens of thousands more than you as they now muster fewer.[2]

About Avidius Cassius himself the emperor says: 'For an eagle is not formidable when in command of an army of daws nor a lion when in command of fawns.' An interesting by-product of such statements in ancient sources is the conviction, firmly rooted in the modern literature, that western soldiers were indeed superior to those of the East, an opinion not born out by the eventual survival of the various parts of the empire. However, it is not the prejudices of modern scholars which should concern us here, but rather the question of social identity implied in such ancient statements. What was Marcus Aurelius supposed to mean when he, a Roman emperor, disparaged 'Cilicians, Syrians, Jews and Egyptians'? Were they inhabitants of specific provinces? Provinces were administrative units which often ignored existing social organization, as is most obvious from the frequent re-arrangement of provincial borders in the East in the first

---

[1] *CIL* III 86.
[2] Dio lxxi 25, 1–2: ὑμᾶς γε ὦ συστρατιῶται χρὴ θαρρεῖν. οὐ γάρ που κρείττους Κίλικες καὶ Σύροι καὶ Ἰουδαῖοι καὶ Αἰγύπτιοι ὑμῶν οὔτε ἐγένοντό ποτε οὔτε ἔσονται, οὐδ' ἂν μυριάκις πλείους ὑμῶν, ὅσῳ νῦν ἐλάττους εἰσίν, ἀθροισθῶσιν.

and second centuries. Did Marcus refer to speakers of a language of
their own? 'Cilician' was not a language and many, or most Syrians,
Jews and Egyptians spoke Greek in the second century A.D. The Jews
had a distinct religion of their own, but that did not apply to the
other groups.

The question to be asked first is what bound, or was felt to bind
such groups together. Language was certainly one factor, as is clearly
illustrated by the graffito opposing *Latin* speaking Romans to Syrians. But in other cases religion was the element which determined
common identity. To Marcus Aurelius, again, Ammianus attributes
the following: 'For Marcus, as he was passing through Palestine on his
way to Egypt, being often disgusted with the malodorous and rebellious Jews, is reported to have cried with sorrow: "O Marcomanni,
O Quadi, O Sarmatians, at last I have found a people more unruly
than you."'[3] Here the Jews are singled out for abuse as a group.
This is worth noting, for many or most ethnic groups disappear after
their absorption into the empire.[4] For instance, following the formation of the province of Arabia the Nabataeans are no longer mentioned and the Idumaeans are last described as an extant people by
Josephus. However, the Jews and the Samaritans continued to exist.
In the late second century they are both said to have rebelled. 'Iudaeos
et Samaritas rebellare conantes ferro coercuit' (undated but following Niger's defeat).[5] The Jews and Samaritans, unlike the Nabataeans
and Idumaeans, were extant in that period to the extent that they
could rebel. They had a religion of their own which distinguished
them from the polytheistic environment in Judaea. The latter is anonymous and the only way in which we can refer to these people is by
describing them as inhabitants of the province of Judaea/Palaestina
or as citizens of the various cities in that province. There is no parallel in the East for the process which transformed names of tribes
into names of cities, so common in Gaul.

---

[3] Ammianus xxii 5.5: Ille enim cum Palaestinam transiret, Aegyptum petens,
Iudaeorum fetentium et tumultuantium saepe taedio percitus, dolenter dicitur ex-
clamasse: 'O Marcomanni o Quadi o Sarmatae, tandem alios vobis in<qui>etiores
inveni.' Cf. M. Stern, *Greek and Latin Authors on Jews and Judaism* (Jerusalem, 1974–
84), ii, no. 506 with comments on p. 606.
[4] Cf. F. Millar, 'Empire, Community and Culture in the Roman Near East: Greeks,
Syrians, Jews and Arabs', *Journal of Jewish Studies* 38 (1987), 143–64, esp. pp. 153 ff.
[5] Orosius vii, 17, 30; cf. Eusebius, *Chron. Sev.* V, Iudaicum et Samariticum bellum
motum. Cf. E. Mary Smallwood, *The Jews under Roman Rule, from Pompey to Diocletian:
A Study in Political Relations* (Leiden, ²1981) 488, n. 7.

It is the aim of the present paper to trace the effect of the transformation of Judaea into a Roman province on the social identity of various groups in the area. This question is part of the larger topic already mentioned: what was the common identity of peoples which had lost their independence following their incorporation into the system of Roman provinces.

Common Ancestors

In antiquity the traditional means of indicating an ethnic relationship was the adoption or invention of common ancestors. Thus Areios, king of Sparta, is cited as writing to the High Priest Onias:

> It has been learned from a letter regarding the Spartiates and the Jews that they are brothers and related through descent from Abraham.[6]

The 'People of Pergamon' describe a somewhat more distant relationship in the following terms:

> ... remembering that in the time of Abraham, who was the father of all Hebrews, our ancestors were their friends, as we find in the public records.[7]

It would be interesting to know what sort of documents the Spartiates and the People of Pergamon found in their archives, to confirm such statements. Gentile authors, writing in Latin and Greek, emphatically mention Abraham as the ancestor of the Jews. For instance Apollonius Molon: 'Abraham died of old age, while to Gelos and a native woman there were born eleven sons, and a twelfth one Joseph. His grandson was Moses'.[8] Note also the attempt to link the name 'Hebrew' to Abraham, made by Claudius Charax: 'Hebrews. Thus are called Jews after Abramon, as Charax says'.[9]

---

[6] 1 Mac. 12, 20–23, cf. Josephus, *Ant.* xii, 4, 10 (225–227). For present purposes the question of the authenticity or the origin of these documents is not the issue, but the fact that they are cited in historical works of the period.

[7] Decree of the People of Pergamum, cited by Josephus, *Ant.* xiv, 10, 22 (247–255); esp. 255.

[8] Apollonius Molon, *de Iudaeis*, *ap.* Eusebius, *Praeparatio Evangelica*, ix, 19, 1–3 (first cent. B.C.; Stern, *Greek and Latin Authors*, i, no. 46).

[9] Claudius Charax of Pergamum *ap.* Stephanus s.v. Ἐβραῖοι. οὕτως Ἰουδαῖοι ἀπὸ Ἀβράμωνος, ὥς φησι Χάραξ (second cent. A.D.), Stern, ii, no. 335 with comments on p. 161. Cf. Nicolaus of Damascus, *apud* Josephus, *Ant.* i, 7, 2 (159–160), (Stern 83):

 Common ancestors could not only be adduced, but also disclaimed in order to acknowledge or disavow relationships. Josephus' accusation of Samaritan opportunism in this respect is well known:

> When they see the Jews prospering, they call them their kinsmen, on the ground that they are descended from Joseph and are related to them through their origin from him, but when they see the Jews in trouble they say that they have nothing whatever in common with them . . . and they declare themselves to be alien residents of another race (μετοίκους ἀλλοεθνεῖς).[10]

The case of the Jews and Samaritans was unusual in the ancient world because these two peoples had related monotheistic religions. On the other hand, the manipulation of ancestors to give substance to a political relationship was not unusual in itself. It may also be observed in the case of the Idumaeans. Judah the Maccabee fought 'the sons of Esau' in Idumaea.[11] What was unusual in the ancient world was the collective conversion of the Idumaeans to the religion of the victors which followed this war.[12] Josephus' criticism of Nicolaus of Damascus is also relevant. Nicolaus claimed that Antipater the Idumaean's family belonged to the leading Jews who came to Judaea from Babylon.[13] According to Josephus, he said this merely to please Herod. Nicolaus thus provided Herod with Jewish ancestors which would have turned him into a real Jew, according to the norms of the period, an identity which the conversion to Judaism of his ancestors could not provide. The aristocratic Josephus rejected these claims as fabrications.

 While the status of Herod may have been dubious in the eyes of the Jewish priestly class it is clear that the Idumaeans totally disappear from our records after the first century A.D. Idumaea is occasionally mentioned in Latin sources instead of Judaea,[14] but the Idumaeans lost their identity as a people, unlike the Jews and Samaritans.

'But not long after, he left this country also with his people for the land then called Canaan but now Judaea, where he settled, he and his numerous descendants. . . .'

[10] Josephus, *Ant.* ix 288–291, esp. 291.

[11] 1 Mac. 5, 1; cf. Jos. *Ant.* xii, 8, 1 (328): 'falling upon the sons of Esau, the Idumaioi' cf. E. Schürer, *The History of the Jewish People in the Age of Jesus Christ,* revised ed. by G. Vermes and F. Millar (Edinburgh, 1979), ii, 2, n. 4.

[12] Josephus, *Ant.* xiii, 9, 1 (257 f.).

[13] Josephus, *Ant.* xiv, 1, 3 (8–9); cf. *BJ* i 123.

[14] See Latin sources *ap.* Stern: index.

The New Testament

In the New Testament Judaea is seen as inhabited by Jews, Samaritans and Gentiles (ἔθνα) 'Go nowhere among the Gentiles, and enter no town of the Samaritans, but go rather to the lost sheep of the house of Israel.'[15] The major social division is that between Jews and Gentiles: 'If he refuses to listen to them, tell it to the church; and if he refuses to listen even to the church, let him be to you as a Gentile an a tax collector (ὁ ἐθνικὸς καὶ ὁ τελώνης)'.[16] The enmity between Jews and Samaritans is also obvious: 'And he sent messengers ahead of him, who went and entered a village of the Samaritans, to make ready for him; but the people would not receive him, because his face was set toward Jerusalem'.[17] What is most striking, however, is that besides Jews and Samaritans no other people is mentioned by name apart from the inhabitants of certain cities. In the districts of Tyre and Sidon in Phoenicia a woman is described alternatively as 'Canaanite' or as 'Hellenis' and Syrophoenician by birth.[18] The use of the term 'Canaanite' is interesting. It occurs also on coins of the second century B.C. in Phoenician characters: 'Laodicea in Canaan' (Berytus, apparently).[19] Another possibility is that the term here derives from the Old Testament and thus did not apply to the social reality of the first century A.D. It was the old Biblical term for a Gentile living in the Land of Israel and as such it would have been understood by Jews in the Roman period. The second term, 'Hellenis', refers to contemporary language and culture and reflected the actuality

---

[15] Matthew 10, 5: Εἰς ὁδὸν ἐθνῶν μὴ ἀπέλθητε, καὶ εἰς πόλιν Σαμαριτῶν μὴ εἰσέλθητε· πορεύεσθε δὲ μᾶλλον πρὸς τὰ πρόβατα τὰ ἀπολωλότα οἴκου Ἰσραήλ.

[16] Matthew 18, 17: ἐὰν δὲ παρακούσῳ αὐτῶν, εἰπὲ τῇ ἐκκλησίᾳ· ἐὰν δὲ καὶ τῆς ἐκκλησίας παρακούσῃ, ἔστω σοι ὥσπερ ὁ ἐθνικὸς καὶ ὁ τελώνης. cf. 20, 25: Οἴδατε ὅτι οἱ ἄρχοντες τῶν ἐθνῶν κατακυριεύουσιν αὐτῶν καὶ οἱ μεγάλοι κατεξουσιάζουσιν αὐτῶν. 'You know that the rulers of the Gentiles lord it over them, and their great men exercise authority over them. . . .'

[17] Luke 9, 52.

[18] Matthew 15, 21: Καὶ ἐξελθὼν ἐκεῖθεν ὁ Ἰησοῦς ἀνεχώρησεν εἰς τὰ μέρη Τύρου καὶ Σιδῶνος. καὶ ἰδοὺ γυνὴ Χαναναία ἀπὸ τῶν ὁρίων ἐκείνων ἐξελθοῦσα ἔκραζεν λέγουσα, Ἐλέησόν με, κύριε, υἱὸς Δαυίδ· ἡ θυγάτηρ μου κακῶς δαιμονίζεται. 'And Jesus went away from there and withdrew to the district of Tyre and Sidon. And behold, a Canaanite woman from that region came out and cried, "Have mercy on me, O Lord, Son of David; my daughter is severely possessed by a demon"'. Cf. Mark 7, 26 for the alternative expressions: ἡ δὲ γυνὴ ἦν Ἑλληνίς, Συροφοινίκισσα τῷ γένει.

[19] *British Museum Catalogue of Greek Coins, Phoenicia*, pp. 1 ff.; 51–52. For the Phoenicians in this period: F. Millar, 'The Phoenician Cities: a Case-Study of Hellenisation', *Proceedings of the Cambridge Philological Society* 209/NS 29 (1983), 55–71.

of the period. The third, however, is a vague indication of origin, an ethnic concept which can have been used only because the author knew how his readers would have understood it. Yet the very fact that such terms could coexist shows that old social patterns were dissolving. An epigram which beautifully illustrates this process commemorates Dalmatius, grandson of Tiron who had been *beneficiarius* of the governor κατὰ ἔθνος Φοινίκων.[20] This is the province of Syria Phoenice, not 'the people of the Phoenicians'. In other cases it is harder to be certain—what was Herodian's intention when he wrote that Julia Maesa (from Emesa) was 'of Phoenician descent, from the city named Emesa in Phoenice'?[21] Possibly here too the Roman province of Phoenice is meant. Heliodorus, the author of *Aethiopica*, also describes himself 'a Phoenician from Emesa'.[22]

The dissolution of ethnic barriers may have been a reality, but it was also part of the ideology of early Christianity, a proselytizing movement which, unlike Judaism, ignored ethnic identity. This is clear from many passages. When visiting Cornelius, a centurion in Caesarea, Peter said: 'You yourselves know how unlawful it is for a Jew to associate with or visit any one of another nation (ἀλλοφύλῳ); but God has shown me that I should not call any man common or unclean'.[23] The same moral is conveyed in stronger terms still by the story of the Good Samaritan.[24] The Jewish priest and the Levite avoided contamination from the victim of a bandit-attack and left ·him lying on the road. A Samaritan took care of him and thus proved his real neighbour. The message is that ethnic ties are not meaningful in themselves. Its impact is assured by the common knowledge that the attack, and the behaviour of the priest and the Levite were to be expected, but the behaviour of the Samaritan would have been entirely surprising.

Of particular interest is the use in the New Testament of the term

---

[20] P. Le Bas - H. Waddington, *Inscriptions grecques et latines recueillies en Grèce et en Asie Mineure*, iii (Paris, 1870), 2432: Τίρωνος ἀρτιεπὴς υἱωνος φίλος ὄλβιος τε, ὅς ποθ' ἡγεμόνος βενεφικιάριος κατὰ ἔθνος ἔπλετο Φοινίκων, Δαλμάτιος. . . .

[21] Herodian v, 3, 2: Μαῖσα ἦν τις ὄνομα, τὸ γένος Φοίνισσα, ἀπὸ Ἐμέσου καλουμένης οὕτω πόλεως ἐν Φοινίκῃ· In the sequel Herodian observes that the name Elagabalus was Phoenician.

[22] Heliodorus *Aethiopica* 41.4.4: ὃ συνέταξεν ἀνὴρ Φοῖνιξ Ἐμισηνός, τῶν ἀφ' Ἡλίου γένος, Θεοδοσίου παῖς Ἡλιόδωρος.

[23] Acts 10, 28: ἔφη τε πρὸς αὐτούς, Ὑμεῖς ἐπίστασθε ὡς ἀθέμιτόν ἐστιν ἀνδρὶ Ἰουδαίῳ κολλᾶσθαι ἢ προσέρχεσθαι ἀλλοφύλῳ·

[24] Luke 10, 30 ff.

'Hellenes' or 'Hellenists' ('Ελληνισταί) already mentioned. It is not always easy to determine what is meant by the word, for it is used without explanation. In Judaea it usually refers to Greek speaking Jews. It is a term denoting language, not ethnic origin. This is clearly the case when Paul preached in Jerusalem and argued with the Hellenists there.[25] Outside Judaea it usually refers to Greek speaking Gentiles. Thus we read that Stephen, when travelling to Phoenicia, Cyprus and Antioch, spoke only to Jews, but others, coming from Cyprus and Cyrene to Antioch, addressed Hellenists also.[26] The term here again refers to language and not origin, but it is clear from the context that Gentiles are meant.[27] The expression assumed a special meaning in an internal Christian context where a conflict is described between the 'Hellenists' among the disciples and the 'Hebrews'.[28] The Hellenists are non-Jewish Christians and the Hebrews are Christians of Jewish origin.

It is to be noted that here the term 'Hebrews' is used, which refers to language, rather than 'Ioudaioi', an ethnic concept. When Paul was suspected of being an Egyptian rebel he replied in Greek that he was a Jew ('Ιουδαῖος) and a citizen of Tarsus.[29] (His Roman citizenship was mentioned only afterwards when it became advantagious to emphasize his legal status).[30] In a later period Eusebius still calls Christian Jews *Hebraioi* as against unconverted Jews for whom he employs the term *Ioudaioi*.[31]

In the previous century Mommsen assumed that, after the First Revolt, the Jews lost their status as a recognized people (gens/ἔθνος)

---

[25] Acts 9, 29.

[26] Acts 11, 19 ff.

[27] In Acts 14, 1 a distinction is made between Jews and ἕλληνες. Some people from both groups accepted the preaching of Paul and Barnabas but others did not, so the apostles were attacked by unbelieving Jews and Gentiles (ἔθνα). Cf. Acts 19, 10: τοῦτο δὲ ἐγένετο ἐπὶ ἔτη δύο, ὥστε πάντας τοὺς κατοικοῦντας τὴν Ἀσίαν ἀκοῦσαι τὸν λόγον τοῦ κυρίου, Ἰουδαίους τε καὶ Ἕλληνας. '. . . so that all the inhabitants of Asia heard the word of the Lord, Jews and Hellenes'. Also: 19, 17. There is an apparent exception in 21, 28: Paul is accused of bringing Ἕλληνας into the Temple, i.e. Gentiles. This, of course, was in Jerusalem, where the term, as argued above, refers to Greek speaking Jews. It is only apparently an exception, however, for the person concerned was Trophimus the Ephesian, that is, a man from Asia Minor.

[28] Acts 6, 1: Ἐν δὲ ταῖς ἡμέραις ταύταις πληθυνόντων τῶν μαθητῶν ἐγένετο γογγυσμὸς τῶν Ἑλληνιστῶν πρὸς τοὺς Ἑβραίους.

[29] Acts 21, 37: εἶπεν δὲ ὁ Παῦλος, Ἐγὼ ἄνθρωπος μέν εἰμι Ἰουδαῖος, Ταρσεὺς τῆς Κιλικίας, οὐκ ἀσήμου πόλεως πολίτης·

[30] Acts 22, 25.

[31] Ἑβραῖοι: Eusebius, *HE* iv 5; cf. 6: τοὺς ἐκ περιτομῆς ἐπισκόπους.

in the Roman empire.[32] This theory, once influential, is now no longer accepted,[33] for the Jews continue to be alluded to as a *gens* or ἔθνος in Greek and Latin sources of the late first and second centuries. Note, for instance, inscriptions from Smyrna which mention the *laos* of the *Ioudaioi* after A.D. 70.[34] Tacitus refers to them as a 'kind of men' while they were still in Egypt, but as a people (*gens*) in Judaea, both in the past and in his own days.[35] Suetonius, Arrian and Appian also call them 'a people'.[36] Origen speaks of them as an ἔθνος in his discussion of the position of the Patriarch.[37]

There can be no doubt, therefore, that the Jews continued to be regarded as a people, both in Judaea and elsewhere. Regarding other groups, however, the situation is less clear. Tacitus says of Tiberius Alexander: '*regebat eiusdem nationis*'. The term *eiusdem* indicates that Alexander came from Egypt himself, but it is interesting that a Roman province should be called a *natio*. It might indicate that Tacitus still considered the Egyptians a people under Roman rule, but it is more likely that the term is used here instead of *provincia*, just as the term *ethnos Phoinikon* was seen to indicate the province of Syria Phoenice. A similar question may be asked when Jerome says of Malchus that he was *Syrus natione et lingua*.[38] Malchus, then, spoke Syriac rather than Greek. But in what sense was Syria his *natio*? If there was a Syriac language the Syrians may have been perceived to form a common nation, but it is more likely that the term indicates his province of origin. Or it could have been a geographical term, as indicated by the sequel: *ut revera ejusdem loci indigena*. The conjunction of the concept of a people and a Roman province in the fourth century is illustrated by the usage of the *Historia Augusta*, which speaks of 'Palaestini' when referring to the inhabitants of the province of that name.[39] Of course, a number of modern states still bear names that go back to the nomenclature of Roman provinces.

---

[32] *Gesammelte Schriften* (1902), iii, 389–422.
[33] Schürer, iii, 114, n. 28 concedes that Mommsen's position has some justification. Smallwood, *The Jews under Roman Rule*, 342, 344, rejects it altogether.
[34] Schürer iii, 90.
[35] *Hist.* v, 3, 1: *genus id hominum* (in Egypt); 4, 1: *gentem* (in Judaea); 5, 1 *gens* (contemporary); 8, 2 (under Antiochus Epiphanes); 13, 4 (under Titus).
[36] Suetionius, *Domitian* 12, 2: *gens*; Arrian, *Parthica*, F79 Roos: ἔθνος; Appian, *Syriaca* 50, 252.
[37] *Ep. ad Afric.* 14 (*PG* xi 81).
[38] *Vita Malchi* 42 (*PL* 23, 54).
[39] *SHA* Niger 7, 9: *Pal<a>estinis*. Smallwood, *The Jews under Roman Rule*, 484, commenting on this passage and the spurious statement it contains, says that surely

When we reach the period of well-established Roman rule it is clear that city, language and religion are unambiguous concepts. The terms *natio* and *ethnos* are ambivalent, however, indicating sometimes a people, sometimes a province (or a region). It would seem that the important factor determining social identity was not so much real or imagined common descent from ancestors, but rather language, lifestyle, religion and culture, as illustrated by the following phrase of Strabo, who wrote in the age of Augustus: 'Not that they are barbarians still, they have for the most part adopted the Roman way, both in language and lifestyle, and some of them in their form of government also.'[40] Strabo here discusses western peoples, where being non-Roman implied belonging to the Barbarians. A different approach may be observed in the work of Cassius Dio, a Roman senator from Nicaea in Asia Minor, writing in Greek in the third century. While describing the imperial cult as instituted by Augustus he relates that the emperor ordered 'the Romans resident [in Ephesus and Nicaea] to honour [Rome and the Divus Iulius], but the foreigners, whom he called *Hellenes*, he allowed to consecrate sanctuaries for himself, namely the Asians in Pergamon and the Bithynians in Nicomedia.'[41] In the sequel he refers to 'the Hellenic nations . . . and the others who are subject to the Romans'. Dio, then, makes a clear distinction between Romans and subject peoples who included the Greek speaking (nations). The first division was mostly a matter of status, the second of language. Thus it remains true that language was one of the most important identifying factors for Dio.

In the social structure of the empire the Jews formed an exception because for them common identity was not a matter of language— Jews could speak Hebrew, Aramaic, Greek or Latin—but of religion and kinship. It was the second part of this package which the Christians rejected, thus assuring themselves a better chance of expansion among the Gentiles in the Roman empire.

---

the Jews are meant. This is possible but cannot be the case when *Pal<a>estini* are mentioned in SHA *Severus* 14, 6 and 17, 1; cf. the comments in Stern, ii, 623; 625.

[40] Strabo iv i, 12 (186 f.), speaking of south-eastern Gaul: τοὺς ταύτη βαρβάρους, οὐδὲ βαρβάρους ἔτι ὄντας, ἀλλὰ μετακειμένους τὸ πλέον εἰς τὸν τῶν Ῥωμαίων τύπον καὶ τῇ γλώττῃ καὶ τοῖς βίοις, τινὰς δὲ καὶ τῇ πολιτείᾳ.

[41] Dio li 20. 6 f.: Καῖσαρ δὲ ἐν τούτῳ τά τε ἄλλα ἐχρημάτιζε, καὶ τεμένη τῇ ἐν Ῥώμῃ καὶ τῷ πατρὶ τῷ Καίσαρι, ἥρωα αὐτὸν Ἰούλιον ὀνομάσας, ἔν τε Ἐφέσῳ καὶ ἐν Νικαίᾳ γενέσθαι ἐφῆκεν· αὗται γὰρ τότε αἱ πόλεις ἔν τε τῇ Ἀσίᾳ καὶ ἐν τῇ Βιθυνίᾳ προετετίμηντο. καὶ τούτους μὲν τοῖς Ῥωμαίοις τοῖς ἀρ' αὐτοῖς ἐποικοῦσι τιμᾶν προσέταξε· τοῖς δὲ δὴ ξένοις, Ἕλληνάς σφας ἐπικαλέσας, ἑαυτῷ τινα, τοῖς μὲν Ἀσιανοῖς ἐν Περγάμῳ τοῖς δὲ Βιθυνοῖς ἐν Νικομηδείᾳ, τεμενίσαι ἐπέτρεψε.

Postscript

Ethnicism as a topic is now even more in fashion than it was when this article was written and that was many years before it was published. For communal and cultural identities the second part of F. Millar, *The Roman Near East* (1993) is now indispensable. These matters are also central in the works of D. Mendels, *The Rise and Fall of Jewish Nationalism* (New York, 1992); A. Kasher, *Jews, Idumaeans and Ancient Arabs* (Tübingen, 1988).

It may be appropriate to add a few words about the Idumaeans. An interesting document has recently been published, namely an Aramaic ostracon inscribed with a marriage contract, dated 176 B.C., i.e. precisely the period of interest for the present study.[1] The document records the marriage between QWSRM son of QWSYD and Arsinoe, daughter of QWSYD, son of QWSYHB. Qos is usually considered an Edomite theophoric element, on the strength of a statement of Josephus to the effect that the Idumaeans worship Qos.[2] Edom or Idumaia, however, is not explicitly mentioned in any surviving part of the text on the ostracon. The authors note a resemblance between this text, the Jewish marriage contracts found in Israel (the documents from the Judaean desert), and the Demotic ones found in Egypt. This, they observe, indicates that different ethnic groups that inhabited Palestine and Egypt were influenced by Aramaic common law. The question then is whether we can be certain that all people in Maresha who bore such names would have described themselves as Edomites. We have now explicit evidence that groups of Phoenician settlers called themselves Sidonians, including those inhabiting Maresha (above, article 1), but what is the real significance of adopting names with the element QWS? Can we be certain that anyone who received such a name would describe himself as an Idumaean? Or would he be described by others as one?[3] Would Sidonians in Maresha con-

---

[1] H. Eshel & A. Kloner, 'An Aramaic Ostracon of an Edomite Marriage Contract from Maresha, dated 176 B.C.E.', *IEJ* 46 (1996), 1–22. The text is dated 136 according to the Seleucid era.

[2] Josephus, *Ant.* xv, 7, 9 (253) Κοστόβαρος ἦν γένει μὲν Ἰδουμαῖος, ἀθιώματος τῶν πρώτων παρ' αὐτοῖς καὶ προγόνων ἱερατευσάντων τῷ Κωζαι· θεὸν δὲ τοῦτον Ἰδουμαῖοι νομίζουσιν. 'Costobar was an Idumaean by origin, the most highly placed among their leaders, and a descendant of priests of Cos. This is the god whom the Idumaeans worship.'

[3] The authors, p. 1, describe Maresha as 'the capital of Idumaea during the Second Temple period'. I am not entirely certain that this is an appropriate descrip-

ciously abstain from giving their children such names? It is clear, in
ny case, that the Idumaeans were considered to be a people in this
eriod, although it is, as often, interesting to note how little the name
ould mean to us if we had not had the text of Josephus. They are
ot mentioned by Philo or in the New Testament,[4] while Josephus has
38 references. In the Greek historical literature they are mentioned
a few times, in the first century B.C. by Diodorus[5] and Strabo[6] and
in the imperial period by Appian.[7] In Latin literature the region
appears in the elder Pliny's description of the area[8] Josephus attributes
to Antigonos a unique epithet describing his enemy Herod, '. . . an
Idumaean, that is: a half-Jew. . . .'[9] Thus we encounter in a first-
century B.C. quarrel a concept which normative Judaism has never
recognized.

---

tion of the status of the town. There is no indication that it had, in any sense, jurisdiction over the surrounding countryside.

[4] Marc 3.6 mentions Idumaea as a geographical region, together with the Peraea,
Galilee and the territories of Tyre and Sidon.

[5] Diodorus, xix.95.2: ἀπὸ τῆς Ἰδουμαίας ἐπαρχίας; xix.98.1: κατὰ μέσην τὴν σατρα-
πείαν τῆς Ἰδουμαίας.

[6] Strabo xvi 2, 2, 8; 34, 2.

[7] Appian, *Mith.* 499.4; *B.C.* v 8, 7, 75.

[8] Pliny, *NH* v, 68, 3 etc. Note also references in Martial, *ep.* ii, 2, 5; Vergil, *Georgica*
iii 12. Servius' comments on this passage shows the extent to which Idumaea had
been forgotten in his time: *idvmaeas palmas abundantes, quantae sunt apud Idumen, civitatem
Phoenices: Lucanus 'et arbusto palmarum dives Idume'. et aliter: Idumaei gens est Syriae. quidam
Idumaeas palmas ab Idyma, quae est urbs Lydiae palmarum ferax, dictas volunt. plerique Idumam
Syriae Iudaeae civitatem tradunt.*

[9] Josephus, *Ant.* xiv (403) attributes to Antigonos the claim ὡς παρὰ τὴν αὐτῶν
δικαιοσύνην Ἡρώδῳ ὤσουσιν ἣν βασιλείαν ἰδιώτω τε ὄντι καὶ Ἰδουμαίῳ, τουτέστιν
ἡμιιουδαίῳ, δέον τοῖς ἐκ τοῦ γένους οὖσι παρέχειν ὡς ἔθος ἐστὶν αὐτοῖς.

18

ORIENTALS AND JEWS IN THE HISTORIA AUGUSTA:
FOURTH-CENTURY PREJUDICE AND STEREOTYPES

Cessent Syri ante Latinos Romanos: these are the words of a contentious
traveller scratched in the rocks of the Wadi Mukatteb in Sinai.[1] This
graffito reflects the opinion of a Latin speaking Roman proclaiming
the superiority of his people over the Syrians. The implication of the
pronouncement is that only those who spoke Latin were true Romans,
that Syrians, that is, speakers of Aramaic,[2] were not, and that there
was an uneasy relationship between the two groups. Naturally, the
graffito is undated. Recently a Greek graffito was discovered not far
from the Latin one, in the Hisma, proclaiming: 'Romans always win.
I, Lauricius, wrote "Hail Zenon"'.[3] It is not surprising that one should
find a Greek graffito in the region, identifying the Romans as the
conquerors of the world. However, the same Zenon was greeted on
yet another graffito seen nearby: 'Greetings Zenon, son of QYMT,
Tribune, with (the) good for ever.'[4] The Roman officer Zenon did
not only have have writers of Aramaic among his friends, he himself
had a father with an Arabic name. These texts, then, reflect a sense
of superiority held by those who identified with Roman power and
the Latin language while, at the same time, they are evidence of the
mixed culture prevailing in the area.

There is no shortage of dated literary passages reflecting similar
sentiments. Thus we find the emperor Marcus Aurelius encouraging
his western troops when they were about to fight the eastern army
of Avidius Cassius—in the words of Cassius Dio:

> You, at least, fellow soldiers, ought to be of good cheer. For Cilicians,
> Syrians, Jews and Egyptians have certainly never proved superior to

---

[1] *CIL* III 86.

[2] Jerome, *vita Hilarionis* 22; 25: 'Syriac' is used for Aramaic including Palestinian
Aramaic. 'Syri' therefore are 'Speakers of Aramaic'.

[3] R.G. Tanner, *ZPE* 83 (1990), p. 185.

[4] *Op. cit.*, p. 184; *ADAJ* 26 (1982), 199–209: SLM. ZYNWN BR QYMT KLYRK
BTB L'LM.

you and never will, even if they should muster as many tens of thousands more than you as they now muster fewer.[5]

About Avidius Cassius himself the emperor says: 'An eagle is not formidable when in command of an army of jackdaws nor a lion when in command of fawns.' These words were spoken during a civil war, when an ambitious general made an attempt to usurp the throne, but the rhetoric unhesitatingly turns this into a contest between eastern and western troops. The Jews are mentioned in the first passage as one of the degenerate peoples of the Near East.

Most of the texts to be discussed here express western prejudices against the East, but there are also eastern pronouncements claiming superiority over other peoples. For example, the following lines from Porphyry, a native of Tyre and pupil of Plotinus, known for his interest in Judaism (232/233 to the beginning of the fourth century):

> Steep is the road and rough that leads to heaven, / Entered at first through portals bound with brass. / Within are found innumerable paths, / Which for the endless good of all mankind / They first revealed who Nile's sweet waters drink. / From them the heavenward paths Phoenicia learned, Assyria, Lydia, and the Hebrew race. . . .

> For the road to the gods is bound with brass, and both steep and rough; the barbarians discovered many paths thereof, but the Greeks went astray and those who already held it even perverted it. The discovery was ascribed by the god to Egyptians, Phoenicians, Chaldeans (for these are Assyrians), Lydians and Hebrews.

> Only Chaldees and Hebrews wisdom found / In the pure worship of a self-born God.

Thus the Jews are mentioned in association with the Phoenicians, Assyrians, and Lydians as having found the road to heaven and wisdom, the road which the Greeks failed to discover.

In the fourth century Libanius, in a speech in praise of Antioch, asserts the superiority of his own, Greek city over Roman towns.[6] He refused to learn Latin. When his fellow Antiochene Ammianus, who, of course, wrote Latin, referred to 'both languages' there could be no misunderstanding that he meant Greek and Latin.[7]

---

[5] Dio lxxi, 25, 1.

[6] *Antiochikos (Or.* 11); note also his contempt for the new senators of Constantinople, parvenus who did not know Greek (i 76), cf. J. Matthews, *The Roman Empire of Ammianus* (1989), 70 f.; *Western Aristocracies* (1975), 105–7.

[7] Ammianus xviii, 5, 1: 'utriusque linguae litteras sciens', with comments by Matthews, *loc. cit.*

Syrians

Despite the amalgamation of various peoples into the structure of the empire, and despite the dissolution of pre-existing ethnic links, hostility and prejudice did not disappear. It is only to be expected that we should encounter much disparagement of various peoples considered 'barbarians'. More significant for our understanding of the functioning of the empire as an integrated state, however, are instances of hostility towards the East in the western part of the empire. The terms in which such hostility is expressed can also tell us something about cultural stresses and the categories of social identity that were felt to be relevant at the time.

An interesting by-product of hostile prejudices in ancient sources is their widespread acceptance in the modern literature on the subject.[8] Thus we often read that western soldiers were indeed superior to those from the East. This is an opinion not borne out by the eventual survival of the various parts of the empire. One further example will suffice. T. Mommsen observed that it might be worthwhile to study the history of Latin literature in Berytus 'a Latin island in the sea of oriental Hellenism'.[9] This is almost innocuous compared to those who followed this notion: Cumont cites Mommsen, but gives the expression a racial twist: 'Latin islands in the Semitic ocean'.[10] Vittinghoff takes this another step further and speaks in terms which suggest 'Kulturkampf'.[11] The idea of a soft, lascivious but sophisticated East as opposed to cold and hard Rome is deeply rooted in modern western culture, and this in itself may be a survival of Roman attitudes. We find it in Latin Crusader sources on Syrians,[12] and afterwards.[13]

---

[8] Isaac, *The Limits of Empire* (1990), 20 f.

[9] *Römische Geschichte* v 459: 'Vielleicht darf die Geschichte der lateinischen Litteratur für Berytus, die Lateinische Insel im Meer des orientalischen Hellenismus, den Ernst wissenschaftlicher Arbeit in Anspruch nehmen.'

[10] *C.A.H.* xi 626.

[11] Vittinghoff, *Römische Kolonisation* (1952), 134 f.: 'Den einzigen grossen Sieg einer römischen Kolonie gegen die hellenistisch-östliche Umwelt hat in Syrien die alte Hafenstadt und Veteranenkolonie Berytus . . ., eine "lateinische Insel im semitischen Ozean", errungen'.

[12] William of Tyre, *Historia rerum in partibus transmarinis gestarum* xxii 15, in *RHC, Hist. Occ.* i (1844), p. 1091: 'Syri, qui apud nos effeminati et molles habentur'; Jacques de Vitry, *Historia orientalis seu hierosolymitana*, in *Gesta dei per Francos*, i, ed. J. Bongars (1611), 1089: 'Prorsus imbelles et praeliis velut mulieres nutiles'. This is taken at face value by R.C. Smail, *Crusading Warfare 1097–1193* (Cambridge, 1956), 53.

[13] Shakespeare's Antony and Cleopatra, itself based on North's translation of Plutarch, is built on such contrasts. For instance Act i, sc. iv (3–7): 'From Alexandria /

However, our major concern in this paper is with the question of social relationships and cultural stress implied in such ancient statements rather than with the prejudices of modern scholars.

In the *Historia Augusta*, and particularly in the 'minor lives' there are a substantial number of slurs, meant as such and aimed at ethnic groups within the empire, notably Jews and other easterners, such as Syrians in general, Antiochenes, and Arabs. It could be argued that this is merely typical of this unusual author, but it is also possible that common attitudes of mind are more freely expressed in this work than in the writings of serious historians.[14] At least it tells us something about the author, his origin and the social and intellectual climate in which he produced his curious work. Comparison with similar forms of prejudice in the second and third centuries may show whether it is a phenomenon of a particular age or not.[15] Furthermore, it is important to keep in mind when evaluating specific historical pronouncements in the *Historia Augusta*, that the author regularly inserts ethnic slurs under the guise of historical information.

We have seen above that Cassius Dio attributes derogatory remarks about the eastern troops to Marcus Aurelius. This attitude was quite common. Tacitus' description of the Syrian army when Corbulo took over command is a case in point.[16] While it may have been true that these troops were in bad shape, the fact that there was a great deal of prejudice against Syrians should also be taken into consideration.

This is the news: he fishes, drinks, and wastes / The lamps of night in revel; is not more manlike / Than Cleopatra; nor the queen of Ptolemy / More womanly than he . . .' (55 f.) 'Antony / Leave thy lascivious wassails. When thou once / Was beaten from Modena, where thou slew'st / Hirtius and Pansa, consuls, at thy heel / Did famine follow, whom thou fought'st agains, / Though daintily brought up, with patience more / Than savages could suffer. . . . and all this. . . . Was borne so like a soldier, that thy cheek / So much as lank'd not.'

[14] The modern literature about the *Scriptores Historiae Augustae*, it sources, author, value and many other aspects is massive. For the work in context: R. Syme, *Ammianus and the Historia Augusta* (Oxford, 1968); R. Syme, *The Historia Augusta—A Call for Clarity* (Bonn, 1971). Further references: Stern, vol. ii, pp. 612 f.

[15] For a related subject: Jan Burian, 'Der Gegensatz zwischen Rom und den Barbaren in der Historia Augusta', *Eirene* 15 (1977), 55–96.

[16] Tacitus, *Annales* xiii 35: 'quippe Suria transmotae legiones, pace longa segnes, munia castrorum Romanorum aegerrime tolerabant etc.' Mrs Susan Weingarten points out to me that there is an obvious similarity of the slurs on Syrians to the speech that Cassius Dio attributes to Boudicca, attacking the *Romans* whom she accuses of bathing in hot water, whoring, drinking, with taunts of homosexuality and music-loving added to the list: Dio lxii, 6, 2–5. These clearly were stock slurs and the Romans are, for the benefit of the Roman readers of Cassius Dio, represented as Easterners in the eyes of the Iceni. There is a hint of the same idea in the speech

As I have pointed out elsewhere,[17] Corbulo was fighting a difficult mountain war in the Armenian highlands with troops which had been accustomed to service in Syria. This territory is hard for any army and it may be relevant to cite observations from an account of more recent warfare in the same region: 'A notable lesson of the successive Russo-Turkish wars over the same terrain and under similar climatic conditions is the progressive capacity of man to endure and overcome hardships imposed by the natural conditions.'[18] This suggests that perhaps the troops only had to undergo a natural process of acclimatization.

Like Dio, the *Historia Augusta* attributes derogatory remarks about Syrian troops to Marcus Aurelius, in a spurious letter:

> I have given Avidius Cassius the command of the Syrian legions, for they are abandoned to luxury and living the life of Daphnis; and Caesonius Vectilianus has written that he found these very legions all accustomed to bathe in hot water.

The implication is clear: Syrians are degenerate and poor soldiers. In their equally spurious answer the prefects write:

> You made the right decision, My Lord, when you put Cassius in command of the Syrian legions. Nothing benefits soldiers who have been living like Greeks so much as a man who is rather stern.

It is remarkable to encounter such anti-Greek sentiment in an author writing more than half a millennium after the incorporation of Greece into the empire. The expression *Graecanici milites* seems to be without parallel. It is reminiscent of the verb *pergraecari* i.e. 'to live like the Greeks, to revel, carouse', although this is attested only in pre-classical comedy.[19] Hostility towards Syrians is here expressed in the age-old, traditional anti-Greek terminology. We should note that these Syrians were troops from the province of Syria, rather than speakers of Syriac or Aramaic, as in the graffito cited above.

The author of the *Historia Augusta* uses similar language in a speech attributed to Severus Alexander addressing mutinous soldiers, in Antioch:

---

that Tacitus attributes to Calgacus, *Agricola* 32: 'An eandem Romanis in bello virtutem quam in pace lasciviam adesse creditis? . . .'

[17] *The Limits of Empire*, 24 f.
[18] W.E.D. Allen and P. Muratoff, *Caucasian Battlefields* (Cambridge, 1953), 7.
[19] I am grateful to Netta Zagagi for this reference.

> Soldiers of Rome, your companions, my comrades and fellow-soldiers, are whoring and drinking and bathing and, indeed, conducting themselves in the manner of the Greeks.

Here again the eastern troops are accused of degenerate behaviour and 'living like Greeks'. The *Historia Augusta* also mentions Antioch as the location of Verus' dissipation in the years when others were fighting his war for him, stating explicitly that low forms of entertainment are characteristic of this city, of Syria in general and of Alexandria.[20] The assumption is that the entertainment usually found in big cities anywhere is immoral and characteristic of the East. It is thought to belong to a Greek, decadent way of life that had been considered un-Roman ever since the days of the republic.[21] Singing and dancing on the stage were the ultimate disgrace of which Caligula and Nero and some aristocrats were guilty in the eyes of conservative Roman noblemen.[22]

Whatever the actual quality of life in eastern cities may have been, these are not objective descriptions of realities in the Roman east, but expressions of subjective hostility. What we can learn from such pronouncements is not that Syrians were degenerate, but that there were tensions between various cultures of the Roman empire with fear of the large cities of the East whose population was often hard to control.

It is remarkable that disparaging remarks regarding Syrians are found not only in the Latin literature, but also in the work of an author writing in Greek, Herodian, mainly in connection with the civil war of 193:

> Straight away they began to press Niger with requests to be allowed to take a personal part in the campaign. Syrians, being characteristically erratic people, are always ready to upset established rule.

According to Herodian, during the civil war in 193, Niger 'gave himself over to a life of useless luxury and enjoyment with the Antiochenes, spending his time on festivals and spectacles.' In a speech attributed to Septimius Severus we find the stereotype about eastern troops repeated:

---

[20] *SHA, Verus* 8, 11: 'adduxerat secum et fidicinas et tibicines et histriones scurrasque mimarios et praestigiatores et omnia mancipiorum genera, quorum Syria et Alexandria pascitur voluptate, prorsus ut videretur bellum non Parthicum sed histrionicum confecisse.' Cf. *SHA, Marcus Antoninus* 8, 12.

[21] Cicero, *Pro Murena* 6, 13: 'Saltatorem appellat L. Murenam Cato.'

[22] Suetonius, *Caligula* 54; *Nero* 20 f.; Tacitus, *Ann.* xiv 15 f.; cf. R. Syme, *Tacitus* (1958), 515 f.

Syrian troops live a life of luxury and are incapable of fighting. 'It is elegant, witty remarks that the Syrians are good at, particularly the people at Antioch'.[23] This, of course, is rhetoric, and represented as such, but Herodian himself believed in such statements. He describes a military tribune as a 'man of common sense—he was a Syrian by origin, and Easterners are rather clever. . . .' It is interesting to note that intelligence is associated with effeminate characteristics, while the true masculine fighter is thought to be rather straightforward and guileless.

So far all the passages cited have been connected with the army in Syria and the presumed effect of their presence there on their fighting qualities. We shall now turn to the *Historia Augusta* for pronouncements made in a different context.

> He [Alexander] preferred it to be thought that he derived his descent from the Roman people, for he was ashamed at being called a Syrian, particularly because on the occasion of a certain festival, the people of Antioch, the Egyptians, and the people of Alexandria had irritated him with taunts, as they are wont to do, calling him a Syrian *archisynagogus* and a high priest.[24]

For our present purposes it is irrelevant whether Severus Alexander was ever taunted in this manner, and whether he really was ashamed of being Syrian.[25] The passage is cited as an expression of anti-oriental sentiment in the late fourth century, and is most remarkable in its automatic assumption that being of Syrian origin and being Roman are mutually exclusive qualities. Syrians are not Romans, a sentiment

---

[23] Herodian, ii, 10, 6–7. Cf. iii, 4, 1: 'The support of the army helped Niger, but they were far inferior to the Illyrian troops in experience and quality'. The Illyrians are characterized elsewhere, ii, 9, 11: they have a fine physique and are good fighters, but are dull and stupid.

[24] *SHA, Severus Alexander* 28, 7, 'volebat [sc. Alexander] videri originem de Romanorum gente trahere, quia eium pudebat Syrum dici, maxime quod quodam tempore festo, ut solent, Antiochenses, Aegyptii, Alexandrini lacessiverant conviciolis, et Syrum archisynagogum eum vocantes et archiereum.' For comments, Stern, ii 630. This clearly reflects a hostile response to Alexander's respect of Jewish privileges, *ibid.*, 22, 4. There is no need to search for a rational explanation of why he was called an archisynagogus, cf. references in Stern, *loc. cit.* Schürer, ii 436, n. 40, notes that it is probable, but not absolutely certain that the phrase alludes to a Jewish rather than heathen *archisynagogus*; cf. Momigliano, *Athenaeum* N.S. 12 (1934), 151–3. There can be no doubt that a Jewish official is meant, for in a rather similar passage, *SHA, Quadrigae Tyrannorum* 8, 2 ff. (see below) explicit reference is made to a *archisynagogus Iudaeorum*.

[25] Alexander's shame may well be another of the author's witticisms. As will be seen below, Septimius Severus is said to have been ashamed as well, of his African origin, because his sister did not speak Latin.

expressed also in the graffito cited in the beginning of this article. There is also the interesting conflation of Alexander's Syrian origin and his alleged support of the Jews, apparent from the fact that he was called an *archisynagogus*.

In the passage just cited Alexander is represented as being ashamed of his origins.[26] The implications of being Syrian are expressed by the author in one of his spurious exchanges with the emperor Constantine.[27]

> You are wont to ask, great Constantine, how it could have happened that a man who was a Syrian and an alien became so great an emperor, while so many of Roman origin and so many from other provinces were found to be evil, impure, cruel, base, unjust, and lustful.

Once again the implication is that Syrians are not Romans but foreigners and that they are supposed to be a morally inferior people. It should be emphasized that expressions of such sentiment are neither incidental nor confined to this particular life. Elsewhere Claudius Pompeianus, Marcus' son-in-law and an Antiochene, is described as a foreigner (*peregrinus*).[28] Syrians are not only degenerate and frivolous, they lack the basic qualities that supposedly characterized Romans ever since the days of the early republic: *fides*,[29] and *gravitas*.[30]

Egyptians

So far the Syrians seem to have been the favourite target of literary slurs. The longest and most hostile tirade against the people of the East in the Historia Augusta, however, may be found in the *Quadrigae Tyrannorum*, in a spurious letter about the Egyptians, attributed to Hadrian, preceded by lavish disparagement: 'Among them, indeed,

---

[26] The statement that Alexander was ashamed of his origin is also repeated in *SHA, Severus Alexander* 44, 3 and 64, 3.

[27] *Op. cit.*, 65, 1: 'Soles quaerere, Constantine maxime, quid sit quod hominem Syrum et alienigenam talem principem fecerit, cum tot Romani generis, tot aliarum provinciarum reperiantur improbi, impuri, crudeles, abiecti, iniusti, libidinosi.' Cf. 68, 4: 'hi sunt qui bonum principem Syrum fecerunt, et item amici mali, qui Romanos pessimos etiam posteris tradiderunt, suis vitiis laborantes.'

[28] *SHA, Avidius Cassius* 10, 4: (epistula Faustinae ad Marcum): '. . . . Pompeianus gener et senior est et peregrinus.' *Marcus Antoninus* 20, 6: 'filiam suam . . . grandaevo equitis Romani filio Claudio Pompeiano dedit [sc. Marcus] genere Antiochensi. . . .'

[29] *SHA, Aurelian* 31: 'Rarum est ut Syri fidem servent, immo difficile.'

[30] *SHA, Tacitus* 3, 5: 'iam si nihil de Persicis motibus nuntiatur, cogitate tam leves esse mentes Syrorum ut regnare vel feminas cupiant potius quam nostram perpeti sanctimoniam.'

are Christians and Samaritans and those who are always dissatisfied
with the present although they enjoy excessive liberty. . . .' The letter
continues in a similar vein:

> Those who worship Serapis there, are [in fact] Christians, and those
> who call themselves bishops of Christ, are [in fact] devotees of Serapis.
> There is no Jewish archisynagogus, no Samaritan, no Christian presbyter,
> who is not an astrologer, a soothsayer, or a master of wrestlers. When
> the Patriarch himself visits Egypt, he is forced by some to worship
> Serapis, by others to worship Christ. They are a most seditious sort of
> people, most deceptive, most injurious; their city is wealthy, rich, and
> fertile and no one is idle. . . . Their only god is money, and this the
> Christians, the Jews, and all people adore.

There are several points of interest in this text. The author disapproves
of eastern religions among which he (a late fourth-century author)
still includes Christianity and that of the Samaritans, one of two
references to this people,[31] which reflects their increased prominence
in the fourth century. The author insists on the confusion which, he
claims, was characteristic of these peoples. Thus the (Jewish) Patriarch is compelled to worship Christ and Serapis when visiting Egypt.[32]
This reminds us of the alleged taunts of the people of Antioch, the
Egyptians, and the people of Alexandria who are supposed to have
called Severus Alexander a Syrian *archisynagogus* and a high priest.
The view that eastern peoples are seditious and frivolous has also
been encountered above among the sources regarding the Syrians.[33]
The identification of Jews with astrologers and the like goes back to
Hellenistic tradition and the republican period:[34] in 139 B.C. both
Jews and astrologers were expelled from Rome.[35] On the other hand,
the notion that easterners in general and Jews in particular are ava-
ricious and grasping has lasted till the present day.

Jews

The Jews have been mentioned frequently above, because they were
one of the main targets of slurs in the *SHA* aimed at Orientals in

---

[31] For the other, below, p. 277.
[32] Stern, ii, p. 639, points out that the Patriarch mentioned must be the Jewish
one, since he is described as being compelled to worship Christ and Serapis.
[33] Herodian ii, 7, 8–9; *SHA, Tacitus* 3, 5.
[34] See Vettius Valens and various references cited by Stern, ii, 173 f.
[35] Valerius Maximus, *Facta et Dicta Memorabilia* i, 3, 3 (Stern, i, no. 147, pp. 357–360).

general. There are two passages concerning Jews in particular worth citing here.[36]

> And sometimes at his banquets [Elagabalus] served ostriches, saying that the Jews had been commanded to eat them.[37]

This may be one of the many instances of deliberate obfuscation on the part of the author, for Jews are, in fact, forbidden to eat ostriches,[38] but he may not have known this. The point of the joke may have been merely that Jews are described as having been commanded to eat something exotic, while in fact they were known as people who abstained from perfectly normal fare like pork. The passage in which it occurs describes Elagabalus' religious mania, which aimed at including all major religions in his cult. Elsewhere Elagabalus is said to have demanded that the religions of the Jews and Samaritans and the rituals of the Christians should be transferred to the temple of Elagabalus on the Palatine, so that the priesthood of Elagabalus would include the mysteries of all forms of worship.[39]

The other reference to the Jews which ought to be discussed here is the following:

> At this time the Jews started a war because they were forbidden to mutilate their genitals.[40]

This statement is famous because it is the only source which appears to state explicitly that the cause of the Bar Kokhba war in the reign of Hadrian was a prohibition of circumcision.[41] Whatever the merit of this theory, it is worth noting that the SHA does not mention circumcision, but mutilation. The implication is that this was a ludicrous rebellion, for who in his senses would go to war because he

---

[36] There are 16 passages in Stern, vol. ii, pp. 612–40 which contain references to the people of Palestine, to Jews and Judaism. I only discuss the two which are relevant for the present discussion.

[37] SHA, Heliogabalus 28, 4: 'Struthocamelos exhibuit in cenis aliquotiens, dicens praeceptum Iudaeis ut ederent.'

[38] R. Syme, Ammianus and the Historia Augusta (1968), points out that the SHA shows an 'abnormal interest in ostriches.'

[39] SHA, Antoninus Heliogabalus 3, 4–5.

[40] Hadrian 14, 2: 'moverunt ea tempestate et Iudaei bellum, quod vetabantur mutilare genitalia.'

[41] The subject has been much debated. Cf. Schürer, i, 536–40; Smallwood, The Jews under Roman Rule, 429–31; Stern, ii, comments on pp. 619–21, all with extensive bibliography. Note also the articles (cited by Stern) of J. Geiger, Zion 41 (1976), 139; M.D. Herr, ibid., 43 (1978), 1–.

was forbidden to mutilate his genitals? It is a double reversal of the normal state of affairs, reminding us of the claim that the Jews were commanded to eat ostriches, discussed above. This is a view of Judaism which goes far back: 'To secure his influence over his people for the future, Moses introduced novel religious practices, the opposite of those of all other peoples. The Jews consider profane all that is sacred for us; on the other hand they permit all that is sinful for us.'

The statement about the origins of the Bar Kokhba war ridicules the war as such and it is therefore worth considering whether this does not call into question its trustworthiness.[42] The equation of circumcision with mutilation is found also in the work of a contemporary Christian author, John Chrysostom.[43]

The first passage about Elagabalus and the ostriches simply makes the point that Jewish dietary laws are ridiculous, while the reference to the Bar Kokhba war reinforces the image of the Jews, among other eastern peoples, as being both capricious and seditious.

Saracens

The Saracens or nomads inhabiting the desert areas in the east attract no attention in the Historia Augusta. Their name occurs only once, in a spurious story about Niger, where they are mentioned as people who abstain from alcohol;[44] they are clearly a remote people of no great interest from the perspective of the author of the *Historia Augusta*.

So far the peoples of the east. The hostile pronouncements in the *Historia Augusta* have been discussed at length because it is arguable that these show, in an uninhibited and jocular style, prejudices and animosity that were current among the intended readers of the *Historia Augusta* in this period. Moreover, it has been seen that such attitudes

---

[42] The Jews are mentioned frequently in other passages in the *SHA*, but these are not immediately relevant for the present discussion, see Stern for all the sources.

[43] John Chrysostom, *Homilia adversus Judaeos*, PG 48, col. 845. Chrysostom is quoting here Paul: *Philippians* 3, 2: βλέπετε τοὺς κύνας, βλέπετε τοὺς κακοὺς ἐργάτας, βλέπετε τὴν κατατομήν. ἡμεῖς γὰρ ἐσμεν ἡ περιτομή, οἱ πνεύματι θεοῦ λατρεύοντες. . . . 'Look out for the dogs, look out for the evil-workers, look for those who mutilate the flesh. For we are the true circumcision, who worship God in spirit. . . .' I owe this reference to Susan Weingarten.

[44] *SHA, Pescennius Niger* 7, 7–9. This seems to be the first source which mentions abstention from alcohol among the pre-Islamic Arabs. But a dedication from A.D. 132 mentions the god Shaiʿ al-Qaum who does not drink wine (*CIS* ii 1973).

are found even among Greek authors. Ammianus, another late fourth-century author, who wrote Latin but came from Antioch, writes without hesitation:

> After [Eutherius] had become head chamberlain, he would sometimes even castigate even Julian, (saying) that he had been raised in an Asiatic lifestyle and was therefore capricious.

This passage occurs in a eulogy of Eutherius and is clearly cited with approval. The same reproaches of Julian recur in a totally different context. When Julian's army suffered from a lack of food in Gaul his troops assailed him 'calling him an Asiatic, a Greekling and a deceiver, and an oaf with a pretence of learning'.[45] This is cited by Ammianus as the invective of a mutinous army, but it shows how widespread was the hostility against the eastern peoples of the empire amongst those of the west. We see, again, the equation of Asiatic with Greek and the explicit assumption that the characteristics of both are idle pretensions and dishonesty. It is furthermore important to note that these stereotypes were accepted by literary authors no less than by common soldiers.

The attitudes described are best seen in perspective when they are compared with utterances about other peoples: the inhabitants of Africa, Gauls, and barbarians.

Africans

In a few passages in the *Historia Augusta* the old accusation of *Punica fides*, i.e. faithlessness, is brought up.[46] That is a familiar *topos*. Otherwise derogatory remarks are confined to two aristocrats from Africa, of which the best known is the statement about the sister of Septimius Severus:

> His sister from Leptis came to visit him, and, since she hardly spoke Latin, the emperor was very much ashamed.

There is no way of proving this is nonsense, but the story is at least highly unlikely, for the family of Septimius Severus had held equestrian

---

[45] Ammianus xvii, 9, 3: '. . . Asianum appellans Graeculum et fallacem, et specie sapientiae stolidum.'

[46] *SHA, Maximini* 18, 1: (Maximinus in speech) 'Afri fidem fregerunt. nam quando tenuerunt?' *SHA, Gordian* 14, 1: (sim.) '. . . Afri fidem Punicam praestiterunt. . . .' Also: 15, 1.

rank for many generations, and Leptis Magna had received colonial status in the reign of Trajan.[47] It is indeed possible that Severus himself had an 'African accent',[48] but it is at least as likely that this is merely another of the author's witticisms. Above we have seen that Severus Alexander also is described as having been ashamed of his provincial background. The *Historia Augusta* seems to imply in its various remarks about African aristocrats that they could scarcely be accepted as belonging to the real Roman nobility. 'Clodinus Albinus came of a noble family, although he was a native of Hadrumetum in Africa.' It should be noted that Hadrumetum was a Roman colony, seat of the proconsular legate.

There is thus no indication that the author of the *Historia Augusta* had strong prejudices about Africa similar to those that he clearly expresses about easterners. There is, however, the persistent tendency to deny the provincials of both Syria and Africa their identity as true Romans.

Gauls

> Saturninus was a Gaul by origin, one of a people that is always very labile and eager to create an emperor or an empire.

This is the only expression of its kind in the whole work and should not be taken as any more than a reference to historical events in the third century.

Barbarians

> [Maximinus Thrax] came from a village in Thrace bordering on the barbarians and he was indeed the son of a barbarian father and mother, the former, they say, being a Goth, the other from the Alani. At least, it is said that his father was named Micca, his mother Ababa.[49]

---

[47] Leptis Magna: A. Birley, *Septimius Severus* (1971), 26–43. For the use of Latin in the Roman colonies of the East, Isaac, *Limits of Empire*, Chapter VII.

[48] *SHA, Severus* 19, 10: '. . . canorus voce, sed Afrum quiddam usque ad senectutem sonans.' For Septimius Severus and his formal schooling: Birley, *Septimius Severus*, 60–3.

[49] *Maximini* 1, 5–7: '[Maximinus] hic de vico Thraciae vicino barbaris, barbaro etiam patre et matre genitus, quorum alter e Gothia, alter ex Alanis genitus esse perhibetur. et patri quidem nomen Micca, matri Ababa fuisse dicitur.' Cf. Jordanes, *de Rebus Geticis* xv 83 who clearly copied the *SHA*.

The first point to be noted is that we have here yet another instance of the author's favourite joke of confusing identities.[50] Maximinus came from Thrace, but Thrace nowhere bordered on 'the barbarians', in the late second century, for Moesia and Dacia lay north of it.[51] The names of his parents are pure invention, barbaric creatures created for entertainment, like Severus' Punic speaking sister. Indeed the *Historia Augusta* claims that Maximinus could hardly speak or understand any Latin.[52] Other barbarian characteristics attributed to him are credulity,[53] and rashness.[54]

Apart from these few passages about Maximinus, descriptions of barbarians are of little interest to this author, unlike some other writers.[55]

To sum up, in the *Historia Augusta* Africans, Thracians and Gauls are mentioned incidentally, but only when an emperor or high officer came from these peoples. The source then finds it entertaining to represent such men as foreigners rather than true Roman aristocrats. Its attitude towards eastern peoples is entirely different. They are mentioned frequently and in varying contexts. They are described as foreigners, not Romans. They lack stability, *fides*, Latinitas, fighting qualities. All this is particularly true for Syrians who are described as decadent, not warlike, a people without *fides* or *gravitas*: they lack all the qualities exhibited by true Romans. Both the Syrians and the Egyptians are occasionally confused with Jews, Christians or Samaritans: an indication of muddled notions about identity and religion. This reflects a long tradition, but the difficulty is that the *Historia Augusta* almost always levels such accusations in a wholly or partly fictitious context, and it is difficult to judge where we have *genuine* prejudice as opposed to intentional obfuscation. Yet the same notions are found in many other authors of the first to the fourth centuries, notably in Ammianus, a Latin writing soldier from Antioch. There is every reason to assume that the *Historia Augusta* represents attitudes and hostile prejudices that were in fact quite common, but are

---

[50] The most remarkable case is the fact that he invented six spurious authors for his own work.

[51] Perhaps this is just geographical ignorance and not a deliberate joke.

[52] *SHA, Maximini* 2, 5: 'hic adulescens et semibarbarus et vix adhuc Latinae linguae, prope Thracica. . . .' Also: 9, 3–5.

[53] *Ibid.*, 9, 5.

[54] *Ibid.*, 12, 3 'habuit enim hoc barbaricae temeritatis. . . .'

[55] Herodian, for instance: i, 3, 5 with references on p. 15, n. 3 of the LCL edition (Whittaker); i, 6, 9 with reference on p. 36, n. 1.

expressed more freely in spurious biographies than in genuine works of historical scholarship. Finally we may note that the author of the *Historia Augusta* wrote not long before the division of the empire into a western and an eastern part. I should like to suggest that this division was partly the result of stresses between the aristocracies of the two parts and these then may be reflected in the attitudes here described.

So we see that the inscription from Sinai cited at the beginning of this article: 'Cessent Syri ante Latinos Romanos' reflected the attitude of many members of the army and aristocracy in the West. It is thus possible that the division of the empire into Latin speaking and Greek speaking parts resolved tensions of which we are insufficiently aware.

Bibliography

Birley, A., *Septimius Severus* (London, 1971).
Isaac, Benjamin, *The Limits of Empire: The Roman Army in the East* (Oxford, 1990, ²1992).
Matthews, J., *Western Aristocracies and Imperial Court, A.D. 364–425* (Oxford, 1975).
——, *The Roman Empire of Ammianus* (London, 1989).
Momigliano, A., 'Severo Alessandro Archisynagogus. Una Conferma alla Historia Augusta', *Athenaeum* N.S. 12 (1934), pp. 151–3.
Schürer, E., *The History of the Jewish People in the Age of Jesus Christ (175 B.C.– A.D. 135)*, revised and ed. by G. Vermes, F. Millar and M. Goodman, i–iii (Edinburgh, 1973–1987).
Smallwood, E. Mary, *The Jews under Roman Rule from Pompey to Diocletian: A Study in Political Relations* (Leiden, ²1981).
Stern, M., *Greek and Latin Authors on Jews and Judaism*, i–iii (Jerusalem, 1974–84).
Syme, R., *Ammianus and the Historia Augusta* (Oxford, 1968).
Tanner, R.G., 'Greek Epigraphy in South Jordan', *ZPE* 83 (1990), 183–193.
Vittinghoff, F., *Römische Kolonisation und Bürgerrechtspolitik unter Caesar und Augustus* (Wiesbaden, 1952).

Postscript

The subject of this paper belongs, again, to a category of topics that are nowadays discussed very frequently. However, this paper does not discuss Hellenisation, Romanisation or acculturation. It is concerned with a quite specific phenomenon, namely the way a fourth-century author looked at Eastern peoples. This is of some interest in itself and also because of the unique importance of the *Historia Augusta*. Since this source contains much information that is to be found nowhere else, every effort to see it in context is worthwhile.

19

EUSEBIUS AND THE GEOGRAPHY
OF ROMAN PROVINCES

Summary

Several recent studies discuss the limitations of ancient cartography and geographical method as an instrument of Roman military planning. The present article considers the evidence regarding the mapping of individual provinces with special reference to Eusebius, *Onomasticon of Biblical Place Names*, a list of Biblical place names and their identification with late-third-century locations in Palestine. The *Onomasticon* contains references to three aspects of Roman government: (1) It refers to state roads (but not to other highways). (2) It mentions military garrisons of the late third century. (3) It has information on the territories of cities founded or reorganized by the Roman authorities after the annexation of Judaea (but not on territories of cities already existing at the time). Eusebius is not familiar with the essence of Ptolemaean cartography, does not know the use of coordinates and did not produce a map of the area that he studied. It is clear that Eusebius used material in the governor's office in Caesarea and the limitations inherent in his work reflect those of the material which he used.

Military decisions at all levels are determined partly by geographical considerations. Planners of a major campaign are influenced by the geographical tools at their disposal no less than officers at a lower level on an everyday basis. The latter have to decide where to establish a small police fort, or the best route to follow through a hilly area, inhabited by hostile villagers.

In recent years questions about the limitations of ancient geography have been raised as part of a debate about Roman planning at the highest level, the so-called 'Grand Strategy'. Modern theories about an ancient Grand Strategy take it for granted that the Romans had concept of topographical realities which was clear and accurate enough to allow them to conceive of the general military situation in the broadest possible strategic terms. However, it has been suggested that ancient geography was far less developed than is often assumed. To deny the Romans advanced geographical insights is to deny them a Grand Strategy. The debate about the nature of Roman military planning has therefore branched off into another field of great importance in its own right: the limitations of ancient geography or, more precisely, the quality of the geographical tools at the disposal of Roman military officers.

The polemical character of this debate has to some extent obscured the fact that all military planning involves geography. Even if the existence of a Roman 'Grand Strategy' is denied, military decisions still were the result of planning which involved considerations of topography. The adequacy of geographical information was a factor which influenced the outcome of military undertakings.

Among some ancient geographers this was clearly recognized. It is expressed by Strabo in his introductory chapter (*Geog.* i 1.17), where he lists several major disasters which were the result of a lack of geographical information. The most recent of his examples are the Parthian campaigns of Crassus and Antony and a defeat in Germany (no doubt that of A.D. 9): 'The Barbarians fought local battles in swamps, in inaccessible forests, and in deserts and made what was near seem far away to their ignorant enemies and they kept them in ignorance of the roads, stocks of foodstuffs and other necessities.' Strabo considers geography a necessary tool for the ruler.

For Ptolemy 'geography' is a 'graphic representation of the whole known part of the world, along with things occurring in it' (*Geography* i 1.1). His work, unlike those of Pliny and Strabo, was an intellectual exercise in mapping the world (Dilke, 1987, 183). It has been shown conclusively that Ptolemy himself used literary sources when he had no earlier map at his disposal, but his work is conceptually cartographic. Whether he published maps himself is hardly relevant, for his material allows anyone who understands the principle of a grid to reconstruct the maps envisioned in the text. Ptolemy has no other aim than this. He does not attempt to persuade his readers that his work serves the needs of the wider public. Strabo, on the other hand, goes to much trouble to prove that his book is useful for the average educated public (*Geog.* i 1.22). He asserts that the ruler needs geography (i 1.18) and that Homer was the first geographer (i 1.2 ff.), a pronouncement inconceivable in the work of Ptolemy, who attempted to be scrupulous in his selection of sources. The Elder Pliny produced a compilation of scattered facts, dedicated to Titus and meant to be 'useful rather than enjoyable'.[1] Pomponius Mela observes that geography is not only arduous in itself, but repugnant to style.[2]

---

[1] Pliny, *NH, Praef.* 16: ... *qui ... utilitatem iuvandi praetulerunt gratiae placendi.*
[2] *Chorographia* 1.1: *impeditum opus et facundiae minime capax.*

We are faced with two antithetical traditions in ancient geography: the first comprised Ptolemy and his predecessors, such as Marinus of Tyre, pure academics—in the modern sense of the term—whose aim was to produce a true graphic representation of the entire world, a world-map; the other, utilitarian tradition saw in geography a primarily descriptive means of supplying statesmen and generals with the information they needed. They worked with texts rather than maps and sometimes their interests were focused on literature and linguistics rather than practicalities (Lee, 1993, 83 f.; Whittaker, 1994: chap. 1). Seneca quoted with approval the view that we should not trouble to investigate things that it is neither possible nor useful to know, such as the cause of the tides or the principle of perspective (Demetrius Cynicus *apud* Sen., *Ben.* 7.1.5–6, cited by Dodds 1951: 249). There is no indication that these two traditions ever came together in antiquity. Paradoxically then, those who understood the principles of map-making were interested in this only as an intellectual venture, while those who practiced geography to serve the rulers were not much interested in maps.

Modern military movements of any kind are invariably planned with the aid of reliable maps of the appropriate scale (e.g., 1:50.000). The commander of a small patrol will never enter enemy territory without a set of maps which show him the state of the roads, the topography, and the spread of settlement. He will also note on his maps whatever he knows about the distribution of hostile forces in the area. He needs such maps because he has to know where he can move with his vehicles, what kind of terrain he will cross, and what sort of population and enemy forces he may have to face, and what kind of support he may expect. For longer undertakings he must have information about the availability of water and food.

If we leave aside the requirements of modern technology, all this information was equally important to a Roman officer. This is the kind of information Vegetius advises the good commander to prepare before any campaign (III 6, ed. Lang, p. 75). Vegetius here discusses the needs of an army on the move. Those did not include maps of the entire Mediterranean, which would be required nowadays for large-scale planning. It is not likely that the average commander had such material, in Vegetius' time or during the principate. Vegetius speaks of the past when '*sollertiores duces*', the more expert commanders, had not only verbal, but also illustrated itineraries of the roads in the provinces of the Empire—'*itinera provinciarum*'. Vegetius was clearly thinking of road maps of the provinces of the empire, not of information about enemy territory, not even of proper maps of the provinces. Any military commander needs maps, or he must know the area himself, or depend on others who do. This is also to a large extent implied by Vegetius. The old commanders had *itineraria picta* so that they could pick the right road not only through mental deliberation, but while seeing it with their eyes (*ut non solum consilio mentis verum aspectu oculorum viam profecturus eligeret*). Vegetius then goes on to describe more extensively how the commander should handle local guides. Once again, Vegetius is talking about warfare in the provinces, not about foreign campaigns. Information about terrain beyond the provincial boundary was undoubtedly worse.

It is clear that senatorial or equestrian officers of the principate, who served relatively short periods in various parts of the empire, were usually not familiar with the terrain. They would therefore depend on long-serving centurions for information about the terrain. This inevitably dictated the quality of their planning, since the possible range of an officer's decisions is restricted by the quality of the information he receives.

It is the aim of this paper to discuss the availability in antiquity of information at the level of provincial commanders. It is important to know what kind of material a Roman legate would find upon his arrival in a province. What kind of geographical information would be provided in writing? Or (to give a specific example) if he received information that the inhabitants of a certain village resorted to banditry or refused to pay taxes, what could he know about the location and accessibility of the village without asking someone else who knew the terrain? Quite possibly the textual information was good. We have sufficient ancient geographical texts to form an idea of what kind of descriptive sources could be produced. Maps and itineraries, however, are scarce for all of antiquity and normally aim to give information at a global level. The very scarcity of ancient maps and itineraries itself means that every argument about the material can be turned on its head. Whenever a deduction is drawn from the Peutinger Table or the *Itinerarium Burdigalense* an argument can be produced to counter it. It can be assumed that there existed a different kind of global map, which is now lost, or there may have been regional sources which gave an entirely different perspective.

Regional Geography: Eusebius

In the view of Ptolemy (*Geog.* i 1) regional geography was a semantic impossibility. Geography is concerned with the entire world and that was his field. A different discipline, 'chorography' (χωρογαφία), studies parts of the world in isolation and in full detail, describing 'for instance ports, villages, peoples, rivers and their tributaries etc.' (Whittaker 1994: 12). This would indeed have been of interest to administrators and officers, but we have not much ancient material of this sort to form an impression of its quality.

However, there is one source which should be discussed in this connection, namely Eusebius' *Onomasticon of Biblical Place Names*. This is a unique mine of information about a limited area of the Roman Empire. It is unique because it is the only text which is concerned, solely and consistently, with regional matters. The *Onomasticon* is exceptional in antiquity by any standard because of the sheer quantity of facts that it provides about a very small part of the Empire. It covers parts of the Roman provinces of Judaea/Palaestina, Arabia and Syria. It contains more than 900 lemmata, which refer to 29 cities and hundreds of villages. Eusebius mentions the location of settlements along 20 roads and knows of the presence of military garrisons at 11 sites. The aim of the work is to focus not primarily on the cities, but on biblical sites, most of which were villages and small places. While cities regularly serve as a point of reference, the setting of the work is essentially rural rare in classical texts. The work has been studied intensively by scholars interested in the Holy Land, but it is not a book which has received much attention from historians of the Roman Empire. Yet it is a rare source, giving us an insight in the level of detailed geographical knowledge and understanding in a provincial capital, rather than at the centre of the empire.

It is uncertain when Eusebius (ca. 260–ca. 340) wrote his *Onomasticon*. It is usually assumed that the work was written c. 330 (Klostermann, 1904, pp. ix–x), but Barnes, (1975, 412–5; 1981, 110 f.) argued that it was written around 293. Eusebius' aim was to clarify Biblical topography in the geographical terms of his own age. The work is essentially a list of Biblical place names and their identifications with late 3rd-c. locations, primarily cities and villages, but other prominent features such as mountains, plains, deserts and rivers are included. It is, therefore, not only an invaluable source of information on third-century Palestine, but also the most detailed ancient geographical work about any part of the Roman Empire. Eusebius was bishop of Caesarea, seat of the provincial governor, and therefore well placed to use any geographical material to be found in the governor's archive. We should keep in mind, however, that Eusebius did not aim to provide a source-book for administrative historians of the Roman Empire. His terms of reference were primarily practical and he used therefore points of reference which were obvious for a contemporary public. These would be administrative or topographical realities.

Eusebius and Cartography

It should be mentioned first that there is no indication in the *Onomasticon* that it was accompanied by a map of any kind when originally published. In this respect it resembles the works of Strabo and Pliny (or, in modern terms, that of Schürer, old and new versions). Eusebius usually tries to locate a site in relation to a public road (Noth, 1943). This kind of information is generally accurate and to the point, and related to the structure of ancient *itineraria*: the information is verbal, not graphically represented, but the linear distances along roads which he gives are correct. When sites cannot be pinpointed in relationship to roads, Eusebius resorts to less precise methods such as the distance from geographical features like mountains (e.g. Mount Tabor), valleys, or significant sites (e.g., Legio in the Jezreel Valley. Legio had been a legionary base but did not yet have city status, and it was situated near an important crossroads). Often he measures a distance from a city and gives a general direction: north, south, east or west, where for instance 'north' can mean anything between west and east. An alternative method is a vague indication that a site lies 'between' two cities which he names (cf. Snodgrass 1987: chap. 3).

Eusebius, Ptolemy and the Madaba Map

Eusebius does not know of the use of co-ordinates, even though he wrote 150 years after Ptolemy published his 'Geography'. Eusebius himself may have looked at maps, but it is absolutely impossible to draw any map based on the information he provides. In this connection we must refer to the 6th-c. mosaic map at Madaba. Clearly this map relies heavily on Eusebius' *Onomasticon*, for many captions cite Eusebius (Avi-Yonah, 1954). While a map based on Ptolemy's work results in a network of dots on a grid, the Madaba Map offers the spectator a bird's eye view of the Holy Land as seen towards the east. Towns are drawn out of scale as if seen in perspective from the air, resembling the cities on the Peutinger Table and those on the maps accompanying the manuscripts of the *Notitia Dignitatum*. The distortions are as remarkable as those on the Peutinger Map. Hundreds of kilometres between Gaza and the Nile Delta are compressed into the same space as tens of kilometres west of the Jordan. The scale of the map becomes gradually larger towards the edges. While the centre of the map that had to contain much information is drawn at a small scale, the periphery is shown as precisely that—the larger environment which could be drawn at a much bigger scale. The compiler of the Madaba Map copied textual information from Eusebius but took no account of the distances shown in the Onomasticon. In this respect the Madaba Map resembles the Peutinger Table which is not drawn to any scale, although it is full of indications of distance. In the case of the Peutinger Table, it has occasionally been claimed that it owes its elongated form to having been inscribed on a papyrus roll, or less plausibly, to the elongated shape of its supposed distant ancestor, Agrippa's world map, which had to fit a portico in which it was placed. The same cannot be claimed for the Madaba Map. The distortions are the result not of necessity but of the aims of the map-maker. He wanted to draw the Holy Land as seen through the eyes of a single person high from the west, above the Mediterranean, looking eastwards.

One cannot blame Eusebius for the fact that the Madaba Map is not drawn at a uniform scale, for Eusebius did not produce a map. His unawareness of the use of coordinates, however, is clearly a feature inherent to his method. For Eusebius any given site can be located only in relation to one or two other points. In the work of Ptolemy, on the other hand, any given point can be located in relation to all other points in his grid. In other words: Eusebius will give the distance between A and B, and between X and Y, but this does not allow us to work out the distance between A and Y, something which in Ptolemy's system can be done without difficulty. This had serious practical consequences for military planners must know all possible routes to a given point.

To sum up, Eusebius was not familiar with the ideas of Ptolemaean cartography. He did not produce a map of the Holy Land and the sixth-century map which used the *Onomasticon* as a source reflects essentially the same conceptual framework as the Peutinger Table, although it is not a road-map. Apparently in Eusebius' time regional cartography was not much different in quality from global geography as represented by the Peutinger Table, the *Itinerarium Antonini*, or the works of Strabo and others. The material here discussed relates to the Holy Land only. However, what we know of other maps of more restricted areas—those accompanying the *Notitia Dignitatum* or the *Agrimensores*—reinforces the impression that the Romans did not regularly use maps drawn to scale for surfaces larger than a single town or its fields. These conclusions tie in with the work of P. Janni, who observed that the ancient approach to geography was essentially linear (Janni, 1984; Purcell, 1990; Lee, 1993, 81–90). This clearly has consequences for what we must assume to have been the level of planning at, say, a governor's headquarters.

Two interconnected points must be made here. Not only map-making, but also using maps are techniques which must be learnt. In modern times this is a part of the primary school curriculum to familiarize children with maps on various scales: local maps, maps of their own state or country, continent, and the whole world. The mental translation of two dimensional graphic representations into larger surfaces of the same proportions, whatever the scale, is an acquired skill. There is nothing in the ancient literature to show that this was a common art in antiquity, and the extant maps suggest that Ptolemy's work never gained wide popularity. This leads to the second point. Modern maps convey a true sense of topography and relief through contour lines. It requires experience and training to make a mental translation of an accurate modern map with contour lines into an image of the reality on the ground, yet every officer in a modern army is taught how to do this. Evidently ancient cartographers never developed a technique to depict relief on maps in a fairly accurate manner. The Peutinger Table makes no difference in its representation of high hills and the Caucasus Mountains. Even the handbooks of the Roman land surveyors cannot do better than to draw pictures of hills and mountains adjacent to the plans of surveyed areas (Dilke 1971: 191–72; Whittaker 1994: 19–21).

Eusebius and his Sources

Eusebius nowhere specifies the contemporary sources from which he derived his information. So far the conclusions have been primarily negative: there was no regional cartography in the modern sense of the word. This leaves us with the question of what kind of information Eusebius, or any other official or officer in a provincial capital, had at his disposal. We may assume that Eusebius, one of the most influential men in the province, a scholar with an interest in geography, collected facts in whatever way he could.

The question of Eusebius' contemporary sources has been a subject of debate. Thomsen and Klostermann suggest that Eusebius must have used lost written sources. They have no doubt that these were official itineraries and lists (Klostermann, 1904, xvi; Thomsen, 1903). This is possible, but Eusebius does not say so. In the *Onomasticon* Eusebius only mentions the Bible and New Testament, and gives no sources for contemporary information. Jerome's Latin translation of the work is totally dependent on Eusebius' Greek and gives hardly any independent information. When Eusebius disagrees with information he has obtained, he uses vague expressions like 'they say' or 'it is being told' (20, 10: φασίν; 168, 15: λέγεται εἶναι), which suggest, if anything, oral information. The discussion of Eusebius' sources has to stand on its own, for we have no information about what kinds of documents were generally available in the archives of a 4th-c. provincial capital. R. Haensch, in his recent comprehensive study of these archives (1992, esp. 264), assumes that they included lists of auxiliary units and their stations. Neither Haensch nor the literature which he cites contain any proof of the existence of such lists, although there can be little doubt that they existed. For the existence of *itineraria*, the only evidence is Vegetius iii 6.

Kubitschek criticized Thomsen's (and Klostermann's) hypothesis regarding Eusebius' sources (Kubitschek, 1905, followed by Barnes, 1981, 108 f.). Thomsen then responded, restating his position with a slight modification (Thomsen, 1906). This position was later pursued further by Beyer (1931, esp. 214–7; 1933) and taken to extremes by M. Avi-Yonah (1977, 127–9). Thus, we are faced with two antithetical approaches: Thomsen and his followers assume that Eusebius used official documents in Caesarea which may be traced through the fabric of the *Onomasticon*. Kubitschek and Barnes assume that the work is the result of personal knowledge and oral information. Both contentions are hypotheses rather than the result of systematic study. We shall argue that methodical study of all the information in the *Onomasticon* may reach a more satisfactory insight in the nature of Eusebius' sources. This in turn should help in the interpretation of the material which is represented in his work.

As argued elsewhere (Isaac, 1978; Isaac & Roll, 1982), misunderstandings as to the structure of the work and the quality of the information it contains have led to over-interpretation. Consequently distorted maps have been drawn of the administrative division of Palestine in the Roman and Byzantine periods. This is not a topic to be pursued here. However, the *Onomasticon* itself may still shed some light on the availability of literary material and Eusebius' use of it. Here, as so often with unique sources, my claim must rest on an analysis only of internal and implicit evidence. I shall argue that the conclusions to be drawn from the information contained in the *Onomasticon* are of general interest, because they say something about the organization of administrative and geographical material in a provincial capital. This in turn has consequences for our thinking about military planning in the Roman Empire at large.

In what follows I shall try to limit as much as possible the discussion of details of local Palestinian historical geography.[3] However, some discussion is necessary here, for if Eusebius used documentary material—as distinct from oral information—his work must reflect explicit information on the Roman administration of the area. The *Onomasticon* contains references to three aspects of Roman government: (a) public roads, (b) garrisons, and (c) city-territories. I shall now argue that this is a selection of references which is determined not by coincidence or random factors. The selection, it will be seen, can be explained satisfactorily only when it is assumed that they derive from Roman documents.

(a) *Public Roads*

The *Onomasticon* contains more than 30 references to 20 roads in Palaestina, Arabia and Syria. Usually this takes the form of a statement that a site 'is x miles from A as one goes to B.' These references are particularly instructive for the material which the author

---

[3] Full treatment of the subject is envisioned in a book about Palestine after the Bar Kokhba war by Aharon Oppenheimer and myself.

uses, for all the roads he mentions were part of the public road-system. Roman state roads were marked with milestones and mile-stones have been found along each of the Roman roads mentioned in the *Onomasticon*.[4] This point may be pursued a little further. Be-sides the network of Roman state roads, there is a system of ancient roads, often well-constructed, which was not part of the public road-system. Such roads, although paved and sometimes even provided with watch-towers, were not provided with milestones, as will be seen on the *TIR*. Roads of this type are never mentioned by Eusebius, not even in lemmata dealing with sites along them. A few examples will suffice: Thecoa (86, 12), Ziph (92, 19), Maon (130, 12) and Chermala (118, 5), are all three sited along the road from Bethlehem to the south. This is a remarkably well constructed road along the eastern edge of the Hebron Mountains, provided with watch towers, but without milestones. Chermala (Chermula, Karmelos) is mentioned as a military garrison by Eusebius (and in *Not. Dig. Or.* xxxiv 20), but without mention of the road. Beer Sheva (Bersabe, Beer-sheba), also a military site (Eusebius 50, 1; *Not. Dig. Or.* xxxiv 18), was a cross-roads of two important roads, both of which lack milestones. Again, Eusebius does not mention these roads. Other examples are Menois (130, 7) on the road from Gaza to Nessana and Chorazin (174, 23) on the road from Beth Saida (Julias) to Ptolemais. In Provincia Arabia Eusebius lists Zoora (Zoar, 42, 1) and Mefa (Umm er-Resas, 128, 21) as military stations without mentioning that they lay on important roads, namely the east-west road south of the Dead Sea and the desert road, parallel to and east of the *Via Nova Traiana*.

It is clear then, that Eusebius, although well informed about the roads which were part of the public system, had no knowledge of other important, well-paved roads which did not belong to the state. All the same, he regularly mentions sites which were situated along them, sometimes even adding that there was a garrison. It is clear that this is not the kind of information which he would have ob-served himself while traveling through the region, or which he would have received orally from local informants. He must have worked with a written source which gave partial and specific information. The obvious conclusion is that he found in Caesarea a reliable list of public roads. Such a list would not have told him how to reach Beer

---

[4] Milestones are indicated on the newly published sheet of the *TIR*; note also the bibliography in Graf, Isaac and Roll, 1992.

Sheva, for instance, but it apparently contained some information about major arteries in the neighbouring provinces.

The conclusion that Eusebius' source at the governor's office would not have contained information on roads that were major surfaced highways but not state roads may seem rather astonishing. Yet the quantity of evidence on which it is based leaves no doubt. The area with which we are concerned measures roughly 220 km N-S and 60 to 75 km E-W. The Roman road-network is quite dense and the numbers of milestones discovered during a century of survey activity is large. The network of roads provided with milestones measures, very roughly, 1450 km or 975 miles. A total of 180 mile-stations has been identified, representing more than 550 milestones. This includes all of the roads mentioned by Eusebius, apart from the Ascalon—Azotus road.[5] Three roads which Eusebius mentions in the province of Arabia are also marked with milestones. Our information on the network of state roads in the area is therefore quite sound and we can confidently distinguish between the former and the surfaced highways which were not state roads. There is no doubt that Eusebius only refers to the former.

There is a complementary point of interest in all this, namely the significance of Roman milestones. Comparison of roads mentioned (or not mentioned) by Eusebius with the distribution of Roman milestones along roads in the area demonstrates that these markers do represent formal organization. This of course has always been assumed, but there was little to prove the point, since there are no texts which clarify the function of milestones (Pekáry, 1968: *passim*; Isaac, 1992, 108–112; 304–9). The inscriptions on milestones represent a form of imperial propaganda, but this was not the primary reason why the stones were set up along roads. We now know that the capital of one province, Caesarea, had lists with information on the roads which were provided with milestones, but they ignored others. This has consequences for the interpretation of the distribution of milestones in other provinces. For our purposes, however, it is interesting to observe that a new Roman governor in Caesarea probably found himself in the same position as Eusebius: he would

---

[5] This road ran through sand dunes and, like other roads near the sea, has not been found. It should be noted that a few (three) stretches of roads have been identified by one milestation only. It is therefore possible that a few more such cases will be discovered in future, but this would not affect my conclusions regarding Eusebius.

have a list showing him how to travel along the public roads, but this list ignored well-paved secondary roads.

(b) *Garrisons*

Eusebius' *Onomasticon* contains statements about 11 garrisons. His facts are up-to-date; he does not refer to garrisons which we know to have been in the area in the 2nd-c., but were withdrawn by the end of the 3rd. As with the road-system, his information extends also to the province of Arabia. His references to garrisons at the places he mentions do not identify the units by name, apart from the Tenth Legion at Aela. The reason for this omission must be that such information was irrelevant to his aims, but there can be little doubt that this type of information was available in Caesarea. It is possible, but not necessarily the case, that he himself was aware of the location of garrisons in the province. He may have found an army list in Caesarea or even a kind of predecessor of the *Notitia Dignitatum*.

(c) *City Territories*

The third category to which Eusebius refers regularly is again of great interest: the territories of cities. There are 29 villages for which he specifically states to which city territory they belong. This has inspired many scholars to use the *Onomasticon* for the study of the administrative division of Palaestina at this period.

Avi-Yonah assumed that the indications of distance in Eusebius' *Onomasticon* were taken from an unknown road map which must have been based strictly on the administrative organization of the province. Wherever Eusebius gives the distance from a city to a village, this village is presumed by Avi-Yonah to have been within the territory of that city. Thus, building one hypothesis on another, Avi-Yonah published maps that showed in detail the presumed boundaries of all the city territories of Palestine (Avi-Yonah, 1977; also: 1973: esp. cols. 414–27 with map on p. 418; his contribution to Jones 1971, esp. pp. 276–280). Avi-Yonah's approach holds that each indication of distance to a city is an implicit statement to the effect that the point in question belonged to that city. In other words, if Eusebius says that village X lies 20 miles from city Y, then X lies in the territory of Y. I prefer to assume that only explicit statements can be used as a basis for interpretation. The *Onomasticon* contains more information about the territory of Eleutheropolis and its vicinity (13 attributions) than about any other city west or east of the Jordan. I shall therefore cite some examples taken from the material relating to this city.

The first guideline in the interpretation should be that, if Eusebius says that village A lies in the territory of X, then we may believe him, but if he merely says that village B lies 15 miles from city X, this does not necessarily mean that it was in the territory of X. Yet, with due caution two further assumptions may be made regarding such *lemmata*:

(1) When it is clear from explicit statements in the *Onomasticon* that Eusebius had information on the territory of a given city and when he says that a village is 'near' this city, then it is probable that it belonged to the city. In such a case Eusebius simply omits making an explicit statement because it would have been superfluous. Thus, when he says that Bethsur (52, 4), lies 1 mile from Eleutheropolis, it would be unreasonable to conclude that it was not in the territory of Eleutheropolis, merely because Eusebius fails to spell this out. Eusebius frequently refers to the territory of Eleutheropolis. There are places 20 miles from the city which he attributes to its territory. These explicit statements make sense, because it was not evident that relatively remote villages belonged to the city.

(2) If Eusebius says that village C lies 15 miles from Z, without adding that it was in the territory of Z, and if the farthest extent of the territory of Z is less than 15 miles, according to the evidence in the *Onomasticon* then it is probable that C did not lie in the territory of Z and that Eusebius was aware of this. For instance, Esthemo (Eshtemo'a, E-Samo'a, M.R. 156.089) is 'in the territory of Eleutheropolis' (86, 20; also 26, 11). The distance from Eleutheropolis is about 30 km (20 miles). Ietheira (88, 3; 108, 2), also 20 miles from Eleutheropolis, is not described as belonging to Eleutheropolis. This is Yathir, (Kh. 'Attir, M.R. 151.084), 6 km south-west of Eshtemo'a. It makes sense that the former place would belong to Eleutheropolis and the latter not, for the former lies in the hills south of Hebron and the latter at the edge of the desert. Another example may be taken from another city, Neapolis (Nablus, Shekhem): Thebes (modern Tubas, M.R. 184.192) is described as 13 miles/c. 19 km from this city and in its territory, on the road to Scythopolis (100, 13). The village of Aser, was, according to Eusebius, 15 miles/c. 22 km

from Neapolis on the same road (26, 23). This place can be identified with modern Tayasir, (M.R. 187.194), 11.5 miles/17 km from Neapolis.[6] It is reasonable to assume that the boundary of the territory of Neapolis was between Thebes, said to belong to it, and Aser, which is not described as belonging to it. The furthest extent of the territory to the northeast would then have been between 13 and 15 miles.

Eusebius does not usually bother specifying that settlements very close to a city belonged to the territory of that city. This is understandable. In many, or most cases where he explicitly mentions dependency, the settlements were not near the city, but closer to the boundary of the city territory. Eusebius never says this, but we can deduce it from a systematic comparison of villages mentioned as belonging to a particular city with more distant sites mentioned in relation to the same city. Where we have sufficient information, as with Eleutheropolis, we can distinguish villages still belonging to the territory from those just beyond the boundary of its jurisdiction.

A crucial question is why Eusebius frequently and systematically refers to the territories of some cities, and not at all to those of many others, some of which he must have known well. It is likely that this is connected with the sources which he used. We must keep in mind that the arrangement of the work was decided by the books of the Bible and the sites mentioned there. The *Onomasticon* represents a Biblical framework on which a 3rd-c. collection of geographical and administrative facts has been superimposed. Yet it remains an indisputable fact that Eusebius ignores city territories in large parts of the country. He often gives the distance from Scythopolis, an important city, without ever referring to its territory. As observed above, he attributes one village on the Neapolis-Scythopolis road to Neapolis but is silent about the attribution of the next village which apparently did not belong to Neapolis and thus almost certainly belonged to Scythopolis. He regularly mentions cities on the coast: Caesarea, the provincial capital where he was bishop, Joppe, Ascalon and Gaza, but never refers to the territory of any of these cities. The *Onomasticon* regularly refers to villages in relation to cities across the Jordan, but here too it does not mention city-territories in those parts.

It is true that the selection of sites was dictated by the Biblical

---

[6] *Itinerarium Burdigalense* 587, 1 (*CCSL* 175, 13): '*Aser, ubi fuit villa Iob*', 16 miles from Scythopolis. Cf. Abel, 254. For this section of the road: P. Welten, *ZDPV* 81 (1965), 138–65.

material. Yet it is undoubtedly significant that all positive information about territories derives from six cities in the hill country in the interior. Eusebius nowhere refers to city territories in the coastal plain or the valleys in the interior (the Valley of Jezreel, of Scythopolis, and the Jordan Valley). Yet he mentions cities there, and many villages in these areas, at least some of which must have belonged to those cities.

The question to ask about the cities for which he gives concrete information about their territories is: What do they have in common? These cities are: Eleutheropolis (Beth Guvrin), Neapolis (Nablus, Shechem), Sebaste (Samaria), Aelia Capitolina (Jerusalem), Diospolis (Lydda, Lod), Diocaesarea (Sepphoris). The chief characteristic is that they all were founded, or refounded and reorganized after the annexation of Judaea as a Roman province. While those founded by the Roman authorities would not previously have had territory of their own, the cities which were refounded would have had their territories reorganized and redivided. There are a few apparent exceptions which can be explained. The territory of Sebaste, founded originally by Herod, probably was reorganized on one or both of two occasions. It could have occurred following the First Jewish Revolt when neighbouring Neapolis was founded; alternatively, territorial changes may have been made when Septimius Severus punished Neapolis and rewarded Sebaste for their respective attitudes during the civil war in 193.[7] A number of omissions from Eusebius' list can also be explained. Caesarea received colonial status in the seventies, and Flavia Joppe (Jaffa) received a new name in the same period. However, these were changes in status of existing cities and would not have entailed changes in their territories, for they were not accompanied by the introduction of new settlers or changes in the status of neighbouring territories. Also missing is Nicopolis (Emmaus), which received city status in the reign of Elagabalus. Nicopolis can hardly have received a large territory, for it was surrounded on all sides by existing cities which retained their territories: Aelia, Diospolis, Eleutheropolis, and Jamnia.

---

[7] Colonial status for Sebaste: Paulus, *Dig.* L 15, 8, 7: 'The divine Severus gave the city of Sebaste colonial status' (*Divus quoque Severus in Sebastenam civitatem coloniam deduxit*). Colonial coinage: Hill, *BMC, Palestine*, xxxix, 80, nos. 12 f. The latest precolonial coinage dates to 201/2: Kindler and Stein, *Bibliography*, 222–9. Neapolis was punished: *SHA, Severus*, 9, 5: 'He also deprived the citizens of Neapolis in Palestine of city status because they has long supported Niger with their arms' (*Neapolitanis etiam Palaestinensibus ius civitatis tulit, quod pro Nigro diu in armis fuerunt*).

An interesting point is the absence of any reference to the territory of Ptolemais-Acco. Ptolemais was an ancient town (Schürer, ii, 121–5), but there is epigraphic proof that the territory was reorganized following the establishment of a Roman veteran colony there in the reign of Claudius (Isaac, 1992, 322 f.; 344). This is clear from the discovery of a centuriation stone in the territory (Meyer, 1983–4; Avi-Yonah, 1946, 86 n. 3: '*Pago Vicinal(i)*'). Eusebius must have been familiar with the city and with all sites along the coast road to Tyre and Antioch. The reorganization of the territory in the reign of Claudius could have been documented in the offices of the provincial governor. Several villages are mentioned in connection with Ptolemais (for which see 30, 10) without any reference to territory. Achzeiph (Akhziph, Ecdippa), 9 miles (actually 14 km) from Ptolemais on the road to Tyre, definitely belonged to the territory of Ptolemais. Sycaminum (Shiqmonah, 108, 30) is a well-known site, frequently mentioned in the ancient literature, which has long been under excavation (Avi-Yonah, Gazetteer, 98; *NEAEHL* IV: 1373–78); it lies on the coast near the northern tip of Mount Carmel and belongs to the Province of Syria Phoenice and hence to the territory of Ptolemais according to all definitions:[8] *Ibi est mons Carmelus, ibi Helias sacrificium faciebat. mutatio Certha . . . milia viii. Fines Syriae Finices et Palestinae. civitas Caesarea Palestina id est Iudaea milia viii.*[9] The same would be true for Magdiel (130, 21), 5 north of Dor. Eusebius mentions both as villages on the road from Caesarea to Ptolemais without referring to territory. All three villages would be familiar to anyone who ever travelled from Caesarea to Tyre and thus certainly to Eusebius.

These were three sites which clearly belonged to the territory of Ptolemais, but Eusebius did not describe them as such, although it was territory next to the city where he lived. The reason is obvious: Ptolemais belonged to the neighbouring province and any material on it would not have been found in the offices of the governor of Palaestina, but in those of the neighbouring province to which Ptolemais belonged. These were in Antioch in the 1st c. and in Tyre

---

[8] The *Itinerarium Burdigalense* 584, 8–585, 4 (O. Cuntz ed., *Itineraria Romana* [Leipzig 1929], p. 94; ed. Geyer & Cuntz, *CCSL* 175, p. 12) explicitly marks the border between the provinces of Syria Phoenice and Palaestina at Certha, 8 miles south of Sicaminos (Shiqmona) and an equal distance N. of Caesarea.

[9] 'There is Mt. Carmel where Helias made his sacrifice. Mutatio Certha . . . at eight miles. The boundary of Syria Finice and Palaestina. The city of Caesarea Palestina, that is Judaea, at eight miles.'

in the 3rd. The absence of information on the territory of Ptolemais thus fits the assumption that Eusebius used lists present in the office of the governor of Palaestina. It would be inexplicable if one assumes that he picked up oral information while travelling in the area.

This is an argument from silence, but the conclusions, based on an analysis of all 29 references to city territory are consistent: Eusebius mentions territory only in connection with cities in Judaea/Palaestina whose territories were established by the Roman government. He fails to refer to the territories of long existing cities or those founded in the period of the Herodian dynasty before the final annexation of Judaea as a Roman province. Eusebius worked with lists that took account only of changes affecting the city territories in Judaea between the First Jewish Revolt and his own time. He had information only on the territories of those cities which the Roman authorities had founded, or refounded. Apparently he did not have information on the territories of cities founded before the final annexation of the province[10] or those in neighbouring provinces, even if he knew them well, such as Ptolemais. Since the *Onomasticon* is the only work of its kind, we cannot check these conclusions through comparison with other sources. However, this interpretation of the material is entirely consistent and does not result in the internal contradictions which bedevil other approaches.

The conclusions should dictate our views of the material which he used. We may discard the theory that he used only (or almost exclusively) oral information or personal knowledge. There is no conceivable reason why contemporary informants should tell him only about the territories of cities in Judaea and not in Syria or Arabia, which had been founded or refounded under Roman rule. The only rational explanation is that he used specific kinds of written sources.

Since Eusebius lived in Caesarea, the provincial capital, where he was bishop, this should tell us something about the nature and limitations of the provincial archives. Eusebius must have used whatever he found in the archives in Caesarea, if it contributed towards his purpose of explaining to his readers the location of a contemporary place which he identified with a Biblical site.

---

[10] There is one apparent exception: Asor, described as a village east of Ascalon and in its territory (20, 3). Ascalon was an ancient and important city, definitely not founded or refounded by Rome. The explanation is that, for Eusebius, Ascalon was synonym with traditional 'Philistia': Φυλιστιείμ ἡ νῦν Ἀσκαλὼν καλουμένη, καὶ ἡ περὶ αὐτὴν χώρα τῆς Παλαιστίνης ἐπίσημος (166.18).

Eusebius: Conclusions

The information found in the *Onomasticon* is not a random collection of facts, but selected according to principles which can be traced. Eusebius used material which contained full information about the network of Roman public roads in the provinces of Palaestina and Arabia. Whenever he could, he marked the position of a site vis-à-vis the road-network. Milestones have been found along each of the roads which he mentions and he does not mention any roads which were not provided with milestones. This shows that he did not collect his information while travelling through the country or asking questions from private persons. He obviously found fairly accurate verbal '*itineraria*' and various other kinds of lists.

If a site was not near a public road of which he knew, he gives distances from towns or important features. While his distances are often correct, he is incapable of giving a precise location in such cases. His concepts are 'north, west, south, east', whereby each of these directions can refer to a range of 180°. He did not have maps, or any kind of system which allowed an accurate definition of the position of rural sites unconnected with the Roman road-system. Often he gives quite accurate distances between points of reference and villages, the exact location of which he cannot give.

His work also contains up-to-date information concerning the army presence in both provinces. Eusebius did not attempt to give a full survey of roads or army stations in both provinces. It is clear, however, that the material which he used contained full information about public roads and army-sites in both Arabia and Palaestina.

Eusebius frequently gives information on city-territories, but his information is consistently incomplete. He has information only on the territories of cities in Judaea/Palaestina and not on those of cities in the neighbouring provinces. This again fits the assumption that he used documents in the office of the governor in Caesarea. It would be important for officials to know about the road-network and distribution of troops in neighbouring provinces, but the organization of cities and their territories were strictly a provincial matter. In Judaea Eusebius only mentions territories of cities which were founded or reorganized by the Roman authorities after the definitive annexation of the province. From this it may be concluded that the archives in the provincial capital had no lists of the extent of older city-territories. We hear of a census in Judaea in A.D. 6/7 which caused a revolt (Schürer, i, 258 f.; 399–427). Apparently it did not result in the production of a full survey and the proper mapping of city-territories for the provincial archive. This fits the impression one gathers from the Babatha archive (Lewis, 1989). Babatha lived in a small village, Mahoza, somehow connected with a large village, Zoar, which itself belonged to the territory of Petra (*P.Yadin* 12, 14, 15). When Babatha filed her returns for the provincial census in Arabia in 127, she did so, not in Petra, but at a government office in Rabbath Moab, which was closer to her home village (*P.Yadin* 16). For the provincial census it was irrelevant to which city her home village belonged. This has implications for what we may assume about provincial archives and administrative organization.

There is no indication anywhere in the *Onomasticon* that the author ever saw a proper map of the provinces that he studied. He does not know the use of co-ordinates in locating a point in a two-dimensional plane. If a site does not lie on a road, he can only show its location as a rough approximation.

Conclusions

The conclusions based on an analysis of the structure of Eusebius' *Onomasticon* have implications for other provinces, for there is no reason to assume that Judaea, a small province, was mapped less thoroughly than other areas. When Eusebius wrote his work most of Judaea had been a province for three centuries.

This has a bearing on how we envisage Roman officers at work. A modern commanding officer has tools that allow him to take decisions regarding actions in terrain which he has never seen. He may take wrong decisions, but the tools are there. An ancient officer had no such instruments: either he knew the terrain because he had seen it himself, or he depended on others who had. Trajan's Column shows the emperor engaged in all kinds of activities, but never while looking at a map. He is frequently depicted in contact with locals, including both allies, and captive enemies.[11] Recent generals and warlords, on the other hand, are often painted and photographed looking at maps. This is no coincidence. The map symbolizes a commander's control over the terrain in which he operates. He moves

---

[11] Lepper & Frere, 1988, scenes lxviii, xc, cxviii, cxxx, cxli.

a toy soldier 10 cm across the map and consequently a whole battalion is transferred 5 km in the field. Ancient iconography does not know the map as a symbol of anything. The *Notitia Dignitatum* contains primitive maps to indicate the extent of some commanders' authority, but on the illustrations in the manuscripts no maps appear as the attribute of anyone's power. As symbols of office we find the paraphernalia of bureaucracy, military shields and other insignia.

The level of ancient cartography is important not only for an evaluation of Roman military and political thinking at the highest level; it is essential for an understanding of the conceptual tools used locally and regionally by ancient administrators and officers. It is hard to prove the absence of cartographic documentation at a regional level, as it is usually impossible to prove that something did not exist. The present paper, however, has shown that Eusebius, bishop of Caesarea in the early 4th c., used written documentation and that this documentation was remarkably incomplete. He had accurate information about sites along the system of Roman public roads, but he knew nothing about other roads, even if we now know them to have been well constructed and in use. Eusebius had information about territories of cities founded under Roman rule, but he did not have such material for the cities which already existed at the time of the annexation of Judaea as a Roman province. He was unaware of the concept of a grid which is the basis of Ptolemy's work. For Eusebius the only precise way of locating a place was its relationship to a Roman road. If a site was not near a road he had only the crudest and vaguest means of explanation at his disposal. This does not mean that Eusebius was ignorant. It means that his information was essentially verbal and not graphic. This was not an idiosyncracy of Eusebius, but reflects the level of geographical documentation at the disposal of Roman officials. Roman officers did not have the means to learn the topography of terrain which they themselves had not seen. What they did not see with their own eyes they had to learn from others who had been there. This inevitably made them more dependent on their long-serving local cadre than any modern commander would care to be.

Bibliography

Abel, F.-M., 1967. *Géographie de la Palestine*, II (3rd ed., Paris).
Avi-Yonah, M., 1946. 'Newly Discovered Greek and Latin Inscriptions', *QDAP* 12: 84–102.
——, 1954. *The Madaba Map* (Jerusalem).
——, 1972. *RE* Supplementband xiii, s.v. 'Palaestina', 321–454.
——, 1976. *Gazetteer of Roman Palestine* (Jerusalem).
——, 1977. *The Holy Land: From the Persian to the Arab Conquest (536 B.C.–A.D. 640), A Historical Geography* (Revised Edition, Grand Rapids, MI).
Barnes, T. (1975) 'The Composition of Eusebius' *Onomasticon*' *JTS* n.s. 26: 412–5.
——, 1981. *Constantine and Eusebius* (Cambridge, MA).
Beyer, G., 1931. 'Das Stadtbegiet von Eleutheropolis im 4. Jahrhunderts n. Chr. und seine Grenznachbarn', *ZDPV* 54: 209–71.
——, 1933. 'Die Stadtgebiete von Diospolis und Nikopolis im 4. Jahrh. nach Chr. und ihre Grenznachbarn', *ZDPV* 56: 218–53.
Dilke, A.O.W., 1971. *The Roman Land Surveyors: an Introduction to the Agrimensores* (Newton Abbot).
——, 1985. *Greek and Roman Maps* (London).
——, 1987. 'The Culmination of Greek Cartography in Ptolemy', Harley & Woodward (ed.), History of Cartography, I: 177–200.
——, 'Maps in the Service of the State: Roman Cartography to the End of the Augustan Era', *ibid.*, 201–211.
——, 'Itineraries and Geographical Maps in the Early and Late Roman Empires', *ibid.*, 234–57.
——, 'Cartography in the Byzantine Empire', *ibid.*, 258–75.
Graf, D., Isaac, B. & Roll, I., 1992. *The Anchor Bible Dictionary*, ed. D.N. Freedman, vol. 5: 782–7, s.v. 'Roman Roads'.
Haensch, R., 1992. 'Das Statthalterarchiv', *Zeitschrift der Savigny-Stiftung für Rechtsgeschichte* 109/222: 209–317.
Isaac, B., 1992. *The Limits of Empire: the Roman Army in the East* (2nd ed., Oxford).
——, 1978. 'Milestones in Judaea: from Vespasian to Constantine', *PEQ* 110: 47–60.
—— & Roll, I., 1982. *Roman Roads in Judaea*, i: *The Legio-Scythopolis Road* (*B.A.R.*, Oxford).
Janni, P., 1984. *La mappa e il periplo. Cartografia antica e spazio odologico* (Rome).
Jones, A.H.M., 1971. *The Cities of the Eastern Roman Provinces* (2nd ed., Oxford).
Klostermann, E. (ed.), 1904. *Eusebius, Das Onomastikon der biblischen Ortsnamen* (Leipzig, repr. Hildesheim, 1966).
Kubitschek, W., 1905. 'Ein Strassennetz in Eusebius' *Onomasticon*', *JÖAI* 8: 119–127.
Lee, A.D., 1993. *Information & Frontiers: Roman Foreign Relations in Late Antiquity* (Cambridge).
Lepper, F. & Frere, S., 1988. *Trajan's Column: A New Edition of the Cichorius Plates* (Gloucester).

Meyer, J., 1983/4. 'A Centurial Stone from Shavei Tziyyon,' *Scripta Classica Israelica* 7: 119–25, with an appendix by Applebaum: 125–8.

NEAEHL: The new encyclopedia of archaeological excavations in the Holy Land, ed. E. Stern (Jerusalem, 1994).

Nicolet, C., 1991. *Space, Geography, and Politics in the Early Roman Empire* (Ann Arbor).

Noth, M., 1943. 'Die topographischen Angaben im Onomasticon des Eusebius', *ZDPV* 66: 32–63.

Pekáry, T., 1968. *Untersuchungen zu den römischen Reichsstrassen* (Bonn).

Purcell, N., 1990. 'Maps, Lists Money, Order and Power', *JRS* 80: 178–82.

Schürer, E., 1973–9. *The history of the Jewish people in the age of Jesus Christ* (*175 B.C.–A.D. 138*) I–III (rev. ed., G. Vermes and F. Millar) (Edinburgh).

Sherk, R.K., 1974. 'Roman geographical exploration and maps,' *ANRW* II.2: 534–62.

Snodgrass, A.M., 1987. *An archaeology of Greece* (Berkeley).

Thomsen, P., 1903. 'Palästina nach dem Onomasticon des Eusebius', *ZDPV* 26: 97–188.

TIR—Tabula Imperii Romani, Iudaea/Palaestina: Eretz Israel during the Hellenistic and Byzantine Periods, eds. Tsafrir, Y. & Di Segni, L., Roll, I. [roads], Tsuk, T. [aqueducts] (Israel Academy of Sciences, 1994).

Welten, P., 1965. 'Bezeq,' *ZDPV* 81: 138–65.

Whittaker, C.R., 1994. *Frontiers of the Roman empire. A social and economic study* (Baltimore).

Postscript

When this article was written I was unaware of the article by D.E. Groh about the *Onomasticon* of Eusebius.[1] Groh accepts Barnes' early date for the work and adds further arguments in favour of such a date (between the Chronicon and the first edition of the Ecclesiastical History). He analyzes formulae, to distinguish them from Josephus and Pausanias.[2]

After I wrote my article, two books have appeared about political and military intelligence. That of Austin and Rankov[3] covers the period from the Second Punic War till the Battle of Adrianople, and Lee's monograph discusses intelligence in the Later Roman Empire.[4] Both works appeared before it was possible to take account of the present article, in so far as it is relevant, and both, of course, cover a much wider range of topics. However, since it was my aim to express a specific and rather essential point about the conceptual level of ancient geography, it will be useful to see in how far there is agreement.

Austin and Rankov stress that in reading ancient historiography, one has to make allowance for considerable simplification for the benefit of the uninformed readers. This would have affected the description of topography, strategy, tactics.[5] That may be true, but should not lead us to believe that at a conceptual level, ancient geography is far more sophisticated than it appears to be in the sources. In any case, it does not affect the analysis in this article of Eusebius' geography. Nor does it affect many precise and lucid conclusions of Austin and Rankov themselves. On Caesar's work on the Gallic War they note that it shows to what extent the commander on the spot was responsible

---

[1] D.E. Groh, 'The *Onomasticon* of Eusebius and the Rise of Christian Palestine', in E.A. Livingstone (ed.), *Studia Patristica* 18, 1, *Papers of the Ninth International Conference on Patristic Studies, Oxford 1983* (Kalamazoo, MI, 1985), 23–31. I also failed to mention C.U. Wolf, 'Eusebius of Caesarea and the Onomasticon', *Biblical Archaeologist* 27 (1964), 66–96.

[2] εἰς ἔτι νῦν is used by Eusebius, but not by Josephus and Pausanias.

[3] N.J.E. Austin & N.B. Rankov, *Exploratio: Military and Political Intelligence in the Roman World from the Second Punic War to the Battle of Adrianople* (London, 1995).

[4] A.D. Lee, *Information and Frontiers: Roman Foreign Relations in Late Antiquity* (Cambridge, 1993).

[5] Austin & Rankov, p. 2. They refer to C.B.R. Pelling, 'Caesar's battle descriptions and the defeat of Ariovistus', *Latomus* 40 (1981), 741–66.

for acquiring his own intelligence (p. 98). They contribute a most interesting analysis of Cicero's activity in Cilicia (102–7): 'The shocking picture which emerges is of an *ad hoc* approach, greatly at the mercy of the political leanings of native princes, personal relations with other Roman officials and rumour, and with no standing system of intelligence collection.'

Lee pays a good deal of attention to what he regards as strategic intelligence (pp. 106–42). He examines the information available to both sides in a number of episodes and lists items of information which he considers important: knowledge of handicaps (109–112) and knowledge of military preparations (112–119). However, his examples are concerned only with the most basic forms of information: the enemy is waging war elsewhere, or has a rebellion at home, or the enemy is massing troops for a major campaign. Lee considers it essential for the level of intelligence in the Later Roman period that the empire that was to be invaded knew of enemy plans in advance (p. 118). He then discusses a number of other invasions and analyzes them, 'looking for conclusive evidence of absence of information movement' (120–8). He concludes that there are very few cases where it can be proved that there was no advance knowledge of an impending invasion. We are clearly not engaged in the same debate, for I would have been surprised if major invasions had been organized in antiquity *without* the other power knowing it. During the principate, cities were informed early of imperial expeditions because of the many preparations that had to be made for large-scale troop movements and/or imperial visits.[6] Under such circumstances, how would the enemy *not* know something was afoot? It is generally agreed that there were spies in antiquity. The most famous ones are found in the book of Joshua. Yet no one would claim a Grand Strategy for Joshua. Lee states that 'the organisational sophistication of the empire hardly needs discussion . . .' (p. 32). Even if it were true—some of us feel that the subject does require discussion—this is quite a misleading pronouncement for readers who think in terms of twentieth-century sophistication. Modern military intelligence is

---

[6] H. Halfmann, *Itinera Principum* (Stuttgart 1986), 129–42; 207. In Judaea milestones were set up in 129 in preparation for Hadrian's visit in August 130. Note also R. Ziegler, 'Civic coins and imperial campaigns' in D. Kennedy (ed.), *The Roman Army in the East* (*JRA* Supp. 18, 1996, Ann Arbor, MI, 1996), 119–34.

unthinkable without a firm and organizational separation between collecting data and analysis. Information is not an objective fact, but something that is acquired, passed on and interpreted. This is generally recognized in our times, but was not an existing notion in antiquity. It is a point which Lee ignores in his book.

Israel Shatzman, *Scripta Classica Israelica* 16 (1997), 288 f. notes: 'There might be one flaw in the argument of Isaac, however. If the *Onomasticon* was written around 293 (cf. T. Barnes, *JThS* 26, 1975, 412–5), which Isaac seems to accept, it is quite doubtful that at that time Eusebius had access to the archive of the Roman governor of Palestine.' This is certainly a point worth considering and I would tend to raise three arguments to reinforce my views: 1) Eusebius calls himself bishop of Caesarea in the Introduction to the *Onomasticon*. This calls into question the early dating of the work or, if regarded as a later addition, certainly proves editorial activity when Eusebius was bishop. 2) The very point of my paper is that the kind of material found in the *Onomasticon*, whenever it was written, can only derive from formal written documentation. 3) Jerome's Latin translation of the *Onomasticon* was made when Christians definitely had free access to the governor's archive. Yet Jerome's additions or comments on Eusebius' text do not suggest anywhere that he had access to written material of a different kind from that used by Eusebius. To sum up: my argument that Eusebius' *Onomasticon* reflects the geography of his age is not affected by arguments about the date of its composition.

ARABIA AND SYRIA

20

THE DECAPOLIS IN SYRIA:
A NEGLECTED INSCRIPTION*

Decapolis is the name of a group of cities east of the Jordan, from Philadelphia in the South to Damascus in the North.[1] The term occurs in various sources from the first century A.D. onwards.[2] These sources do not indicate what the term represents or what the cities had in common. It has been assumed that the Decapolis was a league of free cities somehow attached to the Roman province of Syria when it was established by Pompey in 63 B.C.[3] In a recent study, however, S. Thomas Parker emphasized that our sources do not say that the Decapolis was a league or confederation.[4] He concludes that the term Decapolis had only geographical significance. It would simply have served as a convenient appelation for a group of Greek cities. Parker is right in pointing out that the Decapolis is never described as a league or confederation. But it is something else again to deny the term any formal or administrative content, merely because our literary sources are vague.

A century ago an inscription was discovered which allows us to be somewhat more precise. In a useful article Am. Hauvette-Besnault published the results of his survey of the cities of the Thracian Chersonnese.[5] At Madytos (then Maito, now Eceabat) he found two fragments of one inscription which reads as follows:[6]

---

* For various comments I am grateful to Professors G.W. Bowersock, Chr. Habicht, F.G.B. Millar, M.M. Roxan, M. Speidel, and Sir Ronald Syme.

[1] See now: E. Schürer, The History of the Jewish People in the Age of Jesus Christ (ed. G. Vermes and F. Millar), vol. ii (1979), 125 ff.

[2] For the sources see Schürer, loc. cit.; H. Bietenhard in ANRW ii, 8, 220 ff.; S. Thomas Parker (below, n. 4). See also IGR iii 1057 of A.D. 134.

[3] Schwartz, Nachr. Göttingen Gesellsch. der Wissensch., phil.-hist. Kl. (1906), 375 ff. did not believe in a league but produced another theory. E. Schürer, Geschichte des Jüdischen Volkes im Zeitalter Jesu Christi, ii (1907), 148–9 did accept the idea of a league or confederation and he was followed by most scholars who expressed an opinion on the subject. For references see Schürer ii (supra, n. 1) and Parker (infra, n. 4).

[4] Journal of Biblical Literature 94 (1975), 437–441; Schürer, vol. ii (1979), loc. cit. agrees with Parker's conclusion.

[5] 'Sur quelques villes anciennes de la Chersonnèse de Thrace', BCH 4 (1880), 506 ff.

[6] Ibid., 507–9 = A. Dumont-Homolle, Mélanges d'Archéologie (1892), 450,

fragment a:

> 1 . . .] πατρὸϲ ἐπιτρόπου Θρᾴ[κηϲ],
> πεμφθέντι ἐπὶ ϲτρατολογίαν ἀπὸ Ῥωμ[αίων]
> εἰϲ τὴν αὐτὴν ἐπαρχείαν, χειλιάρχῳ [—

fragment b:

> 1 . . .] Α, ἐπάρχῳ [εἴλ]ηϲ Β̄ Παννονίων [ἡγη-]
> [ϲα]μένῳ Δεκαπόλεωϲ τῆϲ ἐν Ϲυρίᾳ τετει[μη-]
> μένῳ δώροιϲ ϲτρατιωτικοῖϲ πᾶϲιν ἔν τε τῷ
> [Δ]ακικῷ πολέμῳ [—.

There is no hope of our getting a second reading of the inscription. Ch. Picard and A.J. Reinach re-visited the site and found that fragment b had disappeared, while fragment a was used as a stepping stone in the church, which caused damage to the inscription.[7] The reading, as it stands, has been accepted by Cagnat and Árpád Dobó but Domaszewski prefers to read ἀπὸ Ῥώμ[ηϲ] in l. a 2 which is preferable, [(λογιϲα]μένῳ in b 2–3 and τετει-μένῳ in b 3–4.[8] The inscription is not mentioned in any of the works discussing the Decapolis.

These then are the remnants of an inscription describing the career of an unknown equestrian officer. When his father was procurator of Thrace he was sent as officer in charge of recruitment to his father's province, a rather interesting piece of information.[9] Next he served as tribune in an unknown unit. Thereafter he became prefect of the ala ii Pannoniorum. His posting in the Decapolis will be discussed below. At some stage in his military career he received decorations.

First the date. The Dacian war in which the officer was awarded

---

n. 111c = *IGR* i no. 824 = Árpád Dobó, Inscriptiones extra fines Pannoniae Daciaeque repertae ad res earundem provinciarum pertinentes (⁴1975), nos. 345; 804; also: A. von Domaszewski, Die Rangordnung des Römischen Heeres (²1967), 138; 285. See now: J. Krauss, Die Inschriften von Sestos und die Thrakischen Chersones (Inschriften Griechischer Städte aus Kleinasien) (Bonn, 1980), no. 53, p. 96. Krauss reads in l. 1: Λ.O.O ‖ ‖ ‖ ατροϲ ἐπι[τ]ρο [. . .] which he translates 'dem Procurator . . .?, der von den Römern in dieselbe Provinz geschickt wurde, um Soldaten auszuheben, dem Tribun. . . .' It is not likely that a procurator would serve as a dilectator (see Brunt, *infra*, n. 10). Moreover we would expect a reference to a posting as tribune of a cohort at this stage of the career (*v. infra*). In l. 4 Krauss suggests: ἐ[π]άρχ[ῳ εἴλ]ηϲ oder ἐ[π]άρχ[ῳ χῶρτ]ηϲ. The second alternative is impossible.

[7] *BCH* 36 (1912), 307.

[8] See n. 6.

[9] For the antecedents of equestrian officers see: E. Birley, 'The Equestrian officers of the Roman army' in: Roman Britain and the Roman Army (1953), 139 ff. For conscription in the Roman imperial army, see P.A. Brunt, Scripta Classica Israelica 1 (1974), 90 ff.; for dilectatores, see p. 101 with n. 53.

decorations can be either Domitian's (A.D. 85–8), or one of the two campaigns of Trajan (101–2; 105–6). Picard and Reinach assume without further explanation that Trajan's campaigns are meant.[10] Dobó believes the officer was decorated as prefect of the ala ii Pann., because this unit is known to have served in both Trajan's Dacian campaigns.[11] This assumption raises difficulties. The particle τε in b 3 shows that reference was made to two wars. The missing war is likely to have been the civil war in 89. The Emperor who awarded the decorations is not named. That too points to Domitian, not Trajan (compare *ILS* 1016). We might restore: ἔν τε τῷ [Δ]ακικῷ πολέμῳ [καὶ ἐν τῷ Γερμανικῷ πολέμῳ].[12] Once it is admitted that the officer was decorated after serving in the Dacian and civil wars of Domitian his career is easily understood. He served as prefect of a cohort in the first half of the Dacian war (85–6) and was sent as officer in charge of recruitment to the province where his father was governor. He was transferred to Germania Inferior before the beginning of the Dacian campaign in 88. In Germania Inferior he served as tribune in one of the units which suppressed the revolt of Saturninus, governor of Germania Superior. The officer's supreme commander was the provincial governor A. Lappius Maximus. Immediately after the revolt Maximus was rewarded for his loyalty with the governorship of the major province of Syria.[13] Maximus took our officer with him to Syria, to serve as commander of the ala II Pannoniorum, which we know to have been in Syria at that time.[14] The ala was transferred

---

[10] *V. supra*, n. 7.

[11] *Op. cit.* (*supra*, n. 6), no. 345, n. 1.

[12] Krauss, too, restores [καὶ ἐν . . .]. Cf. *ILS* 1006 for a reference to the civil war of 89 as 'bellum Germanicum'. The Suebo-Sarmatian war of 92 probably also appears on inscriptions as 'bellum Germanicum', see: *CIL* iii 7397 and *ILS* 2710. But in that year the officer from Madytos was in Syria (*v. infra*). For the chronology of the Dacian and civil wars under Domitian, see: Syme, *CAH* xi 168 ff. It may be observed that on inscriptions, decorations received in war need not be mentioned immediately after the command in which they were earned, see e.g. *ILS* 1352 = *AÉ* 1968, 419.

[13] For Antonius Saturninus, see now R. Syme, *JRS* 68 (1978), 12 ff. For the career of Lappius Maximus, see: *PIR* V², 84 and B. Gerov. Klio 37 (1959), 213–15. He is attested as governor of Syria on two diplomata of May 91, see: M.M. Roxan, Roman Military Diplomas 1954–1977 (1978), nos. 4 and 5 (= Gerov, *op. cit.*) and on the dedications from the theatre of Gerasa, 90/1 J. Pouilloux, Liber Annuus 28 (1977), 246–54; 29 (1979), 276–8.

[14] See two diplomata of November 88: *CIL* xvi 35 and *JRS* 29 (1939), 28 ff. As noted in the comments on *CIL* xvi 35, the ala may have been transferred to the East with the legion V Macedonica, c. 56/7 (cf.: Ritterling, *RE* xii 1559, s.v. Legio) or with the IV Scythica, shortly before 62 (Ritterling, *op. cit.*, 1574).

to Moesia Superior in or before 93.[15] The anonymous officer apparently stayed in Syria with Lappius Maximus and received a post in the Decapolis. This then is the case of a senatorial office holder, transferred from one province to another, who took a trusted equestrian officer with him.[16]

Before discussing the officer's post in the Decapolis another remark must be made on the date of the inscription. Trajan's Dacian campaigns cannot be meant, because before the end of the second campaign much of the Decapolis was incorporated in the new province of Arabia, established in 106.[17] The equestrian office in 'The Decapolis in Syria' ceased to exist in that year. It would still have been possible that the officer was decorated after the first Dacian war (101–2) and then transferred to the Decapolis, but as noted above, he must have served in two wars. We may conclude again that he served under Domitian.

The next question is the function of the officer in the Decapolis. Hauvette reads [ἡγηcα]μένῳ which exactly fills the lacuna. Domaszewski alone reads [λογιcα]μένῳ which to me seems meaningless in this context. The verb ἡγεῖcθαι refers to provincial governors of equestrian rank, as pointed out by Pflaum.[18] It is used in this sense for the equestrian governors of Judaea before 67.[19] Such a governor would, in this period, have been a prefect or procurator (with a salary of 60 or 100 HS). This was not an exceptional promotion for a former commander of an ala.[20] The Decapolis would then have been an

---

[15] The ala II Pann. is attested in Moesia Superior on the diplomata of A.D. 93, 100 and 103/7 (CIL xvi, 39; 46 and 54). In 110 it was in Dacia (CIL xvi 163).

[16] E. Birley, op. cit. (supra, n. 9), 147–8, argues that governors or legionary legates, on transfer to other provinces, regularly may have taken selected equestrian officers with them.

[17] Milestone-inscriptions show that all roads south and west of Bostra belonged to the province of Arabia, see P. Thomsen, ZDPV 40 (1917), passim; C.B. Welles apud C.H. Kraeling, Gerasa, city of the Decapolis (1938) (the milestones); S. Mittmann, ZDPV 80 (1964), 113 ff.; for Scythopolis in Judaea, see the milestones cited by me in: PEQ 110 (1978), 47 ff. There is no justification for the apparent reservation of J.-P. Rey-Coquais, JRS 68 (1978), 54, n. 124, who says that Philadelphia, Gerasa and probably Dion 'auraient été attribuées' to Arabia. We may add that Pella did not belong to Syria either, cf. Schürer, vol. I (1973), pp. 153–8.

[18] H.-G. Pflaum, Les carrières procuratoriennes équestres sous le Haut-Empire Romain (1960–1), 822–3 with references in note 5.

[19] Ant. xviii, 1, 1 (2): 'Coponius (. . .) a man of equestrian rank was appointed governor (ἡγηcόμενοc) over the Jews with full authority.' See also: xviii, 3, 1 (55–5); cf.: E. Schürer, op. cit. (supra, n. 1), vol. i (1973), 359, n. 27.

[20] Pflaum, op. cit. (supra, n. 18), 285, n. 4. E. Birley, op. cit. (supra, n. 9), 146 ff.,

administrative unit attached to Syria, just as Judaea before 67. There is no proof as yet, but it seems the best explanation of the evidence. The inscription certainly proves that, around A.D. 90, there was an equestrian official in a district of Syria named 'The Decapolis'. The origin of the term Decapolis may have been geographical only, but in the second half of the first century it certainly was an administrative unit in the Roman empire.[21]

Two questions remain to be answered. First, when was the Decapolis so organized and, second, is there more evidence regarding these matters?

In 63 B.C. Pompey took from Jewish territory the non-Jewish towns east of Jordan. These were declared free and placed under the immediate jurisdiction of the governor of the new province of Syria.[22] All the cities of the Decapolis used the Pompeian era for their coinage.[23] Sex. Julius Caesar, as governor of Syria (47–46 B.C.), appointed Herod strategos of Coele-Syria.[24] The Decapolis was part of Coele-Syria.[25] Coele-Syria, then, appears as a district of Syria under a strategos appointed by the provincial governor. After Herod's death one piece of information is of some interest. The Greek cities of Gaza, Gadara and Hippos were detached from Judaea (the territory now assigned to Archelaus) and were made an annex (προcθήκη) of Syria.[26] This,

---

has pointed out that equestrian officers regularly had a part to play in the civil administration of the provinces and that this explains why they so frequently rose to places of responsibility in the central and provincial administration. The unknown officer from Madytos was son of a procurator, had been loyal during the civil war of 88/9 and this should explain his promotion to procurator of a higher rank in the province where he had served as a cavalry commander (from c. 89 till 92 at the latest). For equestrian governors see: A.H.M. Jones, Studies in Roman Government and Law (1960), 115 ff.; F. Millar, Historia 13 (1964), 180 ff.

[21] The reference to the Decapolis on an inscription of 134 (supra, n. 2) must be geographical only.

[22] Ant. xiv, 4, 4 (74; 76); BJ i, 7, 7 (155); cf. Schürer, op. cit. (supra, n. 1), vol. i (1973), 240.

[23] Schorer, loc. cit. (supra, n. 1); Rey-Coquais, op. cit. (supra, n. 17), 45–7. Gadara of the Decapolis calls the year of Pompey's reorganization 'Year 1 of Rome' (op. cit., 45, n. 19).

[24] Jos., Ant. xiv, 9, 5 (180); BJ i, 10, 8 (213); for Sextus Caesar, see Schürer, vol. i (1973), 248.

[25] For the name Coele-Syria, see: E. Bikerman, RB 54 (1947), 256 ff.; M. Stern, Greek and Latin Authors on Jews and Judaism, vol. i (1974), 14; Rey-Coquais, JRS 68 (1978), 53–4 (in the second century).

[26] Ant. xvii, 11, 4 (320); BJ ii, 5, 3 (97). Cf., on the other hand, the verb ὑποτάccειν used in Ant. xiv, 4, 4 (74) and BJ i, 7, 7 (155). After the death of Sohaemus, king of the Ituraeans and of Agrippa I, their peoples were 'provinciae Syriae additi' according to Tacitus, Ann. XII 23. But in Hist. v, 9, 5 we are told that Claudius 'Iudaeam

or course, refers only to three cities. But the term προϲθήκη is the same as that used later to describe Judaea when it was attached to Syria under its own equestrian governor, after the deposition of Archelaus in A.D. 6.[27] Since Gadara and Hippos were cities of the Decapolis bordering on Judaea, it is not impossible that at this time other cities of the Decapolis also were organized as an 'annex' of Syria under a special official. For the time being this remains a theory.

It may be added that there is evidence that, under the Flavians, the authority of the governor of Syria was recognized in Gerasa of the Decapolis. The names of two governors, one of them Lappius Maximus, are recorded on inscriptions in this city.[28] In the same period, however, the relative independence of Gerasa is reflected by an inscription in honour of the Nabataean king Rabbel II (76–106).[29]

Other inscriptions of these years may be mentioned in this connection. First the gravestone, found in Carnuntum, of Proculus the Son of Rabilus, Col(lina tribu) from Philadelphia (Amman).[30] Proculus served as optio in the Coh. II Italica c(ivium) R(omanorum) which was part of a detachment of the Syrian army led to the west, apparently in 69. The gravestone was set up by his brother Apuleius. As noted by Kraft he probably was recruited by Corbulo in 62, since he died, presumably in 69, after serving for seven years. Corbulo was in charge of Syria from 60 till 63.[31] Another soldier from Philadelphia certainly was recruited by Corbulo, Domitius Domiti f., who was granted citizenship in 88 while still serving as an eques of the

provinciam equitibus Romanis aut libertis permisit.' Rey-Coquais, *op. cit.*, 49 interprets this as meaning that Ituraea also became a province under a procurator. In any event, it is clear that ancient authors are vague about what it means to 'belong to' the province of Syria.

[27] See the discussion in Schürer, *op. cit. (supra,* n. 1), vol. i (1973), 360 and nn. 35–6 cf. *Ant.* xvii, 13, 5 (355) and xviii 1, 1 (2).

[28] *V. supra,* n. 13; Welles, *op. cit. (supra,* n. 17), no. 50; cf.: G.W. Bowersock, *JRS* 63 (1973), 138. See also Welles, *op. cit.,* nos. 2 and 49 mentioning priests of Tiberius and Nero in 22/3 and 67/8 respectively.

[29] Welles, *op. cit.,* no. 1 and Kraeling's comments on p. 38.

[30] *CIL* iii 13483a cf. p. 2328, 32 = *ILS* 9168 = *CSIR,* Österreich I 4; see also Schürer, *op. cit. (supra,* n. 1), i (1973), 365, n. 54 and K. Kraft, Zur Rekrutierung der Alen und Kohorten an Rhein und Donau (1951), 196. The inscription is also discussed by M.P. Speidel, in a paper to be published in Ancient Society (1981).

[31] *PIR²,* D 142; for Corbulo see R. Syme, *JRS* 60 (1970), 27–39 = Roman Papers II (1979), 805–24. Corbulo was retinendae Armeniae praepositus as governor of Cappadocia and Galatia in 54 (Tac., Ann. XIII 8, 1). Shortly after the death of Ummidius Quadratus in 60 he also became governor of Syria (Ann. XIV 26). In 61 Cappadocia went to Caesennius Paetus and Corbulo retained Syria with the legions III, VI and X 'and the old troops in Syria' (priorque Suriae miles, Ann. XV 6). In 63 Corbulo returned to Cappadocia and another governor went to Syria.

cohors II (Syrorum) sagittaria (equitata) milliaria.[32] The date of the diploma shows that he was recruited in 62/3. He dropped his semitic name for that of his commander, Cn. Domitius Corbulo. Dr. Roxan notes that the earliest record of his unit is the diploma of 88 found at Banasa in Mauretania.[33] It is now clear that this unit was part of Corbulo's army in Armenia. Like the II Italica it went to the west in 69. While the II Italica returned to Syria afterwards,[34] the II Syrorum was transferred to Mauretania where units of this type were needed to quell the tribal revolts recorded for the seventies and eighties.[35] We may note the different background of the brothers Proculus and Apuleius on the one hand and of Domitius on the other. The former had Roman names and served in a citizen-unit, which returned to Syria. The latter was given a Latin name only after he joined the army in a unit of specialized Arab archers. While all were recruited in Philadelphia the former presumably were Hellenized townsmen, the latter may have been a rural recruit.

Finally it is worth noting that Proculus belonged to the tribe Collina in spite of the fact that one would normally expect Quirina because Claudius, Nero and the Flavian emperors assigned their new citizens to that tribe.[36] This may well have been a regional matter, since two other Philadelphians, as well as citizens from Gerasa and Gadara are of the tribus Collina.[37]

---

[32] CIL XVI 159. The formula 'qui militant' indicates that he was still serving, cf. John C. Mann, Epigraphische Studien 9 (1972), 231–241, Type II: describing soldiers who were still serving and already veterans. Domitius was still serving and not yet a veteran ('equiti', not 'ex equitis'). Accordingly he had been in the army no more than c. 25 years. These and other references in the following notes I owe to the kindness of Dr. M. Roxan.

[33] For this unit see M.M. Roxan, Latomus 32 (1973), 847.

[34] See CIL XVI 35 of A.D. 88.

[35] Cf. M. Rachet, Rome et les Berbères, Collection Latomus, Vol. 110 (1970), Chapter III, 144–154.

[36] See Birley, op. cit. (supra, n. 9), 162.

[37] For Philadelphia see AÉ 1949.198 and CIL III 6580, 2 v. 33; for Gerasa and Gadara, see J.W. Kubitschek, Imperium Romanum tributim descriptum (1889), 259. It must be noted, however, that at least one citizen from Philadelphia in Lydia also belonged to Collina cf. CIL III 7103. For this city see Chr. Habicht, JRS 65 (1975), 75. Other soldiers from the Decapolis in the first century: the recipient of CIL xvi 15, A.D. 71. This was a soldier in the Misene fleet from Gerasa who received citizenship after his discharge and must therefore have been recruited early in the reign of Claudius. M. Spedius M.f. Corbulo from Hippos might have been the son of a soldier recruited by Corbulo (Roxan, Roman Military Diplomas, no. 9, A.D. 105). Finally, Flavius Cerealis from Gerasa may have served under Cerealis in the Jewish War, 66–70 (Welles, op. cit., supra note 17, no. 119, an inscription set up by his son in 115/6).

To sum up: possibly under Augustus and certainly in the Flavian period the Decapolis was organized as an administrative unit of the province of Syria. It was fully integrated in the empire, as appears from the recruitment of peregrine and citizen-soldiers into the Syrian army. After the establishment of the province of Arabia in 106 the cities of the Decapolis found themselves in three different provinces. Any reference to the Decapolis relating to this period can only have geographical significance, unless the inhabitants felt they had something in common in spite of administrative partition.

Postscript

Several othere inscriptions help to gain a somewhat better under-standing of the value of the notion 'Decapolis'.[1]

1) Διοδώρου Ἡηλιοδώρου ἀπὸ Συριακῆς Δεκαπόλεως Γαδάρων ταφεών.[2] The inscription is of unknown provenance, perhaps from Rome.

2) A dedication from Tayibeh in Palmyrene to Zeus Megistos Keraunios made in 134 by Ἀγαθάνγελος Ἀβιληνὸς τῆς Δεκαπόλεος.[3]

3) An important and interesting inscription refers to the city of Nysa-Scythopolis as 'one of the Hellenic cities in Coele-Syria'.[4] In this connection it is worth mentioning an inscription from Trachonitis dedicated by 'The Hellenes in Danaba'.[5]

Note also: P.-L. Gatier, 'Philadelphia et Gerasa du royaume Nabatéen à la Province de l'Arabie', in P.-L. Gatier & J.-P. Rey-Coquais (eds.), *Géographie historique au Proche-Orient* (Paris, 1990), 159–170.

Although this article appeared in 1981, mention could not yet be made at the time of the major work by A. Spijkerman, *The Coinage of the Decapolis and the Provincia Arabia* (Jerusalem, 1979). Note further:

Y. Meshorer, *City-Coins of Eretz-Israel and the Decapolis in the Roman Period* (Jerusalem, 1985).

P. Freeman, 'The Nabataeans and the Decapolis', P. Freeman and D. Kennedy, *The Defence of the Roman and Byzantine East* (Oxford, 1986), 785–96.

R. Wenning, 'Die Dekapolis und die Nabatäer', *ZDPV* 110 (1994), 1–35.

---

[1] P.-L. Gatier, 'Décapole et Coelé-Syrie: deux inscriptions nouvelles', *Syria* 67 (1990), 204–6.

[2] *SEG* 1980.1801.

[3] Waddington 2631; *IGR* iii 1057, cf. Gatier, *op. cit.*, p. 205.

[4] G. Foerster and Y. Tsafrir, 'Nysa-Scythopolis. A New Inscription and the Titles of the City on its Coins', *Israel Numismatic Journal* 9 (1986–7), 53–8: τῶν κατὰ Κοίλην Συρίαν Ἑλληνίδων πόλεων. See the comments by Gatier, at 205 f. and Alla Stein, in her unpublished Ph.D. thesis (Tel Aviv, 1991).

[5] M. Sartre, in *L'epigrafia del villaggio*. Actes du VIIᵉ colloque international Borghesi à l'occasion du cinquantenaire d'*Epigraphica* (Forli, 27–30 septembre 1990), A. Calbi *et al.* (edd.) (Faenza, 1993), 133–5; *AÉ* 1993.1636 from Dhunaybeh (Danaba) Οἱ ἐν Δαναβοις Ἕλληνες Μηνοφίλῳ εὐνοίας ἕνεκεν. It is suggested that this might be con-nected with the Herodian settlers in Trachonitis.

21

TAX COLLECTION IN ROMAN ARABIA: NEW EVIDENCE
FROM THE BABATHA ARCHIVE

The Document

Inner Text

ἐγγεγραμμένον καὶ ἀντιβεβλημένον ἀντίγραφον πιτακίου ἀπογραφῆς
προκειμένης ἐν τῇ ἐνθάδε βασιλικῇ, καὶ ἔστιν ὡς ὑποτέτακται.

Outer Text

ἐγγεγραμμένον καὶ ἀντιβεβλημένον ἀντίγραφον πιτακίου ἀπογραφῆς προκειμένης ἐν τῇ ἐνθάδε βασιλικῇ, καὶ ἔστιν ὡς
5 ὑποτέτακται· ἐπὶ Αὐτοκράτορος Καίσαρος θεοῦ Τραιανοῦ Παρθικοῦ
υἱοῦ θεοῦ Νέρουα υἱωνοῦ Τραιανοῦ Ἀδριανοῦ Σεβαστοῦ ἀρχιερέως με-
γίστου δημαρχικῆς ἐξουσίας τὸ δωδέκατον ὑπάτου τὸ τρίτον, ἐπὶ
ὑπάτων Μάρκου Γα⟨ου⟩ίου Γαλλικανοῦ καὶ Τίτου Ἀτειλίου Ῥούφου
Τιτι-
ανοῦ πρὸ τεσσάρων νωνῶν Δεκεμβρίων, κατὰ δὲ τὸν τῆς νέας
10 ἐπαρχείας Ἀραβίας ἀριθμὸν ἔτους δευτέρου εἰκοστοῦ μηνὸς Ἀπελ-
λαίου ἐκκαιδεκάτη ἐν Ῥαββαθμωβοις πόλει. ἀποτιμήσεως
Ἀραβίας ἀγομένης ὑπὸ Τίτου Ἀνεινίου Σεξστίου Φλωρεντείνου
πρεσβευτοῦ Σεβαστοῦ ἀντιστρατήγου, Βαβθα Σίμωνος Μαωζηνὴ τῆς
Ζοαρηνῆς περιμέτρου Πέτρας, οἰκοῦσα ἐν ἰδίοις ἐν αὐτῇ Μαωζα,
15 ἀπογράφομαι ἃ κέκτημαι, συνπαρόντος μοι ἐπιτρόπου Ἰουδάνου
Ἐλαζάρου κώμης Αἰνγαδδῶν περὶ Ἰερειχοῦντα τῆς Ἰουδαίας οἰ-
κοῦντος ἐν ἰδίοις ἐν αὐτῇ Μαωζα· κῆπον φοινικῶνος ἐν ὁρίοις
Μαωζων λεγόμενον Αλγιφιαμμα σπόρου κρειθῆς σάτου ἑνὸς
κάβων τριῶν τελοῦντα φοίνικος συροῦ καὶ μείγματος σάτα δεκα-
20 πέντε πατητοῦ σάτα δέκα στεφανικοῦ μέλαν ἐν λεπτὰ τριάκοντα γείτονες ὁδὸς καὶ θάλασσα, κῆπον φοινικῶνος ἐν ὁρίοις Μαωζων λεγόμενον Αλγιφιαμμα σπόρου κρειθῆς κάβου ἑνὸ⟨ς⟩ τελοῦντα τῶν γεινομένων καθ᾽ ἔτος καρπῶν μέρος ἥμισυ γείτονες
μοσχαντικὴ κυρίου Καίσαρος καὶ θάλασσα, κῆπον φοινικῶ-

25 νος ἐν ὁρίοις Μαωζων λεγόμενον Βαγαλγαλὰ σπόρου κρειθῆς
σάτων τριῶν τελοῦντα φοίνικος συροῦ καὶ νοαρου κόρον ἕνα
πατητοῦ κόρον ἕνα στεφανικοῦ μελαίνας τρεῖς λεπτὰ τριάκοντα γείτονε[ς κλ]ηρονόμοι Θησαίου Σαβακα καὶ
Ἰαμιτ Μανθανθου, κῆπον φοινικῶνος ἐν ὁρίοις Μαωζων
30 λεγόμενον Βηθφααραια σπόρου κρειθῆς σάτων εἴκοσι τελοῦντα φοίνικος συρ[ο]ῦ καὶ νοαρου κόρους τρεῖς πατητοῦ κόρου[ς
δύο στεφανικοῦ μελαίνας ὀκτὼ λεπτὰ τεσσαράκοντα πέντε γείτονες Θαμαρὴ Θαμοῦ καὶ ὁδός. ἑρμηνεία ὑπογραφῆς· Βαβθα Σίμωνος ὄμνυμι τύχην κυρίου Καίσαρος καλῇ πίστει ἀπογε-
35 γράφθαι ὡς προγέγραπ[τα]ι. Ἰουδάνης Ἐλαζάρου ἐπιτρόπευ[σ]α καὶ
ἔγρα-
ψα ὑπὲρ αὐτῆς. [2nd hand] ἑρμηνεία ὑπογραφῆς τοῦ ἐπάρχου· Πρεῖ-
σκος ἔπαρχος
ἱππέων ἐδεξάμην τῇ πρὸ μιᾶς νωνῶν Δεκεμβρίων ὑπατίας Γαλλι-
κ[αν]οῦ [καὶ Τιτιανο]ῦ.

Translation

Inner Text

Verified exact copy of a document of registration which is displayed
in the basilica here, and it is as appended below.

Outer Text

Verified exact copy of a document of registration which is displayed
in the basilica here, and it is as appended below.

In the reign of Imperator Caesar divi Traiani Parthici filius divi Nervae
nepos Traianus Hadrianus Augustus pontifex maximus tribuniciae
potestatis XII consul III, in the consulship of Marcus Gavius Gallicanus
and Titus Atilius Rufus Titianus four days before the nones of December, and according to the compute of the new province of Arabia
year twenty-second, month Apellaios the sixteenth, in the city of
Rabbath-Moab. As a census of Arabia is being conducted by Titus
Aninius Sextius Florentinus, legatus Augusti pro praetore, I, Babtha
daughter of Simon, of Maoza in the Zoarene [district] of the Petra
administrative region, domiciled in my own private property in the
said Maoza, register what I possess (present with me as my guardian

being Judanes son of Elazar, of the village of En-gedi in the district
of Jericho in Judaea, domiciled in his own private property in the
said Maoza), viz. within the boundaries of Maoza a date orchard
called Algiphiamma, the area of sowing one saton three kaboi of
barley, paying as tax, in dates, Syrian and mixed fifteen sata, 'splits'
ten sata, and for crown tax on 'black' and thirty sixtieths, abutters a
road and the Sea; within the boundaries of Maoza a date orchard
called Algiphiamma, the area of sowing one kabos of barley, paying
as tax a half share of the crops produced each year, abutters *moschantic*
estate of our lord Caesar and the Sea; within the boundaries of Maoza
a date orchard called Bagalgala, the area of sowing three sata of
barley, paying as tax, in dates, Syrian and Noaran(?) on koros, 'splits'
on koros, and for crown tax three 'blacks' and thrity sixtieths, abutters heirs of Thesaios son of Sabakas and Iamit son(?) of Manthanthes;
within the boundaries of Maoza a date orchard called Bethphaaraia,
the area of sowing twenty sata of barley, paying as tax, in dates,
Syrian and Noaran(?) three kaboi, 'splits' two koroi, and for crown
tax eight 'blacks' and forty-five sixtieths, abutters Tamar daughter of
Thamous and a road.

Translation of subscription: I, Babtha daughter of Simon, swear by
the *genius* of our lord Caesar that I have in good faith registered as
has been written above. I, Judanes son of Elazar, acted as guardian
and wrote for her. [2nd hand] Translation of subscription of the
prefect: I, Priscus, prefect of cavalry, received [this] on the day before
the nones of December in the consulship of Gallicanus and Titianus.

On the back, individual signatures (in Nabataean)   *right edge*
    'Abdu son of Muqimu, witness   Babatha
    Manthanta son of Amru, witness
    'Awd'el son of _____, witness
    Yoana son of 'Abd'obdat Makhoutha, witness
    Shahru son of _____, witness

This document, almost completely preserved, represents a copy of
an original document, dated 2 and 4 December A.D. 127, which was
preserved in the basilica at Rabbath-Moab, a city east of the Dead
Sea, in what was then the province of Arabia. In it Bab(a)tha declares
the landed property she owns in her home village, for the provincial
census ordered by the governor of the province. This property consisted of four groves of date palms, identified by name and location.
The taxes paid in kind and in money are listed for each grove. The

Greek text and the translation printed here are those published by
Naphtali Lewis in his *editio princeps* of the documents from the Bar
Kokhba period found in the Judaean Desert.[1] The aim of this paper
is to show how the document as published affects existing views of
the process of taxation in a Roman province.

This text is unique because it is the only document of its kind
(outside Egypt)[2] which enables a precise reconstruction of the procedure followed by the inhabitants of a Roman province when they
had to declare their landed property to the authorities. There are a
few sources with explicit statements about taxation, notably Hyginus[3]
and Ulpian[4] as well as a number of passing references in other authors.[5]
The interpretations given to these passages have been varied and
there is no consensus among scholars, apart from the recognition
that practices differed between provinces. This is an important point,
for it means that whatever may be deduced from the current document
is not necessarily valid for all other provinces. However, we think
some aspects which give us information on important mechanisms of
Roman government are worth considering here because they bear
upon basic questions about the functioning of ancient empires. This
is the reason why the current journal seems the proper venue for
this discussion. The document also throws light on other aspects of
the history of the Roman provinces which will not be discussed in
this paper: the role of equestrian officers in provincial administration,
ancient agriculture, the position of Jews in the province of Arabia, etc.

The document states that a census of Arabia was conducted by
the provincial governor, i.e. lists were prepared and up-dated for the

---

[1] *The Documents from the Bar Kokhba Period in the Cave of Letters: Greek Papyri*, ed. by
Naphtali Lewis, *Aramaic and Nabataean Signatures and Subscriptions* (Jerusalem, 1989), No.
16, pp. 65–70, with introduction and comments. The documents published in this
volume will be referred to as *P.Yadin*. In this paper Lewis' reading and translation
are accepted *in toto*. The text and translation are given here, because the volume
containing them will not be accessible to many readers of this journal.

[2] For Roman Egypt: N. Lewis, *Life in Egypt under Roman Rule* (Oxford, 1983), ch. 8,
pp. 156–84; D. Rathbone, 'Egypt, Augustus and Roman Taxation', *Cahiers du Centre G. Glotz* 4 (1993), 81–112. For Roman taxation in general: L. Neesen, *Untersuchungen zu den direkten Staatsabgaben der römischen Kaiserzeit (27 v. Chr.–284 n. Chr.)* (Bonn
1980).

[3] Hyginus Gromaticus, *Constitutio Limitum*, Corpus Agrimensorum Romanorum,
Opuscula Agrimensorum Veterum, ed. C. Thulin, (1971), 168, 9; English translation:
B. Levick, *The Government of the Roman Empire: A Sourcebook* (London, 1985), 70 f.

[4] Ulpian, *Digest*, ed. T. Mommsen, P. Kruger, A. Watson (1985), 50, 15, 4; 50,
15, 1, both translated in Levick, *op. cit.*, 72 f.

[5] Discussed by Neesen, *op. cit.*, 54–60.

purpose of taxation throughout the province.[6] The taxpayer himself had to submit the necessary information, which was then checked and confirmed by the responsible officials. There is, however, no indication that the veracity of this declaration was verified on the spot at this stage. Furthermore, a third-century legal source states unambiguously that the declarations had to be made in the chief town of each taxation district, for that is the district where taxes had to be paid: 'A man who possesses land in another city territory has to declare it in the city where the land is, for tax raised on land should lighten the burdens of the city in whose territory the land is in ownership.'[7] The implication of this statement is that there was no immediate correlation between the total of the taxes collected by a city and the sum to be paid into the imperial treasure. Important for the interpretation of the current document is that it clearly follows a different practice: in this case the declaration was not made in the city where the land was, for in the document it is stated, again unambiguously, that the property which Babatha possessed was situated 'in Maoza in the Zoarene [district] of the Petra region'. Thus, while the inhabitants of the village were subject to the civil jurisdiction of the council of Petra, as shown by *P.Yadin* 12 and 27, the declaration for the census was made not in the city of Petra, south-east of Maoza, but in Rabbath-Moab, north-east of it. As the editor notes, Maoza was far closer to Rabbath-Moab (about 75 km along the road) than to Petra (more than twice that distance).[8] This was a good reason for Babatha to go to the nearer city, but it raises questions as to how the system worked in this sort of situation. We now know that Babatha was not an exception, for recently a document was published containing fragments of a similar declaration of landed property made by someone else, also from Maḥoza, for the same officer and thus, apparently, in the same city.[9] Like Petra, Rabbath-Moab served as

---

[6] Neesen, 33–44; E. Schürer, *The History of the Jewish People in the Age of Jesus Christ*, i, revised and edited by G. Vermes & F. Millar (Edinburgh 1973), 401–4; older literature: Kubitschek, s.v. 'Census', *RE* III, cols. 1914–1918; provincial census under the Empire: J. Marquardt, *Römische Staatsverwaltung* II (²1884), 204–23; Mommsen, *Römisches Staatsrecht* II, i (³1887), 1091–5; Kubitschek, 1918–22; Egypt: C. Préaux, *Recherches sur le recensement dans l'Egypte romaine* (1952); Lewis, *Life in Egypt under Roman Rule*, 156 ff.

[7] *Digest* 50.15.4.2: I<s> uero, qui agrum in alia ciuitate habet, in ea ciuitate profiteri debet, in qua ager est: agri enim tributum in eam ciuitatem debet leuare, in cuius territorio possidetur. The translation given here is that of B. Levick (above, n. 4).

[8] Lewis, *op. cit.*, 69.

[9] H. Cotton, *Zeitschrift für Papyrologie und Epigraphik* 85 (1991), 264; 99 (1993), 117;

an assize city, i.e. a city where the provincial governor regularly held court,[10] but this is not connected to the organization of taxation and city territories. It is interesting in itself that the declaration was received by a cavalry commander (*eparchos hippeon*), who was probably the commander of an *ala* (a battalion). Thus we see that a military officer was engaged in administrative duties in a town, only two decades after the organization of the province of Arabia. We note, too, that his attestation had to be translated from the Latin.

The declaration contains a verbal description of the landed properties concerned: an identifying name, the size, the taxes to be paid, and the abutters. It is clear that there was no plan or map in existence, a point which reinforces the opinion held by some scholars that the Romans were not 'map-minded'.[11] The description given in the present document contains all the elements required in the relevant law, formulated by Ulpian in the third century: 'name of each estate; in what city territory and parish it is; two nearest neighbours; acreage of the arable land sown within the previous ten years; number of vines the vineyard has; olives, acreage and number of trees; acreage of meadowland mown within the previous ten years; pasture-lands, estimated acreage; likewise woodland for felling.'[12] In the present case, however, the extent and productivity of the orchards are described using only traditional units of measurement like those found in the Old Testament and the Talmud.[13] There is no indication in the census

---

also: 105 (1995), 176, two fragments of a text which derives from the same area as the current document (Nahal Hever, west of the Dead Sea). An unknown man, son of Levi made the declaration and Priscus, prefect, received it on 27 April 127.

[10] This is clear from, e.g. *P.Yadin* 25. See on these matters B. Isaac, 'The Babatha Archive: A Review Article', *Israel Exploration Journal* 42 (1992), 62–75; this article was critically discussed by N. Lewis, 'The Babatha Archive: A Response', *Israel Exploration Journal* 44 (1994), 243–6, but Lewis' arguments do not touch upon issues discussed in the current paper.

[11] B. Isaac, *The Limits of Empire: The Roman Army in the East* (Revised ed., Oxford 1992), 401–6; 447 f. An exceptional discovery are the cadastral documents found at Orange: A. Piganiol, *Les documents cadastraux de la colonie romaine d'Orange. Gallia*, Suppl. 16 (Paris 1962).

[12] Trans. Levick, *Digest* 50.15.4.2: 'nomen fundi cuiusque: et in qua ciuitate et in quo pago sit: et quos duos uicinos proximos habeat. et <ar>uum, quod in decem annos proximos satum erit, quot iugerum sit: uinea quot uites habeat: oliuae quot iugerum et quot arbores habea<n>t: pratum, quod intra decem annos proximos sectum erit, quot iugerum: pascua quot iugerum esse uideantur: item siluae caeduae.'

[13] Lewis, comments on p. 69. Hyginus, referred to above, states that 'On all these types of land tax has been fixed by their productivity per *iugerum*' and Ulpian in the Digest also uses the Roman *iugerum* as the standard unit of measurement. In Arabia, apparently, no effort was made to force the inhabitants to declare their

declaration that the area was ever measured by professional Roman land-surveyors. Babatha registered three orchards that paid a fixed quantity of produce and crown tax in money. One paid a share of the produce without crown tax. The reference to crown tax is interesting, for this usually appears as an extraordinary supplementary tax and not a regular income tax.[14] In the present document, however, it appears as a fixed amount to be paid in money on some types of property. Another point worth mentioning here is that the document represents both the registration of property, made by the owner, and the assessment by the authorities of the taxes to be paid. There is, in other words, no trace here of a separation of registration (*descriptio*) and valuation (*aestimatio, census*) which some scholars believe to have existed.[15] These are further indications how much uncertainty there is regarding such matters and how varied practices in different provinces and different periods may have been.[16]

Apart from these smaller points, the document also raises more important questions about the process of tax collection to which we shall now turn our attention. As already noted, it is clear that Babatha and her guardian Judanes went to Rabbath-Moab for the registration of land which was situated within the territory of Petra. We may assume that Judanes himself also registered his own property in the village of Maoza on that occasion, for he is said to have lived 'in his own private property in the said village' (l. 17). The same procedure was probably followed in the case of the newly published papyrus (above, n. 9). The owner of the property made the declaration which was translated into Greek and he or she confirmed the veracity of the statement under oath. The Roman equestrian officer subscribed in Latin and the original of the document was then preserved in the local basilica which served as an archive. A copy of the original was made

---

property in Roman terms, even though the declaration had to be submitted in Greek.

[14] Neesen, *op. cit.*, 142; Isaac, *op. cit.*, 301 f. and now H. Cotton, *ZPE* 100 (1994), 553.

[15] Neesen, 42–4. Note also p. 48, where it is observed that Hyginus (referred to in n. 3) does not make it clear who was responsible for the valuation, those who made the declaration themselves, or the authorities: 'Ebenso ungewiß und in der Forschung umstritten ... ist zudem die Frage, *wer* eigentlich im Falle solcher.... Geld-Bodenabgaben die "Abschätzung" vornehmen sollte: der Deklarant selbst, nämlich im Anschluß an die Erklärung (professio) seiner Landgüter nach genauer Größe und Abauart sowie z.T. vielleicht Güte; oder die zuständige Zensus-Behörde, nachdem sie die professio, also die Aufzählund und Beschreibung der Güter, erhalten und möglicherweise überprüft hatte?'

[16] A point emphasized by Neesen, 44 f.; 55 f.

for the tax-payer and the authenticity of this copy confirmed by five witnesses who signed on the back (in Nabataean).

The first point to be made is that the declaration was accepted in good faith, for, as already observed, the description of the property is based on traditional units of measurement and not on those employed by Roman surveyors[17] and there is no indication in the text of the declaration that the information ever had been verified or would be verified by Roman officials. This is in keeping with the law as formulated in the third century and reconfirmed in the sixth: 'The person registering is to make all the estimates himself.'[18] The second point to be stressed is that the original of the declaration was kept in Rabbath-Moab and not in Petra. Yet there can be no doubt that the city of Petra was responsible for levying the taxes on its territory and their transfer to the Roman provincial authorities. In the Roman empire this was one of the essential tasks of the cities.[19] If Babatha and others, living in Maoza, registered their property in one city, but had to pay taxes to another, this raises the question of how the system worked. As matters stand, it appears that the information about Babatha's property was in one city, while the tax had to be collected by another. Moreover, the information available was only that provided by the taxpayer, without verification on the spot by the authorities.

There are two possible solutions to this problem. The first is to assume that copies of all declarations like Babatha's were sent to the cities which needed the information. In this case a copy would have been made of the original in the basilica in Rabbath-Moab and then sent to Petra to be filed with other declarations of landed property in the city territory. This information would then have been used by the city council when it exacted tribute for the Roman authorities. However, there are serious, and probably decisive objections to this theory. Firstly, there is nothing at all in the text which suggests that further copies were made and sent elsewhere. The opening sentence

---

[17] O.A.W. Dilke, *The Roman Land Surveyors: An Introduction to the Agrimensores* (Newton Abbot, 1971).

[18] Ulpian, *Digest* 50.15.4.1: 'omnia ipse qui defert aestimet.'

[19] This is explicitly stated by Ulpian in *Digest* 50, 15, 4, 2 (cited above); by Papinian in the *Digest* 50, 1, 17, 7: 'Exigendi tributi munus inter sordida munera non habetur et ideo decurionibus quoque mandatur.' 'The function of exacting tribute is not classified as degrading and for that reason is also entrusted to members of city councils.' (trans. Levick, p. 75 and see further passages translated there, pp. 75–9). It follows implicitly from the extensive lists of cities enjoying various rights and immunities given by Ulpian in the *Digest* 50, 15, 1.

of the document only says that it is a copy of a document displayed in the basilica here (i.e. in Rabbath-Moab). The entire text suggests that this was strictly a transaction between Babatha with her guardian and the Roman officer who received the declaration. The city authorities were not involved. More important, if we assume that copies of all declarations regarding property in other cities were sent to the relevant archives, this assumes the existence of an extensive bureaucracy at either the provincial level or that of the city-councils. All we know about the administration of the Roman provinces in the second century, apart from Egypt, suggests that there was no such bureaucratic apparatus. This impression is reinforced by the present text. As we know from other sources, the provincial census was held occasionally, possibly once every ten years.[20] In Arabia this was probably the third census since the annexation of the province in 106. Babatha's declaration was received by a Roman officer, the commander of a cavalry unit, who happened to be stationed in the city for what cannot have been more than a few years. There was thus no civil service which took care of the procedure and it is hard to believe that the equestrian officer who signed the subscription would also be responsible for having copies prepared and sent elsewhere. Moreover, it is clear from all relevant sources that the registration of property and the resulting determination of the tax to be paid was a process altogether separate from the actual collection of the taxes. These respective functions were clearly performed by separate bodies, i.e., in the first instance, the provincial government and, in the second, the city. The possibility that one city sent copies of census declarations to another should therefore almost certainly be discarded.

This leaves us with an alternative explanation: the representatives of the city authorities who collected taxes in Zoara and Maoza did not themselves have copies of the census declarations filed in Rabbath-Moab. This may be surprising, but it is not impossible. The certified copies held by the declarants, such as Babatha, were valid documents, showing the taxes assessed by the provincial authorities. They bound both the owner of the property and those who levied the taxes. It is thus quite possible that they served to protect the owners against excessive or random demands from the city authorities, who were in a position to impose their own estimation if they were not shown a valid and up-to-date copy of a declaration. If this represents the process

---

[20] References in n. 6, above.

of tax payment in Arabia at the time the procedure was simple and crude, but it may have worked for an empire which did not possess an elaborate state apparatus. It would prevent systematic extortion at minimum costs to the empire, while taking care of the regular flow of income to the authorities. The function of the copy of the declaration, such as the one obtained by Babatha, would then be somewhat similar to that of military diplomata. These were validated copies of the decision, recorded in Rome, regarding a grant of citizenship and *conubium* to veteran soldiers. For the soldier, the diploma was the only means available to prove his status wherever he was in the provinces, for there were no lists of all Roman citizens of the Empire in the capitals of the provinces.

A series of related documents, published just when this paper went to press may very well confirm, or at least reinforce this interpretation.[21] Document I of this series, a 'Receipt for tax on dates'[22] is particularly relevant. Dated 29 January 125 it says:

> [—] son Judah and his friends to Menaḥem son of Iohannes greetings. We received from you the amount due for dates, which you owe to to our Lord the Emperor in Maḥoza for the eighteenth year (of the province). On account of which we have now received from you through Sammouos son of Simon four blacks and fifty-eight lepta-units. Written in Maḥoza. . . .

As pointed out by the editor, the sum due to the Emperor must have been either tax or rent and it was almost certainly the former.[23] This document, then, shows that amounts due to the state were collected at the local level by Jewish villagers through a middle-man who was also a Jewish villager.[24] A deed of gift of landed property (November, A.D. 129) in this archive specifies the taxes payable to 'the account of the fiscus of our Lord'.[25] The taxes, in other words,

---

[21] H. Cotton, 'The Archive of Salome Komaise Daughter of Levi: Another Archive from the "Cave of Letters"', *ZPE* 105 (1995), 171–208. I am grateful to Prof. Cotton for showing me the text of her publications in advance.

[22] First published in *ZPE* 100 (1994), 550; published with the entire archive in *ZPE* 105 (1995), 174 f.

[23] See the editor's discussion of this question on pp. 202 f., à propos lines 28–29 of document IV, published there. This document is a deed of gift of what was clearly private land for which tax, and not rent was due. No. V is a similar receipt in Aramaic, dated January of 131, to be published by Ada Yardeni.

[24] Sammouos son of Simon, the middle-man, himself owned property in Maḥoza, as appears from document IV, lines 14–15 = lines 35–36, p. 186 f.

[25] *Op. cit.*, No. IV, p. 187, lines 28–30.

were not collected by cities, but by villagers at several levels, who transferred them to the cities, from where they went to the provincial authorities. The only direct contact between the tax payer and the authorities was when the tax payer declared his property during a census. The copy of his declaration obtained on that occasion served as legal documentation for transactions which took place at the lowest level every year, till the next census. Presumably the use of local middle-men who knew the properties (and units of measurements) concerned meant that the central authorities had a built-in mechanism for verifying the census declarations.[26]

It will be clear that the evidence from Arabia does not necessarily tell us much about organization in other provinces, or about in Arabia in other periods. There is, however, no reason to assume that it was unique. It is, therefore, instructive as an example of how a large and primitive Empire could function without an elaborate state apparatus. At minimum costs in terms of manpower and bureaucracy it provided a rudimentary form of protection for the individual against exploitation, while guaranteeing the authorities a steady income from taxation.

---

[26] As pointed out to me by Susan Weingarten.

Postscript

R. Bagnall, 'Notes on Egyptian Census Declarations' *BASP* 27 (1990), 1–14, followed by four more instalments.

M. Broshi, 'Agriculture and Economy in Roman Palestine: Seven Notes on Babatha's Archive', *IEJ* 42 (1992), 230–40. Taxes are discussed on pp. 235–9.

22

INSCRIPTIONS FROM SOUTHERN JORDAN

(Review Article)

M. Sartre, *Inscriptions grecques et latines de la Syrie, Tome xxi, Inscriptions de la Jordanie, Tome iv: Pétra et la Nabatène méridionale, du wadi al-Hasa au golfe de ʿAqaba* (Paris, Paul Geuthner, 1993), 206 pp., 51 Plates, indices.

Recently the Roman Near East in general and Roman Arabia in particular have become the subject of intensive study after years of relative neglect.[1] The literature includes various works of interpretation, reports on archaeological activity and one major collative project: the publication of a corpus of Greek and Latin inscriptions from Syria, with separate volumes devoted to the inscriptions from Jordan. The current volume, which is part of this series, follows two earlier publications: volume xiii.1 devoted to the inscriptions of Bostra (in modern Syria), provincial capital of Arabia and legionary headquarters[2] and Volume xxi 2, collecting the inscriptions of the central region of Jordan.[3] These works represent the activities of French scholars who are part of a tradition going back to the travels of W.H. Waddington in the sixties of the previous century.[4] In their present format these books give us far more than just the basic material required in a corpus (photographs, texts, bibliography and critical apparatus). The work reviewed here contains a geographical introduction, a very useful historical survey with extensive bibliography, introductions for each geographical sub-section, French translation for each inscription and extensive commentary. All of these reflect the high professional standards we have come to expect of this project.[5]

---

[1] See now F. Millar, *The Roman Near East: 31 B.C.–A.D. 337* (Cambridge, Mass., 1993).

[2] *IGLS* xiii 1, Bostra, ed. M. Sartre.

[3] *IGLS* xxi 2, ed. P.-L. Gatier.

[4] W.H. Waddington, *Inscriptions grecques et latines de la Syrie* (2 vols., Paris, 1870).

[5] It would have been desirable to include more maps in a volume which gives the reader such generous measure in other respects. A map of Petra and its vicinity, for instance, would have been helpful.

Inscriptions from Petra

Petra and Bostra

It may be useful for a review in this Journal to give some historical comments on the material which is now easily accessible. More than half of the inscriptions, 93 out of a total of 156, derive from the ancient Nabataean capital, Petra. It is not surprising to learn that most inscriptions belong to the period before the second half of the second century, for Petra did not prosper in the later period (pp. 30 f.), although there are now reports of Byzantine papyri discovered there. The contrast with the material from Bostra is interesting: the dated material from Bostra is distributed over not much more than a hundred years, roughly the mid-second to mid-third century. However, some dated building inscriptions there belong to a later period: from 259/260 to Justinian. Petra has produced one building inscription (Byzantine) and a few Byzantine grave inscriptions. By contrast, the Byzantine towns of the Negev have produced hundreds of inscriptions which contain formulas related to those found in Southern Jordan.[6] This once again emphasizes the remarkable expansion of prosperous settlement in the Negev in the Byzantine period. It is important to realize that there was no parallel development in the region east of the Aravah.

It is further remarkable that only one inscription antedates the Roman annexation (No. 54) and this is also one of the two bilingual texts from Petra, in Greek and Nabataean.[7] Bilingual texts, it should be noted, are rare anywhere in Arabia:[8] in Bostra Nabataean and Greek are combined in two texts (9003, 9412); Greek and Latin on one imperial dedication (9409).[9] Both Gerasa and Ziza have each one Nabataean—Greek inscription.[10] Yet bilingual inscriptions are frequent in the Hauran, Palmyra and among the Jewish inscriptions of Palestine. The publication of a full corpus like this makes us more than ever aware of the complexity and diversity of what is now

---

[6] See the observations and references on p. 144, discussing formulas in grave inscriptions: many parallels are found between Southern Jordan and the Negev, different formulas in Northern Jordan.

[7] The other bilingual inscription is No. 28, perhaps a dedication to Dousares.

[8] See Millar, *The Roman Near East*, Chapter 11.

[9] See below for a remarkable bilingual text from Wadi Ram.

[10] Kraeling, *Gerasa*, p. 371, no. 1 (A.D. 81); *IGLS* xxi, 2, no. 154.

commonly called 'the epigraphic habit'.[11] Petra has produced 93 inscriptions as compared with Bostra's 472. In Bostra many of the inscriptions were set up by the military authorities or by individual soldiers. As already noted, these belong primarily to the second half of the second century, and the first half of the third. The contrast with the current volume is striking. While there are quite a few military inscriptions from Petra, the major army bases in the south are remarkable for the absence of written documents. Udhruh has produce one non-military inscription (pp. 158–161) and at Aela (Aqaba), base of the *Legio X Fretensis* from the late third century onwards, a total of seven inscriptions have been found.[12] One of these, No. 150, is a fragmentary Latin building inscription, dated 324–6.[13] At the Tetrarchic(?) legionary base at Lejjun which has been under excavation for years, not a single inscription has yet been found. Thus, whatever the reason, in the second and third centuries the military at Bostra left behind numerous inscriptions, while their successors in the fourth century, further to the south, failed to do so. Yet there can be no doubt that fourth-century legions had an administration based on paper-work. In this connection it may be recalled that there is very little extant epigraphical documentation of the substantial military presence that was stationed in eastern Cappadocia in the Flavian period.

Epigraphy and the Army

But the new volume is by no means lacking in information about military matters. There are enough inscriptions to state with some confidence that there was a cohort of the *III Cyrenaica* based in Petra for some time.[14] As usual with military inscriptions of the High Empire, most of these are in Latin.[15] An important inscription of the

---

[11] After the famous article by R. MacMullen, 'The Epigraphic Habit in the Roman Empire', *AJP* 103 (1982), 233–46.

[12] Pp. 183–191, nos. 150–156.

[13] For discussion of the discoveries at Aqaba see also: E.A. Knauf & C.H. Brooker, *ZDPV* 104 (1989), 179–181; D. Whitcomb, *ZDPV* 106 (1990), 156–61.

[14] No. 44: the *Cohors Au(relia)*. It is interesting to see that legionary cohorts could have names instead of numbers. Also: Nos. 19; 47 (an *optio* of the legion); 52 (an *eques* of the legion).

[15] No. 19 is in Greek and No. 61, a fragmentary grave inscription in Greek contains a reference to the legion. I am not certain why the editor says that the inscription refers to the son or daughter of a soldier rather than the soldier himself.

mid-fifth century from Petra (No. 50) mentions a *numerus* of Τερτιοδαλ-
ματεῖς which may have been based there at the time.

Inscriptions sometimes furnish information about recruitment. This
is certainly the case with Arrianos (No. 55) whose Greek verse epitaph records the fact that he died from illness in his twenty-seventh
year of military service.[16] It is probably also true for Marcus Ulpius
Andromachos, the son of Ulpius Diogenes, commander of the *Ala II
Auriana* (No. 49, Greek) who was buried in Petra, for his unit is known
to have been based in Cappadocia. His ancestors must have been
granted citizenship at the time of the annexation of the province. He
himself would have been one of the few equestrian officers whose
provenance was from the province of Arabia. We would note here
that is important to distinguish between possible evidence of recruitment as opposed to possible evidence of a garrison. Thus *IGLS* xxi
2, Nos. 26 and 30 almost certainly indicate that recruits from Philadelphia or its territory served in the legion *X Fretensis* in Palestine
and went home after their discharge.[17] There is no need at all to
believe that there was a vexillation of the *X Fretensis* in Philadelphia,
for there is an inscription attesting the presence of the Arabian legion
III Cyrenaica in the city.[18] To return to Petra, inscription No. 36 may
furnish valuable evidence of the existence of a local militia patrolling
the roads near the city, as observed by the editor.[19] Evidence of local
militias in the Near East is relatively rare, although it may be supposed that it was a widespread institution. All this is interesting additional evidence of the military presence in cities, typical of the
disposition of troops in the Near East.[20]

Governors and Financial Procurators

Another point worth commenting on is the distribution of inscriptions testifying to the presence of provincial governors in cities in

---

[16] The length of his service may suggest that he was an auxiliary.

[17] Gatier, *IGLS* xxi 2, p. 55: 'Il faut penser que la légion 10ᵉ Fretensis a des
troupes (une vexillation?) à Philadelphie au début du IIIᵉ siècle'. Gatier himself observes
on p. 117 with n. 96 that there is epigraphical evidence of recruitment in Philadelphia, referring to *AÉ* 1953.74 and *ILS* 9168.

[18] *IGLS* xxi 2, 34: a funerary inscription for the wife of a centurion. Note also
No. 117 in honour of a centurion of the same legion, set up by the city of Madaba.

[19] Comments on pp. 116 f.

[20] B. Isaac, *The Limits of Empire: the Roman Army in the East* (Oxford, ²1992), chapters 1, 3 and 6.

Arabia. There 22 of those in Bostra, for obvious reasons, for it was the provincial capital and the base of the legion which the governor commanded.[21] They are dedications made, in so far as they can be identified, by: the city (1), soldiers (12), family and private persons (2). The governor appears as dedicant on two others.[22] These inscriptions range in date from the reign of Hadrian to the reign of Gallus Caesar. Furthermore there are four third-century building inscriptions from Bostra, describing the governor as responsible for the erection of fortifications.[23] The governor is also mentioned, but less frequently, at Gerasa.[24] Gerasa probably also had a garrison.[25] At Philadelphia one dedication made by a legate and one inscription in honour of another legate have been found.[26] In the reign of Hadrian regular visits by the governor to Petra are attested in the Babatha archive.[27] Inscriptions 1–8 show that these still took place in the early third century. Inscription No. 45 is noteworthy because it is a dedication to the first governor of Arabia, C. Claudius Severus, who is mentioned in the well-known letter of Julius Apollinarius, written in 107. Apollinarius mentions work carried out by soldiers of his legion in the vicinity of Petra, presumably connected with the *Via Nova Traiana*.[28] No. 51 is the funerary inscription of the governor T. Aninius

---

[21] *IGLS* xiii 1, pp. 135–158, Nos. 9063–82. 9081 and –2 are a pair in honour of a governor and his son. 9083 honours a governor of Syria-Palaestina, perhaps indicating that the man (his name is lost), came from Bostra, as suggested by Sartre. However, that would make him the only attested senator originating from the province of Arabia: cf. G.W. Bowersock, 'Roman Senators from the Near East: Syria, Judaea, Arabia, Mesopotamia', *Tituli* 5 (1982), 651–68.

[22] 9060, –62; see also 9086.

[23] 9105, –6 belong to the series discussed by H.-G. Pflaum, 'La fortification de la ville d'Adraha d'Arabie', *Syria* 29 (1952), 307–30; cf. Isaac, *op. cit.*, 133 f. This represents a programme whereby the fortifications of Bostra, Adraa and Soada (Dionysias) were strenghtened in the sixties and seventies of the third century. 9108, –9 from 278–9 and 282–3 may be related; also: *IGLS* xxi 2, 179 from Dibon (Dhiban) in Moab, dated 245–6, which is a little earlier than the other texts of this series. I take no account here of milestone inscriptions, or texts which merely state that a building was erected in the time of a specific governor.

[24] The governor of Syria appears on building inscriptions of A.D. 90/91: at this date Gerasa belonged to this province: J. Pouilloux, *Liber Annuus* 27 (1977), 246–54; 29 (1979), 276–8; Kraeling, *Gerasa*, No. 50. The governor of Arabia: e.g. Nos. 160–2, 165, 170.

[25] Isaac, *op. cit.*, 346.

[26] *IGLS* xxi 2, 11, a dedication to *IOM Conservatori* of A.D. 143; 25.

[27] N. Lewis, *The Documents from the Bar Kokhba Period in the Cave of Letters* (Jerusalem, 1989), Nos. 14, 23, 25.

[28] P. Mich 466, cf. M. Speidel, *ANRW* ii 8, 691–3. Note also inscription No. 46 from Petra, a fragmentary dedication to a governor made by the city.

Sextius Florentinus, who is also mentioned in *P.Yadin* 16 from 127.[29] As the editor notes, most of the inscriptions testifying to the presence of the governor in Petra antedate the mid-second century.[30] He attributes this to an initial interest in the old Nabataean capital which subsequently declined.

One inscription (No. 48), from the third or fourth century, set up by the 'metropolis and metrocol(onia)' honours a financial procurator. The distribution of inscriptions in honour of this official in Arabia is also interesting. At Gerasa there are six inscriptions honouring the procurator and another set up by the *cornicularius* of the procurator.[31] In contrast, a procurator is mentioned on only one text from Bostra,[32] and this is an exceptional case, for it is a dedication made by the powerful Timesitheus who served both as procurator and as acting governor. The inscription can be dated to the period of the joint rule of Elagabalus and Severus Alexander (A.D. 221/2). This is possibly the context of the grant of colonial status to Bostra, first recorded on coins of the reign of Severus Alexander.[33] It is quite likely that Petra received the same status about the same time. Petra issued colonial coins before Bostra, under Elagabalus,[34] but that gives us merely a *terminus ante*, for cities did not issue coinage every year. Whether Bostra received colonial status at the end of Elagabalus' reign or early in the reign of Severus Alexander, it is possible that the grant of this status was the result of a single decision made in the reign of Elagabalus, for there is no other city which received colonial status in the reign of Severus Alexander. For the province of

[29] No. 51, with comments on pp. 86 f.; For *P.Yadin* 16: Lewis, *op. cit.*, 65–70. This is a census declaration which attests the presence of a cavalry commander at Rabbat Moab.

[30] P. 29.

[31] C.H. Kraeling, *Gerasa: City of the Decapolis* (New Haven, 1938), Nos. 173, 175–9, 207 f.; cf. Isaac, *op. cit.*, 345 f., where it is suggested that this city was the seat of the procurator, a situation resembling that of Britain in the first century, when Camulodunum was the capital and London seat of the procurator (*RIB* 12; Tacitus, *Ann.* xiv 38).

[32] No. 9019 with comments on pp. 90 f. No. 9085 mentions a subprocurator.

[33] A. Spijkerman, *The Coins of the Decapolis and Provincia Arabia* (Jerusalem, 1978), pp. 80 f., Nos. 48 ff.; A. Kindler, *The Coinage of Bostra* (Warminster, Wilts., 1983), 8 f.; M. Sartre, *Bostra, des origines à l'Islam* (Paris 1985), 76 f.; F. Millar, 'The Roman *Coloniae* of the Near East: A Study of Cultural Relations', in H. Solin & Mika Kajava (eds.), *Roman Eastern Policy and Other Studies in Roman History* (Helsinki, 1990), 52.

[34] Spijkerman, p. 236, nos. 55 f. S. Ben-Dor, 'Petra Colonia', *Berytus* 9 (1948–49), 41–3; Millar, *op. cit.*, 51 f.

Arabia the governorship of Timesitheus, which spanned both reigns, forms an appropriate setting.

We have noted above that there are not many Byzantine inscriptions, especially when compared with the numbers from the Byzantine towns in the Negev and central Jordan. This apparently reflects the unimportance of the town in this period.[35] A remarkable and very well-known text is provided by the only building inscription in this volume, recording the dedication of an old Nabataean tomb as a Christian church in 446 by the bishop Jason[36] in the presence of the *numerus* of the *Tertiodalmateis*, already mentioned. Related to this is the epitaph of a man who was almost certainly Jason's son, set up in 447 (No. 63). The texts cut in the rock of an hermitage quite near the city (Nos. 75, 76) are also instructive for the history of Petra in the Byzantine period.

Other Sites

So far the inscriptions from Petra. The remainder of the inscriptions, Nos. 94–156, are grouped in regional sections moving from north to south. First comes Wadi al-Hasa—more remarkable for its archaeological remains than its inscriptions. However there is an interesting graffito cut in the rock near the spot where the desert route crosses Wadi al-Hasa (No. 94); it mentions a δρομεδ[ά]ρις. Nearby the editor saw a site, perhaps a fort, named Qasr al-Abyad. The *gentilicium* of the camelrider is Flavius, which suggests a date in the fourth century or after. He could then have served in one of the various units of *equites* recorded in the *Notitia Dignitatum Or.* xxxiv. For those interested in the Babatha documents the section on the Ghawr al-Safi could have been interesting, for this is the area of Zoara, which is subject of many of the papyri. There are, however, only two inscriptions from this region, curiously dated 387 and 388 respectively, although they are not connected (pp. 133–7, Nos. 105 f.). The scarcity of inscriptions in this area is not really surprising, for the Babatha documents themselves clearly point to the limited literacy of Babatha herself and others who appear in the documents.

---

[35] See the survey and references to literary sources and archaeological material on pp. 30 f.

[36] List of known bishops from Petra: pp. 83 f.

Phaeno is famous as the penal colony town which received Christians condemned during the persecution of 303–313.[37] What we know about the history of this copper mining town is conveniently summarized in the introductory section, pp. 139–2. The names of several bishops are recorded in the fifth and sixth centuries. It had two churches and the few inscribed tombstones found on the spot contain formulas which are part of the Byzantine repertoire of the Negev. In this connection it is worth observing that a Christian epitaph found at Aela shows a relationship with usage in Egypt rather than Syria.[38]

Finally there are the inscriptions found in the remote South-East, the Hisma.[39] A Greek graffito cut in the rock says: Ῥωμέοι ἀεὶ νικῶσιν. Λαυρίκιος ἔγραψα. Χαῖρε Ζήνων (No. 138) ('The Romans always win. I, Lauricius, wrote "Hail Zenon"'). It is almost certainly the same Zenon who is greeted on another graffito nearby: 'Greetings Zenon, son of QYMT, Tribune, with (the) good for ever.'[40] The Roman (auxiliary?) officer Zenon had a father with an Arabic name and friends who could write both Greek and Aramaic. These texts, then, reflect a sense of superiority held by those who identified with Roman power while at the same time they are evidence of the mixed culture prevailing in the area. In the same region is the Nabataean sanctuary of Wadi Ram (pp. 173–182, inscriptions nos. 139–49). The Roman military are represented by a *duplicarius*, responsible for the construction (139). A man named Ulpius (140) may also have been a soldier. Two emperors and a governor are mentioned on a fragmentary Latin inscription, one of the remotest texts of its kind. Finally, one of the very few bilingual (Greek and Nabataean) inscriptions mentions one of the builders: 'Ouabalas, also named Abomanos, son of Abdomanos, son of Aialos, from Phaeno, builder.'[41] Rome's impact on the remote desert area is obvious, yet in the end we still cannot say how far the epigraphic material is representative of local culture.

---

[37] Pp. 139–148, nos. 107–114.

[38] No. 156 with comments on pp. 190 f.

[39] For this region and its inscriptions: pp. 165–82. It may noted that no inscriptions have been found at the important site of Humaymah (pp. 167 f., no. 133 is a milestone, no. 134 is illegible and no. 135 was found 5 m east of the site.

[40] W.J. Jobling and C. Bennett, *ADAJ* 26 (1982), 199–209: *šlm Zynwn br Qymt klyrk bb l'lm*.

[41] No. 141: Μνησθῇ Ουαβαλας ὁ κα[ὶ] Αβδομαν[ο]ς Αβδομανου τοῦΑιαλο[υ Φ]αινησιος ἀ(ρχ)[ιτέκτων]. *[dkrt*] lt [w w]hb*lhy dy mtqr* 'bd'mnw [br] 'bd'mnw [br] 'ylw [br] 'bd'bdt br qynw fyny bny'.*

Postscript

Recent publications:

P.M. Bikai & V. Egan, 'Archaeology in Jordan', *AJA* 100 (1996), 28–30, at p. 531: Latin inscriptions found in secondary use in Petra (no text given, to be published by Z.T. Fiema) a *signifer* to the *praefectus* of the *Ala II Ulpia Auriana,* a unit stationed in Cappadocia.

J. Wilson, and E.E. Myers, 'Low-altitude aerial photography at Petra' in: *The Roman and Byzantine Near East: Some Recent Archaeological Research* (*JRA* Supp. 14, Ann Arbor, MI, 1995), 279–86.

Z.T. Fiema *et al.,* 'The Petra Church Project: interim report, 1992–1994', *ibid.,* 287–303.

THE ROMAN ARMY, GENERAL

23

THE MEANING OF *LIMES* AND *LIMITANEI* IN ANCIENT SOURCES*

It is a commonplace of modern scholarship that the Roman Imperial Army frontier areas was organized in *limes*-systems: fortifications
linked by roads along a fixed boundary, marked in many, but not
all, parts of the empire by a river or an artificial obstacle: indeed,
the term *limes* is often used as though it were self-explanatory.[1] The
term is certainly used in ancient sources; thus while the literature
may furnish only fragmentary information on the army and its activities along the border, it does at least apparently provide us with
a name to which to link the material remains. Over the past four
decades conferences on Roman frontier studies have regularly been
held, often under the title '*Limes* Congress'.

It was when the study of army organization in the frontier areas
developed in the nineteenth century that the term *limes* came to be
accepted as referring to a system of defence in use along the border
of the empire from the first century onward. Mommsen was, it seems,
the first to attempt to define the meaning of the term,[2] or, if not the
first, certainly the most influential. Although his theory was not uni-
versally accepted,[3] it is generally taken for granted that the term
indicates permanent defensive structures or a formal military and
administrative organization. The relevant entry in *P-W* states without hesitation that under the Empire the term *limes* came to signify
a hermetically closed border.[4] Or one could cite an influential book
on the Roman army: 'The conception of a system of forts and supply

---

* I am grateful for advice and comments to Glen Bowersock, Averil Cameron,
Tony Honoré, John Mann and Fergus Millar.
[1] Most of the literary and epigraphical sources cited here are listed by Forni,
Dizionario Epigrafico IV, 2, s.v. *limes*, 1074 ff. (1959) and in *TLL* VII, 2, fasc. ix,
p. 1415; see also Fabricius, *RE* XIII, s.v. It is possible that I have missed inscriptions published after 1959, after which perusal of *L'Année épigraphique* had to suffice;
the term *limes* appears frequently there in the notes but only twice in the texts
themselves: *AÉ* 1964, 197; 1967, 555, both boundary stones.
[2] Th. Mommsen, 'Der Begriff des Limes', *Gesammelte Schriften* v (1908), 456–64.
[3] See below, p. 130.
[4] Fabricius, *RE* XIII, 572–5.

bases, with planned communications, belongs entirely to the Empire. The idea that there was a controllable limit to the extension of Roman authority was first enunciated by Augustus. The adequate protection of the frontier areas, in the face of the movements and pressure of barbarian peoples, became an increasing preoccupation of succeeding emperors'.[5] Modern studies do not hesitate to describe as a *limes* any set of Roman forts encountered in a frontier-zone. Syme wrote in 1936: 'This was the term which soon came to be applied to each and all of the frontiers of the Empire. . . . The essential of a *limes*, then, is a road with watch-towers or forts along it.'[6]

Since the term is so widely used by historians and archaeologists it is obviously important to know what we mean by it ourselves, and more important still to have a clear idea of how the Romans used it. Theories invariably start from the presumed meaning of the term in antiquity. It is particularly important to consider whether the notion of 'defence against barbarians' is as closely associated with the word *limes* as is generally supposed. This paper therefore attempts to trace the use of *limes* in ancient texts following a roughly chronological order. It will be argued that the common translation of the term as 'defended border' is incorrect for every period. Moreover, since our common view of the nature of the units of *limitanei* in the late empire derives directly from the accepted meaning of the term *limes*, a discussion of the former term will also follow (pp. 139–46).

I. *Meanings of the Term* Limes

In the republican period and in the works of Cicero and Caesar the normal terms to denote 'the boundary of the empire' were *fines* and *termini*. In the early imperial period, *limes* is used as follows:

---

[5] G. Webster, *The Roman Imperial Army* (1979), 46; see further Forni's definition, *op. cit.* (n. 1), 1080: 'Nel significato di "frontiera fortificata e stesa a difesa dell'impero romano", in senso molto lato e per niente affatto corrispondente all'idea moderna di confine come line ideale contrassegnata da cippi o altro. . . .' Usually, however, it is considered unnecessary to explain what the term means, either in ancient sources or as used in modern studies.

[6] R. Syme, *CAH* XI (1936), 182 f. Hence M.P. Speidel writes in *Studien zu den Militärgrenzen Roms* III, *13. Internationaler Limeskongress, Aalen 1983, Vorträge* (1986), 657, of the forts on the eastern shore of the Black Sea: 'While one is certainly justified to call this well defined sector of the Roman frontier the *limes Ponticus*, from a strategic point of view it may be better to speak of it as the Caucasus frontier'. In a

A. *Military Road*

1. Velleius II, 120 (Tiberius in A.D. 10):

> arma infert quae arcuisse pater et patria contenti erant; penetrat interius, aperit limites, vastat agros, urit domos, fundit obvios. . . .

> He attacked the enemy whom his father and country would have been content to hold in check; he penetrated farther inland, opened up roads, destroyed fields, burned houses, routed those in his way. . . .

Tiberius constructed military roads in enemy territory during a campaign of conquest in difficult terrain. 'Aperit' is used frequently to indicate road-construction.[7]

2. Tacitus, *Ann.* I, 50 (Germanicus in A.D. 14):

> at Romanus agmine propero silvam Caesiam limitemque a Tiberio coeptum scindit, castra in limite locat, frontem ac tergum vallo, latera concaedibus munitus.

> But the Roman commander, in a forced march, passed through the Caesian forest, opening up a road which Tiberius first constructed [or: 'which Tiberius had begun to construct'] and placed his camp on the road, fortifying its front and rear with an earthen wall, the flanks with a palisade.

Here the term *limes* refers to one of the structures mentioned in (I). Germanicus in A.D. 14, used a military road constructed by Tiberius in A.D. 10. He 'cut' a road through the forest. It has been objected that 'scindit' cannot be used in this sense or that the *zeugma* which results is too harsh.[8] It is suggested that Germanicus crossed a fortified line constructed in enemy territory 'designed to mark off and defend territory to which Rome laid claim'. But it is not possible to mark off and defend what has not even been conquered.[9] Suggestions like these ignore the realities of war in antiquity. 'Scindit' evokes the image of a road constructed through a heavily forested area where

---

note Speidel refer to V.A. Lefkinadze, Pontijski Limes, *Drevnei Historij* (1969), 75–93, though he points out that neither term is attested.

[7] Cf. Florus II, 27: Drusus (also in Germany) 'invisum atque inaccessum in id tempus Hercynium saltum patefecit'. 'Aperuit et stravit' is found on milestones; see below, p. 131.

[8] Cf. F.R.D. Goodyear, *The Annals of Tacitus* I (1972), pp. 315–17. Cf. Statius, *Silvae* IV, 3, 41: 'rescindere limites' (of the Via Domitiana); Lucretius II, 406: 'rescindere vias'.

[9] See the remarks by A. Oxé, *BJb* 114 (1906), 128.

safe movement and communications are the primary concern of an attacking force.

3. *Ann.* II, 7 (Germanicus in A.D. 16):

> et cuncta inter castellum Alisonem ac Rhenum novis limitibus aggeribusque permunita.

> All the land between the fort of Aliso and the Rhine was now completely secured with new military roads and causeways.

The plural makes it clear that this was a system of military roads constructed throughout the region, to allow movement of army units in newly invaded land, not a single fortified line meant to prevent foreigners from entering a peaceful area. The term *aggeres* is explained in another passage of Tacitus: in A.D. 15 Germanicus sent Caecina ahead, 'ut occulta saltuum scrutaretur pontesque et aggeres umido paludum et fallacibus campis imponeret' ('to explore unknown forests and to construct bridges and causeways over humid swamps and treacherous fields').[10] These are military roads constructed in marshland on embankments, just as *limites* are military roads built through woodland. Dio LVI, 19, 1 relates that the troops of Quintilius Varus A.D. 9 suffered even before the Germans attacked, because they had to fell trees, build roads and construct bridges where required. The essential difference between this campaign and the others was that Varus' troops had to prepare the roads as the army as a whole was advancing in enemy territory. Normally such engineering activities are undertaken by units preceding the main body of troops, which can then march quickly to their destination.

4. Frontinus, *Strat.* I, 3, 10:

> Imperator Caesar Domitianus Augustus, cum Germani more suo e saltibus et obscuris latebris subinde impugnarent nostros tutumque regressum in profunda silvarum haberent, limitibus per centum viginti milia passuum non mutavit tantum statum belli, sed et subiecit dicioni suae hostes, quorum refugia nudaverat limitibus . . . actis.

> When the Germans according to their custom continuously attacked our forces from their forests and unknown hiding places and would have a safe retreat into the depths of the woods, the emperor Caesar Domitian Augustus, with the aid of a hundred and twenty miles of

---

[10] *Ann.* I, 61, 2. See also the 'aggeres et pontes' constructed during the campaign against the Frisians, IV, 73, 2.

military roads, not merely changed the course of the war, but sub-
jected the enemies whose refuges he made accessible with the roads
which he constructed.

The situation is similar to that in (I). The construction of military roads
penetrating enemy territory enables the Roman troops to move safely.[11]

5. Tacitus, *Germ.* 29, 4, on the Agri Decumates:

> levissimus quisque Gallorum et inopia audax dubiae possessionis solum
> occupavere; mox limite acto promotisque praesidiis sinus imperii et pars
> provinciae habentur.

> The most useless Gauls, made audacious by poverty, occupied these
> lands of precarious ownership; subsequently a road was constructed,
> garrisons were moved forward and they are now reckoned an outlying
> recess of the empire and part of the province.

The reference is to the same campaign as in (4) and may be taken
to indicate the same strategy. Garrisons linked by a system of military roads consolidated the conquest of the region. The term *limes*
here has no connection with border or frontier defence.[12]

Passages (1)–(5) derive from first- and early second-century sources
and refer to four first-century campaigns in Germany. All describe
the same strategy of making difficult terrain accessible for the Roman
army by constructing roads. The word *limes* here does not mean
'boundary' or 'fortified line' and the context is one of conquest, not
defence.[13] The Romans, when campaigning across the Rhine, will

---

[11] For the interpretation of this passage see below, n. 14, with Syme, *CAH* XI,
162 f. H. Schönberger, *JRS* 59 (1969), 159, strangely reverted to the assumption
that Frontinus meant to say that lateral barriers were constructed. See further
F. Millar, *Britannia* 13 (1982), 14.

[12] Cf. J.D.C. Anderson, *Tacitus Germania* (1938), *ad loc.*, p. 149: '*Limitem agere* is one
of the technical expressions for driving such a road. . . .' See also Virgil, *Aen.* X,
513: 'proxima quaeque metit gladio latumque per agmen ardens limitem agit ferro'
('he made his way through the enemy ranks').

[13] See further Oxé, *art. cit.* (n. 9), 99–133, a study more often cited than read.
See in particular the conclusions at 121 f.: 'Nur zuweilen . . . übernimmt der Limes
die Funktion der Grenze . . . der Limes selbst ist nie ein gefestigter Weg, geschweige
denn eine Befestigung mit Palisaden oder Wall mit Graben. . . . Zum schluss mag
nur noch betont werden, dass dem reinen Begriff des Limes die man ihm oft
angedichtet hat, völlig fremd sind: Grenze, Befestigung, Querweg'. These passages
are similarly interpreted by Fabricius, *op. cit.* (n. 4), 572–5. However, in the discussion which follows, Fabricius ignores the conclusions to be drawn from his own
interpretation of the sources. Similarly Forni, *op. cit.* (n. 1), 1079; A. Piganiol, *Quintus
Congressus Internationalis Limitis Romani Studiosorum* (1963), 119–22. Mommsen, *op. cit.*

have been careful not to repeat the mistakes which had led to the 'clades Variana'; indeed, Dio makes it clear that insufficient preparatory care for communications in forests and marsh-land was one of the causes of the disaster.[14] It must be noted that these were not paved Roman roads marked with milestones, but tracks cut through forests. Strangely, perhaps, there are no instances of *limes* used in this sense in later sources; no obvious explanation presents itself, apart from the relative scarcity of descriptions of offensive warfare in well-wooded country.

6. At least one (fragmentary) inscription seems to use the term *limes* in the sense of military road, *CIL* III 3157 (cf. 8663; 14239/4) of A.D. 179:

> Val(erius) Val(ens) v[et(eranus)] ex (centurione) limite[m] pub(licum) praeclus(um) . . . aperuit.

> Valerius Valens, veteran and ex-centurion opened up the public way which was inaccessible.

B. *Boundary*

1. Tacitus, *Agr.* 41, 2:

> nec iam de limite imperii et ripa, sed de hiberniis legionum et possessione dubitatum.

> It was no longer the land- and river-boundaries of the empire, but the winter quarters of the legions and the ownership of territories which were in danger.

Here Tacitus uses the word in a wholly different sense: 'the land boundary of the empire', as opposed to *ripa*, 'river boundary'. This is not a military technical term,[15] but derives from surveyors' vocabulary.[16]

(n. 2), 459, misinterpreted all these passages in an effort to define the term on the basis of surveyors' vocabulary.

[14] See n. 4 above. Note also Vegetius' observations on the dangers of marching on a narrow road: 'melius est praecedere cum securibus ac dolabris milites et cum labore aperire vias' ('it is preferable that soldiers lead the way with hatches and pickaxes and laboriously open up roads') (III, 6).

[15] Cf. Siculus Flaccus, *Grom.* 163, 24: 'Territoria inter civitates, id est municipia et colonias et praefecturas, alia fluminibus finiuntur, alia summis montium iugis ac deuergiis aquarum alia etiam lapidibus positis praesignibus, qui a privatorum terminorum forma differunt: alia etiam inter binas colonias limitibus perpetuis derigentur'. Here a continuously demarcated boundary is meant as opposed to boundary stones set at intervals.

[16] It is curious that Mommsen does not cite this passage (see n. 13).

2. *SHA, vita Hadr.* 12:

> in plurimis locis, in quibus barbari non fluminibus sed limitibus divi-
> duntur, stipitibus magnis in modum muralis saepis funditus iactis atque
> conexis barbaros separavit.

> In many areas were the barbarians are separated [from the empire]
> not by rivers but by land-boundaries he [sc. Hadrian] shut them off
> with high stakes planted deep in the earth and fastened together so as
> to form a palisade.

Although we cannot be certain that the *SHA* reflects second-century
terminology,[17] it is clear that the word *limites* is used here in the
same sense as in the previous example. It has indeed been claimed
that this is an instance of the meaning 'fortified boundary', but the
reference is rather to a land-boundary which was subsequently reinforced with a palisade. From the wording it is clear that it was called
limes before Hadrian built a permanent structure to mark it as such.
Further, a clear distinction is made between river- and land-boundaries:
only the latter are called *limites*. Nor, one may add, is any mention
made of forts or other military installations (cf. below, c. 6).

3. *Itinerarium Antonini* (O. Cuntz, *Itineraria Romana* I, (1929))
(*a*) p. 71, 464:

> Iter Britanniarum. . . . A limite, id est a vallo, Praetorio.[18]

> The itinerary in Britain. . . . From the boundary, that is from the wall,
> to the Praetorium.

(*b*) p. 16, 111:

> Item a Capua Equo Tutico ubi Campania limitem habet.

> Also, from Capua to E.T. where the boundary of Campania is.

(*c*) p. 10, 73:

> Item iter quod limitem Tripolitanum per Turrem Tamalleni a Tacapes
> Lepti Magna ducit.

The boundary (*limes*) of the province of Britain serves as *caput viae*; by
way of explanation ('id est') it is added that the border was marked
by the wall. In other words, the boundary is described as 'the wall';
that does not mean, however, that *limes* means anything but provincial

---

[17] Forni, *op. cit.* (n. 1).
[18] For discussion see A.L.F. Rivet and Colin Smith, *The Place-Names of Roman Britain*
(1979), 154–6.

boundary. It may be noted that the Wall is never referred to as *limes* in inscriptions, but always as *vallum*—e.g. *RIB* 2034; 2200; 2205. It is of interest to note that the same source uses the word for a boundary within Italy (that of Campania), where, of course, no defence system existed in this period. This usage then reflects third-century terminology.[19]

4. *ILS* 451, *Acta Arv.*, II August A.D. 213:

> [The Emperor] per limitem Raetiae ad hostes extirpandos barbarorum [sc. terram vel sim.] introiturus est. . . .

> The Emperor is about to cross the border of Raetia into barbarian [lands] in order to destroy the enemy.[20]

5. R.G. Goodchild and J.B. Ward Perkins, *JRS* 39 (1949), 91 (*AÉ* 1950, 128), A.D. 244–6:

> [The Emperor Philip and his son] regionem limi[tis Ten]theitani partitam et [eius] viam incursib(us) barba[ro]rum constituto novo centenario [—] prae[cl]useru[nt]. . . .[21]

The inscription is badly mutilated, but it seems sufficiently clear that it refers to 'the border region of Tentheos and the road through it(?) which were closed(?) to barbarian raids'. While the reference is obviously to military activity, there is nothing to suggest that the term *limes* means more than simply 'boundary' (or, possibly, 'borderland').

6. *CIL* VIII 22765 (*ILS* 8923), A.D. 262/3:

> [The Emperor Gallienus] castra coh(ortis) viii Fidae opportuno loco a solo instituit operantibus fortissimis militibus suis ex limite Tripolitano.

> (The Emperor Gallienus) established a new fort of the cohort VIII Fida on a suitable site through the toil of his bravest soldiers from the *limes* of Tripolitania.

---

[19] See *TLL*, s.v., for a few additional cases where *limes* is clearly used to mean the boundary of the empire.

[20] G.W. Bowersock doubts whether in Latin *crossing* the border would be expressed by *per* and wonders whether *limes* could mean 'borderland' in the present passage. This is possible, but perhaps support for my rendering may be found in Caes., *BG* III, 26: 'Hostes undique circumventi desperatis omnibus rebus se per munitiones deicere et fuga salutem petere intenderunt'.

[21] For discussion see J.F. Matthews in R. Goodburn and P. Bartholomew (eds.), *Aspects of the Notitia Dignitatum* (1976), 157–86, esp. 170 f. For the meaning of *centenarium* see R.P. Duncan-Jones, *Chiron* 8 (1978), 548, 552–6.

We have here two third-century inscriptions which use the term *limes* to indicate the imperial boundary. Again, (6) cannot support the claim the *limes* refers to military works or organization. In inscriptions *limes* is always geographically defined, and even when using the term to mean 'boundary', none of the sources discussed speaks of it as something constructed or laid out. Where it is stated that the *limes* was 'made', the term is used in the sense of military road.

The term *limes*, then, is not used in this period to indicate permanent defensive structures or formal military and administrative organization, as is assumed in the modern literature.[22] To speak of a *limes* in this sense is therefore incorrect; by the same token '*Limes* congresses' should rather be called congresses of Roman Frontier Studies.[23]

It may be added that Mommsen, on the basis of an etymological discussion of the term, proposed the wild hypothesis that the *limes* always had a dual structure, consisting of a strip of land marked on both sides, with both an 'inner' and an 'outer' border.[24] Despite some criticism,[25] this notion was widely accepted, for instance by Brünnow and Domaszewski, who proceeded to search for the inner and outer *limes* in Arabia, under a misconception which has long bedevilled the study of the eastern provinces.[26] However, misconceptions about the *limites* go further back than Mommsen.[27]

---

[22] Pelham, below, n. 25. See also references above, p. 125 and n. 3.

[23] As indeed they usually are in Britain.

[24] Mommsen, *op. cit.* (n. 2), 456–64: 'Es scheint den Limes-forschern wenig zum Bewusstsein gekommen zu sein, dass der Limes seinem Wesen nach bei allen sonst möglichen Verschiedenheiten, eine irgendwie markierte zweifache Grenze, eine äussere und eine innere fordert'.

[25] *Essays by H.F. Pelham*, ed. F. Haverfield (1911), in the paper 'The Roman Frontier System', 164–78, esp. 168–9. Pelham, however, went on to say that 'there is no doubt that "limes", like "march", was frequently used to include not only the frontier line with its defences, but also the territory stretching along both sides of it'.

[26] Forni, *op. cit.* (n. 1), *passim*; R. MacMullen, *Soldier and Civilian in the Later Roman Empire* (1963), 39 n. 53. A. Poidebard, *La trace de Rome dans le désert de Syrie: Le limes de Trajan à la conquête arabe* (1934), thought he could recognize in the Strata Diocletiana an inner line of defence and farther eastward an outer line. Later R. Mouterde and A. Poidebard, *Le Limes de Chalcis, organisation de la steppe en haute Syrie romaine* (1945), claimed to have discovered two lines farther north, an inner *limes* east of Chalcis and an outer one on the Euphrates. In the Negev M. Gichon traced two lines: *Studien zu den Militärgrenzen Roms, Vorträge des 6. Limes-Kongresses* (1967), 175 ff.; id.; *Roman Frontier Studies 1979* (1980), 852–5; see also, K.C. Gutwein, *Third Palestine* (1981), 309–11. In Africa: J. Baradez, *Fossatum Africae* (1949), 358–60; in Mesopotamia: R.E.M. Wheeler, *Roman Frontier Studies 1949* (1952), 112–29; esp. 127. For criticism see W. Liebeschuetz, *Studien zu den Militärgrenzen Roms* II (1977), 487–99, esp. 488 f.;

For the terminology actually used in the second century to indicate military structures see, for instance, *CIL* III 3385, discussed by
A. Alföldi, *Archaeologiai Értesitö* 3/2 (1941), 40–8:[28]

> Imp(erator) Caes(ar) M(arcus) Aur(elius) [Commodus] Antoninus Aug-
> (ustus) Pius Sarm(aticus) Ger(manicus) Brit(annicus), pont(ifex) max(imus),
> trib(unicia) pot(estate) VI., imp(erator) IIII., co(n)s(ul) IIII., p(ater) p(atriae),
> ripam omnem burgis a solo exstructis, item praesidi(i)s per loca op-
> portuna ad clandestinos latrunculorum transitus oppositis munivit per
> [L. Cornelium Felicem Plotianum] leg(atum) pr(o) pr(aetore).

The Emperor Commodus 'fortified the whole riverbank with new
towers and forts placed on suitable sites to prevent covert crossings
of raiders', etc.

Military terms encountered in this inscription are *burgi, praesidia,
munivit* and *latrunculi*. The word *limes* is missing. For *burgi* see Alföldi,
47 f.;[29] for the term *latrunculi* (hit-and-run raiders), *ibid.*, 42–6. The
term *ripa* is frequently attested in literature and epigraphy.[30] It occurs

---

G.W. Bowersock, *HSCP* 80 (1976), 219–29; B. Isaac, *HSCP* 88 (1984), 191 with nn.
103 and 104. Most recently S. Thomas Parker, *Romans and Saracens* (1986), 6, argued
for the existence of 'a broad, fortified zone, not a single fortified line' in Arabia.
Elsewhere, however, he speaks of a 'main *limes*' and a 'secondary line of defence'
(p. 142).

[27] See P. Bartholomew, *Britannia* 15 (1984), 179 n. 45: 'The text of Ammianus
XXVIII, 5, 1 provides an illustration of the dubious authenticity of "*limes*". According to Clark and the other modern editors, the object of the Saxon attack on north-
east Gaul in 370 was "*Romanum limitem*". But the reading of M (which survives at
this point) is "*Romanum limitem*"; and M is followed by V. "*Limitem*" appears only as
a correction in an inferior fifteenth-century manuscript, and in Ghelen. This indicates the readiness with which Renaissance scholars thought of "*limites*" in the context
of late Roman military operations.... The decision of modern editors to accept
"*limitem*" instead of the better attested "*militem*" must appear distinctly questionable.'
For a similar case see Seeck, *Not. Dig. Oc.* V, 126: 'Comites limitum infrascriptorum',
where all the MS read: '*militum*'; cf. Bartholomew, *Britannia* 10 (1979), 370. The
search for fortresses sometimes leads to even more peculiar conclusions. Gutwein,
op. cit. (n. 26), translates 'ex divisione praesidium Palaestinae' (Jerome, *Quaestiones in
Genesim* 21:30, *PL* XXIII, 969) as 'a recent division of fortifications'. Jerome, *Vita
Hilarionis* 18 (*PL* XXIII, 35) tells the edifying story of 'Orion vir primarius et ditissimus
urbis Aelae, quae mari Rubro imminet, a legione possessus demonum'; this then is
taken as a reference to the Legion X Fretensis based at Aela.

[28] For further references see also A. Mócsy, *Pannonia and Upper Moesia* (1974), 196 f.

[29] Cf. *DE* I, s.v. *burgus*, 1053 f.; IV (1962), s.v. *limes*, 1089 f.; MacMullen, *op. cit.*
(n. 26), 38 f., 57. See also the article on *burgarii* and the *cursus publicus* by M. Labrousse,
Mélanges d'archéologie et d'histoire 55 (1938), 151–67.

[30] E.g. Pliny, *Pan.* 82, 4. It is used in the Antonine Itinerary in a list of stations
along the Euphrates between Satala and Melitene, see J. Crow in *The Defence of the
Roman and Byzantine East, Proceedings of a Colloquium held at the University of Sheffield in
April 1986*, ed. P. Freeman and D. Kennedy (1986), 81 f.

in the title of various commanders: the *praefecti ripae fluminis Euphratensis* (*ILS* 2709), *Danuvii* (*ILS* 2737 in Pannonia, *AÉ* 1926, 80 in Moesia), *Rheni* (Tacitus, *Hist.* IV, 55, cf. 26; 64).[31] They were probably military officers with a local, territorial command rather than one over a specific unit; moreover, the examples given all seem to entail combined activity on land and at sea or on the river. The same would have been true of the *dux ripae* attested at Dura-Europos before the middle of the third century.[32] Relevant for the present discussion is the absence of any comparable reference to an officer in charge of a *limes*.

Milestones on the Trajanic road in Arabia read:

> redacta in formam provinciae Arabia viam novam a finibus Syriae usque ad mare rubrum aperuit et stravit. . . .

> (Trajan) having organized Arabia as a province opened up and paved a new road from the boundary of Syria to the Red Sea.

The reference is, however, to the organization of the *provincia* and the construction of a paved road, not to any *limes*.[33] Finally, as noted above, Hadrian's wall in Britain is never referred to as a *limes*.

It is true that there existed during the principate a vague notion that the empire was made secure by troops stationed at the frontier. Aristides, *Roman Oration*, 80–4, spoke of a defensive system based on an outer ring of permanent camps; and a century later, Herodian II, 11, 5 made the anachronistic statement that 'Augustus . . . fortified the empire by hedging it around with major obstacles, rivers and trenches and mountains and deserted areas which were difficult to traverse' (Loeb trans.). But these are indeed vague pronouncements

---

[31] Tacitus, *Hist.* IV, 26: 'dispositae per omnem ripam stationes quae Germanos vado arcerent'. The *praefecti* are discussed by J.F. Gilliam, *TAPhA* 72 (1941), 157–75. He compares them with other *praefecti*, those in command of the *ora maritima* in Mauretania (*CIL* XI, 5744); the *ora Pontica* (Pliny, *Ep.* X, 21; 86a) and the *Baliorum insulae* (*ILS* 9196). To the evidence in Gilliam's paper add *AÉ* 1968, 321: a *praefectus ad ripam* (sc. *Rheni*) under Claudius and Nero.

[32] Gilliam points out that, unlike the later *duces*, this officer was subordinate to the governor of Syria. Of interest for the later meaning of the word *limes* is that the term *ripa* can also be used for a fiscal district, e.g. on an inscription from the *agora* of Palmyra, which mentions a *curator ripae superioris et inferioris*, see Gilliam, *op. cit.*, 165 n. 35; 174 f. It is not clear what was the difference between this *dux ripae* and the *praefecti* attested elsewhere.

[33] See the catalogue of milestones by P. Thomsen, *Zeitschr. D. Pal. Ver.* 40 (1917), 1 ff. *Aperuit* is only partly applicable, for most of the road followed the alignment of an ancient caravan-route marked by Nabataean road-stations.

which merely convey the sense that good government secured the empire against foreign enemies.

Aristides, *ibid.*, 67, emphasized that the Roman army was not based in cities in the interior, unlike that of the Athenians. Aristides wrote as a citizen of a city of Asia Minor, where this was true in the second century. He could not have said so in the fourth century. Even for his own day Aristides is clearly incorrect if we think of cities in Syria and Palestine. Moreover, he wrote in the reign of Antoninus Pius when the security of the empire rather than achievements in war would be stressed by those who supported the emperor's policy. Herodian's statement occurs in a rhetorical excursus that explains why the Italians were terrified at the approach of Septimius Severus with his Pannonian troops. Augustus, he says, excluded Italians from the army and stationed mercenaries at the frontier to act as a barricade for the Roman Empire.

On the other hand, the uselessness of such obstacles as a means of defence against foreign enemies is emphasized in a number of late-third and early fourth-century texts. These texts are of interest in that they reveal a change in the meaning of *limes*, which, even though its exact form is not always easy to discern, coincides roughly with the major reorganization of the Roman army in the reigns of Diocletian and Constantine.

Panegyrici Latini X (II) 7, 3 (A.D. 298, addressed to Maximianus):

> Atqui Rhenum antea videbatur ipsa sic Natura duxisse, ut eo limite Romanae provinciae ab immanitate barbariae vindicarentur.
>
> In the past Nature itself seemed to have traced the course of the Rhine so that it might mark the boundary and protect the Roman provinces against the ferocity of the barbarians.

It is clear that the term here means 'boundary'.[34] The passage suggests that in the past only the river, a natural obstacle, kept out the barbarians, because the army was too feeble to do so. Now, thanks to the military power exercised by Maximianus, the river has become irrelevant, for Roman power extends across the river.[35] This was a panegyrical *topos*: whereas in the past only natural obstacles

---

[34] For a similar use of the term see XI (III), 5, 4 (addressed to Maximianus in A.D. 291): 'transeo limitem Raetiae repentina hostium clade promotum'.

[35] The passage goes on to state that the same happened in the East, where Syria had only the Euphrates for protection until the Persian kingdoms spontaneously surrendered themselves to Diocletian.

protected the empire against barbarian attack, now it is the mere presence of the emperor, who extended military power far beyond the boundary of the old provinces.

It is important to note that the text nowhere states that the empire was defended, either in the miserable past or in the blessed present, by a system of fortifications. In contrast to the earlier texts the river-boundary is now also referred to as *limes*. It must be kept in mind, however, that these are literary, not formal administrative texts.

It will be clear now that the term *limes* was used rarely during the principate; it does not appear on inscriptions before the third century. This stands in striking contrast to the later period, when it was extremely common. In the second and third century it means 'demarcated boundary' rather than 'defended border'. However, the major conclusion to be drawn from perusal of the available texts is that no term for a 'defended border' existed. It remains to be seen how *limes* was used during the late empire, after the army reorganization of Diocletian and Constantine.

C. *Border District (fourth century and later)*

In the following passages from the *Panegyrics* the term *limes* already seems to be used in the later sense of frontier district.

1. *Pan. Lat.* VIII (V) 3, 3 (A.D. 297, addressed to Constantius):

> Partho quippe ultra Tigrim redacto, Dacia restituta, porrectis usque ad Danubii caput Germaniae Raetiaeque limitibus. . . .

> The Parthian has been sent back beyond the Tigris, Dacia restored, the *limites* of Germany and Raetia have been extended as far as the source of the Danube. . . .

The *limites* of Germany and Raetia that extended as far as the sources of the Danube could be the imperial boundary or frontier districts. The verb *porrigo*, used in the passive for 'to stretch out, to extend', may suggest that an area, not a line is meant.[36]

2. *Ibid.* VI (VII), 11 (addressed to Constantine in A.D. 310 and discussing the safety of the border area against attacks by Franks across the Rhine):

---

[36] Cf. Pliny, *NH* IV, 12, 58: 'Creta inter ortum occasumque porrigitur', and other examples.

> Contra hinc per intervalla disposita magis ornant limitem castella quam protegunt.

The forts established at fixed intervals adorn rather than protect the *limes*.

The meaning of the term here is not immediately clear.[37] It could refer to the boundary of the empire, but 'frontier district' is more appropriate since the forts, seen as distinct from the *limes*, are more likely to protect a district than the boundary itself.[38]

3. *Ibid.* XII (IX):

> 21, 5 (addressed to Constantine in A.D. 313): perrexisti ad inferiorem Germaniae limitem; 22, 5: in superiore limite.

When mention is made of 'the lower *limes* of Germany' and the 'upper *limes*', the terms are obviously used as substitute for the old *provincia*.

4. Ausonius, *Gratiarum Actio* II, 7 (A.D. 379):

> . . . Imperatori fortissimo: testis est uno pacatus in anno et Danuvii limes et Rheni.

> . . . a most powerful emperor: witness the *limes* of the Danube and of the Rhine, pacified in one year.

Since the *limites* of the Danube and of the Rhine are said to be pacified, this is better rendered 'frontier district' than 'boundary'.[39]

From the fourth century onwards, *limes* is used so frequently that a selection has to be made:

5. *CIL* III 12483; *ILS* 724:

> [Constantine's three sons] locum in parte limitis positum, gentilium Gotho[ru]m temeritati semper aptissimum, ad confirmandam provincialium [s]uorum aeternam securitatem erecta istius fabri[c]ae munitione clauserunt latru[nc]ulorumque impetum perennis mun[imi]nis dispositione tenuerunt adcurante Sappone v.p. duce limites Scythiae.

---

[37] Cf. *TLL*, s.v. under the heading *fines extremi imperii Romani*.

[38] Similarly, *ibid.*, 13, 3: 'omnemque illum limitem non equestribus neque pedestribus copiis sed praesentiae tuae terrore tutatus es: quantoslibet valebat exercitus Maximianus in ripa' ('you have protected that whole *limes* not with cavalry nor with infantry but with the terror inspired by your presence: Maximianus on the riverbank is worth an army ever so great'). The *limes*, then, is seen as distinct from the riverbank; cf. the similar argument in the case of the 'limitis . . . custos', below, p. 137.

[39] Cf. *ibid.* XVIII, 82: 'tu Gratiane, tot imperii limites, tot flumina et lacus, veterum intersaepta regnorum . . . celeriore transcursu evoluis'.

[They] blocked a site lying in a part of the *limes* always exposed to the temerity of the Gothic foreigners, in order to guarantee the eternal security of their provincials, by the construction of a fortified building and they have stopped the onslaught of raiders by the arrangement of an enduring fortification through the care of Sappo, *dux* of the Scythian *limes*.

The term *limes* is now attested as a fomal administrative concept denoting a frontier district administered by a military commander (*dux*). The inscription records the erection of a military structure in a part of the *limes*, but this term, taken by itself, does not indicate any specific form of military organization or complex of fortifications. It has an exclusively administrative content.[40]

6. Ammianus, XXIII, 5, 2 (Cercusium):

> Quod Diocletianus exiguum antehoc et suspectum, muris turribusque circumcedit celsis, cum in ipsis barbarorum confiniis interiores limites ordinaret, document* ... per Syriam Persae, ita ut paucis ante annis cum magnis provinciarum damnis.

The text is incomplete but the meaning of *limes* is clear: Diocletian organized the remote border districts.[41] We may note again the distinction made between *limes* and frontier. Two translations which I consulted clearly reflect the development of ideas about the Roman frontier. The Loeb translation by J.C. Rolfe, first published in 1940, writes: '. . . at the time when he was arranging the inner lines of defence on the very frontiers of the barbarians. . . .' The new translation by Walter Hamilton, published in 1986, shows the influence of Luttwak's ideas: '. . . when he was organizing defences in depth on our actual frontier with the barbarians.' But even if it is accepted that term 'defence in depth' correctly describes Roman strategy, there

---

[40] Contrast Forni, *op. cit.* (n. 1), 1081: 'Nel basso impero, in seguito allo sdopiamento delle competenze militari e civili, e ancora in età Giustinianea il concetto di limes venne allargato fino a comprendere, in aggiunta alle strade alle fortificazioni e alle truppe vaste territori affidati all'amministrazione militare'. P. Mayerson, *BASOR* 262 (1986), 35–47, esp. 39, denies that the term has a formal, administrative content and refers to the U.S. concept of a 'frontier': 'that part of a country which forms the border of its settled or inhabited regions' (as defined in the Oxford English Dictionary). This suggests that it is an informal geographical notion. In later sources, such as Malalas, the term is indeed used informally, but there is no doubt that the term *limes* has a formal meaning in the fourth century and afterward.

[41] See also Ammianus XV, 8, 6: 'rupta limitum pace' and other passages cited in the *Thesaurus*. For the city of Cercesium see Oppenheimer *et al.*, *Babylonia Judaica* (1983), 377–82.

is no evidence whatever that the Romans themselves expressed it in this manner.

7. Ammianus, XXXI, 3, 5:

> Munderichem ducem postea limitis per Arabiam.
>
> Munderich, later *dux* of the Arabian *limes*.

It may be noted that this is the first of two references to a *limes* in Arabia, the other being that by Rufinus (below); *per* strengthens the impression that the *limes* is something spread over part of the province rather than a line or zone at the edge of it.

8. Festus, *Breviarium* XIV, ed. Eadie, p. 57:

> et per Traianum Armenia, Mesopotamia, Assyria et Arabia provinciae factae sunt ac limes Orientalis supra ripas Tigridis est institutus.
>
> and Trajan made Armenia, Mesopotamia, Assyria and Arabia provinces and established the eastern *limes* beyond the banks of the Tigris.

Festus discusses Trajan's activities in the terminology of his own times.[42] He describes the organization of new provinces and concludes that the eastern border district was now east of the Tigris. He was thinking of frontier districts under a *dux* such as existed in his own time. Such districts, mentioned in *Not. Dig. Oc.* v (and cf. *Or.* XXVIII), can co-exist without problem with subject peoples beyond the frontier. This is particularly clear in the following passage.

9. *Ibid.*:

> [Under Diocletian] Mesopotamia est restituta et supra ripas Tigridis limes est reformatus, ita ut quinque gentium trans Tigridem constituarum dicionem adsequeremur.
>
> Mesopotamia was restored and beyond the banks of the Tigris a *limes* was re-established, so that we gained sovereignty over five peoples beyond the Tigris.

The submission of the five peoples was a consequence of the reconstitution of the frontier district across the Tigris. Cf. XXV: '(Persae) Mesopotamiam cum Transtigritanis regionibus reddiderunt.'[43] '(The Persians) returned Mesopotamia with the regions beyond the Tigris.'

---

[42] Equally anachronistic is the *dux limitis* mentioned in *SHA, Tyr. Trig.* 3, 9; 29, 1; *Aurelian* 13, 1.

[43] Cf. Eadie's comments on p. 148 with references to Petrus Patricius, fr. 14

10. *SHA, Tyr. Trig.* 26 (on the Isauri):

> in medio Romani nominis solo regio eorum novo genere custodiarum quasi limes includitur, locis defensa, non hominibus.

> This, although in the middle of the empire, is enclosed by a novel kind of guard post, as though it were a frontier district, being defended not by men, but by the nature of the country.

This is mistranslated in the Loeb edition: 'for indeed their district, though in the midst of lands belonging to the Romans, is guarded by a novel kind of defence, comparable to a frontier-wall, for it is protected not by men, but by the nature of the country.'[44] It is not the 'kind of defence' which is compared with a *limes*, but their region. The passage does not refer to any boundary wall and emphasizes that the area is defended by nature, not by men.[45] Fortifications are not mentioned.[46]

11. It should be noted that Byzantine Greek sources often use the Latin term, although there was also a Greek equivalent: *eschatia*, 'the remote regions'. Three examples will suffice:

(a) Zosimus XXXIV, 1–2:

> τῆς γὰρ Ῥωμαίων ἐπικρατείας ἀπανταχοῦ τῶν ἐσχατιῶν τῇ Διοκλητιανοῦ προνοίᾳ κατὰ τὸν εἰρημένον ἤδη μοι τρόπον πόλεσι καὶ φρουρίοις καὶ πύργοις διειλημμένης. . . .

> Thanks to the foresight of Diocletian . . . the *eschatia* of the empire were everywhere occupied by cities, forts and towers.[47]

(*FHG* IV, 188 f.) and Ammianus, XXV, 7, 9, where the same region with five peoples is mentioned. Needless to say, nowhere are military structures referred to. The river Indus mentioned in this source is the Tigris, cf. Aurelius Victor, *de Caesaribus* 13, 3; also, Eutropius VIII, 3, 2. It may be added that Malalas, *Chron.* XII (Dindorf, 307) refers to the 'Indolimiton', where Theophanes speaks of 'Inner Persis' (*Chron. ad ann.* 5793 (A.D. 293)) and Eutropius, *Brev.* 9, 25, of 'ultimas regni solitudines'.

[44] Similarly: J. Rougé, *REA* 68 (1966), 284 f.

[45] Cf. the passages from *Pan. Lat.*, cited above, pp. 132–3.

[46] In two other passages in the *SHA limes* apparently has the same meaning: *Vita Probi* 14, 5: 'nisi si limes Romanus extenderetur et fieret Germania tota provincia'; *Aurelian* 10, 2: 'limites restitueret'. In both cases, however, it is possible that 'boundary' is meant.

[47] For further discussion of this passage, see my forthcoming book, *The Limits of Empire: The Roman Army in the East.*

(b) Suidas, *Lexicon*, s.v. (ed. Adler, I, 2, p. 432):

> Ἐσχατιά· τὰ πρὸς τοῖς τέρμασι τῶν χωρίων ἐσχατιὰς ἔλεγον, οἷς γειτνιᾷ εἴτε ὄρος εἴτε θάλασσα.

> The zones near the frontier of the land are called *eschatia*, which are bounded by a mountain or the sea. . . . Again, Diocletian, when considering the state of the empire thought it necessary to strengthen all *eschatia* with sufficient forces and to build forts.

To my knowledge this is the only extant definition of what the word *limes* might mean. It is significant that the military aspect is not mentioned in the definition itself, but only as a historical footnote. It has been suggested that this may possibly derive from Zosimus.[48]

(c) Procopius, *Anecdota* XXIV, 12–13:

> In the past the Roman emperors stationed numerous soldiers everywhere in the frontier districts of the state (τῶν τῆς πολιτείας ἐσχατιῶν) in order to guard the frontiers of the empire (τῶν ὁρίων τῆς Ῥωμαίων ἀρχῆς), etc.

Here a distinction is made between the *eschatia*, i.e. the *limites*, where soldiers were stationed, and the *horia*, the boundaries of the empire, which the soldiers guarded.

A similar distinction is already made in third-century Palmyrene inscriptions which mention persons who came to 'the frontier zone' or to 'the limits of the frontier zone'.[49]

12. Malalas, *Chronographia*, ed. Dindorf, 308 (also discussed below, p. 141):

> Ἔκτισε δὲ καὶ εἰς τὰ λίμιτα κάστρα ὁ αὐτὸς Διοκλητιανὸς ἀπὸ τῆς Αἰγύπτου ἕως τῶν Περσικῶν ὅρων.

> Diocletian built forts in the *limita* from Egypt to the border with Persia (i.e. in the outer districts).

A clear distinction is made between *limites* and the frontier. The phrase indicates that the term *limes* refers to specific districts where forts are built rather than to the system of forts itself.

---

[48] See Eunapius, *FHG* IV, p. 14. D. van Berchem, *L'Armée de Dioclétien et la réforme constantinienne* (1952), 115.

[49] J. Teixidor, *Syria* 40 (1963), p. 33, no. 1 (an inscription from Qasr Ḥelqum on the road from Palmyra to Hit which commemorates those who were with Abgar the son of Hairan in the frontier-zone (BQST'). J. Starcky, *Syria* 40 (1963), 47–55 (an inscription from a road-station on the same route which commemorates 'Abgar son of Shalman son of Zabdibol, who came to the limits of the frontier-zone (BRṢ QST')'). See also Matthews, *op. cit.* (n. 21), 168 f.

13. Malalas, 295 f., describes the raid into Syria by Shapur I. He reached Antioch through 'the *limes* of Chalcis'. This term is found nowhere else and yet was chosen as the title of a well-known study by Mouterde and Poidebard.[50]

However, van Berchem has already argued, rightly, that what is described there is not a defence system on the frontier, as the authors claimed, but a road system in the interior.[51] If we further admit that Malalas meant no more than 'the hinterland' or 'steppe' of Chalcis, all difficulties are resolved. Diodorus Siculus speaks of Chalcis as a town 'in the frontier area of Arabia'.[52] Jerome and others refer to monasticism in the 'desert of Chalcis'.[53] Jerome cites Malchus, born in Nisibis, who left his home town: 'et quia ad Orientem ire non poteram, propter vicinam Persidem, et Romanorum militum custodiam, ad Occidentem verti pedes. . . . Perveni tandem et eremum Chalcidos . . .' ('and because I could not go east because of the vicinity of Persia and the Roman military garrison I went westward . . . finally I reached the desert of Chalcis . . .'). Malchus, a native of northern Mesopotamia, naturally wanted to travel in those parts, but could not do so because a closed border ran through the country. Jerome clearly distinguishes between the military zone in Mesopotamia and 'the desert of Chalcis' far to the west. Malalas used another geographical term for the same region. It may be noted that there is not a single military inscription in the area, whereas there are numerous civilian Byzantine inscriptions.[54] Finally, Procopius attributes to al-Mundhīr the statement that in this region 'there is neither a fortified city, nor an army worth mentioning.'[55]

To my knowledge there is no passage anywhere in Byzantine sources which states that a *limes* was built or constructed. Reference is made to structures in the *limes* as distinct from the *limes* itself. It should be noted that the so-called 'strata Diocletiana' is known by this name

---

[50] See n. 26.

[51] Van Berchem, *L'Armée*, 5 f.

[52] Fr. 21, *FHG* II, p. xvii. Tryphon concentrated his troops and encamped near the city of Chalcis (cited by Mouterde and Poidebard, *op. cit.* (n. 26), 4–5).

[53] Jerome, *Vita Malchi* 3 (*PL* XXIII, col. 56 f.); Theodoret, *HE* IV, 28, ed. Parmentier, 268, 8; for further references see Mouterde and Poidebard.

[54] See the collection in Mouterde and Poidebard. Note in particular the inscription recording work carried out by private individuals at the fort of el Bab, 71–3, 187 f., *MUSJ* 22 (1939), 65 n. 1; and the fortified *horreum* at et Touba where a similar inscription has been found, 197–201. There is one inscription in honour of Justinian, no. 39 on p. 209.

[55] Procopius, *BP* I, 17, 34.

because the term appears on milestones, but that no mention is made of any *limes*.[56]

14. *Ibid.*, 434: used as in (2).

15. *CTh* VII, 13, 15 and *CJ* I, 27, 13: administrative term denoting frontier district.

16. *Not. Dig. Or.* XXVIII:

> comes limitis Aegypti. sub dispositione viri spectabilis comitis rei militaris per Aegyptum [of units stationed in Memfis, Babilon, Pelusium, etc.].

This is the only *limes* mentioned in the *Not. Dig. Or.*; its meaning is similar to that in (15). In the *Not. Dig. Oc.* many are listed in North Africa. J.C. Mann points out to me that there is no reference here to forts along a frontier line. There was rather a system of roads (with fortifications), as there had been since the time of Augustus.

17. Rufinus, *HE*, II, 6:

> Mavia Sarracenorum gentis regina, vehementi bello Palaestini et Arabici limitis oppida atque urbes quatere, vicinasque simul vastare provincias coepit.

> Mavia, queen of the Saracen people, battered in a fierce war the towns and cities of the *limes* of Palaestina and Arabia and began at the same time to ravage the neighbouring provinces.

In referring to the *limites* and the towns and cities of Palaestina and of Arabia, Rufinus indicates the elements which constituted these provinces: the urbanized area, that is, the cities and their territories on the one hand, and the frontier district on the other.

18. *IGLS* V, 2704 (Khān el-Abyaḍ):

> limitis ur[biu]mque fortissimae custus (*sic*) [i.e. the *dux Foenicis*].

The *dux Foenicis* is commander and administrator of the cities and their territories and of the frontier district. This is virtually the same formulation as in the previous passage. If the term *limes* itself had denoted a system of fortifications meant to protect the province it would make no sense to speak of 'the protector of the *limes*'.

---

[56] Cf. M. Dunand, *Revue Biblique* 40 (1931), 227–48.

19. F.M. Abel, *RB* 29 (1920), 120–2; A. Alt, *Zeitschr. D.Pal. Ver.* 46 (1923), 64 (*SEG* VIII, 296; sixth century):

Οὐδὲ λιπὼν λιμίτοιο Παλεστ(ίνης) χθόνα δῖαν Δωρόθεος γεράων πέλεν ἄμμορος ἐκ βασ[ι]λῆος

Even after leaving the holy land of the *limes* of Palaestina Dorotheus still has a share in the distinctions from the King.

The inscription marked the funerary monument of a dignitary. The context is not military, but refers to the region where the dead man had been active. The use of the term here is close to meaning simply 'the land of Palestine'.[57]

20. Ammianus, XIV, 8, 5:

Orientis vero limes in longum protentus et rectum ab Euphratis fluminis ripis ad usque supercilia porrigitur Nili, laeva Saracenis conterminans gentibus, dextra pelagi fragoribus patens. . . .

The *limes* of Oriens stretching from the banks of the Euphrates to the Nile, bordering on the left on the Saracens and to the right exposed to the waves of the sea. . . .

The term here is used as roughly the equivalent of the Diocese of Oriens. This diocese was indeed composed of the provinces along the eastern frontier, but it is obvious that *limes* as a technical term never included an area of such size. It is used here in a non-technical sense to describe the eastern frontier zone.[58]

21. Ammianus, XXIII, 55:

Proximos his limites possident Bactriani. . . .

The neighbouring lands belong to the Bactrians.

Ammianus here speaks of lands far from the Roman empire, and *limes* is obviously not associated with anything Roman.

---

[57] Abel: 'Bien qu'il a quitté la divine terre de la frontière de Palestine D. a pourtant sa part au distinctions du Basileus.' Alt: 'D. wird schwerlich ein einfacher limitaneus gewesen sein. . . . Türstutz eines Grabgebäudes . . . dessen Errichtung auf Staatskosten [?] war vielleicht die letzte königlichen Ehrung für den im Dienst an der palästinensischen Limes gebliebenen Mann. Der Lobpreis des "göttlichen Landes" ist höffentlich mehr als eine poetische Floskel.' Could the king of the inscription be God rather than the emperor? The phrase would then allude to the man's name, Dorotheus.

[58] It may be noted that it occurs in a chapter full of poetic and rhetorical expressions. The term *limiton* is also taken over into Syriac: see Michael the Syrian, *Chron.* IX, 16 and 26 on the region of the Balīkh and the Khabūr (pillaged by al-Mudhīr).

22. Malalas, 30 and *Chron. Pasch.* 77, in telling the story of Europa and the bull, state that Agenor and his sons waged war 'in the *limes*'.

23. Malalas, 143; 426:

> King Solomon founded Palmyra 'in the *limes*'.

This may be compared with another passage in Malalas: Justinian gave the *comes* of the Orient in Antioch orders to reconstruct Palmyra, 'a city of Phoenike in the *limes*'.[59] He financed the restoration of churches and public buildings and 'ordered a number of soldiers to be stationed there with the *limitanei* and the duke of Emesa to guard the empire and Jerusalem'. Then follows a rambling discussion of Palmyra in the time of David. A similar statement is found in Theophanes: 'a city of Phoenike Libanensis in the inner *limes*, named Palmyra'.[60] Here it is specifically stated that the duke at Emesa was transferred to Palmyra for the protection of the Holy Places. These authors are vague on geographical and military matters and their statements should not be pressed in detail.

24. Malalas, 206:

> Antiochus Epiphanes, beaten by Ptolemy, fled 'to the *limes*'.

25. Malalas, 230 f.:

> The Magi, having visited Jesus and his mother in Bethlehem, eluded Herod's wrath by choosing 'another road through the *limes* and escaped to Persian lands'.

There is more, but these examples should suffice to prove that, in the early Byzantine period, the term came to mean simply 'the eastern desert', i.e. a geographical concept without administrative or military associations. Even the Roman origins of the term had been forgotten.

II. *The Term* Limitanei

In the late empire part at least of the troops serving on the frontier were called *limitanei*. A reconsideration of the meaning of *limes* will

---

[59] Malalas, p. 425, clearly derived from Josephus, *Ant.* VIII, 6, 1 (154).
[60] Theophanes, *Chron.* ad ann. 6020 (A.D. 520), p. 267.

therefore also be relevant for that of *limitanei*; since the nature and organization of these forces have been a subject of controversy, it may be useful to review the available information.

Mommsen was of the opinion that the Roman troops serving on the frontier were, from the third century onwards, a peasant militia, farmers who cultivated lands allotted to them by the government and performed guard duties in addition.[61] This view was generally accepted,[62] although W. Seston and A.H.M. Jones argued against it,[63] and their arguments were accepted by a number of scholars.[64] Usually, however, they are ignored or disbelieved.[65] Luttwak, for instance, admits that there is much controversy, yet continues: 'One thing, however, is certain: in the course of the fourth century, the full-time troops that had guarded the borders using mobile and offensive tactics gave way to part-time peasant soldiers (*limitanei*) who farmed their own assigned lands and provided a purely local and static defense'. As in the case of *limes*, it will be useful to review, in roughly chronological order, the sources which refer to, or are taken to refer to, *limitanei*.

For the army in the period we have three categories of evidence: (i) the *Notitia Dignitatum*, which gives us information of a formal nature

---

[61] Th. Mommsen, 'Das römische Militärwesen seit Diocletian'. *Gesammelte Schriften* VI, 209–11.

[62] See for instance R. Grosse, *Römische Militärgeschichte von Gallienus bis zum Beginn der byzantinischen Themenverfassung* (1920), 63–70; H. Delbrück, *Geschichte der Kriegskunst im Rahmen der politische Geschichte* (1921), 231; E. Stein, *Geschichte des spätrömischen Reiches* I (1928), 90 believes the process started under Septimius Severus; M. Rostovtzeff, *The Social and Economic History of the Roman Empire*, second ed. by P.M. Fraser (1952), 426 with n. 50; L. Dillemann, *Haute Mésopotamie orientale et pays adjacents* (1962), 104. Van Berchem, *L'Armée*, 19–24, did not accept the pre-Diocletianic reference.

[63] W. Seston, *Historia* 4 (1955), 286–91 = *Scripta Varia* (1980), 483–90; A.H.M. Jones, *The Later Roman Empire* (1964), 649–53; see also S. Mazzarino, *Aspetti sociali del quarto secolo* (1951), 330–40, who argued that there is no evidence for the existence of farmer-soldiers in the fourth century.

[64] G. Clemente, *La 'Notitia Dignitatum'* (1968), 319 with n. 1; E.W. Gray, *Proceedings of the African Classical Associations* 12 (1973), 24; T. Cornell and J. Matthews, *Atlas of the Roman World* (1982), 172.

[65] The entry on *limitanei* in *RE*, Suppl. XI (1968) contains no reference to Jones. D. Oates, *Studies in the Ancient History of Northern Iraq* (1968), 94; MacMullen, *op. cit.* (n. 26), 13 n. 34 and, in general, chapter 1; id., *Constantine* (1969), 43 f.; A. Piganiol, *L'Empire chrétien* (second ed., 1972), 365; A. Chastagnol, *L'Evolution politique, sociale et économique du monde romain, 284–363* (1982); J.S. Johnson in M.W.C. Hassall and R.I. Ireland (eds.), *De Rebus Bellicis* (1979), 68; S. Williams, *Diocletian and the Roman Recovery* (1985), 97, 207, 213; E.N. Luttwak, *The Grand Strategy of the Roman Empire* (1976), 170–3; see also A. Ferrill, *The Fall of the Roman Empire* (1986), 49; Parker, *op. cit.* (above, n. 26), 149–52.

on the command structure and distribution of army units; (ii) literary
sources containing scattered pronouncements on military affairs, and
(iii) the material remains of forts and roads, sometimes datable epi-
graphically. However, the information provided by these sources is
combined in modern scholarship to build hypotheses about strategy
and tactics from Diocletian to the Arab conquest, a legitimate method
only if the deficiencies of each source are fully taken into account.
The *Notitia* is full of information, but is a bureaucratic list, while
anyone who uses such literary sources as Malalas or Zosimus without further understanding of their limitations is likely to be seriously
misled. On the other hand, although the remains of military installations may be of great interest, it is a fallacy to assume that one can
always easily understand why a particular site was chosen for a fort.

There are two main problems, frequently discussed in combination:
first, the nature of the reforms instituted by Diocletian and Constantine
respectively; second, the organization of the fourth-century army
following these reforms. This paper is concerned with these matters
only in so far as they touch on the position of the *limitanei* and on
the measures which led to the creation of such forces.

Some of the scattered references in literary sources are discussed
below. But first, Ammianus, in an incompletely preserved passage
(XXIII, 5, 1–2), says that Diocletian fortified Cercesium when he
organized the 'inner *limites*' near the borders with the barbarians as
a response to the Persian raids into Syria.[66] But the nature of the
reform is not clear, apart from fortifying at least one city. Zosimus
II, 34, 1, says that Diocletian made the empire impenetrable to
barbarians by stationing troops in cities, *castella* and towers in the
frontier zones. He goes on to say that Constantine demolished this
system by withdrawing the troops from the frontier to cities in the
interior which did not need them.

It must be admitted that these are vague and unspecific statements
which tell us no more than that Diocletian was responsible for the
construction and manning of military installations in the frontier
areas. Zosimus clearly exaggerates the merits of Diocletian's work—
the frontier was never impenetrable—and is notoriously hostile toward Constantine. As regards the East his statement is simply untrue.
There had always been garrisons in cities, and there were troops in

---

[66] See above, p. 134.

border towns before Diocletian and after Constantine. Further, there were border troops beyond the settled area after Constantine.

The sources taken to refer to *limitanei* are as follows:

1. *SHA, Severus Alexander*, XVIII, 58, 4:

> sola, quae de hostibus capta sunt limitaneis ducibus et militibus donavit, ita ut eorum essent si heredes eorum militarent.

> Lands taken from the enemy he gave to the *duces* and soldiers in the frontier districts stipulating that they woud remain theirs if their heirs served in the army.

Though Mommsen, followed by others, accepted the statement at face value,[67] this is one of the less reliable *Lives* in the *SHA*, and the reference to *duces* shows that we have here at best a reflection of later practice.[68] It will be clear from what has been said above that *limes* was not a formal administrative term before the end of the third century; in the fourth century and later it was used for a frontier district, and in the course of time, applied informally to the whole frontier region. It must be assumed that the same is true of the adjective *limitaneus*, which need mean no more than 'of, or pertaining to, the *limes*'. In principle, therefore, *limitaneus* can be used in three distinct ways: (*a*) as an adjective used in a non-technical or informal context; (*b*) *limitaneus (miles)*, (wider sense) a soldier stationed in the *limes*, i.e. one who served under the command of a *dux limitis*;[69] (*c*) (special sense) a farmer who serves in a territorial militia. In the present passage, it is clear that while reference is first made to 'the commanders and soldiers stationed in the *limes*' in general, Severus Alexander is indeed represented as being the emperor responsible for the measures which led to the creation of farmer-soldiers, *limitanei* in the special sense.

---

[67] Mommsen, *Militärwesen*, 200; Rostovtzeff, *op. cit.* (n. 62), 377; Stein, *op. cit.* (n. 62), 90. Rejected by A. Alföldi, *Archaeologiai Értesitö* I (1940), 234. Van Berchem, *L'Armée*, 21, 41 considered it prudent not to rely on the statement. A.R. Neumann, *RE*, Suppl. XI, s.v. *limitanei*, 876, admits that the reference to *duces* is anachronistic, but relies on the statement as partial support for his theory that the *limitanei* existed in some form since the second century. Grosse, *op. cit.* (n. 62), 63 assumed that the reference reflects the situation in the fourth century. Seston, *op. cit.* (n. 63), argued that the *limitanei* did not exist as farmer-soldiers in the time of Diocletian.

[68] J.C. Mann, *Legionary Recruitment and Veteran Settlement during the Principate* (1983), 67 suggests that the passage refers in fact to veterans, not to serving troops.

[69] Pointed out by van Berchem, *op. cit.* (n. 48), 34, 101.

At issue here is not the question whether soldiers owned land in fact, but the credibility of the formal institution by the imperial authorities of a frontier militia which expected soldiers to work their own land as farmers. One can admit the probability of the former without accepting alleged evidence for the existence of the latter.[70]

2. Eumenius, *Panegyrici Latini* IX, 18, 4 (A.D. 298):

> Nam quid ego alarum et cohortium castra percenseam toto Rheni et Histri et Eufratae limite restituta.

> Why should I enumerate the forts of *alae* and cohorts restored throughout the *limes* of the Rhine, of Histrus and the Euphrates?

A very vague reference to the restoration of the military infrastructure in various sections of the imperial border following earlier catastrophes. It does not suggest that any drastic reorganization took place (note the term *restituta*), but rather supports J.C. Mann's conclusion that Diocletian's army reforms represented consolidation rather than innovation. Mann observed that, by the time of Diocletian's abdication, the frontier system of the principate could still be recognized— strengthened and intensified but not essentially altered.[71] In fact Eumenius refers to the troops on the frontier as *alae* and *cohortes* and does not tell us anything about *limitanei*.

3. Malalas, ed. Dindorf, 308 (above, p. 136):

> [Diocletian also founded *castra* in the *limites* from Egypt to the Persian border] τάξας ἐν αὐτοῖς στρατιώτας λιμιτανέους, προχειρισάμενος καὶ δοῦκας κατὰ ἐπαρχίαν ἐνδοτέρω τῶν κάστρων καθέζεσθαι μετὰ πολλῆς βοηθείας πρὸς παραφυλακήν. καὶ ἀνήνεγκαν τῷ βασιλεῖ καὶ τῷ Καίσαρι στήλας ἐν τῷ λιμίτῳ τῆς Συρίας.

> He stationed there *limitanei* and appointed *duces* in each province for service in the forts to stand guard with a strong force. For the emperor and Caesar they erected stelae in the *limes* of Syria.

Van Berchem observes, no doubt correctly, that the stelae are the milestones set up in these years.[72] However, he misinterprets ἐνδοτέρω by translating it 'en deça des forts,' or 'en retrait du limes'. In fact

---

[70] For soldiers as farmers see MacMullen, *op. cit.* (n. 26), chapter 1.
[71] J.C. Mann in *CBA Research Report No. 18: The Saxon Shore*, ed. D.E. Johnson (1977), 11.
[72] Van Berchem, *L'Armée*, 17–18.

it means quite simply 'in the forts'.[73] Van Berchem then concludes that under Diocletian the *dux* did not command the border troops. Yet it is highly dubious whether Malalas could be expected to provide such technical information on army organization under Diocletian, even if the text had contained a straightforward statement. Further, there is hardly any evidence otherwise of the existence of *duces* as the regular commanders of border troops before Constantine,[74] and John Lydus suggests in fact that it was his innovation.[75]

Malalas refers to the well-known fact that in these years numerous forts and roads were built and others restored in the remote semi-desert in the East. When he says that they were manned by troops under the command of provincial *duces*, this may be partly true or it may be an anachronism. Most important for the present discussion is that the term *limitanei* is used in the wider sense. Malalas does not suggest that they were part-time soldiers who cultivated the land.

4. *CTh* VII, 20, 4 (17 June, A.D. 325): arrangements for exemption from taxation of various categories of troops:[76]

    (a) *comitatenses, ripenses, protectores*
    (b) *alares et cohortales*

The status of (a) was more favoured than that of (b). Reference is made to an earlier enactment where the *ripenses* had an intermediate status:

    (a) *comitatenses*
    (b) *ripenses*
    (c) *alares et cohortales*

Distinctions are made between (i) death in service, (ii) death after retirement as a *veteranus* honourably discharged, (iii) death after discharge

---

[73] See, for instance Josephus, *Ant.* XV, 11, 3 (401): 'within this wall (ἐνδοτέρω δὲ τούτου [sc. τοῦ τείχους]) and on the very summit (of the Temple Mount) ran another wall of stone'. Cf. LSJ, s.v.; H. Stephanus, *Thesaurus Linguae Graecae* III, 1041 f.

[74] For criticism of van Berchem's interpretation see also Mann, *op. cit.* (n. 71), 12 with n. 8, observing that permanent ducates are attested under Diocletian only in Valeria, Scythica, and Augusta Euphratensis.

[75] John Lydus, *De Mag.* II, 11. Cf. Aurelius Victor, *liber de Caesaribus* 41, 12: 'Quo excruciato, ut fas erat, servili aut latronum more, condenda urbe formandisque religionibus ingentem animum avocavit (sc. Constantinus), simul novando militiae ordine'.

[76] I am grateful to Professor Tony Honoré for clarification. J.C. Mann has discussed the term *ripenses* and the development of the various categories of troops in two articles: *CBA Research Report No. 18* (above, n. 71), 11–15 and in R. Goodburn and P. Bartholomew (eds.), *Aspects of the Notitia Dignitatum* (1976), 2.

before completion of the full term of service. *Comitatenses, ripenses* and *protectores* are to be on level so far as (i) is concerned; *alares* and *cohortales* are on a lower level of exemption. It is not clear what the position was before this enactment. As regards (ii), *ripenses veterani* are assimilated to *comitatenses veterani.* Apparently *alares* and *cohortales veterani* are on the same level of exemption. Regarding (iii), *ripenses* are put on a level with *comitatenses* only if discharged because of wounds.

This is the earliest text to mention *ripenses.*[77] It is frequently asserted, without argument, that the *ripenses* were later called *limitanei.*[78] Not only is there no evidence for this; there is no reason to assume that the *ripenses* were indeed soldiers-farmers. The confusion is caused by the assumption, as a matter of course, that *limes* denotes every kind of fortified frontier, for although *ripa*, as noted above, is attested as a formal term from the second century onward, the terms *ripa* and *limes* are not mutually interchangeable.

The *Notitia Dignitatum, Or.* XXXIX and XL, mentions *legiones riparienses* on the Danube. In the West several provinces are described as *ripariensis* or *ripensis*: Pannonia Secunda (XXXII), Valeria (XXXIII), Noricum (XXXIV, 13), [Gallia] Riparensis (XLII, 13). It is quite possible that the troops in these districts also had the status of *ripenses.*

5. *Riparienses milites* are mentioned in *CTh* VII, 4, 14 (1 December, A.D. 365).

6. *CTh* VII, 22, 8 (15 February, A.D. 372) stipulates that soldiers whose physical condition is inadequate for service with the field army (*comitatenses*) can be eligible for *militia ripensis.*

7. *CTh* VII, 13, 7, 3 (2 June, A.D. 375) discusses exemption from capitation taxes of:

(*a*) . . . qui comitatensibus numeris fuerit sociatus
(*b*) ii qui in ripa per cuneos auxiliaque fuerint constituti.

The phrase cited under (*b*) is probably a circumlocution for *ripenses.* This will be a reference to the *cunei equitum* and auxiliary infantry forces service in the provinces described by the *Notitia* as *ripariensis* or *ripensis*—the legionary troops are not mentioned.

---

[77] For discussion see van Berchem, *L'Armée*, 83–7. *SHA, Aurelian* XXVI, 38, 4: 'hi compressi sunt septem milibus Lemberiorum et ripariensium et castrianorum et Daciscorum interemptis', is merely another of the *SHA*'s anachronisms.
[78] For instance in *RE, ibid.*

8. *CTh* VII, 1, 18 (*CJ* XII, 35, 14) (19 March, A.D. 400):

> non solum de comitatensibus ac palatinis numeris ad alios numeros milites transferri non licere, sed ne ipsid quidem seu de comitatensibus legionibus seu de ripariensibus castricianis ceterisque, etc.

Soldiers may not be transferred from any branch of service to another. It may perhaps be argued that transfer of farmer-soldiers to another type of unit—had they been included in this list—would not merely have been forbidden, it would be impossible. More important, nothing in these texts suggests that we are faced with anything but regular troops.

9. Various fourth-century enactments are concerned with the supplies of subsistence allowances to troops in the *limes* by civilians in the hinterland, and regulate the responsibility for transport of the supplies: *CTh* XI, 1, 11 (A.D. 365); VII, 4, 15 (A.D. 369); XI, 1, 21 (A.D. 385); *CJ* XI, 60, 1 (A.D. 385); XI, 62, 8 (A.D. 386). It should be obvious that troops which received such allowances were not expected to produce their own supplies.

10. *CTh* VII 4, 30 (23 March, A.D. 409) = *CJ* XII, 37, 13:

> Limitanei militis et possessorum utilitate conspecta per primam, secundam ac tertiam Palaestinam huiuscemodi norma processit, ut pretiorum certa taxatione depensa speciorum inte[r]mittatur exactio. Sed ducianum officium Versamini et Moenoni castri nomine salutaria st[a]tuta conatur evertere. . . .

> In view of the interests of soldiers of the frontier districts and of landowners in First, Second and Third Palestine a ruling has been issued that, when taxes have been paid at a fixed rate, exaction of payment shall be suspended. But the office of the *dux* in the name of the forts at Versaminum and Moenonium attempts to nullify this salutary statute. . . .

Essential in this text is the contrast between *pretia* and *species*. If assessments in money are paid, no exactions in kind are permissible. This is repeated later (*speciorum exactio* v. *adaeratio statuta*) and, despite appearances, is in the interest of the landowners, not the soldiers.

The *limitanei milites* referred to are not farmer-soldiers, but 'soldiers serving in a frontier command', as opposed to those in the field army. For the discussion of the meaning of the term *limes* it is of interest to see that there were such soldiers not only in Third Palestine, which included the Negev and the desert of Southern Jordan, but also in

First and Second Palestine nowhere near any kind of frontier. Even if it is admitted that the term *limes* meant no more than 'frontier district', it is hard to see how any part of First or Second Palestine could have been so designated. We must, therefore, assume that the *limitanei milites* referred to are a specific category of soldiers under the command of the *dux* who had as the area of his command the three provinces of Palestine. An administrative meaning should be given to *limitanei milites* in this text; these soldiers were not necessarily ever stationed in an area described as *limes*.[79]

This is also clear from an episode recorded by Cyril of Scythopolis. Upon the request of Sabas, Justinian instructed the *dux Palaestinae* to transfer funds for the construction of a fort, which was to protect the monasteries in the Judaean desert (that is, in Palaestina Prima, far from what is usually called the *limes* in the Negev). After its construction the *dux* was ordered to put a garrison in it.[80] This shows again that the *dux* was responsible for security throughout the Palestinian region.

11. Fragments of imperial edicts from Beer Sheva: A. Alt, *Die griechischen Inschriften der Palästina Tertia westlich der Araba* (1921), nos. 1–4, pp. 4–8; cf. Ch. Clermont-Ganneau, *Recueil d'archéologie orientale* V (1902), 13–147 and further, Alt, *op. cit.*

The amounts to be paid in coin, instead of supplies in kind as *annona*, are specified for the various communities listed. There is nothing in the reference to 'devoted *limitanei*' to suggest that they were farmer-soldiers. The laws cited above under (9) and (10) were measures which attempted to protect civilians against greed on the part of bureaucrats and soldiers.[81] It is possible that the Beer Sheva edict had the same purpose.[82] A comparable text from Cyrene actually

---

[79] Grosse, *op. cit.* (above, n. 62), 66, already pointed out that part of the *limitanei* were not stationed in frontier zones, such as Isauria and Upper Egypt.

[80] Cyril of Scythopolis, *Vita S. Sabae* 73, ed. Schwartz, 178.

[81] Similarly, Justinian's novel 102 regarding Arabia.

[82] Alt, p. 5, would then have missed the point in his translation: '[Es sollen ihre Abgaben entrichten die . . . der] jeweiligen Duces, sowie die treuergebenen unter [-stellten] Grenzsoldaten [und die übrigen Steuerpflichti]gen Jahr für Jahr in folgender Weise'. It is not impossible that the [??] of the Duces and the soldiers were to receive payment instead of paying others. Similar texts from the reign of Anastasius were found in Arabia, see E. Littman *et al.*, *Publications of the Princeton University Archaeological Expedition to Syria, in 1904–1905* III, *Greek and Latin Inscriptions* A2 (Leiden, 1910), p. 33, frs 15–19; *IGLS* XIII, 1, no. 9046; J. Marcillet-Jaubert, *ADAJ* 24 (1980), 122 f.; D. Kennedy, *Archaeological Explorations* (1982), 44–8: a text concerned with the payment of penalties by officials, which makes reference to, among others, 'those in

specifies the functions of these troops (*SEG* IX, 356, paras. 11, 14)—
essentially police—and guard duties; they controlled movement in
and out of the frontier districts. In fourth-century Mesopotamia such
duties were carried out by *stationarii* (Ammianus XVIII, 5, 3). That,
of course, was not novel: in the second century the same duties were
carried out by auxiliary troops.

12. The first enactments regarding land held by the military date to
the fifth century. They are not numerous and it is important to establish what can actually be learnt from the texts.

(*a*) *CTh* VII, 15, 1 (29 April, A.D. 409) discusses:

> terrarum spatia, quae gentilibus propter curam munitionemque limitis
> atque fossati antiquorum humana fuerant provisione concessa.
>
> Lands which had been granted to *gentiles* (natives) for the care and
> protection of the frontier district and the *fossatum* by a benevolent pro-
> vision of past generations.

If such lands are held by others these persons are responsible for the
care of the *fossatum* and the protection of the *limes*. Otherwise the
land must be transferred to natives or to veterans.

The law deals with a specific situation in Africa[83] and has no general
validity. Even in Africa it is not concerned with lands held and worked
by regular border troops (*limitanei* are *not* mentioned). They were held
by natives, many of whom had apparently abandoned their land.
The purpose of the law is to establish that anyone working the land
would be bound by the same conditions as the original natives. It is
clear that we are faced with the organization of some sort of militia,
but it is an organization distinct from that of the *limitanei*, who are
not mentioned in this text.

(*b*) *CTh* VII, 15, 2 (7 March, A.D. 423):

> Quicumque castellorum loca quocumque titulo possident, cedant et
> deserant, quia ab his tantum fas est possideri castellorum territoria,
> quibus adscribta sunt et de quibus iudicavit antiquitas.
>
> 'Anyone who holds the lands of military forts under any title shall
> withdraw and abandon such property', etc. Any private person who is

---

charge in the *limes* of Palaestina and of Euphratensis' (i.e. Commagene). For the
Beer Sheva edict see also P. Mayerson, *ZPE* 64 (1986), 141–8.

[83] See Matthews, *loc. cit.* (above n. 21).

found holding the territory of forts will be liable to capital punishment and confiscation of property.

The application of this law, enacted in the east at Constantinople, is not confined to any particular province. It does not prove that land was assigned to army units, but shows rather that territories of forts were assigned to authorized persons who might, for example, be veterans. The two laws cited above both deal with lands originally assigned to specific groups which had been abandoned and taken over by others. The status of the land is, however, altogether different. Those who took possession of land assigned originally to *gentiles* had to fulfil certain obligations if they wanted to keep the property, but in principle they might keep it. On the other hand, it was absolutely forbidden for private individuals to hold military land. This is the first post-Diocletianic text which refers to land assigned to army units,[84] but it certainly does not allow any conclusions about the transformation of regular troops into a peasant militia, let alone a hereditary militia.

(c) *NTh* XXIV, 1, 4 = *CJ* I, 60, 3 (12 September, A.D. 443):

> agros etiam limitaneos universis cum paludibus omnique lure, quos ex prisca dispositione limitanei milites ab omni munere vacuos ipsi curare pro suo conpendio atque arare consueverant, et si in praesenti coluntur ab his, firmiter ac sine ullo concussionis gravamine detineri.

> All the lands in the border districts with marsh-lands and of every status which, according to previous regulations, the soldiers in the border districts were accustomed to work themselves and to cultivate for their own profit, exempt from any compulsory service. . . .[85]

It is often stated that lands such as these were called 'fundi limitrophi'. As already observed by Jones, that is misleading and incorrect.[86] *CJ* XI, 60 has the following heading: 'de fundis limitrophis et terris et paludibus et pascuis limitaneis vel castellorum'. Three categories of property are clearly distinguished: (a) lands which must provide supplies to the army in the frontier districts; (b) property belonging to forts; (c) property worked by the troops in the *limites*. Then follow the

---

[84] For Military land in the earlier period in the western provinces see F. Vittinghoff, *Ac. Naz. Lincei* 194 (1974), 109–24.

[85] For references to supplies to the *limes* see above, with *CTh* VIII, 4, 6 (358); *CJ* XII, 8 (386).

[86] Jones, *op. cit.* (n. 63), 651.

texts of three separate laws: (1), dated A.D. 385, refers to 'possessiones quae ad limitem frumenta conveherent', that is category (*a*); (2) *CTh* VII, 15, 2, cited above, dated A.D. 423, category (*b*); (3), the current text of A.D. 443, category (*c*). But category (*c*) is not that of 'fundi limitrophi'; accordingly *CJ* XI, 60 contains no evidence on the existence of 'farmer-soldiers' before 443.

This is in fact the first reference to lands worked by soldiers for their own use and profit. It occurs in a lengthy measure aimed at checking corruption and neglect in the frontier zones throughout the East. Specific complaints are noted: the corruption of *duces*, military units not kept at the appropriate strength, insufficient training and exercise, forts and river patrol boats not kept in good repair, extortion of soldiers and native allies by the higher officers and their staff. Then follows the clause which emphasizes that lands granted to soldiers in the frontier area for their own use may not be transferred to others.

It is clear from this passage that in the fifth century soldiers in the frontier zone were allowed to work their own land. It is important, however, also to note what may not be deduced from it. There is nothing, for instance, to indicate that the status of these soldiers as *limitanei* was hereditary. Veterans' sons in all branches of the army had to serve, but not necessarily in the same type of unit as their fathers. It is misleading, moreover, to speak of a 'peasant militia'. Nor does this text by itself justify the statements common in modern works to the effect that the level of training and expertise of the army seriously deteriorated in this period. Complaints about the current state of affairs must always be assessed with some scepticism; after all, there is no lack of similar complaints about the deterioration of army discipline in earlier periods.[87] Nor, even if the description of the *limitanei* as a 'peasant militia' were correct, would it necessarily follow that they were poor soldiers.[88] Belisarius, for instance, used *limitanei* from Phoenicia-Libanensis for offensive operations in Mesopotamia.[89] Some of the best armies were and are militias and that

---

[87] See Jones, *op. cit.*, 663 for the suggestion that the *limitanei* and the *comitatenses* were equally poor soldiers.

[88] For reservations see also Luttwak, *op. cit.* (n. 65), 172 f., and for discussion of the quality of frontier soldiers in the late empire, G.E.M. de Ste. Croix, *The Class Struggle in the Ancient Greek World* (1981), 261 ff.

[89] This is to be inferred from Procopius 11, 16, 17; see also 1, 13, 5, 11, 8, 2; 11, 19, 33. W. Liebeschuetz, *Studien zu den Militärgrenzen Roms* II (1977), 497, assumes

includes the Roman army of the republic. The same scholars who
sadly observe the deterioration of the frontier troops into no more
than a static militia often credit Roman veteran colonies of the republic and early empire with the pacification of huge areas. Surely
both assumptions must be reconsidered.

(d) *CJ* I, 27 (A.D. 534): Justinian's instructions regarding the reorganization of Africa following the reconquest.

In paragraph 8 it is specified that in addition to the *comitatenses*,
limitanei are to be stationed in forts, soldiers 'who can defend the
forts and the towns of the *limes* and cultivate the land so that other
provincials who see them in those parts will settle there. . . .' As observed by Luttwak, Justinian restored the pattern of organization as
it had been in the fifth century, which perhaps indicates that it had
not been totally unsatisfactory. The *limitanei* are expected to take care
of local defence without the support of the field army; they cannot
have been regarded as a totally inadequate fighting force.

Conclusions

To sum up, the following can be said of the use of the term *limes* in
antiquity:

   I. A limited number of literary sources referring to Germanic
campaigns in the first century use the term in describing the construction of military roads.

   II. From the late first century till the third century it is used to
indicate a demarcated land border of the empire. As such it does
not refer to military structures or frontier organization, nor was it
used to indicate a river boundary. In this sense the term is not in
fact often encountered before the fourth century.

   III. From the fourth century onward it is the formal term used to
designate a frontier district under the command of a *dux*. It denoted
an administrative concept, again unconnected with the military structures which may have existed in the area. The *limes* is always men-

---

that this force was separate from the *limitanei*, because these were intended for defence of their immediate locality. However, the troops from Phoenicia Libanensis
used by Belisarius were intended for the defence of their own province, as emphasized by Procopius, who represents Belisarius' step as unusual. Moreover, the conclusion of this paper is that all troops under the command of a *dux limitis* were
limitanei.

tioned as distinct from the frontier of the empire. In no single case is a *limes* described as something made or constructed, although the term is now used very frequently. The change in meaning coincides with the reforms of Diocletian and Constantine. In the course of time it came to be used as a geographical concept (instead of an administrative one), to indicate the eastern desert. The association with institutions specifically Roman was lost.

IV. More important, there is in Latin no term to indicate what modern frontier studies describe as a *limes*, a defended border. It must then be asked whether in many instances the military organization, as represented by the physical remains, should be explained along different lines. In other words, there can be no justification for calling any chain of forts in a frontier area a *limes*.

V. The *limitanei* of the late empire were not peasant farmers. They were simply units under the command of a *dux limitis*. That is not a novel conclusion, yet it needs to be reiterated, since the old theory, already discarded by Jones, is still repeated. *Limitanei* is a term first attested in A.D. 363 (*CTh* XII, 1, 56), in a text which applies to all troops assigned to specific border regions (*limites*) under the command of *duces*. The term *limitaneus* is, in fact, only attested after the appearance of mobile field armies and in order to distinguish frontier forces from them. Before that the term was not needed because the bulk of the army was on the frontiers anyway.

The first source that indicates that *limitanei* worked their own land, assigned to them by the authorities, dates to A.D. 443. There is no evidence that this seriously affected their professional qualities, and it is consequently misleading to speak of a peasant militia as though this necessarily has qualitative implications.

VI. A revised interpretation of the meaning of *limes* has consequences for the function of the *limitanei*. The commander in charge of a specific *limes* must now be considered to have held a purely territorial command, not a functional one. The *limitanei* were simply soldiers serving anywhere in the area assigned to the relevant *dux* and their duties were not necessarily connected with frontier defence. The task of these troops was to take care of road security, mainly in the frontier districts, but they could be stationed elsewhere as well. They controlled movement across the imperial border and were expected to keep their district under control in times of disturbances. The existence of such units is not an indication of the deterioration of the army as a whole, any more than is the existence of a police apparatus in any other state.

Postscript

While this paper is cited very frequently, its conclusions are quite often ignored or misunderstood by those who cite it, even when they do not express explicit disagreement. This postscript may serve as an opportunity to clarify its intention and to add some arguments against those who disagreed with the conclusions.

The first point made in the article, is that the term 'limes' was not frequently used in the first three centuries A.D. When it was used it designated simply the border of the province. It certainly was not a term used for a 'defended border' or 'defended frontier line' (about the occurrence of the term in mid-third century Africa something will be said below). It is my contention that this has consequences, even if one takes into account the limitations of semantics. If there was no term in second-century Latin for what modern archaeologists call a 'limes' it is quite possible that the entire concept is an anachronistic construct. It is uncomfortable for those who spend their working lives studying what they call a 'limes' to remain without a usable term for their object of study, and they tend to ignore the conclusion, even when they cite the paper.

The second point is the significance of the term in its formal and administrative sense in the Late Roman period. The article argues that this is precisely what it became in that period, namely a formal and administrative concept, but the meaning of the term 'limes' still is often misunderstood. It is my contention that the term reflects a re-organization of the chain of command in the provincial armies. Before the fourth century the basis of army-organization was the province. Garrisoned provinces were governed by senatorial legates who served as judges and military commanders. The units under their command were legions and auxilia and the legates acted as direct commanders of the officers in command of the units stationed in their provinces. There was no intervening grade and there is no evidence that the units of the provincial armies were grouped in any way or organized on any other basis than their belonging to a specific province. Indeed, it has been suggested in the past that auxiliary units might have been attached to legions. In other words, equestrian commanders of auxiliary units would somehow have been answerable to the senatorial legates who themselves commanded legions and served under the higher command of the provincial governor.[1] This then would have made the legionary legates territorial commanders, to some extent. However, there is no sound evidence that this ever was the case. It must be admitted that this was no more than a speculation by modern scholars who considered this a likely proposition, but could find no support for it in the sources.

The state of affairs just described remained true only as long as the troops served as a provincial army. On campaign other rules might apply, when the troops were organized as an expeditionary army. The one element of organization that was conspicuously non-existent before the fourth century, is that of a territorial sub-division of the provincial armies. There were no commanders of the troops in specific areas within a province who answered to the governor, but were higher in the chain of command than the unit commanders. As observed in the paper, re-published above, there were a few exceptions to this general pattern, namely the commanders of specific 'river-banks', who, apparently, had a territorial command under the over-all authority of the relevant provincial governors. Apart from these local exceptions, also discussed below, however, it is generally true that the only form of territorial organization in the Roman army of the principate was the division into provinces. All this is relevant for the present discussion, since the consequence is that there was no formal division between inland and frontier zone. In terms of military hierarchy, the frontier zone was not organized as a separate command. The garrisons at the centre were commanded by the governor, just like those near the frontier. The result is that the '*limes*' was not a reality in the military hierarchy and organization.

In the present paper I maintain that this is one of the essential differences between the army of the principate and that of the Later Roman Empire. In the latter period the frontier army, as distinct from the *comitatenses*, was indeed organized on a territorial basis. This was an organizatory framework distinct from that of the civilian provinces, whose governors were no longer the commanders in chief of the troops in their areas. There were now military officers in charge of the troops within a defined geographical area. The commanders had

---

[1] E.g. G.L. Cheesman, *The Auxilia of the Roman Imperial Army* (Oxford, 1914, repr. 1971), 49–52; see article 24, below.

the title of *dux* and the term used for their area of command was *limes*, always used in conjunction with a geographical name. A *limes* could be bigger than a province and it included all of its territory, not merely the frontier zone or area of confrontation with an external enemy. Thus the *limes Palaestinae* encompassed the three civilian provinces of that name and included the entire area of those provinces. The essence, then, of the term *limes* is that it indicates a form of army-organization. It refers to the chain of command but not to the function of the troops. It is not a term that describes physical structures, forts, defence works, roads and related features, but a term indicating army bureaucracy. As such it occurs in official and legal documents, in the *Notitia Dignitatum*, in legal sources and on inscriptions. Consequently the modern scholarly literature is justified in using the term for this period. However, it is still erroneous to use it in the sense of something that was built or that was visible in the field. It is not a term that should be used by archaeologists for the structures they excavate.

The issue is made complicated by another sense in which later Roman literary sources use the term. As an informal, colloquial expression it is used from the fourth century onward, in a vague sense of 'frontier zone', indicating a wide area at the edge of an organized community. As such it is also used for other periods and regions and does not have a specific Roman or military connotation. Obviously, use of the term for a specific form or Roman military organization is unjustified and incorrect.

Let us look briefly at the issue of imperial boundaries that came up in a recent publication. D. Potter has discussed an arch placed in Germanicus' memory at the grove of Mt. Amanus.[2] Lebek, fr. I 22: *alter ianus in montis Amani iugo, quod est in [—sive (seu) qui] alius aptior locus Ti. Caesari Aug. principi nostr[o videretur in regionibus quarum] curam et tutelam Germanico Caesari ex auctori[tate senatus p.R. lege demandasset?].* This monument, says Potter, marked the limit of Rome's power. It is an interesting suggestion. However, there is nothing in the text itself to support this theory. It will therefore appeal only to those who tend to believe that there existed monuments marking the boundaries of Rome's power or that the Romans would have cared to set up such

---

[2] D.S. Potter, 'The *Tabula Siarensis*, Tiberius, the Senate, and the Eastern Boundary of the Roman Empire', *ZPE* 69 (1987), 269–75.

monuments. I claim that the very notion of empire, as conceived by the Romans, precluded the setting up of such monuments.[3]

Next, several inscriptions which I missed, or which were published recently may be discussed profitably for the light they throw on the development of the term 'limes'.

ILS 8855 (from Bithynia):

> ... [ἐπίτροπον] ... [Σεβαστ]οῦ χώρας Σ[ου]μελοκεννησίας καὶ [ὑπ]ερλιμι-
> τανῆς, ἐπί[τροπον τ]οῦ αὐτοῦ Σεβαστοῦ ἐπα[ρ]χίας Γαλατίας καὶ τ[ῶν]
> συνεγγὺς ἐθνῶν. . . .

I missed this inscription in my discussion of the meaning of 'limes'. It shows that at the time there was a procurator responsible for tribal territory (part of the *Agri Decumates*) 'beyond the *limes*', a term which is here clearly used for the provincial boundary. In this inscription this term cannot designate a district, since it says that the procurator was based beyond it. The context is administrative and financial, and possibly, but not necessarily, also military. Since the honorand was responsible, in his capacity as procurator, for an area 'beyond the *limes*' it follows that the concept *limes* itself also refers to an administrative and financial boundary. This is true, whether or not this procurator had troops under his command. Thus the term *limes* can here only be interpreted as a line distinguishing between two forms of administration: provincial and extra-provincial. The inscription therefore lends significant support for the argument that the term '*limes*' did *not* signify a military border in this period.

A different explanation is required for an interesting group of three building inscriptions from North Africa, recently discussed very well by Y. Le Boheq.[4] The first of these, found at Bu Njem and dated A.D. 248, reads as follows:[5]

---

[3] For a claim that there were no such markers, see *Limits of Empire*, 396–8.

[4] Y. Le Boheq, 'La genèse du *limes* dans les provinces de l'Empire romain', *Revue historique de droit français et étranger* 69 (1991), 307–330. On p. 315 the argument of the present article is misunderstood and thoroughly misrepresented.

[5] This is the reading given by Le Boheq, pp. 308 f. (whence *AÉ* 1992.1758), based on R. Rebuffat, 'L'inscription du *limes* de Tripolitaine' *Libya Antiqua* 15–16 (1978–79), 125–38. The inscription was first published with a slightly different reading by R. Rebuffat, 'Le "limes" de Tripolitaine', *Town and Country in Roman Tripolitania: Papers in honour of Olwen Hackett*, ed. by D.J. Buck and D.J. Mattingly, (BAR Int. Series 274), 1985, 127–41 (*AÉ* 1985.849).

[Im]pp(eratoribus) dd(ominis) nn(ostris) Philipp[is] / [Aug]g(ustis duobus), M. Aurel(io) Cominio / Cassiano leg(ato) Augg(ustorum duorum) pr(o) pr(aetore), c(larissimo) v(iro), / et Lucretio Marcello v(iro) e(gregio), proc(uratore) Augg(ustorum) nn(ostrorum duorum), praeposito / limitis Tripolitanae, / C Iulius Do[n]atus, dec(urio) / alae Flavi[a]e Philip / pianae, pr[ae]fectus / a dd(ominis) nn(ostris duobus) Augg(ustis) [——] prae / fuit vex[illationi] / Golensi et [——], / Imp(eratoribus) Philippo III et Phi / lippo II co(n)s(ulibus).

This inscription, then, mentions the emperors of the year 248, a legate of Numidia and, serving under him, a procurator who was *praepositus* of the *limes Tripolitanae*. The inscription was set up by a *decurio* who acted as commander of a vexillation.

Next there is the famous inscription, discussed also in the article above.[6]

IRT 880 (*AÉ* 1950, 128):

Imp(erator) Caes(ar) [M. Iulius Philippus, invictu[s, ——], / et [M. Iul(ius) Philippus, C]aesar n(oster), (ou -obilissimus), regionem limi[tis Ten] / theitani partitam et u [——]iam incursib(us) barba[ro] / rum, consituto novo centenario [——] / [——] as praecluserunt, Cominio Cassiano, leg(ato) Aug(usti) / pr(o) pr(aetore), Gallican[o . . .], v(iro) e(gregio), / praep(osito) limitis, cura / Maximi DOMO [——]SIA, trib(uno).

In the year 246–7 the legate of Numidia had an equestrian official under his command who was *praepositus* of the *limes Tentheitanus*. A tribune served under the latter.

Thirdly, there is a building inscription set up in 263 at Ras el Ain:

CIL VIII 22765; *ILS* 8923; *IL Tun.* 3:

Imp(erator) Caes(ar) [[P. Licinius Gallienus]], pius, felix, invictus, / Aug(ustus), Germanicus, Persicus maximus, pontifex / maximus, trib(unicia) p(otestate) XII, co(n)s(ul) V, p(ater) p(atriae), proco(n)s(ul), castra coh(ortis) / VIII Fidae opportuno loco instituit, / operantibus fortissimis militibus suis ex limi / te Tripolitano.

According to the text 'soldiers from the *limes Tripolitanus*' built an army camp.

---

[6] Cf. G. Di Vita-Evrard, 'Regio Tripolitana: a Reappraisal', in D.J. Buck & D.J. Mattingly, *Town and Country in Roman Tripolitania: Papers in Honour of Olwen Hackett*, BAR 274, Oxford 1985), 143–63; the same author has made suggestions for alternative readings in *Actes du ive colloque sur l'histoire et l'archéologie de l'Afrique du Nord*, Strasbourg, 1988 (Paris, 1991), 427–44 (*AÉ* 1991.1621a). See also Rebuffat, *op. cit.*, 129; Le Bohec, *op. cit.*, 318 f.

It is clear that these three inscriptions use the term *limes* in a formal sense. It is used for a district where an equestrian officer is in command and where soldiers are based.[7] An essential difference between the status of this commander and the later *duces* is that the equestrian officer was subject to the higher authority of the provincial legate. His status is best compared with that of the *dux ripae* attested at Dura-Europos before the middle of the third century (mentioned in my own article above) and with the *praefecti ripae* of various rivers, also mentioned above. These *praefecti* too were regional commanders, but of lower rank than the procurators in Tripolitania. In the present connection it may be mentioned again (cf. note 32 of the article above) that the term *ripa* can also be used for a fiscal district. The combination of military command and financial responsibility may also be presumed for the procurators who were *praepositi limitis Tripolitanae*, as observed by Le Bohec.[8] That they were in charge of certain building operations should not surprise, nor the fact that they had combined military and financial responsibility. After all, there had been governor-procurators with troops since the early first century.

One or two inscriptions from Arbal in Mauretania show that there too an imperial procurator acted as *praepositus limitis*.[9] From an inscription of A.D. 301 it is clear that this official was still in place in the Tetrarchic period.[10]

---

[7] This is a different interpretation of *AÉ* 1950.128 and *CIL* VIII 22765 from the one given in the article reprinted above.

[8] P. 322: 'Dans cette hypothèse, le *limes* de secteur, incontestablement district frontalier, mais aussi zone à défendre, aurait und double origine: financière et militaire. . . .' This is entirely convincing, but why the presence of soldiers proves it to be a 'zone à défendre' is not obvious. The presence of soldiers somewhere does not prove they were defending something. Similarly, P. Trousset, 'La frontière romaine: concepts et représentations', in P. Brun, S. van der Leeuw and C.R. Whittaker (eds.), *Frontières d'Empire: Nature et signification des frontières romaines* (Nemours 1993), 115–120, at 116, claims that these inscriptions show the *limes* to have been 'la ligne d'arrêt ou plutôt la zone de contrôle où étaient campées les légions ou les unités d'auxiliaires qui protégaient les provinces.' If anything these inscriptions show that they refer to a district, not a line, and they say nothing about protecting the provinces.

[9] *CIL* VIII 9790; *ILS* 3251: *Dianae Victrici / C Jul Maximvs / Proc Aug / Praepositus Limitis. CIL* VIII 9791 is possibly a bad copy of the same inscription, cf. Rebuffat, p. 135; Le Bohec, 324 f.

[10] *CIL* VIII 9025: *[Victori]ae Aug(ustae) san / ct(a)e deae, L. / Iulius [.] / f(ilius) Capito, / AIARIS / praeposi / tus limi / tis cum / suis o / mnibus / f(ecit) {a}(nno) / p(rovinciae) CCLXII.*

How does the evidence from North Africa fit in with the conclusions of the article reprinted above? By the middle of the third century, apparently, there were a few isolated areas of provincial land organized in a manner not attested before. While these remained part of the responsibility of the provincial governor, local commanders in charge of a military force were appointed with the rank of procurator. Such districts were called a *limes*. The term itself, the title of the procurator (*praepositus*) or the presence of troops says nothing about the function of the troops. They may have been engaged in local police duties, police action beyond the provincial boundary or any of the other regular activities of armed forces. There is good evidence of centurions entrusted with regional responsibility for the administration, justice and police-duties.[11] It certainly cannot be claimed that these texts show the term *limes* to have indicated a fortified frontier. What is clear, is that *limes* now is a military and administrative term designating the status of a particular area of provincial land, an early form of regional command. This is a different use from that encountered in earlier texts of the first and second centuries, where the term occasionally designates the provincial boundary, a meaning still encountered in the inscription of 213 which states that 'the Emperor is about to cross the border of Raetia into barbarian [lands] in order to destroy the enemy.'[12] It is also quite different from the current and wide-spread meaning in the fourth century and afterwards, when it designates a military district or regional command only, unconnected with the framework of civilian provinces. While the *praepositi limitis* of the third century were subject to the provincial governors, the later *duces* were not. Thus the inscriptions from third-century North Africa represent early and rare instances of a form of organization that was, to may be recognized afterwards in altered shape in many parts of the empire, from the fourth century onwards. Finally, it may be observed that there is nothing in these texts that refers to a defended boundary or to defence works.

---

[11] For the *centurio regionarius: Limits of Empire* (second edition), 442; R. Alston, *Soldier and Society in Roman Egypt: A Social History* (London and New York, 1995), 86–96; also: B. Campbell, *The Roman Army, 31 B.C.–A.D. 337: A Source Book* (London A.D.–A.D. 1994), nos. 286–8, pp. 172 f.

[12] *ILS* 451, *Acta Arv.*, mentioned above. Le Bohec, 323 f., seems to understand the inscription as referring to a district.

Several papers discuss the meaning of the term '*limes*' during the
Later Roman Empire:

P. Mayerson, 'A Note on the Roman *Limes*: "Inner" versus "Outer,"'
  IEJ 38 (1988), 181–3 = *Monks, Martyrs, Soldiers and Saracens* (1994),
  301–3.
id., 'The Meaning of the word *Limes* (λίμιτον) in the Papyri', *ZPE* 77
  (1989), 287–91 = *Monks, Martyrs* . . ., 308–12. Mayerson observes
  that in all attested instances, with the exception of four, discussed
  in detail, the word appears as part of the title of the *comes* together
  with the name of the province. He concludes that *limes* is not a
  formal term. As argued in the article on the meaning of 'limes',
  above, I agree that this is the case in late Roman and early Byzantine authors such as Malalas, etc., where the term is used in a
  vague and general sense of 'frontier zone'. However, this cannot
  be maintained for Late Roman works of a formal nature, such as
  the Notitia, for legal texts and inscriptions, where, in my opinion,
  it is a term for a regional command. The same would be true
  when the term is used used in papyri, coupled with *comes* and *dux*.
M. Casevitz, 'Sur *eschatia*. Histoire du mot', in Aline Rousselle (ed.),
  Frontières terrestres, frontières célestes dans l'antiquité (Paris, 1995) 19–30.

24

HIERARCHY AND COMMAND-STRUCTURE IN THE ROMAN ARMY[1]

The military hierarchy and the military command-structure represent two different aspects of army organization. While the former expresses a set of social relations in the barracks, the latter determines the way an army functions as an organized fighting force. For the individual, the positions he occupied in the hierarchy during the course of his career reflect his social status as a Roman soldier and afterwards in civilian life. Thus these are listed on many public and private inscriptions and have provided the material for extensive research by modern scholars, ever since von Domaszewski published his major study, *Die Rangordnung des römischen Heeres*. The combined study of literary sources and inscriptions has done much to clarify the relationships between ranks in all parts of the Roman army, although there are problems which remain to be solved and others which may never be solved on the available evidence.

Elucidation of the hierarchy, however, does not necessarily help in understanding the command-structure, or chain of command, although obviously there must always be some connection between rank and function in a large organization. While our sources abound in references to specific ranks in the army, they provide far less information about what the people holding these ranks were actually doing, in war or in peace-time. Systematic study has therefore focused more on the hierarchy than on functions or command-structure. It is the aim of this paper to show that there are various unresolved problems with regard to the chain of command in the Roman Imperial Army, from the first till the fourth centuries, which need to be addressed if we want to understand the basic principles of its organization.

Every army, ancient or modern, needs a chain of command to convey the orders of its general to the individual soldiers. The command structure depends on the system which groups soldiers into the units

---

[1] School of History, Tel Aviv University, Ramat Aviv 69978, Israel.

which, when combined, make up the fighting force. We should like to deal here with the specific question of which officer filled the gap between the legionary legate, who commanded almost 6000 men, and the legionary centurion, who commanded 80. The principle of a chain of command is clearly defined in some of our sources and can occasionally be seen as functioning in practice. Onasander, in the middle of the first century A.D., observes that the general should transmit his orders through officers.[2] Julius Caesar frequently describes himself as giving orders through his *legati* and *tribuni*, or addressing his centurions.[3] Very few sources, however, give specific information about the command-structure in peace-time, or the order of battle when the army acted as a fighting force. This distinction has to be made, for on the battle-field the army operates on a massive scale, while in peace-time its constituent units maintain themselves independently and often operate on a small scale.

First, however, brief mention should be made of the organization of the republican legion. It seems that, originally, the legion was an administrative unit, not a tactical one.[4] As described by Polybius (vi 24) the legion was divided into thirty maniples,[5] each commanded by two centurions,[6] assisted by two optiones (δύ' οὐραγούς) and two standard-bearers (σημαιοφόρους). There is no suggestion in Polybius that the maniple was subdivided into tactical units of centuries, commanded by their own officers: the two centurions are said to command 'a half maniple'.[7] The term '*centuria*' or its equivalent does not exist. There is no reference to any other unit above the level of the maniple and the cohort is nowhere mentioned. Each legion had six tribunes, but these had no specific function in the chain of command, but were experienced officers in this period (vi 19–20; 27, 4). Polybius' description of the Roman army camp suggests that there

---

[2] Onasander, *strategicus*, 25.

[3] Caesar, *BG* iv 23; vii 52; also: v 37; vi 7.

[4] Livy 8, 8–10; 14.

[5] Polybius gives four synonyms for the term maniple (vi 24, 5): καὶ τὸ μὲν μέρος ἕκαστον ἐκάλεσαν καὶ τάγμα καὶ σπεῖραν καὶ σημαίαν. . . . It follows that the term σπεῖρα is used here for a maniple rather than a cohort, as in the Early Empire, or as in Polybius xi 23 (below, n. 20).

[6] The officers of the maniple are called 'centurions' or 'taxiarchoi': τοὺς δ' ἡγεμόνας (ἐκάλεσαν) κεντυρίωνας καὶ ταξιάρχους.

[7] The maniple has two officers, says Polybius, because it should never be without a commander. If there are two centurions each commands one half of the maniple, but if there is one, he commands the entire maniple.

was no legionary commander between the supreme commander and the tribunes.[8] Apart from this important factor, the essential features of the later chain of command, to be described below, are thus already visible. The Greek phalanx of the Hellenistic period was organized along entirely different lines, if we may trust Asclepiodotus, *Tactics* ii, 8 (who was followed by Aelian and Arrian).[9] It was subdivided into a strict hierarchy of equal units, each commanded by its own officer, down to the level of a *lochos* of 16 men.[10]

We shall now turn to the Order of Battle in the period of the Principate.

The Order of Battle

Our information about the Order of Battle is very sketchy, and refers almost exclusively to the highest level of officers. Vegetius describes various formations and explains 'where the supreme commander should stand, where the second-in-command, where the third....' The first should stand 'between cavalry and infantry on the right flank', the second in the middle, the third on the left flank.[11] The first should have with him reserve cavalry mixed with light-armed infantry, etc. There is no further specification of the tactical units which might make up the fighting force or of their commanders. Information at a similar level is given in Arrian's *acies contra Alanos*. In battle the legate of the fifteenth legion would command the entire right flank with the cavalry. The left flank would be commanded by

---

[8] Polybius vi 27, 4: ἐξ ὑπαρχόντων χιλιάρχων ἐν ἑκάστῳ στρατοπέδῳ κατὰ τὸν ἄρτι λόγον, δυεῖν δὲ στρατοπέδων ὄντων τῶν Ῥωμαϊκῶν ἀεὶ μεθ᾽ ἑκατέρου τῶν ὑπάτων, Φανερὸν ὅτι δώδεκα χιλιάρχους ἀνάγκη συστρατεύειν ἑκατέρῳ τῶν ὑπάτων.

[9] For Aelian see: H. Köchly & W. Rüstow, *Asclepiodotos' Taktik; Aelianos' Theorie der Taktik der Griechische Kriegsschriftsteller*, vol. 2.1 (Leipzig, 1855, repr. Osnabrück); for Asclepiodotus, the more recent Loeb ed.

[10] Only the *phalanx* and the *hekatontarchia* (century), however, are said to have supernumeraries, which for the latter unit, included a herald, signal-man, and a bugler (Asclepiodotus, vi 3).

[11] Vegetius, iii 18: *In quo loco primus dux stare debeat, in quo secundus, in quo tertius. Dux, qui praecipuam sustinet potestatem, inter equites et pedites in parte dextra stare consuevit.... Hic de equitibus supernumerariis mixtis peditibus expeditis adversariorum sinistrum cornu, qui contra ipsum stat.... Secundus dux in media acie ponitur peditum, qui eam sustentet et firmet.... In sinistra parte exercitus tertius esse dux debet, satis bellicosus et providus, quia sinistra pars difficilior est.*

the tribunes of the twelfth.[12] Julius Caesar likewise provides general information: legates command legions (*BG* i 52). His commanders are legates and a *quaestor* (iv 13). As already mentioned, orders are transmitted through *legati* and *tribuni* (iv 23; vii 52). Arrian also records in some detail the marching order of his troops (*acies* 5), but for our purposes it will suffice to note that separate mention is made of the legate, *praefectus castrorum*, tribunes and the five centurions of the first cohort.

Since all this does not get us very far, the next step must be to see what is recorded about the command-structure in peace-time. Vegetius (ii 7) gives the ranks and titles of various officers, but he gives no information about the chain of command. He then (ii 8) lists the centurions commanding the first legionary cohort. Whatever the value of this information, he is not aware of the concept that there should be a commander of the entire cohort, either the senior centurion, or anyone else.[13] We shall return to this point below. Later (ii 10) Vegetius refers to a different kind of cohort, commanded by experienced tribunes or *praepositi*, which apparently reflects fourth-century organization,[14] since *tribuni* were not experienced career officers and did not command legionary cohorts during the principate. Vegetius again refers to his own time when he mentions *draconarii*,[15] but appears to be aware of the situation in the high empire 'when cohorts were divided into centuries, each with their own standards,[16] stressing the importance of the centurions who were responsible for training and individual equipment (iii 14).[17]

---

[12] Arrian, *acies contra Alanos* 24: ἡγείσθω δὲ τοῦ μὲν δεξιοῦ κέρως παντὸς σὺν τῷ ἱππικῷ Οὐάλης, ὅσπερ καὶ τῆς πεντεκαιδεκάτης Φάλαγγος ἡγεμών ἐστιν· τοῦ δὲ ἀριστεροῦ οἱ χιλίαρχαι τῆς δωδεκάτης; cf. E. Ritterling, 'Zur Erklärung von Arrians Ektaxis', *Wiener Studien* 34 (1902), 359–72.

[13] The primus pilus commanded four centuries (of the first cohort) '*quin non solum aquilae praeerat, verum etiam quattuor centurias, hoc est quadringentos milites, in prima acie gubernabat.*' The *primus hastatus* commanded two centuries, the *princeps* a century and a half, the *secundus hastatus* a century and a half, the *triarius prior* a century. The concept of the *primus pilus* as commander of the first cohort is obviously lacking here, whether or not it was the case.

[14] In the fourth century 'tribune' was the commonest title and was often used loosely for all commanding officers: A.H.M. Jones, *The Later Roman Empire: A Social, Economic and Administrative and Survey* (Oxford, 1964, repr. 1973), 640.

[15] Vegetius ii 13, cf. Jones, 1264.

[16] *Qui nunc centenarii vocantur*, cf. Jones, 258. For the standards, see below.

[17] Vegetius' detailed description of the rotating advancement of centurions within the legion has been much discussed. However this need not concern us here, since it is an arrangement which concerns hierarchy and status rather than the chain of

Both Onasander (3) and Vegetius (iii 9) consider it essential that the general should have a council of advisors.[18] However, these are persons chosen by himself. It is not a statutory body and it is not integrated into the command structure. The composition of Caesar's council varied: it could include legates, tribunes, sometimes *primi ordines* (centurions of the first cohort) or even all centurions (*BG* i 40; v 28).[19]

The Command of the Legionary Cohort

The legionary cohort appears relatively late as a unit. It is referred to first in the Second Punic war.[20] The context, however, suggests that it is mentioned only when it served as an ad-hoc formation removed from the legion to which it belonged.[21] This is still the case in the late second century B.C., at the time of the *Bellum Iugurtinum*[22] and even in the wars of Julius Caesar legionary cohorts are only mentioned as units, when they were temporarily removed from their legion for special duties.[23]

From the mid-first century onward the special position of the centurions of the first cohort is clear from the ancient literature and inscriptions.[24] The senior centurion of the first cohort, the *primus pilus*, had special responsibilities and a higher status than all the other cen-

---

command. Vegetius ii 21; cf. A. von Domaszewski, *Die Rangordnung des römischen Heeres* (2nd ed. by B. Dobson), (Köln, 1967), xxiii–xxv; 90–7.

[18] Vegetius iii 9: '*Praecipua ars et utilitas ducis est, ut adhibitis ex universo exercitu scientibus belli et sapientibus vis. . . .*'

[19] Before deciding whether to destroy the temple in Jerusalem Titus held a council of war with all the senior commanders down to the level of tribunes: Josephus, *BJ* vi, 4, 3 (237 f.).

[20] Polybius xi 23: (. . .) καὶ τρεῖς σπείρας-τοῦτο δὲ καλεῖται τὸ σύνταγμα τῶν πεζῶν παρὰ Ῥωμαίοις κοόρτις-(. . .); 33.1.3: (. . .) πρὸς δὲ τοὺς εἰς τὸν αὐλῶνα καταβεβηκότας ἄθρους ἄγων ἐκ τῆς παρεμβολῆς ἐπὶ τέτταρας κοόρτις προσέβαλε τοῖς πεζοῖς τῶν ὑπεναντίων.

[21] I owe this observation to Mr. Ido Hecht, to whom I am grateful for useful conversations on the subject of this paper.

[22] Sallustius, *Iug.* 51 3.

[23] For instance: Aulus Hirtius, *BG* vii, 2, 2: (. . .) *binis cohortibus ad impedimenta tuenda relictis reliquum exercitum in copiosissimos agros Biturigum inducit.* Caes. *BC* ii, 39, 1: *Curio cum omnibus copiis quarta vigilia exierat cohortibus v castris praesidio relictis.* Also: *BC* ii, 18, 2; iii, 89, 2; *B.Afr.* 6 5; 9 1; 10 1; 11 3, etc.

[24] Domaszewski/Dobson, *op. cit.*, xxiv. See for instance Caesar, *BG* i 41; v 44: *centuriones qui primis ordinibus appropinquarent;* vi 40: centurions from the *inferiores ordines* promoted and transferred to the *superiores ordines* of another legion; *BC* iii 53: a centurion in the eighth cohort who was made *primus pilus;* Arrian, *acies* 5; *ILS* 2452: '*Primi ordines et centuriones et evocatus. . . .*'

turions, as is immediately apparent from the size of his lodgings in permanent legionary bases. It is nowhere suggested, however, that the *primus pilus* commanded the first cohort of the legion, as we have already observed. This brings us to the central question in this paper: who, if anyone, commanded legionary cohorts? It has been argued that 'the cohort had no particular officers or staff, as it was a tactical rather than an administrative unit'.[25] This raises two questions: (1) What kind of a unit was a legionary cohort? (2) If it was a tactical unit, what was the necessary officer corps for such a unit? Since the legionary cohort clearly did not have a staff of its own, we have to consider how a tactical unit operates in battle. Obviously, before it can function it has to be trained. The elements of training and experience were of supreme importance in ancient armies, because the lack of sophisticated means of communications meant that the ancient commander had far less control than his modern counterpart over the troops during the actual fighting.[26] Both training and operations require planning and co-ordination. A group of soldiers cannot function as a unit in battle without co-ordination of communications and extensive practice. If it has to operate independently in any way, in battle or in times of peace, it will also need co-ordinated logistics, intelligence and the administration of manpower. If a unit is part of a larger unit it may rely heavily on the administrative cadre of the larger unit, but the reverse, the sub-unit handling all administration for the larger unit, probably would not work.

We have extensive information about the legionary command and about the existence of *centuriae* of 80 men under the command of centurions. But what happened at the level of a legionary cohort? In terms of a modern army that would mean that there would be, say, company commanders and their staff, but not officers corresponding to commanders of battalions. While the former are usually captains, the latter are generally lieutenant-colonels, a difference of two ranks. This is in keeping with the essence of the chain of command, which means that officers of superior rank, in command of larger units, have the authority to issue orders to officers of lower rank who command the sub-units which together make up the larger unit. The very purpose of a ranking system is to give one man greater authority than several

---

[25] G. Webster, *The Roman Imperial Army* (London, 1969), 120–1.
[26] See, for instance, the events described by Caesar in *BG* ii 20 with his comments there.

others together. If one legionary cohort, consisting of six centuries, acted as a tactical unit, one man must have had greater authority than the six centurions commanding the centuries. This is true in all bureaucratic organizations, but nowhere more so than in an army, where the decisions taken affect victory or defeat, life or death. In other words, the cohort should have had a commander of higher rank than a centurion. Yet such an officer is not mentioned in any literary or epigraphic source.

Some scholars have suggested that the senior centurion of each cohort acted as commander of the cohort.[27] This suggestion was made without reference to any evidence and without much thought as to what it implies. Roman society in general, and the army in particular, was definitely more class- and rank-conscious than modern counterparts. The wife of a military tribune who had committed adultery with a mere centurion was deemed to have disgraced her rank and that of her husband.[28] The implication is that it would have been less of a disgrace if she had had a relationship with a man of her own social class. The sharp differentiation between the social status of the various ranks is clear from the diffences in size of the living-quarters in permanent camps. In this connection it should be observed that there were two kinds of centurions' lodgings: larger ones for the centurions of the first cohort and small ones for all others. The first centurions of cohorts ii–x had lodgings of the same size as the other centurions of those cohorts. There is nothing here to confirm the suggestion that they had greater authority.[29] As already mentioned, the special status of the centurions of the first cohort is also clear from literary sources and inscriptions.[30] Yet all centurions, including

---

[27] H.M.D. Parker, *The Roman Legion* (Oxford, 1923; repr. 1980), 202: 'The chief duty of the centurions was, of course, the command of their own century, and, if promoted to be *pilus prior*, the command of the cohort in which they held that post'; J. Kromayer & G. Veith, *Heerwesen und Kriegsführung der Griechen und Römer* (Munich, 1928), 400: 'der rangälteste, d.h. der *prior* des Triariermanipels, führte naturgemäss im Gefecht das taktische Kommando'. M. Grant, *The Army of the Caesars* (London, 1974), 73, seems to accept this suggestion.

[28] Pliny, *ep.* vi 31.

[29] H. von Petrikovits, *Die Innenbauten römischer Legionslager während der Prinzipatszeit* (Opladen 1975), 62–4. The smallest centurions' houses measure about 240 m². Frequently they measure between 290–390 m². The houses of the centurions of the first cohort are twice the size of those of the other centurions. At Inchtuthil the house of the *primus pilus* was bigger than that of the other centurions of the first cohort (*ibid.*, fig. 11, 1).

[30] It is, however, a matter of dispute whether the *pili priores* of cohorts ii–x were

those of the first cohort, were *caligati* and thus of a lower class than all equestrian and senatorial officers.[31] The existence of a complicated hierarchy within the group of legionary centurions is of less significance than the gap between all of them and the equestrian officers of the Roman army.[32] The suggestion advanced by Parker, according to which the senior centurion of each cohort acted as commander of the cohort, implies, in fact, that the Roman army worked with a system of *primi inter pares* for its officers. There is no evidence that this is a workable principle for any army and it would have been totally uncharacteristic of the Roman army. There is indeed no indication in the available evidence that any centurion had the authority to act as commander of a legionary cohort, even though they were military professionals, while the equestrian and senatorial officers were amateurs.[33]

There is no indication that legionary centurions ever commanded more than the 80 or so men who normally made up a century. This may be further illustrated by the evidence regarding the command of detachments. Commanders of legionary combat vexillations were senatorial officers till the reign of Marcus Aurelius, i.e. *tribuni laticlavii* or higher officers.[34] From the reign of Marcus Aurelius onwards, we find equestrian officers with this function, and from Septimius Severus' reign, *primipilares* are mentioned as commanders of legionary combat vexillations.[35] Auxiliary combat vexillations were always commanded

included among the *primi ordines*. On balance it seems they were not. References ap. J.F. Gilliam, 'The *ordinarii* and *ordinati* of the Roman Army', *TAPA* 71 (1940), 127–48, esp. 128, n. 2 '*Roman Army Papers*', 1–22, esp. p. 2, n. 2.

[31] Gilliam, '*Milites caligati*', *Roman Army Papers*, 43–51: auxiliary centurions were *milites caligati* at least till the time of Severus Alexander. Legionary centurions were almost certainly *caligati* at least till the mid-third century. This excludes centurions of equestrian status (*ex equite Romano*) who received an appointment as centurion direct instead of climbing through the ranks like other centurions. Cf. Domaszewski/Dobson, *Die Rangordnung*, xxi.

[32] For the hierarchy of centurions: Domaszewski/Dobson, xxiii–xxv; 90–7.

[33] B. Dobson, 'The *Rangordnung* of the Roman Army' in D.J. Breeze & B. Dobson, *Roman Officers and Frontiers* (Stuttgart, 1993), 129–204, esp. 136. Caesar, *BG* i 39, records that he had brought with him a number of senior officers without military experience, out of friendship: on one occasion they spread unnecessary panic *(hic primum ortus est a tribunis militum, praefectis reliquisque, qui ex urbe amicitiae causa Caesarem sicuti non magnum in re militari usum habebant.)* Occasionally there was a reliable officer among them, e.g. *BG* iii 5.

[34] R. Saxer, *Untersuchungen zu den Vexillationen des römischen Kaiserheeres von Augustus bis Diokletian, Epigraphische Studien* 1 (Köln & Graz, 1967), 120 f. Only senatorial governors could command vexillations sent to other provinces.

[35] Saxer, *loc. cit.* For an early exception see: B. Dobson, *Die Primipilares. Entwicklung*

by equestrian officers. The commanders of labour vexillations were usually centurions if they numbered about 80 men. When several legionary detachments were combined or an auxiliary unit added, the centurions served under the command of a higher officer.[36] Legionary centurions, then, did not normally command more than approximately a century independently. Since detached units of the size of a cohort were never commanded by centurions, there is no support here for the assumption that legionary centurions could command cohorts.

A further point which should be raised is the matter of communications, which are essential if groups of soldiers are to operate effectively in war. On the battle-field communication was effected by use of trumpets and standards. There were auditory signals given by the trumpet (*tuba* or *cornu*) to draw attention to the visual ones, the standards (Caesar, *BC* iii 46; 90). Within the legion there was a hierarchy of two types of standards: the legionary eagle and the centurial *signa*.[37] The latter showed the soldiers of each century where they had to go. Thus expressions indicating movement of *signa* are used in Roman literature to describe movements of troops. The *signa* were the focus of movement in battle. In an emergency soldiers would follow whichever standard they saw, rather than searching for their own unit, or they would panic, because they did not know where their own standards were.[38] When troops were hard pressed and lost courage 'the standards were crowded together' so that the soldiers hampered each other.[39] The standards of the Roman army have been studied by Domaszewski, who reached the conclusion that the legion-

---

und Bedeutung, Laufbahnen und Persönlichkeiten eines römischen Offiziersranges (Köln, 1978), no. 94.

[36] Saxer, 129–31: legionary or auxiliary tribunes, procurators. An excellent example of such a combined vexillation is *ILS* 2483; Saxer, no. 294, with extensive comments on pp. 97–9. Three exceptions are nos. 207, 214 and 266, where centurions command composite detachments.

[37] *Bellum Hispaniense* 7, 4: '*aquilas et signa habuit xiii legionum.*' Ibid., 18, 3 a *signifer* uses 'signum' as the equivalent for 'century': '*eodem tempore signifer de legione prima transfugit, et innotuit ... suo signo perisse homines xxxv. ...*'

[38] *BG* ii 21. Cf. vi 37: panic in an army camp: the soldiers did not know where the *signa* where, or where they had to assemble.

[39] *BG* ii 25; *BC* i 71. The former passage has been criticized by John Keegan, *The Face of Battle: A Study of Agincourt, Waterloo and the Somme* (Penguin, 1978), 64 f., but this is not quite fair. While it is true that Caesar is usually the dominant figure in his own work, the battles which he describes are quite often real ones. It may be added that the heroic feat which he describes as saving the battle in *BG* ii 25 is repeated to no effect in *BC* iii 69.

ary centuries had *signa*, but that cohorts did not.[40] This was supported by Mommsen, who agreed that legionary cohorts had no standards and also stressed that auxiliary units of similar size did have *signa*: *alae* of cavalry certainly had them and auxiliary cohorts almost certainly.[41] This is logical, for auxiliary cohorts and *alae* certainly functioned as separate units in war and in peace-time.[42] This then leaves the legionary cohort without the means to act as a tactical unit. To solve this problem it has been suggested that the *signum* of the leading centurion also served as a standard for the entire cohort.[43] This is a hypothesis similar to the one concerning the command structure: since legionary cohorts had no commanders, it was assumed that the senior centurion must have acted in this capacity. Similarly, since legionary cohorts had no standards, it was suggested that the *signifer* of the first century in the cohort must have filled the gap. These assumptions are both unlikely for the same reasons. The commander of a group of centuries must be a man of higher rank than the individual centurions and the standard of a single century cannot at the same time be used as the standard for an entire cohort without causing dangerous confusion on the battle field.[44] There is no reason to assume that there was a hierarchy of two kinds of *signa*. The *vexillum* (banner) served as standard for *ad hoc* formations (*BG* vi 36; 40).[45] Even if these arguments are not accepted, it remains true that there is no support in the literature for the hypotheses explaining the absence of commanders of cohorts and their *signa*.

---

[40] A. von Domaszewski, Die Fahnen im römischen Heere. Abhandlungen des archäologisch-epigraphischen Seminares der Universität Wien (Vienna, 1885), repr. in: Aufsätze zur römischen Heeresgeschichte (Darmstadt, 1972), 1–79, esp. 21–24; Webster, [1985] *op. cit.* note 19, 133–9, musical instruments: 140.

[41] Th. Mommsen, 'Zu Domaszewski's Abhandlung über die römischen Fahnen', *Gesammelte Schriften* 6 (Berlin, 1920), 134–44; esp. 135 f.; dissent: Kubitschek, *RE* ii A (1923), s.v. 'signifer', cols. 2348–58, esp. 2352.

[42] This conclusion was further reinforced by Speidel in his discussion of an apparent exception, a *signifer leg iii Ital. coh. i et ii.* The exception is indeed apparent only because the unit was part of an expeditionary force: M. Speidel, 'Legionary Cohorts in the Structure of Expeditionary Armies', *Roman Army Studies* i (Amsterdam, 1984), 65–75.

[43] G. Veith in Kromayer & Veith, *op. cit.* note 20, 404: 'Dabei ist nach Analogie der Kommando Verhältnisse ganz gut denkbar, dass das *signum* des vom ranghöchsten Zenturio kommandierten Triarier-manipels zugleich das *signum* der Kohorte schlechtweg und dann wohl als solches sichtbar gekennzeichnet war.'

[44] G. Webster, *op. cit.* note 19, 134–40.

[45] *Vexilla* could be used as signal flags for all purposes: *BG* ii 20; *B. Alex* 45 . . . *vexillo sublato, quo pugnandi dabat signum* . . . [on board ship].

One final point may be made in this connection: In the descriptions of Julius Caesar's wars and elsewhere there is a remarkable number of cases where legionary centurions appear to act on their own, taking private initiatives, without regard for the men they were supposed to lead. Yet it is not suggested that this caused immediate confusion among the centuries, or that this was improper behaviour for centurions.[46] If these descriptions are true and if actions like these were typical of centurions, the conclusion appears to be then that the movements of Roman soldiers in battle were, to a large extent, predetermined by past training and experience.[47] If centurions were dispensable at times, although they are the attested backbone of the Roman legion, it is more easily understood that the legion could function without the commander of the cohort—whose existence is nowhere attested. It is then likely that cohorts, when acting as part of the legion on the battle-field, were not expected to move independently.[48] Paradoxically, this may again leave us with the possibility, not recorded in the literature, that the centurions who made up a cohort took their lead from the chief-centurion of the cohort, while moving on the battle-field. This, however, would not have made the chief-centurion into anything resembling the commander of a battalion, for it does not entail that he had a clearly defined function in the chain of command.

To sum up: it has long been recognized that the regular legionary cohort had no administrative functions and hence no administrative officials. We must now add that it had no commander and no standard of its own and hence no independent tactical function. The legionary cohort, in other words, did not have an independent existence, but was a way of grouping centuries in the barracks and on the battle field. As observed above, the republican legion also did not have any tactical unit intervening between the level of the legion and that of the maniple (double century). Moreover, even the legion itself did not have a commander in the time of Polybius.

This has consequences for our views of the command structure of the Roman army and for our understanding of the way in which the

---

[46] *BG* v 44; vi 38; 40; vii 47; B. Hisp. 23, 3–4; Josephus i, 18, 1 (351); vi, 1, 8 (81).

[47] This seems to be suggested by Caesar himself in *BG* ii 20.

[48] I am not aware of any descriptions of legionary cohorts acting independently in battle. Exceptions are perhaps *BG* v 25 and *BC* ii, 41, 6, both cases when the initiative had unfortunate results.

legion operated as a fighting force. Between the commander of the
legion and the sixty legionary centurions there was no intervening
officer with operational responsibility for a battalion-type unit. This is
a gap much greater than usually thought. Of course any tribune could
be ordered by the legate to act as commander of part of the legion, in
battle or in peace-time, just as Arrian made a legionary legate commander of the entire right flank, including the legate's own legion
and the cavalry (above, p. 390). However, these are *ad hoc* decisions
which do not reflect the permanent command structure. There is no
evidence of any kind that the military tribunes in the republican or
imperial legion had permanent operational responsibility for specific
cohorts. The tribunes were attached to the legate and had no properly
defined function in the chain of command. Of course, this does not
exclude the possibility that they would be given responsibility in battle,
but such decisions appear to have been made on an *ad hoc* basis.

On the battle-field then, the legion was essentially a force consisting of sixty centuries, some of them of double size.[49] How this worked
in practice is an important question which lies beyond the scope of
this article. A relevant observation may be found in Asclepiodotus'
Tactics ii 9: 'For when the file consisted of eight men, eight files
constituted the square, which alone of all the detachments, by reason of the equal length of the sides of the formation, could hear
equally well the commands from every quarter and so was properly
called a company; when, however, the file was later doubled, the
battalion (*syntaxiarchia*) constituted the square, and, as a consequence,
included the supernumeraries.'[50] According to this author then, a unit
of 64 men was most easy to control in the circumstances of his age.
This number is not far removed from the size of a Roman century.
The legion was certainly a far less flexible tool than units of similar
size in recent history and it may have been less manoeuverable than
we might suppose.

There is a similar problem below the level of the century. In modern
armies companies are split into smaller units, platoons or squads,
which have their own officers serving under the company commander.

---

[49] For the size of the first cohort: Domaszewski/Dobson, *op. cit.* note 15 p. xxiv;
D.J. Breeze, 'The Organization of the Legion: The First Cohort and the Equites
Legionis', Breeze & Dobson, *Roman Officers and Frontiers*, 65–70. The evidence from
the legionary base at Inchtuthil is decisive.

[50] Trans. Loeb, Aeneas Tacticus, Asclepiodotus, Onasander, pp. 259 f.

Roman centuries were divided into *contubernia*, familiar from the excavations of Roman camps.[51] This, however, appears to have been an arrangement for the barracks only, for it is not reflected in the composition of the officer corps. Within the century the *principales* are the *signifer, optio* and *tesserarius*.[52] Their functions are well known and there is no need to discuss them here. The point at issue is that there were no commanders of *contubernia* or of any other sub-unit of the *centuria*. The century of eighty men was clearly the smallest constituent part of the legion, and was not split up into smaller tactical units. This again would be considered unworkable in a modern army.

Finally we must note a similar problem at a higher level which has often been discussed, namely the relationship between legions and auxiliary units within the provincial command. It is often supposed that in those provinces where both legionaries and auxiliaries were stationed, a group of auxiliary units was formally as well as in practice attached to each legion.[53] However there is no evidence of such a formal attachment. On one occasion Tacitus refers to 'the eight cohorts of Batavians, auxila of the fourteenth legion',[54] and we find the formula '*legio . . . et auxilia eius*' in a very few cases.[55] These instances, however, are too rare to form the basis for hypotheses regarding provincial organization in general.

It must be stressed that there is no evidence between the first and third centuries, of the existence of any form of territorial command within the provinces. Such an organization, however, did exist in the fourth century when it is attested in abundant references to *limites* and their commanders.[56] The existence of a regional military command-structure in this later period is clear from legal sources, inscriptions, and the *Notitia Dignitatum*, although the term *limes* itself has usually been misunderstood as referring to the physical aspect of

---

[51] von Petrikovits, *op. cit.* note 22, 36–43 with fig. 2, 3; 121.

[52] D.J. Breeze, 'The Organization of the Career Structure of the *immunes* and *principales* of the Roman Army' in Breeze & Dobson, *Roman Officers and Frontiers* (Stuttgart, 1993), 11–58.

[53] G.L. Cheesman, *The Auxilia of the Roman Imperial Army* (Oxford, 1914, repr. 1971), 49–52.

[54] Tacitus, *Hist* i 59: *et erant in civitate Lingonum octo Batavorum cohortes, quartae decimae legionis auxilia. . . .*

[55] *CIL* viii 2637; xiii 8017; iii 3228.

[56] B. Isaac, 'The Meaning of "Limes" and "Limitanei" in Ancient Sources'. JRS 78 (1988), 125–147; The Limits of Empire: The Roman Army in the East, (Oxford, ²1992), 161, 208–213.

frontier fortifications rather than military organization. The essence of the system is clear: a territorial commander, the *dux limitis* had direct authority over all the units of *limitanei* in his district. The system was separate from that of the civilian administration, a separation which did not exist in the provincial administration from Augustus till the late third century. Moreover, in the fourth century the military organization did not coincide geographically with the civil administration. Thus we see that the area under the command of the *Dux Palaestinae* covered three civilian provinces and extended in range beyond them (when he acted, for instance, in the Red Sea).[57]

There is no indication in the available material before the fourth century that the legions and auxilia operated in peace-time under any unified command other than that of the provincial governor. When modern scholars attach auxilia to legions they attempt to solve a question with an hypothesis for which there is no evidence—just as in the case of the missing commanders of legionary cohorts and their missing standards. Apparently the system worked reasonably well because the various units had routine tasks which they could carry out satisfactorily.

To return to the chain of command at legionary level: in the period of the principate there was an element missing without which no modern army could function. Yet the Roman army did function, perhaps because the decisions which had to be made in battle at lower levels were simpler than those made in modern warfare. Whatever the explanation, there are two conclusions to this paper. Firstly, the command structure of the Roman army is a subject in its own right which cannot be discussed as a mere subordinate topic to the problems of the hierarchy. Secondly, serious consideration of the command structure, from the governor down to the individual soldier, has to take into account the existence of what we in our age would consider essential gaps in the pyramid.

---

[57] J.F. Gilliam has shown that a form of territorial command existed in a few areas along rivers and some coastal areas in earlier periods: 'The *Dux Ripae* at Dura', *TAPA* 72 (1941), 155–75 '*Roman Army Papers*', 23–41. The examples known seem to have entailed combined activity on land and at sea or on the river. However, unlike the later *duces* the earlier territorial commanders were subordinate to provincial governors.

Postscript

Note the interesting recent work by A. Goldsworthy, *The Roman Army at War: 100 B.C.–A.D. 200* (Oxford, 1996). Relevant is in particular chapter 1, which deals with organization and unit organization. On p. 15 Goldsworthy observes that without a commander a unit cannot function as a tactical unit. So far we agree. He then concludes that it would seem eminently reasonable to assume that the senior centurion, the *pilus prior*, acted as commander of the cohort. Here we disagree.

25

AN OPEN FRONTIER

> Frontier policy is of the first practical importance, and has a more
> profound effect upon the peace or warfare of nations than any other
> factor, political or economic; there is yet no work or treatise in any
> language which, so far as I know, affects to treat the subject as a
> whole. . . . You may ransack the catalogues of libraries, you may search
> the indexes of celebrated historical works, you may study the writings
> of scholars, and you will find the subject almost wholly ignored.[1]

By the time Lord Curzon wrote these words Roman historians had
been studying the Frontiers of the Roman Empire for quite some
time. However, they had considered the essence of the problem as
little as the academics Curzon was referring to. Curzon, however,
was unaware of the work of the German geographer Ratzel, who
made a determined effort to produce a set of laws for predicting the
behaviour of states in respect of boundaries. Ratzel believed that each
state had an idea of the possible limits of its territorial dominion and
he called this idea 'space conception'. Ratzel's view on the space
conception of states followed logically from his belief that the state
was like a living organism which grew and decayed. These ideas had
a profound influence on Roman historians in Germany and, through
them, on those in other countries. For Ratzel the border was a dy-
namic feature and only fixed in position during a temporary halt in
political expansion. Thus he argued that the territory of a state should
never be regarded as definite. The people of a state press against the
boundaries of the state area, trying to force them wider. 'The area
of a state expands as its culture develops (Der Raum der Staaten
wächst mit der Kultur). . . . The lower the cultural level, the smaller
will be the territory of the state, so that the size of a state becomes
a measure of its culture. No primitive people has ever created a
large state, nor even one equivalent in area to an intermediate German state [von der Grösse eines deutschen Mittelstaates], Ratzel, 1896,

---

[1] Lord Curzon, *Frontiers*, 4.

98 f.' This view, held by many contemporary scholars, assumed that the growth of culture was indissolubly linked with expansion of territory: the state is an organism and growth is normal and necessary in an organism (Ratzel, 1896, 97: . . . 'die einzig richtige Auffassung . . . dass wir es im Staate mit einem organischen Wesen zu tun haben. Der Natur des Organischen widerspricht aber nichts mehr als die Starre Umgrenzung.'). Ratzel does not fail to cite with approval Mommsen's law of nature which dictates the dissolution of politically and culturally underdeveloped peoples by their more developed neighbours.[2]

Such views may be intellectually unproductive and morally repugnant, but it must be recognized that they are still influential, although they are nowadays expressed in more cautious language than that of Ratzel. There are, however, other approaches which are more helpful for our purposes. Thus C.B. Fawcett devotes an entire chapter to the 'zonal character of frontiers' in his book 'Frontiers'.

> The common conception which is expressed in such terms as 'frontier-line' and 'border-line' is a result of the natural human tendency to think of things in sharply defined separate compartments: it is not based on careful observation of the facts (Fawcett, 1918, 17).

> Even for the political frontier this zonal character is a prominent feature. It is through the frontiers of a state that it has relations with other states; and its frontier areas are thereby differentiated from the interior parts of its territory (p. 21).

Fawcett considers frontiers to be essentially transition areas—zones in which the characters and influences of two or more different regions or states come together. He proposes grouping frontiers into the two main classes of zones of separation and zones of intercourse (or of pressure). He suggests that this is a more accurate description than the common classification into 'natural' and 'artificial' frontiers, an approach which has had a profound effect on both politicians

---

[2] Theodor Mommsen, *Römische Geschichte*, iii 220: 'Kraft des Gesetzes, dass das zum Staat entwickelte Volk die politisch unmündigen, das zivilisierte die geistig unmündigen Nachbarn in sich auflöst—kraft dieses Gesetzes, das so allgemeingültig und so sehr Naturgesetz ist wie das Gesetz der Schwere. . . .' Ratzel's views may be found at length in Ratzel, 1897 and 1940. A recent example of such views: '. . . the solid Roman people and empire had more to offer the Mediterranean world than did Carthage, which still practiced human sacrifice regularly and had only a weak derivative culture; this war made it certain that western civilization was to be based on the Greco-Roman outlook' (C.G. Starr, *A History of the Ancient World*, New York, 1965, 487).

and historians of the past few centuries and is still widely accepted.[3]

Those who reject the theories of Ratzel, or those of other 'pattern discoverers' and historical determinists will conclude that attempts to produce a set of reliable theories about international boundaries have failed (Prescott, 1987, 8, cf. p. 11). On the other hand, there has been notably more success in devising a set of procedures or guidelines by which boundaries can be studied. Nevertheless, the procedures which are applicable to the study of modern boundaries are not necessarily applicable to the ancient world.

There are two different ways of viewing the frontiers of the Roman empire. The first studies them from the centre outwards, focusing on material relating to the central government or coming from government circles. The second method concentrates on the periphery itself, working from the margins of the empire inwards. Scholars who are mostly concerned with central government tend to identify with what they perceive as government values and actions, while those who study the provinces are often interested mostly in social and economic developments in the frontier area. Thus we are faced not only with different types of material or varying methods of analyzing facts, but with two different attitudes towards the essence of Empire. The first approach is commonly found in the work of those concerned with Roman political and military history. An offshoot of this is the work of Roman army specialists who study the archaeology of military installations in the provinces. Although they work with material from the provinces they usually prefer to see the subject from the presumed perspective of the Roman authorities and their instruments of empire. We are faced not only with different types of material or varying methods of analyzing facts, but with two diverse attitudes towards the essence of Empire. This was first developed as a field of study in Germany in the nineteenth century. The value of the second approach has been emphasized more recently. It is defined in a programmatic statement by Fergus Millar (1966, 166): 'The Republic, it may be, can be seen from Rome outwards. To take this standpoint for the Empire is to lose contact with reality. Not only the pattern of the literary evidence, or the existence of an immense mass

---

[3] For instance, from the 16th century onwards successive rulers regarded France's desirable boundaries as coinciding with the sea, the Alpine watershed, the Pyrenees, and the Rhine: Pounds, 1951, 1954, also: 1972, 422. The notion of a 'natural boundary' goes back to the eighteenth century: Guichonnet & Raffestin, 1974, 19.

of local documents, but the very nature of the Empire itself, means that it can only be understood by starting from the provinces and looking inward'. Recently C.R. Whittaker, following Owen Lattimore's analysis of the Chinese frontier, has traced the development of the frontier of the western part of the Roman empire through the study of the social and economic history of the periphery.[4]

These two approaches to the study of frontiers are often concerned with entirely different topics, but each in its own way is trying to answer the question of what determined the limits of imperial expansion. Traditional devotees of what are often, erroneously, called '*limes* studies', have argued that decisions made by the imperial authorities at the centre fixed the boundaries of the empire along the lines most suitable for an effective defence of the provinces against outsiders. I have rejected these theories in a recent book about the Roman army in the East (Isaac, 1990). On the other hand, Whittaker, following Lattimore, has argued that social and economic factors at the periphery ultimately determined the range of effective imperial control. As Lattimore puts it: '(ancient civilizations) learned by experiment to discriminate between those territories, resources, and peoples which could be profitably included within their imperial expansion and those which it was better to exclude because military action, administration, and the collection of revenue cost more than they were worth' (Lattimore, 1962, 503 f.).

In the present paper I shall attempt to demonstrate my own views on the subject, and discuss some of the features peculiar to the Roman frontier in the East that must be taken into consideration in any discussion of Roman policy and its impact in the frontier zone. It is undeniable that economic factors are always paramount in determining the farthest limits of imperial expansion. I cannot accept, however, that the social and economic reality of the periphery was a factor in determining the process of decision-making at the imperial court.[5] I would suggest that imperial policy was often dictated by other con-

---

[4] Whittaker, 1989, and cf. his earlier chapter on Trade and Frontiers of the Roman Empire in Garnsey and Whittaker, 1983, 110–27.

[5] There are similar differences in views on bedouinisation: 'From the perspective of history or of the townsmen there is a tendency to see the process as being forced upon the bedouin by the pressure of physical environment, political or economic events or of technology. However, we (and the Rwalah) see the process as being mediated by choices, freely made, and based on moral or ideological principles. The other parameters are there and have an effect on which choices are possible, but the primary consideration is that of morality or ideology' (Lancaster, 1988, 51).

siderations, namely: ideology, the relationship of the emperor with the army, and the need to maintain political control. Priorities may have varied, and we have to allow for the force of short-term greed as opposed to long-term profitability. I should also add that in the Later Roman Empire, traditional ideology was gradually replaced by the ideology of the state religion which had a direct influence on the attitudes of emperors towards every non-Roman people. In the present paper I shall attempt to clarify my own point of view regarding these matters, and discuss a number of peculiarities of the Roman frontier in the East that must be considered by anyone discussing Roman policy and its impact in the frontier zone.

Scholars who argue that Roman frontier policy carefully considered the cost of expansion and refrained from ventures it could ill afford invariably refer to the same limited number of pronouncements made by ancient authors that ostensibly support this assumption. After a lifetime of foreign conquests, Augustus is said to have advised his successor to refrain from further expansion, 'to confine the empire to its (present) limits—either from fear or out of jealousy', adds Tacitus.[6] This statement can teach us something about Augustus towards the end of his life, about Tacitus and what he thought of the recommendation, and perhaps about Tiberius and his policies thereafter, but it does not tell us much about imperial policy in general. Tiberius, it may be noted, may not have initiated foreign wars as emperor, but he did annex a number of key 'client states' in the East: Commagene, Cappadocia, and Hierapolis-Castabala. He may have thought Rome had to consolidate before marching on.

There are a number of Greek authors who favoured restraint. Strabo explicitly and repeatedly claimed that Rome refrained from unprofitable annexation. This shows that the concept existed, but not that it had a decisive impact on imperial policy. The same approach is found in the works of Appian, Aristides, and Pausanias. Those three authors wrote in a period when the ruling emperors did not initiate wars. Besides expressing their own opinion they may have echoed the official policy of their own times, but it cannot be claimed that this represents a consensus through the centuries. On the contrary, these authors are in a minority, and there is no justification in the

---

[6] *An.* i 11: 'addideratque consilium coercendi inter terminos imperii, incertum metu an per invidiam'. Cf. Dio lvi 33, 5–6, whose version reinforces the impression of an elderly ruler who had not recovered from the disaster in Germany.

emphasis laid on their statements in the modern literature. There never was agreement along these lines. At all times there were groups of aristocrats and others denying the validity of the cost/benefit argument, even in times when this argument determined imperial policy. Hence the resistance to Hadrian's policies, and to those of Justinian in his last years. For example in the fourth century we find a speech of Themistius [*Or.* 8, p. 172. 11 ff.] delivered on 28 Mar. 368 celebrating Valens' *Quinquennalia.* Themistius advises Valens that the Empire lacks the resources for constant campaigning.[7]

Imperialism in the Later Roman Empire has recently been the subject of a new study (McCormick, 1986, 78 f.). McCormick observes that the establishment of the Christian Roman empire entailed a decisive increase in triumphal ceremonies, a kind of renaissance of triumph. In the fourth century especially, there were numerous victory celebrations over imperial rivals. Extraordinary significance was attached to such celebrations because an imperial rival was a more dangerous foe and a deeper threat to the throne than Germanic invasions, however damaging these were at a local level.

In the reign of Claudius, Corbulo found it intolerable that the Frisians remained outside his jurisdiction, even though experience had shown that they were a troublesome people, incapable of paying a substantial tribute. He was forced by Claudius to withdraw, but gained Tacitus' sympathy (*Ann.* xi 19 and iv 72–4). Claudius clearly agreed with his predecessor that no efforts should be made to extend direct control far beyond the Rhine. Yet Germanicus, Corbulo and Tacitus were not the only Romans who felt that Germany had to be conquered permanently, not for gain, but as a matter of honour. It has been argued quite plausibly that Domitian's war in Germany (A.D. 83–?85) originally envisaged a far more ambitious advance than the modest one east of the Rhine which was achieved (Schönberger 1969, 158).

From the Roman perspective, John Mann was right in stating that: 'the frontiers congealed around the borders of the empire: they arose by default' (Mann, 1974, 513 f.). Twentieth-century scholars, on the other hand, are now in a position to explain why the Roman empire, in spite of so many efforts, failed to control Central Europe east of the Rhine, or Britain north of Hadrian's wall. These explanations

---

[7] Cf. Heather, 1991, 117.

naturally take into account the social and economic realities that made it impossible for the Roman army and administrators to do there what they did so successfully in Gaul.

Yet it remains essential to recognize that such realities had only a limited impact on the views and actions of the Roman upper class. Similar tensions are found in the history of many Empires: 'From the earliest days of the British connection with India there have been two opposing forces at work, a forward tendency, and a policy which sought to restrict, or to prevent, expansion. Contrary to the wishes of the Directors of the East India Company and of fox-hunting politicians at home, British rule was extended in India, until the mountains of the north-west were reached . . .' (Collin Davies, 1975, 1).

Roman emperors do seem to have realized eventually that large-scale expeditions in Germany east of the Rhine did not bring their predecessors much glory or booty, so they sent their armies elsewhere. In the East, on the other hand, they never conceded the right of the rival empire to exist. A few years before the Islamic conquest took over the Sassanid empire and conquered the Byzantine Orient, east of Anatolia, Heraclius was happily destroying Fire Temples in the middle of Persia, while Persia was occupying large parts of Byzantine *Oriens*. The dynamics of imperial expansion are complex. An empire decaying internally may still be expanding—for example China in the 19th century or the Soviet state recently. There is no direct relationship between internal stability, economic strength and the tendency of empires to expand.

The preoccupation of historians with boundaries does not take account of many actual historical situations. India was not lost to Britain because of foreign invaders. The Soviet Union did not collapse as a result of attacks by foreign barbarians. The Western (not the Eastern) Roman empire was penetrated by foreigners before and after its demise, but it is not obvious that military weakness was the root of the problem. Byzantium lost *Oriens* and Egypt to the Muslims, but unlike the Sassanid Empire the heart of the Byzantine state continued to exist for another 800 years.

Obviously the forces in favour of expansion and an aggressive foreign policy were not equally strong at all times and in all circles. Following periods of intense military effort as in the reigns of Augustus, Nero and the year 69, Trajan, Marcus Aurelius, and Septimius Severus, it would be natural to expect periods of consolidation and restoration. And it is clear that in such periods voices would be heard in favour of a rational military policy. Empires that go on expanding without pause or restraint will soon exhaust themselves.

The traditional notion of Rome's frontier is that the line of a river or a barrier represents four or five different types of boundaries at the same time: military, cultural, political, administrative, and sometimes also ethnic. It could not have been all this. 'To seek for a zone which traverses easily defensible topographical features; which does not violate ethnic considerations by cutting through the territories of closely related tribes; and which at the same time serves as a political boundary is Utopian' (Collin Davies, 1975, 16). In the case of Rome's frontier in the north-west it is clear that the barriers were laid out irrespective of existing topography and that they cut through the territories of closely related peoples. Hadrian's wall was simply the shortest line across the island, the Antonine wall was the shortest line north of Hadrian's wall. The barriers in Germany were straight and ignored topography. Since rivers do not serve as proper barriers it is clear that they were simply the most convenient way of linking bases (Curzon, Fawcett, Collin Davies). The barriers were not a line of defence either. They were meant to hamper movement, as in Germany, or control it, as in Britain. This does not prove that any of them served as a political boundary.

The East

I should now like to turn to a consideration of several phenomena peculiar to the frontier in the East. The topics I should like to look at are, firstly, the relationship between Rome and Parthia/Persia, followed by the relations between Rome and the nomads, and finally, the importance to Rome of the eastern trade.

Rome and Parthia/Persia

When we look at the history of Rome's eastern frontier we see that time and again, between seven and nine times, Roman and Byzantine armies reached the heartland of both the Parthian and Sassanid empires: the region of Ctesiphon/Seleucia. Why could they not hold it? Roman armies looted and plundered the countryside, sometimes even captured parts or all of the twin cities, and then withdrew. What made it impossible or undesirable for the Roman authorities to annex the region? We cannot explain this failure by problems of distance or system of government. The area was ruled by monarchs most of the time and could be governed from Antioch in Syria, as the Seleucids proved. It was densely populated, urbanized and much of it was under cultivation, thanks to a highly developed system of irrigation canals. Trajan indeed made an attempt to annex the entire region and divide it into provinces. This was followed by a major revolt of the Jews in the area, which spilled over into several provinces of the Roman empire: Egypt, Libya, Cyprus, and to some extent Judaea. Was it impossible for Rome to swallow Babylonia with its distinct social and cultural identity? Most of the time Rome enjoyed an obvious military superiority, it hated the other empire, and there was a firm ideological commitment to expansion. Babylonia was wealthy and urbanized. One point we may note is that the Parthian and Sassanian periods witnessed a spectacular growth in settlement as compared with the Achaemenid period when Alexander conquered the area (Adams, 1965, 71–3, Table 19). Whatever the reason, it is clear that, apart from Trajan, Roman generals and emperors who actually reached the region concluded that they could not incorporate it into the empire, and that their only option was to loot and destroy as much as possible before a relatively speedy withdrawal. It is also clear that they did not follow any well-considered plan when they acted thus. Their decisions were almost certainly taken in the course of their campaign as a result of what they saw and experienced.

Rome and the Nomads

It seems to me that much modern thinking about Rome and her relations with the nomads is based on erroneous ideas about the nature of nomadism in the Near East. I would therefore like to begin with some general remarks about the subject.[8] First of all, nomadism was never the dominant culture in the Near East. It was always a marginal phenomenon, a way of existing in regions where cultivation is difficult if not impossible, but which may be profitably exploited by grazing.[9] The dominant culture in the Near East—at least for the

---

[8] References in Isaac, 1990, p. 70, n. 67; add: Patai, 1951; Bacon, 1954; W. & F. Lancaster, 1988. Similar arguments have been offered in discussions of the Roman presence in Africa: Shaw, 1982; Trousset, 1980.

[9] We must distinguish between ancient nomads in the Near East and groups called bedouin in more recent times. Lancaster, 1988, 54 observes: 'For the Rwalah

past five millennia—has been the sedentary agricultural population. These settlers have always been far more numerous than the nomadic groups with whom, however, they always shared significant elements of culture. In the period we are discussing there were two main groups of nomads: Firstly, camel-breeders, who did not cultivate crops but kept some horses. The second group consisted of shepherd tribes who bred sheep and goats, using donkeys and camels for transport. The latter had to remain fairly close to good water sources and thus moved within a more limited territory than the former, who travelled hundreds of miles. Apart from these two main groups, there were various transitional groups whose cultures combined features of both shepherds and camel-breeders as well as features of both nomads and settled populations.

Many historians tend to think of nomads as constantly predatory and expansionist. It can be argued that this is very much an outsiders' view, influenced by the traditional western image of the victorious Moslem and Mongol armies. There is no evidence to show that the nomads in the Syrian and Arabian deserts had the social structures, the aggressive ideology, or the numbers so often ascribed to them. 'Desert logistics are against the aggregations of groups and forces; even hardy bedouin and their camels need nourishment sometimes and a large aggregation could only take place in a extremely good spring' (Lancaster, 1988, 56).

Where actual raids are reported the description is often misleading. The victims have a practical interest in exaggerating their losses, and the tribesmen describe the events from their own perspective which requires cautious interpretation.[10]

All groups are characteristically mutually interdependent. The fully nomadic tribes who raised no crops for themselves depended on sedentary cultivators for agricultural products such as dates or grain,

---

being bedouin means neither economic necessity nor ecological compulsion but a political or ideological decision. The conceptualised expression of the ideology is the genealogy and its economic underpinning is multi-resource'. We do not know whether this was true for the ancient nomads. It is possible that economic necessity and ecological compulsion played a more important role then. In any event, it follows that the term 'bedouin' should be avoided when discussing antiquity. It would be incorrect to use it for people who do not call themselves so.

[10] '. . . a raid might be described as having taken place between "the Rwalah" and "the Fi'dan". At once one assumes a tribal conflict with a cast of hundreds if not thousands . . . on questioning . . . the final total proves to be, perhaps, only a dozen or so men' (Lancaster, 1988, 56).

money and other goods in exchange for livestock, related products, guides and guards. The semi-nomads who raised some crops lived in proximity to both and could, for instance, herd flocks for towns-people and for those nomad tribes who took their camels into the desert in the winter months. In historical times both the sedentary population and the semi-nomads frequently paid tribute to the full nomads. The latter recognized an obligation to protect the goods and personnel of the settlements from depredation. The interaction and interdependence of the nomadic and settled population groups in the Near East has been described as a pattern of symbiosis neces-sitated by the features peculiar to their habitat, which required spe-cialization in exploiting the resources of the area.[11] The symbiosis of pastoralism, cultivation and trade made steppe and arable areas mutually interdependent, and has been one of the characteristic fea-tures of the region through several millennia. Nomadic tribal units existed side by side with, and in close proximity to, villages and cit-ies living on agriculture and trade. In studying the frontiers of the Roman empire we must therefore keep in mind the essential difference between Rome's relations with the nomads in the Near East and in Central Asia. These nomads from Central Asia who faced the Romans in the north and the north-east were horse-riding pastoral peoples, with open territories beyond them. The Near Eastern nomads, on the other hand, always lived in an enclosed desert: to the north-west they faced Rome, to the north-east Parthia/Persia, to the South the sea. There may have been repeated bouts of hostility between the settled population and the nomads, but they were bound together by their mutual dependence. Clashes between such groups, when they took place, are not likely to have involved very many fighters.

In the north Romans and Persians could in theory try to exclude the Central Asian nomads, and keep them out of their empires. In south-western Asia this was never an option. Here regions of great fertility suitable for agriculture are frequently interspersed with areas where cultivation would be difficult, but which may be profitably

---

[11] For the so-called *khuwwah* relationships which worked between different parts of the symbiosis in the case of the Rwala bedouin, Lancaster, 1981; Lancaster, 1988, 57 f.: 'Such contractual relationships seem similar to those mentioned in pre-Islamic times and at the time of the Prophet, thus helping to establish the idea that co-operation between towns and bedouin has a long history, and that the idea of a symbiosis between the two is important for the management of the area. This is certainly how the Rwalah see it today'.

exploited by grazing, while some parts may be utilized either way. These variations in land-use have not always been picked up by scholars looking at modern precipitation charts.

In the Near East, therefore, Rome faced not only Persia, but a population which consisted of widely distinct, but mutually dependent elements. The nomadic groups on their part were in touch with and influenced by both major powers. Neither government could exclude the nomads, and there is no indication that they ever tried. Whatever the function of Hadrian's wall and similar structures in the north-west, or the fossatum in Africa, there is nothing like them in the East. In the East the Romans encountered what was essentially an open frontier.

The question asked by nineteenth century German scholars and their intellectual heirs was: how did Rome exclude the nomads? I would reply that Rome did not and could not exclude them. What we should be asking is to what extent and how Rome included them, and what was the impact of Roman rule on the population in the frontier zone?

I have argued on several occasions that Roman involvement in the desert area was minimal at first and thereafter developed by stages (Isaac, 1990, chapters III and IV). I should like to stress here that these stages went in tandem with periods of militancy towards Persia. Trajan annexed the Nabataean kingdom and fought a major war in Mesopotamia. Under Marcus Aurelius another war was fought in North Mesopotamia. From his reign dates the famous Ruwwafa inscription in which the Thamud in the northern Hijaz recognize the authority of the governor of Arabia. A Roman military presence in the desert parts in the East is first attested under Septimius Severus, who also conquered and annexed N. Mesopotamia and gave Palmyra colonial status. A more pronounced military presence in the desert was the work of the tetrarchs, who also fought in Persia and expanded in the north-east.

This brief summary is based on the interpretation of a combination of literary sources, inscriptions and archaeological material. The material gives no information about motive or aim of Roman actions, and we can do no more than say that a pattern can be distinguished. The actual result was that the nomads in the Near East were faced with an increased military presence peaking in the early fourth century. We do not know as yet whether this was a peaceful process or whether it was accompanied by various forms of violence and expulsions. In the fourth century we have the first reports from Roman sources about predominant Arab tribal chiefs as allies of Rome or Persia. Archaeological evidence shows that quite a number of the structures in the desert, first occupied in the tetrarchic period, were abandoned between the later fourth century and the sixth. This is a clear indication that the heavy presence there was considered unnecessary or too costly or both (Isaac, 1990, 211). Instead Byzantium developed a system of alliances with tribal heads, who received the status of *phylarch* and were subsidized in exchange for their services. This meant that Rome in fact withdrew its army from important sites and relied on allies for security.

An interesting example of one of the places involved is Resapha— Sergiopolis. This site was on the road from Palmyra to Sura on the Euphrates, first laid out with milestones in the reign of Vespasian. Palmyra, nodal point and oasis in the Syrian desert, was formally part of the province of Syria, but in practice it was far more independent than a regular provincial town. In the third century, however, it received the status of a Roman colony with a Roman garrison. After the destruction of Palmyra in the 270's, legions were based at Palmyra and Sura. Later the road-station at Resapha became the base of *Equites Promoti Indigenae* (locally recruited cavalry), a site of Christian pilgrimage and developed into a substantial settlement which was surrounded with walls in the reign of Anastasius.[12] In 540 the citizens withstood a siege by Khusro I without any army support. It is also clear from Procopius' account of the so-called 'strata dispute' in the mid-sixth century that troops had been withdrawn from the entire region by this period. Procopius tells us that the region was under the control of the Ghassanids, Byzantium's Arab allies. In the course of a dispute about grazing lands between nomad chiefs, the Ghassanids argued that the fact that the region was called 'Strata', presumably after the Damascus—Palmyra—Sura road, the so-called 'Strata Diocletiana', showed that it was part of the Roman empire. It is significant that an entire region in the desert derived its name from a Roman highway, an illustration of the importance of such a feature in this type of country. However, the point here is that, in the sixth century, the Ghassanids had to resort to the evidence of

---

[12] Resapha is mentioned by Ptolemy. The *Notitia Dignitatum, Or.* xxxiii 27 (late fourth century) lists it as a military base. Procopius, *Buildings* ii, 9, 3–7, mentions that it was attacked by Saracens and then surrounded with a modest wall.

the name, which shows that there could no longer have been any more tangible evidence of a Roman presence. Next, al-Mundhir, the Ghassanid chief, (569–582) established his headquarters or '*praetorium*' outside the walls of Resapha.[13]

Thus we can distinguish the following stages:

1) The seventies: A Roman road is organized through the desert. We have no evidence of any Roman military units in the region, so the Palmyrenes must have seen to its security.

2) Late second–early third century: A cohort is established at Palmyra.

3) Tetrarchic period: Palmyra and Sura, on the Euphrates, become legionary bases. Resapha was also certainly garrisoned by the end of the fourth century.

4) Early sixth century: Resapha is walled. The military unit was withdrawn between the end of the fourth and the beginning of the sixth century.

5) Sixth century: There appear to be no Roman troops anywhere in the area. The inhabitants of Resapha are on their own when besieged. The surrounding countryside is controlled by the Byzantine Arab allies who establish their headquarters outside Resapha.

We can see here a progression from an absence of Roman involvement to a massive presence, followed by withdrawal at an uncertain date, and a situation where the local population, both sedentary townspeople and pastoral nomads, play a key role in the maintenance of security. It is clear that in such circumstances the concept 'boundary' is meaningless. The Ghassanids were of the Empire, but not necessarily in it in any geographical sense. There is no reason to believe that the presence of two legions in the region resulted in better security than the subsequent arrangement. Of course, this does not mean there was never any armed conflict in the region. But we learn of problems only in the context of major conflict: when Palmyra attempted to establish a breakaway Empire, when the Persian king passed, invading Syria and when the Persian allies instigated the 'Strata Dispute' with the purpose of creating a casus belli.

The process whereby nomad tribes developed into an integral part of the organization of the eastern frontier can never be fully be traced, for contacts between Rome and nomad tribes were not usually

---

[13] Musil, 1928, 260–72; Sauvaget, 1939.

recorded on stone or in the literature. We have occasional glimpses to suggest that this process took place: for instance, the Ruwwafa inscription already mentioned, in which the Thamud, who lived in the northern Hijaz, honour the Emperor Marcus Aurelius, recognize the authority of the governor of Arabia and thank him for settling an internal dispute. Although we can merely guess at the historical processes that led to the state of affairs in the sixth century, it must be stressed that the very role played by the tribal chiefs allied to Rome and Persia is the result of centuries of proximity to and links with the empire. The rise of powerful groups of nomads in the desert between Rome and Persia is itself due to the influence of the empire on the periphery. Again, our information may be scanty, but the increasingly powerful position occupied by tribal chiefs is not the result of an internal development, but a process engendered by Roman and Persian action. And finally, it is highly significant that the Saracen allies of Rome and Persia are described as playing an active role in the wars between the two powers from the fourth century onwards. For in co-opting the Saracens as allies, Rome and Persia themselves created the armies that ultimately took over the Near East.

To sum up this part of my paper, it is has been recognised for some time that the Roman presence had a decisive impact on the social situation in the eastern provinces, through the imposition of Roman law,[14] through the establishment of veteran colonies such as Berytus and Heliopolis, or through the destruction of centres of rebellion such as Jerusalem or Palmyra. It is now evident that a more gradual, but no less conclusive process of social change took place among the tribes inhabiting the frontier zone.

Rome and the Eastern Trade

The high cost of transport over land as compared with shipping has frequently been described.[15] Duncan-Jones has converted the known prices into ratios to allow direct comparison as follows, sea: river: land = 1: 4.9: 28. He compares this with figures for England in the eighteenth century: 1: 4.7: 22.6. Another set of calculations reached

---

[14] Nowhere better illustrated than in the Babatha archive (Yadin Papyri, Lewis, 1989).

[15] E.g. Lattimore, 1962, 'The Frontier in History, 479; Jones, 1974, Chapter II, p. 37; White, 1984, 127–140, discusses technical aspects: Duncan-Jones, 1974, 366–9.

a far higher discrepancy (Künow, 1980, 21–2) sea: river: land = 1: 5.9: 62.5. This higher cost of land transport was due to the fact that the grain-consuming carriers themselves—draught animals or human porters—ate up the margin of profit within a short distance.

The desert was different in this respect. Transport here was relatively cheap because camels could graze on the open steppe while on the march. Carriage by camel is 20% cheaper in Diocletian's Price Edict. This made the trade-routes through the desert in the Near East relatively attractive, all the more so because they were by far the shortest link between the Mediterranean coast and southern Mesopotamia and trade here was primarily trade in valuable merchandise.

For transport through the desert, however, Rome depended on the local people. To begin with, this meant the Nabataeans and the Palmyrenians whose prosperity derived from desert trade. And just how profitable this was, we can still see from the magnificent remains of their cities of Petra and Palmyra. The importance to Rome of these routes is underlined by early road-construction: in the 70's the governor of Syria, Marcus Ulpius Traianus constructed a road from Damascus to Palmyra and thence to Sura on the Euphrates. His son Trajan annexed Nabataea and constructed a road from the north of the new province to the Red Sea. The eastern trade crossed deserts or seas. The essence of control focused therefore on trade routes, lines of communication, way-stations and ports, rather than a specific territory, zone or group of settlements.

Here again we see that the frontier in the East was an open one. We must assume that built up mutual interests between the parties involved. We know that Palmyra had representatives in all the major trade centres in Parthia and maintained a temple of the Augusti at Vologesias (*SEG* vii 135).[16] We hear of several cases when inhabitants of the frontier zone changed loyalty. One Antoninus, in an incident vividly described by Ammianus, went over to the Persians in 359.[17] In 420 'Aspebetus', chief of an Arab tribe which belonged to the Persian sphere of influence, went over to the Romans with his followers and settled in Roman territory. He was accepted as ally and made a high ranking 'phylarch'. As a matter of course he converted to Christianity with his followers and became bishop under the name of Petrus. According to one report (which may be unreliable),

---

[16] R. Mouterde, *Syria* 12 (1931), 105–15.
[17] Ammianus xviii 5.1–3; 10.1; xix 1.3; cf. Matthews, 1989, 68.

Odenathus of Palmyra first made overtures towards Shapur and only when these were rebuffed did he turn against the Persians to become the saviour of the Orient (Petrus Patricius, fr. 10, *FHG* iv 187).

There was much profit in the eastern trade, as we see from Petra and Palmyra, and no doubt Rome gained still more from the trade through Egypt. It is clear, however, that Rome would never sacrifice vital control for considerations of trade. When Palmyra attempted to create a separate eastern empire it was destroyed, despite the services it had rendered for centuries.[18] In the Later Roman Empire trade between the two empires was restricted to a few designated cities to prevent spying (Isaac, 1990, 407). There is no lack of evidence, however, to show that nomads and the local population could not be prevented from crossing the border freely.

The most serious problem of studying ancient trade is the lack of quantitative indices of its volume (Duncan-Jones, 1990, 31). The statements made by Pliny the Elder are quoted again and again: 'In no year does India drain off less than 50 million sestertii from our empire' (Pliny, *NH* vi 26.101). 'And by the lowest reckoning India, China and that peninsula [Arabia] take 100 million sestertii from our empire each year. That is the sum which our luxuries and our own women cost us. For what fraction of these imports, I ask, gets to the gods or to the lower world?' (*NH* xii 41.84). It is highly doubtful whether Pliny actually knew what he was talking about. The tone of Pliny's statements about trade remind us of his xenophobic remarks about Greek doctors. Citing Cato the Elder, he claims that they have sworn to kill all barbarians—'and they are taking money for it besides!' (*NH* xxix 1.1 ff.). Greek doctors with their fancy medicine charge more than our solid Roman practitioners and thus 'vicendo victi sumus' (*NH* xxiv, 1, 4–5). An author who talks about a 'conspiracy' of foreign doctors should not be trusted when he disparages foreign traders.

It is even more difficult to estimate how far trade was taken into consideration by the Roman authorities in their decision-making. We have already seen that when an emperor had to choose between a dangerous Palmyra or no Palmyra at all he opted for the latter. It is

---

[18] The destruction of Palmyra may have been less immediate than the literary sources suggest. A recently published building inscription is dated 279 or 280: As'ad and Gawlikowski, 1986/7; *SEC* 38 (1988), 1579; cf. Starcky and Gawlikowski, 1985, 67, 69 f.

equally clear that governors would go to the trouble of organizing a safe road-system if this was likely to encourage trade. Scholars differ considerably regarding the influence of trade on the rise of Islam. It used to be widely assumed that Mecca's far-flung trading empire played an important role in the early stages of the rise of Islam. This theory has now been rejected and it has been argued that no such trading empire existed (Crone, 1987).

There are many studies summarizing what is known about ancient trade in the east (Crone, 1987; Sidebotham, 1986). We shall now turn to consider the question of the connection between this trade and Roman frontier policy. We know from Strabo that there was a marked increase in the volume of trade through Alexandria after the annexation of Egypt (Strabo ii, 5, 12 (118); xvii, 1, 13 (798)), and it is clear that in the first half of the first century, and under Trajan and Hadrian, roads and installations were constructed in the Eastern Desert of Egypt. These facilitated transportation between the Red Sea ports and the Nile (Sidebotham, 1986, chapter iii). As I have noted elsewhere, these installations look like buildings that in other deserts are often thought to belong to systems of frontier defence. In the eastern desert, however, it is obvious that they belong to a system of protected trade-routes. The military presence in the eastern desert was organized in the form of a regional command, one of the early instances of this form of organization (Sidebotham, 1986, 53; cf. Isaac, 1990, 151 f.).

In the Hellenistic period overland trade was carried from Gerrha on the Persian Gulf to the Mediterranean, but in the Roman period this route was no longer used (Potts, 1990, 85–97). At all times most of the trade was seaborne. As already mentioned, Trajan built a road in Arabia from Bostra to Aela (Elath, Aqaba) on the Red Sea and linked Clysma (Suez) to the Nile by a canal (Sidebotham, 1986, 146 f.), so it is possible that these two ports, to some extent at least, ousted the ports further to the south (Berenice, Myos Hormos and Leuke Kome), in spite of the difficulty of sailing north up the Red Sea.[19] However this may be, it is clear from the literary sources, notably Strabo and the *Periplus*, that most of the eastern trade passed through Alexandria in Egypt. An alternative route, known primarily from archaeological and epigraphical sources, is the one through Palmyra.

---

[19] Casson, 1989; cf. C. Préaux, *Chronique d'Egypte* 53 (1953), 271; Crone, 1987, 25.

Inscriptions from Palmyra show how Palmyra protected the caravan trade through the desert, and record the presence of Palmyrene agents in all the major trade-centres down to the Persian Gulf. We have no evidence for the relative importance of the Egyptian route and the one through Palmyra, nor for any fluctuations there might have been. The latter, as we have already noted, ceased to function with the destruction of Palmyra in the 270's. It is widely assumed that the eastern trade was at its liveliest in the first two centuries A.D. Numismatic evidence from India seems to indicate that, by the end of the third century A.D. it had declined, to peter out after a partial revival in the fourth century (Wheeler, 1951, 345–81, esp. 371 ff.).

There is no other evidence to confirm or modify these assumptions, apart from the impression that the Roman empire, when it became Christian, used far less incense than before. Recent discoveries by Sidebotham at Abu Sha'ar on the Egyptian Red Sea coast show that there was a military station there in the tetrarchic period, presumably involved in securing trade (Sidebotham, 1989). Also in the tetrarchic period, Roman troops were deployed in various bases in the desert of southern Jordan, including the Legio X Fretensis, which was transferred from Jerusalem to Aela. It is possible that part of the function of these troops was to secure the port of Aela and the trade passing through it to the North.

In the fifth century there was a Byzantine customs station on the island of Iotabe in the Red Sea.[20] In the sixth century another dux of Palestine expelled Jews who had occupied the island. These incidents show that there was enough trade to levy profitable customs duties and that military action was needed to maintain control. Another piece of evidence which also shows the link between customs duties and the army is provided by fragments of an edict of Anastasius (*IGLS* xiii no. 9046; cf. Isaac, 1990, p. 288, n. 123). This edict provides that the *dux Palaestinae* be financed from the revenues of the *commerciarius* of Clysma and the *dux Mesopotamiae* from the revenues of the *commerciarius* of the province of Mesopotamia. Once again we see that the eastern trade provided quite substantial sums in duties. By the sixth century the Ethiopians played a key role in the eastern trade of the Byzantines, and there is evidence of Byzantine intervention

---

[20] This island has not been identified. We hear of its existence only because the Byzantine customs officials were at one stage expelled by an Arab chief and reinstated by the dux of Palestine (Isaac, 1990, 247 f.).

in Ethiopia and the Arabian peninsula, presumably with the aim of securing a monopoly of the commercial routes that passed through the area (Rubin, 1989).

Conclusions

Should we, then, look inwards or outwards in our attempts to understand Roman frontier policy? Who or what determined the extent of empire—decision makers at the centre, or social and economic factors at the periphery? It is true that the actual situation at the periphery ultimately determined what could be achieved, but I also maintain that decisions at the centre were often taken regardless of the realities in the Weld. Roman policy was influenced by considerations of a different kind: ideology, internal politics and tensions, lack of information or information of the wrong kind—in short, all the chronic deficiencies common to the politics of a large monarchy in antiquity.

I do not claim that the urge to expand the empire was equally strong at all times and in all circles of Roman society. The Roman tendency to opt for an aggressive military policy went in cycles. There were periods of consolidation following periods of major wars, and there were intellectuals who argued that the empire should absorb only what was profitable. However, throughout the history of the Roman empire, such periods were followed by periods of warfare and, as late as the sixth century, such wars were often initiated by Rome. Roman policy was frequently inspired by considerations that had nothing to do with economics but a lot to do with politics, honour, and, later, religion.

The conflict between Rome and Parthia/Persia is the most significant case: it was endemic in nature, and kept alive, not by the ambition of Persia to expel Rome from the Near East, but by Rome's refusal to tolerate the existence of a rival empire. The regular campaigns to southern Babylonia cannot be analyzed in terms of a rational strategy. They can only be explained as stemming from a conviction that any form of damage to the heartland of the enemy is desirable and worthwhile in itself, even if it does not bring about the far more desirable outcome, the decisive annihilation of the rival empire.

As for Rome and the nomads, I would suggest that society in the Near East consisted of two complementary, but unequal elements. The settled population and the nomads lived in a complex symbiotic relationship, in spite of regular conflict. Geography, economy and social realities in the region never made it possible for Rome to separate the two effectively, or to organize a closed frontier that would exclude the nomads from its territory. However, it is clear that the relationship between Rome and the nomads was not static, but fluctuated over the course of time. The very presence or proximity of Roman and Persian forces at different times had its effect on all the component parts of society, including the nomads. We have seen the role of the nomads in the organization of the desert trade.

The evidence of Roman road-construction and, in some periods, active political or military intervention, shows that Rome did attach a certain degree of importance to the security of the trade routes. However, the inadequacy of the evidence precludes a proper evaluation of the volume of trade along the various routes through the centuries and hence its importance to Rome. Thus it is difficult to say whether considerations of trade normally influenced major policy decisions taken by Rome.

References

Adams, R.Mc., 1965. *Land Behind Baghdad, A History of Settlement on the Diyala Plains.* Chicago & London.

As'ad, K. & Gawlikowski, M., 1986/87. *AAS* 36/37 (1986/1987) [1988], 164–171.

Bacon, E.E., 1954. 'Types of Pastoral Nomadism in Central and Southwest Asia', *Southwestern Journal of Anthropology* 10, 44–68.

Campbell, J.K., 1967. *Honour, Family and Patronage: A Study of Institutions and Moral Values in a Greek Mountain Community.* Oxford.

Casson, L., 1989. *The Periplus Maris Erythraei.* Princeton.

Collin Davies, C., 1975. *The Problem of the North-West Frontier 1890–1908.* Cambridge, 1932; revised ed., London, 1975.

Crone, P., 1987. *Meccan Trade and the Rise of Islam.* Princeton.

Curzon, G.N., 1907. *Frontiers.* Oxford.

Duncan-Jones, R., 1974. *The Roman Economy: Quantitative Studies.* Cambridge.
———, 1990. *Structure and Scale in the Roman Economy.* Cambridge.

Fawcett, C.B., 1918. *Frontiers: A Study in Political Geography.* Oxford.

Febvre, L., 1970. *La Terre et l'évolution humaine: Introduction géographique à l'histoire.* Paris, 1922, reissue: 1970.

Garnsey, P. & Whittaker, C.R., 1983. *The Trade and Famine in Classical Antiquity.* Cambridge.

Guichonnet, P. & Raffestin, C., 1974. *Géographie des frontières.* Presses universitaires de France.

Heather, P.J., 1991. *Goths and Romans: 332–489.* Oxford.

Isaac, B., 1990, ²1992. *The Limits of Empire: the Roman Army in the East*. Oxford.

Jones, A.H.M., 1974. *The Roman Economy: Studies in Ancient Economic and Administrative History*, ed. P.A. Brunt. Oxford.

Künow, J., 1980. *Negotiator et Vectura: Händler und Transport im freien Germanien*. Marburg.

Lancaster, W., 1981. *The Rwala Bedouin Today*. Cambridge.

Lancaster, W. & F., 1988. 'Thoughts on the Bedouinisation of Arabia', *Proceedings of the Twenty First Seminar for Arabian Studies, 28–30 July, 1987*. London.

Lattimore, L., 1962. 'Inner Asian Frontiers: Defensive Empires and Conquest Empires', in: *Studies in Frontier History: Collected Papers, 1928–1958* (London), pp. 501–513.

Lewis, N., 1989. *The Documents from the Bar Kokhba Period in the Cave of Letters, Greek Papyri*, ed. by N. Lewis, *Aramaic and Nabatean Signatures and Subscriptions*, ed. by Y. Yadin & J.C. Greenfield. Jerusalem.

Mann, J.C., 1974. 'The Frontiers of the Principate', *Aufstieg und Niedergang der Römischen Welt* ii, 1, 508–33.

Matthews, J., 1989. *The Roman Empire of Ammianus*. London and Baltimore.

McCormick, M., 1990. *Eternal Victory: Triumphal Rulership in Late Antiquity, Byzantium and the Early Medieval West* (Cambridge, 1986, n.e. 1990).

Millar, F., 1966. 'The Emperor, the Senate and the Provinces', *JRS* 56, pp. 156–66.

Musil, A., 1928. *Palmyrena*. New York.

Patai, R., 1951. 'Nomadism: Middle Eastern and Central Asian', *Southwestern Journal of Anthropology* 7, 401–414.

Potts, D.T., 1990. *The Arabian Gulf in Antiquity*, ii, *From Alexander the Great to the Coming of Islam*. Oxford.

Pounds, N.J.G., 1951. 'The origin of the idea of natural frontiers in France', *Annals, Association of American Geographers* 41, 146–57.

——, 1954. 'France et "les limites naturelles" from the seventeenth to twentieth centuries', *ibid.*, 44, 51–62.

——, 1972. *Political Geography*, New York, Second ed.

Prescott, J.R.V., 1987. *Political Frontiers and Boundaries*. London.

Ratzel, F., 1896. 'Die Gesetze des räumlichen Wachstums der Staaten', *Petermanns Mitteilungen* 42, 97–107.

——, 1897. *Politische Geographie*. Munich & Leipzig.

——, 1940. *Erdenmacht und Völkerschicksal, Eine Auswahl aus seinen Werken*, ed. Generalmajor a.D. Prof. Dr. Karl Haushofer, Stuttgart.

Rubin, Z., 1989. in D.H. French & C.S. Lightfoot, *The Eastern Frontier of the Roman Empire* (Oxford, B.A.R. N° 553), 383–420.

Sauvaget, J., 1939. 'Les Ghassanides et Sergiopolis' *Byzantion* 14, 115–130.

Schönberger, H., 1969. 'The Roman Frontier in Germany: an Archaeological Survey', *JRS* 59, 144–97.

Shaw, B.D., 1982. 'Fear and Loathing: The Nomad Menace and Roman Africa' in C.M. Wells (ed.), *Roman Africa: The Vanier Lectures 1980* (Ottawa), 29–50.

Sidebotham, S.E., 1986. *Roman Economic Policy in the Erythra Thalassa, 30 B.C.–A.D. 217*. Leiden.

—— et al., 1989. 'Fieldwork on the Red Sea Coast: The 1987 Season', *JARCE* 26, 127–166.

Starcky, J. & Gawlikowski, M., 1985. *Palmyre.* Paris.

Trousset, P., 1980. 'Signification d'une frontière: nomades et sédentaires dans la zone du limes d'Afrique', in L. Keppie & W. Hanson (eds.), *Roman Frontier Studies 1979* (B.A.R., Oxford), iii, 931–942.

Wheeler, R.E.M., 1951. 'Roman Contact with India, Pakistan and Afghanistan', in F. Grimes, ed., *Aspects of Archaeology in Britain and Beyond, Essays Presented to O.G.S. Crawford.* London. 345–81.

White, K.D., 1984. *Greek and Roman Technology.* Ithaca, NY.

Whittaker, C.R., 1989. *Les frontières de l'empire romain.* Besançon.

Postscript

Jean-Michel Carrié, 'L'ouverture des frontières de l'Empire romain?' in Aline Rousselle (ed.), *Frontières terrestres, frontières célestes dans l'antiquité* (Paris, 1995), 31–53. This paper with its remarkably similar title was written at approximately the same time, but appeared a little later. Not surprisingly, it contains views similar to those expressed in the current article.

Recent excavations have brought to light interesting information about the site of Resafa. It is now clear that there was first-century (Flavian) occupation on the site.[1] This corresponds very well with the fact, known through the discovery of a milestone dating from the seventies of the first century, that the *Strata Diocletiana* represents a reorganization of a road from Damascus and Palmyra to the Euphrates. The author of the excavation report also has interesting observations on the siting of the town: 'The position of Resafa, on an elevated point in the terrain and the accessibility of water, constitute two criteria that are essential for the location of *castella* in the desert. Along the section of the road south of Sura is the site of Resafa particularly favourable for the water supply because of the confluence of several smaller wadis with a major one, south of the town.'[2]

After the publication of this article the revised English version appeared of *Frontiers of the Roman Empire: A Social and Economic Study* (Baltimore and London, 1994) by C.R. Whittaker. It is indispensable for the questions discussed in this paper.

---

[1] M. Konrad, 'Flavische und spätantike Bebauung unter der Basilika B von Resafa-Sergiupolis', *DM* 6 (1992), 313–402, containing a full report on excavations in Basilica B. Historical discussion on pp. 345–50.

[2] *Op. cit.*, 347.

26

MILITARY DIPLOMAS AND
EXTRAORDINARY LEVIES

It is uncertain to what extent units in the Roman army were kept below strength in peace-time. In this paper it is assumed that the Roman army, like regular standing armies at all times, found itself in need of reinforcement when it had to serve as a war-time army. This would entail the transfer of units from other provinces and extraordinary levies to strengthen units which had been kept below strength. There exist literary and epigraphical sources which mention such levies in passing and this suggests that there would be more but for the reticence or indifference of our sources.

Such levies could be held at various stages of a war: they could be held in advance of planned campaigns,[1] but there were also instances of emergency recruitment when the Romans were surprised, when wars did not proceed as planned, or when losses were unexpectedly heavy.[2] For the present discussion it is irrelevant whether service at such times was compulsory or voluntary.[3] It is important, however, to keep in mind that the Roman imperial army was not organized as a militia, but as a professional standing army. Soldiers who joined the army in times of emergency were not discharged after the end of the campaign for which they had been recruited, but after completing the full term of service imposed on every professional soldier.

---

[1] E.g. Tacitus, ann. 13, 7; 35, 4; Agr. 28, 1; Josephus, b. Iud. 2, 18, 9 (499–502); 3, 1, 3 (8); *IGRR* I 824. A key passage which distinguishes between levies in war and peacetime is Dig. 49, 16, 4, 10. Cf. P.A. Brunt, Conscription and Volunteering in the Roman Imperial Army, Scripta Classica Israelica 974, 90–115; J.C. Mann, Legionary Recruitment and Veteran Settlement during the Principate, London 1983, 50.

[2] Emergency recruitment for the suppression of the revolt of Vindex: Suetonius, Nero 44, 1. For emergency recruitment in the civil war, see: Mann, Legionary Recruitment (cf. n. 1) 13; 29 f.; 52 f. In the East in 116–7: *ibid.* 15; 66. On the Danube in 118–9: *ibid.* 15; 40. For special levies held during the First Jewish Revolt and the Bar Kokhba Revolt see below, pp. 263 f.

[3] Brunt, Conscription (cf. n. 1) 92, assumes that conscription was normal and necessary in war-time. Mann, Legionary Recruitment (cf. n. 1) 50 agrees that 'as late as the early third century not all recruits were volunteers', but disagrees with Brunt in assuming that 'the highest proportion of recruits at all periods seem to have been volunteers'.

This is clear from part of the evidence cited above.[4] Peregrine auxiliaries who were recruited as part of a special levy would accordingly serve twenty-five years or more and receive diplomas. In this
paper I shall attempt to show that some diplomas are understood
better if it is assumed that they were issued to soldiers originally
recruited for specific campaigns. At issue, therefore, are the circumstances at the time of recruitment, not the events which preceded
the award of the diplomas. In the following pages diplomas are listed
which may reflect levies connected with historical events that took
place at the presumed time of enlistment, twenty-five years or more
before the diplomas were issued.

First, diplomas are discussed which offer solid evidence of recruitment for a specific campaign. This is considered to be the case when
the recipient, or units listed can be shown to have participated in a
military campaign, or to have been involved in the reinforcement of
a province, shortly after the presumed time of enlistment. Next, cases
are presented which allow of an interpretation along the lines here
suggested, while there is no definite proof. In all instances discussed
we know that the army in the area was reinforced at the time.
Geographical and chronological coincidence, therefore, justify serious consideration of the second group, where we have no definite
proof of a connexion between enlistment and historical events. No
attempt has been made here to collect systematically evidence from
sources other than diplomata of extraordinary levies of auxiliaries.
This might well be profitable. It is hoped, in any event, that this
paper has convincingly shown that not all diplomas represent routine replacement of dismissed soldiers.

Corbulo's campaigns:
   CIL XVI 33; 159; *RMD* 3; *CIL* XVI 35; 42; *RMD* 9.

Tacitus twice mentions levies held for Corbulo's campaign, in 54
and 58.[5] First to be discussed is *CIL* XVI 42 of 98 from Pannonia.

---

[4] There may have been exceptions such as the Palmyrene archers discharged in
Dacia in 120 and 126 (*CIL* XVI 68; *RMD* 17; 27; 28). As suggested by Prof. Mann,
these may have joined the Roman army by special arrangement for Trajan's Dacian
wars, on the understanding that they would not have to serve as long as regular
auxiliary soldiers.
[5] Ann. 13, 7, 1: *Nero ... inventutem proximas per provincias quaesitam supplendis Orientis
legionibus admovere ... iubet.* Mann, Legionary Recruitment (cf. n. 1) 50, notes that

The recipient is *P. Insteius Agrippae f.* from Cyrrhus in Syria, of the Coh. I Aug. Ituraeorum. The nomenclature is significant. The father, Agrippa, can hardly have been named after Augustus' minister who died in 12 B.C. There is clearly a connexion with one of the two members of the Herodian house who bore that name, either Herod Agrippa or Agrippa II, who both ruled Ituraea.[6] The name Insteius is not very common. There was a tribune of the plebs named M. Insteius in 43.[7] However, the name occurs twice in Tacitus' Annals.[8] In 54 the Parthian king Vologaeses sent hostages to the Romans. They were accepted by a centurion Insteius in the name of the governor of Syria. In 58 Corbulo campaigned in Armenia. The commander himself subdued the most important stronghold. Others were captured by a legate, Cornelius Flaccus and by *Insteius Capito castrorum praefectus*.

Returning to P. Insteius Agrippae f. we may now establish a rough chronology. He received his diploma in 98 and was recruited in the early seventies. He will have been born in the fifties. His father may have been born in the twenties. The name Agrippa may derive from Herod Agrippa, born in 10 B.C., king from 37 till his death in 44.[9] The alternative would be Agrippa II who was made tetrarch in 53.[10] Finally it must be noted that the recipient of the diploma was born in Syrian Cyrrhus, a military base in the north of the province, far from Ituraea.[11]

---

quaesitam here suggests voluntary rather than compulsory recruitment. Ann. 13, 35, 4: *et habiti per Galatiam Cappadociamque dilectus.* . . .

[6] The historian Josephus had a son Agrippa: vita 76. A duovir M. Flavius Agrippa is honoured on an inscription at Caesarea: *CIL* III 12082. The first editor, Zangemeister, *ZDPV* 12, 1889, 25, thought the two were identical, but that is unlikely. Note also Flavius Agrippa on the Hadrianic arch at Gerasa (A.D. 130): C.B. Welles apud C.H. Kraeling, Gerasa, City of the Decapolis, New Haven (Conn.) 1938, no. 58.

[7] *PIR*² I 28. I found no other instances in the first century. Cf. M. Insteius mentioned on *CIL* XVI 55 of 107 and M. Insteius Bithynicus, consul in 162 (*CIL* X 522).

[8] Tacitus, ann. 13, 9, 3 and 39, 2.

[9] See E. Schürer, The History of the Jewish People in the Age of Jesus Christ, I, Rev. and ed. by G. Vermes and F. Millar, Edinburgh 1973, 442 f. and n. 1 for the name; 444; 567 for the career.

[10] For Agrippa II see Schürer, History (cf. n. 9) 471–483.

[11] Cyrrhus lay on the main road connecting the Syrian capital Antioch with the place of crossing the Euphrates at Zeugma, cf. R. Dussaud, Topographie historique de la Syrie antique et médiévale, Paris, 1927, 470 f.; Honigmann, *RE* XII 199–204; E. Frézouls, Recherches historiques et archéologiques sur la ville de Cyrrhus, Ann. Arch. de Syrie 4/5, 1954/55, 89–128. In A.D. 18 it was the base of the legio X Fret., cf. Tacitus. ann. 2, 57, 2.

The following curriculum vitae of father and son is suggested: Agrippa, the father, will have served in an Ituraean unit of Agrippa II—hence the name—which was dispatched to reinforce Corbulo's army in Armenia. He served under the command of Insteius Capito, whose gentile name he gave to his son. He may have been based at Cyrrhus where the son was born. The son joined the Roman army when the Ituraean forces had already been organized as regular auxiliary units. It remains to be asked when he was transferred to Pannonia, where he received his diploma in 98. His unit, the Coh. I Aug. Ituraeorum was already in Pannonia in 80 (*CIL* XVI 26), so it may well have been sent from Syria to this province under Vespasian, between 70 and 80. The garrison of Moesia appears to have been reinforced under Vespasian.[12] Now it may be noted that Titus visited Ituraea and other parts of Syria after the siege of Jerusalem in 70.[13] Shortly afterwards two legions returned from Judaea to their bases in Moesia and Pannonia.[14] If P. Insteius served as long as twenty-eight or twenty-nine years he may have been recruited and sent to Pannonia with his unit at this time. This is, of course, an hypothesis.[15]

A connexion with Corbulo's campaign is clearly attested in the case of *CIL* XVI 159 of 88, as noted in an earlier publication.[16] The recipient, *Domitius Domiti f.* from Philadelphia of the Decapolis dropped his semitic name for that of his commander Cn. Domitius Corbulo. The name of the recipient is decisive in this case. Finally, M. Spedius M. f. Corbulo from Hippos may have been the son of one of Corbulo's recruits (*RMD* 9 of 105).

The Civil War, 69:
CIL XVI 38 of 94 from Dalmatia; XVI 39 of 94 from Moesia.

The date and the origin suggest that these were troops recruited in the Civil War. Tacitus mentions *sex milia Dalmatorum recens dilectus*.[17]

---

[12] See A. Mócsy, Pannonia and Upper Moesia, London 1974, 80 f.
[13] Josephus, b. Iud. 7, 5, 1 (96–9).
[14] Josephus, b. Iud. 7, 5, 3 (116–117).
[15] A suggestion made by Dr. Roxan who kindly read a draft of this paper. I am grateful to Dr. Roxan for her advice and comments.
[16] Isaac, *ZPE* 44, 1981, 72 f. See also the discussion in this paper of *ILS* 9168, the epitaph of another soldier from Philadelphia, recruited in 62 by Corbulo.
[17] Tacitus, hist. 3, 50, 2.

This proves that a levy was held at the time. Tacitus also notes that Moesian troops supported Vespasian.[18] *CIL* XVI 38 from Dalmatia contains a special clause concerning peregrina condicio of soldiers in a unit of Roman citizens. Dr. Roxan kindly pointed out to me that this suggests conscription in an emergency, for one would not otherwise expect to find peregrini in a unit of Roman citizens.[19]

Cerealis' Campaign against the Brigantians in Britain, 71–74:
  CIL XVI 43 of 98 from Britain; 164 of 110 from Pannonia Inferior.

Under Cerealis the garrison of Britain was restored to four legions.[20] The auxilia must also have been augmented. Mann and Dobson argue that the recipient of XVI 43 was a Tungrian going home after service in Britain.[21] *CIL* XVI 164 of 110 from Pannonia Inferior was issued to *C. Petillius C.f. Vindex, Batavus*. The man was a decurio who already had the citizenship. The most attractive explanation is that his father served in the army under the command of Cerealis. Since he was a Batavian it is not likely that he helped to suppress the Batavian revolt in 69. He may have joined the army after the revolt when Cerealis was still in Germania Inferior and accompanied him to Britain, but this cannot be proved.[22]

Domitian's Dacian War, 85–88:
  The Dacian diplomas *CIL* XVI 57; 160; 163 of 110 and *CIL* XVI 164 from Pannonia Inferior, also of 110.

It is clear that these are diplomas issued to soldiers who fought in Dacia under Trajan in 102–105, but this does not exclude their participation in Domitian's war in the eighties as well. Their experience

---

[18] Hist. 3, 5, 9.

[19] *CIL* XVI 53 probably derived from the same constitutio, as argued by Nesselhauf, *CIL* XVI p. 50, supported by Zs. Visy, Acta Arch. Hungarica 36, 1984, 224. For emergency recruitment in the civil war, see Mann, Legionary Recruitment (cf. n. 1) 13; 29 f.; 52 f.

[20] P. Salway, Roman Britain, Oxford 1981, 136 f.

[21] J.C. Mann and B. Dobson, Britannia 4, 1973, 202, n. 52. This is a diploma from Britain, which was found on the territory of the Tungri (at Flémalle near Liège). One of the units listed is the ala I Tungrorum.

[22] Cf. A. Birley, Petillius Cerialis and the Conquest of Brigantia, Britannia 4, 1973, 179–190.

in the earlier Dacian war would have made them particularly qualified
for service in that country, since they were familiar with the terrain
and the enemy's manner of fighting. The Coh. I Brittonum which is
listed on the Dacian diplomas *CIL* XVI 160 and 163 of 110 was in
Pannonia in 85 (*CIL* XVI 31).

Trajan's Dacian Wars, 101–102; 105–106:
   The Dacian diplomas dated between 123–129: *RMD* 26–28; 30–
31; *CIL* XVI 75.

At least one unit listed on XVI 75 was undoubtedly in Dacia during
the Trajanic wars: the Coh. I Hisp. Vet., mentioned on the Moesian
pridianum of 105.[23] Probably all the units named in the diploma
had taken part in the Dacian wars and it is sensible that they would
then have formed part of the garrison of the province.

The Jewish War, 66–70:
   RMD 4 and 5 of 91 from Syria; *CIL* XVI, App. 12.

The recipients of RMD 4 and 5 are Thracians. Dr. Roxan notes in
her comments on RMD, 5 (p. 35, n. 5): 'In view of the probable
date of the recruitment of the *gregalis* (c. 66) he may have been part
of a general levy sent to the East under Nero.' Now, in the autumn
of 66 Cestius Gallus, governor of Syria, is reported to have held a
levy in his own province.[24] Serious trouble broke out in Judaea in
the spring of 66.[25] There may be a connexion, but this cannot be
proved. There is, however, no doubt that in 68–9 men were recruited in Egypt as peregrini and transferred to Judaea for service in
the legio X Fretensis.[26]

---

[23] *BMP* 2851, cf. J.F. Gilliam, The Moesian 'Pridianum', in: Hommages à Albert
Grenier, Bruxelles 1962, 747–756.
[24] Josephus, b. Iud. 2, 18, 9 (502): πλεῖστοι δὲ κἀκ τῶν πόλεων ἐπίκουροι συνελέγησαν.
[25] Schürer, History (cf. n. 9) 485–7.
[26] *CIL* XVI, App. 12; *ILS* 9059. Cf. Mann, Legionary Recruitment (cf. n. 1) 53.

Agricola in Britain, 78–84:
CIL XVI 48 of 103; RMD 8 and CIL XVI 51 of 105.

These soldiers began to serve at the time of Agricola's campaign in Britain. For comparison we may refer to Tacitus' account of the mutiny of the Usipi at this time: *cohors Usiporum per Germanias conscripta et in Britanniam transmissa*.[27] It is clear that these soldiers had recently been conscripted and were sent from Germania to Britain for the war. Since we know that men in other provinces were conscripted for the war in Britain at this time, it is very likely that the same is true for soldiers in Britain known to have begun their service in these years.

The Bar Kokhba Revolt, 132–135:
CIL XVI 106 of 156/7 from Syria; 107 of 157 from Dacia.

Legions from Syria participated in the suppression of the revolt.[28] Syrian auxiliaries who began their service at this time may therefore have been conscripted for the same purpose. CIL XVI 106 was found near Kazanlyk in Thrace. The recipient served in the ala I Ulpia Singularium, a unit known to have formed the garrison of Palmyra, c. 150.[29] It is conceivable that the man was recruited in Thrace in 132, transferred to the East for the war in Judaea, stayed with his unit in Palmyra and returned home after his discharge.

The recipient of CIL XVI 107 came from Caesarea—no doubt the Judaean capital is meant—where he must have joined the army c. 132 when the Bar Kokhba revolt broke out. His name, *Barsimso*, probably is Aramaic.[30] This diploma was found in Jupa in Dacia Superior, the province where the unit was stationed in 144 as well.[31]

---

[27] Tacitus, Agr. 28, 1. See also Dio 56, 20 and cf. Salway, Roman Britain (cf. n. 20) 139 ff.

[28] Cf. IGRR III 174; 175. For a list of units known to have been in Judaea at the time, see Schürer, History (cf. n. 9) 547–9, n. 150. See also B. Isaac and A. Oppenheimer, Journal of Jewish Studies 36, 1985, 56 n. 100.

[29] AÉ 1933, 210 and 211. Cf. H.-G. Pflaum, Les carrières procuratoriennes équestres sous le Haut-Empire romain, Paris, 1960, no. 155, p. 367.

[30] BRŠMŠ is attested at Palmyra, CIS III 2,3911. Cf. Βαρσιμος: IGLSyr 1533; perhaps Β[α]<ρ>σάμσο[υ]: IGLSyr 2407; Σαμσαῖος: Gerasa, no. 136. Barsimso could also be a Latinized form of the Jewish name 'Bar Shimshon', 'son of Samson', but the Biblical name Samson is not attested in this period.

[31] CIL XVI 90.

In 100 the unit was based in Moesia Superior.[32] It is possible that Barsimso joined the unit when it served in the East from 132–135 and stayed with it when it moved to Dacia. These suggestions cannot be proved, but it may be noted that levies in Transpadana under Hadrian undoubtedly are to be connected with the Bar Kokhba Revolt.[33]

Lucius Verus' Parthian War, 162–165:
RMD 69 of 186 from Syria-Palaestina.

The legio VI Ferrata from Syria-Palaestina took part in this war.[34] An inscription from Bostra shows that in Arabia legionaries were recruited in 163.[35] It may tentatively be suggested that auxiliaries were recruited in Syria-Palaestina for this war.

---

[32] *CIL* XVI 46.
[33] See *ILS* 1068; *AÉ* 1955, 238 + 1969/70, 633. Cf. J.F. Gilliam, *AJP* 77, 1956, 359 ff. and Mann, Legionary Recruitment (cf. n. 1) 46 f. who also refers to *ILS* 8828.
[34] *PIR²* A 754.
[35] *IGLSyr* 9067.

THE LATE ROMAN ARMY

27

THE ARMY IN THE LATE ROMAN EAST:
THE PERSIAN WARS AND THE DEFENCE
OF THE BYZANTINE PROVINCES

I. *Byzantium and Persia*

In 572 the Turks attacked Persia 'and laid it waste, and sent an embassy to Justin to urge him to join them in their war against the Persians. They asked him to show his friendship to the Turks by joining them in destroying the common enemy. In this way, with the Turks attacking from one direction and the Romans from another, the Persians would be destroyed. Aroused by these hopes, Justin thought that the power of the Persians would easily be overthrown and brought to nothing.'[1]

Menander the Guardsman is in this passage one of the few ancient authors who explicitly states the aim of one of the many wars fought by Rome and Persia. In another fragment of Menander's text we read that Justin 'was confident that if he made war he would destroy Khusro and himself give a king to the Persians. With these unrealistic threats he dismissed Sebokhth [the Persian envoy]'.[2]

It is usually assumed that the successful destruction of Persia and the conquest of large parts of the Roman East by the Muslim armies were at least partly made possible by the long and fierce wars in the sixth and seventh centuries which decisively weakened the two empires. Although this is very likely it is necessarily an impressionistic assumption, for we cannot objectively measure the resources, military and material, that were at the disposal of the two powers in the 630's, as compared with other periods, nor can we form an accurate and reliable impression of the political will in both states at the time of the Islamic conquest. Yet this is one of the important subjects that

---

[1] R.C. Blockley, ed., trans. and comm., *The History of Menander the Guardsman* (Liverpool, 1985), Fr. 13, 5 (p. 146). Cf. H. Turtledove, 'Justin II's Observance of Justinian's Persian Treaty of 562', *Byzantinische Zeitschrift* 76 (1983), 292–301.

[2] Fr. 16, 1 (Blockley, p. 154).

should be discussed in a workshop on States, resources and armies in the eastern Mediterranean from the late sixth century to the rise of the 'Abbasids.

In this paper I shall discuss two questions connected with these problems.

(1) What was the role played by material and military resources in the process of decision-making when Byzantine emperors fought Persia in the sixth and seventh centuries? Were considerations of material gains and losses more important than ideology and glory in defining the aims of policy and warfare? In this connection something will have to be said about the recurring conflicts over payment of Byzantine subsidies to allies and neighbouring peoples.

(2) Conflicting conclusions have been drawn regarding the state of the Byzantine army in the provinces. In previous publications I have argued against the theory that the troops in the frontier districts (*limitanei*) were a peasant militia, maintaining that these were troops functioning as an army in every respect. The question to be considered here is whether there is evidence of a significant reduction in the number and quality of units and men in the frontier districts in the fifth and sixth centuries.[3] Specific issues that should be considered include: (a) Procopius' claim that Justinian disbanded the standing army in the provinces.[4] I shall argue that correlation of various literary sources may clarify to some extent what kind of troops were present in Palestine in the fifth and sixth centuries, though not, perhaps in the seventh. (b) Conclusions based on archaeological exploration to the effect that many military sites in Palaestina III and Arabia were abandoned in the fifth and sixth centuries.

As noted, the passages cited above are unusual in ancient literature in that they explicitly state that a Byzantine emperor went to war with Persia in the hope and expectation of destroying the rival state. Our source, however, Menander the Guardsman, makes it clear that he thought the emperor Justin's threats unrealistic. Contemporary sources report that Justin was unbalanced—he is said to have gone hopelessly mad after receiving the news of the loss of Dara.[5] To

---

[3] B. Isaac, 'The Meaning of *Limes* and *Limitanei* in Ancient Sources', *JRS* 78 (1988), 125–47; *The Limits of Empire: The Roman Army in the East* (1990), 208–13; 287 f.

[4] Procopius, *Secret History* xxiv, 12–14; cf. Isaac, *Limits of Empire*, 210–212.

[5] John of Ephesus, *HE* iii 4; cf. vi 5; Theophylact iii, 11, 3–4.

some extent, however, this madness may be merely an extreme reaction which essentially reflects the spirit of the age. John the Lydian
(sixth century), surely no madman, does not hesitate to say that
Anastasius' greatest deed was the construction of Dara ... 'unless
God by the former's hand had heavily fortified it at the throats of
the Persians, long ago the Persians would have seized the domains
of the Romans inasmuch as these are adjacent to them.'[6]

Even though he was unbalanced, Justin's aggressive policies *vis à
vis* foreign peoples were approved in general, by Corippus, John of
Ephesus, Menander the Guardsman, and Agathias.[7] Historians of this
period tend to think in terms of 'total war'. Justin hoped to destroy
Persia and the Persians were assumed to have similar aims. For instance, Agathias[8] explains that Persian annexation of Lazica (ancient
Colchis, western Georgia of today) would have been dangerous, as
Justinian understood, for the Persians could then sail up the Euxine
with impunity and probe deep into the heart of the Roman Empire.[9]
It is remarkable and significant that Agathias, and perhaps indeed
Justinian, could see the importance of this entire region only in terms
of access and invasion routes. Agathias at least could not conceive of
it as having importance for its own sake.[10] It is true, however, that
it must have been to the advantage of the Roman Empire that
Parthia/Persia had no maritime access to the Mediterranean.

It is significant that the literature of this period reflects attitudes of
far greater hostility towards Persia than is apparent in earlier centuries.

---

[6] John Lydus, *On Powers or The Magistracies of the Roman State*, ed. and trans. Anastasius C. Bandy (Philadelphia, 1983), 47, p. 206.

[7] Corippus, *in Laudem Iustini*, ed. and trans. Averil Cameron (London, 1976), iii
231–402; John of Ephesus, *HE* vi 24; Menander: discussion in Blockley, introduction,
p. 23; see especially fr. 8; 9, 1; note 92; Agathias: Averil Cameron, *Agathias* (Oxford,
1970), 124–130; Similar attitudes: John Lydus, *de Magistratibus*, e.g. 33, p. 184 (Bandy).
Only Theophylact Simocatta, iii 9, condemns Justin which fits in with his general
attitude of enthusiastic approval of a good fight if only it was successful from his
point of view.

[8] *Hist.* ii, 18, 7.

[9] Also: Theophanes, *Chronographia*, p. 291 de Boor = AM 6095 (September 1,
602–Aug. 31, 603): the Persian king Khusro hoped to conquer the Roman empire
by deception ... most of all by inciting unexpected enemies and ravaging Roman
lands.

[10] As a matter of interest: John the Lydian says the reverse (33–4, ed. Bandy,
186–7): '... it is expedient, says Celsus, to attack them by surprise and to initiate
the attack especially through Colchis ... for its rough terrain is inaccessible to the
Persians because they are horse-borne. ...' Celsus was wrong, for the Persians actively campaigned in Lazica (Colchis) in the reign of Justinian and afterwards.

Let me give a few examples. Agathias is remarkable for his extreme
anti-Persian rhetoric.[11] But he is not the only one. Procopius also
shows violent hostility to Khusro.[12] The Persians were considered
perverse, as appears from accusations of incest.[13] They did not bury
properly the dead, and exposed the sick.[14] They were incapable of
understanding or producing genuine philosophy.[15]

An interesting case is that of the recurring accusations of savage
and barbaric punishment inflicted by Persian kings, notably on their
own generals. We read this about Khusro and his generals Nakho-
ragan[16] and Shahin. Of the latter we learn that he was flayed and
his skin made into a bag—'a painful and violent death', as Nicephoros
helpfully explains.[17] Elsewhere, however, we learn that Shahin in fact
remained in service another ten years.[18] Agathias further claims that
Shapur was the first to inflict this form of punishment, namely on
the captive Roman Emperor Valerian, which was '. . . confirmed by
the testimony of several historians. . . .' In fact, none of the earlier
historians mentions this at all.[19] Zosimus mentions only Valerian's
capture.[20] The *Epitome de Caesaribus*, (late fourth–early fifth century)
and Orosius (early fifth century) say Valerian grew old in shameful
captivity: the Parthian king used him as footstool.[21] Two Christian
authors have Valerian flayed *after* his death.[22] A gruesome end for
Valerian would have appealed to Christian authors because Valerian
had been an active persecutor of the Christians. Thus, when Agathias
claims that Valerian was flayed alive, this must be seen as a bogus
horror story, designed to portray the Persian king as particularly cruel

---

[11] *Hist.* ii 22.
[12] *BP* ii, 9, 8–9; cf. the comments by Averil Cameron, *Agathias* (Oxford, 1970),
44; 116.
[13] Agathias ii, 24, 1; 31, 6–9; comments: Cameron, *Agathias*, 92.
[14] Cf. Averil Cameron, 'Agathias on the Sassanians', *Dumbarton Oaks Papers* 23–24
(1969–1970), 78–80 with comments on 90 f.
[15] *Ibid.*, 28–30. King Khusro was interested, but a naive barbarian all the same;
Cf. Cameron, *art. cit.*, 114 f.
[16] Agathias iv, 23, 2.
[17] Nicephoros, *Breviarium*, 7 (Cyril Mango, *The Patriarch Nicephorus: Short History*,
ed., comm. and trans. [Washington, DC, 1990], with comments at p. 177).
[18] Theophanes, *Chron.*, 315 de Boor 315.
[19] *RE* xiii s.v. Licinius (Valerianus), col. 492 for full references.
[20] Zosimus i, 36, 2.
[21] *Epitome de Caesaribus* 32, 6; Orosius, *Adversus Paganos* vii, 22, 4.
[22] Lactantius, *De mortibus persecutorum* v 3–6 (late third–early fourth century); Petrus
Patricius (A.D. 500–565), 13 (*FHG* iv 188).

and barbaric. This is not to deny that generals may have been treated shabbily by their monarchs. That happened in the Roman empire as well.[23]

To sum up this part of my argument, it is clear that authors of the sixth and seventh centuries are fiercely hostile towards Persia, to a degree not encountered in earlier ages. It may at least be presumed that this reflects attitudes widespread at the time. It is likely that this in itself influenced Byzantine policies *vis à vis* Persia.

In this connection it is of some interest that the idea that the two empires should live together in mutual understanding is expressed only in speeches attributed by Byzantine authors to Persian ambassadors.[24] In Byzantium, then, there was a mood of fierce hostility towards Persia. This went together with an ideology which held that the ruler's military successes confirmed his right to rule.[25] As expressed by Procopius: 'war and the royal office are agreed to be the greatest of all things among mankind'.[26] 'The imperial majesty should not only be decorated with arms but also armed with laws, that there may be good government in times both of war and of peace. . . .' Thus the opening phrase of Justinian's *Corpus Iuris Civilis* elucidates the priorities of state.[27] I would argue that this was not a spiritual and political climate in which considerations of the availability of resources played an important role in the process of decision-making about war and peace.

---

[23] In Byzantium: Justinian's treatment of Belisarius and that of Narses by Justin II. In Persia Hormisdas humiliation of his general Vahram caused a civil war (Theophylact iii, 8, 1–3).

[24] Niceph., *Brev.*, 6, ed. Mango, pp. 44, 46: speech of Persian general Shahin. He emphasizes that war between Rome and Persia cannot lead to anything worthwhile for either party. Theophylact i, 15, 3–10; Petrus Patricius, fr. 13, ed. Müller, *FHG* iv 188. Memorandum from the Persian king Kavah to Heraclius in the *Chronicon Paschale*, p. 735 Bonn ed.; cf. N. Oikonimides, 'Correspondence between Heraclius and Kavadh-Siroe in the Paschal Chronicle (628)', *Byzantium* 41 (1971), 269–81.

[25] Michael McCormick, *Eternal Victory: Triumphal Rulership in Late Antiquity, Byzantium and the Early Medieval West* (Cambridge, 1986, 1990).

[26] Procopius, *BP* i, 24, 26. This is a pronouncement made in a speech attributed to the senator Origenes. It is immaterial here whether Procopius expresses his own views or those he attributes to an influential senator. Cf. also the preface to Agathias, *Histories*, preface, 1.

[27] 'Imperatoriam maiestatem non solum armis decoratam, sed etiam legibus oporte esse armatam, ut utrumque tempus et bellorum et pacis recte possit gubernari'. Cf. W.E. Kaegi Jr., *Some Thoughts on Byzantine Military Strategy* (Brookline, MA, 1983), *The Hellenic Studies Lecture*, 3.

Tribute and Subsidies to Foreign Peoples

An issue that comes up again and again in the diplomacy of this period is the payment of subsidies or tribute by Byzantium to neighbouring peoples.[28] These payments were undoubtedly often very costly. However, there are numerous instances when the decision not to pay proved to be far more expensive than the alternative would have been. Furthermore, such a decision was more often inspired by considerations of honour than by financial strictures. This was clearly the case when Julian refused to give subsidies to the Saracens beyond the Tigris, precisely when he needed their support for his Persian campaign in 363.[29] The issue is central in all the works that discuss the policies of Justinian in his last years and those of Justin II.[30] There are two remarkable features in these discussions: firstly the approval of Justin's steadfast refusal to make payments, even though the result was disastrous. 'The present Emperor wishes to be an object of the greatest fear to all'.[31] Justin spoke 'like a king'.[32] Menander considers Justin to have been clever, when he refused to pay subsidies to the Persian allies, the Lakhmids, even though the only tangible result of this refusal was that the territory of the Ghassanids, the Roman allies, was ravaged by the Persian allies while Justin left his federates unprotected.[33] Secondly, there is no concrete consideration anywhere of the actual costs and benefits accruing to the state as a result of the payment or non-payment of such subsidies.

When Byzantine emperors did pay tribute it was usually considered essential that it not be called tribute, but 'an exchange of gifts' or a voluntary non-recurring donation. The very notion that the Byzantine state should pay for services rendered was considered barely tolerable or even intolerable. Payments were part of the fifth-century agreements between Rome and Persia, 'but the kings of the Persians have been sending ambassadors and receiving money for their needs;

---

[28] Discussed by Z. Rubin, 'Diplomacy and War in the Relations Between Byzantium and the Sassanids in the Fifth Century A.D.', in P. Freeman and D. Kennedy (ed.), *The Defence of the Roman and Byzantine East* (BAR, Oxford, 1986), 677–95; Isaac, *Limits of Empire*, 231, 245, 248, 260 f., 264.

[29] Ammianus xxv, 6, 10. Cf. Julian, *Caesars* 329a [Budé ed. ii, where Constantine is being ridiculed because he paid tribute to the Barbarians.

[30] Above, n. 1.

[31] Menander, Fr. 9, 1, (c. 565).

[32] Fr. 12, 7.

[33] Fr. 9, 3.

but it was not as tribute that they received it as many thought'.[34] The refusal of Zeno and Anastasius refusal to pay tribute resulted in the first of a long series of wars.[35] Khusro demanded an annual subsidy from Justinian for guarding the Darial pass (and because the Romans maintained Dara as a fortress city). Khusro emphasized that this was not tribute but payment for services rendered, 'similar to the payments made to Huns and Saracens so that they may guard your land unplundered for all time.' Justinian agreed.[36] In Menander's account of negotiations Roman ambassadors again and again insist on this point.[37]

In the course of the Islamic conquest subsidies and tribute played a decisive role on three occasions. According to Theophanes 'some of the nearby Arabs received a small subsidy from the Emperor for guarding the mouths of the desert. At that time a eunuch came to distribute the soldiers' wages. [In 633] the Arabs came to get their pay, as was customary, but the eunuch drove them away, saying, "The Emperor hardly gives money to his soldiers; much less to you, dogs!" The oppressed Arabs went to their fellow-tribesmen and showed them the route to the land of Gaza, which is the mouth of the desert for Mt. Sinai and is very rich.'[38] In this case Theophanes apparently did not consider the Byzantine attitude and the refusal to pay rational or responsible. The text reads as if at least part of the responsibility for the catastrophe that followed is thus conveniently attributed to an anonymous and arrogant courtier.

Following their decisive victory at the Yarmuk the Muslims took Damascus and campaigned against Egypt. Cyrus, bishop of Alexandria,

---

[34] Joshua the Stylite 8, trans. Wright, 7. 'Even in our days Peruz, the king of the Persians because of the wars that he had with the Kush'naye or Huns, very often received money from the Greeks, not however demanding it as tribute . . .', *ibid.*, 9.

[35] Cf. Rubin, 'Diplomacy and War'; Isaac *Limits of Empire*, 261–2.

[36] Procopius, *BP* ii, 10, 21–4.

[37] Menander, Fr. 6, 1, Blockley, pp. 69, 82 (A.D. 562); Fr. 9, 1, Blockley, pp. 98–102 (c. 565?).

[38] Theophanes, *Chron.*, 335 f. de Boor = AM 6123 (A.D. 631–2). Niceph., 20, ed. Mango, 68, trans., p. 69, has a different version: 'The charge was that he (sc. Sergios *kata Nketan*) had persuaded Herakleios not to allow the Saracens to trade from the Roman country and send out of the Roman State the 30 lbs. of gold which they normally received by way of commercial gain; and for this reason they began to lay waste the Roman land.' Cf. commentary at p. 187. See in general F. MacGraw Donner, *The Early Islamic Conquests* (Princeton, 1981), 115–117; P. Mayerson, 'The First Muslim Attacks on Southern Palestine', *Transactions of the American Philosophical Association* 95 (1964), 155–99.

then made a treaty which promised that Egypt would provide them with 200,000 *denarii* per year.[39] Heraclius intervened and forbade the making of payments, even though Cyrus had assured him that the imperial taxes would not be affected and Heraclius had no means of protecting Egypt. The Muslims attacked and levied tribute. Thus Egypt is said to have been lost because the emperor refused to allow tribute to be paid by provinces which he could not protect anyway.

The emperor apparently did not consider this a catastrophic mistake. In 636/7 the governor of Osrhoene 'came to Iad at Chalcis and arranged to pay 100,000 *nomismata* per year if the Arabs would not cross the Euphrates.'[40] Heraclius again intervened and deposed the governor. In 638–9 'Iad crossed the Euphrates and conquered all of Mesopotamia. Thus another province for which the empire had fought intermittently during half a millennium was lost because the emperor forbade the payment of tribute in order to maintain his honour and dignity. One does not sense that the ancient literature condemns Heraclius. When he died of a repugnant illness this was considered punishment for his incestuous marriage to his niece, not for losing the entire diocese of *Oriens* and Egypt.[41]

Heraclius' Persian Campaigns

I shall now argue that indifference to the fate of the provinces may be detected even in the conduct of the war that was considered Heraclius' greatest triumph, his Persian campaigns in the 620's.[42]

---

[39] Theophanes, 338 de Boor = AM 6126 (A.D. 634–635). Practically the same story is found in Michael the Syrian (ed. and trans. J.-B. Chabot), II, 425, and in other Syriac chronicles. A parallel account is given by Niceph. 23, cf. comm. Mango, 188 f.

[40] Theophanes, 338 de Boor = AM 6128.

[41] Niceph. 27.

[42] The literature is very extensive: G. Ostrogorsky, *Geschichte des Byzantinischen Staates* (Munich, 1940), 54–63; Eng trans. J.M. Hussey, *History of the Byzantine State* (Oxford, 1968, trans. of third ed.), 92–106; A. Pernice, *L'imperatore Eraclio* (Firenze, 1905), 111–179; A.N. Stratos, *Byzantium in the Seventh Century*, i: *602–634* (Eng. trans., Amsterdam, 1968), 135–44, 151–72; 197–234; N. Oikonomides, 'A Chronological Note on the First Persian Campaign of Heraclius (622)', *Byzantine and Modern Greek Studies* 1 (1975), 1–9; see also references in John Haldon, *Byzantium in the Seventh Century* (Cambridge 1990), 41–53. Clive Foss, 'The Persians in Asia Minor and the End of Antiquity', *The English Historical Review* 90 (1975), 721–47 repr. in his *History and Archaeology of Byzantine Asia Minor* (Aldershot, 1990): the archaeological record, especially the numismatic material. For a historiographical study of two of the sources

Following the loss of control over Egypt, all of *Oriens*, and parts of Anatolia between 604 and 620, Heraclius himself took to the field and began a counter offensive. Heraclius constantly acted as supreme commander in the field, which is remarkable. This had been customary in the Early Empire from the second century onward, but was no longer usual from the fourth century onward. As observed by Theophanes,[43] Heraclius found 'that the Roman state had become exhausted. The Avars were devastating Europe and the Persians had trampled on Asia, captured its cities, and destroyed the Roman army in their battles. As he considered these problems, Heraclius was at a loss what could be done. . . .' He took care of essentials first: military organization, training and religion.[44] His subsequent actions are more surprising to me than other modern commentators seem to find them.

Heraclius, like every general since Pompey, took the war as far into Persia as he could. According to an entirely familiar pattern he marched eastwards through Lazica/Colchis, Armenia and into northwest Persia (Persarmenia). He then moved to the southwest, to Mesopotamia, campaigning along the tributaries of the Tigris, the Greater and Lesser Zab and the Diyala, till he reached Ctesiphon. This is a unique achievement, for previous generals campaigned either in the north-east or in Mesopotamia and even so, many got their army in trouble on the way. In fact, Heraclius reached approximately the same farthest points as Mark Antony and Julian together without suffering the fate of either man. This was unquestionably great generalship. It is less clear what Heraclius thought to accomplish in doing so. Our sources relate with relish that he destroyed cities and overturned

---

(Niceph. and Theoph. (Syncellus)), Paul Speck, *Das geteilte Dossier* (Berlin/Bonn, 1988). Further sources: George of Pisidia, who was an important source for Theophanes, ed. and trans. A. Pertusi, *Giorgio di Pisidia: Poemi* (Ettal, 1959), *Expeditio Persica* I. It is clear that Theoph. used at least one other source, a chronicle presumably, since there is duplication in his account, one version giving geographical details that are missing in George of Pisidia. For the Armenian history of Sebêos I have had to depend on the translation by F. Macler, *Histoire d'Héraclius par l'évêque Sebêos* (Paris, 1904).

[43] Theophanes, *Chron.*, 299–300 de Boor = AM 6103 (A.D. 611–12), trans. Turtledove.

[44] George of Pisidia, *Expeditio Persica* i 139–153; ii 22 ff.; 45–8; Theophanes, AM 6113 (621–2), de Boor, 302 f. Military re-organization: J.F. Haldon, *Byzantine Praetorians*. In the religious sphere Heraclius activated the 'effigy of the God-man which hands did not paint'. Cf. Averil Cameron, 'The History of the Image of Edessa: The Telling of a Story', in *Harvard Ukrainian Studies: Okeanos, Essays presented to Ihor Ševčenko*, 7 (1983), 90 f.; *ead. The Sceptic and the Shroud*, Inaugural Lecture, King's College London, 1980. Another such effigy raised Byzantine morale before the battle with Persian troops at Solachon in 586: Theophylact ii, 2, 4–6.

fire temples. The farthest point in the north-east he reached was
Ganzak where he destroyed a major shrine.[45] From there he marched
on, destroying temples, cities and the royal residence at Dastagerd,
till he reached the neighbourhood of Ctesiphon. Having reached this
region, he ravaged it and, like so many Romans before him, withdrew.

This then was highly satisfactory: effective revenge for the Persian
raids in the Roman provinces. Just as the Persians had destroyed
churches and sacked Roman cities, so Heraclius destroyed fire temples,
and ravaged the Persian cities and countryside. In the meantime,
however, Egypt, Palaestina and Syria were occupied by the Persians.
Why did Heraclius not make it his first priority to liberate the occupied provinces? It is possible, of course, to fancy that there was a
sophisticated strategy, unknown to the chroniclers, a plan to strike at
the trunk of Persian power rather than the branches, but that ignores
the simple fact that Heraclius followed the centuries-old, traditional
route and course of action of Roman commanders invading Persia—
or Persian commanders invading the Roman provinces. There is
evidence that Heraclius attempted to bring about the conversion of
the Persians.[46] The emperor, however, did not develop a plan suited
to the special circumstances of the moment: for the first time since
the days of Zenobia of Palmyra, Rome had lost effective control over
much of the Near East.

Not long before, in the 570's Roman armies, following a victory
over Persian troops, had marched to the Caspian and 'ravaged and
pillaged everything in their path, and what they encountered became a victim of destruction.'[47] In 580 Byzantine troops crossed the

---

[45] Theoph. 308 de Boor; Niceph. 12. One of these sanctuaries, where Khusro
stayed before the arrival of Heraclius was Gazacon, cf. Georgius Cedrenus i,
721–2, *PG* 121, 789 f. Gazacon is Ganzak, almost certainly to be identified with
Takht-i-Sulaymn, southeast of Margha, west of Zengan in Media Atropatene. In 31
B.C. Mark Antony besieged but failed to take 'Phraata', presumably the same place.
In 589/90 the Persian general Bahram Chobin tried in vain to lure the Roman
commander Romanus from Albania into Persarmenia by moving to 'Canzacon',
Theophylact iii, 7, 2. For the site, A. Oppenheimer, *Babylonia Judaica in the Talmudic
Period* (Wiesbaden, 1983), 120–126.

[46] C. Mango, 'Deux études sur Byzance et la Perse Sassanide, II: Héraclius,
Sahrvaraz et la vraie croix', *Traveaux et Mémoires* 9 (1985), 105–118. Mango points
out (p. 111) the puzzling fact that the occupied Byzantine provinces were not restored until July 629, a year after the end of the war, even though the Persian
general, Sahrvaraz did, in fact, collaborate with Heraclius.

[47] Theophylact iii, 15, 1, trans. of Michael and Mary Whitby, *The History of
Theophylact Simocatta* (Oxford, 1986).

Tigris to ravage the interior of Media and they 'pillaged the fertile and most fruitful areas of the Persians; after spending the whole of the summer season in the slaughter of Persians, they ravaged Media, and wrought extensive destruction.'[48] Although the geography of these campaigns is confused it is clear that Heraclius operated in both these regions, marched again into the Persian heartland and caused as much destruction as he could. The apparently obvious conclusion is that Heraclius found it more important to attack Persia and cause havoc there than to put his own house in order. The successes of Heraclius tend to obscure what his priorities were. I would not want to suggest that the Persian strategy was more sophisticated than that of the Byzantine commanders. Both powers operated at the same conceptual level, if we can trust the sources which are all Byzantine. What they had in common was that they did not distinguish between military targets, the destruction of which would help to win the war, and civilian targets, which should have been of secondary interest to any commander aiming at disarming the enemy.

George of Pisidia makes a comparison between Heraclius and Scipio Africanus.[49] Three colleagues have independently suggested to me that this proves the former's strategic aims. The point clearly seems an attractive one and has rather important implications, so it must be considered. In fact, all we have here is an allusion to the most famous Republican victor, the saviour of the Roman state, in a panegyric. If this is cited as evidence of a planned strategy, it can only reinforce the impression that ancient sources fail to produce a clear sense of what we call rational strategic thinking. Indeed, the work of George of Pisidia does not contain any concrete information about the movements of the Byzantine army. Heraclius, moreover is not compared only with Scipio, for elsewhere in this author's work the emperor is compared with Moses,[50] obviously without any thought of strategy, and reference is made to Xerxes and the Spartans.[51] The author presumably had read Herodotus and Polybius or Livy, but there is no indication that he knew much about military affairs. Furthermore: the parallel shows the opposite of what modern scholars want to read in it, for Scipio first expelled the Carthaginians

---

[48] Theophylact iii, 17, 4.
[49] George of Pisidia, *Heraclias* i 97–99, ed. Pertusi, p. 244, comm. at p. 266.
[50] *Expeditio Persica* i 135; iii, 415, 421.
[51] *Expeditio Persica* ii 303 ff.

from Spain and only then attacked them in Africa, while Heraclius attacked the Persian homeland bypassing the occupied provinces.[52] The invocation of the name of Scipio is of the same order as the eternal desire of emperors fighting in the East to emulate Alexander.[53]

It would, of course, be interesting to know what Heraclius may have known about previous wars with Persia. Elsewhere I have argued that the information ancient generals had about the expeditions of their predecessors was very limited and was not conceptually different from the accounts we ourselves read in the ancient literature.[54] It may be useful to cite an additional example in support of this thesis: Libanius considers it worth explaining that Julian prevailed upon his officers at staff meetings in Mesopotamia by producing 'books of generals of bygone days' and reading from their accounts. Thus he persuaded them not to march through the desert by citing the example of Crassus.[55] Julian also knew about the existence of a canal linking the Euphrates with the Tigris (the Naarmalcha) from an unknown ancient source, but it is clear that his knowledge was restricted to the mere fact of the existence of such a waterway.[56] All that an emperor fighting in Mesopotamia had at his disposal was the ancient literature in a better state of preservation than we have it. There were no military archives in Rome or Constantinople and we must avoid foisting modern military concepts on ancient warfare.

It remains to be asked what in fact Heraclius, and so many of his predecessors had in mind. Hans Delbrück was the first to make the useful distinction between a strategy of annihilation and one of attrition: the one aiming at disarming the enemy, and the other at

---

[52] It is interesting to note that P. Cornelius Scipio Africanus Maior was modelling himself either on Alexander or on Cyrus and, like Caesar later, was 'refusing' the title of King: Elisabeth Rawson, 'Caesar's Heritage: Hellenistic Kings and their Roman Equals', *JRS* 65 (1975), 154.

[53] Trajan: Dio lxviii, 29, 1; Julian: *Caesars* 333A. Alexander appears also in George of Pisidia, *Heraclias* i, 113–116; *Expeditio Persica* iii 48 f.

[54] *Limits of Empire*, 404–6.

[55] Libanius, *Or.* xviii 233, referring probably to Plutarch, *Crassus* 20–31. George of Pisidia, too, is familiar with the lives of Plutarch (*Heraclias* i 110 ff).

[56] Libanius, *ibid.*, 245 says Julian knew about the channel from books and made enquiries from captives, the usual method of gathering information; cf. Ammianus xxiv 6,1; Zosimus iii 24 says local people attributed one branch of this waterway to Trajan. Cf. comments by F. Paschoud, *Zosime, Histoire Nouvelle*, vol. ii (Paris, 1979), 167–73; J. Matthews, *The Roman Empire of Ammianus* (London, 1989), 149–55. Foerster assumes that Julian knew about the canal from Herodotus i 193, rather than Polybius v 51. I would consider it more likely that he had read a work written in the Roman period, such as Pliny *NH* v 90 or Arrian's *lost History of Parthia*.

exhausting him, or weakening his will to resist. It is not clear that Byzantine commanders made this distinction and formulated a well-defined plan when they set out to cause economic damage to the enemy. The impression is that any form of destruction of enemy resources, whether military or civilian was felt to be a good thing. The ultimate aim of such campaigns is rarely described explicitly, apart from the acquisition of glory. When it is, the destruction of the enemy state is clearly hoped for. Thus Libanius envisioned in 363 that following Julians campaign the Persian empire would lie in ruins and its territory be administered by Roman governors.[57] It is a mere assumption frequently asserted by modern authors that emperors marching to Ctesiphon only hoped to change the balance of power.

The concomitant of ravaging enemy territory is the acquisition of booty, which is not mentioned very often in ancient literature in spite of its importance.[58] The work of Theophylact, however, is an exception because it fairly frequently refers to the capture of booty and its division.[59]

To sum up this part of my paper:

(1) The actions of Heraclius in his wars with Persia are a vivid illustration of what I have argued elsewhere: that the defence of the provinces was not a matter of high priority in the formulation of imperial policy, even at times of great danger. Honour, the majesty of empire, and religion came first. It was more important to humiliate the enemy than to disarm him.

(2) The acquisition and destruction of resources were indeed of central importance in ancient diplomatic relations and warfare. However, these were means of enhancing the dignity of empire and humiliating the enemy, rather than instruments of empire in their own right. If we can trust our sources we must conclude that material resources were first of all of symbolic importance and, to a far lesser degree, a commodity to be husbanded as a means of control and political power. If these conclusions are correct they may help

---

[57] Libanius, *Or.* xviii 1.

[58] Isaac, *Limits of Empire*, 380–2.

[59] Theophylact i, 14, 1; note that in i, 14, 10 the word 'glory' is used as a synonym for booty; cf. iii, 14, 10: 'glorious booty'. Particularly interesting is ii, 6, 10–11, the only parallel I know, to Titus' victory parade described in Josephus, *BJ* vii, 1, 3 (14 f.). Note also Theophylact iii, 6, 10–14; 16; vi, 7, 6–8; 8, 1–3: a conflict about the division of booty; vi, 11, 3; 21 etc.

to explain why none of the wars between Byzantium and Persia were decisive in any modern sense.

II. *The Byzantine Army in Palestine*

The first confrontation between a Muslim army and the Byzantine empire took place in southern Palestine. It would therefore be interesting to know more about the Byzantine troops in that area. The nature of the armed forces in the eastern provinces, however, is also of more general interest. It so happens that there are a number of literary sources providing information about army units in Palestine which is unavailable for other provinces. I shall attempt to show that correlation of these sources gives more information about this part of the Byzantine army than we thought we had. It cannot be shown that this is immediately relevant for the seventh century, but even some clarification for the sixth may be of value.

This part of the paper considers a subject related to the issues discussed [in this volume] by Michael Whitby, but there are significant differences. When Whitby argues that he does not detect any significant decline in the overall size of armies in the late sixth century,[60] his numbers derive from information provided by literary evidence and focuses on forces on campaign and on the battlefield. In the following part of this paper the peace-time garrison in one province only is considered and the evidence derives from a combination of inscriptions, papyri, and archeological material. The literary sources have the advantage that they provide numbers, but we cannot be certain that their figures are accurate. The material from southern Palestine discussed here does not offer exact numbers of forces on the battlefield but, if interpreted correctly, provides fairly reliable information on the standing army in times of peace. Neither Whitby, nor I have found concrete information about the army in the seventh century.

---

[60] Whitby, 'Recruitment in Roman Armies...', in Averil Cameron (ed.), *The Byzantine and Early Islamic Near East*, iii, *States, Resources and Armies* (Princeton, 1995), chapter 2, 61–124.

Literary Sources

(a) Eusebius' *Onomasticon* of Biblical place-names, lists a number of places that were garrisoned. We cannot know whether this is a full list, but it is one based on local and up-to-date information for the early fourth century.

(b) The *Notitia Dignitatum Orientis*. The lists for Palaestina and Arabia may be taken to represent the army organization of the late fourth century.

(c) *The Beer Sheva Edicts*. Early this century a group of inscriptions was found in Beer Sheva, representing fragments of at least one, probably of several imperial edicts. The date is uncertain and could be anything from the early fourth century to the reign of Anastasius. van Berchem (below) has argued that they were issued before 443. There are five fragments, one of them (No. 4) consisting of three pieces which fit together:

> (1) F.-M. Abel, *RB* n.s. 6 (1909), 88–104, with discussion and comments.
> (2) Ch. Clermont-Ganneau, *RB* n.s. 3 (1906), 412–32 = *Recueil d'archéologie orientale* 7 (1906), 257–84: publication with extensive commentary.
> (3) H. Vincent, *RB* 12 (1903), 275–7; Ch. Clermont-Ganneau, *Recueil d'archéologie orientale* 5 (1903), 129–147: discussion comments.
> (4) F.-M. Abel, *RB* 12 (1903), 425–9 (fr. 4b); R. Savignac, *RB* n.s. 1 (1904), 84–7 (fr. 4a); Clermont-Ganneau, *RB* n.s. 3 (1906), 87–91 (frgs. 4 a, b, c, with brief discussion).
> (5) F.-M. Abel, *RB* 29 (1920), 123–4; 260–65; *SEG* viii 282 with further references.

The text of nos. 1–4, but not that of no. 5, is given with brief comments in A. Alt, *Die griechischen Inschriften der Palaestina Tertia westlich der 'Araba* (Berlin & Leipzig, 1921), 4–13.[61]

The nature of these texts has been discussed by van Berchem.[62] They are lists of place-names, followed by amounts to be paid to the *dux Palaestinae* and his office. Van Berchem has shown, and there is no need to repeat his arguments, that these sums do not represent the *annona militaris* paid by the civilian population of the province for

---

[61] Recent discussions usually refer to Alt with the result that fragment no. 5 is overlooked and that many of Clermont-Ganneau's valuable remarks are ignored and so are the lucid conclusions of van Berchem.

[62] D. van Berchem, *L'armée de Dioclétien et la réforme constantinienne* (Paris, 1952), 33–36.

the benefit of the troops, but, on the contrary, part of the *annona* paid by the soldiers of the provincial army to the duke and his office. In the mid-fifth century it became a legal requirement for the *limitanei* to make a contribution to the duke and his office of the *annona* which they received (see below). Before this period it apparently was common practice, though considered unfair and illegal.[63] This, then was a tax imposed on the 'most loyal *limitanei*' mentioned at the beginning of fr. no. 1. Thus the place-names listed on the inscriptions represent the bases of military units rather than civilian settlements.[64] It is therefore legitimate—and will prove to be useful—to compare these lists with the military sites mentioned in Eusebius' *Onomasticon* and the *Notitia*.

Van Berchem pointed out that the contribution made by the *limitanei* to the duke and his office was fixed in 443 at one twelfth of the *annona* which the soldiers received.[65] At the same time it was stipulated that the Saracen allies and other tribes were exempt from such payments. Since one of the Beer Sheva inscriptions mentions the tribal chiefs in the Constantinian imperial domain among the contributors, it is not likely that this particular text is of a date later than 443.[66]

(d) The papyri discovered at Nessana: C. Kraemer, *Excavations at Nessana*, iii, *Non-Literary Papyri* (Princeton, 1958). The papyri, most of which date to the sixth century, are referred to as P.Colt. Of these

---

[63] The reality before 443 is reflected in *C.Th.* vii, 4, 28–9; cf. *CJ* xii, 38, 12. It is clear also from the *SHA*, *Pescennius Niger* iii 6–8. It does not matter here that the information about Niger in this passage is probably invented. The interest of the text for us is that, when the author wrote his work in the late fourth century, it was customary for for *tribuni* to accept donations from soldiers and to make deductions (*stellaturae*) from the soldiers rations. Similarly: *SHA*, *Severus Alexander* xv 5: 'annonam militum diligenter inspexit. tribunos, qui per stellaturas militibus aliquid tulissent, capitali poena adfecit'. Severus Alexander may have done nothing of the sort, but the author did not invent the abuses of power which he describes.

[64] As observed by van Berchem, *l'Armée*, 34, in one entry, Zoar, distinction is made between the contribution to be made by the soldiers at Zoar and *a(po) koin(ou) Zoor(on) ton suntel(eston)*. It is possible that the latter represent the heirs of *limitanei* with local property.

[65] Theodosius, *Nov.* xxiiii 2 of Sept. 12, A.D. 443 (*CJ* i, 46, 4, 2).

[66] Related texts, almost certainly of later date, are the edicts of Anastasius, found in Cyrenaica and on fragments in Arabia: for the text from Cyrenaica, W.H. Waddington, *IGLS* iii (Paris, 1870), no. 1906; G. Oliverio, *Il decreto di Anastasio I su l'ordinamente politico-militare della Cirenaica* (Bergamo, 1936). One of the clauses stipulates that the duke and his office will receive one twelfth of the *annona militaris* collected for the troops. For the fragments from Arabia, M. Sartre, *IGLS* xiii, i, (Bostra) no. 9046 with comments on pp. 116 f. For the Constantinian domain, cf. below.

the most relevant is P.Colt 39.[67] This document contains a fragmentary double list of villages in the northern Negev with two sums of money set against each name, the second being a fixed rate of the first. Lionel Casson has shown that this list must represent military organization since: (1) Seven out of nine places are known from other sources to have had garrisons. (2) The locations are in two separate provinces: Palaestina I and III. (3) The sites named are of entirely disparate status: some of them being small villages, others big ones and one of them, Elusa, perhaps a provincial capital. (4) As will be noted again below, the figures given for each locality roughly correspond to the size of the garrison where this is known from other sources. It is less clear what precisely is represented by the figures, since the headings of the two lists are missing.

A comparison of some of the elements in the various lists produces a number of interesting conclusions. Two sites are *not* mentioned in Eusebius and in the *Notitia*, but are present on the Beer Sheva inscriptions and in P.Colt 39: Mampsis[68] and Elusa. That is to say, these are absent in the fourth century lists and present in those of the fifth–sixth century. Three others are mentioned only in P.Colt 39: Eboda (Avdat), Nessana and Sobila.[69] One important site is mentioned only in the Beer Sheva texts and in Ptolemy: Adroa (Udruḥ) in southern Jordan. It is clear then that the Negev towns which prospered in the Byzantine period, particularly in the fifth and sixth centuries, are not mentioned as army sites in the lists dating from the fourth century, but they do appear in the later ones. In the case of Avdat and Nessana we know from the archaeological material and the other Nessana papyri that a garrison was located there in this period. It seems legitimate to conclude that these places

---

[67] For this document, see L. Casson, 'The Administration of Byzantine and Early Arab Palestine', *Aegyptus* 32 (1952), 54–60 and the comments in Kraemer, *Nessana*, pp. 119–25.

[68] Mampsis is mentioned in Eusebius, *Onomasticon* 8, 8, but not as a place with a garrison. A soldier of the *cohors I Augusta Thracum* was buried there, probably early in the second century: A. Negev, *IEJ* 17 (1967), 46–55; J.C. Mann, *IEJ* 19 (1969), 211–14; cf. M. Speidel, *ANRW* ii, 8, 710. Recent publications which I could not take into account at the time of writing: A. Lewin, *Studi sulla città imperiale nell' oriente tardo antico* (Rome, 1991); Y. Tsafrir, L. Di Segni, J. Green, *Tabula Imperii Romani: Judaea/Palaestina* (Jerusalem, 1994).

[69] Sobila occurs on the Madaba Map in the area of the 'Salton Gerariticon' (see below, note on Birsama). It has tentatively been identified with Kh. Zubala, at Grid Ref. 126091, very roughly half-way between Gaza and Carmel. It is otherwise unknown.

received garrisons in the period when they became prosperous towns.

The case of Adroa (Udruḥ) is interesting. This is a legionary base in southern Jordan of roughly the same size as the other legionary base in those parts, al-Lajjun.[70] Udruh was certainly occupied into the sixth century, but it is not clear when it was organized as a legionary base. In the absence of decisive archaeological information it may at least be suggested that this happened after the redaction of the *Notitia* list (late fourth century) and before the publication of Beer Sheva fr. no. 2 (first half of the fifth century?). If true, this contradicts the theory that the military presence in Third Palestine was characterized by a culmination in the early fourth century and a straightforward, gradual reduction during the next three centuries.[71] What can be said with certainty at this stage, is that al-Lajjun was abandoned in the sixth century, and the legionary base at Aela before the Islamic conquest. Some places—Birosaba (Beer Sheva),[72] Birsama,[73] Zoar,[74] Moleatha (Malaatha, Malhatha)[75]—occur consistently

---

[70] For Udruh: D.L. Kennedy & D.N. Riley, *Rome's Desert Frontier from the Air* (London, 1990), 131–33; D. Kennedy, *Journal of Roman Archaeology* 5 (1992), 'The Roman Frontier in Arabia (Jordanian Sector), 473–89, esp. 480–2'. S. Thomas Parker, the excavator of al-Lajjun, has calculated that this base could hold between 1000 and 1,500 men.

[71] See the conclusions reached by S. Thomas Parker, *Romans and Saracens: A History of the Arabian Frontier* (Winona Lake, Indiana, 1986); *id.* (ed.), *The Roman Frontier in Central Jordan: Interim Report on the Limes Arabicus Project 1980–1985* (BAR, Oxford, 1987). Cf. the cautionary remarks by David Kennedy, 'The Roman Frontier in Arabia (Jordanian Sector)', *Journal of Roman Archaeology* 5 (1992), 473–89 esp. 478–85.

[72] Eusebius, *On.* 50, 1–2; *Not. Dig. Or.* xxxiv 18: *Equites Dalmatae Illyriciani.* It is not mentioned on the Beer Sheva inscriptions, but it was the site where they were found, cf. Abel, *RB* 12 (1903), 425, for a sketch map; also: R. Savignac, *RB* NS 1 (1904), 84–85. It is mentioned as Birosaba on P.Colt 39. I share the doubts of the excavator that the building on Tel Sheva represents the Byzantine military post, V. Fritz, 'The Roman Fortress' in Y. Aharoni (ed.), *Beer Sheba I: Excavations at Tel Beer-Sheba, 1969–1971 Seasons* (Tel Aviv, 1973), 83–9; cf. Kennedy & Riley, *Rome's Desert Frontier*, 162 f. The Byzantine inscriptions were found c. 5 km to the west in a field of ruins destroyed by modern building early this century. Little is known about Byzantine Beer Sheva, archaeologically, but it has produced many inscriptions and lay on an important crossroads.

[73] *Not. Dig. Or.* xxxiv 22: *Equites Thamudeni Illyriciani; CTh.* vii, 4, 30 of A.D. 409, Mart. 23: 'Sed ducianum officium sub Versamini et Moenoeni castri nomine salutaria st[a]tuta conatur evertere.' P.Colt 39: Birsamis. For the identification of the sites listed in the *Notitia* F.-M. Abel, *Géographie de la Palestine* ii 180–4, and references, below. For Birsama a tentative identification is Kh. el-Far, now H. Beer Shema, G.R. 1059.0741. On this site a Byzantine church has been excavated with splendid inscribed mosaics: D. Gazit & S. Lander, 'St. Stephan's Church at Beer-Shema, Northern Negev', *Qadmoniot* 25 (1992), 33–39 (preliminary and partial publication). One of these mentions 'Gerara'. This is visible only on a photograph published by these authors in the on-board magazine of El Al: S. Lander & D. Gazit, 'The Lost Church of St. Stephen', *Israelal* 46/November–December (1992), 9–16, photograph on

in the various lists. Apart from Beer Sheva, these places were less important settlements. They were small or medium-sized villages and, perhaps apart from Birsama, significant road-stations. The *duke* had offices at Birsama and at Menois, mentioned in a law of 409. The latter place is not mentioned in the later documents.[76] Finally it should be noted that Chermula, Menois and Birsama were not in the Negev proper, but in the southern part of First Palestine. Chermula (Carmel) was in an area which was settled by Jews.[77]

There are then five or six military posts in the Negev and southern Palaestina I, attested in both the fourth century and the sixth.[78] Furthermore, in the north-eastern and central Negev there are four small road-forts that cannot be identified with any site mentioned in ancient texts: Mezad Thamar,[79] Ein Boqeq,[80] Upper Zohar,[81] and

---

p. 14. 'Gerar' is the ancient name of the region referred to by Eusebius, *On.* 60, 7, and by the Madaba Map as *Gerara, Geraritikon Salton*. Georgius Cyprius, *Descriptio Orbis Romani* (ed. H. Gelzer, 1890), 1027, has an entry *Salton Geraritikos*, or *Barsamon* under the heading *Palaestina I*. It should be noted that this region, presumabaly an imperial domain, was in First Palestine, north of Beer Sheva. Cf. Abel, *Géographie*, ii, 173; 443. Another site mentioned in P.Colt 39, Sobila, was in the same region.

[74] Zoar, south-east of the Dead Sea, is mentioned regularly in the Babatha archive (late first–early second centuries) as a village in the district of Petra. There is no mention of a military presence: N. Lewis (ed.), *The Documents of the Bar Kokhba Period in the Cave of Letters: Greek Papyri* ed. by N. Lewis (Jerusalem, 1989). Eusebius, *On.* 42, 1 (garrison); *Not.* xxxiv 26: *Equites sagittarii indigenae.* Beer Sheva fr. no. 1. P.Colt 39 does not mention any place so far east.

[75] Malaatha is mentioned as a tower which served as a refuge to Agrippa I by Josephus, *Ant.* xviii, 6, 2 (147); it is listed by Ptolemy and mentioned by Eusebius, *On.* 14, 3; 88, 4; 108, 3, as a reference point, which reflects its position on a cross-roads. He does not mention a garrison. *Not.* xxxiv 45: *Cohors Prima Flavia.* Nessana, P.Colt 39: Maalatha.

[76] Menois: Madaba Map; Eusebius, *On.* 130, 7 (*polichne*); *Not.* xxxiv 19: *Equites Promoti Illyriciani*; '*Moenoenum Castrum*' in *CTh* (above). To be identified with Kh. Ma'in, NE of Raphia, G.R. 0930.0820, M. Avi-Yonah, *Gazetteer of Roman Palestine* (Jerusalem, 1976), 78, s.v. Maon II. Civil settlement near modern Nirim with remains of synagogue.

[77] Eusebius, *On.* 92, 20 mentions the place as a reference point; 172, 20–22 as a large village with a garrison; cf. also 118, 6. *Not.* xxxiv 20: *equites scutarii Illyriciani*; P.Colt 39: Chermoula.

[78] Beer Sheva, Birsama, Chermula, Elusa, Malhatha. There is no written source attesting a military presence at Eboda (Avdat) in the fourth century, but the military camp of Avdat I antedates the sixth-century citadel and looks like a fourth-century structure.

[79] See references in Isaac, *Limits of Empire*, 193–5. I am not convinced by the tentative identification of Mezad Thamar with 'Thamara' mentioned by Eusebius, *On.* 8, 8. The excavations by M. Gichon have produced evidence of occupation from the end of the third century to the late sixth or early seventh century.

[80] Isaac, *Limits of Empire*, 191. Excavated by M. Gichon, occupied from the second half of the fourth century until the seventh.

[81] R.P. Harper, 'Upper Zohar: A Preliminary Excavation Report' in Freeman &

Ḥorvat Ma'agorah.[82] All four appear to have been occupied throughout the period under discussion. Finally, one small fort, Yotvetah
(Ad Dianam), in the southern Negev, has produced a tetrarchic inscription which mentions an '*alam Costia*', perhaps '*Co(n)s(tan)tia*' or
'*Co(n)s(tan)tia(na)*'.[83] It was abandoned before the end of the fourth
century and that may be the reason why it does not occur in any of
the texts discussed here.

The amounts of the assessments recorded in the Beer Sheva inscriptions and the Nessana papyri correspond roughly to the expected
size of the units listed in these documents, as tentatively suggested by
Kraemer. 'But one may note that, whatever the reason, Chermula
(Carmel, south of Hebron) is here the outstanding town in the area,
that Nessana stood high in the rating and Elusa astonishingly low.'[84]
If we think in terms of the importance of these places as settlements
that is astonishing, but not if we consider the size of the units based
there: At Chermula, *Equites scutarii Illyriciani*, at Nessana a substantial
unit of native cavalry, and at Elusa an *agraria statio*.[85] This leads to
the next question, namely why some settlements had bigger garrisons than others. Why, for instance, did Nessana have a substantial
unit of native cavalry and Elusa a mere *agraria statio*, while the former
was a village in the territory of the latter? A likely explanation is the
location of these places in the road-network. Nessana was the last
Negev settlement on the road into Sinai and Oboda (Avdat) the

---

Kennedy (ed.), *The Defence of the Roman and Byzantine East* (1986), 329–36; also: Isaac,
Limits of Empire, 191–3; Kennedy & Riley, 202 f. It may be contemporary with Ein
Boqeq, but no material has been found that can be securely dated before the fifth
century. There is evidence of Justinianic refurbishment and subsequent occupation.

[82] R. Cohen, *Archaeological Survey of Israel: Map of Sede Boqer-West* (Jerusalem, 1985),
pp. 66–8 (Heb.), 27* (Eng.): with brief remarks about unpublished excavations on
the site. It is a square building with four corner towers, of the same type as Ein
Boqeq and the others, built on earlier (Iron Age, Nabataean) remains. It lies on the
road Avdat-Ḥaluza (Elusa)-Gaza. I would describe it as a fortified road-station in
the desert. It measures 12 × 12 m, towers 4 × 4 m.

[83] *Ibid.*, 188–191. Excavated by Z. Meshel, 'A Fort at Yotvata from the Time of
Diocletian', *IEJ* 39 (1989), 228–238 For the inscription: I. Roll, 'A Latin Imperial
Inscription from the Time of Diocletian Found at Yotvata', *IEJ* 39 (1989), 239–260.
I do not accept the editor's interpretation of the inscription as argued in that paper.
The identification with Ad Dianam from the Peutinger Table seems certain and
rests on the similarity to the Arabic name of the site, Ghadiyan.

[84] Kraemer, *Nessana*, 124. The figures given there are as follows: Chermoula 2337,
Birsamis 1899, Nessana, 1414, Mampsis 1375, Eboda 1356, Birosaba 1153, Sobila
1031, Elusa 792, Malaatha 524.

[85] For Chermula the information derives from the *Notitia*, cited above. The *agraria
statio* at Elusa is mentioned on the Beer Sheva fragment No. 1.

southernmost place in the Negev on the Petra-Gaza road. Another road branched off from there into Sinai. The important town of Elusa also lay on a crossroads, but well to the north and farther from the desert.

Similar factors may have determined the figures on Beer Sheva, fragment No. 2, which contains entries further to the east, in the Aravah and in modern Jordan. To give just one example: by far the highest figure, 65 *nomismata* is assigned to Adroa (Udruḥ), which was a legionary base and by far the biggest unit on this list.[86]

To conclude this part of my paper: a substantial number of military sites in the northern Negev, attested in the fourth were occupied into the sixth or longer. Settlements which prospered in the fifth and sixth century probably received a garrison in that period. The evidence which I have discussed, and the current state of archaeological research, cannot confirm or deny the possibility that there was a reduction of forces at some stage. It is quite clear, however, that there was no full withdrawal and there is, so far, no positive evidence of withdrawal in this region. Theophanes' entry for 631–2 (633) shows that there were sufficient local forces for the vicarius Theodorus 'to gather all the soldiers of the guardposts of the desert' and to repulse a Muslim attack at Mothous (Mu'ta).[87] It should also be emphasized that all the visible structures are very small by the standards of the Early Empire and quite modest when compared with the bigger but still modest structures in Jordan.[88] Whatever the number of occupied sites in the desert areas of Third Palestine, the total number of troops was not large, even when there were two

---

[86] The Beer Sheva fragments contain several references to territories. No. 2 mentions Sobaeia in the territory of Arid(ela); No. 3 mentions the territory of the *Mobenoi*, i.e. Moab, No. 4 the *koinon* of *archiphyloi* of the 'Constantinian *salton*' (cf. above, n. 66), the territories of Arindela and Petra (for the Constant(in)ian domain cf. Georgius of Cyprus, *Descriptio*, ed. Gelzer, 1026). It should be noted that most commentators misinterpret *horion* in these inscriptions as 'boundary'. In the Nessana papyri reference is frequently made to 'Nessana village in the territory of Elusa'.

[87] Theoph., *Chron.* 335 de Boor = AM 6123 (A.D. 631–2).

[88] Mezad Thamar: 38 × 38 m (0.14 ha); Ein Boqeq: 20 × 20 (0.040 ha); Upper Zohar (0.034 ha); Yotvetah (Ad Dianam): 34.5 × 34.8 (0.12 ha); Nessana: 35 × 85 (0.30 ha); Avdat II: 60 × 40 (0.24 ha); the earlier fort at Avdat, which looks tetrarchic, measures 100 × 100 (1 ha) like Daajaniya in southern Jordan; the fourth-century legionary base at al-Lajjun measures 240 × 190 (4.6 ha; that at Udruḥ: 246 × 207 × 248 × 177 m (4.7 ha). Compare this with the full size second century legionary base at Bostra: c. 463 × 363 m (16.8 ha/41.5 acres). Most of these measurements are taken from Kennedy & Riley, *op. cit.*

legions each perhaps 1,500 a 2,000 men.[89] So far these conclusions seem to correspond rather well with Whitby's conclusions from quite different material, although these do not take us beyond the reign of Maurice. It is an interesting question why the Byzantine emperors in general seem to have had such problems in maintaining the size of the army. Large areas of the Near East, and certainly all of Palestine, were more densely populated in the Byzantine period than in any other period before the present century.[90]

Locally Recruited Camel Riders in Oriens

The *Notitia Dignitatum Orientis* has many entries marked *equites Sagittarii Indigenae*.[91] These are of interest, for they were clearly units without a name or a number, unlike the legions and auxiliary units. Other units of *equites* with standard names are still qualified to the extent that no duplication occurs within a given duchy. Thus we find *Equites scutarii Illyriciani* in Phoenice, Syria, Palaestina, Mesopotamia, and Arabia, but there is only one such entry in each of these duchies. The units of native horsemen are the only group that recurs frequently within the duchies, but without any special designation other than the place where they were based. Thus we find four units of *equites sagittarii indigenae* in Palaestina, and two units of *equites promoti indigenae*, each of these identified only by the locality of their base.

This has operational consequences, for it means that such troops were never expected to operate as a unit in larger formations, away from their bases. The men were recruited locally on the understanding that the unit was not to be transferred. This impression is reinforced by the papyri and inscriptions from Nessana which never refer to the unit there by name.[92] In formal documents, such as P.Colt No. 29, a summons issued at Elusa, the provincial capital, individu-

---

[89] Neither legion was there at the time of the Islamic conquest.

[90] For suggestions, Whitby's paper in: *The Byzantine and Early Islamic Near East III. States, Resources and Armies*, eds. A. Cameron, L. Conrad, G. King, (1995), conclusions at pp. 119–24.

[91] They are found under all the headings of the *Notitia* pertaining to the diocese of Oriens, except Isauria; also in the duchy of *Thebais*, but not under the command of the *comes limitis Aegypti*.

[92] P.Colt 15 mentions two brothers who came from Nessana and lived in Rhinocorura in Egypt, serving in the 'Numerus of Very Loyal Theodosians'. Kraemer, pp. 41–2, deduced that this was the unit based in Nessana. I agree with A. Negev, *The Architecture of Mampsis, Final Report*, ii, *The Late Roman and Byzantine Reports* (Jerusalem,

als are identified as 'soldiers at the camp of Nessana'.[93] This shows that there was no other current title or number to identify their unit. In the language of the *Notitia* the unit would have been designated '*Equites sagittarii indigenae, Nessana*', but locally such a designation was of course meaningless.

The papyri distinguish between the base and the village of Nessana, *to kastron* and *he kome*.[94] The soldiers clearly lived in their own houses in the settlements of Nessana and Avdat, for the walled compounds (*kastra*) there contained no barracks or visible living quarters for the troops, unlike the earlier, much bigger base situated near Avdat, which lay outside the town.[95] The military compounds were an integral part of the settlements, forming an architectural unity with the main churches. Whatever went on, apart from administration, in the rather empty space within these compounds, the planning serves to emphasize that the military units were an integral part of the settlements and gave them authority as fortified centres for the surrounding area and as road-stations on important locations.[96] Being garrisoned settlements in a densely inhabited region,[97] however, they fulfilled a function totally different from that of the small and isolated road-stations

---

1988), 1–2, who argues against the identification of the unit at Nessana with the Numerus of Very Loyal Theodosians. He points out that the text of P.Colt 15 could imply that the brothers served in this unit while it was based in Rhinocorura. He is likely to be right, for there is no other reference to this unit in the Nessana papyri.

[93] P.Colt 29, line 4.

[94] P.Colt 16, lines 3–4: ... *en ko[me Nessanois horiou pole]os Elouses ... strat(iotai) apo k]astrou Nesanon....* The village belonged to the territory of Elusa, but the soldiers and their relatives had the advantage of the administrative and judicial services offered by the army unit (no. 19). The tax office, however, was at Elusa.

[95] Avdat I is not reliably dated. Unpublished trial excavations are said to have produced a date in the 1st century A.D., but this camp certainly *looks* like a late third or early fourth-century structure, as observed by Kennedy & Riley, 170–72. For the size of these bases, above.

[96] L. Wooley and T.E. Lawrence, *The Wilderness of Zin* (London, 1914–15), 49: 'The forts there are of Justinian's plan and most probably his work, but only a bureaucratic pedant could have imposed on a desert such incongruous defences, which seem intended rather to complete a theory than to meet a local need'. As I indicated elsewhere, I do not think that such observations bring us closer to an understanding of the meaning of these forts. Wooley and Lawrence do not take account of the prosperity of the northern Negev in the sixth century. To some extent comparable may be Dibsi Faraj (Athis?) on the Euphrates, excavated by R.P. Harper, *DOP* 29 (1975), 319–38; also: Isaac, *Limits of Empire*, 257–9.

[97] Mordechai Haiman, 'Preliminary Report of the Western Negev Highlands Emergency Survey', *IEJ* 39 (1989), 173–191, esp. 189–191, reports on the discovery of scores of farmhouses in the western Negev in the Early Islamic period.

like Mezad Thamar, Upper Zohar, or Ad Dianam (Yotvetah). It is a major problem in the interpretation of archaeological material that it is impossible to know whether such unidentified structures were indeed military sites or merely fortified road-stations.[98] This is a difficulty in large areas of the region, where there are numerous anonymous square buildings clearly belonging to the Later Roman Empire.[99] Generally speaking we should identify as military structures only those that are marked as such by inscriptions or identified with sites known from other sources.

The soldiers in Nessana then, like all the others serving in units of 'native horsemen', were recruited to serve in the garrisons of their home-towns.[100] Several of the papyri show that the soldiers owned houses and landed property in and near their home town. These were privately owned and there is no indication that they cultivated land made available by the state. There is no doubt, however, that the men functioned there as soldiers in the full sense of the word. The fact that the enlisted men were professional soldiers appears from the fact that individual soldiers were detached (and still referred to as 'soldiers of the camp of Nessana, at present in X')[101] Soldiers were detached to Elusa, capital of Third Palestine,[102] to Caesarea, capital of First Palestine,[103] and even to Egypt.[104] This proves that the unit was part of a functioning army structure and an integral part of the provincial army in the period covered by the documents. As background material the decree of Anastasius from Cyrenaica is of interest.[105] It establishes the numbers of soldiers from each unit that may be detached for special service with the duke's office as gatekeepers and guardsmen in the public prison. There are other indications that the army organization was well integrated in the sixth century. A levy of 64 camels imposed on the village of Nessana, most of them for the use of the local unit, specifies that two camels are to be sent to the churches in Characmoba, east of the Dead Sea, a distance of

---

[98] Discussion in *Limits of Empire*, 186–208.

[99] Kennedy & Riley, *passim*.

[100] For my views on the military functions of such troops in the desert areas of the Near East, Chapters IV and V of *The Limits of Empire*.

[101] For instance P.Colt 29, l. 4.

[102] *Loc. cit.*

[103] 36, line 19; 37, lines 5 and 15.

[104] 'to Egypt': 37, lines 33 and 40. It is still possible that no. 15 refers to two soldiers detached to Rhinocorura in Egypt.

[105] Above. See lines 29–36.

almost 150 km.[106] There was, in Nessana, a functioning hierarchy and command structure: P.Colt 35 mentions camels assigned to a *Primicerius, priores, ducici*,[107] and P.Colt 36 an *optioprinceps*, and a doctor.[108] P.Colt 37 gives a list of camel-riders under the command of officers with the rank of *dekarchoi*.[109] The men were no militia, but propertied, professional soldiers, locally recruited and serving in their home town. There can be little doubt that this still was the case by the end of the sixth century. I disagree with Kraemer's interpretation of P.Colt 29 as a summons issued at Elusa, December 23, 590. Kraemer thinks that there was apparently no longer a military court at Nessana, hence the summons from Elusa. He concludes that the unit was disbanded before this date. However, the language of the papyrus does not support this conclusion: 'Flavius . . ., most loyal soldier of the camp at Nessana and at present dwelling here [sc. at Elusa], sends to George son of Ianes, most loyal soldier of the same camp and a native of that place, this affidavit which has the force of a second and third summons. . . .' I would assume that, as the document says, the unit was still there, and that there was another reason why the summons was dispatched from Elusa: namely the fact that the summons was issued by a person living at Elusa (perhaps detached from the unit in Nessana). Thus I conclude that the unit is last attested in Nessana in 590. When it was disbanded we cannot know. If the unit at Nessana was a typical example of this sort of establishment recorded in the *Notitia*, we should expect to find most 'native horsemen' based in or near fairly substantial settlements. For the units listed in Palestine that may well be true in so far as they can be identified.[110] It is possible that elsewhere *alae* and *cohortes* were

---

[106] P.Colt 35, line 12.

[107] Lines 2, 3, 9, 10. Normally *ducici*, like the Latin *duciani* would refer to members of the staff of the *dux*. This is not really suitable here, but I am not quite sure that Kraemer, p. 110, makes it clear what the term does stand for in this context. P.Colt 26 of A.D. 570 is a contract between two *priores* of the *kastron* of Nessana and an officer who is *apo dom(estikon)*.

[108] P.Colt 36 line 13: *d(ia) Stefanou optioprink(ipos)*; l. 15: *Ioannou iatrou*. Note also the *ducici* and the *priores* in lines 2 and 12. An intriguing reference in line 18 of this document is the sum *d(ia) . . . kaut(o)u ton dem(osion) ton trion kastr(on)*. 'The three military' bases presumably were Nessana and two others in the same area, but they cannot be identified. One of them may well be Avdat. It can definitely be deduced that Nessana was one of three functioning bases at the time of the document, said to date to the sixth century.

[109] A *dek(. . .)* is also mentioned in P. 38, cf. comments at p. 116.

[110] Sabaia and Robatha are unidentified. Zodocatha is Sadaqa in southern Jordan, where a spring and remains of a substantial settlement have been seen: Brünow & Domaszewski, *Die Provincia Arabia* i (1904), 469, citing older literature; Parker, *Romans*

more often based in remote areas and less often in settlements.[111]

To conclude, it must be said again that so far there is little evidence of any large-scale systematic reduction of the provincial army in Palestine before the early seventh century. Even if there is evidence of the abandonment of some military sites in the fourth and fifth century we must be cautious in interpreting this as part of a pattern.[112]

The evidence discussed here does not cover the early seventh century. It is clear that by that time the key legionary establishments at al-Lajjun, Aela, and almost certainly that at Udruh had been disbanded. The unit at Nessana was apparently disbanded in, or not long after the last decade of the sixth century.[113] Inscriptions from

---

and Saracens, 99. It is usually assumed that the nearby watchtower was the Byzantine base. One would expect something more substantial. Hauana = Hauara, mentioned also on Beer Sheva, fr. 2, modern Humeima, Kennedy & Riley, 146–8: large fort: 204 × 147 m (3 ha/7.4 acres), a smaller unidentified structure which looks like a Roman *principia* (50 × 60 m) and settlement. Recent publications: J.P. Oleson, 'Humeima Hydraulic Survey, 1980: Preliminary Field Report', *Annual of the Department of Antiquities of Jordan* 23 (1990), 285–311; J.P. Oleson, D.F. Graf and J. Eadie, *Humayma* in: D. Homès-Fredericq and J.B. Hennessy (ed.), *Archaeology of Jordan* II/1 (Leuven, 1989), 270–4; D.F. Graf, 'The "God" of Humayma' in: Z.J. Kapera (ed.), *Intertestamental Essays in Honour of J.T. Milik* (Kraków, 1992), 67–76. Zoar is archaeologically unknown, but it is mentioned as a settlement by Eusebius and in the Beer Sheva inscriptions. The site of Moahile/Moa has not been identified with certainty: Isaac, *Limits of Empire*, 129 f. It may well have been Moyet 'Awad, now called Mo'ah. For the identification of sites in southern Palestine mentioned in the *Notitia*, F.-M. Abel, *Géographie de la Palestine*, (Paris, ³1967), ii, 179 f.; Y. Aharoni, 'Tamar and the Roads to Aila (Elath)', *IEJ* 4 (1954), 9–16; G.W. Bowersock, *Roman Arabia* (Cambridge, MA, 1983), Appendix iv: Ancient Maps of Roman Arabia, 164–86.

[111] See van Berchem's conclusions for Phoenice, *L'armée*, 16. He points out that all but one of the units based along the *Strata Diocletiana*, south of the Rawaq were *alae* and *cohortes*, while those along the parallel system north of the Rawaq were *equites*.

[112] The *Notitia* mentions three legionary bases in Arabia and Palaestina. That gives us three legions in the late fourth century. Udruh was an additional legionary base, not mentioned in the *Notitia*, but occupied in the time of Beer Sheva fr. 2 (undated, fifth-century?). The only base that has been excavated and published properly is al-Lajjun and we do not know when the other three legionary bases in these two duchies were occupied after the end of the fourth century. Units may have been transferred from one base to another. The same is true for smaller units. Even if we are certain that a camp was evacuated (e.g. Yotvetah), we do not know whether the unit was disbanded, or transferred to another place in the same region, or transferred to another province.

[113] Al-Lajjun was finally abandoned in the mid-sixth century as mentioned above. Udruh was occupied well into the sixth century. We must await the report on the excavations there for further archaeological information. For current references and information, Kennedy & Riley, 131–3. It is clear however from Arabic sources that

Beer Sheva 9 f A.D. 605 and 613 mention, respectively, a *scriniarius* and a *tribunus* (Alt, nos. 26 and 27). These are the latest texts attesting thepresene of Byzantine officers in the Negev. It is also clear that the unit at Nessana, and presumably others like it, were a functioning part of the provincial army, even though the unit was locally recruited and fulfilled local police duties. The information we have about Nessana and Avdat (Eboda) illustrate the random nature of the material: The military presence at the latter site is known exclusively from the presence of the fort there, almost a replica of the one at Nessana, and the one reference in P.Colt 39, found among many others at Nessana.

The first part of this paper attempted to consider the priorities of military policies in the period before the Islamic conquest. Our perspective is necessarily determined by the views of literary sources in the centre of the empire. At best we can attempt to ascertain contemporary thinking and values and then look at how these were realized in practice. When the two empires clashed and military campaigns were planned realities in the provinces had little impact on the decisions made by the rulers. So much is clear. The economic realities that were the result of these decisions ultimately determined how feasible imperial policies might be. The limits of the taxability of the provinces had to be faced by every ruler, whether he was interested in the prosperity of his subjects or not. On the whole, however, material resources do not seem to have formed an issue of concern in its own right. The payment of tribute to allies was a matter often measured more in terms of honour and prestige than of cost and benefit. The destruction of enemy resources was an aim of warfare for its own sake, rather than a means of realizing a well-defined strategy.

The second part of this paper attempts to consider the nature of the military presence in one duchy of the Byzantine empire. It is a well-known difficulty of working with local material—archaeological remains and inscriptions—that the link between the major events described by the historians and the artifacts representing local life in the periphery is often hard to trace. We may well accept the Byzantine

---

neither Adruh (Udruh), nor Ayla (Aela) had a substantial garrison by 630: F. McGraw Donner, *The Early Islamic Conquests* (Princeton, 1981), 109, with references at n. 90. Note the brief letter from Moses, bishop of Aela, to Victor son of Sergius in Nessana: P.Colt 51, said to date to the early seventh century.

Table of places mentioned in literary sources

	Place Name	Eusebius	Not. Dig.	Beer Sheva	P.Colt 39
1.	Adroa	−	+	−	−
2.	Aela	+	+	−	−
3.	Beer Sheva	+	+	(+)	+
4.	Birsama	−	+[114]	−	+
5.	Chermula	+	+	−	+
6.	Eboda (Avdat)	−	−	−	+
7.	Elusa	−	+	+	+
8.	Malhatha	(−)	+	−	+
9.	Mampsis	(−)	−	+	+
10.	Menois	(−)	+[1]	−	−
11.	Nessana	−	−	−	+
12.	Sobila	−	−	−	+
13.	Zoar	+	+	+	−

Military posts

14.	Ein Boqeq	Excavated, unidentified.
15.	Lejjun	Excavated, probably mentioned in Not. Dig.
16.	Mezad Thamar	Excavated, probably unidentified.
17.	Upper Zohar	Excavated, unidentified.
18.	Yotvetah	Epigraphically dated, not mentioned in above mentioned sources (Tab.Peut.: Ad Dianam)
19.	Ḥorvat Ma'agorah	Dated by excavation to unspecified LR/Byz. periods. Unidentified.

N. Negev, S. Pal. I		CIV[2]	CV	CVI
3.	Beer Sheva	+/+	+	+
4.	Birsama (Pal. I)	−/+	+	+
5.	Chermula	+/+	−	+
6.	Eboda	?[3]	?	+
7.	Elusa	−/−	+	+
10.	Menois	−/+	+	−
11.	Nessana	−/−	−	+
12.	Sobila	−/−	−	+
North-East and Central Negev				
9.	Mampsis	−/−	+	+
13.	Zoar	+/+	+	?
14.	Ein Boqeq[4]	+	+	+
15.	al-Lajjun[5]	+	+	+
16.	Mezad Thamar[4]	+	+	+
17.	Upper Zohar[4]	+	+	+
19.	Ḥorvat Ma'agorah	Unspecified LR / Byzantine occupation		
Southern Palaestina III				
1.	Adroa (Udruh)[6]	?	+	?
2.	Aela	+	?	?
18.	Yotvetah[7]	+	−	−

[1] Birsama and Menois are mentioned also in *CTh.* vii, 4, 30 of A.D. 409.
[2] Sites are marked twice as attested in (a) Eusebius and (b) *Not. Dig. Or.*
[3] The earlier fort at Avdat is not firmly dated, see n. 78.
[4] Unidentified and not attested in documents. Dating based on archaeological excavation.
[5] Probably to be identified with Betthoro in *Not. Dig. Or.* xxxvii 22 (in the list of Arabia), situated in Jordan, east of the Dead Sea. Dated by excavation.
[6] Attested in Beer Sheva fr.; results of excavations to be awaited.
[7] Tetrarchic inscription and excavation.

literary sources that give us an impression of a Negev manned by very few soldiers and policed to some extent by Arab allies of dubious loyalty. It is also conceivable that the Persian occupation and the wars of the seventh century destroyed part or much of the previous existing infra-structure. By the time of the Islamic conquest there seem to have been very few troops in Palestine: if Theophanes' information is correct there were none in Aila, and near Gaza the Roman army attempted to halt the Muslims with 300 men altogether. Yet from all this it does not follow that during the fifth and sixth century there was a gradual reduction of forces in this area who could have prevented the Islamic conquest, if they had been present.

I would argue that the Byzantine army in the provinces was never capable, or meant to be capable of defence against full scale invasion. In the zone of confrontation with Persia, cities were organized so as to withstand a siege, but the countryside was never defended against penetration by large forces. When Persia attacked, an army had to be sent by the central authorities. Palestine and southern Syria had not been invaded by regular armies from the time of Zenobia in the third century till the Persian conquest in the seventh. The troops that were there, whatever their numbers, were meant to take care of local security and they did so adequately most of the time. They were doing so for centuries even when there was havoc elsewhere in the Empire. The soldiers serving at Nessana could not have withstood the Muslim forces, even if the unit had still been there. The Byzantine collapse in the Near East in the thirties took place because the central authorities were incapable of responding adequately in the 630's, as they had done in the 620's. We would want to know to what extent this was due to a lack of resources or political will and moral support.

Postscript

The unit stationed at Nessana clearly was one of camel-riders. There has been some discussion recently about the function of camel-riders in the Roman army. Reference should be made also to a study by Brent Shaw, who assumes they were used primarily for transport and reconnaissance.[1] This certainly would be true when they were part of a war-time army. In peace-time the regular task of such units was undoubtedly to patrol the desert, where they could protect travellers and caravans.[2] This states in a nut-shell what should be said about the Roman army in the Negev in general. It will be clear that a unit permanently based in the north-western Negev, far from any main road, major population centre and large army base, would have been of limited use for transport. Nessana, however, would have been a natural position for reconnaissance and patrolling in various directions.

A recent paper discusses a well-known crux: Justinian's handling of the *limitanei* as described in Procopius' *Buildings*.[3] As a professional numismatist Casey looks at the evidence from another perspective which is worth taking into account. Rather than concluding that Procopius was right or wrong he suggests that he was right for a limited geographical area. It is an interesting hypothesis, but I feel that there are problems which should be stated explicitly:

(1) Casey's assumption on p. 220 that the availability of coinage should correlate with the flow of coinage to garrisons and that Justinian's cessation of payments to the *limitanei* should ɔe reflected in the coinage record, is itself an hypothesis. It is still possible that the evidence assembled on pp. 216–9, based on indisputable fact, has a different cause. Also: is the assumption, which is undoubtedly true for the west during the Principate, necessarily right for the east in the sixth century? Carrié has argued that in the Byzantine period 'l'armée n'apparait pas comme le principal facteur d'injection et de circulation

---

[1] Brent D. Shaw, 'The Camel in Roman North Africa and the Sahara: history, biology and the human economy,' *Bulletin de l'Institut Fondamental d'Afrique Noire 41, Ser. B, no. 4. Dakar, 1979*, 663–721, repr. in B.D. Shaw, *Environment and Society in Roman North Africa* (Aldershot, 1995), 707–716.

[2] *Limits of Empire*, 59 f.

[3] P.J. Casey, 'Justinian, the *limitanei*, and Arab-Byzantine Relations in the 6th century', *JRA* 9 (1996), 214–22.

monétaire dans l'économie Égyptienne.'[4] The cessation of coinage is seen everywhere in Palestine, and even in Beiruth and Baalbek, far from the known locations of garrisons. This weakens the hypothesis that there is a connection with the cessation of payment to garrisons.

2) Were soldiers paid in bronze coin rather than silver or gold? They would have received improbable quantities of bronze.

3) Is it not possible to think of different reasons for the cessation of bronze coins? One could think of technical reasons: there could have been warfare elsewhere, or perhaps there simply was enough bronze coin in circulation and consequently there was no need of further issues for some time.

4) As the author himself points out, it is difficult to identify the sites of limitanean garrisons. There can be little doubt that one of them, very well known, was Nessana. Precisely at Nessana, however, there is good evidence that the military unit based there continued to exist as such till the early seventh century, as observed in the article above.

Elsewhere the evidence is less good than the author suggests. In any case, the connection with alleged measures taken by Justinian is a speculation and it seems better not to build a theory regarding Procopius' problematic statement on material that itself is hard to interpret.

It is, incidentally, of interest to note that Procopius' statement unambiguously implies that the *limitanei* were regular units.

An interesting piece of evidence, long available and only recently assessed, may be mentioned here. German air photographs, taken in World War I, by units supporting the Turkish army against the British forces, show many sites in Palestine as they were then, before modern development. These have been collected by B.Z. Kedar in a remarkable book.[5] One of these photos shows an area south of the town of Beer Sheva, where the outline of what seems to have been a Roman army camp is clearly visible. The archaeologist P. Fabian located the site and managed to carry out small scale excavations

---

[4] J.-M. Carrié in: *Armées et fiscalité dans le monde antique* (Paris, 1977), 373–93, at 384–5.

[5] B.Z. Kedar, *Looking Twice at the Land of Israel* (Jerusalem, 1991, Heb.).

before the last part of the site was overbuilt. The excavations produced late Roman pottery.[6]

Additional Bibliography

See also the postscripts to Nos. 6, 10 and 19.

W.E. Kaegi, 'Reconceptualizing Byzantium's Eastern Frontiers in the Seventh Century', in R.W. Mathisen & H.S. Sivan, *Shifting Frontiers in Late Antiquity* (Altershot, Hampshire, 1995), 83–92.

---

[6] P. Fabian, 'The Late-Roman military camp at Beer-Sheva: a new discovery', in: *The Roman and Byzantine Near East: Some Recent Archaeological Research* (1995), 235–40. See also M. Abel, 'Inscriptions de Bersabee', *RB* 12 (1903), 425–30, at 427, for references to what clearly was this site.

INDEX

Abdagos/Abdagon ch. 3
Abu Ghosh 204n.
Abu Sha'ar 421
Acha, R. 128
Achzeiph (Akhziph, Ecdippa) 300
Acrabeta 166, 167
ad Dianam 73f., 456
administrative division 165–9
Adroa see Udruḥ
Aela (Aqaba, Elath) 72, 136, 139,
  148, 336, 341, 462n., 466
Aelia Capitolina 50, 80, 82, 99, 194,
  214, 299, *passim*, ch. 8
  colonists of 101
  territory of 90
Aelius Severianus 53
African frontier 158
Africans
  SHA on 279f.
Afula 36
ager publicus 112n.
aggeres 348
agoranomos 95n.
agrariae stationes 147, 456
Agri Decumates 349, 383
agrimensores 291
Agrippa I 102n.
Agrippa II 429
air photographs 468
Akeson 26, 28
Akiba, R. 194n.
Akrabatta 178
ala I Ulpia Dromedariorum 139
ala I Ulpia Singularium 433
ala II Auriana 337, 342
ala II Pannoniorum 315
ala II Ulpia Auriana 157
alares 371f.
Albinus 55f.
Alexander 31, 32
Alexandria 127, 420
al-Mundhīr (Munderich) 142n., 360,
  363, 416
Ammaus see Emmaus
Amorcesus 146
Anastasius 143, 421, 443
  edicts of 452n., 460

ancestors 259f.
Andreas 215
Aninius Sextius Florentinus, T.
  338f.
annona 59, 60, 66, 451f.
Antioch 411
Antiochus Epiphanes 366
Antiochus V Eupator 8, *passim*, ch. 1
Antonine Wall 84
Antoninus 418
Antoninus Pius 46
Antonius Saturninus, L. 86
Apollonia (Arsuf) 15
Aqiva, R. 132, 242, 248, 249
Aquila 183n.
Arabia 419
  annexation of 98f., 139
  garrisons in 135f., 196
  Roman roads in *passim*, ch. 6
  troops recruited from 139
Arabia Felix 126, 127
Arabs 125, 126, 132, 443
Arados 32
Aratius 146
Aravah, milestones in 71–4
Archelais 92n.
Archelaus 115
archisynagogus 274–6
Arindela 457n.
Aristobulias 178
Aristobulus 127
Arminius, revolt of 212, 215
Artemion 215
Ascalon (Ashkelon) 298
Aser (Tayasir) 297f.
Ashkelon 14
Asiatic 279
Asinaeus and Anilaeus 146
Asinius Gallus, C. 78n.
Asinius Pollio Verrucosus 79
Aspebetus 418
assize cities 162
Athena (Allat) 157
Attidius Cornelianus 52
Aufidius Priscus 72
Augustus 126, 128, 129, 406
  advice to Tiberius 407

Auranitis (Hauran) 128
Aurelius Fulvus 45
Avars 445
Avdat see Oboda
Avidius Cassius 257
Azotus (Ashdod) 34

Babatha archive *passim*, ch. 11, 303
Babylonia 411
balsam-plantations 116n., 170
bandits, banditry *passim*, ch. 10
Bar Kokhba 248–250
  not mentioned by Dio 214
Bar Kokhba, revolt of 87, 100,
  105, 106, 117, 132, 174f., *passim*,
  ch. 15, ch. 16
  aftermath of 250f.
  archaeological exploration and
    228–233
  Bar Kokhba a leader of 248–250
  Cassius Dio on see Cassius Dio
  causes of 233–8, 277f.
  coinage of 230
  course of 243–48
  documents from 230f., *passim*,
    ch. 11
  Early Christian authors on 216n.,
    221n.
  final episode of 242
  geographical scope of 243–5
  Greek and Latin sources on
    226f.
  and prior unrest 238–43
  Samaritan chronicles on 227f.
  subterranean hiding places 217,
    231–3, 256
  Talmudic sources 216n., 224–6,
    248f.
Barabbas 130
Batanaea (Bashan) 128, 129, 141,
  335
Batavians, revolt of 213
Batharda 178
Bedouin *passim*, ch. 10
Beer Orah 74
Beer Sheva (Bersabe, Beer-sheba)
  294, 374f. See also Birosaba
  edict(s) from 451, 468, *passim*,
    ch. 27
Beit Dagon 32
Belisarius 377, 441n.
bellum Germanicum 315
Berenice 420
Berytus 91, 97, 127, 270

Beth Guvrin see Eleutheropolis
Beth Shammai 239
Bethar (Battir) 228, 242, 255
Bethbassi 178
Bethsur 297
Betthoro 140n.
bilingual inscriptions 335
Birosaba 454
Birsama (Beer Shema) 454, 455
Bostra 71, 88n., 90nn., 190, 204,
  335f., 338, 434, 457n.
  colonial status of 339
Boudicca, revolt of 212, 214f., 217,
  271n.
boundary
  between Judaea and
    Phoenice 201n., 300
  between Syria-Pal. and Sinai 58n.
boundary-marker 201n.
Brigantes, revolt of 213, 215n.
builder (ἀρχιτέκτων) 341
burganin (burgi) 193n., 354
Byblus 127

Caecina 348
Caesarea 94–8, 116, 166, 204n., 298,
  433, 460, *passim*, ch. 4
Caesareans (auxiliaries) 97, 105
Calama 92
Calgacus 272n.
caligati 395
Caligula 129
camel riders 458–62, 467
camels 412, 417
Camulodunum (Colchester) 214
Canaanite 261
canabae 89, 101
Canatha 132
Caparcotna see Legio
Capernaum 176
capita viarum, selection of 62–5, 351
Cappadocia 407
Caracalla 55, 56f.
Carmel, Mt. 127
Cartimandua 215n.
Cassius Dio 56, 226f., *passim*, ch. 15
census 163, 302f., *passim*, ch. 21
centuria 389, 393
centurio regionarius 163f., 386n.
centurions 163, *passim*, ch. 24
  living quarters of 394
Cercesium 368
Cestius Gallus 43n., 192n.
Chalcis 363

SUPPLEMENTS TO MNEMOSYNE

EDITED BY J. M. BREMER, L. F. JANSSEN, H. PINKSTER
H. W. PLEKET, C. J. RUIJGH AND P. H. SCHRIJVERS

Recent volumes in the series:

152. KNIGHT, V.H. *The Renewal of Epic*. Responses to Homer in the *Argonautica* of Apollonius. 1995. ISBN 90 04 10386 4
153. LUSCHNIG, C.A.E. *The Gorgon's Severed Head*. Studies of *Alcestis, Electra*, and *Phoenissae*. 1995. ISBN 90 04 10382 1
154. NAVARRO ANTOLÍN, F. (ed.). *Lygdamus*. Corpus Tibullianum III. 1-6: Lygdami elegiarum liber. Translated by J.J. Zoltowski. 1996. ISBN 90 04 10210 8
155. MATTHEWS, V.J. *Antimachus of Colophon*. Text and Commentary. 1996. ISBN 90 04 10468 2
156. TREISTER, M.Y. *The Role of Metals in Ancient Greek History*. 1996. ISBN 90 04 10473 9
157. WORTHINGTON, I. (ed.). *Voice into Text*. Orality and Literacy in Ancient Greece. 1996. ISBN 90 04 10431 3
158. WIJSMAN, H.J.W. *Valerius Flaccus*, Argonautica, *Book V*. A Commentary. 1996. ISBN 90 04 10506 9
159. SCHMELING, G. (ed.). *The Novel in the Ancient World*. 1996. ISBN 90 04 09630 2
160. SICKING, C.M.J. & P. STORK. *Two Studies in the Semantics of the Verb in Classical Greek*. 1996. ISBN 90 04 10460 7
161. KOVACS, D. *Euripidea Altera*. 1996. ISBN 90 04 10624 3
162. GERA, D. *Warrior Women*. The Anonymous Tractatus *De Mulieribus*. 1997. ISBN 90 04 10665 0
163. MORRIS, I. & B. POWELL (eds.). *A New Companion to Homer*. 1997. ISBN 90 04 09989 1
164. ORLIN, E.M. *Temples, Religion and Politics in the Roman Republic*. 1997. ISBN 90 04 10708 8
165. ALBRECHT, M. VON. *A History of Roman Literature*. From Livius Andronicus to Boethius with Special Regard to Its Influence on World Literature. 2 Vols. Revised by G. Schmeling and by the Author. Vol. 1: Translated with the Assistance of F. and K. Newman, Vol. 2: Translated with the Assitance of R.R. Caston and F.R. Schwartz. 1997. ISBN 90 04 10709 6 (Vol. 1), ISBN 90 04 10711 8 (Vol. 2), ISBN 90 04 10712 6 (Set)
166. DIJK, J.G.M. VAN. Αἶνοι, Λόγοι, Μῦθοι. Fables in Contexts in Archaic, Classical, and Hellenistic Greek Literature. 1997. ISBN 90 04 10747 9
167. MAEHLER, H. (Hrsg.). *Die Lieder des Bakchylides*. Zweiter Teil: Die Dithyramben und Fragmente. Text, Übersetzung und Kommentar. 1997. ISBN 90 04 10671 5
168. DILTS, M. & G.A. KENNEDY (eds.). *Two Greek Rhetorical Treatises from the Roman Empire*. Introduction, Text, and Translation of the Arts of Rhetoric Attributed to Anonymous Seguerianus and to Apsines of Gadara. 1997. ISBN 90 04 10728 2
169. GÜNTHER, H.-C. *Quaestiones Propertianae*. 1997. ISBN 90 04 10793 2
170. HEINZE, T. (Hrsg.). *P. Ovidius Naso. Der XII. Heroidenbrief: Medea an Jason*. Einleitung, Text und Kommentar. Mit einer Beilage: Die Fragmente der Tragödie *Medea*. 1997. ISBN 90 04 10800 9
171. BAKKER, E.J. (ed.). *Grammar as Interpretation*. Greek Literature in its Linguistic Contexts. 1997. ISBN 90 04 10730 4
172. GRAINGER, J.D. *A Seleukid Prosopography and Gazetteer*. 1997. ISBN 90 04 10799 1
173. GERBER, D.E. (ed.). *A Companion to the Greek Lyric Poets*. 1997. ISBN 90 04 09944 1
174. SANDY, G. *The Greek World of Apuleius*. Apuleius and the Second Sophistic. 1997. ISBN 90 04 10821 1
175. ROSSUM-STEENBEEK, M. VAN. *Greek Readers' Digests?* Studies on a Selection of Subliterary Papyri. 1998. ISBN 90 04 10953 6
176. McMAHON, J.M. *Paralysin Cave*. Impotence, Perception, and Text in the *Satyrica* of Petronius. 1998. ISBN 90 04 10825 4
177. ISAAC, B. *The Near East under Roman Rule*. Selected Papers. 1998. ISBN 90 04 10736 3